THE SOVIET SYSTEM
in THEORY and PRACTICE

Selected Western and Soviet Views

Edited by

HARRY G. SHAFFER

The University of Kansas

 New York

APPLETON-CENTURY-CROFTS

Division of Meredith Publishing Company

THE SOVIET SYSTEM

in THEORY and PRACTICE

To my sons Bernie, Ronnie, and Lennie in the hope that they will learn to approach all problems with open minds, always ready to expose themselves to a wide variety of views before forming their own opinions on any controversial subject.

PREFACE

A few weeks ago I was showing some photographs I had taken in Russia to a class of fifth and sixth graders in an American school. Most of the children came from middle class faculty and professional families. Among my pictures were a number of shots of roads lined with young trees.

A child's hand went up: "Why do they have trees along the road?"

A bit puzzled, I turned the question back to the class: "Why do you suppose they have trees?"

Another child's hand rose for eager answer: "So that people won't be able to see what's going on beyond the road."

A girl had a different idea: "It's to make work for the prisoners."

I asked why some of *our* roads have trees planted along the side.

"For shade," the children said. "To keep the dust down."

Where did the children get the idea that the Russians have different reasons than we have for planting trees?

URIE BRONFENBRENNER,
AMERICAN SOCIAL PSYCHOLOGIST
(From *Saturday Review*,
January 5, 1963)

The Union of Soviet Socialist Republics is a gigantic land that covers one half of Europe and one third of Asia, in all one sixth of the continental surface of the earth. East-West, the country stretches over a distance of 6,000 miles; when the fishermen on the Bering Strait ready their boats at five in the morning, it is midnight on Lake Baikal in Siberia, while the citizens of Moscow are just sitting down to their dinner at 7 P.M. the evening before. Every third tree on earth grows in this vast land which leads the world in reserves of many of the raw materials that are essential for today's industrial societies. More than one hundred peoples and nationalities inhabit the territory of the USSR. Over 225 million strong, her population is exceeded in number only by that of China and India; it increases by about seven every minute, 10,000 every day; and the vast majority of Soviet citizens alive today are expected to be living in the twenty-first century. Two decades ago the Soviet people broke the backbone of Hitler's armies at the gates of Leningrad and on the banks of the Volga, at a cost of more than twenty million lives and incalculable material damage, thereby playing an invaluable part in preventing the would-be master race from enslaving the world (just as their forefathers had turned back and destroyed another would-be conqueror's "grand army," thus paving the way for the subsequent liberation of Europe one and a half centuries ago). Still primarily an agricultural country at the time of the outbreak of World War II, the USSR by the mid 'sixties produces roughly one fifth of the world's industrial output. Second only to the United States in industrial and military might, she has been challenging the United States to an economic race, predicting that by 1980 she will have taken the lead not only in productive output but also in regard to the standard of living of her people.

But the Soviet challenge is not merely economic in nature. With its social ownership of the means of production, its political philosophy of "democratic centralism," and its proclaimed goal of a classless society in which each member works according to his ability and receives according to his need, the Soviet system challenges also the political, the social, and the philosophical structure of Western capitalist and semi-capitalist democracies.

What is this Soviet system whose adherents can be counted in the hundreds of millions, from the jungles of Laos and South Vietnam, from the deserts of Africa and the mountain plateaus of Latin America, to the very hearts of London, Paris, and New York? What is this system— Socialist, Communist, Marxist-Leninist, or whatever it may be called— under which the Soviet people have lived and labored in peace and in war since 1917, and under which they have transformed a semi-feudal, semiliterate, and predominantly peasant Russia into the industrial and military colossus of the Union of Soviet Socialist Republics? How does this system —its institutions, its moral foundation, the hopes it holds for the people living under it—resemble and how does it differ from those of Western societies? What exactly are its accomplishments? What are its major shortcomings? Is it really likely to supersede the economic and political systems of the West, as Marxists have been predicting for over a century?

To find answers to some of the questions above and to evaluate the challenge of the Soviet system we must understand it as it was intended to be by its ideological creators and as it has evolved during its nearly half a century of existence. To gain such understanding, the Western Soviet area specialist studies Soviet source material and the views of Soviet scholars as well as Western interpretations. The purpose of this book of readings is to enable the student to use such an approach in his study of the Soviet system, even though he may not be familiar with the Russian language, nor have the time or the opportunity to dig his way through countless books, pamphlets, monographs, government publications, magazines, and journals in search of appropriate material on both sides. To this end, Western anti-

Marxist or at least non-Marxist views in each chapter are confronted by representative selections translated from the writings of Soviet experts on the respective topics. In five of the eleven chapters, views of Western Marxists are also presented, and on one topic, "On the Question of Stalin," the Chinese Communist view is given a hearing, too. Although necessarily not all-inclusive, the eleven chapters cover a sufficiently wide range of topics to enable the reader to gain some understanding of the most important philosophical, historical, political, economic, and social aspects of the Soviet system. The selections in each chapter were chosen with an eye to their current applicability and with emphasis on broad, general issues rather than technical, specialized detail.

As is to be expected, Western non-Marxist scholars vary more widely in their interpretations of the Soviet system than either Western Marxist or Soviet scholars. Especially in the case of the more controversial aspects of the Soviet system (such as for instance "Freedom and Democracy in the U.S.S.R.") several *Western Views,* often disagreeing with one another on some major points, have been included in this book.

Soviet views are more uniform than either Western or Western Marxist views. But even the Soviet Union is no longer the monolithic structure it used to be in the days of Stalin. Issues varying from the "heredity versus environment" controversy in genetics to the advisability of decentralizing economic decision making, and from the desirability of reducing specialization for children in secondary schools to the merits of restricting art to "socialist realism" are debated widely and openly today. Yet, on basic ideological and major policy issues Soviet scholars still profess strong agreement. The selections under Soviet views are therefore generally representative of officially expressed views and only in rare instances (such as the inclusion of poems by Yevtushenko and the official criticism thereof, or the article "What Soviet Economists Discuss and Why,") was it deemed necessary to indicate areas of disagreement among Soviet authors.

From the selections included in this book, the reader may gain the impression that apart from somewhat more frequent criticism of certain aspects of the Soviet system the views of Western Marxists are very similar to those of their Soviet peers. It should, therefore, be pointed out first that the editor has refrained from including any selections by right-wing anti-Soviet Socialists or by Trotskyists since many of the former would refuse to be classified as "Marxists" altogether (and indeed many of their views are effectively represented by the "liberal" wing of Western opinion) while the latter, whatever the merits of their theories may be, are too few in number and too small in influence among Western Marxists or in the world at large to be included in a book of readings designed to contrast widely prevailing Western and Soviet views. Secondly, the reader should be made aware that with the split of the world Communist movement and of many Communist parties into pro-Soviet and pro-Chinese factions, and with the diminution of control by the Kremlin over Communist parties even within the Soviet bloc, increased deviationism from the prevailing Soviet Party line appears to be in the offing. Finally, it ought to be stressed that the Western Marxists included in this book, in spite of their apparent general approval of the Soviet "experiment," do actually represent a variety of shadings on the Marxist ideological spectrum. Isaac Deutscher, for instance, is an independent British Marxist who has not been affiliated with any political organization since he was expelled from the Communist party in 1932; Italian Marxist Giuseppe Boffa has earned such adjectives as "respected" and "objective" even from such a strongly anti-Communist organization as Radio Free Europe; American Marxist Victor Perlo usually supports the Soviet interpretation of Marxism-Leninism; and Paul M. Sweezy and Leo Huberman, co-editors of the *Monthly Review* ("An Independent Socialist Magazine"), although by no means uncritical of either faction of the Communist movement, have recently arrived at the conclusion that the Chinese Communists are right "on the basic issues in their dispute with the Soviet leaders."

At this point it may be wise to remind the reader that all Soviet material is presented in English translation and that any translation involves choices which may distort the meaning of the original. The Russian word *bit,* for instance, can be translated as "strike," or "beat," *goret* as "burn" or "shine," *krupnyi* as "large" or "important," *lyubit* as "like" or "love." From these few examples it is evident that even the translator who attempts to be objective may impart connotations which were not intended by the original author. The translations in this volume were originally published by a wide variety of intermediaries ranging from agencies of the United States Government to Soviet Embassies in London and Washington, and from non-profit organizations of Western scholars to private organizations registered with the U.S. Department of Justice as agents of a foreign government. Since translators are likely to disagree with one another on how to translate a passage to most faithfully reproduce the meaning of the original text, this editor will refrain from passing judgment on the relative merits of the translations here included.

I wish to express my gratitude to all the authors, publishers, and editors who granted reprinting permissions; to Professors Jan S. Prybyla (Pennsylvania State University), Alec Nove (Glasgow University), Lowell C. Harriss (Columbia University), Warren W. Eason (Syracuse University), D. Velappan (S.T. Hindu College, Nagercoil, India), and to my colleagues Roy Laird, Ronald K. Calgaard, and John Augelli at The University of Kansas who read the table of contents and the introductions to the chapters and made valuable comments and suggestions; to Professor Charles Oldfather (The University of Kansas), Mr. Abraham L. Popper, and Mr. Marshall Marcus (attorneys at law, New York), who offered helpful advice regarding the introduction to the chapter on Soviet Law; to the editors of *Soviet News,* who aided in identifying some of the Soviet authors; to Miss Selma Hoffman who typed part of the manuscript; and to Mrs. Gladys Korthuis who helped with the proofreading. I am especially indebted to my friend and colleague Dr. Oswald P. Backus of The University of Kansas whom I consulted on several occasions while the work was in progress, who read the entire manuscript with great care, and who will find practically all his numerous and invaluable critical suggestions incorporated in the final version of this book. Last, but by no means least, I wish to thank my wife and most severe critic, Dr. Juliet P. Shaffer, for her intellectual stimulation and for the time and effort taken from her own professional work and family obligations to check and recheck several versions of this preface and of the introductions to the eleven chapters for lack of coherence, flaws in logic, and deficiencies in grammar and sentence structure.

As this book goes to press, the Soviet Union has just witnessed a shift in the top ranks of its government and party organizations. The former duties of Nikita Sergeyevich Khrushchev have been assumed by Leonid Brezhnev and Alexi Kosygin.

Khrushchev was born on April 17, 1894 in the village of Kalinova, near Kursk in the Ukraine. He became First Secretary of the Central Committee of the Communist Party of the Soviet Union on September 7, 1953 and Chairman of the U.S.S.R. Council of Ministers (frequently referred to as "Premier" or "Prime Minister") on March 27, 1958. On October 14, 1964, Brezhnev (President of the Presidium of the Supreme Soviet of the U.S.S.R. from May, 1960 to July, 1964 and then Secretary of the Central Committee of the Communist Party of the Soviet Union, second only to Khrushchev) became the new First Secretary. On October 15, 1964, Kosygin (First Deputy Premier since 1960) became the new Soviet Premier.

The full extent of the ideological changes involved in this transfer of power is not yet clear to the rest of the world.

H.G.S.

FOREWORD

It is a pleasure to recommend this careful and stimulating work by my good friend and colleague at The University of Kansas, particularly because I strongly endorse an underlying purpose of this book, namely to encourage students and interested readers to think. Learn by analyzing problems against a solid background of knowledge—that is a method which has merit! One assumes that attention to problems will lead to deeper analysis, more nearly accurate knowledge, and, ultimately, the habit of logical thought.

Will these selections on the Soviet system stimulate deeper analysis? My answer to that question is an unequivocal yes. A reasonably interested and intelligent person will with proper application, I am convinced, respond to the appeal of conflicting judgments on important issues such as those presented here, judgments from Western non-Marxists, from Western Marxists, from Soviet, and, in one case, Chinese Communist sources. Some readers may find the Communist selections tedious, for they are written in a style which is too ponderous. Would that the selections of Soviet origin reflected the same concern for expressing oneself with wit and grace which characterizes the selections from the pens of some of our Western colleagues like Professor Alec Nove of the University of Glasgow. The tediousness of much of Soviet writing style is a built-in handicap which Professor Shaffer can hardly avoid if he is to achieve his purpose, and which the reader must bravely suffer, for the expected rewards. Perhaps Professor Shaffer should be twitted for having laid little stress on economic planning—his own special interest. The section on economic planning is the shortest in the book—a fact which may well cause the unwary to delve too little into that problem. One may, however, excuse Professor Shaffer: after all, he has published a widely adopted companion volume (*The Soviet Economy: A Collection of Western and Soviet Views,* New York, Appleton-Century-Crofts, 1963) in which economic planning is a major focus. As a help to the reader of the present volume, Professor Shaffer has included introductory statements with guidelines to the use of selections and with references to some other sources which, in many cases, the earnest delver would do well to investigate; they should help to make his analysis deeper.

Will these selections stimulate the acquisition of more nearly accurate knowledge of the Soviet Union? To this question, I must also answer yes. But the intelligent reader should be aware that he is faced with a problem: whom should he believe? On examination of the selections contained in this book, he will find that only some information seems to be generally accepted. What shall he do about points of information, let alone points of interpretation, over which there is dispute? He must be careful. He should recognize that on many points he cannot hope to get definitive information at present. He must remember that the very nature of the subject gives rise to strong prejudices which are reflected in many of the selections, and these he must learn to discount. He would do well to bear in mind that some of the selections were prepared originally for propagandistic purposes, and that some translations from Russian are to be trusted more than others: clearly the product of a scholarly, non-profit, non-governmental organization, such as the *Current Digest of the Soviet Press,* is a more reliable source than the product of government-connected and government-supported organizations. I should hope that the reader would not be deceived by some statements: for example, Herbert Aptheker's assertion that there is no prostitution in the Soviet Union or *Novosti*'s implication that all people in the Soviet Union actually secure the minimum housing to which they are legally entitled. It has not been possible for Professor Shaffer to provide the widest possible divergence of opinions by the inclusion of both Western Marxist and strongly anti-Soviet views in all sections, but with the limitations of space, I believe he has chosen wisely. I must leave to the judgment of Soviet specialists whether any truly important issue has been altogether omitted. If the reader bears these points in mind and works diligently, he should acquire much knowledge of considerable accuracy and a true appreciation of the problems involved in obtaining and identifying such knowledge, an asset which is indispensable to analysis of the Soviet system and to analysis in general.

Will these selections lead to more highly developed processes of thought, to the habit of logical thought? I am optimistic.

Oswald P. Backus
Professor of History
Director of Off-Campus Activities
Slavic and Soviet Area Studies
The University of Kansas

CONTENTS

I

COMMUNIST IDEOLOGY AND MORALITY: THE MARXIST-LENINIST BACKGROUND

"Marx's teaching is all-powerful because it is true."

VLADIMIR ILYICH LENIN

"The Soviet system and communist ideology have withstood all kinds of enemy attacks, all tests and trials. We hold firmly to our revolutionary Marxist-Leninist positions. Here we have stood, here we stand and here we shall stand, since these are the only correct positions."

NIKITA S. KHRUSHCHEV

Ever since the dawn of history, there have been men who, dissatisfied with the imperfections of the system under which they lived, advocated the establishment of some new order—an order which they perceived as a fairer, happier, better-functioning society, more conducive to the good life than the one under which they have been born and raised. Many of their proposals may have been oversimplified and unrealistic. Yet, from the days of Plato or Sir Thomas More to the days of Edward Bellamy and H. G. Wells, farsighted dreamers, through their descriptions of what they considered a more perfect world, have had their impact upon modern economic and political movements. Universal free education; equality before the law, irrespective of race, religion, or country of origin; an equitable distribution of wealth and income; the protection of minorities against the tyranny of majorities; the priority of human rights over property rights—these are but a few of the concepts which bear definite traces of Utopian ideas, proposed centuries before they became part of the economic policy, the political philosophy, or the legal reality of one or another twentieth-century human society.

Many of the essential features of what the Soviets like to refer to as "the moral code of the builders of Communism" are also traceable to philosophical and moral concepts developed by Utopians long ago. The common ownership of the means of production, the "end of the exploita-

1

tion of man by man," the perfectibility of man's character, a world united
under one government and eventually functioning without a government—
all these concepts antedate the birth of Karl Marx (1818-1883), the
social philosopher and bearded revolutionist acclaimed by Communists the
world over as the founder of the modern Communist movement.[1] And
yet, to the Communist mind, Marx is the ideological father, not merely in
the sense in which John Locke and Adam Smith are frequently referred to
as the fathers of Western political and economic thought, but perhaps more
in the sense in which Christianity looks upon Christ.

To the Communist mind Marx has always been more, much more,
than a moral philosopher. And, indeed, Marx was not primarily a moral
philosopher who dealt with the "ought to be." Instead, Marx tried to lay
bare the dynamics of social development, tried to discover the laws of
nature prevailing in the *real* world which, independent of man's will, would
lead mankind towards an ever higher form of human society. To the Communist mind, Marx accomplished what he set out to do: he worked out
the only valid explanation of all important historical events, and he
illuminated the path to the future, to a perfect world of abundance, justice,
and freedom for all, a world which will "inevitably" be inherited by the
Communist workingman. "By revealing the laws governing the operation
and development of the forces of nature and society, genuine science can
always foresee the new," proclaims the official Soviet manual on Marxism-
Leninism. "The Marxist science of the laws of social development enables
us not only to chart a correct path through the labyrinth of social contradictions," it continues confidently, "but to predict the course events
will take, the direction of historical progress and the next stages of social
advance." And it concludes optimistically, "Marxists have no fear of the
future. They represent the class to which the future belongs. . . ."[2]
Communists today may disagree with one another as to just exactly what
Marx meant, but they are fully agreed that Marx was right. If errors have
been made, they were not Marx's errors; they could only be errors of
interpretation, "left-wing," "right-wing," "personality-cult-inspired," or
"revisionist" deviations from the "true" path.

An advertisement of some of Marx's works has this to say about the
essence of Marxist philosophy: "Everyone in the Soviet Union, from a
housewife to a high-order scientist, is trained in it. If one does not understand Marxism, one is in the dark about the ideas which represent the
Soviet ideology which motivates the Soviet people."[3] Indeed, for the

---

[1] It should be emphasized that some Western critics consider the ideology of
Communism as one devoid of any moral code, and the system as one "of the devil!"
For an example of such views, see selection No. VIII, 5 below.

[2] *Fundamentals of Marxism-Leninism: Manual,* 2nd rev. ed. Foreign Languages
Publishing House, Moscow, 1963, p. 17.

[3] *ALL ABOUT USSR: A Catalog of Books about the USSR in English, Imported from the Soviet Union,* Catalog Number 26, Cross World Books and Peri-
odicals Inc., Chicago, 1963, p. 17. (Copies of the Catalog are sent out free of
charge on request.)

serious student who wants to obtain a *thorough* understanding of Marxian theories there is no substitute for the study of Marx's original works. But for a brief and clear summary and evaluation of Marxian philosophy, as seen through the eyes of a Western, non-Marxist scholar, it would be difficult to find a better selection than the first one, taken from Robert L. Heilbroner's well-known book, *The Worldly Philosophers*.

When, under the leadership of Vladimir Ilyich Ulyianov (1870-1924), better known as Lenin, the first Marxian-type "Dictatorship of the Proletariat" was established in Russia in 1917, much of Marxian ideology needed to be revised, reinterpreted, added to, or subtracted from— in the light of the momentous development. How could the revolution take place and succeed in a relatively backward country that had not gone through all the "inevitable" stages of development? What was the role of the peasant in a predominantly peasant society before, during, and after the revolution? What was the function of the Communist party? What was the role of the Soviet Union in relation to the World Communist Movement and to the non-Communist nations surrounding her? These and many other questions needed to be answered. The answers officially accepted by Soviet and Chinese Communists alike (although they disagree as to the meaning of many of them) are those given in the voluminous writings of Lenin. It is *Marxist-Leninist* ideology, then, which Communists everywhere acclaim as the "correct" line to which they have been adhering. To its practical application they ascribe the successes of Communist construction in the Soviet Union, Eastern Europe, and Communist China; upon its ability to forecast correctly the future course of events they base their predictions of the advent of a Communist world.

Once again, a detailed study of at least the major writings of Lenin would be essential for a *thorough* understanding of Lenin's contribution to Marxian ideology. The excerpts taken from Gerhart Niemeyer's study and presented as selection No. 2 below can do no more than introduce the reader, in summary form, to Lenin's contribution as seen through the eyes of a Western analyst.

In the third selection under *Western Views,* Harry G. Shaffer compares Communism with Fascism, using Fascist Italy and Nazi Germany, primarily, as illustrations for the latter. Taking to task those who assume that one type of dictatorship is just like any other type, the author concludes that we can no longer "afford the erroneous assumption that Fascism and Communism . . . are but two strands of poison ivy bearing different designations but demanding equal treatment and eradication."

Next, in the two selections under *Western Marxist Views,* two of the foremost Marxists in the United States, Paul M. Sweezy and Leo Huberman, assisted by Sybil H. May, present the case for Marxian Socialism. To them it is both a moral and a scientific case: the advent of Socialism and eventually of Communism is both morally right and scientifically proven to be not only workable but inevitable. In greatest confidence, therefore, Sweezy can say that he is "very glad to leave it to the future to decide" whether Marxists are right or not, while Huberman and May proclaim: "Socialism is not an impossible dream. It is the next step in the process of social evolution. . . ."

In the first, brief selection under *Soviet Views,* Nikita S. Khrushchev points to the persistence of unemployment in the United States as evidence of the correctness of Marx's, Engels',[4] and Lenin's predictions that Capitalism will give way to Socialism and eventually to Communism. "It is only a matter of time . . . ," Khrushchev asserts emphatically.

Marx devoted most of his writings to an attempt to prove the inevitability of the downfall of Capitalism; Lenin elaborated on Marx's few and scattered remarks as to what the societies of the future—the "Dictatorship of the Proletariat" and the "Final Stage" of Communism—would be like. Selection No. 7 consists of a few quotes from Lenin's writings to familiarize the reader, albeit to a very limited degree, with Lenin's train of thought in regard to Communist society during the transitional and the final stages.

In Marxist ideology, any understanding of the development of human society is predicated upon a realization that the economic structure, i.e. the ways in which goods are being produced, is the "foundation" upon which rests the "superstructure" of the political, moral, legal, and cultural framework of society. The very ideas of men, important though they may be, are but a reflection of the economic fabric of their time. In the final selection in this chapter, Victor Afanasyev attempts to clarify this relationship between the foundation and the superstructure of society. By applying Marxist-Leninist analysis, he traces this relationship from prehistoric society to present-day life in the Soviet Union, and he projects it even to the society of the future, the society of "perfect communism."

---

[4] Friedrich Engels (1820-1895), socialist; son of a wealthy manufacturer; Marx's friend, collaborator, and financial supporter.

WESTERN VIEWS

1. THE INEXORABLE WORLD OF KARL MARX *

ROBERT L. HEILBRONER
New School for Social Research

The philosophy [a new philosophy of history developed by Marx] was to take the name of dialectical materialism; *dialectical* because it incorporated Hegel's [1] idea of inherent change, and *materialism* because it grounded itself not in the world of ideas, but on the terrain of social and physical environment.

"The materialist conception of history," wrote Engels many years later in a tract aimed against a German professor named Eugen Dühring, "starts from the principle that production, and with production the exchange of its products, is the basis of every social order; that in every society which has appeared in history the distribution of the products, and with it the division of society into classes or estates, is determined by what is produced and how it is produced, and how the product is exchanged. According to this conception, the ultimate causes of all social changes and political revolutions are to be sought, not in the minds of men, in their increasing insight into eternal truth and justice, but in changes in the mode of production and exchange; they are to be sought not in the *philosophy* but in the *economics* of the epoch concerned."

The reasoning is not difficult to follow. Every society, says Marx, is built on an economic base, is ultimately grounded in the hard reality of human beings who have organized their activities in order to clothe and feed and house themselves. That organization can differ vastly from society to society and from era to era. It can be pastoral or built around hunting or grouped into handicraft units or structured into a complex industrial

---

* Excerpts reprinted from Robert L. Heilbroner, *The Worldly Philosophers*, Rev. Ed., 1961, pp. 119-123 and 129-142, by permission of Simon and Schuster, Inc. Permission for the British Empire by Eyre and Spottiswoode (Publishers) Ltd. Copyright © 1953, 1961 by Robert L. Heilbroner.

[1] George Wilhelm Friedrich Hegel (1770-1831), German philosopher. [Editor's note.]

whole. But whatever the form in which men organize to solve their basic economic problem, society will require a whole superstructure of non-economic activity and thought—it will need to be bound together by laws, supervised by a government, inspired by religion and philosophy.

But the superstructure of thought cannot be selected at random. It must mirror the foundation on which it is raised. No hunting community will evolve or could use the legal framework of an industrial society, and similarly an industrial community obviously requires an entirely different conception of law, order, and government than does a primitive village. Note that the doctrine of materialism does not toss away the catalytic function and creativity of ideas. It only maintains that thoughts and ideas are the *product* of environment, even though they aim to change that environment.

Materialism by itself would reduce ideas to mere passive accompaniments of economic activity. That was not Marx's contention. For the new theory was *dialectical* as well as materialist: it envisaged change, constant and inherent change; and in that never-ending flux the ideas emanating from one period would help to shape another. "Men make their own history," wrote Marx, commenting on the *coup d'état* of Louis Napoleon in 1852, "but they do not make it just as they please; they do not make it under circumstances chosen by themselves, but under circumstances directly found, given, and transmitted from the past."

But the dialectical—the changing—aspect of this theory of history did not depend merely on the interplay of ideas and social structures. There was another and far more powerful agent at work. The economic world itself was changing; the ultimate reality on which the structure of ideas was built was itself constantly in flux.

For example, the isolated markets of the Middle Ages began to lock fingers under the impetus of exploration and political unification, and a new commercial world was born. The old hand mill was replaced by the steam mill under the impetus of invention, and a new form of social organization called the factory came into being. In both cases the ultimate reality of economic life itself changed its form, and as it did, it forced a new social adaptation from the community in which it was embedded.

And once such a change had taken place, it carried with it a whole train of consequences. The market and the factory were incompatible with the feudal way of life—even though they were born amidst it. They demanded a new cultural and social context to go with them. And they helped in that difficult birthing process by creating their own new social classes: the market created a professional merchant class and the factory a proletariat.

But the process of social change was not merely a matter of new inventions pressing on old institutions: it was a matter of new classes displacing old ones. For each society is organized into a class structure, into aggregates of men who stand in some common relationship—favorable or otherwise—to the existing form of production. And social change threatens all of that. As the technical conditions of production change—as factories destroy handicraft industry, for example—the old classes find that their accustomed situation is changing too; those on top may find the ground cut from under them, while those who were on the bottom may be carried higher. We have seen just such an upset of the relative position of social classes in Ricardo's [2] day in England, when the capitalists, riding the wave of the Industrial Revolution, were threatening to usurp the time-honored prerogatives of the landed gentry.

Hence conflict develops. The classes whose position is jeopardized fight the classes whose position is enhanced: the feudal lord fights the rising merchant, and the guild master despises the young capitalist.

But the process of history pays no attention to likes and dislikes. Gradually conditions change and gradually, but surely, the classes of society are rearranged. Amid turmoil and anguish the division of wealth is altered. And thus history is a pageant of ceaseless struggle between classes to partition social wealth. For as long as the technics of society change, no existing division of wealth is immune from attack.

And what did this theory augur for the present? It pointed to revolution—inevitable revolution. For capitalism, according to this analysis, must also consist of a technical base of economic reality and a superstructure of a social class system. And if its technical base was evolving, then necessarily, its superstructure must be subject to increasing strain.

And that is exactly what Marx and Engels saw in 1848. The technical base of capitalism—its anchor in reality—was industrial production. Its superstructure was the system of private property, under which a portion of society's output went to those who owned its great technical apparatus. The conflict lay in the fact that the base and superstructure were incompatible.

Why? Because the base of industrial production—the actual making of goods—was a highly organized, integrated, interdependent process, whereas the superstructure of private property was the most highly individualistic of social systems. Hence the superstructure and the base clashed: factories necessitated social planning, and private property abhorred it; *capitalism* had become so complex that it needed direction but *capitalists* insisted on a ruinous freedom.

The result was twofold. First, capitalism must destroy itself. The planless nature of production must lead to a constant disorganization of economic activity—to crises and slumps and the social chaos of depression. The system was simply too complex; it was constantly getting out of joint, losing step, and overproducing one good while underproducing another.

---

[2] David Ricardo (1772-1823), English economist, follower of Adam Smith (see footnote 4, p. 9) advocate of laissez-faire. [Editor's note.]

Secondly, capitalism would unknowingly breed its own successor. Within its great factories it would not only create the technical base for socialism—mass production—but it would create as well a trained and disciplined *class* who would be the agents of socialism—the embittered proletariat. By its own inner dynamic, capitalism would produce its own downfall, and in the process, it would nourish its own enemy.

It was a profoundly revolutionary insight into history, not only for what it betokened for the future, but for the whole new perspective it opened upon the past. We have come to be familiar with the "economic interpretation" of history, and we can accept with equanimity a re-evaluation of the past with respect to the struggle, say, of the nascent seventeenth-century commercial classes and the aristocratic world of land and lineage. But for Marx and Engels, this was no mere exercise in historical reinterpretation. The dialectic led to the future and that future, as revealed by the *Communist Manifesto*,[3] pointed to an *inevitable* communist revolution which this same dialectic would produce. In somber words the *Manifesto* proclaimed: "The development of modern industry . . . cuts from under its feet the very foundation on which the bourgeoisie produces and appropriates products. What the bourgeoisie therefore produces, above all, are its own grave-diggers. Its fall and the victory of the proletariat are equally inevitable." . . .

"The history of capitalism," Stalin has written, "has entirely confirmed the theories of Marx and Engels concerning the laws of development of capitalist society . . . that must inevitably lead to the downfall of the whole capitalist system." What were those laws? What was Marx's prognosis for the system that he knew?

The answer lies in that enormous work *Das Kapital—Capital*. With Marx's agonizing meticulousness, it is remarkable that the work was ever finished—in a sense it never was. It was eighteen years in process; in 1851 it was to be done "in five weeks"; in 1859 "in six weeks"; in 1865 it was "done"—a huge bundle of virtually illegible manuscripts which took two years to edit into Volume I. When Marx died in 1883 two volumes remained: Engels put out Volume II in 1885 and the third in 1894. The final (fourth) volume did not emerge until 1910.

There are twenty-five hundred pages to read for anyone intrepid enough to make the effort. And what pages! Some deal with the tiniest of technical matters and labor them to a point of mathematical exhaustion; others swirl with passion and anger. This is an economist who has read *every* economist, a German pedant with a passion for footnotes, and an

---

[3] The *Communist Manifesto*, written by Marx in collaboration with Engels, was published in 1848. Originally intended as a statement of objectives of the newly formed Communist League, it turned out to be much more than that: it became an attempt to prove the inevitability of the downfall of capitalism, a call to revolution, a program for the future. [Editor's note.]

emotional critic who can write that "capital is dead labour, that vampire-like, only lives by sucking living labour" and who tells us that capital came into the world "dripping from head to foot, from every pore, with blood and dirt."

And yet one must not jump to the conclusion that this is merely a biased and irascible text inveighing against the sins of the wicked money-barons. It is shot through with remarks which betray the total involvement of the man with his theoretical adversary, but the great merit of the book, curiously enough, is its utter detachment from all considerations of morality. The book describes with fury, but it analyzes with cold logic. For what Marx has set for his goal is to discover the intrinsic tendencies of the capitalist system, its inner laws of motion, and in so doing, he has eschewed the easy but less convincing means of merely expatiating on its manifest shortcomings. Instead he erects the most rigorous, the purest capitalism imaginable and within this rarefied abstract system, with an imaginary capitalism in which all the obvious defects of real life are removed, he seeks his quarry. For if he can prove that the best of all possible capitalisms is nonetheless headed for certain disaster, it is certainly easy to demonstrate that real capitalism will follow the same path, only quicker.

And so he sets the stage. We enter a world of perfect capitalism: no monopolies, no unions, no special advantages for anyone. It is a world in which every commodity sells at exactly its proper price. And that proper price is its *value*—a tricky word. For the value of a commodity, says Marx (and Smith[4] and Ricardo before him), is the amount of labor it has within itself. If it takes twice as much labor to make hats as shoes, then hats will sell for twice the price of shoes. The labor, of course, need not be direct manual labor; it may be overhead labor which is spread over many commodities or it may be the labor which once went into making a machine and which the machine now slowly passes on to the products it shapes. But no matter what its form, everything is eventually reducible to labor, and all commodities, in this perfect system, will be priced according to the amount of labor, direct or indirect, which they contain.

In this world stand the two great protagonists of the capitalist drama: worker and capitalist—the landlord has by now been relegated to a minor position in society. . . . The worker . . . is a free bargaining agent who enters the market to dispose of the one commodity he commands—labor-power—and if he gets a rise in wages he will not be so foolish as to squander it in a self-defeating proliferation of his numbers.[5]

[4] Adam Smith (1723-1790), Scottish economist, father of modern economics. His *Wealth of Nations* is usually accredited as the economic treatise upon which rests the philosophy of a "free enterprise" system. [Editor's note.]

[5] This is a reference to Malthus' theory of population (Thomas Robert Malthus, 1766-1834). Malthus contended that population would always tend to outrun food supply, and that increased incomes would only induce workers to have more children. [Editor's note.]

The capitalist faces him in the arena. He is not a bad fellow at heart, although his greed and lust for wealth are caustically described in those chapters which leave the abstract world for a look into 1860 England. But it is worth noting that he is not money-hungry from mere motives of rapacity: he is an owner-entrepreneur engaged in an endless race against his fellow owner-entrepreneurs; he *must* strive for accumulation, for in the competitive environment in which he operates, one accumulates or one gets accumulated.

The stage is set and the characters take their places. But now the first difficulty appears. How, asks Marx, can profits exist in such a situation? If everything sells for its exact value, then who gets an unearned increment? No one dares to raise his price above the competitive one, and even if one seller managed to gouge a buyer, that buyer would only have less to spend elsewhere in the economy—one man's profit would thus be another man's loss. How can there be profit in the *whole* system if everything exchanges for its honest worth?

It seems like a paradox. Profits are easy to explain if we assume that there are monopolies in the system which need not obey the leveling influences of competition or if we admit that capitalists may pay labor less than it is worth. But Marx will have none of that—this is to be *pure* capitalism which will dig its own grave.

He finds the answer to the dilemma in one commodity which is different from all others. That commodity is labor-power. For the laborer, like the capitalist, sells his product for exactly what it is worth—for its value. And its value, like the value of everything else that is sold, is the amount of labor that goes into it—in this case, the amount of labor that it takes to "make" labor-power. In other words, a laborer's salable energies are worth the amount of socially necessary labor it takes to keep that laborer alive. Smith and Ricardo would have agreed entirely: the true value of a workman is the wage he needs in order to exist. It is his subsistence wage.

So far, so good. But here comes the key to profit. The laborer who contracts to work can only ask for a wage which is his due. What that wage will be depends, as we have seen, on the amount of labor-time it takes to keep a man alive. If it takes six hours of society's labor to maintain a workingman, then (if labor is priced at one dollar an hour), he is "worth" six dollars a day. No more.

But the laborer who gets a job does not contract to work only six hours a day. That would be just long enough to support himself. On the contrary, he agrees to work a full eight-hour, or in Marx's time a ten- or eleven-hour, day. Hence he will produce a full ten or eleven hours' worth of value and he will get paid for only six. His wage will cover his subsistence which is his true "value," but in return he will sell the value which he produces in a full working day. And this is how profit enters the system.

Marx called this layer of unpaid work "surplus value." But it is quite devoid of moral indignation. The worker is only entitled to the *value* of his labor-power. He gets it in full. But meanwhile the capitalist gets the full value of his workers' whole working day, and this is longer than the hours for which he paid. Hence when the capitalist sells his products, he can afford to sell them at *their* true value and still realize a profit. For there is more labor-time embodied in his products than the labor-time for which he was forced to pay.

How can this state of affairs come about? It happens because the capitalists monopolize one thing—access to the means of production themselves. If a worker isn't willing to work a full working day, he doesn't get a job. Like everyone else in the system, a worker has no right and no power to ask for more than his own worth as a commodity. The system is perfectly equitable and yet all workers are cheated, for they are forced to work a longer time than their own self-sustenance demands.

Does this sound strange? Remember that Marx is describing a time when the working day was long—sometimes unendurably long—and when wages were, by and large, little more than it took to keep body and soul together. The idea of surplus value may make little sense in a world where the sweatshop is very largely a thing of the past, but it was not merely a theoretical construct at the time that Marx was writing. One example may suffice: at a Manchester factory in 1862 the average workweek for a period of a month and a half was 84 hours! For the previous 18 months it had been 78½ hours.

But all this is still only the setting for the drama. We have the protagonists, we have their motives, we have the clue to the plot in the discovery of "surplus value." And now the play is set in motion.

All capitalists have profits. But they are all in competition. Hence they try to accumulate and so to expand their scales of output, at the expense of their competitors. But expansion is not so easy. It requires more laborers and to get them the capitalists must bid against each other for the working force. Wages tend to rise. Conversely, surplus value tends to fall. . . .

To Smith and Ricardo the solution to the dilemma lay in the propensity of the working force to increase its numbers with every boost in pay. But Marx has ruled out this possibility. He doesn't argue about it; he simply brands the Malthusian doctrine "a libel on the human race"— after all, the proletariat, which is to be the ruling class of the future, cannot be so shortsighted as to dissipate its gains through mere unbridled physical appetite. But he rescues his capitalists just the same. For he says that they will meet the threat of rising wages by introducing laborsaving machinery into their plants. That will throw part of the working force back onto the street and there, as an Industrial Reserve Army, it will serve the same function as Malthus' teeming population: it will compete wages right back down to their former "value"—the subsistence level.

But now comes the crucial twist. It seems as though the capitalist has saved the day, for he has prevented wages from rising by creating unemployment through machinery. But not so fast. By the very process through which he hopes to free himself from one horn of the dilemma, he impales himself on the other.

For as he substitutes machines for men, he is simultaneously substituting nonprofitable means of production for profitable ones. Remember that in this never-never world, no one makes a profit by merely sharp bargaining. Whatever a machine will be worth to a capitalist, you can be sure that he paid full value for it. If a machine will yield ten thousand dollars' worth of value over its whole life, our capitalist was charged the full ten thousand dollars in the first place. It is only from his living labor that he can realize a profit, only from the unpaid-for hours of surplus working time. Hence when he reduces the number or proportion of workers, he is killing the goose that laid the golden egg.

And yet, unhappy fellow, he has to. There is nothing Mephistophelean about his actions. He is only obeying his impulse to accumulate and trying to stay abreast of his competitors. As his wages rise, he *must* introduce laborsaving machinery to cut his costs and rescue his profit margin—if he does not, his neighbor will. But since he must substitute machinery for labor, he must also narrow the base out of which he gleans his profits. It is a kind of Greek drama where men go willy-nilly to their fate, and in which they all unwittingly cooperate to bring about their own destruction.

For now the die is cast. As his profits shrink, each capitalist will redouble his efforts to put new laborsaving, cost-cutting machinery in his factory. It is only by getting a step ahead of the parade that he can hope to make a profit. But since everyone is doing precisely the same thing, the ratio of labor (and hence surplus value) to total output shrinks still further. The rate of profit falls and falls. And now doom lies ahead. Profits are cut to the point at which production is no longer profitable at all. Consumption dwindles as machines displace men and the number of employed fails to keep pace with output. Bankruptcies ensue. There is a scramble to dump goods on the market and in the process smaller firms go under. A capitalist crisis is at hand.

Not forever. As workers are thrown out of work, they are forced to accept subvalue wages. As machinery is dumped, the stronger capitalists can acquire machines for less than their true value. After a time, surplus value reappears. The forward march is taken up again. But it leads to the same catastrophic conclusion: competition for workers; higher wages, labor-displacing machinery; a smaller base for surplus value; still more frenzied competition; collapse. And each collapse is worse than the preceding one. In the periods of crisis, the bigger firms absorb the smaller ones, and when the industrial monsters eventually go down, the wreckage is far greater than when the little enterprises buckle.

And then, one day, the drama ends. Marx's picture of it has all the eloquence of a description of Damnation: "Along with the constantly diminishing number of the magnates of capital, who usurp and monopolize all advantages of this process of transformation, grows the mass of misery, oppression, slavery, degradation, exploitation; but with this too grows the revolt of the working-class, a class always increasing in numbers, and disciplined, united, organized by the very mechanism of the process of capitalist production itself. . . . centralization of the means of production and socialization of labour at last reach a point where they become incompatible with their capitalist integument. This integument bursts asunder. The knell of capitalist private property sounds. The expropriators are expropriated."

And so the drama ends in the inevitable overthrow which Marx had envisioned in the dialectic. The system—the *pure* system—breaks down as it works upon itself to squeeze out its own source of energy, surplus value. The breakdown is hastened by the constant instability which arises from the essentially planless nature of the economy, and although there are forces at work which act both to prolong and to hasten its end, its final death struggle is inescapable. And if the pure system is unworkable, what possible hope can there be for the real system, with all its imperfections, monopolies, cutthroat tactics, and heedless profit seeking? . . .

What are we to make of his apocalyptic argument?

There is an easy way of disposing of the whole thing. Remember that the system is built on value—labor value—and that the key to its demise lies in that special phenomenon called surplus value. But the real world consists not of "values" but of real tangible prices. Marx must show that the world of dollars and cents mirrors, in some approximate fashion, the abstract world that he has created. But in making the transition from a value-world to a price-world, he lands in the most terrible tangle of mathematics. In fact he makes a mistake.

It is not an irreparable mistake and by going through an even worse tangle of mathematics one can make the Marxist equations come out "right"—one can, that is, explain a correspondence between the prices that really obtain in life and the underlying values in terms of labor-time. But the critics who pointed out the error were hardly interested in setting the scheme aright and their judgment that Marx was "wrong" was taken as final. When the equations were finally justified, no one paid much attention. For regardless of its mathematical purity, the Marxian rigmarole is at best a cumbersome and difficult framework and an unnecessarily laborious method of getting at the required understanding of how capitalism works.

But while we might be tempted to toss the whole analysis to one side because it is awkward and inflexible, to do so would be to overlook its values. Marx, after all, did not strip capitalism down to its barest essentials merely to indulge his bent for abstract argument. He did so because he believed that in the simplicity of a theoretical world the mechanics of the actual world would lie clearly exposed; because he hoped that the very starkness of his model world would highlight tendencies hidden in real life.

And so it did. For all its clumsiness, Marx's model of the capitalist world seemed to *work,* to display a kind of life of its own. Given its basic assumptions—the *mise en scène* of its characters, their motives and their milieu—the situation it presented *changed,* and changed in a way that was foreseeable, precise, and inevitable. We have seen what these changes are: how profits fell, how capitalists sought new machinery, how each boom ended in a crash, how small businesses were absorbed in each debacle by the larger firms. But all this was still within the framework of an abstract world: now Marx applied his findings on paper to the real world about him—the actual world of capitalism, he said, must also display these trends.

He called the trends the "laws of motion" of a capitalist system—the path which capitalism would tread over future time. And the astonishing fact is that almost all these predictions have come true!

For profits *do* tend to fall in an enterprise economy. The insight was not original with Marx, nor do profits fall for the reason he gave—we can dispense with the idea of exploitation contained in the theory of surplus value. But as Adam Smith or Ricardo or Mill pointed out—and as any businessman will vouchsafe—the pressures of competition and rising wages will serve quite as well. Impregnable monopolies aside (and these are few), profits are both the hallmark of capitalism and its Achilles' heel, for no business can *permanently* maintain its prices much above its costs. There is only one way in which profits can be perpetuated: a business— or an entire economy—must grow.

But growth implies the second prediction of the Marxist model: the ceaseless quest for new techniques. It was no accident that industrial capitalism dates from the Industrial Revolution, for as Marx made clear, technological progress is not merely an accompaniment of capitalism but a vital ingredient. Business *must* innovate, invent, and experiment if it is to survive; the business that rests content on its past achievements is not long for this enterprising world. It is interesting to note that recently one large chemical company announced that sixty per cent of its income came from products that were unknown ten years ago; and although this is an exceptionally inventive industry, the relationship between industrial inventiveness and profitability generally holds.

The model showed still two more tendencies for capitalism which have also come to pass. We hardly need document the existence of business cycles over the past ninety years nor the emergence of giant business enterprise. But we might remark on the daring of Marx's prediction. When *Das Kapital* appeared, bigness was the exception rather than the rule and small enterprise still ruled the roost. To claim that huge firms would come to dominate the business scene was as startling a prediction in 1867 as would be a statement today that fifty years hence America will be a land in which small-scale proprietorships will have displaced giant corporations.

It was, all things considered, an extraordinary bit of foresight. And note this: all these changes, vast and portentous as they were, could not have been unearthed purely by examining the world as it appeared to Marx's eyes. For these are historical changes, slow in their unfolding and stretched out over time; as real, but as unnoticeable, as the growth of a tree. It was only by reducing the economic system to a microcosm and then by observing that microcosm in its speeded-up life span that this drift of the future could be apprehended.

It was not, of course, exact. Marx thought that profits would not only fall *within* the business cycle, which they do, but that they would display a long downward secular trend; this does not appear to have taken place. Marx did not stop to consider that the economic particles with which he played had feelings and volitions and consciences that could also change and that they would not therefore behave with the imperturbable predictability of the particles under a chemist's microscope. But for all its shortcomings—and it is far from infallible, as we shall see—the Marxist model of how capitalism worked was extraordinarily prophetic.

But everything that Marx had predicted so far was, after all, innocuous. There remained the final prediction of the model; for as the reader will remember, in the end Marx's "pure capitalism" *collapsed.*

Let it be said at the outset that this prediction as well cannot be lightly brushed aside. In Russia and Eastern Europe capitalism has disappeared; in Scandinavia and Britain it has been partially abandoned; in Germany and Italy it drifted into fascism and emerged from its bath of fire in less than perfect health. Indeed, almost everywhere except in the United States capitalism is on the defensive; and while wars, brute political power, exigencies of fate, and the determined efforts of revolutionaries have all contributed their share, the grim truth is that its demise has largely been for the very reason Marx foresaw: it broke down.

Why did it break down? Partly because it developed the instability Marx said it would. A succession of business crises, compounded by a plague of wars, destroyed the faith of the lower and middle classes in the system. But that is not the entire answer—we too have had our wars and depressions, and capitalism here is very much alive. Something else spelled the difference between survival and destruction: European capitalism failed not so much for economic as for *social* reasons.

And Marx predicted this too!

For Marx recognized that the economic difficulties of the system were not insuperable. Although antimonopoly legislation or antibusiness cycle policies were unknown in Marx's day, such activities were not inconceivable: there was nothing inevitable in the *physical* sense about Marx's vision. The Marxist prediction of decay was founded on a conception of capitalism in which it was *socially* impossible for a government to set wrongs aright; intellectually, ideologically, even emotionally impossible. The cure for capitalism's failings would require that a government would have to rise above the interests of one class alone—and that, as Marx's doctrine of historical materialism revealed, was to assume that men could free themselves from the shackles of their immediate economic self-interest.

And it is just this lack of social flexibility, this bondage to short-sighted interest, which weakened European capitalism. For one who has read the works of Marx it is frightening to look back at the grim determination with which so many nations steadfastly hewed to the very course which he insisted would lead to their undoing. It was as if their governments were unconsciously vindicating Marx's prophecy by obstinately doing exactly what he said they would. When in Russia under the Tsars all democratic trade-unionism was ruthlessly stamped out, when in England and Germany monopolies and cartels were officially encouraged, the Marxist dialectic looked balefully prescient indeed. Even today, when one considers that in France or Italy or Greece capitalist governments still cannot collect the taxes they levy on their own business communities, when one inspects the enormous gulf between rich and poor and sees evidence of the indifference of the former for the latter, then one has the uneasy feeling that the psychological stereotypes which Marx cast in his historical drama were all too truly drawn from life.

And it is these very facts which give us the clue as to why capitalism survived in the United States. We have had our share of reactionaries and revolutionaries. The economic history of the United States contains more than enough exploitation and ugliness. But capitalism here nonetheless evolved in a land untouched by the dead hand of aristocratic lineage and age-old class attitudes. Hence we have faced up to the economic problems of capitalism with social attitudes that sprang from a less hardened heritage: attitudes of experiment and adaptation, a healthy disrespect for too much power, public or private, and a social flexibility that has prevented the development of brittle and die-hard class structures.

It is in these attitudes that the answer to Marxian analysis lies. Marx was not so much "wrong" in his economic vision as he was wrong in assuming that his psychological and sociological preconceptions were fixed and unalterable. The laws of motion which his model of capitalism revealed may still be visible in American capitalism—indeed, they are—but they are faced with a set of remedies which spring from political and social attitudes quite beyond his imagination.

Some of these remedies arise from new attitudes and values on the part of business itself. But the most important remedies come from a different source: the government. As we have seen, for Marx, a government was as inevitably a tool of the capitalist class as a revolutionary proletariat was inevitably a product of factory life. There was reason to form such ideas in the dark atmosphere of England in the 1860's—let us not forget that the world Marx knew, economically and politically, was cruel, cold, and doctrinaire. In too much of Europe it never quite lost that unhealthy cast—and the result for European capitalism was catastrophic. But in the New World new attitudes have emerged: the idea of democracy, the idea of an impartial government seeking to reconcile divergent interests, the idea of a class *struggle* without a class *war*. Our government has often been tinctured with class interest, but it has not been tainted with it to the point of self-destruction. All this would have seemed only a wishful fantasy to Marx.

The fact is that capitalism was capable of developing in many directions. The tragedy is that for much of the world—and for all of the communist world—the stereotypes with which Marx set his plot into motion, the grasping Manchester millowner and the blindly selfish regimes of 1848, are still taken as true likenesses of capitalism everywhere.

But shorn of its overtones of inevitable doom, the Marxist analysis cannot be disregarded. It remains the gravest, most penetrating examination the capitalist system has ever undergone. It is not an examination conducted along moral lines with head-wagging and tongue-clucking over the iniquities of the profit motive—this is the stuff of the Marxist revolutionary but not of the Marxist economist. For all its passion, it is a dispassionate appraisal and it is for this reason that its somber findings must be soberly considered.

To repeat an earlier statement: it is with Karl Marx the Revolutionary that the world has been preoccupied, with Marxism as an intolerant force for the enslavement of free opinion. Certainly that is the immediate battle. And yet it is not with Marx the Revolutionary that capitalism must finally contend. When Khrushchev boasts that communism will "bury" capitalism, it is not military prowess but economic theory which gives him his certitude. In the end the figure who must be proven wrong is Marx the Economist, Marx the finicky scholar who laboriously sought to prove, through the welter of surface distraction, that the essence of capitalism is *self*-destruction. The answer to Marx lies not so much in pointing out the injustices of communism as in demonstrating that in a social atmosphere of which Marx never dreamed, capitalism can continue to evolve and to adapt its institutions to the never-satisfied demands of social justice.

2. THE COMMUNIST IDEOLOGY: LENIN'S CONTRIBUTION *

GERHART NIEMEYER

University of Notre Dame

LENIN'S VIEWS ON CAPITALISM

"Monopoly Capitalism"

Lenin, in his revised description of the present society, derived key ideas from two books: *Imperialism* by J. A. Hobson (1902), which discussed the division of the world among the leading European nations, and *Finanzkapital* by Rudolf Hilferding (1910), which showed how huge banking enterprises controlled vast economic processes. These two ideas Lenin combined into the following picture of the present capitalist society.

The salient feature of modern capitalism is the rule of monopoly. Competition (which Marx said was the basic law of capitalist development) has given way to the concentration of enormous wealth in a few hands.

. . . This transformation of competition into monopoly is one of the most important—if not the most important—phenomena of modern capitalist economy. . . .[1]

Marx asserted that power in capitalist society belonged to the factory owner who could buy the worker's labor power and employ it to produce surplus value. Lenin says that power now is in the hands of the financier. . . .

The concentration of production; the monopoly arising therefrom; the merging or coalescence of banking with industry: this is the history of finance capital and what gives the term "finance capital" its content.[2]

Monopoly, in the form of finance capital, governs the present society in all its aspects. . . .

* Excerpts from *Facts on Communism,* Vol. I (Committee on Un-American Activities, House Document No. 336, 1960) reprinted by permission of the author and the publisher.

[1] V. I. Lenin, "Imperialism, The Highest Stage of Capitalism" (January-July 1916), *Selected Works* (New York: International Publishers, 1943), vol. V, pp. 15, 21, 22.

[2] *Ibid.,* p. 42.

The "Need for Foreign Markets"

The driving power of capitalism, as Lenin describes it, is no longer the need of one capitalist to compete with the other, but the need of the banker-monopolist to export excess capital, obtain more foreign markets, and get them under his exclusive control. . . .

This tendency, according to Lenin, explains not only the political system under which modern (capitalistic) nations live, but also the international political developments on a world scale:

Monopolist capitalist combines—cartels, syndicates, trusts—divide among themselves, first of all, the whole internal market of a country. . . .[3]
[Then] a struggle began which . . . is fittingly called "the struggle for the division of the world." [4]

Division and Redivision of the World

Now, this division of the world is not merely a division of economic spheres of influence, but of political control. This is where imperialism enters.

. . . Imperialism . . . means the partition of the world, and the exploitation of other countries . . . which means high monopoly profits for a handful of very rich countries. . . .[5]

In such a "parasitic" state, even parts of the working class are corrupted and stop being revolutionary. . . .

The New Image of Capitalism

Now Lenin has just about exchanged all the parts of the Marxist structure for new ones and still retained the structure! The "exploiters" are, in addition to factory owners, the rich countries; the "exploited" are, in addition to industrial workers, the colonies. The "chain of bondage" is no longer the sale of labor-power on the commodity market, but the political control of territory, and the economic control of markets. . . .

Thus, without giving up Marx's idea of the irreconcilable class struggle and Marx's condemnation of the present (capitalist) society Lenin managed to explain . . . that capitalism has not yet collapsed because the advanced capitalistic societies found a new field of expansion which yielded them new wealth, that the lot of the people under capitalism has improved at the expense of the colonial populations, and that the upper part of the working class has allowed itself to become "corrupted" into preferring this shared wealth to the cause of the revolution. The latter observation served Lenin also as a means to read his opponents, the social-democratic parties, out of the "proletarian movement.". . .

---

[3] *Ibid.,* p. 61.
[4] *Ibid.,* p. 64.
[5] *Ibid.,* p. 95.

LENIN'S VIEWS ABOUT THE DYNAMICS
OF CAPITALISM

Among Marx's basic concepts was also that of the inevitably catastrophic development of capitalism. Lenin did not abandon this concept,
either, but gave it a new content that seemed compatible with the all but
catastrophic course which capitalism had taken since Marx wrote. Monopoly capitalism, Lenin said, is the "highest stage" of capitalism.

> . . . Monopoly is the transition from capitalism to a higher system.
> . . . Imperialism is the monopoly stage of capitalism.[6]

In other words, the "higher system," socialism, is at hand. But will
it grow organically out of capitalism? Will it emerge peacefully? No,
answers Lenin, it will come as the result of "inner contradictions" in the
capitalist system in combination with a violent struggle between the ruling powers of that system and the "gravediggers" the system has produced
within itself. . . .

"Inherent Contradictions of Imperialism"

There are two kind of "contradictions" which, according to Lenin,
contribute to the downfall of the system: the "contradictions" between the
leading industrial powers, and that between the rich countries and the
emerging power of the formerly colonial areas. . . .

> We ask is there *under capitalism* any means of remedying the disparity
> between the development of productive forces and the accumulation of capital
> on the one side, and the division of colonies and "spheres of influence" by
> finance capital on the other side—other than by resorting to war? [7]
> . . . imperialist wars are absolutely inevitable under *such* an economic
> system, *as long as* private property in the means of production exists.[8]

Thus, Lenin has now combined "war" with "exploitation" as the evil
for which he indicts capitalism.

In the Marxist concept of history, the reader will remember, it appeared inevitable that capitalist society be supplanted by socialist society.
Lenin here adds . . . [that] the downfall of capitalism . . . will be
hastened by the revolutionary action of all the colonial peoples. . . .

Weaknesses of Lenin's Concept

Lenin's picture of the world as an imperialist, predatory, oppressive
system torn by conflict and wars, is, in its way, as impressive at first

---

[6] *Ibid.,* p. 81.

[7] *Ibid.,* pp. 89, 90.

[8] Lenin, Preface to the French and German editions of "Imperialism, The Highest Stage of Capitalism" (July 6, 1920), *Selected Works* (New York: International
Publishers, 1943), vol. V, p. 8.

glance as is Marx's picture of spiralling capitalistic production of wealth and misery. Both have enough support in observable facts to appear plausible. But Lenin's explanation, no less than that of Marx, has been refuted by actual developments. . . . In other words, Lenin's *Imperialism* is—just as little as that of Marx's *Capital*—a true picture of democratic industrial society and its development.

COMMUNISTS IN "PRESENT-DAY SOCIETY"

It is now becoming more and more clear that the end of the sway of capitalism is drawing near in other countries, too, and that capitalism is a system that has outlived its age and is bound to perish. The future is ours! The future is for Marxism-Leninism! The future is for communism! . . .[9]

This view of "present-day society" is not new for Communists. It has been implicit in Communist doctrine from the beginning. . . .

Communist Attitudes Toward "Present-day Society"

. . . The proper attitude of Marxists toward "present-day society" has been the chief issue between Communists and democratic socialists. . . . The revolutionary alternative looks upon "present-day society" as something that is utterly corrupt as well as utterly doomed, so that one need take no interest in its problems other than to the end of hastening its collapse and of detaching the masses from its authorities. This view is the one on which Lenin insisted as the core of communism. . . .

There is no common ground between the Communists and their fellow-citizens . . . for the Communists do not regard themselves as citizens of "present-day societies" and do not share with others the desire to solve "present-day" problems. They have put all their eggs in the basket of the future. . . .

Communists should know that at all events the future belongs to them. . . .[10]

[According to] Communist ideology, Capitalism is . . . the last historical stage before socialism; as a society, it is considered worthless; as a system, it is believed about to tumble down. Revolution is the cause of the future; its adherents look to the future alone and to the present as a mere condition for hastening the advent of the future. . . .

LENIN'S VIEWS OF COMMUNIST REVOLUTION

What Marx left to his followers was the myth of the Socialist Revolution: a great convulsive crisis, a political explosion of the oppressed class

[9] Excerpts from Khrushchev speech November 3, 1958; *New York Times,* Nov. 5, 1958, p. 2.
[10] Lenin, " 'Left-Wing' Communism, An Infantile Disorder" (Apr. 27, 1920), *Selected Works* (New York: International Publishers, 1943), vol. X, p. 144.

of proletarians, which would at one fell swoop end the rule of the bourgeoisie and thus all class societies. . . .

Lenin, while still making full use of the myth of the revolution, saw in practice not one single threshold event that would separate two ages from each other, but rather a protracted struggle extending over an entire epoch, a struggle in which no single event or explosion could accomplish the passage from one age to the other. . . . The period of the struggle extends, in Lenin's views, from the time at which Communist forces organize, through both the bourgeois and socialist revolutions, into an indefinite duration of proletarian dictatorship. . . . Since to Lenin the revolution means not so much a liberating explosion occurring at the point of highest development of capitalism, but rather a protracted class struggle, he made a number of statements which seemed to favor more backward countries as the most suitable theater in which to carry forth this struggle. At any rate, Communist doctrine, evolving from Lenin's concepts, now calls for a concentration of the revolutionary blow on the "weakest link" of the entire "chain" of "imperialism."

Quite logically, then, Lenin expected the revolution in Russia to be decided not solely by the social forces of the proletariat, but rather by the proletariat combined with the peasantry, both led by the party. . . .

The entire world is now pictured as one single system of "imperialist" capitalism in which all countries hang together as by a chain. The fight against this system might concentrate on any point of the chain. No point is decisive. Every attack is an attempt to weaken the system as a whole. This is an entirely new concept of the revolution, as different from Marx's idea as the atom bomb from the battle axe. Stalin acknowledges this. . . .

Marx saw the proletarian revolution coming when "capitalism had fully matured." Lenin sees it when "the decisive battle has fully matured." . . . This recipe does not depend on a highly developed capitalism. As a matter of fact, says Lenin:

> . . . we must be able to reckon with the fact that the world socialist revolution cannot begin so easily in the advanced countries as the revolution began in Russia. . . .[11]

Once Communist power is established, the fight, however, does not stop. The revolution then continues in the form of the "Dictatorship of the Proletariat." The fight goes on against the class enemy, the bourgeoisie:

> . . . whose resistance is increased *tenfold* by its overthrow . . . and whose power lies, not only in the strength of international capital . . . but also in the *force of habit,* in the strength of *small production.* . . .[12]

[11] Lenin, "War and Peace" (Mar. 7, 1918), *Selected Works* (New York: International Publishers, 1943), vol. VII, p. 294.

[12] Lenin, " 'Left-Wing' Communism, an Infantile Disorder" (Apr. 27, 1920), *Selected Works* (New York: International Publishers, 1943), vol. X, p. 60.

Here Lenin changes the last of Marx's concepts which he has still retained, that of the bourgeoisie. For Marx, the bourgeoisie was the capitalistic class, the class which, with the help of capital, developed large-scale production and employed wage laborers. Lenin has shifted the "proletarian" revolution from advanced capitalist countries to backward countries, he has substituted for the proletariat first the combination of proletariat and peasantry and then "all toilers," and now he pins the label of bourgeoisie on the "small producers," which is Communist jargon meaning, in this context, the peasantry. . . .[13]

For Lenin, the "class struggle" goes on even after the "proletarians" (i.e., Communists) have seized power, as long as the former order of society still continues to mold the habits of people. In the "force of habit," certain elements of hostile class rule persist. . . .

In other words, the end of the revolution will come as a "gradual and spontaneous process" of people acquiring perfectly social habits. As long as this has not happened . . . the revolutionary class struggle must continue. . . .

THE COMMUNIST PARTY

The definition of the nature and function of the Communist Party by a whole series of ideological concepts is the central Leninist idea. Marx, in the Communist Manifesto, had declared that "the Communists do not form a separate party opposed to other working class parties. They have no interests separate and apart from those of the proletariat as a whole." . . .

Lenin insisted on a new type of organization. Although this organization is still called a "party," it is not a genuine political party in the sense of considering itself a part of a whole, nor in the sense of functioning mainly for the purpose of organizing voters in a competitive system of politics. Rather, it was from the beginning envisaged as a combat organization, a kind of ideological-military army. . . .

Lenin set up the Communist Party as an "organization of professional revolutionaries." Such an organization is required, according to Lenin, because the class struggle is above all a "political struggle." . . .

The party therefore must be—

. . . A small, compact core, consisting of reliable, experienced and hard-

[13] "Peasantry" is a term used by Marxists to connote the mass of farmers whose production is based on private property but not on the large-scale employment of labor. . . .

Lenin assumes that as long as agricultural production continues in forms that essentially differ from those of factory production it will perpetuate the existence of a peasant class apart from the proletariat, and that from the "mode of life" of the peasantry a "bourgeois consciousness" as well as tendencies toward the renewal of capitalism will continue to emerge.

ened workers, with responsible agents in the principal districts and connected by all the rules of strict secrecy with the organisations of revolutionaries. . . .[14]

It must consist of people—

. . . who will devote to the revolution not only their spare evenings, but the whole of their lives. . . .[15]

"Democratic Centralism"

It follows from the entire concept of the party, its purpose as a combat organization, its foundation of "true" theory, its position as the vanguard of history's movement, that there can be no question of democracy within the party. Lenin, as has already been shown, conceived the party as built "from above" rather than "from below." He coined the term "democratic centralism" to denote the combination of two features already foreshadowed in the relation between the party and the masses; strict guidance from a small center and broad "participation" of large numbers of people in the activities flowing from this guidance. . . .

Later, the principle of "democratic centralism" was made a worldwide requirement for any party that wanted to call itself Communist:

13. The parties affiliated to the Communist International must be built up on the principle of democratic *centralism*. In the present epoch of acute civil war the Communist Party will be able to perform its duty only if it is organised in the most centralised manner, only if iron discipline bordering on military discipline prevails in it, and if its party centre is a powerful organ of authority, enjoining wide powers and the general confidence of the members of the party.[16]

Again, Stalin states the same principle in its most concise and systematic form:

. . . The achievement and maintenance of the dictatorship of the proletariat is impossible without a party which is strong by reason of its solidarity and iron discipline. . . .
The Party represents unity of will, which precludes all factionalism and division of authority in the Party.[17]

The Party as the Priesthood of "Truth"

The logic of all these ideas points to one final conclusion about the party, a conclusion which has not so much been explicitly stated as a theory, but has been implied as a principle in action: *The party alone*

[14] Lenin, "What Is To Be Done?" (1901-1902), *Selected Works* (New York: International Publishers, 1943), vol. II, p. 133.
[15] Lenin, "The Urgent Tasks of Our Movement" (December 1900), *Selected Works* (New York: International Publishers, 1943), vol. II, p. 14.
[16] Lenin, "The Conditions of Affiliation to the Communist International" (July 1920), *Selected Works* (New York: International Publishers, 1943), vol. X, p. 204.
[17] Stalin, "The Foundations of Leninism," *Problems of Leninism* (Moscow: Foreign Languages Publishing House, 1953), pp. 106, 107.

is the possessor of truth. We must recall that truth, for a Communist, is the unfolding movement of social forces, according to the "laws" of history. . . .

The party, in the eyes of Communists, is thus not a mere political expedient but a kind of priesthood administering the truth of history. It is, for Communists, not just an organization but also a spiritual home. At any rate, there can be no other spiritual home for someone committed to the doctrines of the class struggle, the socialist revolution, and the laws of history, as Lenin teaches them.

Functions of the State

The Communist-ruled state has three functions: repression, economic-organizational rule, and cultural-educational rule. . . .[18] This means that, contrary to the function of the state in a normal society, the Soviet state directly organizes *all* activities of human life. . . .

Official Definitions

. . . The Communists cannot escape the promise of eventual stateless freedom, of the "withering away" that has been made by the founders of their movement. Hence, they officially define their totalitarian, dictatorial, and ever increasing state power as something that is more free, more democratic, and closer to the people than other regimes. . . .

The use of the term "democratic" here is based on dogmatic definitions of the character of a state in a given society, rather than on any test as to what extent a regime actually reflects the preferences and values of the people. By definition of historical materialism, a capitalist state *cannot* be democratic, whereas a Soviet state *must* be democratic. . . .

THE ROLE OF THE SOVIET UNION

The Soviet Union is one of the "great powers" in the world. This particular "great power" plays a role in Communist ideology. It figures in that ideology as an instrument of the Communist revolution. It assumed that role when the Communists, having seized control in Russia, decided to consolidate their regime in that country rather than move on toward a chain reaction of revolutions in other countries. Had they chosen to do the latter, the revolution would have been propelled by the combination of Communist parties in all the industrial countries in the world, and Soviet Russia would not have occupied a specially prominent position as the foremost instrument of the revolution. The decision of the Communist leaders first to develop the Russian base rather than to fan out came to

---

[18] G. Glezerman, *Soviet Socialist State* (Moscow: Foreign Languages Publishing House, 1955). These functions can be found summarized in any Soviet textbook. We have chosen here a pamphlet by Glezerman, for purposes of illustration.

be embodied in the doctrine called "socialism in one country," which is now part and parcel of the Communist ideology. . . .

Socialism in One Country

"Socialism in one country" is a formula characterizing a new situation and a new doctrine of the revolution. Marx and Engels, who thought in terms of "society" asserting itself against the distorting and oppressive action of the state, could not see how a socialist society could replace bourgeois society except on a worldwide scale. They did envisage national revolutionary action but felt that socialism would be possible only insofar as national revolutions overthrew bourgeois regimes everywhere. Lenin, too, for most of his political life had looked for revolutions in the industrial countries of the West and had often expressed his conviction that the Bolsheviks could not succeed in their revolution unless helped by successful revolutions elsewhere. Nevertheless, he gave in fact top priority to the problem of consolidating the Bolsheviks' power in Russia. Hence the new thesis which commits Communist ideology to the model of the Russian revolution and to Russia as the model country. . . .

"Peaceful Coexistence"

Applied to the foreign relations of the Soviet Union, this adds up to a strategy of "peaceful coexistence" in a period in which the Soviet Union is still in a "minority position," or, better, "peaceful coexistence" in foreign relations coupled with the exploitation and active promotion of "inherent contradictions" and "fissures" in the non-Communist world.

The principle of "peaceful coexistence" was implied in Lenin's policies, recognized and mentioned by Stalin, and explicitly formulated by Khrushchev. . . .

Lenin insisted on a policy of "compromise" that stemmed from a spirit of irreconcilable struggle together with an appreciation of temporary weakness. He contrasted this with "false compromise" in which the principle of struggle itself was sacrificed. His principle of compromise is the real root of what is now called, in Soviet foreign policy, "peaceful coexistence." . . .

"Coexistence" thus is not a relationship of live-and-let-live, but rather a relationship of hostility coupled with cautious restraint, comparable to the "coexistence" of two boxers who feel each other out while looking for a chance to land their most damaging blows. "Coexistence" is a Communist term for a relationship short of overt war in which a final showdown is being prepared. . . .

Khrushchev thus was right when he said at the Twentieth Congress of the Communist Party of the Soviet Union:

. . . The Leninist principle of the peaceful coexistence of states with different social systems has always been and remains the general line of our country's foreign policy.

It has been alleged that the Soviet Union advances the principle of peaceful coexistence merely out of tactical considerations, considerations of expediency. Yet it is common knowledge that we have always, from the very first years of Soviet power, stood with equal firmness for peaceful coexistence. Hence it is not a tactical move, but a fundamental principle of Soviet foreign policy. . . .[19]

"Inevitability" of War

. . . There is some change in doctrine here, although not in the sense in which wishful thinking about Soviet peacefulness would have it. War is considered no longer "inevitable" because the relative power of the Soviet camp is considered strong enough to bring about revolutionary changes "peacefully" or to discourage resistance to Communist revolutionary advances. This change does not, however, affect the basic assumption that there is a conflict which can end only in complete triumph of one or the other side, and that, moreover, there is a continuing tendency toward war inherent in the system of "imperialism." In other words, what has changed is not the Communist concept of the basic conflict between the "Soviet camp" and the "camp of Imperialism," but rather the estimate of the probability of an open battle between the two. . . .

"Just" and "Unjust" Wars

. . . At present . . . [the] doctrine . . . taught throughout all Communist lands in the official textbook . . . [is]:

. . . The Bolsheviks held that there are two kinds of war:

(a) *Just* wars, wars that are not wars of conquest but wars of liberation, waged to defend the people from foreign attack and from attempts to enslave them, or to liberate the people from capitalist slavery, or, lastly, to liberate colonies and dependent countries from the yoke of imperialism; and

(b) *Unjust* wars, wars of conquest, waged to conquer and enslave foreign countries and foreign nations. . . .[20]

The "Socialist Fatherland"

. . . In Communist doctrine, the significance of the Soviet Union is . . . ideologically defined. The Soviet Union is, first, the "fatherland" of all proletarians and toilers all over the world, second, the constitutional leader of the "socialist camp" and leader-ally of all movements directed against imperialism, and, third, the country whose interests are identical with the interests of mankind.

The Communist Manifesto had stated that "the working men have no country." In 1928, the Communist International declared:

Being the land of the dictatorship of the proletariat and of Socialist con-

[19] Leo Gruliow, ed., *Current Soviet Policies II* (New York: Frederick A. Praeger, Inc., 1957), p. 36.

[20] *History of the Communist Party of the Soviet Union* (Bolsheviks), *Short Course* (New York: International Publishers, 1939), pp. 167, 168.

struction, the land of great working class achievements, of the union of the workers with the peasants and of a new culture marching under the banner of Marxism—the U.S.S.R. inevitably becomes the base of the world movement of all oppressed classes, the centre of international revolution, the greatest factor in world history. In the U.S.S.R., the world proletariat for the first time acquires a country that is really its own, and for the colonial movements the U.S.S.R. becomes a powerful centre of attraction. . . .[21]

The Soviet Union and the "Interests of Mankind"

. . . All human development supposedly is moving forward in the direction marked by the "progress" of the Soviet Union, and all human hope is also alleged to lie in that same direction. On this basis, Communists look upon the interests of the Soviet Union as those of a nation that represents the best hope of all people and cannot have interests opposed to those of all men. . . .

On the grounds of this ultimate identity of the national interests of Soviet Russia with the hopes of mankind, support of the power of Russia is thus declared something that has universal moral significance and ought to be the bounden duty of every "right-minded" person in the world. . . .

3. COMMUNISM AND FASCISM: TWO PEAS IN A POD? *

HARRY G. SHAFFER
The University of Kansas

Born and raised in nations which, under a democratic, free enterprise system, have reached unparalleled economic affluence, the majority of Americans and Canadians have come to regard their political and economic system not only as the very best but as the only acceptable way of life for free men anywhere. Even moderate deviations towards the right or the left have been viewed traditionally with suspicion and apprehension, and changes are incorporated but slowly into the "American Way of Life". The extreme political left and the extreme political right, more often than not, are adjudged but poorly disguised tyrannies, alike in all respects except the

[21] *Programme of the Communist International* [adopted at the forty-sixth session of the Sixth World Congress of the Communist International, Sept. 1, 1928] (New York: Workers Library Publishers, Inc., 1929), p. 63.

* Reprinted from *Queen's Quarterly*, Vol. LXIX, No. 1, Spring, 1962, pp. 146-156, by permission of the publisher.

names of the tyrants. Men like Hitler, Mussolini, Stalin, Khrushchev, Mao Tse-tung, and Castro tend to be treated as if they were identical in their philosophies and actions—all agents of the devil bent on enslaving suffering mankind for essentially similar purposes and by essentially similar means. Such men as Franco, Chiang Kai-shek, and Syngman Rhee, however, have (for reasons of political expediency) at one time or another received the luke-warm if not enthusiastic support of the American government, and the American public has been conditioned to accept them as defenders of Western Democracy with no questions asked.

As of now, well over one-third of the world's population is already within the Communist fold, and many other, smaller nations—both East and West—are ruled over by Fascist-type dictators. Under these circumstances, can we afford the erroneous assumption that Fascism and Communism—the two major radical challenges to twentieth century Capitalist democracies of the liberal and of the more conservative type alike—are but two strands of poison ivy bearing different designations but demanding equal treatment and eradication?

While great centralization of economic and political power, the one party system, and the use of force have been manifestations of Fascist and Communist societies alike, the difference between Fascism and Communism is not merely one of semantics. A *thorough* comprehension of differences would entail a detailed analysis of several societies, past and present. Hitler's Germany, Mussolini's Italy, Peron's Argentina, Franco's Spain and Trujillo's Dominican Republic differ from one another in many aspects of their ideological, political, economic, and social structure, and Khrushchev's Russia, Mao's China, Tito's Yugoslavia, and Castro's Cuba are homogeneous only in the eyes of the most superficial observer. *Fundamental, basic* differences between the extreme political right and the extreme political left, however, should be fully understood by all who live in countries in which—in the field of public policy—the people, to a great extent, still represent "the man behind the man behind the gun".

An outgrowth of Mercantilist ideology of the 16th, 17th, and 18th centuries, Fascism was launched without any philosophy whatsoever, beyond the vague concept that the leader always knows what's best. In its early history, Mussolini himself denied that Fascism had a philosophy, or that it needed one. In 1921, realizing that "If Fascism does not wish to die, or worse still to commit suicide, it must provide itself with a doctrine . . . ," he asked that one be written within two months. Obligingly, Giovanni Gentile, Fascism's foremost "philosopher", wrote his *Origini e Dottrina del Fascismo*. "The doctrine of Fascism," he expounded, "is not a philosophy in the usual sense of the word . . . nor even a detailed and ultimate political doctrine. It has never desired to tie itself down, as far as the future is concerned. It has often announced reforms when the announcement seemed politically feasible, but, nevertheless, it has not felt itself obligated to the actual execution of such reforms. The decisions of the Duce alone are those which must always be . . . carried out."

Once Fascism had gained a foothold in the Western world, it began to develop an ideology that bore clear traces of earlier philosophies. It embodied Machiavelli's and Hobbes' contentions that man is evil and brutish, that he cannot be trusted with liberty and that he must be ruled by force lest confusion and disorder persist. It embraced Nietzsche's views of human weakness and inadequacy (of which Democracy, Christianity, equality, and pacifism are prevalent manifestations) to be overcome only by finding the superman capable to rule. It perverted William James' pragmatism, interpreting it to mean that whatever works is by definition right. Adding German nationalism, founded largely upon John Fichte's early 19th Century writings, Alfred Rosenberg translated it all into the National Socialist "Weltanschauung" of the Aryan master race whose supremacy is threatened by oriental Communism, by Christianity (whose founder was a Jew), and by the decadence of a system of Democracy which rewards mediocrity and permits it to rule.

Fascism, its viewpoint somewhat reminiscent of that of the Tories during the American revolutionary period, denies the ability of people to govern themselves as free men in a democratic society. Mario Palmieri, Italian social scientist, refers to Democracy as "a bastard form of political and social organization. The mass of men," Palmieri proclaims, "is created to be governed and not to govern; is created to be led and not to lead; and is created finally to be slaves and not masters, slaves of their animal instincts, their physiological needs, their emotions and their passions." Mussolini explains that "Fascism asserts the irremediable, fruitful and beneficial inequality of men which can never be leveled permanently by a mere mechanical process such as universal suffrage." And Hitler sums it up and draws the logical conclusion: "There must be no majority decision, but merely a body of responsible persons, and the word 'council' will revert to its ancient meaning. Every man shall have councillors at his side, but the *decision* shall be made by but one man."

The state, the all-powerful state which stands above the law, is the keystone of Fascist doctrine. "The state is not only the present," Mussolini shouted from his balcony, "it is also the past and above all it is the future. Transcending the brief spell of the life of individuals, the state stands for the immanent conscience of the nation." By superimposing the leadership principle upon the theory of the omnipotence of the state, a system is created which, in Hitler's words, is based upon the maxim: "Authority of every leader towards below and responsibility towards above." The role of the *individual* in such a society was perhaps most clearly stated by one of Fascism's best known theoreticians, Alfredo Rocco: "For Fascism, society is the end, individuals the means, and its whole existence consists in using individuals as instruments for its ends."

In the economic sphere, private enterprise—though regulated by the government—is not only permitted but even encouraged, and the profit motive is accepted as one of the guiding incentives for production, second only to the desire to serve one's country. Both in Hitler's Germany and in Mussolini's Italy, private economic activity, though subordinated to the overall goal, was yet the area of greatest individual freedom of action. In this respect, certainly, the changes brought about by the advent of Fascism were less sweeping than those resulting from the passage of state power into the hands of the Bolsheviks in the Soviet Union.

Even in times of peace, Germany's and Italy's Fascist economies were both oriented towards war. This was only partly due to their inherent spirit of nationalism, to their ambitions to build "a German Reich that would last for a thousand years" and to "re-establish what once was the glory of the Roman Empire". It was only partly due to their belief that "might is right" and that, in Hitler's words, "Nothing will ever grant us life or land for our nation, except the power of a victorious sword." It went much further than that. These modern "supermen"—even more than Sparta's ruling classes during the days of antiquity or Europe's knights during the age of Feudalism—looked upon war as desirable for its own sake. "Fascism . . . ," Mussolini wrote in an article for the Italian Encyclopedia, "believes neither in the possibility nor in the utility of perpetual peace. It therefore refutes the doctrine of Pacifism . . . *War alone keys up all human energies to their highest tension and puts the stamp of nobility upon those people who have the courage to face it.*"

In disagreement with the teachings of Fascism, Socialists and Communists of all shades and leanings believe in the perfectibility of all mankind. Man is basically good and capable of being master of his own destiny. Only the economic, social, and political environment (with the stress on "economic") has prevented man from realizing the utmost limits of his capabilities both as a productive and as a social being.

Utopian thinkers and writers usually assumed that a change in environment in and of itself would be adequate to reform immediately what we generally refer to as "human nature". Karl Marx, father of "scientific socialism", was much more realistic. Fully aware that no revolutionary transformation of the economic, political, and social order could possibly usher in the stage of perfect freedom (which he prophesied would be the final destiny of mankind), Marx predicted the advent of an intermediate stage in society's development from Capitalist Democracy to pure Communism. This Intermediate Stage has been referred to by many designations, such as "Socialism" (as contrasted with "Communism"), "the Period of Transition", and, perhaps most frequently, "the Dictatorship of the Proletariat". It is this stage—not "Communism"—which the Soviet Union professes to be in at this moment. (This Marx-Lenin type of Socialism is basically quite different from moderate, evolutionary, or Fabian types of socialism which combine partial socialization of the means of production with Western-type political democracy. England under the British Labour Party or Sweden today would be examples of such moderately socialist democracies.)

Had Marx based his ideology on subjective value judgments, he could never have been recognized as a social *scientist*. Contrary, however, to a viewpoint rather widely held in the Free World, his main argument was *not* that Capitalism was inherently "bad", and that Socialism and Communism were "better". On the contrary, Marx acknowledged in glorious words the accomplishments of bourgeois society which "during its rule of scarce one hundred years [it would be more than two hundred years now] has created more massive and colossal productive forces than have all preceding generations together". Yet, Marx attempted to prove that the Capitalist, free enterprise system was just one of the stepping stones on mankind's arduous climb towards pure Communism. Using dialectic materialism and an economic interpretation of history as his basic philosophies, he developed in over two thousand pages of *Das Kapital* his major theories: the labour theory of value, the subsistence theory of wages, the surplus value concept, the law of decreasing profits, the law of Capitalist accumulation, the theory of the self-perpetuating concentration and centralization of capital, the theory of the increasing misery of the proletariat, a simplified version of the underconsumption-overproduction theory of depressions, and the doctrine of the class struggle. Utilizing these analytical tools with which his name is associated, Marx described Capitalism as a system of production in which economic forces were at work which eventually would lead to its "inevitable" downfall. At the time of the breakdown of the old order, the working class, under the leadership of a well-organized Communist party, would take over the reins of government. Society, not yet ready for pure Communism, would now be transformed politically into a dictatorship of the working class.

In marked distinction to Fascist ideology, no Communist ever proclaimed that a dictatorship would be the *final* goal of mankind. From Marx and Engels to present day Communist writers, this dictatorship is to be but preparatory for the time when, in Lenin's words, "mankind will inscribe on its banners: From each according to his ability, to each according to his needs." A pure Communist society, then, is mankind's promised land; a society without any government, police force, army, or jails; a society in which perfect freedom reigns; a society in which production will have been developed "to the n'th degree"; a society in which man will have been transformed into a "social being" who voluntarily and without special personal reward contributes to the best of his ability and takes from the common stores whatever he needs. It is this hope of an ideal order in which, quoting Lenin, "the *necessity* of observing the simple, fundamental rules of everyday social life in common will have become a *habit*"—it is this promise of a perfect world which Communism holds out to the hundreds of millions of its followers. To them, life under a "temporary" dictatorship does not seem too high a price to pay since most of them have known but little freedom in their native lands and most of their forefathers had lived and laboured under one or another type of tyranny since time immemorial.

In the "Intermediate Stage", all the means of production are gradually taken over by the government and supposedly operated in the interests of the people. The entire economy is, in a sense, transformed into one gigantic corporation in which every citizen is an equal stockholder and in which the government acts as the board of directors. Though gradually declining in importance as, step by step, the last vestiges of Capitalist teachings are replaced by Communist indoctrination, monetary incentives are still utilized as essential economic stimuli. "Work in the U.S.S.R.," states Article 12 of the Constitution of the Soviet Union, "is a duty and a matter of honour for every able-bodied citizen in accordance with the principle: 'He who does not work, neither shall he eat.' The principle applied in the U.S.S.R. is that of Socialism: 'From each according to his ability, to each according to his work.' " In Marx's concept of the Intermediate Stage, *and* in actual practice in the Soviet Union or in Red China today, the more productive worker has a higher income than his less qualified or less industrious comrade. With his higher income he can purchase more of the consumer goods available but he cannot invest his savings, for in Socialist-Communist morality there is no greater crime (once Capitalism has been abolished) than to derive a profit from the labour of another man.

How about "Democracy" under the "Dictatorship of the Proletariat"? Democracy is redefined in theory and, still more, in practice. "Democracy for the vast majority of the people," explained Lenin, "and suppression by force, i.e., exclusion from democracy of the exploiters and oppressors of the people—this is the modification of Democracy during the *transition* from Capitalism to Communism." Democracy for those, then, who go along with the party line, but suppression of "counter revolutionary enemies of the people" is the admitted redefinition of democracy during the "Intermediate Stage". In Marxist-Leninist ideology, the state has always been "and by its very nature always must be" an agency of oppression used by the ruling class to oppress all other classes. This was so when feudal lords ruled over their land and when absolute monarchs held absolute power. This is so, Communism proclaims, when the bourgeoisie rules via universal suffrage which allows the masses, in Marx's words, "once every few years, to decide which particular representatives of the oppressing class should be in parliament to represent and to oppress them". This is also so during the Dictatorship of the Proletariat, when political power has been merely transferred from the bourgeoisie to the proletariat. Only when there are no more classes could, in Marxian philosophy, the state itself "wither away" and make room for a perfect, all inclusive, unlimited democracy.

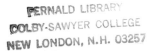

The extent to which Soviet policy conforms to Marxian ideology is a question of major interest to students of the Russian economy. The Soviet leadership asserts that theirs is the only correct interpretation and application of Marxist-Leninist teachings. On the other hand, most social scientists in the Western world, including those of laissez-faire, Keynesian, and Socialist leanings, contend that Marx would turn over in his grave were he to know what had been done to his philosophy in the Soviet Union.

It is admittedly difficult to ascertain the extent to which Soviet history and practice have corresponded with, or deviated from, Marxian theory. Marx had predicted that the Dictatorship of the Proletariat would supersede an advanced phase of Capitalism, but Russia never went through a stage of Industrial Capitalism at all. Early endeavours to eliminate money and to introduce a semi-Communist society from the start were quite contrary to Marx's concept of the "Intermediate Stage" and failed utterly. The era of the N.E.P. (New Economic Policy) ushered in in 1921 was a period of restoration of order which entailed a substantial degree of de-socialization and amounted, in effect, to partial Capitalism. This period of temporary readjustment came to an end seven years later with the introduction of the first Five-Year Plan which saw the Soviet economy move, with renewed vigour, towards more complete nationalization. Yet, even today, the elimination of Capitalist incentives and motivation has been but partially accomplished and private enterprise on a limited scale is still permitted. Non-agricultural private entrepreneurship is limited to small productive units and, as the law prevents a private "businessman" from employing anyone, less than one per cent of the total non-farm output is produced by handicraftsmen in business for themselves. Peasants on state and collective farms, on the other hand, are allowed to devote part of their labour time to their own individual farmsteads, varying in size from one-half to two and one-half acres depending upon the fertility of the soil. These farmsteads account for upwards of twenty per cent of the incomes of that half of the Russian population that is engaged in agricultural pursuits. In violation of Socialist principles, interest is paid on bank deposits and the purchase of government bonds is encouraged. By means of titles ("Hero of Labour"), honours, and recognition, an attempt is being made to substitute gradually "unselfish, Socialist competition" for monetary incentives, but percentage wage differentials in the Soviet Union are still greater than in the United States.

Elections in the Soviet Union are not quite so undemocratic as usually visualized in America. Any recognized, organized association, such as a labour union, a youth organization, a unit of the army, navy, or air force, or a peasant organization—as well as a Communist party cell, of course —has the right to nominate any man or woman for office, regardless of whether he or she is a member of the Communist party. All nominating organizations, then, send their representatives to a convention for the purpose of selecting the one slate of officers submitted to the electorate for a "yea" or "nay" vote—somewhat comparable to the procedure followed by nominating committees in some of our own, democratically run, private clubs. Yet it is difficult for us to conceive that such a procedure could be preferable, from the point of view of political freedom, to our system of national elections.

Most important, probably, is the question as to whether there are any indications that the state has started to "wither away". It is true that certain recent changes seem to point to some reduction of centralized control and authority. For instance, machine-tractor stations (once a powerful weapon of centralized control over collective farms) have been abolished, more authority has been given to local management, and force as a means of exacting compliance with rules and regulations has diminished since Stalin's death. Yet all this is insufficient evidence, at best, that the state has begun to "wither away". Marxian theory, including the promise of the "Final Stage", *is* propounded from first grade classrooms to union halls and mass meetings. Still, the danger that a prolongation of centralized control will perpetuate the dictatorship unquestionably exists, even if we were to grant the sincerity of the leaders' proclamations. The recently adopted party program promised within the next twenty years economic abundance including free medical services, free education, rent-free housing, free water and heating, free public transportation, etc. This, if it were to materialize, would certainly be a great step forward in the direction of a classless society in which goods would be distributed according to needs. But whether it would bring in its wake a simultaneous decrease in the dictatorial powers of the state, only the future can tell.

Western social scientists show relatively little interest in a detailed theoretical analysis or in constructing a model of the "Final Stage", as they consider it Utopian, at least in the foreseeable future. Even Marx did not attempt to describe its composition or operation in any detail. Marxists (utilizing dialectic materialism to prove that all progress results from the clash of opposite forces) find it difficult to explain. How can an era come about in which the synthesis of the new social structure fails to turn into a new thesis, fails to call forth a new antithesis, fails to continue creating the forces which, according to Marx, have shaped the course of mankind's development since the dawn of history? Western fear of Communism, anyhow, is not fear of the visionary "Final Stage" but rather of a dictatorship (whether of the proletarian or the one-man type) which repeatedly has shown its unwillingness to stay within its geographic boundaries.

In a tense Western world, moving uneasily along the brink of a nuclear holocaust, the threat posed by such semi-fascist organizations as the John Birchers, the Christian Crusade, or the Minutemen (who in the name of "fighting Communism" and "preserving Democracy" would destroy all freedom) should not be underestimated. Yet, for many reasons, Communism presents a much greater challenge to the survival of Western Capitalist society, as we know it, than Fascism.

First of all, Fascism today has under its domain but a few relatively small, militarily and economically powerless nations while Communism embraces hundreds of millions of followers in vast areas of the world's potentially most productive regions.

Second, Fascism *could* in theory be non-expansionist, though it has usually refused to be so in practice, while Communism is committed to engulf the entire world. Lest it change its views and aims and give up its promise of the "Final Stage", peaceful coexistence can be but temporary and Khrushchev's expectation of "burying" us takes on added significance (though it must be admitted that Marxian theory would consider an East-West war quite unnecessary, as the downfall of Capitalism is "inevitable" anyhow).

Third, Fascism involves mainly a *political change,* and a re-emergence of some type of Capitalist Democracy is quite possible as evidenced in West Germany and in Italy today. Communism, on the other hand, entails such a *complete change* in the economic, social, and political order of things that a return to a relatively decentralized free enterprise system guided by the objective forces of the market seems highly improbable. Marx meant it when he said: "With us it is not a matter of reforming private property, but of abolishing it; not of hushing up the class antagonism, but of abolishing the classes; not of ameliorating the existing society, but of establishing a new one."

Fourth, the Communist policy of expropriation and nationalization of productive facilities has a strong appeal to the masses in the "hungry countries", and any attempt to return private property to the previous owners is unlikely to be interpreted as a "return to liberty" by the many who have little to gain by it.

Fifth, idealists in the "Free World" are much more likely to be impressed by the high moral principles propagated by Communists than by the base appeals of Fascists. Both ideologies demand unswerving loyalty of their followers. Yet, there is a great difference between the oath of blind allegiance Germans had to swear (not to their cause or ideal, not even to their fatherland, but to the person of the Führer) and the Communist demand for adherence to the party line for the proposed goal of "ending the exploitation of man by man". Compare the Fascist dictatorship based on the right of the strong few to rule over the weaker many, a dictatorship which is the end in itself: compare it with Communist totalitarianism which seeks its justification in being a temporary necessity as a means to a moral end. Compare the Fascist view of the world as one consisting of enemies, of inferiors, of lands to be conquered and dominated by the master race: compare it with the Communist view of a world consisting of masses of peasants and workers to be awakened to their social responsibilities so that they may throw off the yoke of "wage slavery". Compare the Nazi-adopted "Deutschland, Deutschland über alles" (Germany, Germany above everything), and the Italian "crédere, obbedire, combattere" (believe, obey, fight): compare these with the closing words of the Communist International: "The International Party, shall be the Human Race." Compare the admitted, pronounced, and executed policies of Nazi Germany in the area of race and nationality relationships with Article 123 of the Soviet Constitution: "Equality of rights of citizens of the U.S.S.R. irrespective of their nationality or race, in all spheres of economic, government, cultural, political, and other public activity is an indefeasible law. Any direct or indirect restriction of the rights of, or, conversely, the establishment of any direct or indirect privileges for, citizens on account of their race or nationality, as well as any advocacy of racial or national exclusiveness or hatred, and contempt, is punishable by law." Compare Mussolini's view that "all the history of man's civilization, from the caves to civilized or so-called civilized man, is a progressive limitation of liberty": compare this with Marx's economic interpretation of history and its Utopian society of perfect freedom at the end of the rainbow. Indeed, Fascism offers its adherents only one basic "moral" argument, if such it may be called: "I am better than you are, therefore, I should have the right to rule over you." The Communist, on the other hand, is left with the feeling that he devotes his all to the improvement of the lot of suffering mankind. And the argument that words and deeds do not always jibe is easily countered by the contention that they can fail to jibe only if good men refrain from joining the movement.

Finally, Marx (like laissez-faire economists such as Adam Smith, David Ricardo, Jeremy Bentham, and Alfred Marshall, but unlike Fascist writers and philosophers) presents a *scientific* approach towards the solution of mankind's problems and this appeals to intellectuals, irrespective of their agreement, disagreement, or partial agreement with his conclusions. Marx's *Das Kapital* is as thorough and comprehensive a study of economic forces prevalent in Capitalist society as can be found anywhere. One may question his assumptions, one may take him to task for his overemphasis on supply and underemphasis on demand, one may criticize the oversimplification of his competitive model, one may disagree with some of his interpretations of historic, economic, political, and social data collected during three decades of almost incessant study and research. Yet, one cannot help but admire his scientific approach, his attempt to establish scientific truths by logical and by deductive reasoning, his endeavour to utilize scientific inquiries to discover economic laws and to make valid predictions. Nowhere in Fascist literature (with its appeal to emotions, feelings and myth, referred to by Bertrand Russell as the "revolt against reason") can a comparable work be found. It is not surprising, then, that so many strongly anti-Marxist social scientists throughout the world have incorporated one or another of Marx's analytical tools, scientific findings, and economic and political predictions into their own philosophies, thus demonstrating the truth embodied in the German proverb: "Der Weise lernt vom Feinde mehr, als der Narr vom Freunde Heer." (The wise man learns more from the enemy, than the fool from an army of friends.)

*   *   *

The purported *ends* of Communists and Fascists, then, are totally and completely different from each other. Even the "Dictatorship of the Proletariat" is superficially similar to Fascism only in some aspects of its *political* structure, but essentially different in its philosophic approach to the solution of mankind's problems, in the economic structure and social fabric of its society, in its declared goal and at least in some of the ways in which it hopes to achieve it. Last but by no means least, it differs in its material, moral, psychological, and intellectual appeal to individuals and nations the world over. To appreciate these fundamental differences between the extreme political right and the extreme political left is imperative, not merely for the sake of satisfying intellectual curiosity but in the interest of a realistic approach to foreign and domestic problems.

WESTERN MARXIST VIEWS

4. MARXIAN SOCIALISM *

PAUL M. SWEEZY

Co-Editor, Monthly Review

WHAT IS MARXISM?

. . . Marxism is a body of ideas about the nature of the universe, of man, of society, and of history. It bears the name of Karl Marx, a German who was born in 1818 and died in 1883, and who lived the latter half of his life in London. Marx was a man of prodigious learning and enormously powerful intellect, one of the greatest thinkers not only of the nineteenth century but of all recorded history.

* Excerpts reprinted from Paul M. Sweezy, *Marxian Socialism*, Monthly Review Pamphlet Series No. 13, 1956, by permission of the author and the *Monthly Review*.

Marx combined in his system of ideas the realistic philosophy of the English and French Enlightenment, the comprehensive and dynamic point of view of the German idealists and particularly of Hegel, and the hardheaded analysis of the capitalist economy which we owe to the great British classical economists. The result was a brilliant new synthesis which is both highly original and at the same time stands squarely in the mainstream of modern intellectual development from the Renaissance onward. Here, in desperate brevity, are what I understand to be the central elements of the Marxian view of society and history.

The universe is real and existed for eons before there was human life, or for that matter life of any kind, on our planet. Life here on the earth is a natural by-product of the earth's cooling, and humanity is the result of a long process of evolution. In the earliest stages of society, human labor was still so unproductive that it yielded no surplus over and above the requirements of life and reproduction. As long as this was true, men lived in a state of primitive communism—cooperating, sharing, fighting, but not yet exploiting each other.

Later, techniques improved so much that a man could produce a surplus over and above what he needed for himself, and from this dates the beginning of economic exploitation and social classes. When one tribe fought and defeated another, it was now worthwhile to take captive the vanquished and force them to work for the victors. Some men became rulers living off the surplus produced by others; while the actual producers lost their independence and spent their lives toiling for their masters. It was in this way that exploitation of man by man and the division of society into classes originated.

But the form of exploitation has not remained unchanged—indeed, nothing remains unchanged, everything is in a constant state of flux. The exploiters seek to expand the surplus at their disposal, and with this end in view they invent and introduce new and better techniques of production; the exploited seek to improve their condition and therefore carry on a never-ending struggle to enlarge their share of the product. As a result the forms of exploitation change, and with them the whole structure of society. At first it was slavery, in which the laborer is the property of his master. Next came serfdom, in which the laborer has attained a certain degree of freedom but is still tied to the soil. And finally there is wage labor, in which the laborer is legally entirely free but must work for the profit of others because he lacks means of production of his own.

A society based on private ownership of the means of production and wage labor is called capitalism. It came into the world first in England and certain parts of Western Europe, not all at once but gradually and painfully between the sixteenth and nineteenth centuries. It brought with it social and political upheavals, new ways of thinking, and a deep awareness of the vast creative potentials of human labor and industry. Historically speaking, capitalism was a long leap forward. In the words of the *Communist Manifesto*: "It has been the first to show what man's activity can bring about. It has accomplished wonders far surpassing Egyptian pyramids, Roman aqueducts, and Gothic cathedrals; it has conducted expeditions that put in the shade all former migrations and crusades."

But capitalism contains within itself what Marx called contradictions which prevent it from fully realizing the potentials which it was the first to uncover. The capitalist class, comprising those who own the instruments of production and set them in motion, is and must be concerned with making profits, not with the general welfare. Capitalists subordinate other aims to the maximization of profit. In pursuit of this objective, they pay workers as little as they can get away with and steadily introduce labor-saving machinery. The consequence, of course, is to hold down the consuming power of the working class. At the same time, the capitalists restrict their own consumption in the interests of accumulating more and more capital. But accumulating more and more capital means adding to society's productive capacity. We, therefore, have the paradox that capitalism steps on the brake as far as consumption is concerned and on the accelerator as far as production is concerned. This is its basic contradiction, and it cannot be eliminated except through changing the system from one of production for profit to one of production for use.

On the basis of this analysis, Marx believed that it was to the interest of the workers to organize themselves politically in order eventually to gain power and replace capitalism by a system based upon common ownership of the means of production and economic planning, a system to which he and his followers came in time to give the name of socialism. Moreover, Marx had no doubt that the workers would in fact follow this course, and that their growing numbers, importance, and discipline under capitalism would sooner or later ensure their victory. As to *how* the transition would be effected, Marx at first thought that it would have to be everywhere by means of a violent revolution. But as political democracy spread, especially in the English-speaking countries, he modified this view and in the last decades of his life believed that a peaceful and legal transition was quite possible in some countries and under some conditions. "We know," he said in a speech at Amsterdam in 1872, "that special regard must be paid to the institutions, customs, and traditions of various lands; and we do not deny that there are certain countries, such as the United States and England, in which the workers may hope to achieve their ends by peaceful means."

WHAT IS SOCIALISM?

So much then for Marxism. Naturally, my account is oversimplified and very incomplete, but I hope it may serve to give you some idea of the scope and quality of Marx's thought—so different from the impressions which demagogic opponents have always sought to convey. Let us now ask: What is socialism?

Socialism, according to Marx, is the form of society which will succeed capitalism, just as capitalism is the form of society which succeeded feudalism.

The fundamental change would consist in the abolition of private ownership of the means of production. Please note that neither Marx nor (so far as I know) any other modern socialist of importance ever advocated or expected that private ownership of consumer goods would or should be abolished. On the contrary, he favored the multiplication of consumer goods in the hands of the lower-income groups, hence a great extension of private ownership in this sphere.

As to the form of ownership of the means of production which would characterize socialism, Marxists have never been dogmatic. Ownership must be by public bodies, but that does not necessarily mean only the central government: local governments, special public authorities of one sort or another, and cooperatives can also own means of production under socialism. And there can even be a certain amount of private ownership, provided it is confined to industries in which production takes place on a small scale.

A corollary of public ownership of the means of production is economic planning. The capitalist economy is governed by the market, that is to say, by private producers responding to price movements with a view to maximizing their own profits. It is through this mechanism that supply and demand are adjusted to each other and productive resources are allocated to various industries and branches of production. But public bodies have no compelling reason to maximize their profits (though, admittedly, under certain circumstances they may be *directed* to make as much profit as they can). In general, therefore, they must have some other principle to guide their economic conduct, and this can only be the following of a plan which coordinates the activities of all the public bodies.

Now socialists claim that it is precisely the freedom from the necessity to make profits and the coordination of all economic activities by a general plan which allows socialism to overcome the contradictions of capitalism and to develop its resources and technology for the greatest good of the people as a whole. Under such a system, crises and unemployment could only result from bad planning; and while bad planning is certainly not impossible, especially in the early stages of socialist society, there is no reason why planners should not learn to correct their mistakes and to reduce the resulting maladjustments and disproportions to smaller and smaller dimensions.

What about the non-economic aspects of socialism? Here Marx had a well-developed theory. He expected socialism to come first in the more advanced industrialized countries and to build on the political foundations which they had already achieved. Since in such countries the workers were in a majority, he believed that the taking of political power by the working class would mean full democracy and liberty for most of the people, though he also expected that there would be a period of greater or lesser duration when the rights and freedoms of the former exploiters would be subject to certain restrictions. As to the longer-run future, he reasoned that the full development of society's economic potential under socialism would gradually raise the well-being and education of everyone so that eventually all classes and class distinctions would be done away with. When that happened—but not before—the state as a repressive apparatus for dealing with class and other forms of social conflict would "wither away." The final goal of Marx and his followers can therefore be said to be the same as that of the philosophical anarchists. It would be a state of society in which, to quote Marx's words, "the free development of each is the condition for the free development of all" and in which distribution takes place according to the principle "from each according to his ability, to each according to his need."

Others before Marx had had a similar vision of a good society to come—a society of abundance and brotherhood in place of the society of scarcity and alienation which the human race had always been condemned to live in. What particularly distinguished Marx from his predecessors is that he purported to prove that this society of the future, which he called socialism, is not only a dream and a hope but is in fact the next stage of historical evolution. It would not come automatically, to be sure—not as the result of the blind decrees of fate. It would come rather as the result of the conscious, organized activity of working people, the vast majority of mankind. Given this perspective, the task of the humanitarian could only be to devote his energies to educating and organizing the working class to fulfill its historic mission. That, in a word, is what Marxists have been trying to do for nearly a hundred years now.

WAS MARX RIGHT?

Marx's prophetic forecast of the end of capitalism and the opening of a new era in human history was given to the world in the *Communist Manifesto* in 1848. More than a century has passed since. Do the facts of this intervening period permit us to say whether Marx was right or wrong?

In the broadest sense, I do not see how it can be denied that Marx has been brilliantly vindicated. A mighty socialist movement based on the working class grew up during his lifetime. The crises of capitalism, far from abating, grew in intensity and violence, culminating in the holocausts of two world wars. Beginning with the Russian Revolution of 1917, more and more of the earth's population has withdrawn from the orbit of capitalism and has undertaken to reconstruct its economy and society on the basis of public ownership and planning. Today, something like a third of the human race has definitively abandoned private enterprise and, under Communist leadership, is building up a network of planned economies.

But it is not only in Communist-led countries that this is happening, though elsewhere the pace is slower. Since World War II, Great Britain has moved a considerable distance along the road to a socialized economy, and one of the two big political parties is a socialist party. Even more recently, India, next to Communist China the most populous country in the world, has adopted a Five Year Plan which the sober London *Times* calls "India's Socialist Plan."

The fact is that over most of the world's surface the trend is now visibly away from private enterprise and toward public ownership of the means of production, away from market-dominated economies and toward economic planning. Only in the United States and a few countries closely allied to the United States does the trend seem to be in the other direction. Here, it is true, the socialist movement is at a low ebb, and private enterprise is very much in the saddle.

Should we perhaps conclude that Marx was right for the rest of the world but wrong for the United States? Are we the great exception? Or are we merely lagging somewhat behind in a movement which eventually will be as universal as Marx predicted it would? These are crucial questions, especially for us Americans. . . .

There is one respect, and it is an important one, in which Marx was certainly wrong. As I noted earlier, he expected socialism to come first in the most advanced industrial countries. It did not. For reasons having to do with the late 19th- and early 20th-century development of relations between the advanced countries and the colonial and semi-colonial backward countries, the revolutionary movement grew more rapidly and had more opportunities in the backward than in the advanced regions. When the capitalist system was wracked by the destruction and disasters of the two world wars, it broke at its weakest points not at its strongest. Socialism came first to the Tsarist Empire, and spread from there to Eastern Europe and China.

This has, of course, meant that the early stages of the development of socialism have been very different from what Marx foresaw.

The new order could not build directly on the achievements of the old. It had no developed industrial base, no educated and trained labor force, no political democracy. It had to start from scratch and work under conditions of utmost difficulty.

Many people, including Marxists, expected socialism to proceed at once, or at any rate within a short time, to achieve its great goals: an economy of abundance, increasing democracy and freedom for the workers, a richer life for all. It could have happened that way if Britain, Germany, and the United States had been the first great socialist countries. But it could not possibly happen that way in backward Russia standing alone for a whole generation. The industrial base had to be built, and that meant belt-tightening. The Russians had no traditions of democracy and civil liberty, and under the difficult conditions of the '20s and '30s it was natural that a new police state should arise on the foundations of the old Tsarist police state. Moreover, like all police states this one committed excesses and horrors which had little if anything to do with the central tasks of construction the regime had set itself.

Under these circumstances, socialism in practice had little attraction for the people of the advanced countries. The standard of living of those living under it remained abysmally low, and political conduct, both among leaders and between leaders and people, often seemed closer to oriental despotism than to enlightened socialism. It was widely assumed in the West either that the Soviet Union was not socialist at all, or that socialism had been tried and failed.

In the underdeveloped countries, however, the USSR made a very different impression. They saw rapid economic advance, a vast process of popular education, some improvement in living standards—and never having experienced democracy themselves, they hardly noticed its absence in Russia. Communism was imposed on Eastern Europe by the Red Army chasing Hitler back to Berlin, but in China it was the product of a great popular revolution. And it is now expanding its influence throughout the underdeveloped regions of the world. . . .

We come finally to the question of liberty. Here the advanced capitalist countries started with an advantage over the Soviet Union no less enormous than in the field of economics. . . . And yet there is no doubt that the last few years, which happen to be the years since Stalin's death, have witnessed a considerable change in the Soviet world, and the pace of this change has been sharply stepped up. . . .

Suppose socialism shows what Marxists have always maintained, that it is possible to have economic collectivism *and* freedom? Suppose the socialist world overtakes and surpasses the capitalist world not only in production and per capita income, not only in education and science, but also in freedom and respect for the dignity of the individual? What then?

You may think these questions fantastic now. Perhaps. But let me make a suggestion. Let me propose that you file them away in the back of your mind and then bring them out, say once every year, and check the answers you are able to give on the basis of the latest facts available to you. I have no doubt what the answers will be, sooner or later. If I am right, it will be facts and not my arguments that will convince you. And I am very glad to leave it to the future to decide.

5. THE ABC OF SOCIALISM *

LEO HUBERMAN
Co-Editor, Monthly Review

SYBIL H. MAY
Assistant to the Editors

The only thing most Americans know about socialism is that they don't like it. They have been led to believe that socialism is something to be either ridiculed as impractical, or feared as an instrument of the devil.

This is a disturbing situation. It is a mistake to dismiss or condemn so important a subject on the basis of the extremely superficial and biased accounts of it which are now so widespread in the United States. Socialism is a world-wide movement. The millions who hate it in this country are matched by millions in other countries who rejoice in it. No idea has ever caught the imagination of so many people in so short a time.

Socialism has already become the way of life for some 200,000,000 people—the inhabitants of one-sixth of the earth's surface. It is fast becoming the way of life for an additional 600,000,000 people. These two groups together make up approximately one-third of the earth's population. . . .

Marx saw the capitalist system as part of the history of human development. It was neither permanent nor unchangeable. On the contrary, capitalism was an essentially transitory social system which, like every other form of human society, arose out of the system before, developed, would decay and be followed by still another system. For Marx, no human society was static—all were in a constant state of flux and change. His job, as he saw it, was to find out what produced the changes in capitalist society—to discover capitalism's "law of motion." He began by trying to explain it and ended not by apologizing for it, as other econ-

---

* Excerpts reprinted from Leo Huberman and Sybil H. May, *The ABC of Socialism*, 1953, pp. 3, 40-43, and 62-63, by permission of the authors and the *Monthly Review*. The pamphlet, No. 7 in the Monthly Review Pamphlet Series, is a condensation of Leo Huberman, *The Truth About Socialism*, and is edited by Sybil H. May.

omists did, but rather by outlining a guide to action for the forces which would create a better society in the future.

Socialists believe that Marx's picture of capitalist society is sound, that it is closer to reality than the picture drawn by non-Marxist economists. On that point Professor Leontief of Harvard University, though he is himself not a Marxist, had this to say to the members of the American Economic Association fifteen years ago: "If . . . one wants to learn what profits and wages and capitalist enterprises actually are, he can obtain in the three volumes of *Capital* more realistic and more relevant first-hand information than he could possibly hope to find in ten successive issues of the U. S. Census [or] a dozen textbooks on contemporary economic institutions. . . ."

In the same article, Professor Leontief paid tribute to the many predictions made by Marx which have since been fulfilled: "The record is indeed impressive: increasing concentration of wealth, rapid elimination of small and medium-sized enterprises, progressive limitation of competition, incessant technological progress accompanied by the ever-growing importance of fixed capital, and, last but not least, the undiminishing amplitude of recurrent business cycles—an unsurpassed series of prognostications fulfilled, against which modern economic theory with all its refinements has little to show indeed."

It is interesting to note that about the same time that this Harvard professor felt it necessary to suggest to his fellow economics teachers that they could learn much from Karl Marx, another distinguished scholar was offering similar advice to his colleagues in the field of history. In an article in the *American Historical Review* of October 1935, the late Charles Beard, one of America's most eminent historians, wrote: "It may be appropriate to remind those who may be inclined to treat Marx as a mere revolutionary or hot partisan that he was more than that. He was a doctor of philosophy from a German university, possessing the hallmark of the scholar. He was a student of Greek and Latin learning. He read, besides German, his native tongue, Greek, Latin, French, English, Italian, and Russian. He was widely read in contemporary history and economic thought. Hence, however much one may dislike Marx's personal views, one cannot deny to him wide and deep knowledge—and a fearless and sacrificial life. He not only interpreted history, as everyone does who writes any history, but he helped to make history. Possibly he may have known something."

The working class movement in almost every country of the world, striving to achieve social and economic justice, feels that he may have known something.

The colonial peoples of Asia and Africa, basing their struggles for liberation and independence on his teachings, think that he may have known something.

The countries of eastern Europe, attempting to replace anarchic production for profit with planned production for use, believe that he may have known something.

The privileged few in every capitalist country of the world trying desperately to remain secure on their tottering seats of power, tremble with the fear that he may have known something.

The people in a country one-sixth of the earth's surface, having successfully overthrown capitalism and demonstrated that socialism can end class division and enable man consciously to direct his economy for the welfare of all, are certain that he did know something.

We come now to an analysis of socialism. Let us be clear at the outset that believers in socialism do not argue that the change from private to public ownership of the means of production will solve all man's problems—it will not make angels out of devils, nor will it bring heaven on earth. The claim is made, however, that socialism will remedy the major evils of capitalism, abolish exploitation, poverty, insecurity, and war, and make for greater welfare and happiness of man.

Socialism does not mean piecemeal patchwork reform of capitalism. It means revolutionary change—the reconstruction of society along entirely different lines.

Instead of individual effort for individual profit, there will be collective effort for collective benefit.

Cloth will be made, not to make money, but to provide people with clothes—and so with all other goods.

The power of man over man will be diminished; the power of man over nature will be increased.

The capacity to produce abundance, instead of being strangled by consideration of profit-making, will be utilized to the utmost to provide plenty for all.

The overhanging fear of depression and unemployment, of destitution and insecurity, will vanish with the knowledge that planned production for use insures jobs for all, all the time—economic security from the cradle to the grave.

When success is no longer measured by the size of your pile but by the extent of your cooperation with your fellow man, then the rule of gold will be replaced by the golden rule.

Imperialist wars, which result from the profit-makers' hunt for foreign markets where they can sell "excess" goods and invest "excess" capital will come to an end—since there will no longer be "excess" goods or capital, and no profit-makers.

With the means of production no longer in private hands, society will no longer be divided into classes of employers and workers. One man will not be in a position to exploit another—A will not be able to profit from B's labor.

In short, the essence of socialism is that the country will no longer be owned by a few and mismanaged by them for their own benefit, it will be owned by the people and managed by the people for the benefit of the people.

So far we have dealt only with one part of that "essence" of socialism, the part about the country being "owned by the people"—another way of saying public ownership of the means of production. We come now to the second part of that definition—"managed by the people for the benefit of the people." How will that be accomplished?

The answer to that question is *centralized planning*. Just as public ownership of the means of production is an essential feature of socialism, so, too, is centralized planning.

Now obviously centralized planning for a whole nation is a tough job. It's so tough that many people in capitalist countries—particularly those who own the means of production and therefore think capitalism is the best of all possible worlds—are certain that it can't be done. The National Association of Manufacturers, for example, is emphatic on that point—it has repeated it again and again. Here is one of its plainest, most direct sentences on the subject from its "Platform for American Industry" some years ago: "No small group of men can possess the wisdom, foresight and discernment required to plan, direct, and stimulate successfully the activities of all the people."

Now this charge, if true, is extremely serious in any consideration of socialism. For socialist economy *must* be a planned economy, and if planning is impossible, then socialism is impossible.

Is centralized planning possible? In 1928 something happened which took the question of planning out of the realm of guesswork and brought it down to earth. In 1928, the Union of Soviet Socialist Republics set up its First Five-Year Plan. When that was completed, they started their Second Five-Year Plan, and after that, their Third Five-Year Plan (and so it will go, for ever and ever, so long as Russia is socialized—because, as we have seen, a socialist state *has* to have a plan).

Now we need no longer guess whether or not it is possible for a nation to have centralized planning. Now we know. The Soviet Union has tried it. It works. It is possible. . . .

Socialism will not bring perfection. It will not create a paradise. It will not solve all the problems that face mankind.

It is only in artificially created, visionary systems of society, like those of the Utopian Socialists, that sinners become saints, heaven is brought to earth, and a solution is found for every problem. Marxist socialists have no such illusions. They know that socialism will solve only those problems which can be solved at this particular stage in the development of man. More than that they do not claim. But that much, they feel, will result in a vast improvement in our way of life.

The conscious planned development of the commonly owned productive forces will enable socialist society to attain a far higher level of production than was possible under capitalism. Socialism eliminates capitalist inefficiency and waste—particularly the waste of idle men, machinery, and money in needless depressions; it abolishes the even costlier waste of men and materials in capitalist wars, through the establishment of international peace; it accelerates the speed of technical progress; socialist science, unhampered by capitalist consideration of profit-making as the first and most important goal, makes tremendous strides forward. The standard of living for all is raised as increased production increases the quantity of goods available.

The entire change in the mode of life brings a change in the people who live that life. At first, man will carry with him into socialist society much the same outlook on life and work that he had in capitalist society. Steeped in the competitive atmosphere of capitalism he will not readily accustom himself to the cooperative spirit of socialism; soaked in the capitalist ideology of selfishness he will not quickly switch to the socialist principle of service to his fellow man. This unreadiness to change will even be true of many who have everything to gain from the change from capitalism to socialism; it will, of course, be particularly true of those former ruling class capitalists who lose their wealth and power in the transition from private to public ownership of the means of production.

But as the new socialist system of planned production for use takes root, changes take place in the attitude and development of the people. The capitalist taint in their mental and spiritual outlook fades away and they are reoriented in the spirit of socialism. The new generation, born and bred in the new society, becomes as used to the socialist way of life as the old generation formerly was to the capitalist.

The propagandists for capitalism would have us believe that socialism means the end of freedom. The truth is the exact opposite. Socialism is the beginning of freedom. Socialism is freedom from the evils which most sorely afflict mankind—freedom from wage slavery, poverty, social inequality, insecurity, race discrimination, war.

Socialism is an international movement. Its program in every country of the world is the same—to substitute for the barbaric competitive system, the civilized cooperative commonwealth; to establish the society of the brotherhood of man in which the welfare of each is realized in the welfare of all.

Socialism is not an impossible dream. It is the next step in the process of social evolution. Its time is now.

SOVIET VIEWS

6. MARX, ENGELS, AND LENIN WERE RIGHT: CAPITALISM IS DOOMED *

NIKITA S. KHRUSHCHEV

Former First Secretary, Central Committee of the Communist Party of the Soviet Union and Former Chairman of the U.S.S.R. Council of Ministers

. . . The number of workers and employees in our country [the U.S.S.R.] has increased by 12,900,000, or 24.2%, in the past four years. There has been no unemployment in the Soviet Union for a long time. Each Soviet person enjoys the right to work and is paid by society according to the quantity and quality of his work. But in the United States of America unemployment has increased by 1,900,000 in this period, and the unemployed now constitute a huge army of 5,000,000 people. In addition, millions of Americans are partly unemployed.

The composition of the Soviet Union's population has become so much younger that there are now very few people who have a concrete idea of what unemployment means. In order to understand what it is like, you must get into the unemployed man's skin, as the saying goes, must experience the full hopelessness of his situation. He comes home; his family is waiting for him—his wife and children—but he has no hope of getting a job the next day and easing their difficult conditions. And this happens when a healthy man wants to work and when there are jobs he could do, but there is no work for him because there is over-production in the country. It is not because everyone in the country is well fed and well clothed that this overproduction exists, but because the purchasing power of the population has fallen, because many people are destitute and cannot buy even the absolute necessities. Therefore there is no market for many goods. This is the vicious circle of capitalism, whose essence was well described by Marx, Engels and Lenin.

The capitalists cannot renounce such procedures. You cannot, after all, persuade a tiger to start eating grass; it cannot do this, since it is carnivorous. You cannot persuade a monopolist, a capitalist, cannot demonstrate to him that communism is better than capitalism. What do we mean by "persuade" him? We mean persuade him to give up his capital, to turn over the enterprises he calls "mine" into the possession of the people, so that the working people will start calling them "ours."

Where will you find a capitalist who will voluntarily give up his riches?

Such a transfer of wealth into the hands of the people can be brought about only by a working class that, organized into a close family, takes power into its hands. In order to achieve this successfully, the working class needs a party that can organize it and lead it along the right path. This party, as the experience of history shows, can only be the Communist Party. Only then is the victory of the working class possible, and this victory will come, it will come, it will come!

No prayers, no handouts will enable the capitalists to buy off the victory of communism! It is only a matter of time. . . .

There are journalists from bourgeois countries present here. Of course, they will immediately write that Khrushchev is calling for world revolution, for world communism, and that therefore peaceful coexistence is impossible, and so forth.

Write what you will, gentlemen! You, after all, want the victory of capitalism. Why, then, do you want to deprive me of the same right to propagandize world communism? Where are the equal terms here? . . .

7. LENIN ON COMMUNIST SOCIETY *

From capitalism mankind can pass directly only to socialism, i.e., to the social ownership of the means of production and the distribution of products according to the amount of work performed by each individual. Our Party looks farther ahead: socialism must inevitably pass gradually into communism.

* Quotations from the writings of V. I. Lenin. Selected, rearranged, and reprinted from *Soviet Union*, No. 158, 1963, p. 14.

We must take all the culture capitalism left us and build socialism from it. We must take all the science and technology, all the knowledge and the arts. Without that we cannot build the life of communist society.

In the last analysis, productivity of labour is the most important, the principal thing for the victory of the new social system. . . .

The economic basis for the complete withering away of the state is such a high stage of development of communism that the antithesis between mental and physical labour disappears; and, consequently, there disappears one of the principal sources of modern social inequality—a source, moreover, which cannot on any account be removed immediately by the mere conversion of the means of production into public property, by the mere expropriation of the capitalists.

Socialism will shorten the working day, will raise the masses to a new life, will create such conditions for the majority of the population as will enable everybody without exception to perform "state functions", and this will lead to the complete withering away of every form of state in general.

And as soon as equality is achieved for all members of society in relation to ownership of the means of production, that is, equality of labour and equality of wages, humanity will inevitably be confronted with the question of advancing farther, from formal equality to actual equality, i.e., to the operation of the rule, "from each according to his ability, to each according to his needs".

In striving for socialism we are convinced that it will develop into communism and, hence, that the need . . . for the subordination of one man to another, and of one section of the population to another, will vanish altogether since people will become accustomed to observing the elementary conditions of social life without violence and without subordination.

The communist organisation of social labour, the first step towards which is socialism, rests, and will do so more and more as time goes on, on the free and conscious discipline of the toilers themselves who have thrown off the yoke both of the landlords and capitalists.

We shall work to eradicate the accursed rule: "every man for himself and god for us all", to eradicate the habit of regarding work only as a duty, and of regarding as legitimate only such work as is paid for at certain rates. We shall work to inculcate in people's minds, to convert into a habit, to introduce in the daily life of the masses, the rule: "all for each and each for all"; the rule: "from each according to his ability, to each according to his needs"; gradually but steadily to introduce communist discipline and communist labour.

The state cannot wither away completely until society implements the rule: "from each according to his ability, to each according to his needs", i.e., when people become so accustomed to observing the basic rules of social life and when their labour is so productive that they will voluntarily work according to their ability.

8. BASIS AND SUPERSTRUCTURE OF SOCIETY *

VICTOR AFANASYEV

A modern building must have a foundation for its tall, heavy, often complex superstructure to rest upon.

Human society has a certain resemblance to a building. It, too, must have a "foundation," or, as Marxists put it, a basis—the economic relations which necessarily evolve between people in the process of producing material values.

Thus, the term "basis of society" refers to the relations of production between people, the economic structure of their society. This structure or basis makes it possible for us to determine who owns the means of production (the raw materials and implements of labor)—society as a whole or a particular group of people, what relationship (cooperation or domination) exists between the people in this society, how the material values are shared.

It is this basis also that determines the society's superstructure—the sum total of its ideas, theories, attitudes and its related ideological (political, legal, moral, cultural, religious and other) institutions and organizations.

Marxists think of the history of human society as a process of development and consecutive replacement of five socioeconomic orders: primitive-communal, slave, feudal, capitalist and socialist. Each of these societies

* Excerpts reprinted from *USSR,* September, 1963, pp. 38-39 by permission of the publisher.

had its particular economic structure, its basis or "foundation" upon which it built a corresponding superstructure.

Let us take primitive communal society—"the childhood of the human race," Engels called it in his book *The Origin of the Family, Private Property and the State*. With his primitive tools and weapons (club, stone, spear, bow) early man could not cope with a rigorous nature if he lived alone. Joint hunting, fishing, building of shelters, etc., made for cooperation of a kind and even a certain division of labor—that between men and women. Everything such communities gathered was distributed equally among its members.

So we see that it was communal (social) property upon which the production relations (basis) of primitive society were founded. There was no exploitation of man by man in that society and, consequently, its super-structure—its system of attitudes, theories and institutions—could do without instruments of compulsion, that is to say, without a state.

With the appearance of metal tools and weapons and a division of labor which led to the exchange of agricultural, livestock and handicraft products, some members of society, generally the tribal chieftains, began to acquire private property. Classes emerged—the rich and the poor, the slaveowners and the slaves—and an entirely new type of society developed. Thus, the primitive-communal society with common ownership of prop-erty was replaced by a slave society with private property. The new rela-tions of production, or basis, as we call it, gave birth to new ideas and institutions, to a superstructure suited to these new relations. Notice that this superstructure safeguarded the slaveowners' rule over their slaves. That was not simply coincidence. The slaveowners—the wealthy class in that society—owned the means of production, and, as Marx put it, the class that is the dominating economic force of a society is also its dominat-ing ideological force.

Similarly, the basis and superstructure were replaced when society moved from the slave to the feudal system and from the feudal to the capitalist system. In spite of the enormous difference between these three socioeconomic orders as regards the level of development of their produc-tive forces, their production relations were all based on private property and reflected the opposition of class interests, the antagonism between the oppressed and the oppressors.

It could not have been otherwise. Not when the life of the propertied classes—the slaveowners, feudal lords and capitalists—was as different from the life of the classes that had been deprived of the ownership of the means of production—the slaves, serf-peasants and workers—whose labor had created all of the society's material values, as heaven is from earth. And naturally, there was a corresponding difference in their class views on life, on society and the state, on the rights and duties of man, on good and bad, justice, honor, etc.

Thus the antagonism in a society's production relations is always reflected in its superstructure, in other words, the superstructure always conforms to the basis.

Economic relations are important not only because they determine the development of the ideas and institutions of society but because changes in these relations produce corresponding changes in the social superstructure. The development of society and the changes it undergoes are a continuous process. But the changes in the superstructure run especially deep when one type of production relations is replaced by another through social revolutions. Marx called social revolutions the "locomotives of history," and Lenin designated them "holidays of the oppressed and exploited."

In the course of revolutionary changes, the political domination of the old class is ended and the rule of a new class established. The old state machinery is replaced by a new system of political and legal institutions. People's thinking changes then much faster than it usually does—old ideas and views are discarded for new ones that conform to the new economic relations. Lenin wrote that in a revolutionary epoch the "old" superstructure explodes and a new one is created by the self-activity of various social forces.

However, while Marxism maintains that all superstructures depend on the economic "foundation," it does recognize that they have a certain independence.

This independence is manifest in the continuity of many ideas and conceptions even after the old basis is replaced by a new one. However, the old superstructure, as an entity, as a system of ideas and institutions, ceases to exist when its basis is destroyed.

Only those elements of the old superstructure that conform to and serve the interests of the new ruling class are carried over to the superstructure of the new society. For instance, every newly formed society in which the means of production remain private property holds on to the ideas, concepts and the relevant political and legal institutions that preserve the exploitation of man by man. The superstructure of a society may also retain certain elements which time cannot destroy—great works of art and literature, for example.

The relative independence of the superstructure is also evident in the fact that, having originated from a given economic foundation, the superstructure actively influences the development of that economic basis. The ideas, theories and attitudes, reflecting the changes that are continuously taking place in the basis, shape the activities of people and thus influence the direction in which society moves.

Take for illustration as significant an event in the history of mankind as the Great October 1917 Socialist Revolution. Was it the result simply of a certain level of development of Russia's productive forces? No, of course not. The Revolution would never have triumphed if Russia's working class had not accumulated the political experience it did, had not gone through the hard school of revolutionary struggle, and had not made the poorest peasantry its ally. Neither can we imagine the victory of this Revolution without the Communist Party—its leader and militant general staff.

Of course, in the final analysis the Great October Revolution was the expression of economic necessity, but this necessity manifested itself both in the political struggle of the opposing classes and in the activities of the Communisty Party, which had been waging uncompromising war against the Russian bourgeoisie and all varieties of opportunists. In short, the development of society is the interaction of economics with politics, ideology, and every other aspect of social life. However, it is the economic basis which is fundamental here and which sets the pattern for the development of society.

HOW IS THE STRUCTURE OF SOCIALISM BUILT?

The socialist mode of production is based on public property. It could not then have existed under capitalism, where private property is sovereign.

The experience of the Soviet Union and of other socialist countries has demonstrated the political rule of the working class to be an indispensable condition for creating a socialist society. Once it controls all the basic means of production, the proletarian state organizes the planned construction of a socialist economy in town and countryside. We see then that the new basis does not arise spontaneously, but is steadily built to a plan drafted by the socialist state.

With the victory of socialism and the establishment of a socialist basis, the process of forming a socialist superstructure is completed. It should be noted, however, that some of the elements of the socialist superstructure (unlike the basis) can already be seen under capitalism. Indeed, Marxist-Leninist theory, the party of the working class, the Soviets of Workers' Deputies, trade unions, proletarian ethics, progressive literature and art came into being when the capitalist basis was still dominant in Russia. These superstructural phenomena developed, of course, not in response to, but in spite of the wish of the ruling classes. The very existence of these elements of a socialist superstructure demonstrated the profound contradictions of the capitalist production relations in Russia.

After the Great October Socialist Revolution, these elements, together with the achievements of world science, culture and philosophy of all the foregoing social epochs, were incorporated into the superstructure of the socialist society. . . .

The formation of a comprehensive system of socialist ideas and institutions took several decades. The completion of this system of political, legal, esthetic, ethical, scientific and philosophic concepts and its relevant institutions—the socialist state, the Communist Party, trade unions, Young Communist League, cultural, educational, sports and other organizations —marks the victory of socialism.

COMMUNISM AND SELF-GOVERNMENT

. . . As the USSR progresses toward communism—a classless social order—the superstructure of ideas and institutions will gradually lose its class character and assume a nationwide character. . . .

Some of the functions previously exercised by state agencies are now carried out by public bodies. The trade unions, for instance, handle all social insurance matters, supervise the health resorts and rest homes, and are in charge of physical culture and sports. People's public order squads, comrades' courts and public control committees help the militia, the courts and the procurator's office to enforce the law.

In the very near future places of entertainment, libraries, clubs and other cultural establishments are to be administered by public organizations.

Further changes in the superstructure will be taking place as the material and technical basis of communism is built up, as socialist production relations are transformed into communist production relations, and as the people's communist consciousness is further developed. . . .

II

STALIN: GREAT LEADER OR CRUEL DESPOT?

"There was an interesting difference between Lenin and Stalin: Lenin forgave his enemies, Stalin killed his friends."

NIKITA S. KHRUSHCHEV

"Stalinism is the only true Marxism-Leninism."

LOZARI NREGI
ALBANIAN DELEGATE TO AN
INTERNATIONAL CONFERENCE OF WORLD
WAR II PARTISANS IN ROME

"In abusing Stalin, Khrushchev is in fact wildly denouncing the Soviet system and state. His language in this connection is by no means weaker but is actually stronger than that of such renegades as Kautsky, Trotsky, Tito, and Djilas."

EDITORIAL DEPARTMENTS OF
COMMUNIST CHINA'S *People's Daily*
AND *Red Flag*

For almost three decades—from the death of Lenin in 1924 to his own death in 1953—Joseph Stalin (1879-1953) ruled the Soviet Union with an iron hand, often as tyrannically as any oriental potentate had ever ruled over his subjects. Eliminating his former comrades-in-arms one by one, Stalin first turned against the Trotskyist radicals who favored the immediate support of world-wide revolutions, as opposed to his plan to perfect "socialism in one country," the U.S.S.R., and then to proceed from there. Having defeated the left-wing opposition and driven Trotsky [1] into exile in 1928 (where he was assassinated eleven years later, presumably on Stalin's orders), Stalin then turned against the "right-wing opportunists and bourgeois nationalists." Opposed to radical collectivization and industrialization at the expense of current consumption, these "right-wing deviationists" favored a more gradual introduction of changes, at a speed that would not call forth the bitter antagonism of the peasants. The leaders of

[1] Leon Trotsky, 1877-1940, Soviet Commissar of War from 1918 to 1925.

these moderate forces, men like Bukharin,[2] had almost all been active revolutionists during the days of the establishment of the Soviet Union, had fought on Lenin's side against the White Russians and the foreign armies, and had given their full support to Stalin in his fight against the Trotskyites. Now their turn had come. During the purges of the 1930's, one after another faced charges of treason and eventually the firing squad.[3]

In the meantime Stalin proceeded to pursue his goal of rapidly industrializing the Soviet Union. Opposition was ruthlessly shattered; peasants who refused to cooperate with the collectivization program or the enforced delivery of grain to the state at almost confiscatory prices were shipped to Siberia by the hundreds of thousands; and improvements in living standards were postponed,[4] since all available resources not absolutely required to meet minimum consumption needs were utilized to build up the military and industrial might of the U.S.S.R. The sacrifices exacted from the population at large and from the peasantry in particular were appalling, but some of the objectives were undoubtedly achieved. Even today, almost a quarter of a century later, it is not easy to form a judgment as to whether, within the framework of the type of planned economy that was being built, more permissive policies would have led to equally rapid industrialization. If not, could a less-well-prepared U.S.S.R. have withstood the brutal onslaughts of the Nazi war machinery and turned the tide in World War II against the would-be master race bent on enslaving the world?

Under the given conditions, then, was Stalin an historical, objective necessity? Although by no means in complete disagreement, Alec Nove and Leopold Labedz cross swords on this issue under *Western Views* below.

Throughout the days of his regime, in classrooms and assembly halls, in newspapers, books, and radio broadcasts, on the stage and on the screen, Stalin was hailed as the benevolent father and magnanimous mentor, the protector of the socialist motherland, the "greatest genius of mankind." Whatever he personally may have contributed or failed to contribute to the war effort, it was under his leadership that the Nazi invaders were driven from Soviet soil and the red flag carried deep into the heart of Europe. By the end of World War II, Stalin was acclaimed by one and all in the U.S.S.R. as the "wise leader and military commander," the "organizer of victory." The first selection under *Soviet Views* gives a few examples of the glorification of Stalin during his lifetime.[5]

---

[2] Nikolai Ivanovich Bukharin, 1888-1938.

[3] Some but by no means all of those purged have since been cleared posthumously of all charges.

[4] In fact, living standards dropped sharply during the early 1930's, and some Western economists would argue that the 1928 levels were not reached again until as late as 1955.

[5] The phrases in quotes were titles bestowed upon Stalin by Khrushchev. See *Soviet World Outlook: A Handbook of Communist Statements,* Department of State Publication 6836, released July, 1959, p. 43.

Soon after the end of World War II, Stalin once again turned against his former friends and comrades. If his "excesses" had ever been in any way "justifiable" in pre-War days to eliminate political opponents and speed the process of industrialization, their recurrence at a time at which a unified nation had come to accept its new social order as the best way of life and him as its revered leader could be ascribed only to paranoic suspicion. Doubtful of the loyalty of even his closest associates, Stalin returned to the terror tactics of the 1930's. Thousands of faithful party members and ardent supporters of Soviet Communism were arrested on the slightest suspicion, tried before mock courts, and summarily executed for crimes to which all of them "confessed." Did other party leaders, men like Khrushchev, know about all of this? Here is Khrushchev's answer:

> The question arises whether the leading cadres of the Party knew about, for example, the arrests of people in that period. Yes, they did. But did they know that absolutely innocent people were arrested? No, they did not. They believed Stalin and could not dream that repressions could be used against honest people devoted to our cause.[6]

Stalin died in 1953, and a nation mourned the leader who had guided its destiny for an entire generation. His body was placed next to that of Lenin in the Soviet Union's most hallowed shrine, the Mausoleum in Red Square, and millions filed by in the days and months and years that followed. "At Stalin's funeral many, including myself, were in tears," Khrushchev admitted frankly. "These were sincere tears, for although we knew about some of Stalin's shortcomings, we believed in him." [7]

At the Twentieth Party Congress, in 1956, came the now famous secret session in which Khrushchev denounced Stalin. Here is Nathaniel Weyl's description of the proceedings, taken from his introduction to the English translation of Khrushchev's speech:

> We know something of the atmosphere in which Khrushchev's speech was delivered. Sixteen hundred delegates to the Party Congress met behind locked doors. Not even foreign Communist fraternal delegates were permitted inside. The address lasted until four in the morning. Khrushchev reportedly broke down in tears four times; some thirty delegates fainted or had seizures.
>
> This was not a cold, Machiavellian performance, but an intensely emotional and disturbing ritual in which men who had lived in fear, under terror, in a miasma of lies spoke out to an audience which was also partly guilty. . . .
>
> . . . When they learned what sort of man Stalin had actually been, when they were told about crimes which they had perhaps previously heard rumors of, but had tried to deny even in the privacy of their own thoughts, clearly they could not dissociate themselves emotionally or morally as if they had been mere bystanders and not participants and accomplices.[8]

---

[6] From a speech by Nikita S. Khrushchev, delivered on March 8, 1963. Translated in *Current Soviet Documents,* April 5, 1963, p. 13.

[7] *Ibid.,* p. 15.

[8] Nathaniel Weyl's Introduction to *The Anatomy of Terror,* Public Affairs Press, 1956, p. 14.

The second selection under *Soviet Views* consists of excerpts from Khrushchev's condemnation of Stalin. It should be noted, however, that Stalin was taken to task only for having brought about the execution of *loyal* comrades on trumped-up charges. Stalin's purges of left- and right-wing deviationists are still officially approved by the Party. Here is the way the most recent Soviet edition of the *History of the Communist Party of the Soviet Union* reports Stalin's actions against his political opponents:

. . . As an outstanding theoretician and organizer, he led the fight against the Trotskyists, Right-wing opportunists, and bourgeois nationalists, against the intrigues of the capitalist encirclement. He rendered great services not only in ensuring the victory of Socialism in the U.S.S.R., but also in developing the world Communist and liberation movement. This naturally earned him great prestige and popularity. However . . .[9]

The denunciation of Stalin was undertaken for the declared purpose of assuring that "phenomena of this kind would never again arise in the Party and country." [10] If ever Stalinist methods and practices were to be discontinued, if ever Stalinist attitudes and approaches were to be changed, the Stalin myth had to be unmasked for, in the words of an eminent American author, editor, and social critic,

. . . Stalin was not just a tyrant who brought a reign of terror and suppression to the Russian people. He exerted a profound influence on the form and direction of the Communist Party, on approaches to major problems, on the thought patterns of the people. And before the effects could be extirpated, the cause had to be clearly defined.[11]

Once Stalin had been exposed, the Soviet Union and all the Eastern European bloc countries, except Albania, proceeded to erase one by one the vestiges of the Stalin cult. His pictures were taken down; his statues were removed from their pedestals; the names of streets, places, towns, collective farms, and cooperative and state enterprises were changed. Even the hallowed name of Stalingrad, where the Nazi armies met their first major defeat, was changed to Volgograd. In the meantime, the accusations against Stalin mounted in vigor and bitterness. To this very day, in issue after issue of the leading Soviet papers and historical journals there appear obituaries on the anniversaries of the birth of former leading Communists, eulogizing their contributions to the cause, and ending in words such as these: "His [V. P. Zatonsky's] devotion to the ideals of Marxism-Leninism, his unusual courage and heroism, his close ties with the people, his internationalism, the purity of his actions and thoughts—all this was unjustly deleted from history, along with his name, in the period of the Stalin

[9] *History of the Communist Party of the Soviet Union,* Foreign Languages Publishing House, 1960, pp. 670-671.
[10] *Ibid.,* p. 670.
[11] Norman Cousins, "Listening to Ivan Denisovich," *Saturday Review,* February 9, 1963, p. 18.

cult." [12] Sometimes the phrasing is simpler but no less revealing: "Yuri Mikhailovich perished in 1941, a victim of the repressions of the cult of the individual." [13]

By the time the Twenty-Second Party Congress met in 1961, the Party was ready to take the final step: Stalin's body was removed from the Lenin Mausoleum and his remains were reduced to ashes. Most of the Communist world approved, but the Chinese Communists (and their Albanian comrades) didn't. The latter did not sanctify Stalin, who for years had refused to support their struggle against the Chiang Kai-shek regime. They did not pronounce him faultless. They admitted that he had erred, and they did not even deny that "innocent people . . . were wrongly convicted." But, balancing his accomplishments against his shortcomings, they proclaimed that he was "primarily correct" and that his faults had been "secondary." The last selection of this chapter is an exposition of the Chinese Communist point of view.

WESTERN VIEWS

1. WAS STALIN AN "HISTORICAL NECESSITY"?

a. Was Stalin Really Necessary? *

ALEC NOVE

University of Glasgow

Stalin has suffered a dramatic post-mortem demotion, and a monument to his victims is to be erected in Moscow. The present Soviet leadership is thus disassociating itself publicly from many of the highly disagreeable features of Stalin's rule, while claiming for the Party and the Soviet

[12] *Voprosii istorii KPSS*, No. 9, September, 1963. Translated in *The Current Digest of the Soviet Press*, October 9, 1963, p. 23.

[13] *Izvestia*, August 27, 1963. Translated in *The Current Digest of the Soviet Press*, September 18, 1963, p. 41.

* Reprinted from *Encounter*, April, 1962, pp. 86-92, by permission of the author and the publisher.

system the credit for making Russia a great economic and military power. Is this a logically consistent standpoint? How far was Stalin, or Stalinism, an integral, unavoidable, "necessary" part of the achievements of the period? How much of the evil associated with the Stalin system is attributable to the peculiar character of the late dictator, and how much was the consequence of the policies adopted by the large majority of the Bolshevik party, or of the effort of a small and dedicated minority to impose very rapid industrialisation on a peasant country?

To ask these questions is of interest from several standpoints. Firstly, in trying to answer them we might be able to see a little more clearly the meaning of such misused terms as "determinism," causality, or the role of personality in history, and so continue to explore some of the problems which E. H. Carr presented in so stimulating a way in his Trevelyan lectures. Secondly, an examination of the circumstances which brought Stalin to power and led to—or provided an opportunity for—crimes on a massive scale is surely of very practical interest, since it might help in understanding how to avoid a repetition of these circumstances, particularly in those underdeveloped countries which are being tempted by their very real difficulties to take the totalitarian road.

To some people, the word "necessary" smacks of "historicism," of a belief in inevitability, or suggests that the author wishes to find some historic justification, a whitewash to be applied to Stalin and his system. This is far from being my intention. "Necessity" is used here with no moral strings attached. If I say that to travel to Oxford it is necessary to go to Paddington station, this implies no approval, moral or otherwise, of the service provided by the Western Region of British Railways, still less of the project of making the journey to Oxford. It is simply that *if* I wish to do A, it involves doing B.

It is true that there may be alternatives. One might, for instance, do not B but C, or D. Thus I could go to Oxford by car, or by bus. However, it could be that these physically possible methods are not in fact open to me; I may not own a car, and shortage of time precludes taking the bus. Thus a judgment on the "necessity" or otherwise of an action in pursuit of a given purpose requires some consideration of what could have been done instead.

The range of choice is not, in practice, limited only by what is *physically* possible. There are also actions which are excluded by religious or ideological principle. For example, it is not in fact open to a rabbi to eat a ham sandwich or an orthodox Hindu to eat cow-meat. Thus if an "alternative" happens to involve such acts, it is not *for them* an alternative at all. This is because, were they to act otherwise, they would cease to be what they in fact are. A rabbi does not eat pork; were he to do so, he would not be a rabbi. The fact that he is a rabbi would also affect his outlook, his "freedom" to choose between alternative modes of conduct, where religious law is less strict: for instance, there is nothing in the Talmud or in Deuteronomy about smoking on the Sabbath, but rabbis would tend to be the kind of people who, faced with this "new" problem, would give the answer "no."

Thus, to come nearer our subject, there may have been a number of solutions to the problems posed by Russia of the 'twenties which the Communists could not have chosen because they were Communists, and in considering the practical alternatives before them we have to bear this in mind. In doing so, we are by no means driven to any generalisations about the "inevitability" of the Russian revolution or of the Bolshevik seizure of power, and *a fortiori* we need not assume that non-Bolsheviks could not have found some other ways of coping with the problems of the period. (Indeed, though the problems would still have been acute, they might in important respects have been different.) Before his assassination in 1911, the last intelligent Tsarist prime minister, Stolypin, expressed the belief that his land reform measures would create in about twenty years a prosperous peasantry which would provide a stable foundation for society and the throne. No one will know if he would have been right, if he had not been murdered, if the Tsar had been wise, if Rasputin had not existed, if the war had not broken out. . . . But of what use is it to indulge in such speculations? A 19th-century Russian blank-verse play provides, if somewhat inaccurately, a relevant comment:

> *If, if, if grandma had a beard,*
> *She would be grandpa. . . .*

In assessing the choices open to the Bolsheviks in, say, 1926, the events before that date must be taken as given. The real question, surely, is to consider the practical alternatives which Stalin and his colleagues had before them.

In doing so, we should certainly not assume that what happened was inevitable. "Necessity" and "inevitable" are quite distinct concepts, though some critics seem to confuse them. Two simple and probably uncontroversial propositions will illustrate this: it was necessary for 18th-century Poland to make drastic changes in its constitution if she were to survive as an independent state; and for China around 1890 a strong, modernising government was urgently necessary if many disasters were to be avoided. Yet the "necessary" steps were not taken and the disasters occurred. Unless we believe that whatever was not avoided was for that reason unavoidable, we would wish to examine the actions which men took, their choices between *available* alternatives, and see whether viable alternatives in fact existed.

At this point, many historians—at times one feels E. H. Carr is among them—tend to brush aside impatiently any talk of what might have been;

they are concerned, they would claim, with chronicling and explaining what was. Curiously, this line is often taken both by those who believe in strict historical determinism, *i.e.,* that what happened *had* to happen, and by those who consider history to be merely a chronological series of events, *i.e.,* that by implication *anything* could have happened. Both these apparently opposite extremes agree in not examining the actual possibilities as they were seen by the statesmen of the period. Yet how can one speak meaningfully of the reasons for, or causes of, any political act unless one implicitly or explicitly considers what could have been done instead? In other words, we must be concerned with freedom of choice, or its converse, necessity, whether we like it or not, unless we hold either that freedom of choice is infinite or that it is non-existent.

There are several more things to be said on the subject of "necessity." One of these concerns what might be called consequences of consequences, or indirect effects. For example, it is difficult to marry a wife without simultaneously acquiring a mother-in-law. Or, moving nearer to our subject, a sergeant is an unavoidable element in an army, and the needs of discipline involve giving him powers over his men which he is likely to abuse. Bullying N.C.O.'s are likely to be found if an army exists, and so, given the necessity for an army, they become an inevitable consequence of its existence, just as the mother-in-law is an unavoidable appendage of a "necessary" wife. Thus, getting still nearer to the point, a situation which requires many bureaucrats, or which gives exceptional power to many policemen, may bring into action certain forces, certain behavioural tendencies, which are typical of bureaucrats or policemen and which, though not needed or desired as such, cannot in the circumstances be avoided.

The saying that "you cannot make omelettes without breaking eggs" (or its Russian equivalent: "if you chop trees, the chips fly") has been used so often as an excuse for excesses and crimes, that we sometimes forget that you really *cannot* make omelettes without breaking eggs. . . .

Now on to Stalin, or rather to Stalinism, since the idea of "necessity" does not of course mean that the leader had to be a Georgian with a long moustache, but rather a tough dictator ruling a totalitarian state of the Stalinist type. What were the practical alternatives before the Bolsheviks in the late 'twenties, which contributed to the creation of the Stalinist régime, or, if one prefers a different formulation, gave the opportunity to ambitious men to achieve so high a degree of absolutism?

The key problem before the Bolsheviks concerned the linked questions of industrialisation and political power. They felt they had to industrialise for several reasons, some of which they shared with non-Bolshevik predecessors. Thus the Tsarist minister, Count Witte, as well as Stalin, believed that to achieve national strength and maintain independence, Russia needed a modern industry, especially heavy industry. The national-defence argument, re-labelled "defence of the revolution," was greatly strengthened by the belief that the Russian revolution was in constant danger from a hostile capitalist environment, militarily and technically far stronger than the U.S.S.R. Then there was the belief that the building of socialism or communism involved industrialisation, and, more immediately, that a "proletarian dictatorship" was insecure so long as it ruled in an overwhelmingly petty-bourgeois, peasant, environment. There had to be a large increase in the number and importance of the proletariat, while the rise of a rich "kulak" class in the villages was regarded as a dangerous (or potentially dangerous) resurgence of capitalism. It was clear, by 1927, that it was useless to wait for "world revolution" to solve these problems. These propositions were common to the protagonists of the various platforms of the middle 'twenties. Thus even the "moderate" Bukharin wrote: "If there were a fall in the relative weight of the working class in its political and its social and class power, . . . this would subvert the basis of the proletarian dictatorship, the basis of our government." [1] He too spoke in principle of the "struggle against the kulak, against the capitalist road," and warned of the "kulak danger." [2] He too, even in the context of an attack on Zinoviev and the "left" opposition, argued the need for "changing the production relations of our country." [3]

Until about 1927, a rapid rise in industrial production resulted from (or, "was a result of") the reactivation of pre-revolutionary productive capacity, which fell into disuse and disrepair in the civil war period. However, it now became urgent to find material and financial means to expand the industrial base. This at once brought the peasant problem to the fore. The revolution had distributed land to 25 million families, most of whom were able or willing to provide only small marketable surpluses. Supplies of food to the towns and for export fell, peasant consumption rose. Yet the off-farm surplus must grow rapidly to sustain industrialisation, especially where large-scale loans from abroad could scarcely be expected. As the "left" opposition vigorously pointed out, the peasant, the bulk of the population, had somehow to be made to contribute produce and money, to provide the bulk of "primitive Socialist accumulation."

The arguments around these problems were inextricably entangled in the political factional struggles of the 'twenties.[4] The moderate wing, led by Bukharin, believed that it was possible to advance slowly towards in-

---

[1] "The Results of the United Plenum of the Central and Control Commissions of the Party" (1927).

[2] Speech on "The Results of the 14th Party Congress" (5th January, 1926).

[3] Speech to the XXIII special conference of the Leningrad provincial party organisation (1926).

[4] See A. Erlich: *The Soviet Industrialisation Debate* (Harvard, 1960) for a most valuable account of the interaction between the debates and the economic realities of the period. The account given here is necessarily oversimplified.

dustrialisation "at the pace of a tortoise," [5] a pace severely limited by what the peasant was willing to do voluntarily. This was sometimes described as "riding towards socialism on a peasant nag." The logic of this policy demanded priority for developing consumers' goods industries, to make more cloth to encourage the peasants to sell more food. At first, Stalin sided with the moderates.

The case against the Bukharin line was of several different kinds. Firstly, free trade with the peasants could only provide adequate surpluses if the better-off peasants (*i.e.,* those known as *kulaks*) were allowed to expand, since they were the most efficient producers and provided a large part of the marketable produce. Yet all the Bolshevik leaders (including, despite momentary aberrations, Bukharin himself) found this ideologically and politically unacceptable. A strong group of independent, rich peasants was Stolypin's dream as a basis for Tsardom. It was the Bolshevik's nightmare, as totally inconsistent in the long run with their rule or with a socialist transformation of "petty-bourgeois" Russia. But this made the Bukharin approach of doubtful internal consistency. This was understood at the time by intelligent non-party men. Thus the famous economist Kondratiev, later to perish in the purges, declared in 1927: "If you want a higher rate of accumulation . . . then the stronger elements of the village must be allowed to exploit (the weaker)," in other words that the "kulaks" must expand their holdings and employ landless labourers.[6] The "peasant nag" could not pull the cart; or it, and the peasant, would pull in the wrong direction.

A second reason concerned the pace of the tortoise. The Bolsheviks were in a hurry. They saw themselves threatened by "imperialist interventionists." Even though some war scares were manufactured for factional reasons, the Party as a whole believed that war against them would come before very long. This argued not merely for speed, but also for priority to *heavy* and not light industry, since it provided a basis for an arms industry. Still another reason was a less tangible but still very real one: the necessity of maintaining political *élan,* of not appearing to accept for an indefinite period a policy of gradualism based on the peasant, which would have demoralised the Party and so gravely weakened the régime. It was widely felt, in and out of Russia, that by 1927 the régime had reached a *cul-de-sac.* I have in front of me a contemporary Menshevik pamphlet published abroad, by P. A. Garvi,[7] which describes its dilemma quite clearly, and indeed the political and economic problem was extremely pressing: to justify its existence, to justify the Party dictatorship in the name of the proletariat, a rapid move forward was urgent; but such a move forward

[5] Paper read at a plenum of the Agricultural Economics Research Institute, Moscow, 1927.

[6] Bukharin's words, speech of 5th January, 1926.

[7] *Zakat bolshevisma* (Twilight of Bolshevism) (Riga, 1928).

would hardly be consistent with the "alliance with the peasants" which was the foundation of the policy of the moderates in the 'twenties. Stalin at this point swung over towards the left, and his policy of all-out industrialisation and collectivisation was a means of breaking out of the *cul-de-sac,* of mobilising the Party to smash peasant resistance, to make possible the acquisition of farm surpluses without having to pay the price which any free peasants or free peasant associations would have demanded. He may well have felt he had little choice. It is worth quoting from the reminiscences of another Menshevik, who in the late 'twenties was working in the Soviet planning organs: "The financial base of the first five-year plan, *until Stalin found it in levying tribute on the peasants, in primitive accumulation by the methods of Tamerlane,* was extremely precarious. . . . (It seemed likely that) everything would go to the devil. . . . No wonder that no one, literally no one, of the well-informed economists, believed or could believe in the fulfillment (of the plan)." [8]

It does not matter in the present context whether Stalin made this shift through personal conviction of its necessity, or because this seemed to him to be a clever power-manœuvre. The cleverness in any case largely consisted in knowing that he would thus strengthen his position by becoming the spokesman of the view which was widely popular among Party activists. The "leftists," destroyed organisationally by Stalin in earlier years, had a considerable following. Stalin's left-turn brought many of them to his support—though this did not save them from being shot in due course on Stalin's orders. It is probably the case that he had at this time genuine majority support within the Party for his policy, though many had reservations about certain excesses, of which more will be said. But if this be so, the policy as such cannot be attributed to Stalin personally, and therefore the consequences which flowed from its adoption must be a matter of more than personal responsibility.

Let us examine some of these consequences. Collectivisation could not be voluntary. Rapid industrialisation, especially with priority for heavy industry, meant a reduction in living standards, despite contrary promises in the first five-year plans. This meant a sharp increase in the degree of coercion, in the powers of the police, in the unpopularity of the régime. The aims of the bulk of the people were bound to be in conflict with the aims of the Party. It should be added that this conflict is probably bound to arise in some form wherever *the state* is responsible for financing rapid industrialisation; the sacrifices are then imposed by political authority, and the masses of "small" people do not and cannot provide voluntarily the necessary savings, since in the nature of things their present abstinence

---

[8] N. Valentinov, in *Sotsialisticheskii Vestnik* (New York), April, 1961. (Emphasis mine.)

cannot be linked with a future return which they as individuals can identify. However, this possibly unavoidable unpopularity was greatly increased in the U.S.S.R. by the sheer pace of the advance and by the attack on peasant property, and, as we shall see, both these factors reacted adversely on production of consumers' goods and so led to still further hardships and even greater unpopularity. The strains and priorities involved in a rapid move forward required a high degree of economic centralisation, to prevent resources from being diverted to satisfy needs which were urgent but of a non-priority character. In this situation, the Party was the one body capable of carrying out enormous changes and resisting social and economic pressures in a hostile environment; this was bound to affect its structure. For a number of years it had already been in process of transformation from a political into a power machine. The problems involved in the "revolution from above" intensified the process of turning it into an obedient instrument for changing, suppressing, controlling.

This, in turn, required hierarchical subordination, in suppression of discussion; therefore there had to be an unquestioned commander-in-chief. Below him, toughness in executing unpopular orders became the highest qualification for Party office. The emergence of Stalin, and of Stalin-type bullying officials of the sergeant-major species, was accompanied by the decline in the importance of the cosmopolitan journalist-intellectual type of party leader who had played so prominent a role earlier.

The rise of Stalin to supreme authority was surely connected with the belief among many Party members that he was the kind of man who could cope with this kind of situation. Of course, it could well be that Stalin tended to adopt policies which caused him and his type to be regarded as indispensable, and he promoted men to office in the Party because they were loyal to him. Personal ambition, a desire for power, were important factors in shaping events. But this is so obvious, so clearly visible on the surface, that the underlying problems, policy choices and logical consequences of policies need to be stressed.

Let us recapitulate: the Communists needed dictatorial power if they were to continue to rule; if they were to take effective steps towards industrialisation these steps were bound to give rise to problems which would require further tightening of political and economic control. While we cannot say, without much further research, whether a Bukharinite or other moderate policy was impossible, once the decision to move fast was taken this had very radical consequences; the need for a tough, coercive government correspondingly increased. Given the nature of the Party apparatus, the mental and political development of the Russian masses, the logic of police rule, these policies were bound to lead to a conflict with the peasantry and to excesses of various kinds. Thus, given the premises, certain elements of what may be called Stalinism followed, were objective "necessities." In this sense, and to this extent, Stalin was, so to speak, operating within the logical consequences of Leninism.

It is an essential part of Lenin's views that the Party was to seize power and use it to change Russian society; this is what distinguished him from the Mensheviks who believed that conditions for socialism should ripen within society. Lenin also suppressed opposition parties and required stern discipline from his own followers. (It is impossible to ban free speech outside the Party without purging the Party of those who express "wrong" views within it.) Indeed Lenin promoted Stalin because he knew he was tough, would "prepare peppery dishes," though he had last-minute regrets about it. While it would be going too far to describe Stalin as a true Leninist, if only because Lenin was neither personally brutal nor an oriental despot, Stalin undoubtedly carried through some of the logical consequences of Lenin's policies and ideas. This remains true even though Lenin thought that the peasant problem could be solved by voluntary inspiration, and would probably have recoiled at the conditions of forced collectivisation.

Is it necessary to stress that this does not make these actions right, or good? Yes, it is, because so many critics assume that to explain is to justify. So it must be said several times that no moral conclusions follow, that even the most vicious acts by politicians and others generally have causes which must be analysed. We are here only concerned to disentangle the special contribution of Stalin, the extent to which Stalinism was, so to speak, situation-determined. This is relevant, indeed, to one's picture of Stalin's personal responsibility, but in no way absolves him of such responsibility. If in order to do A it proves necessary to do B, we can, after all, refuse to do B, abandon or modify the aim of attaining A, or resign, or, in extreme circumstances—like Stalin's old comrade Ordzhonikidze—commit suicide.

But Stalin's personal responsibility goes far beyond his being the voice and leader of a party majority in a given historical situation. For one cannot possibly argue that all the immense evils of the Stalin era flowed inescapably from the policy decisions of 1928-29. In assessing Stalin's personal role in bringing these evils about, it is useful to approach the facts from two angles. There was, first, the category of evils which sprang from policy choices which Stalin made and which he need not have made; in other words we are here concerned with consequences (perhaps necessary) of unnecessary decisions. The other category consists of evil actions which can reasonably be attributed to Stalin and which are his direct responsibility.

Of course, these categories shade into one another, as do murder and manslaughter. In the first case, the evils were in a sense situation-determined, but Stalin had a large hand in determining the situation. In the second, his guilt is as clear as a politician's guilt can be.

The most obvious examples of the first category are: the brutality of collectivisation and the madly excessive pace of industrial development. In each case, we are dealing with *"excessive excesses,"* since we have already noted that collectivisation without coercion was impossible, and rapid industrialisation was bound to cause stresses and strains.

Take collectivisation first. Some over-zealous officials were presumably bound to overdo things, especially since the typical Party man was a townsman with no understanding or sympathy for peasants and their problems. But these officials received orders to impose rapid collectivisation, to deport *kulaks,* to seize all livestock, and Stalin was surely the source of these orders. The deportation of the *kulaks* (which in reality meant anyone who voiced opposition to collectivisation) removed at one blow the most efficient farmers. There had been no serious preparation of the measures, no clear orders about how a collective farm should be run. Chinese experience, at least before the communes, suggests that milder ways of proceeding are possible. In any event, the attempt to collectivise all private livestock ended in disaster and a retreat. It is worth reproducing the figures from the official handbook of agricultural statistics:

LIVESTOCK POPULATION (MILLION OF HEAD)

	1928	1934
Horses	32.1	15.4
Cattle	60.1	33.5
Pigs	22.0	11.5
Sheep	97.3	32.9

Yet already by 1934 private livestock holdings were again permitted, and in 1938 over three-quarters of all cows, over two-thirds of all pigs, nearly two-thirds of all sheep, were in private hands. This is evidence of a disastrous error.

Its consequences were profound. Peasant hostility and bitterness were greatly intensified. For many years there were in fact no net investments in agriculture, since the new tractors merely went to replace some of the slaughtered horses. Acute food shortage made itself felt—though the state's control over produce ensured that most of those who died in the resulting famine were peasants and not townsmen. But once all this happened, the case for coercion was greatly strengthened, the need for police measures became more urgent than ever, the power of the censorship was increased, freedom of speech had still further to be curtailed, as part of the necessities of remaining in power and continuing the industrial revolution in an environment grown more hostile as a result of such policies. So Stalin's policy decisions led to events which contributed greatly to the further growth of totalitarianism and the police state.

The same is true of the attempt to do the impossible on the industrial front in the years of the first five-year plan. Much of the effort was simply wasted, as when food was taken from hungry peasants and exported to pay for machines which rusted in the open or were wrecked by untrained workmen. At the same time, the closing of many private workshops deprived the people of consumers' goods which the state, intent on building steelworks and machine-shops, was quite unable to provide. Again, living standards suffered, the hatred of many citizens for the régime increased, the N.K.V.D. had to be expanded and the logic of police rule followed. But Stalin had a big role in the initial decisions to jump too far too fast.[9] (It is interesting to note that Mao, who should have learnt the lessons of history, repeated many of these mistakes in China's "great leap forward" of 1958-59, which suggests that *there are certain errors which Communists repeatedly commit,* possibly due to the suppression, in "antirightist" campaigns, of the voices of moderation and common sense.)

One of the consequences of these acute hardships was isolation from foreign countries. Economists often speak of the "demonstration effect," *i.e.,* of the effect of the knowledge of higher living standards abroad on the citizens of poor and under-developed countries. This knowledge may act as a spur to effort—but it also generates resistance to sacrifice. Stalin and his régime systematically "shielded" Soviet citizens from knowledge of the outside world, by censorship, by cutting off personal contacts, by misinformation. The need to do so, in their eyes, was greatly increased by the extent of the drop in living standards in the early 'thirties.

But we must now come to Stalin's more direct contribution to the brutality and terrorism of the Stalin era.

There was, firstly, his needless cruelty which showed itself already in the methods used to impose collectivisation. The great purges were surely not "objectively necessary." To explain them one has to take into account Stalin's thirst for supreme power, his intense pathological suspiciousness, *i.e.,* matters pertaining to Stalin's personal position and character. These led him to massacre the majority of the "Stalinist" central committee elected in 1934, who had supported or at the very least tolerated Stalin's policies up to that date. The facts suggest that they believed that relaxation was possible and desirable; many of them seem to have died for the crime of saying so. Nor was there any "police logic" for the scale and drastic nature of the purges. Indeed, the police chiefs figured prominently among the victims. True, there was a kind of "snow-

---

[9] N. Jasny, in his *Soviet Industrialisation, 1938-52* (Chicago, 1961), has much to say about the chaotic planning of the early 'thirties.

balling" of arrests, which might have got out of control in 1938, but this was due largely to the effect of the terror on the police, who had to show zeal or go under. Nor can any "necessity" explain the post-war repressions, the death of Voznesensky, the so-called "Leningrad affair," the shooting of the Jewish intellectuals, the "doctors' plot." Stalin played so prominently a personal role in establishing a reign of terror in the Party and the country that he must bear direct responsibility even where executions were the result of false information supplied to him by his subordinates for reasons of their own.

The atmosphere of terror had, of course, far-reaching consequences in every sphere of Soviet life. It became particularly grotesque and purposeless in the last years of Stalin, when the social and economic developments, plus victory in war, provided the Soviet régime with a much firmer base among the people, so that a considerable part of the discontent was the result, rather than the cause, of repressive measures. Many obviously overdue reforms had to await his death. As did Tsar Nicholas I, a century earlier, Stalin was able to delay "necessary" changes.

Many other examples can be given of the personal role of Stalin. On the economic front, the miserable state of the peasants in 1953 was due largely to Stalin's obstinate refusal to face the facts and listen to serious advice. He contributed greatly to wasteful and grandiose schemes to "transform nature," and to a wasteful and grandiose style of architecture. In the military field, history will, I think, support Khrushchev's accusation that Stalin's inability to see the signs of a German attack, his unwillingness to allow preparations, his massacre of the best Soviet officers, all made a personal contribution to the Russian disasters of 1941. Stalin personally insisted on his own deification, the rewriting of history, the creation of myths. Some myths were based on lies which he himself publicly uttered. For instance, in 1935 he announced: "We have had no poor for two or three years now"—and this when bread had reached the highest price, in relation to wages, that it had ever attained in Soviet history. Or equally ridiculous was his claim, in 1947, that Moscow "had completely abolished slums." In this personal way he made impossible all serious discussion either of living standards or the housing problem, just as his wildly false assertions about "Bukharin and Trotsky, agents of Hitler and the Mikado," made the writing of Soviet history impossible in Russia. One could argue that the myth about "voluntary collectivisation" was an objectively necessary lie, in the sense of transcending Stalin's personality; indeed, this lie figures in the Party programme adopted by the 22nd Congress last November. But Stalin's lies went very much beyond this, and beyond the distortions and myths which can be ascribed to other politicians in other countries.

Throughout Russia, officials at all levels modelled themselves on

Stalin, and each succeeded in imposing more unnecessary misery on more subordinates, stultifying initiative, penalising intelligence, discouraging originality. The price of all this is still being paid.

The urgent need to prepare for war has often been advanced as an excuse for Stalin's industrial "tempos" and for the terror. This can hardly be accepted. In the worst years of social coercion and over-ambitious plans, *i.e.,* 1929-33, Hitler was only just climbing to power, and Comintern policy showed that he was not then regarded as the main enemy. It is possible that Stalin was liquidating all potential opponents in the Purges of 1936-38 as a precaution in case war broke out, though this seems doubtful for a variety of reasons. But it is quite false to use the result of the war as ex-post-factum justification of Stalinism. Perhaps, with less harsh policies, the greater degree of loyalty in 1941 would have offset a smaller industrial base? In any event the Purges not only led to the slaughter of the best military officers but also halted the growth of heavy industry.

The attentive reader will have noticed that this analysis has some features in common with Khrushchev's. Before 1934, Stalin had been carrying out policies which commanded the assent of a majority of the Party and which, like collectivisation, had been accepted as necessary and irreversible by the bulk of Party members, whatever their reservations about particular mistakes and acts of brutality. However, after that date he took more and more personal, arbitrary measures, massacred much of the Party, behaved like an oriental despot. It is true that he was also arbitrary before 1934, and that he took some wise decisions after that date; but there is a case for placing a qualitative change around then.

But this is by no means the end of the matter. It is not only a question of making some obvious remarks concerning Khrushchev's own role during the terror. Of much more general significance is the fact that the events prior to 1934, including the building-up of Stalin into an all-powerful and infallible dictator (by men many of whom he afterwards massacred), cannot be disassociated from what followed; at the very least they provided Stalin with his opportunity. This is where the historian must avoid the twin and opposite pitfalls of regarding what happened as inevitable, and regarding it as a chapter of "personalised" accidents. At each stage there are choices to be made, though the range of possible choices is generally much narrower than people suppose. In 1928 any practicable Bolshevik programme would have been harsh and unpopular. It might not have been *so* harsh and unpopular but for choices which need not necessarily have been made. If before 1934, *i.e.,* in the very period of maximum social coercion, Stalin truly represented the will of the Party, and Khrushchev argues that he did, some totalitarian consequences logically follow. One of these, as already suggested, is the semi-militarised party led by a

Fuehrer, a dictator, because without an unquestioned leader the consequences of the policies adopted could not be faced.

But, even if it is true that the triumph of a dictator may be explained by objective circumstances which certainly existed in the Soviet situation, the acts of a dictator once he has "arrived" involve a considerable (though of course not infinite) degree of personal choice. Those who gave him the opportunity to act in an arbitrary and cruel way, who adopted policies which involved arbitrariness and coercion on a big scale, cannot ascribe subsequent events to the wickedness of one man or his immediate associates and claim that their hands are clean, even indeed if they were shot themselves on Stalin's orders. The whole-hog Stalin, in other words, was not "necessary," but the possibility of a Stalin was a necessary consequence of the effort of a minority group to keep power and to carry out a vast social-economic revolution in a very short time. And *some* elements of Stalinism were, in those circumstances, scarcely avoidable.

The serious problem for us is to see how far certain elements of Stalinism, in the sense of purposefully-applied social coercion, imposed by a party in the name of an ideology, are likely or liable to accompany rapid economic development even in non-Communist countries.

For it is surely true that many of the problems tackled by Stalin so brutally are present elsewhere, though events in the U.S.S.R. were, of course, deeply affected by peculiar features of Russia and of Bolshevism. The West should indeed emphasize the high cost in human and material terms of a Stalin, and show that the rise of such a man to supreme power in the Soviet Union was, to use the familiar Soviet-Marxist jargon phrase, "not accidental." Indeed, some Western historians who normally write "personalist" and empiricist history will begin to see the virtues of an approach they normally deride as "historicist"; they will analyse Soviet history to establish patterns, regularities, "necessities" which lead to Stalin. By contrast, an embarrassed Khrushchev will be—is being—forced to give an un-Marxist emphasis to personal and accidental factors.

But, of course, we must not confine our search for "necessities" in history only to instances which happen to serve a propagandist purpose. This would be a typically Soviet approach to historiography, only in reverse. It is particularly important to think very seriously about the interrelationship of coercion and industrialisation, about the nature of the obstacles and vicious circles which drive men to think in totalitarian terms. Unless we realise how complex are the problems which development brings, how irrelevant are many of our ideas to the practical possibilities open to statesmen in these countries, we may unconsciously drive them towards the road which led to Stalin. They cannot be satisfied with "the pace of a tortoise."

b. Was Stalin Really Necessary?:
a Comment *

LEOPOLD LABEDZ
Associate Editor, Survey

Alec Nove's article, "Was Stalin Really Necessary?" is very stimulating. Although his answer to the basic question posed is not quite clear,
one can agree with most of what he says. Still, my own inclination is to
say "Quite, quite unnecessary!" and so I should like to make a few comments on the way Nove handled the three central issues:

1. What is the meaning of historical necessity?
2. Was the forcible collectivisation necessary?
3. Was the Great Purge linked with the 1929-31 economic upheaval
or was it only a consequence of Stalin's "excesses"?

1. Nove argues that historical necessity is not historically immanent
(why exactly is it historical?) but is to be understood as the existence of
objective and subjective factors limiting the range of possible choice. The
subjective factors are concerned with the Aristotelian essences of those taking decisions. "A rabbi does not eat pork; were he to do so, he would not
be a rabbi." Similarly: "there may have been a number of solutions to the
problems posed by Russia of the 'twenties which the Communists could
not have chosen because they were Communists." That may be true, but
if historical necessity is so defined then each régime carries within it its
own "inevitability." The Indian Congress Party, for instance, cannot do
certain things without ceasing to be an Indian Congress Party, and Soviet
Russia's "historical necessities" are thus irrelevant to it by definition. Is
this the conclusion Mr. Nove wanted to draw? He rightly rejects Marxist
"historical inevitability," but then in his reasoning the belief in it is surely
a subjective factor without which the Soviet Communists would not be
Communists. It thus follows that, however mistaken and however "volun-
taristic" their acts, they are in Nove's scheme in a sense all "necessary" by
definition. This is, of course, part of a genuine paradox; but it largely rests
on how the words "possible" and "necessary" are defined. Is this begging

* Reprinted from Leopold Labedz, "Nove on Stalin," *Encounter,* August, 1962,
pp. 93-94, by permission of the author and the publisher.

the whole question? If "really necessary" is not the same as "historically necessary," why is it not?

2. The answer to the second question is given in the affirmative: Yes, Nove argues, forcible collectivisation was necessary. This is not the answer implied by Gomulka, and Khrushchev himself admitted at the 22nd Congress the possibility of a different road to socialism in countries "where peasants are deeply attached to private property." The Polish Communists have quickly reproduced this passage offering a doctrinal legitimation of their present practice. If this is so, doesn't it cast doubt on the "necessity" of Stalin's forcible collectivisation? Peasants everywhere are attached to their property; so were they in Russia. It is interesting to compare Nove's conclusions on the subject with those given in the official Polish Communist theoretical journal *Nowe Drogi* (No. 12, 1961):

> Apart from objective factors there are also subjective factors. There are no situations in which the Party or the individuals do not have possibility of choice, in which definite problems cannot be solved by different methods, less costly, and avoiding many unnecessary sufferings and negative effects.

Would Nove reject this in favour of the Khrushchevian justification of Stalin's "necessities" (*minus* his "excesses")? Is there not enough evidence that the whole monstrous character of Soviet collectivisation was connected more with *political* than with economic necessities?

3. According to Nove, forcible collectivisation stemmed from objective necessities and only its excesses (which Stalin also condemned) resulted from subjective factors and indirect effects. This apparently is not the case with the great purges of 1936-38. In his view, "the great purges cannot possibly be derived from any 'objective necessity' arising from past policies. They can be derived from Stalin's thirst for supreme power, his intense pathological suspiciousness."

This is an astonishing argument. It is enough to look at the record (for example, in the chapter on the subject in Leonard Schapiro's history of *The Communist Party of the Soviet Union*) to see that historical evidence points to a precisely opposite conclusion. The Great Purge was more than intimately linked with the past policies of forcible collectivisation. Nobody, of course, would deny Stalin's "thirst for power," but this was also an operative factor in the previous instances. "Given the nature of the system," Stalin had at each stage been taking decisions which largely conditioned his subsequent actions (and "Stalin would not be Stalin, if he had done otherwise").

Collectivisation may be regarded either as an end in itself, or as a means to secure industrial growth. In the former case, the problems besetting Soviet agriculture today cast doubt on the economic rationality of collectivisation; in the latter case, in the perspective of 1931, Stalin may well have felt that the drastic method of squeezing agriculture in order to build industry quickly may be the only one, but three decades later this does not seem so certain and there is no reason to fall into the trap of *post hoc ergo propter hoc* type of reasoning. In any case the economic perspective is not the only one. What may seem economically necessary may not be "really necessary" if the human price to be paid is too high. It is only too easy to confuse retrospectively doctrinal necessity with economic necessity and then make it into a "historical necessity".

The exclusively economic perspective probably accounts for Nove's conclusion on the great purges. "Objective necessity" in this context means for him more or less plausible economic reasons; and these, he seems to suggest, may have justified drastic steps in 1931 but not after 1934 when the economic situation improved. But in political perspective there were apparently reasons more compelling than the economic one for Stalin to act as he did.

For an economist there may be a temptation to qualify economic reasons as "objective necessity", but not political reasons. This reflects a certain economic determinism. It is an oversimplification to regard Stalinism as just a function of the necessities of industrialisation in "backward Russia". Stalin had risen to power before his "second revolution" and not as a result of it. There is no historical reason to confer an economic justification on his would-be imitators in the underdeveloped countries, however harsh may be the conditions of the industrial "take-off" in them.

c. Was Stalin Really Necessary?: a Rejoinder *

ALEC NOVE
University of Glasgow

It is always a pleasure to cross swords with my old friend Leopold Labedz, who never fails to be a stimulating opponent. He takes me to task for my judgment of the necessity or otherwise of Stalin. I do not deny the validity of some of his comments, but on occasion he seems to misunderstand what I was trying to say. My article was concerned, first, to discuss the personal role of Stalin, *i.e.,* the extent to which his terror régime was situation-determined; secondly, I was concerned to identify the extent to

* Reprinted from Alec Nove, "Was Stalin Necessary?", *Encounter,* November, 1962, pp. 93-94, by permission of the author and the editor.

which the situation itself, including the horrors of forced collectivisation, flowed from the existence of a Communist dictatorship which was trying to industrialise a predominantly peasant country quickly. I do not pretend that these are the only questions which should be asked in a survey of the political and economic history of the Soviet Union. Nor indeed are they the kind of questions which permit of a definitive answer. They are, nonetheless, matters which are interesting to discuss.

I do not quite understand the point of Labedz's criticism of my discussion of necessity. He both accepts and rejects the proposition that the choices of politicians are limited by their own ideological attitudes and beliefs. Surely, if one is trying to identify the role of an individual, it is significant to identify the ideological limitations on his choice which would apply not only to him but also to the overwhelming majority of his party comrades. For example, no leader of the British Labour Party is in a position to de-nationalise an existing nationalised industry, and this is surely an elementary political fact. A Conservative is less limited in this respect, though no doubt he would be precluded by his beliefs from advocating certain solutions which would be acceptable to the Labour Party. All this is obvious, and I do not see why the same kind of logic cannot be applied to the choices available to the Bolsheviks. Labedz complains that "if historical necessity is so defined, then each régime carries with it its own inevitability." The word "inevitability" is his, not mine. It does carry with it its own limitations on the range of practicable choices. He points out that, if my logic were valid, the Indian Congress Party must be seen as having a different field of choices from that which was or would be available to the Communists. A minute's reflection would cause him to see that this is not only the case, but self-evidently the case. Why is this a criticism?

Labedz also asserts that I expressed the view that "forcible collectivisation was necessary." In doing so he again shows a misunderstanding of the subject of my article, which was Stalin and not collectivisation as such. I carefully made the point that non-Communists would have found some totally different solution; I also quite specifically left open the question of the possible viability of alternative policies. What I tried to do was to stress the considerations which led to the decision to impose collectivisation, looking for the impersonal logic of events, noting that the bulk of the Communist Party, including former oppositionists, rallied round the Party in its campaign against the peasants. All this is relevant to the assessment of Stalin's personal role. I also noted that voluntary collectivisation was a non-starter in the circumstances, and that in those same circumstances forced collectivisation would be associated with excesses. The actual methods used, not without a great deal of personal encouragement from Stalin, led to excesses and brutalities on a vast scale. What happened then is not part of any model for underdeveloped countries to follow. It is rather a terrible warning, and I never suggested otherwise.

Labedz roundly asserts that I deny any connection between collectivisation and the great purge. Perhaps he would re-read my article, where I devote much space to establishing the connection between the harshness and brutalities of collectivisation and the increasing intensity of police repression. But the events which followed Kirov's death, and especially the great massacres of 1936-38, were no *necessary* consequence of the events before 1934. Labedz seems to overlook the distinction between a causal connection and a necessary connection, though admittedly the distinction is never absolute, but is rather one of degree. *Of course* the events of 1929-34 were part of the essential background of the purges. But was it a logical consequence of collectivisation for Stalin to massacre the majority of the members of his own faction, the very men who carried collectivisation through? Is there not some evidence for the proposition that this massacre followed an attempt by his colleagues to restrain Stalin's growing arbitrariness and blood-letting? True, the earlier events created an atmosphere in which a mass purge became possible. However, as recent Chinese experience suggests, disastrous "leaps forward" can sometimes be followed by a sinking of differences in an effort to put matters right, rather than by mass shootings.

Labedz would seem to ascribe to me the belief that I accept only economic and social logic, and not a political logic of events. This is surely not the case. The desire of the Communist leadership to maintain itself in power was an essential element in the choices which they made, including the decision to collectivise. The relative importance of this aspect of the decision is a matter on which legitimate disagreement is possible, but I nowhere denied that this was a significant factor. Did the events of 1936-38 follow from political necessity? If they did, and I failed to allow for this, I am guilty of error. However, despite carefully reading Schapiro's book, I still believe that what I called the "whole-hog Stalinist terror" was primarily aimed at securing the absolute dictatorship of Joseph Stalin, over the Party and everyone else. (Schapiro's chapter on the purges is entitled: "Stalin's Victory Over the Party"!) I say this while entirely accepting the proposition that political logic led to toughness and to numerous restrictions on human freedom. It is true that the power manœuvring of Stalin did indeed have its own logic and its own "irregularities." However, since my paper was concerned with identifying Stalin's personal role, I naturally treated actions in furtherance of Stalin's career as attributable to Stalin rather than to the impersonal logic of events. I am surprised that Labedz should be so insistent on historical inevitability and the inexorable march of History, etc., etc. On other occasions he and those who think like him seem to take a somewhat different view of the role of personality.

d. *Was Stalin Really Necessary?:*
a Reply to the Rejoinder *

LEOPOLD LABEDZ

Associate Editor, Survey

Having formulated the problem "of the necessity or otherwise of Stalin", Alec Nove is still reluctant to give an explicit answer to his own question, despite my promptings. Instead, he tries to turn the tables by reversing the charge and accusing me of being "insistent on historical inevitability and the inexorable march of History". I admire his polemical skill, but one should not exaggerate: not only have I not expressed in my letter anything remotely connected with such argument, it was most emphatically directed against it.

Nove dissociated himself in his article from historicism; nevertheless, he did betray a certain tendency towards determinism. Apart from the general Krushchevian character of his analysis (which he admits), implying the "necessity" of Stalin before 1934, there was a somewhat selective impatience with historical "might-have-beens" ("If, if, if grandma had a beard, she would be grandpa") and also the familiar, though qualified, stress that "we sometimes forget that you really *cannot* make omelettes without breaking eggs".

We also sometimes forget that those who accept the "necessary evil" in history, eventually tend to stress more and more the "necessity" and less and less the "evil". It is all too easy to dismiss historical "might-have-beens" in the name of "realism"; but those who reject historical determinism cannot dismiss them in principle. If it is admitted that we have our choices in facing the problems of today, the same surely must apply to the problems of yesterday. Hence, unless we believe in historical inevitability, we have to accept the idea of historical "might-have-beens". Nove's arguments reflect less a consistent method of analysis than an attitude of mind.

It is ironical that he should insist so much on the necessity of collectivization now that Khrushchev himself told an American journalist that

* Hitherto unpublished manuscript. Originally prepared for the Dallin-Brzezinski seminar at the Russian Institute of Columbia University, it has been slightly revised by the author, especially for publication here. Included herein by permission of the author.

"We are paying now for Stalin's mistakes in agriculture" (*New York Times,* April 26, 1962). Replying to the Chinese attacks, the Yugoslav Communists emphatically rejected the necessity of collectivization, saying that it "would provoke an open conflict between the state and the peasants" (*Komunist,* November 7, 1963). Indeed, this has been the case in all the countries of the Soviet bloc where it was imposed upon the countryside. A public opinion poll recently conducted among the Polish farmers amply confirms it: only 2.2 percent among them are ready to accept the collective farm as a solution of the agricultural problems (*The Polish Sociological Bulletin,* No. 1, 1963).

The "necessity" of Stalinist collectivization cannot be seriously argued on economic grounds, and even less so on social grounds. It is only "necessary" for political reasons and then it is *post hoc* dressed up as a "historical necessity". The subsequent "ideological superstructure" is buttressed by the doctrinal myth of historical inevitability. Nove does not believe in it, but he falls into some methodological fallacies usually connected with it.

His definition of "necessity" may not in his view be historicist, but in effect it reintroduces inevitability through the back door. If subjective ideological belief makes for him an action "necessary" (not characteristic, or appropriate, or likely, but necessary), then in case of Bolsheviks it is also *ipso facto* inevitable, because of their belief in historical inevitability. We are all aware of the Popperian "self-fulfilling prophecy" but that should make it easier to avoid the pitfalls of "historical necessity". Indeed, Nove's reasoning simply confuses the probability of action and its necessity. It is pointless to argue at one and the same time, as Nove did in his article, that forcible collectivization was necessary for the Communists and then to declare that after all there is always a choice: one can even "like Stalin's old comrade Ordzhonikidze—commit suicide". The chief architect of the forcible collectivization would have been somewhat perplexed by this combination of the logic of historical determinism with the existentialist free choice. He was never reluctant in breaking eggs, but his actions were supported, as Djilas reports, by a belief in their "historical inevitability" and because of this, within the framework of Nove's own formulation, his range of choice was limited and *his* suicide did not enter into it.

The confusion stems from postulating "essences" of the actors on the historical scene in analysing their political actions. It is perfectly obvious that their ideological beliefs make some actions more likely than others; still, they can change their ideological beliefs, and within a given ideological framework there is also a margin of choice. Not only non-Communists would have found a different solution to the problem of industrialization, many Communists would have done it too. Nove refers to Erlich's book on the Soviet industrialization debate, but he seems to have completely missed its main point, which contradicts his own. Erlich points out that none of the various proposals discussed in the Soviet economic debates between 1924 and 1928 was eventually implemented and that the participants in these debates, all of them Communists, perished in the great purge.

All of them—Left, Right, or Center—operated under the assumption that in the sphere of economic policy there are resistances of material which call not for a smashing knock-out blow but for some kind of coexistence of heterogeneous socio-economic setups for a long time to come.

However, when Stalin eliminated the Left and then the Right opposition, the time for economic arguments was over, and they were replaced by what Erlich calls "the meat-axe technique". Butchers may well be economically more necessary than economists, but one must not jump to conclusions about their historical necessity. Economic goals can be reached in a variety of ways and 'great leaps forward' are not always successful. Yet certain types of omelettes cannot be made without breaking eggheads—and economists, of all people, should remember this. Erlich's conclusion shows that, unlike Nove, he is well aware of it:

The rapid-fire industrialization and sweeping collectivization were not merely devices of economic policy, but means of extending the direct control of the totalitarian state over the largest possible number within the shortest time.

In the light of this conclusion by another economist, the inconsistency of Nove's analysis is all the more striking. His treatment of the great purge stands in contrast to his attitude towards collectivization. The latter was, but the former was not "objectively necessary". Thus the logic of 'necessity' is applied to the economic but not to the political sphere. One can reject it in both cases, as I do; or rationalize them in both cases, as Stalin did; but one cannot apply it in one case, but not the other, without committing a methodological fallacy.

SOVIET VIEWS

2. PAGES FROM THE PAST: A GARLAND OF STALINISMS *

The Sun . . .
The heart of every Soviet citizen is warmed by his love of Stalin. In all languages of the world, humanity glorifies his name, the name of the promoter of popular happiness, of the head of working humanity.
PRAVDA, DECEMBER *10, 1949.*

The Father . . .
He is friend of the sun
He will disarm all his foes.
Your name is on our lips,
Your heart is in our hearts,
Your will in our deeds.
Stalin, the father, has sixteen daughters—
Sixteen loving Republics.
PRAVDA, DECEMBER *11, 1949.*

The Ubiquitous . . .
Stalin! Always we hear in our souls his dear name. And here, in the Kremlin, his presence touches us at every step. We walk on stones which he may have trod only recently. Let us fall on our knees and kiss those holy footprints.
FROM ZEMLIA RUSSKAIA [RUSSIAN LAND], BOOK PUBLISHED BY KOMSOMOL, *1946.*

Author of Creation . . .
O Great Stalin, O Leader of the Peoples,
Thou who didst give birth to man,
Thou who didst make fertile the earth,
Thou who dost rejuvenate the centuries,
Thou who givest blossom to the spring . . .
PRAVDA, AUGUST *28, 1936.*

Omnipotent (?) Sire . . .
I love a young woman with a renewed love and I shall perpetuate myself in my children—all thanks to Thee, great educator Stalin. . . . And when the woman I love presents me with a child, the first word it shall utter will be: Stalin.
PRAVDA, FEBRUARY *1, 1935,* QUOTING A WRITER BY NAME OF AVDIENKO.

That naughty Yossif . . .
. . . I feel no more than in my twenties since Stalin taught me to understand the meaning of life and art. . . .
IZVESTIA, DECEMBER *2, 1936,* QUOTING A VENERABLE SOVIET ACTRESS.

He drives . . .
Stalin is the driver of the locomotive of history.
PRAVDA, DECEMBER *26, 1939.*
He personally . . .
. . . foresees and determines the plan for the development of our country for long historical periods. . . .
PRAVDA, DECEMBER *21, 1949.*

. . . examined all the main questions of Soviet technical history. . . .
RADIO MOSCOW, DECEMBER *28, 1949.*

. . . attended to gas conversion in Moscow.
MOSCOW BOLSHEVIK, APRIL *9, 1949.*

. . . [was responsible] for planting eucalyptus trees on the coast of the Black Sea, cultivating melons in the Moscow

---

* Reprinted from *Problems of Communism*, March-April, 1963, p. 87, by permission of the United States Information Agency.

region and extending the cultivation of branched wheat. . . .

PRAVDA, DECEMBER 21, 1949.

. . . bestows daily attention on the development of public health. . . .

MEDICAL WORKER, NOVEMBER 5, 1952.

. . . inspires Soviet male and female physical culturists to achieve new successes in sport for the glory of the great socialist Homeland.

PRAVDA, MAY 26, 1952.

He is . . .
. . . the greatest Marxist, the great Leninist, the brilliant continuer of the great cause of Marx-Engels-Lenin. . . .

SOVIET STATE AND LAW,
No. 4, 1950, P. 79.

. . . the greatest scholar of our epoch. . . .

PRAVDA, NOVEMBER 25, 1946.

. . . the creator of the Soviet Armed Forces, the great military leader of modern times . . . the creator of the progressive Soviet military science. . . .

N. BULGANIN IN PRAVDA,
DECEMBER 21, 1949.

. . . the greatest man on our planet.

K. VOROSHILOV, IN STALIN AND THE
ARMED FORCES OF THE USSR,
MOSCOW, 1951, P. 81.

. . . the best that humanity possesses. For Stalin is hope; he is expectation; he is the beacon that guides all progressive mankind. Stalin is our banner! Stalin is our will! Stalin is our victory!

NIKITA SERGEYEVICH KHRUSHCHEV, AS
QUOTED IN PRAVDA, JANUARY 31, 1937.

3. AN ANATOMY OF TERROR *

NIKITA S. KHRUSHCHEV

Former First Secretary, Central Committee of the Communist Party of the Soviet Union, and Former Chairman of the U.S.S.R. Council of Ministers

The objective of the present report is not a thorough evaluation of Stalin's life and activity. Concerning Stalin's merits, an entirely sufficient number of books, pamphlets and studies had already been written in his lifetime. The role of Stalin in the preparation and execution of the Socialist Revolution, in the Civil War, and in the fight for the construction of Socialism in our country is universally known. Everyone knows this well. At the present we are concerned with a question which has immense importance for the Party now and for the future—(we are concerned) with how the cult of the person of Stalin has been gradually growing, the cult which became at a certain specific stage the source of a whole series of exceedingly serious and grave perversions of Party principles, of Party democracy, of revolutionary legality. . . .

* From Khrushchev's 1956 address to the Twentieth Party Congress of the Communist Party of the Soviet Union. Excerpts reprinted from *The Anatomy of Terror*, 1956, by permission of the Public Affairs Press.

In December 1922 in a letter to the Party Congress Vladimir Ilyich [Lenin] wrote: "After taking over the position of Secretary General Comrade Stalin accumulated in his hands immeasurable power and I am not certain whether he will be always able to use this power with the required care." . . .

Vladimir Ilyich said: "Stalin is excessively rude, and this defect, which can be freely tolerated in our midst and in contacts among us Communists, becomes a defect which cannot be tolerated in one holding the position of the Secretary General. Because of this, I propose that the comrades consider the method by which Stalin would be removed from this position and by which another man would be selected for it, a man, who above all, would differ from Stalin in only one quality, namely, greater tolerance, greater loyalty, greater kindness and more considerate attitude toward the comrades, a less capricious temper, etc." . . .

As later events have proven, Lenin's anxiety was justified: in the first period after Lenin's death Stalin still paid attention to his [i.e., Lenin's] advice, but later he began to disregard the serious admonitions of Vladimir Ilyich.

When we analyze the practice of Stalin in regard to the direction of the Party and of the country, when we pause to consider everything which Stalin perpetrated, we must be convinced that Lenin's fears were justified. The negative characteristics of Stalin, which, in Lenin's time, were only incipient, transformed themselves during the last years into a grave abuse of power by Stalin, which caused untold harm to our Party.

We have to consider seriously and analyze correctly this matter in order that we may preclude any possibility of a repetition in any form whatever of what took place during the life of Stalin, who absolutely did not tolerate collegiality in leadership and in work, and who practiced brutal violence, not only toward everything which opposed him, but also toward that which seemed to his capricious and despotic character, contrary to his concepts.

Stalin acted not through persuasion, explanation, and patient cooperation with people, but by imposing his concepts and demanding absolute submission to his opinion. Whoever opposed this concept or tried to prove his viewpoint, and the correctness of his position—was doomed to removal from the leading collective and to subsequent moral and physical annihilation. This was especially true during the period following the XVIIth Party Congress, when many prominent Party leaders and rank-and-file Party workers, honest and dedicated to the cause of Communism, fell victim to Stalin's despotism. . . .

Stalin originated the concept "enemy of the people." This term automatically rendered it unnecessary that the ideological errors of a man or men engaged in a controversy be proven; this term made possible the usage of the most cruel repression, violating all norms of revolutionary legality, against anyone who in any way disagreed with Stalin, against those who were only suspected of hostile intent, against those who had bad reputations. . . .

Stalin . . . used extreme methods and mass repressions at a time when the revolution was already victorious, when the Soviet state was strengthened, when the exploiting classes were already liquidated and Socialist relations were rooted solidly in all phases of [the] national economy, when our Party was politically consolidated and had strengthened itself both numerically and ideologically. It is clear that here Stalin showed in a whole series of cases his intolerance, his brutality and his abuse of power. Instead of proving his political correctness and mobilizing the masses, he often chose the path of repression and physical annihilation, not only against actual enemies, but also against the Party and the Soviet government. Here we see no wisdom but only a demonstration of the brutal force which had once so alarmed V. I. Lenin.

Lately, especially after the unmasking of the Beriya gang, the Central Committee looked into a series of matters fabricated by this gang. This revealed a very ugly picture of brutal willfulness connected with the incorrect behavior of Stalin. As facts prove, Stalin, using his unlimited power, allowed himself many abuses, acting in the name of the Central Committee, not asking for the opinion of the Committee members nor even of the members of the Central Committee's Political Bureau; often he did not inform them about his personal decisions concerning very important Party and government matters. . . .

Stalin's willfulness vis-à-vis the Party and its Central Committee became fully evident after the XVIIth Party Congress which took place in 1934.

Having at its disposal numerous data showing brutal willfulness toward Party cadres, the Central Committee had created a Party Commission under the control of the Central Committee Presidium; it was charged with investigating what made possible the mass repressions against the majority of the Central Committee members and candidates elected at the XVIIth Congress of the All-Union Communist Party (Bolsheviks).

The Commission has become acquainted with a large quantity of materials in the NKVD archives and with other documents and has established many facts pertaining to the fabrication of cases against Communists, to false accusations, to glaring abuses of Socialist legality—which resulted in the death of innocent people. It became apparent that many Party, Soviet and economic activists, who were branded in 1937-1938 as "enemies," were actually never enemies, spies, wreckers, etc., but were always honest Communists; they were only so stigmatized and often, no longer able to bear barbaric tortures, they charged themselves (at the order of the investigative judges—falsifiers) with all kinds of grave and unlikely crimes. The Commission has presented to the Central Committee Presidium lengthy and documented materials pertaining to mass repressions against the delegates to the XVIIth Party Congress and against members of the Central Committee elected at that Congress. These materials have been studied by the Presidium of the Central Committee.

It was determined that of the 139 members and candidates of the Party's Central Committee who were elected at the XVIIth Congress, 98 persons, i.e., 70 percent, were arrested and shot (mostly in 1937-1938).

The same fate met not only the Central Committee members but also the majority of the delegates to the XVIIth Party Congress. Of 1966 delegates with either voting or advisory rights, 1108 persons were arrested on charges of anti-revolutionary crimes, i.e., decidedly more than a majority. This very fact shows how absurd, wild and contrary to common sense were the charges of counter-revolutionary crimes made out, as we now see, against a majority of participants at the XVIIth Party Congress. . . .

Stalin deviated from the clear and plain precepts of Lenin. Stalin put the Party and the NKVD up to the use of mass terror. . . . This terror was actually directed not at the remnants of the defeated exploiting classes but against the honest workers of the Party and of the Soviet State; against them were made lying, slanderous and absurd accusations concerning "two-facedness," "espionage," "sabotage," preparation of fictitious "plots," etc. . . .

Now when the cases of some of these so-called "spies" and "saboteurs" were examined it was found that all their cases were fabricated. Confessions of guilt of many arrested and charged with enemy activity were gained with the help of cruel and inhuman tortures.

At the same time Stalin, as we have been informed by members of the Political Bureau of that time, did not show them the statements of many accused political activists when they retracted their confessions before the military tribunal and asked for an objective examination of their cases. There were many such declarations, and Stalin doubtless knew of them.

The Central Committee considers it absolutely necessary to inform the Congress of many such fabricated "cases" against the members of the Party's Central Committee elected at the XVIIth Party Congress. . . .[1]

Only because our Party has at its disposal such great moral-political strength was it possible for it to survive the difficult events in 1937-1938 and to educate new cadres. There is, however, no doubt that our march forward toward Socialism and toward the preparation of the country's defense would have been much more successful were it not for the tremendous loss in the cadres suffered as a result of the baseless and false mass repressions in 1937-1938. . . .

Facts prove that many abuses were made on Stalin's orders without reckoning with any norms of Party and Soviet legality. Stalin was a very

[1] Now follow some specific examples of such allegedly fabricated cases. [Editor's note.]

distrustful man, sickly suspicious; we knew this from our work with him. He could look at a man and say: "Why are your eyes so shifty today," or "Why are you turning so much today and avoiding to look me directly in the eyes?" The sickly suspicion created in him a general distrust even toward eminent Party workers whom he had known for years. Everywhere and in everything he saw "enemies," "two-facers" and "spies."

Possessing unlimited power he indulged in great willfulness and choked a person morally and physically. A situation was created where one could not express one's own will.

When Stalin said that one or another should be arrested, it was necessary to accept on faith that he was an "enemy of the people." Meanwhile, Beriya's gang, which ran the organs of the state security, outdid itself in proving the guilt of the arrested and the truth of materials which it falsified. And what proofs were offered? The confessions of the arrested, and the investigative judges accepted these "confessions." And how is it possible that a person confesses to crimes which he has not committed? Only in one way—because of application of physical methods of pressuring him, tortures, bringing him to a state of unconsciousness, deprivation of his judgement, taking away of his human dignity. In this manner were "confessions" acquired. . . .

The power accumulated in the hands of one person, Stalin, led to serious consequences during the Great Patriotic War. . . .[2]

All the more shameful was the fact that after our great victory over the enemy which cost us so much, Stalin began to downgrade many of the commanders who contributed so much to the victory over the enemy, because Stalin excluded every possibility that services rendered at the front should be credited to anyone but himself. . . .

Not Stalin, but the Party as a whole, the Soviet Government, our heroic army, its talented leaders and brave soldiers, the whole Soviet nation—these are the ones who assured the victory in the Great Patriotic War. . . .

The magnificent and heroic deeds of hundreds of millions of people of the East and of the West during the fight against the threat of Fascist subjugation which loomed before us will live centuries and millennia in the memory of thankful humanity. . . .

Comrades, let us reach for some other facts. The Soviet Union is justly considered as a model of a multi-national State because we have in practice assured the equality and friendship of all nations which live in our great Fatherland.

All the more monstrous are the acts whose initiator was Stalin and

[2] Now follows a long list of accusations charging Stalin with incompetent leadership and with many errors in the conduct of the war. Special stress was put on the "grievous consequences" resulting from the unjustified annihilation of military commanders and political leaders. [Editor's note.]

which are rude violations of the basic Leninist principles of the nationality policy of the Soviet State. We refer to the mass deportations from their native places of whole nations, together with all Communists and Komsomols without any exception; this deportation action was not dictated by any military considerations.

Thus, already at the end of 1943, when there occurred a permanent break-through at the fronts of the Great Patriotic War benefiting the Soviet Union, a decision was taken and executed concerning the deportation of all the Karachai from the lands on which they lived. In the same period, at the end of December 1943, the same lot befell the whole population of the Autonomous Kalmyk Republic. In March 1944 all the Chechen and Ingush peoples were deported. . . . The Ukrainians avoided meeting this fate only because there were too many of them and there was no place to which to deport them. Otherwise, he would have deported them also.

Not only a Marxist-Leninist but also no man of common sense can grasp how it is possible to make whole nations responsible for inimical activity, including women, children, old people, Communists and Komsomols, to use mass repression against them, and to expose them to misery and suffering for the hostile acts of individual persons or groups of persons.

After the conclusion of the Patriotic War the Soviet nation stressed with pride the magnificent victories gained through great sacrifices and tremendous efforts. The country experienced a period of political enthusiasm. The Party came out of the war even more united; in the fire of the war Party cadres were tempered and hardened. Under such conditions nobody could have even thought of the possibility of some plot in the Party.

And it was precisely at this time that the so-called "Leningrad Affair" was born. As we have now proven, this case was fabricated. Those who innocently lost their lives included Comrades Voznesensky, Kusnetsov, Rodionov, Popkov, and others. . . .

Stalin became even more capricious, irritable and brutal; in particular his suspicion grew. His persecution mania reached unbelievable dimensions. Many workers were becoming enemies before his very eyes. After the war Stalin separated himself from the collective even more. Everything was decided by him alone without any consideration for anyone or anything.

This unbelievable suspicion was cleverly taken advantage of by the abject provocateur and vile enemy, Beriya, who had murdered thousands of Communists and loyal Soviet people. . . .

The willfulness of Stalin showed itself not only in decisions concerning the internal life of the country but also in the international relations of the Soviet Union.

The July Plenum of the Central Committee studied in detail the reasons for the development of conflict with Yugoslavia. It was a shameful role which Stalin played here. The "Yugoslav Affair" contained no problems which could not have been solved through Party discussions among comrades. There was no significant basis for the development of this "Affair"; it was completely possible to have prevented the rupture of relations with that country. This does not mean, however, that the Yugoslav leaders did not make mistakes or did not have shortcomings. But these mistakes and shortcomings were magnified in a monstrous manner by Stalin, which resulted in a break of relations with a friendly country. . . .

Let us also recall the "Affair of the Doctor-Plotters." Actually there was no "Affair" outside of the declaration of the woman doctor Timashuk, who was probably influenced or ordered by someone (after all, she was an unofficial collaborator of the organs of State security) to write Stalin a letter in which she declared that doctors were applying supposedly improper methods of medical treatment.

Such a letter was sufficient for Stalin to reach an immediate conclusion that there are doctor-plotters in the Soviet Union. He issued orders to arrest a group of eminent Soviet medical specialists. He personally issued advice on the conduct of the investigation and the method of interrogation of the arrested persons. He said that the academician Vinogradov should be put in chains, another one should be beaten. Present at this Congress as a delegate is the Former Minister of State Security, Comrade Ignatiev. Stalin told him curtly, "If you do not obtain confessions from the doctors we will shorten you by a head."

Stalin personally called the investigative judge, gave him instructions, advised him on which investigative methods should be used; these methods were simple—beat, beat, and once again beat.

Shortly after the doctors were arrested we members of the Political Bureau received protocols with the doctors' confessions of guilt. After distributing these protocols Stalin told us, "You are blind like young kittens; what will happen without me? The country will perish because you do not know how to recognize enemies."

The case was so presented that no one could verify the facts on which the investigation was based. There was no possibility of trying to verify facts by contacting those who had made the confessions of guilt.

We felt, however, that the case of the arrested doctors was questionable. We knew some of these people personally because they had once treated us. When we examined this "case" after Stalin's death, we found it to be fabricated from beginning to end.

This ignominious "case" was set up by Stalin; he did not, however, have the time in which to bring it to an end (as he conceived that end), and for this reason the doctors are still alive. Now all have been rehabilitated; they are working in the same places they were working before; they treat top individuals, not excluding members of the Government; they have our full confidence; and they execute their duties honestly, as they did before.

In organizing the various dirty and shameful cases, a very base role was played by the rabid enemy of our Party, an agent of a foreign intelligence service—Beriya, who had stolen into Stalin's confidence. . . .[3]

Beriya was unmasked by the Party's Central Committee shortly after Stalin's death. As a result of the particularly detailed legal proceedings it was established that Beriya had committed monstrous crimes and Beriya was shot.

The question arises why Beriya, who had liquidated tens of thousands of Party and Soviet workers, was not unmasked during Stalin's life? He was not unmasked earlier because he had utilized very skillfully Stalin's weaknesses; feeding him with suspicions, he assisted Stalin in everything and acted with his support. . . .

Comrades! The cult of the individual has caused the employment of faulty principles in Party work and in economic activity; it brought about rude violation of internal Party and Soviet democracy, sterile administration, deviations of all sorts, covering up of shortcomings and varnishing of reality. Our nation gave birth to many flatterers and specialists in false optimism and deceit.

We should also not forget that due to the numerous arrests of Party, Soviet and economic leaders, many workers began to work uncertainly, showed over-cautiousness, feared all which was new, feared their own shadows and began to show less initiative in their work. . . .

Comrades!

If we sharply criticize today the cult of the individual which was so widespread during Stalin's life and if we speak about the many negative phenomena generated by this cult which is so alien to the spirit of Marxism-Leninism, various persons may ask: How could it be? Stalin headed the Party and the country for 30 years and many victories were gained during his lifetime. Can we deny this? In my opinion, the question can be asked in this manner only by those who are blinded and hopelessly hypnotized by the cult of the individual, only by those who do not understand the essence of the revolution and of the Soviet State, only by those who do not understand, in a Leninist manner, the role of the Party and of the nation in the development of the Soviet society.

The Socialist revolution was attained by the working class and by the poor peasants with the partial support of middleclass peasants. It was attained by the people under the leadership of the Bolshevik Party. Lenin's great service consisted of the fact that he created a militant Party of the working class, . . . became its experienced leader, and led the working masses to power, to the creation of the first Socialist State.

[3] Now follows an account of some of the crimes allegedly committed by Beriya. (Beriya, by the way, is often spelled "Beria" in English transliteration. See, for example p. 331.) [Editor's note.]

You remember well the wise words of Lenin that the Soviet State is strong because of the awareness of the masses that history is created by the millions and tens of millions of people.

Our historical victories were attained thanks to the organizational work of the Party, to the many provincial organizations, and to the self-sacrificing work of our great nation. These victories are the result of the great drive and activity of the nation and of the Party as a whole; they are not at all the fruit of the leadership of Stalin, as the situation was pictured during the period of the cult of the individual.

If we are to consider this matter as Marxists and as Leninists, then we have to state unequivocally that the leadership practice which came into being during the last years of Stalin's life became a serious obstacle in the path of Soviet social development. . . .

Some comrades may ask us: Where were the members of the Political Bureau of the Central Committee? Why did they not assert themselves against the cult of the individual in time? And why is this being done only now?

First of all we have to consider the fact that the members of the Political Bureau viewed these matters in a different way at different times. Initially, many of them backed Stalin actively because Stalin was one of the strongest Marxists and his logic, his strength and his will greatly influenced the cadres and Party work.

It is known that Stalin, after Lenin's death, especially during the first years, actively fought for Leninism against the enemies of Leninist theory and against those who deviated. Beginning with Leninist theory, the Party, with its Central Committee at the head, started on a great scale the work of Socialist industrialization of the country, agricultural collectivization and the cultural revolution. At that time Stalin gained great popularity, sympathy and support. The Party had to fight those who attempted to lead the country away from the correct Leninist path; it had to fight Trotskyites, Zinovievites and rightists, and the bourgeois nationalists. This fight was indispensable. Later, however, Stalin, abusing his power more and more, began to fight eminent Party and government leaders and to use terroristic methods against honest Soviet people. . . .

In the situation which then prevailed I have talked often with Nikolai Aleksandrovich Bulganin; once when we two were traveling in a car, he said, "It has happened sometimes that a man goes to Stalin on his invitation as a friend. And when he sits with Stalin, he does not know where he will be sent next, home or to jail."

It is clear that such conditions put every member of the Political Bureau in a very difficult situation. And when we also consider the fact that in the last years the Central Committee Plenary sessions were not convened and that the sessions of the Political Bureau occurred only occasionally, from time to time, then we will understand how difficult it was for any member of the Political Bureau to take a stand against one or another injust or improper procedure, against serious errors and short-comings in the practices of leadership.

* * *

Comrades: We must abolish the cult of the individual decisively, once and for all; we must draw the proper conclusions concerning both ideo-logical-theoretical and practical work.

It is necessary for this purpose:

First, in a Bolshevik manner to condemn and to eradicate the cult of the individual . . . and to fight inexorably all attempts at bringing back this practice in one form or another.

To return to and actually practice in all our ideological work the most important theses of Marxist-Leninist science about the people as the creator of history and as the creator of all material and spiritual good of humanity, about the decisive role of the Marxist Party in the revolutionary fight for the transformation of society, about the victory of Communism.

In this connection we will be forced to do much work in order to examine critically from the Marxist-Leninist viewpoint and to correct the widely spread erroneous views connected with the cult of the individual in the sphere of history, philosophy, economy and of other sciences, as well as in the literature and fine arts. It is especially necessary that in the im-mediate future we compile a serious textbook of the history of our Party which will be edited in accordance with scientific Marxist objectivism, a textbook of the history of Soviet society, a book pertaining to the events of the Civil War and the Great Patriotic War.

Secondly, to continue systematically and consistently the work done by the Party's Central Committee during the last years, a work character-ized by minute observation in all Party organizations, from the bottom to the top, of the Leninist principles of Party leadership, characterized, above all, by the main principle of collective leadership, characterized by the observation of the norms of Party life described in the Statutes of our Party, and finally, characterized by the wide practice of criticism and self-criticism.

Thirdly, to restore completely the Leninist principles of Soviet Social-ist democracy, expressed in the Constitution of the Soviet Union, to fight willfulness of individuals abusing their power. The evil caused by acts vio-lating revolutionary Socialist legality which have accumulated during a long time as a result of the negative influence of the cult of the individual has to be completely corrected.

Comrades!

The XXth Congress of the Communist Party of the Soviet Union has manifested with a new strength the unshakable unity of our Party, its cohesiveness around the Central Committee, its resolute will to accom-plish the great task of building Communism. And the fact that we present in all their ramifications the basic problems of overcoming the cult of the individual which is alien to Marxism-Leninism, as well as the problem of liquidating its burdensome consequences, is an evidence of the great moral and political strength of our Party.

We are absolutely certain that our Party, armed with the historical resolutions of the XXth Congress, will lead the Soviet people along the Leninist path to new successes, to new victories. . . .

CHINESE COMMUNIST VIEWS

4. ON THE QUESTION OF STALIN *

EDITORIAL DEPARTMENTS OF THE "PEOPLE'S DAILY" ("RENMIN RIBAO") AND THE "RED FLAG" ("HONGQI")

The question of Stalin is one of worldwide importance which has had repercussions among all classes in every country and which is still a subject of much discussion today, with different classes and their political parties and groups taking different views. It is likely that no final verdict can be reached on this question in the present century, but there is virtual agreement among the majority of the international working class and of the revolutionary people, who disapprove of the complete negation of Stalin and more and more cherish his memory. This is also true of the Soviet Union. Our controversy with the leaders of the CPSU [1] is with a section of people. We hope to persuade them in order to advance the revolutionary cause. This is our purpose in writing the present article. . . .

The great Soviet Union was the first state of the dictatorship of the proletariat. In the beginning, the foremost leader of the party and the government in this state was Lenin. After Lenin's death, it was Stalin. After Lenin's death, Stalin became not only the leader of the party and government of the Soviet Union but the acknowledged leader of the international communist movement as well.

---

* Excerpts reprinted from *Peking Review*, Sept. 20, 1963, pp. 8-15.
[1] Communist Party Soviet Union. [Editor's note.]

It is only 46 years since the first socialist state was inaugurated by the October Revolution. For nearly 30 of these years Stalin was the foremost leader of this state. Whether in the history of the dictatorship of the proletariat or in that of the international communist movement, Stalin's activities occupy an extremely important place. The Chinese Communist Party has consistently maintained that the question of how to evaluate Stalin and what attitude to take toward him is not just one of appraising Stalin himself; more important, it is a question of how to sum up the historical experience of the dictatorship of the proletariat and of the international communist movement since Lenin's death.

Comrade Khrushchev completely negated Stalin at the 20th Congress of the CPSU. He failed to consult the fraternal parties in advance on this question of principle, which involves the whole international communist movement, and afterwards tried to impose a fait accompli on them. Whoever makes an appraisal of Stalin different from that of the leadership of the CPSU is charged with "defense of the personality cult," as well as "interference" in the internal affairs of the CPSU. But no one can deny the international significance of the historical experience of the first state of the dictatorship of the proletariat, or the historical fact that Stalin was the leader of the international communist movement; consequently, no one can deny that the appraisal of Stalin is an important question of principle involving the whole international communist movement. On what ground, then, do the leaders of the CPSU forbid other fraternal parties to make a realistic analysis and appraisal of Stalin?

The CCP [2] has invariably insisted on an overall, objective, and scientific analysis of Stalin's merit by the method of historical materialism and the presentation of history as it actually occurred, and has opposed subjective, crude, and complete negation of Stalin by the method of historical idealism and the willful distortion and alteration of history.

The CCP has consistently held that Stalin did commit errors, which had their ideological as well as social and historical roots. It is necessary to criticize the errors Stalin actually committed, not those groundlessly attributed to him, and to do so from a correct stand with correct methods, but we have consistently opposed improper criticism of Stalin, made from a wrong stand and with wrong methods.

Stalin fought Tsarism and propagated Marxism during Lenin's lifetime; after he became a member of the Central Committee of the Bolshevik Party headed by Lenin he took part in the struggle to pave the way for the

[2] China's Communist Party. [Editor's note.]

1917 revolution; after the October Revolution he fought to defend the fruits of the proletarian revolution.

Stalin led the CPSU and the Soviet people, after Lenin's death, in resolutely fighting both internal and external foes, and in safeguarding and consolidating the first socialist state in the world.

Stalin led the CPSU and the Soviet people in upholding the line of socialist industrialization and agricultural collectivization and in achieving great successes in socialist transformation and socialist construction.

Stalin led the CPSU, the Soviet people, and the Soviet Army in an arduous and bitter struggle to the great victory of the antifascist war.

Stalin defended and developed Marxism-Leninism in the fight against various kinds of opportunism, against the enemies of Leninism, the Trotskiyites,[3] Zinovievites, Bukharinites and other bourgeois agents.

Stalin made an indelible contribution to the international communist movement in a number of theoretical writings which are immortal Marxist-Leninist works.

Stalin led the Soviet party and government in pursuing a foreign policy which on the whole was in keeping with proletarian internationalism and in greatly assisting the revolutionary struggles of all peoples, including the Chinese people. Stalin stood in the forefront of the tide of history guiding the struggle, and was an irreconcilable enemy of the imperialists and all reactionaries.

Stalin's activities were intimately bound up with the struggles of the great CPSU and the great Soviet people and inseparable from the revolutionary struggles of the people of the whole world.

Stalin's life was that of a great Marxist-Leninist, a great proletarian revolutionary.

It is true that while he performed meritorious deeds for the Soviet people and the international communist movement, Stalin, a great Marxist-Leninist and proletarian revolutionary, also made certain mistakes. Some were errors of principle and some were errors made in the course of practical work; some could have been avoided and some were scarcely avoidable at a time when the dictatorship of the proletariat had no precedent to go by.

[3] The name is usually spelled "Trotsky," but in this translation from the Chinese it is spelled "Trotskiy" throughout the text. [Editor's note.]

In his way of thinking Stalin departed from dialectical materialism and fell into metaphysics and subjectivism on certain questions, and consequently he was sometimes divorced from reality and from the masses. In struggles inside as well as outside the party, on certain occasions and on certain questions he confused two types of contradictions which are different in nature—contradictions between ourselves and the enemy and contradictions among the people—and also confused the different methods needed in handling them. In the work led by Stalin of suppressing the counterrevolution, many counterrevolutionaries deserving punishment were duly punished, but at the same time there were innocent people who were wrongly convicted, and in 1937 and 1938 there occurred the error of enlarging the scope of the suppression of counterrevolutionaries. In the matter of party and government organization, he did not fully apply proletarian democratic centralism and, to some extent, violated it. In handling relations with fraternal parties and countries he made some mistakes. He also gave some bad counsel in the international communist movement. These mistakes caused some losses to the Soviet Union and the international communist movement.

Stalin's merits and mistakes are matters of historical, objective reality. A comparison of the two shows that his merits outweighed his faults. He was primarily correct, and his faults were secondary. In summing up Stalin's thinking and his work in their totality, surely every honest communist with a respect for history will first observe what was primary in Stalin. Therefore, when Stalin's errors are being correctly appraised, criticized, and overcome, it is necessary to safeguard what was primary in Stalin's life, to safeguard Marxism-Leninism which he defended and developed.

It would be beneficial if the errors of Stalin, which were only secondary, are taken as historical lessons so that the communists of the Soviet Union and other countries might take warning and avoid repeating those errors or commit fewer errors. Both positive and negative historical lessons are beneficial to all communists, provided they are drawn correctly and conform with and do not distort historical facts. . . .

The leaders of the CPSU have accused the CCP of defending Stalin. Yes, we do defend Stalin. When Khrushchev distorts history and completely negates Stalin, naturally we have the inescapable duty to come forward and defend him in the interests of the international communist movement.

In defending Stalin, the CCP defends his correct side, defends the glorious history of the first state of the dictatorship of the proletariat, which was created by the October Revolution; it defends the glorious history of struggle of the CPSU; it defends the prestige of the international communist movement among working people throughout the world. In brief, it defends the theory and practice of Marxism-Leninism. It is not only the Chinese communists who are doing this; all communists devoted to Marxism-Leninism, all staunch revolutionaries, and all fair-minded people have been doing the same thing.

While defending Stalin, we do not defend his mistakes. Long ago the Chinese communists had first-hand experience of some of his mistakes. Of the erroneous "left" and right opportunist lines which merged in the CCP at one time or another, some arose under the influence of certain mistakes of Stalin's, insofar as their international sources were concerned. In the late twenties, the thirties and the early and middle forties, the Chinese Marxist-Leninists represented by Comrades Mao Tse-tung and Liu Shao-chi resisted the influence of Stalin's mistakes; they gradually overcame the erroneous lines of "left" and right opportunism, and finally led the Chinese revolutionary to victory.

But since some of the wrong ideas put forward by Stalin were accepted and applied by certain Chinese comrades, we Chinese should bear the responsibility. In its struggle against "left" and right opportunism, therefore, our party criticized only its own erring comrades and never put the blame on Stalin. The purpose of our criticism was to distinguish between right and wrong, learn the appropriate lessons, and advance the revolutionary cause. We merely asked the erring comrades to correct their mistakes. If they failed to do so, we waited until they were gradually awakened by their own practical experience, provided they did not organize secret groups for clandestine and disruptive activities.

Our method was the proper method of inner-party criticism and self-criticism; we started from the desire for unity and arrived at a new unity on a new basis through criticism and struggle, and thus good results were achieved. We held that these were contradictions among the people and not between the enemy and ourselves, and that therefore we should use the above method.

What attitude have Comrade Khrushchev and other leaders of the CPSU taken toward Stalin since the 20th Congress of the CPSU?

They have not made an overall historical and scientific analysis of his life and work but have completely negated him without any distinction between right and wrong. They have treated Stalin not as a comrade but as an enemy. They have not adopted the method of criticism and self-criticism to sum up experience but have blamed Stalin for all errors, or ascribed to him the "mistakes" they have arbitrarily invented. They have not presented the facts and reasoned things out but have made demagogic personal attacks on Stalin in order to poison people's minds.

Khrushchev has abused Stalin as a "murderer," a "criminal," a "bandit," a "gambler," a "despot of the type of Ivan the Terrible," "the greatest dictator in Russian history," a "fool," an "idiot," and the like. When we are compelled to cite all this filthy, vulgar, and malicious language, we are afraid it may soil our pen and paper.

Khrushchev has maligned Stalin as "the greatest dictator in Russian history." Does this not mean that the Soviet people lived for 30 long years under the "tyranny" of "the greatest dictator in Russian history" and not under the socialist system? The great Soviet people and the revolutionary people of the whole world completely disagree with this slander!

Khrushchev has maligned Stalin as a "despot of the type of Ivan the Terrible." Does this not mean that the experience that the great CPSU and the great Soviet people provided over 30 years for people the world over was not the experience of the dictatorship of the proletariat but that of life under the rule of a feudal "despot?" The great Soviet people, the Soviet communists, and Marxist-Leninists of the whole world completely disagree with this slander!

Khrushchev has maligned Stalin as a "bandit." Does this not mean that the first socialist state in the world was for a long period headed by a "bandit?" The great Soviet people and the revolutionary people of the whole world completely disagree with this slander!

Khrushchev has maligned Stalin as a "fool." Does this not mean that the CPSU which waged heroic revolutionary struggles over the past decades had a "fool" as its leader? The Soviet communists and Marxist-Leninists of the whole world completely disagree with this slander!

Khrushchev has maligned Stalin as an "idiot." Does this not mean that the great Soviet Army which triumphed in the antifascist war had an "idiot" as its supreme commander! The glorious Soviet commanders and fighters and all antifascist fighters of the world completely disagree with this slander!

Khrushchev has maligned Stalin as a "murderer." Does this not mean that the international communist movement had a "murderer" as its teacher for decades? Communists of the whole world, including the Soviet communists, completely disagree with this slander!

Khrushchev has maligned Stalin as a "gambler." Does this not mean that the revolutionary peoples had a "gambler" as their standard-bearer in the struggles against imperialism and reaction? All revolutionary people of the world, including the Soviet people, completely disagree with this slander!

Such abuse of Stalin by Khrushchev is a gross insult to the great Soviet people, a gross insult to the CPSU, to the Soviet Army, to the dictatorship of the proletariat and to the socialist system, to the international communist movement, to the revolutionary people the world over, and to Marxism-Leninism.

In what position does Khrushchev, who participated in the leadership of the party and the state during Stalin's period, place himself when he beats his breast, pounds the table, and shouts abuse of Stalin at the top of his voice? In the position of an accomplice to a "murderer" or a "bandit?" Or in the same position as a "fool" or an "idiot?"

What difference is there between such abuse of Stalin by Khrushchev and the abuse by the imperialists, the reactionaries in various countries, and the renegades of communism? . . .

Especially noteworthy is the fact that, while they abuse Stalin in every possible way, the leaders of the CPSU regard Eisenhower, Kennedy, and the like "with respect and trust." They abuse Stalin as a "despot of the type of Ivan the Terrible" and "the greatest dictator in Russian history," but compliment both Eisenhower and Kennedy as "having the support of the absolute majority of the American people!" They abuse Stalin as an "idiot," but praise Eisenhower and Kennedy as "sensible!"

On the one hand they viciously lash at a great Marxist-Leninist, a great proletarian revolutionary, and a great leader of the international communist movement, and on the other they laud the chieftains of imperialism to the skies. Is there any possibility that the connection between these phenomena is merely accidental and that it does not follow with inexorable logic from the betrayal of Marxism-Leninism?

If his memory is not too short, Khrushchev ought to remember that at a mass rally held in Moscow in January 1937 he himself rightly condemned those who had attacked Stalin, saying: "In lifting their hand against Comrade Stalin, they lifted it against all of us, against the working class and the working people! In lifting their hand against Comrade Stalin, they lifted it against the teachings of Marx, Engels, and Lenin!" Khrushchev himself repeatedly extolled Stalin as an "intimate friend and comrade-in-arms of the great Lenin," as "the greatest genius, teacher, and leader of mankind," and "the great, ever-victorious marshal," as "the sincere friend of the people" and as his "own father."

If one compares the remarks made by Khrushchev when Stalin was alive with those made after his death, one will not fail to see that Khrushchev has made a 180-degree turn in his evaluation of Stalin.

If his memory is not short, Khrushchev should of course remember that during the period of Stalin's leadership he himself was particularly active in supporting and carrying out the then prevailing policy for suppressing counterrevolutionaries. . . .

Why does Khrushchev, who was in the leadership of the party and the state in Stalin's period and who actively supported and firmly executed the policy for suppressing counterrevolutionaries, repudiate everything done during this period and shift the blame for all errors on to Stalin alone, while altogether whitewashing himself?

When Stalin did something wrong, he was capable of criticizing himself. For instance, he had given some bad counsel with regard to the Chinese revolution. After the victory of the Chinese revolution he admitted his mistake. Stalin also admitted some of his mistakes in the work of purifying the party ranks in his report to the 18th Congress of the CPSU in 1939.

But what about Khrushchev? He simply does not know what self-criticism is; all he does is to shift the entire blame on to others and claim the entire credit for himself.

It is not surprising that these ugly actions of Khrushchev's should have taken place when modern revisionism is on the rampage. As Lenin said in 1915, when he criticized the revisionists of the Second International for their betrayal of Marxism: "In our time, when words previously spoken are forgotten, principles are abandoned, world outlook is discarded, and resolutions and solemn promises are thrown away, it is not at all surprising that such a thing should happen."

As the train of events since the 20th Congress of the CPSU has fully shown, the complete negation of Stalin by the leadership of the CPSU has had extremely serious consequences. It has provided the imperialists and the reactionaries of all countries with exceedingly welcome anti-Soviet and anticommunist ammunition. Shortly after the 20th Congress of the CPSU the imperialists exploited Khrushchev's secret anti-Stalin report to stir up a worldwide tidal wave against the Soviet Union and against communism. The imperialists, the reactionaries of all countries, the Tito clique, and opportunists of various descriptions all leaped at the chance to attack the Soviet Union, the socialist camp, and various communist parties; thus many fraternal parties and countries were placed in serious difficulties.

The frantic campaign against Stalin by the leadership of the CPSU enabled the Trotskiyites, who had long been political corpses, to come to life again and clamor for the "rehabilitation" of Trotskiy. In November 1961 at the conclusion of the 22d Congress of the CPSU, the international secretariat of the so-called Fourth International stated in a "Letter to the 22d Congress of the CPSU and Its New Central Committee" that in 1937 Trotskiy said a monument would be erected to the honor of the victims of Stalin. "Today," it continued, "this prediction has come true. Before your congress the first secretary of your party has promised the erection of this monument."

In this letter the specific demand was made that the name of Trotskiy be "engraved in letters of gold on the monument erected in honor of the victims of Stalin." The Trotskiytes made no secret of their joy, declaring that the anti-Stalin campaign started by the leadership of the CPSU had "opened the door for Trotskiyism" and would "greatly help the advance of Trotskiyism and its organization—the Fourth International."

In completely negating Stalin, the leaders of the CPSU have motives that cannot bear the light of day.

Stalin died in 1953; three years later the leaders of the CPSU violently attacked him at the 20th CPSU Congress, and eight years after his death they again did so at the 22nd Congress, removing and burning his remains. In repeating their violent attacks on Stalin, the leaders of the CPSU aimed at erasing the indelible influence of this great proletarian revolutionary among the people of the Soviet Union and throughout the world and at paving the way for negating Marxism-Leninism, which Stalin had defended and developed, and for the all-out application of a revisionist line.

Their revisionist line began exactly with the 20th Congress and became fully systematized at the 22nd Congress. The facts have shown ever more clearly that their revision of the Marxist-Leninist theories on imperialism, war and peace, proletarian revolution, and the dictatorship of the proletariat, revolution in the colonies and semicolonies, the proletarian party, and so on, is inseparably connected with their complete negation of Stalin.

It is under the cover of "combating the personality cult" that the leadership of the CPSU tries to negate Stalin completely.

In launching "the combat against the personality cult," the leaders of the CPSU are not out to restore what they call "the Leninist standards of party life and principles of leadership." On the contrary, they are violating Lenin's teachings on the interrelationship of leaders, party, class, and masses, and contravening the principle of democratic centralism in the party.

Marxist-Leninists maintain that if the revolutionary party of the proletariat is genuinely to serve as the headquarters of the proletariat in struggle it must correctly handle the interrelationship of leaders, party, class, and masses, and must be organized on the principle of democratic centralism. Such a party must have a fairly stable nucleus of leadership, which should consist of a group of long-tested leaders who are good at integrating the universal truth of Marxism-Leninism with the concrete practice of revolution. . . .

Lenin was absolutely right in saying that "not a single class in history has achieved power without producing its political leaders, its prominent representatives able to organize a movement and lead it." He also said: "The training of experienced and most influential party leaders is a long-term and difficult task. But without this, the dictatorship of the proletariat, its unity of will, will remain a phrase."

The CCP has always adhered to the Marxist-Leninist teachings on the role of the masses and the individual in history and on the interrelationship of leaders, class, and masses, and upheld democratic centralism in the party. We have always maintained collective leadership; at the same time, we are against belittling the role of leaders. While we attach importance to this role, we are against the dishonest and excessive eulogy of individuals and exaggeration of their role.

As far back as 1949 the CCP Central Committee, at Comrade Mao Tse-tung's suggestion, took a decision forbidding public celebrations of any kind on the birthdays of party leaders and the naming of cities, streets, or enterprises after them. This consistent and correct approach of ours is fundamentally different from the "combat against the personality cult" advocated by the leadership of the CPSU.

It has become increasingly clear that in advocating the "combat against the personality cult" the leaders of the CPSU do not intend, as they themselves claim, to promote democracy, practice collective leadership, and oppose exaggeration of the role of the individual, but have ulterior motives.

What exactly is the gist of their "combat against the personality cult?"

To put it bluntly, it is nothing but the following:

1—On the pretext of "combating the personality cult," to counterpose Stalin, the leader of the party, to the party organization, the proletariat, and the masses of the people;

2—On the pretext of "combating the personality cult," to besmirch the proletarian party, the dictatorship of the proletariat, and the socialist system;

3—On the pretext of "combating the personality cult," to build themselves up and to attack revolutionaries loyal to Marxism-Leninism so as to pave the way for revisionist schemers to usurp the party and state leadership;

4—On the pretext of "combating the personality cult," to interfere in the internal affairs of fraternal parties and countries and strive to subvert their leadership to suit themselves;

5—On the pretext of "combating the personality cult," to attack fraternal parties which adhere to Marxism-Leninism and to split the international communist movement.

The "combat against the personality cult" launched by Khrushchev is a despicable political intrigue. Like someone described by Marx, "he is in his element as an intriguer, while a nonentity as a theorist."

The open letter of the CPSU Central Committee states that "while debunking the personality cult and fighting against its consequences," they "put high the leaders who . . . enjoy deserved prestige." What does this mean? It means that, while trampling Stalin underfoot, the leaders of the CPSU laud Khrushchev to the skies. They describe Khrushchev, who was not yet a communist at the time of the October Revolution and who was a low-ranking political worker during the civil war, as the "active builder of the Red Army." They ascribe the great victory of the decisive battle in the Soviet patriotic war entirely to Khrushchev, saying that in the battle of Stalingrad "Khrushchev's voice was very frequently heard" and that he was "the soul of the Stalingraders."

They attribute the great achievements in nuclear weapons and rocketry wholly to Khrushchev, calling him "cosmic father." But as everybody knows, the success of the Soviet Union in manufacturing the atom and hydrogen bombs was a great achievement of the Soviet scientists and technicians and the Soviet people under Stalin's leadership. The foundations of rocketry were also laid in Stalin's time. How can these important historical facts be obliterated? How can all credit be given to Khrushchev? They laud Khrushchev who has revised the fundamental theories of Marxism-Leninism and who holds that Leninism is outmoded as the "brilliant model who creatively developed and enriched Marxist-Leninist theory." . . .

According to the leaders of the CPSU, after the October Revolution put an end to capitalism in Russia there followed a "period of the personality cult." It would seem that the "social system" and "the ideology and morals" of that period were not socialist. In that period the Soviet working people suffered "heavy oppression," there prevailed an "atmosphere of fear, suspicion, and uncertainty which poisoned the life of the people," and Soviet society was impeded in its development.

In his speech at the Soviet-Hungarian friendship rally on 19 July 1963, Khrushchev dwelt on what he called Stalin's rule of "terror," saying that Stalin "maintained his power with an axe." He described the social order of the time in the following terms: ". . . in that period a man leaving for work often did not know whether he would return home, whether he would see his wife and children again."

"The period of the personality cult" as described by the leadership of the CPSU was one when society was more "hateful" and "barbarous" than in the period of feudalism or capitalism.

According to the leadership of the CPSU, the dictatorship of the proletariat and the socialist system of society which were established as a result of the October Revolution failed to remove the oppression of the working people or accelerate the development of Soviet society for several decades; only after the 20th Congress of the CPSU carried out the "combat against the personality cult" was the "heavy oppression" removed from the working people and "the development of Soviet society" suddenly "speeded up."

Khrushchev said: "Ah! If only Stalin had died 10 years earlier!" As everybody knows, Stalin died in 1953; 10 years earlier would have been 1943, the very year when the Soviet Union began its counteroffensive in the great patriotic war. At that time, who wanted Stalin to die? Hitler!

It is not a new thing in the history of the international communist movement for the enemies of Marxism-Leninism to vilify the leaders of the proletariat and try to undermine the proletarian cause by using some such slogan as "combating the personality cult." It is a dirty trick which people saw through long ago.

In the period of the First International, the schemer Bakunin used similar language to rail at Marx. . . . In the period of the Second International, the renegade Kautskiy used similar language to rail at Lenin. . . . In the period of the Third International the renegade Trotskiy similarly used such language to rail at Stalin. . . . The modern revisionist Tito clique also uses similar words to rail at Stalin, saying that Stalin was the "dictator" in a system of absolute personal power.

Thus, it is clear that the issue of "combating the personality cult" raised by the leadership of the CPSU has come down through Bakunin, Kautskiy, Trotskiy, and Tito, all of whom used it to attack the leaders of the proletariat and undermine the proletarian revolutionary movement.

The opportunists in the history of the international communist movement were unable to negate Marx, Engels, or Lenin by vilification, nor is Khrushchev able to negate Stalin by vilification. As Lenin pointed out, a privileged position cannot insure the success of vilification. Khrushchev was able to utilize his privileged position to remove the body of Stalin from the Lenin Mausoleum, but try as he may, he can never succeed in removing the great image of Stalin from the minds of the Soviet people and of the people throughout the world. Khrushchev can utilize his privileged position to revise Marxism-Leninism one way or another, but try as he may, he can never succeed in overthrowing Marxism-Leninism which Stalin defended and which is defended by Marxist-Leninists throughout the world.

We would like to offer a word of sincere advice to Comrade Khrushchev. We hope you will become aware of your errors and return from your wrong path to the path of Marxism-Leninism.

Long live the great revolutionary teachings of Marx, Engels, Lenin, and Stalin!

III

SOVIET LIFE TODAY: SOME INTRODUCTORY OBSERVATIONS

"With its example the USSR inspires people everywhere in their struggle to build a new life."
NIKITA S. KHRUSHCHEV

To millions of pro-Soviet Communists the world over, the Union of Soviet Socialist Republics represents the ray of light in an otherwise rather dark world, the beacon of hope, the fulfillment of a dream, the promise of a marvelous future for all mankind. Here is a symbol to be looked up to; an example to be followed; the first land in which the scourge of unemployment, "wage slavery," and "the exploitation of man by man" has been abolished forever; the first land in which the means of production belong to all the people and are operated in their interest by their elected government. It is a land of promise, a land with a rapidly rising standard of living, in which no man can get rich at the expense of his fellow man. It is a land on the verge of achieving the ultimate in human accomplishments, for has not Khrushchev proclaimed solemnly that "the present generation of Soviet citizens shall live under Communism," while the best he could hold out to the less fortunate inhabitants of the United States was a prediction that "your grandchildren shall live under Communism."

But there are millions of others to whom the Soviet Union presents a quite different image. They see it as a gigantic slave labor camp, ruled over by tyrannical masters bent on enslaving all of mankind. They see it as a nation ever ready to stir up revolutions in the "Free World," to pit brother against brother and countryman against countryman in an effort to divide and conquer. They see the Communist leaders as men willing to take advantage of any opportunity to further their goal, unhesitatingly willing to lie, to cheat, to kill in order to advance their cause.

What is the Soviet Union *really* like? Is it heaven on earth? Is it a living hell? Or is it, perhaps, somewhere in between, a country with considerable accomplishments to its credit, and with severe shortcomings on the debit side of the ledger? It is hoped that this book will shed a little light upon these questions, that it will give the reader some insight into Soviet life today, as he becomes better acquainted with Western and Soviet views on a variety of topics concerning present-day Soviet society. This chapter is intended as a preliminary survey. Many points, merely touched upon here, will be examined at greater length in chapters to come.

In the first selection under *Western Views,* William Henry Chamberlin compares the Soviet Union in 1963 with the Soviet Union a decade before, at the time of Stalin's death. He does not deny that some changes have taken place in the standard of living and in the conduct of the affairs of government. But Chamberlin sees any improvements primarily as "surface changes," and he warns that "the Soviet Union retains all the characteristics of a totalitarian state."

Alec Nove, next, cautions the reader to beware of extreme views. Maintaining that "Russians and Americans have some pretty fantastic views about one another," he sees the Soviet Union neither as a "totalitarian slave state" nor as a nation that "is or has become free." He does not claim that the U.S.S.R. is "just, free, or affluent," but he does see progress.

In the final selection under *Western Views,* Urie Bronfenbrenner relates how he discovered, during a trip to the Soviet Union, that many of the views held by Americans about the U.S.S.R. are likewise held by Soviet citizens concerning the United States. A careful analysis of this "mirror image" leads him to the conclusion that there are "serious distortions by *both* parties of realities on either side."

In the selection under *Western Marxist Views,* Herbert Aptheker paints a favorable picture of life in the Soviet Union. Answering in the affirmative the question as to whether the Soviet Union is a progressive society, he tries to show how backward the country was when the Soviet government took over in 1917, how far it has come since then in spite of the frightful losses incurred during World War II, and how confidently it can look towards a better future. Assuring us that the Soviet Union believes in democracy and peace, Aptheker proposes that we accept the challenge and "see, as friends and brothers, who can contribute most to the happiness and well-being of mankind!"

The picture magazine *USSR* is published monthly by the Soviet Embassy in the USA under a reciprocal agreement between the governments of the United States and the Soviet Union—an agreement which provides for the publication and circulation of the magazine *USSR* in the United States and the magazine *Amerika* in the Soviet Union.[1] The selection under *Soviet Views* below has been compiled from the Question and Answer Section of several issues of *USSR*. Rearranged under six sub-headings, the selection provides Soviet answers to some of the questions frequently asked by Westerners interested in life in the U.S.S.R.

---

[1] As of January 1965, the name of the magazine *USSR* has been changed to *Soviet Life.*

WESTERN VIEWS

1. U.S.S.R.: HOW MUCH CHANGE SINCE STALIN? *

**WILLIAM HENRY
CHAMBERLIN**

Associate Editor, The Russian Review

Ten years have passed since Josef Stalin died and what has turned out to be the Khrushchev era began. There have unmistakably been some changes in Soviet internal conditions and also in the style of the government and in its methods of conducting foreign affairs. At the same time the basic characteristics of the totalitarian state have remained. If there have been some striking surface changes, the old French proverb, "Plus ça change, plus c'est la même chose" still holds good for many fundamental aspects of the system that was introduced by Lenin and perfected by Stalin. One may perhaps get a clearer perspective on present-day Russia and its relation to the United States, and to the outside world in general, by considering first the elements of change, then the indications of continuity.

Life for the Soviet citizen has, on balance, become easier. Food and clothing are available in larger quantity and greater variety. Housing remains an outstanding problem; but huge blocks of new apartments have gone up on what were formerly the outskirts of Moscow and, to a smaller degree, in provincial towns.

The sinister knock on the door in the early hours of the morning, the warning of arbitrary arrest and summary banishment to a concentration camp, has become less frequent. Many prisoners in Stalin's enormous network of slave labor concentration camps have been released and conditions for those who are still there have been made somewhat less barbarously inhuman. Mass deportations, often applied to whole nationalities or large groups of the population under Stalin, have ceased.

---

* Excerpt reprinted from *The Russian Review*, July, 1963, pp. 227-234, by permission of the publisher.

Police controls are constant and vigilant; but it may be said that the Soviet Union has advanced from a terror state, comparable with the regimes of Genghiz Khan, of Tamerlane, of Ivan the Terrible, to a very strict police state.

It should also be emphasized that the improvement in material conditions is relative, not absolute. The Soviet Union remains far behind the United States and Western Europe in such staple aspects of the standard of living as food, clothing and housing, still more, perhaps, in the thousand and one little comforts and amenities which get scant consideration in a planned economy. And during the milder post-Stalin era in Russia, Europe, especially the countries of the Common Market, was moving ahead at a galloping pace. Thirty years after Stalin proclaimed that, as a result of industrialization and collective farming the Soviet Union would "overtake and outstrip the leading capitalist nations" there is little evidence that this goal will ever be realized. The old joke of the Soviet citizen who says to the state planners, "When we come abreast of America, just let me off; I don't want to go any further" has not lost its biting edge.

This is also true as regards one of the more recent Soviet "anecdotes." A Soviet professor, boasting of achievements in the conquest of outer space and suggesting that Soviet citizens will soon be able to go to Mars, Venus and the moon, is interrupted by the timid voice of a student: "Yes, but when will we be able to go to Vienna?" Foreign travel, almost completely forbidden except to officials under Stalin, is now allowed for limited groups of the Soviet population. One can see busloads of Soviet tourists, carefully shepherded by Communist guides, in Paris and Brussels and other European capitals; a few such groups have come to America. But foreign travel is a privilege, not a right, and is still a tiny trickle, compared with the annual outpouring of travelers from America, England, France and Germany.

Khrushchev's personal style, as a dictator, is very different from Stalin's. The latter enhanced the sinister quality of his terrorist rule by secluding himself in the Kremlin, meeting very few foreigners, especially in the last years of his life. Khrushchev, by contrast, is a backslapping, gregarious type, who makes the round of embassy cocktail parties, mingles freely with journalists, exchanging jokes with them, invites foreign guests to his summer villa on the Black Sea.

In foreign affairs Khrushchev, under the soothing names of peace and co-existence, has recommended a gradual, zigzag, nibbling advance toward the Communist goal of world domination. Of course it should be remembered that Stalin was reluctant to risk direct confrontation of Soviet with Western troops. He preferred to make war, as in Korea, by proxy.

A meeting with a foreigner is no longer, as it was in Stalin's time, a likely passport to a concentration camp. And in the Khrushchev era there has been more freedom of literary expression, although at a slow pace, the process of thaw being interrupted by many freezes, such as Khrushchev's recent warning to intellectuals that the authority of the Community Party is supreme in cultural affairs and that such subjects as Stalin's concentration camps should not receive too much attention.

Something of the terror which even the dead Stalin inspired may be gauged from the fact that three years passed before Khrushchev delivered, behind closed doors, a carefully expurgated account of his crimes, that there was a lapse of eight years before Stalin's embalmed body was removed from the Lenin Mausoleum and that a decade had to pass before one of Stalin's greatest crimes against humanity, his huge system of slave labor camps, where overwork, cold and hunger took a fearful toll of lives, could be described in print in the Soviet Union in a novel by a former inmate.

Some of the harsher labor regulations of Stalin's period, the penalty of imprisonment for lateness at work, the forbidding of the worker to change his job without permission, have been repealed or modified. After the terrific tensions of the Stalin tyranny Soviet citizens have begun to breathe more freely.

However, the Soviet Union retains all the characteristics of a totalitarian state, with a single political party, or rather a ruling caste, monopolizing power and governing with the aid of unlimited one-sided propaganda and as much repression as seems necessary. Soviet elections are still farces, with a single list of candidates to vote for and no means of expressing dissent or opposition.

The Iron Curtain is no mere figure of speech. The Soviet authorities make a heavy investment of human and technical resources to jam foreign broadcasts.[1] Moscow is the only large European capital where the leading newspapers of America, Great Britain, France and other non-Communist foreign countries may not be bought.

The status of the peasants remains what it has been since collective farming was forced on them thirty years ago. They are serfs in the power of the state, with no freedom in deciding what they should plant or how much they should receive for their labor, although, again like serfs before 1861, they possess the limited freedom of cultivating little plots of land, which, incidentally, supply Moscow and other cities with a high proportion of vegetables and fruits. The trade-unions are merely part of the apparatus of the dictatorship; there is no free collective bargaining as to wages and working conditions.

Along with the relaxation of some of Stalin's harsher measures there has been, in recent years, a considerable extension of the death penalty. In May, 1961 this could be imposed for treason, espionage, sabotage, first degree murder and banditry. Later it was extended to large scale economic

---

[1] At the time this book goes to press, Voice of America and BBC broadcasts are no longer being jammed in the USSR. [Editor's note.]

offenses and forgery, then to infringement of currency regulation, and made retroactive. There is also the tyranny of organized youth groups which go about interfering with so-called anti-social behavior, speculation, Western hairdos, "decadent" jazz. And there is the hypocritical practice of publishing alleged enthusiastic letters from workers applauding such measures as the repudiation of government bonds and the raising of meat and milk prices.

It is Soviet foreign policy that is of most direct concern to America. Khrushchev never tires of repeating attractive words like peace and co-existence. Certainly every rational human being prefers peace to war and free societies have no reason to fear the results of co-existence, if by this word one understands the peaceful competitive development of Communist and non-Communist societies with no attempt by either to impose their system by force.

Before the Berlin Wall was put up by the East German Communists there was a kind of co-existence between the German Federal Republic, committed to free political institutions and an individualist economic system, and the "German Democratic Republic," a satellite replica of Soviet political and economic institutions. The result of this experiment in co-existence was that 3.7 million Germans fled from East to West, that the population of the Soviet Zone, between 1948 and 1960, declined by about 2 million (it is probably the only area in the world to report a 10 percent decline in population during this period) and that the only means which the East German rulers found to stop this terrific drain in manpower was to seal off their territory with barbed wire, watchtowers, mine-fields and armed guards with orders to shoot to kill anyone trying to escape from this huge penitentiary.

Free movement everywhere in the world, in Asia as in Europe, has always been away from Communist-ruled areas. But genuine free co-existence, in the sense of free movement of men and ideas across the demarcation line between the Communist and the non-Communist world, is the last thing Khrushchev would permit. On any other assumption, why the elaborate defensive apparatus of the Iron Curtain? Some revealing comments in the program of the 22nd Congress of the Soviet Communist Party, held in the autumn of 1961, show what Khrushchev really means by co-existence:

"Peaceful co-existence affords more favorable opportunities for the struggle of the working class in the capitalist countries and facilitates the struggle of the peoples of the colonial and dependent countries for their liberation. . . .

"The Communist Party of the Soviet Union and the Soviet people as a whole will continue to oppose all wars of conquest, including wars between capitalist countries, and local wars aimed at strangling people's emancipation movements, and consider it their duty to support the sacred struggle of the oppressed peoples and their just anti-imperialist wars of liberation."

In other words, co-existence is a synonym not for peace, but for strictly one-sided war, for "just anti-imperialist wars" which may be interpreted as wars for the spread of Communism. Or, as an American Soviet specialist, Philip Mosely, puts it:

"In the Soviet view peaceful co-existence is the current policy in an epoch, more or less prolonged, during which so-called capitalism (any non-Communist regime) is to be compelled to retreat from one position to another until it gives up the ghost."

And Khrushchev's praise of peace is constantly punctuated by threats of nuclear annihilation, directed against all who oppose his will. Since the Suez crisis of 1956 he has threatened twenty countries 110 times with Soviet missiles. In the summer of 1961 he threatened to blow up the Acropolis. More recently, in an insulting letter to Chancellor Adenauer of the German Federal Republic, he warned that West Germany would "burn like a candle" in the event of war. He has repeatedly, fortunately without success, tried to frighten the United States out of standing by its treaty obligations to the Chinese Nationalists and out of its commitment to defend the freedom of West Berlin. His attempt, accompanied by elaborate deception, to install offensive missiles in Cuba is too recent to be forgotten. His behavior, both in Cuba and in Berlin, recalls a characterization of Russian policy by the famous British Foreign Secretary Lord Palmerston in 1853:

"The policy and practice of the Russian government have always been to push forward its encroachments as fast and as far as the apathy or want of firmness of other governments would allow it to go, but always to stop and retire when it met with decided resistance, and then to wait for the next favorable opportunity to make another spring on its intended victim."

A European diplomat once expressed the opinion, in a private conversation, that Khrushchev, although outwardly more amiable than Stalin, is really a more dangerous adversary, because his actions are less predictable. And, both in foreign and in domestic policy, the era of Khrushchev has been a time of curious zigzags, suggesting a man who is being pushed in several directions by different forces. Even since November, 1958 Khrushchev has been threatening off and on to oust the Western powers from West Berlin. But he has never, up to the present time, judged it expedient to make a decisive spring on this intended victim. A most dangerous experiment in brinksmanship in Cuba, when challenged, was followed by retreat.

These and other alternations of policy indicate the pressure of conflicting considerations, of the need for peace, if only to insure more favorable conditions of Soviet economic development, and of considerations of Communist dogma, voiced by his increasingly critical Chinese ally. This same zigzag course has been followed in home policy, where there has been an attempt to eliminate the more brutal and generally detested aspects of Stalinism without endangering the totalitarian structure of the Soviet state. It may be that, just because he has, within very narrow limits, tried to be a reformer, Khrushchev, despite his more relaxed pose, is running greater political risks than Stalin, with his grim, unvarying Asiatic terrorist despotism. On the danger of reform for an autocratic regime that wise and brilliant political philosopher, Alexis de Tocqueville, offered these observations:

"It is not always as a result of a country going from bad to worse that a revolution occurs. It very often happens that a people which had supported the most oppressive rule without a murmur, and as if unconscious of it, should reject it with violence the moment its pressure is reduced. The system of government which is destroyed in a revolution is nearly always an improvement on the one which immediately preceded it, and experience shows that the most dangerous moment for a bad government normally occurs at the point where it begins to improve itself." . . .

2. THE U.S.S.R.: MYTHS AND REALITIES *

ALEC NOVE

University of Glasgow

Once in the course of a discussion I was asked whether, in my view, the Russians misunderstood America more, or less, than the Americans misunderstood Russia. After some reflection—the answer is by no means obvious—I expressed the opinion that possibly the American view is the more unbalanced. By the American view I certainly do not mean that of American experts on the Soviet Union. On the contrary, American specialists on this subject are generally extremely well-informed, and analyze and present the facts with a remarkable lack of bias. It is with the non-specialists that I am concerned; the politically conscious man-in-the-street, or even intellectuals who specialise in other subjects. Here one encounters views

* Reprinted from the *Lawrence Daily Journal World,* Jan. 21, 1963, by permission of the author and the publisher. (The *Lawrence Daily Journal World* is the daily paper of Lawrence, Kansas, the home of The University of Kansas. During the fall semester, 1962/63, Professor Nove was Visiting Professor at The University of Kansas.)

that seem to be wildly off the mark, even more so than some peculiar views about the United States which are held in Russia.

The reader may well be surprised by such a judgment, will rightly wish to know the reasoning behind it. Is it not a fact, he might ask, that a Soviet citizen is presented by his authorities with a highly slanted and propagandist view of the world in general, and of the United States in particular? Is he not almost wholly cut off from access to outside sources of information? Is not the American who wishes to study Soviet reality able to do so from the several different points of view, which are freely accessible to him? All this is true, and yet . . .

The first point to make is that the Soviet citizen has long ago learnt to take the official propaganda with a pinch of salt, and particularly when it is describing the "miserable life" which the masses are supposed to lead in western countries. In my own conversations in the Soviet Union, I formed the impression that many citizens over-compensate for the propaganda, and possibly believe that conditions of life in the west are better than in fact they are.

> The Russians have always had an inferiority complex about their general level of culture and technique. They regard themselves as inferior in table manners, women's fashions, automobile design and even science. Only last week I was reading a report from a foreigner resident in Moscow to the effect that some Russians were doubtful whether Gagarin really circled the globe! As the example is meant to suggest, the feeling may exist even if it is unfounded. There is a general predisposition to believe that everything in the West is likely to be better than anything Russian. The loud official propaganda to the contrary is partly to be explained by the need felt to combat this tendency. One of the effects of official efforts to conceal the truth is to heighten the curiosity which the majority of Soviet citizens feel about what is really going on in the West.

It is worth mentioning in passing that the failures of official propaganda in this matter are just one small example of the limitations of indoctrination. A good deal of the misunderstanding of what goes on in Russia is caused by the misuse of such terms as totalitarianism, brainwashing and slavery. After watching the brilliantly made movie, "The Manchurian Candidate," I wondered what proportion of the audience had been brainwashed into believing its underlying assumptions about brainwashing. I also wondered whether the repeated presentation of fiendishly clever Russo-Chinese indoctrinators does not have the effect of unnecessarily making the enemy seem "ten feet tall." In fact, Soviet attempts at indoctrination are usually conducted with great lack of imagination, and are appallingly dull. On occasion this fact is referred to in the Soviet press. I recall a cartoon in *Krokodil* concerning the notorious inadequacy of anti-religious propaganda. The drawing shows a priest talking to a woman cleaner in his church. The following is the conversation:

CLEANER: I hear that an intelligent lecturer on atheism is being sent to our district.
PRIEST: Do not worry, my dear. Miracles do not happen.

Another point to make is that the Soviet educated classes have a considerable knowledge of, and a very great interest in, Western literature. It used to be said that they believed that England is still the country described by Dickens, since under Stalin only pro-Communist living writers were translated, with comparatively few exceptions. This is no longer the case. Many modern American and British writers are known and admired. It is true that selection of material for translation remains slanted. For example, Graham Greene is known to the Soviet public only by "The Quiet American" and "Our Man in Havana." Nonetheless the improvement in the past ten years is unquestionable. Though human contact with Westerners is still far from free, there is much more of it, and a growing number of Soviet citizens, no doubt carefully screened, actually travel abroad as tourists. They tell their friends, when they return, what they have seen. With mass arrests a thing of the past, people do talk much more freely than was possible a few short years ago. Also many people listen to foreign broadcasts, despite efforts at jamming some programs. There is no difficulty in buying a radio set with short wave reception.

Needless to say, it is not being argued that the Soviet citizen has an accurate picture of life in the West, still less that his government wishes him to have one. But the American citizen's picture of the USSR may be even less accurate.

What are the most commonly held erroneous views found in the United States? The first and most pervasive is a persistent refusal to accept that Stalin is dead. Some excellent western writers have given a most vivid and basically truthful picture of the Stalin terror, and in most people's minds that picture has not been replaced by any other. Those who study the Soviet Union do know, of course, that terror is relaxed, that the concentration camps have been largely emptied, that no one appears to have been shot for a political offense since 1954 (an all-time record, this, under Communist rule).[1] But much of the public does not seem to know. One can judge this by the kind of propagandist material which is thought to have a popular appeal in this country. Films such as "We will bury you" seem to

---

[1] Between the time Professor Nove wrote this article and the time this book went to press, one such execution did take place when convicted Soviet spy, Col. Oleg Penkovsky, faced a firing squad on March 16, 1963. [Editor's note.]

be based on the idea that mass arrests of terrified slaves in the streets of Moscow are an everyday occurrence. I doubt if such a film could be shown in London, as it would probably be laughed off the screen. Here it appeals, as do certain extreme right statements, to a ready-made belief that Khrushchev is Stalin, or even, as Joseph Alsop prefers to call him, Hitler, and therefore Evil incarnate. At the level of "mass culture," i.e. in pulp magazines, this attitude towards the Russians takes the form of picturing degenerate monsters in Soviet army uniforms whipping half-clad maidens, to cite an example which was on sale a couple of weeks ago. (How can one explain such vicious rubbish to a well-meaning visitor from the East?)

By contrast, there is very little interest indeed in Soviet literature in the United States. Admittedly a good deal of it is rather dull, but this is far from explaining the fact that for the vast majority of literate Americans the only book written in Russia for the past twenty years is Doctor Zhivago.

It is lack of interest, of any real curiosity, rather than lack of information, which may be at the root of misunderstandings. Sensible interpretations of the USSR do get published, of course, in large paper-back editions. They do little to alter the commonly-held view. Perhaps this rests on a psychological need to see the enemy as a devil, to disregard evidence which modifies the picture of a slave state ruled by professional criminals. I sometimes feel that this attitude has a basically honorable explanation. Decent people are apt to be worried about a situation in which bombers and ICBM's are apparently poised ready for the slaughter of many millions of fellow human beings, and it is certainly easier to reconcile oneself with this if one is dealing with devils.

The "totalitarian slave state" caricature simply does not correspond to reality. Russian people laugh, love, go to football games, quarrel, cheat, complain, travel in overcrowded subways and behave like normal human beings most of the time. Even the higher authorities have some human failings, of which vodka is obviously one. In practice it is physically impossible for Moscow to order everyone's lives, even though from time to time it has tried to do so. Perhaps Stalin got nearer to paralyzing spontaneous human activity than anyone did before him. However, most fortunately, he died ten years ago.

Some American liberals, conscious of the false view of Russia held by so many of their countrymen, swing to the other extreme, and maintain that the Soviet Union is or has become free. This is going too far altogether. The Communist monopoly of power is a fact, arbitrary and unjust actions by party officials do occur, freedom of speech and assembly is very seriously restricted, the arts are still subject to the party supervision, "elections" to representative bodies are completely meaningless. There are ways of ensuring communist control over political and social life without actually shooting anyone. While people are not hungry, the food is often of poor quality, with certain items unavailable for months at a time. Although much building is certainly going on, the housing problem remains very acute, and it is perhaps hard to visualize the human miseries caused by the appalling overcrowding. While the Russian church is active and is not directly persecuted, the situation of a regular church-goer is not a comfortable one. He is free to go, but this will certainly not help his career. I have heard of students dismissed from a teacher's training college for attending church, on the grounds that they may pass on their beliefs to school children. And the toleration extended to the Orthodox and Baptist churches does not cover smaller Christian sects, some of whose members invaded the American embassy in Moscow last month. Jews, too, have much to complain about.

It is not that the USSR is just, free, or affluent. It is none of these things. The point is that it is evolving, that the changes are on the whole in a desirable direction, and that we must in no circumstances regard Soviet society as being frozen into some kind of unchangeable totalitarian mold. It is remarkable how many things that were forbidden or unavailable a few years ago have become part of normal life. There are open controversies in such diverse fields as literature, economics, music. The Communist leadership's attempt to prevent showings of abstract art elicited protest letters signed by large numbers of Soviet intellectuals, which were referred to in the press, an event inconceivable ten years ago (though the fact of the party's interference is a reminder of the limitations of change). Or to take examples of a more material kind: In 1959 I saw for the first time that white and black bread is available free with meals in unrestricted quantity in Soviet restaurants. In earlier periods the customers would have put it in their pockets. And we recall (perfectly true) stories of Russian soldiers stealing watches when they reached Central Europe in 1945. They were worth their weight in gold in the soldiers' imagination, because such things were simply unavailable to the ordinary man in Russia. Yet today watches and also cameras have become plentiful, as any visitor to the USSR can see. So, alongside many shortages, inconveniences, oppressive regulations, there is progress.

Lastly, it is worth stressing one point which seems to me significant. We rightly deplore the fact the Communist governments of such countries as Hungary or East Germany have been put there by the Russians. Their policies reflect the Moscow line rather than the needs of their own countries. In fact this is a serious source of weakness of Communist parties in the satellites: Nationalist sentiments are against them. But clearly we cannot see Russia itself in the same light. If Budapest obeys Moscow, Moscow obeys whom, or what? The Soviet Communist party, while of course not democratically expressing the views of the citizens, does express in many ways the deep nationalist sentiments which penetrate Russian society and the Communist leadership itself. Despite all ideology, national interest is a powerful force. The Communist leadership has many unlovely features. . . . But even the unlovely features are very Russian—just as there is, close beneath the surface among Soviet intellectuals, another and much more attractive Russian tradition, inherited from the humanistic ideas so well expressed in 19th century literature.

Both Russians and Americans have some pretty fantastic views about one another. I know of no instrument which can measure degrees of fantasy, so the views expressed above can neither be qualified nor proved right. But in a sense the errors which the Russians make are the more excusable. The American government does not, unlike its Russian counterpart, make active efforts to prevent its people from learning about the other side.

3. THE MIRROR IMAGE IN SOVIET-AMERICAN RELATIONS: A SOCIAL PSYCHOLOGIST'S REPORT *

URIE BRONFENBRENNER
Cornell University

I should explain by way of introduction that I was in the Soviet Union during the summer of 1960, about a month after the U2 incident. The primary purpose of my trip was to become acquainted with scientific developments in my field, which is social psychology. But in addition to visiting laboratories at universities and institutes, I wanted also to become acquainted with *living* social psychology—the Soviet people themselves. It was my good fortune to be able to speak Russian. I was traveling with a tourist visa on a new plan which permitted me to go about alone without a guide. Accordingly, after spending the first two or three days of my visit in a particular city at scientific centers, I would devote the remaining days to walking about the town and striking up conversations with people in public conveyances, parks, stores, restaurants, or just on the street. Since

* Excerpt reprinted from *The Journal of Social Issues,* Vol. XVII, No. 3, 1961, by permission of the author and publisher.

foreigners are a curiosity, and I was obviously a foreigner (though, I quickly learned, not obviously an American), people were eager to talk. But I also went out of my way to strike up conversations with people who weren't taking the initiative—with fellow passengers who were remaining silent, with strollers in the park, with children and old people. Or I would enter a restaurant deciding in advance to sit at the third table on the left with whoever should turn out to be there. (In Soviet restaurants it is not uncommon to share a table with strangers.)

These conversations convinced me that the great majority of Russians feel a genuine pride in the accomplishments of their system and a conviction that communism is the way of the future not only for themselves but for the rest of the world as well. For several reasons my Soviet journey was a deeply disturbing experience. But what frightened me was not so much the facts of Soviet reality as the discrepancy between the real and the perceived. At first I was troubled only by the strange irrationality of the Soviet view of the world—especially their gross distortion of American society and American foreign policy as I knew them to be. But then, gradually, there came an even more disquieting awareness—an awareness which I resisted and still resist. Slowly and painfully, it forced itself upon me that *the Russian's distorted picture of us was curiously similar to our view of them—a mirror image.* But of course our image was real. Or could it be that our views too were distorted and irrational—a mirror image in a twisted glass?

It was—and is—a frightening prospect. For if such reciprocal distortion exists, it is a psychological phenomenon without parallel in the gravity of its consequences. For this reason, the possibility deserves serious consideration.

Let us then briefly examine the common features in the American and Soviet view of each other's societies. For the Russian's image I drew mainly not on official government pronouncements but on what was said to me by Soviet citizens in the course of our conversations. Five major themes stand out.

1. *They* are the aggressors.

The American view: Russia is the warmonger bent on imposing its system on the rest of the world. Witness Czechoslovakia, Berlin, Hungary, and now Cuba and the Congo. The Soviet Union consistently blocks Western proposals for disarmament by refusing necessary inspection controls.

The Soviet view: America is the warmonger bent on imposing its power on the rest of the world and on the Soviet Union itself. Witness American intervention in 1918, Western encirclement after World War II with American troops and bases on every border of the USSR (West Germany, Norway, Turkey, Korea, Japan), intransigence over proposals to make Berlin a free city, intervention in Korea, Taiwan, Lebanon, Guatemala, Cuba. America has repeatedly rejected Soviet disarmament proposals while demanding the right to inspect within Soviet territory—finally attempting to take the right by force through deep penetration of Soviet air space.

2. *Their* government exploits and deludes the people.

The American view: Convinced communists, who form but a small proportion of Russia's population, control the government and exploit the society and its resources in their own interest. To justify their power and expansionist policies they have to perpetuate a war atmosphere and a fear of Western aggression. Russian elections are a travesty since only one party appears on the ballot. The Russian people are kept from knowing the truth through a controlled radio and press and conformity is insured through stringent economic and political sanctions against deviant individuals or groups.

The Soviet view: A capitalistic-militaristic clique controls the American government, the nation's economic resources, and its media of communication. This group exploits the society and its resources. It is in their economic and political interest to maintain a war atmosphere and engage in militaristic expansion. Voting in America is a farce since candidates for both parties are selected by the same powerful interests leaving nothing to choose between. The American people are kept from knowing the truth through a controlled radio and press and through economic and political sanctions against liberal elements.

3. The mass of *their* people are not really sympathetic to the regime.

The American view: In spite of the propaganda, the Soviet people are not really behind their government. Their praise of the government and the party is largely perfunctory, a necessary concession for getting along. They do not trust their own sources of information and have learned to read between the lines. Most of them would prefer to live under our system of government if they only could.

The Soviet view: Unlike their government, the bulk of the American people want peace. Thus, the majority disapproved of American aggression in Korea, the support of Chiang Kai Shek, and, above all, of the sending of U2. But of course they could do nothing since their welfare is completely under the control of the ruling financier-militaristic clique. If the American people were allowed to become acquainted with communism as it exists in the USSR, they would unquestionably choose it as their form of government. ("You Americans are such a nice people; it is a pity you have such a terrible government.")

4. *They* cannot be trusted.

The American view: The Soviets do not keep promises and they do not mean what they say. Thus while they claim to have discontinued all nuclear testing, they are probably carrying out secret underground explosions in order to gain an advantage over us. Their talk of peace is but a propaganda maneuver. Everything they do is to be viewed with suspicion since it is all part of a single coordinated scheme to further aggressive communist aims.

The Soviet view: The Americans do not keep promises and they do not mean what they say. Thus they insist on inspection only so that they can look at Soviet defenses; they have no real intention of disarming. Everything the Americans do is to be viewed with suspicion (e.g., they take advantage of Soviet hospitality by sending in spies as tourists).

5. *Their* policy verges on madness.

The American view: Soviet demands on such crucial problems as disarmament, Berlin, and unification are completely unrealistic. Disarmament without adequate inspection is meaningless, a "free Berlin" would be equivalent to a Soviet Berlin, and a united Germany without free elections is an impossibility. In pursuit of their irresponsible policies the Soviets do not hesitate to run the risk of war itself. Thus it is only due to the restraint and coordinated action of the Western alliance that Soviet provocations over Berlin did not precipitate World War III.

The Soviet view: The American position on such crucial problems as disarmament, East Germany, and China is completely unrealistic. They demand to know our secrets before they disarm; in Germany they insist on a policy which risks the resurgence of a fascist Reich; and as for China, they try to act as if it did not exist while at the same time supporting an aggressive puppet regime just off the Chinese mainland. And in pursuit of their irresponsible policies, the Americans do not hesitate to run the risk of war itself. Were it not for Soviet prudence and restraint, the sending of U2 deep into Russian territory could easily have precipitated World War III.

It is easy to recognize the gross distortions in the Soviet views summarized above. But is our own outlook completely realistic? Are we correct, for example, in thinking that the mass of the Soviet people would really prefer our way of life and are unenthusiastic about their own? Certainly the tone and tenor of my conversations with Soviet citizens hardly support this belief.

But, you may ask, why is it that other Western observers do not report the enthusiasm and commitment which I encountered?

I asked this very question of newspaper men and embassy officials in Moscow. Their answers were revealing. Thus one reporter replied somewhat dryly, "Sure, I know, but when a communist acts like a communist, it isn't news. If I want to be sure that it will be printed back home, I have to write about what's wrong with the system, not its successes." Others voiced an opinion expressed most clearly by representatives at our embassy. When I reported to them the gist of my Soviet conversations, they were grateful but skeptical: "Professor, you underestimate the effect of the police state. When these people talk to a stranger, especially an American, they *have* to say the right thing."

The argument is persuasive, and comforting to hear. But perhaps these very features should arouse our critical judgment. Indeed, it is instructive to view this argument against the background of its predecessor voiced by the newspaperman. To put it bluntly, what he was saying was that he could be sure of getting published only the material that *the American people wanted to hear*. But notice that the second argument also fulfills this objective, and it does so in a much more satisfactory and sophisticated way. The realization that "Soviet citizens *have* to say the right thing" enables the Western observer not only to discount most of what he hears, but even to interpret it as evidence in direct support of the West's accepted picture of the Soviet Union as a police state.

It should be clear that I am in no sense here suggesting that Western reporters and embassy officials deliberately misrepresent what they know to be the facts. Rather I am but calling attention to the operation, in a specific and critical context, of a phenomenon well known to psychologists —the tendency to assimilate new perceptions to old, and unconsciously to distort what one sees in such a way as to minimize a clash with previous expectations. In recent years, a number of leading social psychologists, notably Heider (1958), Festinger (1957), and Osgood (1960), have emphasized that this "strain toward consistency" is especially powerful in the sphere of social relations—that is, in our perceptions of the motives, attitudes, and actions of other persons or groups. Specifically, we strive to keep our views of other human beings compatible with each other. In the face of complex social reality, such consistency is typically accomplished by obliterating distinctions and organizing the world in terms of artificially-simplified frames of reference. One of the simplest of these, and hence one of the most inviting, is the dichotomy of good and bad. Hence we often perceive others, be they individuals, groups, or even whole societies, as simply "good" or "bad." Once this fateful decision is made, the rest is easy, for the "good" person or group can have only desirable social characteristics and the "bad" can have only reprehensible traits. And once such evaluative stability of social perception is established, it is extremely difficult to alter. Contradictory stimuli arouse only anxiety and resistance. When confronted with a desirable characteristic of something already known to be "bad," the observer will either just not "see" it, or will reorganize his perception of it so that it can be perceived as "bad." Finally, this tendency to regress to simple categories of perception is especially strong under conditions of emotional stress and external threat. Witness our readiness in times of war to exalt the virtues of our own side and to see the enemy as thoroughly evil.

Still one other social psychological phenomenon has direct relevance for the present discussion. I refer to a process demonstrated most dramatically and comprehensively in the experiments of Solomon Asch (1956), and known thereby as the "Asch phenomenon." In these experiments, the subject finds himself in a group of six or eight of his peers all of whom are asked to make comparative judgments of certain stimuli presented to them, for example, identifying the longer of two lines. At first the task seems simple enough; the subject hears others make their judgments and then makes his own. In the beginning he is usually in agreement, but then gradually he notices that more and more often his judgments differ from those of the rest of the group. Actually, the experiment is rigged. All the other group members have been instructed to give false responses on a predetermined schedule. In any event, the effect on our subject is dramatic. At first he is puzzled, then upset. Soon he begins to have serious doubts about his own judgment, and in an appreciable number of cases, he begins to "see" the stimuli as they are described by his fellows.

What I am suggesting, of course, is that the Asch phenomenon operates even more forcefully outside the laboratory where the game of social perception is being played for keeps. *Specifically, I am proposing that the mechanisms here described contribute substantially to producing and maintaining serious distortions in the reciprocal images of the Soviet Union and the United States.*

My suggestion springs from more than abstract theoretical inference. I call attention to the possible operation of the Asch phenomenon in the Soviet-American context for a very concrete reason: I had the distressing experience of being its victim. While in the Soviet Union I deliberately sought to minimize association with other Westerners and to spend as much time as I could with Soviet citizens. This was not easy to do. It was no pleasant experience to hear one's own country severely criticized and to be constantly out-debated in the bargain. I looked forward to the next chance meeting with a fellow Westerner so that I could get much-needed moral support and enjoy an evening's invective at the expense of Intourist and the "worker's paradise." But though I occasionally yielded to temptation, for the most part I kept true to my resolve and spent many hours in a completely Soviet environment. It was difficult, but interesting. I liked many of the people I met. Some of them apparently liked me. Though mistaken, they were obviously sincere. They wanted me to agree with them. The days went on, and strange things began to happen. I remember picking up a Soviet newspaper which featured an account of American activities in the Near East. "Oh, what are they doing now!" I asked myself, and stopped short; for I had thought in terms of "they," and it was my own country. Or I would become aware that I had been nodding to the points being made by my Soviet companion where before I had always taken issue. In short, when all around me saw the world in one way, I too found myself wanting to believe and belong.

And once I crossed the Soviet border on my way home, the process began to reverse itself. The more I talked with fellow Westerners, especially fellow Americans, the more I began to doubt the validity of my original impressions. "What would you expect them to say to an American?" my friends would ask. "How do you know that the person talking to you was not a trained agitator?" "Did you ever catch sight of them following you?" I never did. Perhaps I was naive. But, then, recently I reread a letter written to a friend during the last week of my stay. "I feel it is important," it begins, "to try to write to you in detail while I am still in it, for just as I could never have conceived of what I am now experiencing, so, I suspect, it will seem unreal and intangible once I am back in the West." The rest of the letter, and others like it, contain the record of the experiences reported in this account.

In sum, I take my stand on the view that there *is* a mirror image in Soviet and American perceptions of each other and that this image represents serious distortions by *both* parties of realities on either side. . . .

WESTERN MARXIST VIEWS

4. IS THE SOVIET UNION A PROGRESSIVE SOCIETY? *

HERBERT APTHEKER

*Director, American Institute for
Marxist Studies*

How shall one define a progressive society? The definition would have to include comparison with other societies and would have to include some firm criteria not themselves wholly relative. . . . Is the Soviet Union a progressive society? Our search for an answer must include an effort to compare the present society of the USSR with that which the revolution creating it replaced; it must include an effort to compare that society with the societies which historically have surrounded the European and the Asian components of the USSR; it must include a comparison of that society with the global community as a whole and as it is today, encompassing what are referred to as the "most advanced" societies on earth. It must simultaneously consider whether or not the society reflects a release of the productive capacities within it and whether or not the society enhances the well-being of the members constituting it.

One may also demand of a progressive society today that it be one which is positively associated with the historic efforts to eliminate colonialism and that its general stance in the international arena be one which favors peace and impedes war.

It is my view that the overwhelming weight of all the evidence is in the direction, in all these respects, of an affirmative reply.

Soviet Russia inherited a land whose economy was among the most

* Reprinted from *Political Affairs,* April, 1963, pp. 45-51, by permission of the author and the publisher.

The text of the article reprinted here represents the affirmative side of a debate on the topic "Is the Soviet Union a Progressive Society?" The debate was sponsored by the Student Council of the College of Liberal Arts of Howard University, Washington, D.C., and took place on March 20, 1963. The negative side was taken by Mr. Saul Mendelson, a member of the National Executive Committee of the Socialist Party of the United States. Professor Emmet Dorsey, Chairman of the Department of Government at Howard University, served as moderator.

backward in Europe—and one which had been devastated by war, so that industrial production in 1918 was only 20 per cent of what it had been in 1913. Its population was about 65 per cent illiterate, Church and State had been one and both had been the most medieval in Europe, the Empire had been a prison-house of nations with racism, anti-Semitism and colonial-style subjugation, especially of the Asian people, all official and chronic and intense features of government and society.

The society inherited by Soviet Russia was one having a death rate comparable to that then afflicting India and China; an educational system of a totally elitist character confined to the barest minority of the top classes and marked by obscurantist emphasis, while the general technical level was among the lowest in the world.

In all these respects—production, health, education, cultural level—the present society is incomparably superior to the one it replaced . . . Here we wish to affirm that as to the first test of a progressive society—how it compares with the one it replaced—the evidence leads to the conclusion that the accomplishments of the USSR justify one in saying that its creation was one of the greatest strokes for human advancement in all history.

If one applies another test of the meaning of a progressive society—comparing the USSR with its neighbors—its historic compeers—I think the evidence would confirm that the old Poland and the old Hungary and the old Rumania, and the old Baltic states, and the old Bulgaria—all of them quasi-fascist and monarchical states until the end of World War II, when they, too, were revolutionized—were in every respect really backward and regressive societies. I think that if one compares the USSR with its other neighbors he finds that to the south, "Turkey is in Crisis" to quote the title of the article by Gabriel Gersh in the *Christian Century,* Feb. 20, 1963, where one will read of a land with chronic and massive unemployment, with luxury rampant and starvation widespread, where 65 per cent of the people are illiterate, where half the villages are without schools, and where, as the author summarizes, "the country is in a pre-revolutionary condition." Moving along to Iran and Iraq and Pakistan and India, also neighbors of the USSR—largely the same situation prevails—mass illiteracy, mass poverty, mass hunger—very much like the Russia prior to the USSR! In China—until the revolution of 1949—comparable conditions existed, worsened by chronic warfare and almost incredible governmental corruption and chaos.

These are the neighbors of the USSR and in another test of what is meant by a progressive society—a comparison *vis-à-vis* those nations making up its part of the world—I think again, the evidence indubitably and overwhelmingly supports the proposition that the USSR is such a society and that the Revolution creating it again must be hailed as a decisive event in the forward march of the human race.

How will the USSR fare if it is put to another test—namely, comparing it with the most highly developed and the most advanced of the capitalist nations—our own? Before detailing this, one must state that even posing it—and it is being posed every day now, by the President and the CIA and Congress and every newspaper in the land—is a tremendous tribute to the phenomenal growth of the Soviet Union. It is only thirty years since the United States decided to admit even the existence of the USSR. And while two world wars served to enrich the United States, they —plus the interventions—served to devastate the land of the Soviets. It cannot be overemphasized that in considering the USSR today one is considering a land which for about one-fourth of its life has had to wage war, a land which suffered seventeen million dead in World War Two, a land which saw 50 per cent of its homes, in its European areas, utterly destroyed by the Nazis; let this be burned into the brain of anyone who undertakes a comparison between the United States and the USSR today—for then and only then can he understand what a tribute to the latter such an undertaking actually represents.

The astonishing fact is—and it is a sobering fact for any American— that in a whole series of significant indices the USSR stands today ahead of the USA. Illiteracy is higher in the USA today than in the USSR; the death rate is higher in the USA than in the USSR; the USSR leads the world in the publication of books; the USSR has the highest ratio of libraries per population in the world today; while 40 per cent of all crime in the United States is committed by those under 18, the comparable percentage in the USSR is 5 per cent; while in the "free world" the "call girl" profession and prostitution are institutionalized and spreading, in the USSR they are unknown; while in the USA over 50 per cent of all hospital beds are occupied by the mentally ill, the figure for comparable ailments in the USSR is less than 10 per cent.

The rate of growth of industrial production is about three times greater than that of the USA, and this ratio was maintained again in 1962; the result is that in certain industrial products—steel and cement, for example —the USSR has already caught up with the United States and overall it is closing the gap at a swift pace. Simultaneously, its economy is unmarked by cycles and crises, its working people are unplagued by unemployment, and the development of automation is a blessing rather than a blight and a menace.

While in racism and pornography the United States stands preeminent in the world, the USSR has been substantially cleansed of both.

In seeking to eliminate some of the most pressing of its social problems—that of housing, for example—exacerbated as that was by World War II—the USSR leads the world in its massive home-construction program; indeed, in the last five years, it has succeeded in providing new housing for fully one-fourth of its whole population. And in the purification of its legal and political system—especially since the worst abuses associated with the years just before, during and after World War II (with the onset of the Cold War)—the Soviet Union has made impressive advances, according to the testimony of most observers, both American and European. Further, in the direction of enhancing individual freedom and democratic rights, the motion of society in the USSR during the past decade has been a most positive one, in contrast with the situation in the United States, so that, here, too, even in a formal sense, an American will have to exert himself very strongly against the Smith Act and the McCarran Act and the Landrum-Griffin Act and the House Un-American Activities Committee and Senator Eastland's Internal Security Committee, and so forth, if this country of parliamentary democracy and of the Bill of Rights is not to see that tradition utterly trampled into the dust.

Let us present some of the statements from distinguished Americans—clearly non-subversive by any standards other than those set by Mr. Welch. *On economic advance:* S. L. A. Marshall, in *The New Republic* (Feb. 3, 1958), "The USSR is marching toward superiority in over-all productiveness while we move at a crawl." Walter Lippmann: "The fact of the matter is that the growth of the Soviet economy has been amazing" (column of June 10, 1958).

On Education: Claude M. Fuess, formerly headmaster of Phillips Academy in Massachusetts: "The Russians have realized for some years the necessity of guiding every child as far along the educational path as he is qualified to go, of identifying talent early and cultivating it to the utmost, rewarding scholarship and research, and making teaching a reputable, dignified profession" (*Saturday Review,* Feb. 1, 1958). Alvin C. Eurich, president of the State University of New York: "Soviet education today combines the rigorous European system with the mass education of the United States—a phenomenal attempt. . . . The accomplishments of the Russian educational system are exceedingly impressive" (*The Atlantic,* April 1, 1958). Marc Raeff, professor of history, Clark University in Massachusetts: "Reading [in the USSR] is the national pastime; everybody reads in great amounts, bookstores and libraries are always full, and books literally sell like hot cakes in the streets, in theatres, in museums, stores, railroad stations. Learning is highly valued, thirst for knowledge is great, seriousness of purpose is universal" (*N. Y. Times Magazine,* June 22, 1958). Lawrence G. Derthick, U.S. Commissioner of Education: "What we have seen has amazed us in one particular. We were simply not prepared for the degree to which the USSR, as a nation, is committed to education as a means of national advancement. Everywhere we went we saw indication after indication of what we could only conclude amounted to a total commitment to education.

"Our major reaction therefore is one of astonishment—and I choose the word carefully—at the extent to which this seems to have been accomplished" (*N. Y. Times,* June 14, 1958).

On science—in which the evidence before one's eyes is so overwhelming that we offer but one witness—Professor Jerome Wiesner, of MIT, after stating that in science in general the USSR is second to none and that in certain areas—he named meteorology, oceanography and metallurgy—the country has no peer, declared: "The Soviets have a view of science as an integral part of their society. They are pioneers. To the intellectual, the frontier is not the land but the mind, and the Soviet leaders seem to understand this. Because they appreciate the long-term implications of the development of science for the growth of their society, they are able to make determined long-range commitments to train people, build universities, laboratories, and institutes on a grand scale" (essay in *Soviet Progress and American Enterprise,* New York, 1958).

On health, official UN data show: the mortality rate in the USSR is lower than in the USA; longevity in the USSR is equal to that in the USA; in the number of physicians in proportion to population the USSR is far ahead of the USA; and in the number of hospital beds, while the USSR is still behind, her rate of growth has been more than twice as rapid as has been that in the USA.

The testimony as to the particularly favored position of *children* in the USSR is universal and uncontradicted so far as I know. *The advanced position of women*—who have achieved a status of equality never approached before by any society—also is a matter of fact universally agreed to and again, so far as I know, uncontroverted. On this last point, one of the most recent American reporters to confirm it was Mrs. Jewell R. Mazique, a distinguished graduate of this [Howard] University, and columnist for the *Afro-American* chain of newspapers.

The developing *role of trade unions* in the Soviet Union, and their active and real participation in the political and economic and productive life of the nation has been confirmed and documented at length in the book issued by the International Labor Office of Geneva after a study on the spot and published in 1960.

As to *culture,* one has had in the USSR the most colossal revolution in all history, for a people hitherto largely illiterate has been brought not only to full literacy, but it has been raised to the highest cultural level in the world. As Ossia Trilling, vice-president of the International Association of Theatre Critics, stated: "In no city in the world can one see so much Shakespeare, Ibsen, Wilde, Schiller, Ostrovsky, Chekhov, and so on, in one week as in Moscow" (*N. Y. Times,* Jan. 26, 1958). Wrote Howard Taubman of the *N. Y. Times* in the summer of 1958, after an extended stay in the USSR: "There is a genuine dedication to artistic ideals in the Soviet Union. There is a pervasive love of beauty. There is an exhilaration in the skill and virtuosity of highly trained performers. There is respect for the creative vocation. The people are being taught unremittingly to take pride in art as in learning. . . . To be cultured is regarded as one of the highest goods."

In *international affairs,* I think the record proves, from the Decree of Peace issued as its first act by the revolutionary Soviet Russia in 1917 to its leadership in getting the United Nations to adopt unanimously in 1959 the declaration for general and complete disarmament, the USSR has been in the forefront of the battle against war and against fascism. Her record in the international sphere—from Italy's rape of Ethiopia to fascism's ravishment of Spain to Japanese imperialism's war upon China, to her decisive role in breaking the back of fascism when that monster was led under Hitler's banners—consistently has been a record of support of the forces of democracy and peace and opposition to the forces of reaction and war. This was true in her struggle against war in 1917, and it is true in her support of the Cuban Revolutionary Government against the attacks, invasions, insults, and provocations of the United States. I think that the works of Professors J. P. Morray, F. L. Schuman, D. F. Fleming, and Arnold Toynbee sufficiently demonstrate this truth; I have myself labored to document it in the recent work, *American Foreign Policy and The Cold War* (New York, 1962).

The "secret" explaining the basic domestic and international record of the USSR—it is a secret alas, only in the United States—is the fact that socialism exists there; the private ownership of the means of production has been eliminated—the exploitation of man by man has been terminated. Heaven did not result, nor did hell, but great improvement did result, and a considerable fragment of this globe was revolutionized. The system triumphant there has brought great progress to its people, helped save humanity, and is being instituted—of course, with necessary national differences—in other parts of Europe, in Asia, and now, in America.

Of course, one's evaluation of the Soviet Union is not simply an academic exercise. Mr. Richard Nixon, in 1957, when he was Vice-President, affirmed that the USSR was civilization's main threat and insisted that "we are in a war today" with that threat. Vice-Admiral Charles R. Brown, addressing the Navy League in October, 1958, said: "World War III has long since started, whether we'll admit it or not," and the Admiral went on to name the USSR as the foe.

The Admiral and the former Vice-President may be impatient to attempt the destruction of the USSR. But is that country—described by leading American figures and eyewitnesses in the terms already brought before you—is that country really the enemy of the peoples of the United States?

Rather, in the case of most of those who have described the tremendous advances made in the Soviet Union, the conclusion drawn has been that these advances should stimulate us to improve ourselves. Certainly, this is the conclusion which was drawn by the late Mrs. F. D. Roosevelt; by Walter Lippmann, by Howard Taubman, by Professor Marc Raeff.

Professor Harold J. Berman, of Harvard University—an outstanding authority on Soviet law, and recently having lectured at the University of Moscow—has said that the main point in the world as it is today, given the forward sweep of its socialist sector, is that here in our own country we must concentrate on the achievements of "justice, mercy and morality," and that we must match in a way consonant with our own national genius, "the spirit of service, self-sacrifice, and common purpose," that the peoples of the USSR in their way have brought to their country.

Here is a kind of contest that is worthy of the finest national feeling and profoundest love of country of which any of us—citizens of the USA or of the USSR—are capable. Come, let us see, as friends and brothers, who can contribute most to the happiness and well-being of mankind!

SOVIET VIEWS

5. INFORMATION U.S.S.R. *

NOVOSTI PRESS AGENCY

a. *Some Questions of General Interest*

QUESTION: *What is the average life span in the USSR?*
ANSWER: The average is 69 years. For men it is 64 and for women—72. In pre-revolutionary Russia the average life span was only 32.

QUESTION: *Is is true that in the Soviet Union patients have to go for medical treatment to doctors to whom they are "attached"?*
ANSWER: No, that's not the case at all. It is true that every doctor is attached to a particular district comprising several city blocks, or to an equivalent rural district, both to treat patients and to look after people so they stay healthy.

* Selected from the Question and Answer Sections of the February 1962, March 1962, May 1962, January 1963, February 1963, March 1963, April 1963, and May 1963 issues of *USSR* by permission of the publisher.

There are more than 400,000 physicians in the Soviet Union today, or 19 for every 10,000 of the population, enough so that people who need medical attention can get it at a clinic or a hospital in their neighborhood. There is nothing, however, to prevent a patient from picking out the particular doctor he prefers at the clinic. Serving as consultants in the clinics are leading specialists, including professors at medical colleges. Consultations, like all other forms of medical service, are free. Patients may also go to any central clinic or medical research institute, where they also treat patients without charge.

Should a patient be dissatisfied with the diagnosis of a particular doctor at his district clinic, he may go to a pay clinic, to be found in all of the larger towns, or to a private practitioner, of whom there are a good many.

QUESTION: *How many libraries are there in the Soviet Union?*
ANSWER: 382,000. They hold 1.89 billion books.

QUESTION: *Are many books by American writers published?*
ANSWER: From 1918 to 1961 the country's publishing houses printed a total of 102 million copies of 2,863 books by American writers. These works, moreover, were translated into 50 languages of the peoples of the USSR. It is noteworthy that the Soviet Union, according to UNESCO, stands first in the volume of translated literature.

QUESTION: *We would like to know the price of various products and goods in the Soviet Union. Can you give us some of them?*
ANSWER: By all means. A loaf of bread costs 14 kopecks; a pound of potatoes, five kopecks; a pound of meat, one ruble; a quart of milk, 28 kopecks; four ounces of ice cream, 22 kopecks; a package of cigarettes, slightly more than 15 kopecks. A long-playing phonograph record costs one ruble 10 kopecks (90 kopecks equal one dollar).[1]

QUESTION: *What is the housing situation in the Soviet Union?*
ANSWER: In the past five years every third person in the country has moved into a new home. However, we do not consider the housing problem solved, and large-scale construction is going on all the time. When U.S. Secretary of the Interior Stewart Udall visited the Soviet Union, he commented with surprise on the huge scale of housing construction. In Bratsk, a new Siberian town rising near a hydroelectric power station, he saw many attractive apartment house developments that were, he said, as solid and well built as similar American projects.

[1] There are 100 kopecks to one ruble (often spelled "kopeks" and "rouble," respectively, in transliteration). [Editor's note.]

By the way, in the two minutes it takes the reader to finish this page [in the original journal], ten Soviet families will have been handed keys to newly built apartments.

QUESTION: *What are these new apartments like?*
ANSWER: For the most part they are efficiencies and one- and two-bedroom apartments with from 160 to 485 square feet of living space, exclusive of hallways, kitchen and bathroom. Rent and utilities average four per cent of the family income. Repairs are made at state expense.

QUESTION: *What is the rent for a one-bedroom apartment in the USSR?*
ANSWER: The rent for a one-bedroom apartment with all conveniences, including telephone, costs from 12 to 13 rubles a month.

QUESTION: *Who pays for the upkeep of houses and apartments?*
ANSWER: Houses owned by cooperatives and individual citizens are maintained at their own expense, but the state helps out with easy-term loans and with building materials for repairs. The maintenance of houses owned by the state are financed out of the public consumption fund, and the tenants pay rent. Rent is very low and covers no more than half the upkeep. It runs from three to five per cent of family income. The plan for the next 20 years is to gradually cut even these modest rents to the vanishing point and to supply housing and utilities—gas, electric, central heating, etc.—free of charge. The intention is also to provide various free public services, including municipal transportation.

QUESTION: *We read that there is no unemployment in the USSR. How did you achieve full employment?*
ANSWER: This is a result of socialist transformations that took place in our country. Our industry, farming, transport, educational and medical systems develop on the basis of a unified state plan and constantly demand more and more workers. As early as 1930 there was no unemployment in the Soviet Union. Between 1928 and 1937 the number of factory and office workers more than doubled. The demand for manpower grows with every year because of the tremendous amount of construction going on. We are building new towns and villages, farms, factories, mines, power plants and railways. In the past four years 3,700 large new enterprises were put into operation.

We should point out that the large-scale mechanization and automation taking place cannot lead to unemployment. Automatic machines make work easier, help raise labor productivity and release workers for other jobs where they are needed. Automation helps to shorten working hours without cutting wages and will eventually give the Soviet people the world's shortest working day.

QUESTION: *How many hours a day do people in the Soviet Union work?*
ANSWER: Either seven or six hours a day, or 41 or 36 hours a week respectively. In offices the working day generally begins at 9 A.M. and ends at 5 P.M., with an hour off for lunch. In factories with only a single shift work begins at 8 A.M. and ends at 4 P.M., also with an hour for lunch. Where there is a second shift, it starts at 4 P.M. People in the more hazardous trades—iron and steel workers, chemical workers, coal miners, and such—work six hours a day. In accordance with the new Program of the Communist Party of the Soviet Union there will be another cut in the workday to six and five hours in the near future.

QUESTION: *May Soviet workers declare a strike?*
ANSWER: While strikes are not forbidden, the idea of striking makes no sense to Soviet workers because they would be striking against themselves. In the Soviet Union the means of production belong to the whole of society, that is, they have been nationalized, and the fruits of people's labor, too, belong to society in general. Distribution is governed by the principle, "From each according to his ability, to each according to his work." And immense amounts of money are spent by the state for such social services as free education and free medical services. Hence, any loss caused by a strike would be borne by the working people themselves.

This does not mean that there can be no dispute between workers and management or that everything is so perfect that workers never have any grievances. Where disagreements do arise, they are settled at a plant by the trade union committee, with the committee's decision binding on the management. The infrequent case where management does not agree to the decision is carried to the courts. There is a rule in the Soviet Union that "the collective is never wrong." Accordingly, wherever workers voice their dissatisfaction with some action of the management, they get the support of the trade union, the Party and other local organizations, and the press.

QUESTION: *Do young people who want to marry require the consent of their parents?*
ANSWER: The law makes no such provision, but young people usually obtain such consent. Like anywhere in the world, there are young people who ask their parents' consent and some who do not, who marry against the will of their parents. When that happens, the parents make the best of the situation. No Soviet young men or women are threatened with the fate of Romeo and Juliet, at any rate.

QUESTION: *What is the attitude in your country toward a woman who has been married three times?*
ANSWER: The same as yours: Any man will think thrice before he decides to become her fourth husband.

b. Some Questions Concerning the Distribution of Income

QUESTION: *Will you describe the system of distribution of material benefits in the Soviet Union?*
ANSWER: Since all industrial enterprises and state farms are publicly owned, their income is public property. Add the income of the collective farms, and you have the total national income.

A quarter of the national income is spent to augment and develop the country's industry, transport and agriculture; to expand and modernize existing enterprises and build new ones. This is paid for out of the accumulation fund.

The remaining three-quarters of the national income makes up the consumption fund. It is spent for the material and cultural needs of the citizen.

The consumption fund is subdivided into the wage fund and the public consumption fund.[2]

QUESTION: *Since the public consumption fund serves as an indirect addition to wages, wouldn't it be simpler and better to raise wages directly?*
ANSWER: Simpler perhaps, but not better. Our country operates on the principle of socialism—"From each according to his abilities, to each according to his work." This means that every able-bodied person receives equal pay for equal work, irrespective of sex, age, race or nationality. A person's earnings depend on the quantity and quality of work he does.

People vary in stamina and skill. Some workers are stronger, capable of greater effort and endurance, and can therefore do more. Workers with more skill do a better job. Consequently their earnings are higher and they have more cash income to spend to satisfy whatever personal needs they have. Besides that, there is the difference in size of families, number of wages earners and so on. All these things make for inequalities in material well-being which will be gradually ironed out as we move toward

---

[2] The public consumption fund is that part of the consumption fund that is distributed according to needs, irrespective of a person's contribution to production. Free schooling and free medical treatment are examples of services provided out of the public consumption fund. [Editor's note.]

the communist principle of distribution—"From each according to his ability, to each according to his *needs*."

When we come to the public consumption fund, this material inequality does not operate. Higher wages do not help a man to give his children a better education or to get more qualified medical attention, let us say. In Western countries the quality of these services depends entirely on the amount the family earns and can afford to spend. Our approach is altogether different. The public consumption fund is distributed by the communist principle—according to needs. If you have children, they go to school. If you are ill, you get free medical attention, hospitalization, surgery or whatever else is indicated. When you grow old, you get an old age pension. The public consumption fund meets people's needs regardless of the quantity and quality of the work they do. It makes all Soviet citizens equal with regard to educational opportunity, medical care and the other services the public consumption fund supplies. . . .

QUESTION: *Is anything withheld from the worker's pay for medical care, education and other such free services?*
ANSWER: No, all these services are financed by state funds allocated in the national budget. Most of the state funds come from the profits of state factories and farms. Only a very small proportion—some seven or eight per cent—comes from income taxes. . . .

QUESTION: *About how much, would you say, do these various services, translated into income, add to the average family budget?*
ANSWER: Economists estimate that the social services mentioned above and such other items as reduced rates for sanatorium and resort accommodations and nursery and kindergarten care at a very modest fee actually add about 25 per cent to a worker's yearly income. . . .[3]

c. Some Questions About Soviet Education

QUESTION: *Will you tell us something about the educational system of the USSR?*
ANSWER: All schools, from the elementary grades to the university, are public; there are no private or religious schools in the Soviet Union.

The three most characteristic features of the school system are:

1. Tuition is free at all levels.

2. The system is uniform. There is an absolute continuity of the

---

[3] Quite a few Soviet and Western Marxist economists would consider this estimate too low. See, for example, selection VI. 3 below. [Editor's note.]

various rungs of the educational ladder. No school leads to a blind alley from which the student cannot progress to the university level.

    3. The teaching is done in the students' native language. Soviet schools teach their students in 59 of the languages spoken by the peoples of the USSR. Textbooks and study aids are published in all these languages.

QUESTION: *How much do Soviet students pay for dormitory accommodations?*
ANSWER: From one and a half to two rubles a month. Most Soviet students receive scholarships that average 30 rubles a month.

QUESTION: *Is it true that those who study by correspondence receive an additional paid vacation?*
ANSWER: Yes. That's true for students of both correspondence and evening institutes. The length of these vacations vary from 20 to 40 calendar days, depending on the year of study and whether it is evening or correspondence. Students in their senior year have an additional day off each week to study, also with pay. When they have to prepare a diploma project or thesis, students get a four-month paid vacation, and when they have to take state exams, a paid vacation of 30 calendar days. Tuition, as you probably know, is free in all schools. There are about a million students in the evening and correspondence divisions.

QUESTION: *I understand that the Soviet Union trains more engineers than the United States. Is that so?*
ANSWER: Yes. In 1960 the Soviet Union trained 120,000 engineers, and the United States 38,000. So far as we know, last year's ratio was the same.

QUESTION: *What are the basic aims of communist education?*
ANSWER: Our schools aim to instill in the child a love for work and an understanding of his responsibility as an individual in a collective society; in other words, to teach the child how to use his abilities and talents in behalf of society.

    We want our children to have initiative, to be courageous, not to shirk hardship, to recognize weakness and errors and correct them, to be truthful and self-disciplined.

    One of our major aims is to give our children a feeling of internationalism, to teach them respect for peoples of other countries and nationalities.

    To bring up man with a capital M, adults who combine high moral and spiritual stature with physical perfection—that is the goal of every Soviet teacher.

d. Some Questions About the Government

QUESTION: *How are elections to the Soviets of Working People's Deputies held?*
ANSWER: Elections are held on the basis of universal, equal and direct suffrage by secret ballot.

All citizens of the USSR who have reached the age of 18 (except insane persons), regardless of their race, nationality, sex, religion, education and domicile, are included in the list of voters in their residential districts. If a voter has moved since the last election, is sick or is traveling, he gets an absentee ballot entitling him to vote where he is. Lists of voters are posted a month before the election. On election day the voter goes to the nearest polling place. These are located in schools, colleges, clubs, theater lobbies and auditoriums of scientific institutions. There he presents any identification document and receives a ballot. He may cast his vote for the candidate. If he chooses to, he may use the voting booths provided for that purpose. He then drops his ballot in the sealed ballot box.

Voting starts at 6 A.M. and ends at midnight, when the election commission begins to tally the votes. This commission consists of people from local factories, collective farms and institutes. The election results are turned over to the Central Election Commission.

QUESTION: *What is the Soviet equivalent of the American Congress or the British Parliament? How is it elected and what are its powers?*
ANSWER: The USSR Supreme Soviet is the country's highest legislative body. The present Supreme Soviet has 1,443 deputies. . . . They are elected for a four-year term by secret ballot cast by all citizens who have reached the age of 18. The Supreme Soviet has two chambers with equal rights. The Soviet of the Union is elected on the basis of one deputy for every 300,000 citizens and represents the interests of all the people of the country, regardless of their nationality. The Soviet of Nationalities represents the specific interest of the more than 100 nationalities and peoples who live in the Soviet Union. The USSR Supreme Soviet legislates for the country, appoints the USSR Council of Ministers and adopts the national economic plans and the national budget.

QUESTION: *What trades or professions do your legislators come from?*
ANSWER: Industrial workers and farmers make up more than 46 per cent of the deputies to the Supreme Soviet of the republics; office workers,

17 percent; managers of factories and shops, 2.5 percent; teachers, scientists and those working in the arts, 7 percent. The USSR Supreme Soviet, our national parliament, has approximately the same composition. Of the slightly less than two million deputies in town and village Soviets, 45 percent work in industry, agriculture, transport and the like. The rest are scientists, educators, writers, artists and office workers.

QUESTION: *Does the Soviet Union have an office equivalent to the American presidency?*
ANSWER: In the Soviet Union the functions of president are carried out by a collective body—the Presidium of the USSR Supreme Soviet. The Presidium, which acts for the Supreme Soviet between sessions and is accountable to it, consists of 33 people: the President of the Presidium . . . 15 Vice Presidents (one for each of the 15 union republics), a Secretary, and 16 members at large. The Presidium is elected at a joint session of both chambers of the Soviet parliament.

e. Some Questions Concerning the Communist Party

QUESTION: *Your magazine told us that there are 10 million members of the Communist Party in the Soviet Union. Do they join the Party individually or collectively?*
ANSWER: Applicants for Party membership must apply individually. Any worker, farmer or intellectual who accepts the Program and Rules of the CPSU and has reached the age of 18 may join the Party. We should add that young people up to the age of 20 are accepted in the Party only through the Young Communist League.

The prospective member must submit the recommendation of three members who have been in the Party for at least three years and have known the applicant as a coworker for at least one year. These members are responsible to the Party for the objectivity of their data on the personal and political qualifications of the applicant. The applicant submits the necessary recommendations to the primary Party organization, i.e., to the Communist Party organization at his place of work. His acceptance is discussed at a meeting of this organization, where each member freely expresses his opinion. The question is then decided by a simple majority vote of raised hands. The decision must be approved by the district committee of the CPSU before it becomes final.

The applicant is first accepted as a candidate member. It is only after a year has elapsed and the candidate has proved himself worthy that he is accepted as a full member of the Communist Party.

QUESTION: *What kind of jobs do Party members hold and what wages do they receive?*
ANSWER: More than 40 percent of the members of the Party are factory workers, more than 22 percent are collective farmers, and the rest are office workers, professionals and students. Like everyone else, they receive the prevailing wage for the jobs they hold. Wages vary only with level of work and the individual's qualifications: Party members have no special privileges in this respect or in any other. Moreover, Party members assume an obligation to serve the people and voluntarily undertake the hardest and least rewarding jobs. We could cite thousands of cases of Party members asking to be transferred to lower-paid jobs where they can, by example and greater experience, help a weak or lagging team turn out more and better work. . . .

QUESTION: *Do people who are not members of the Communist Party hold important jobs?*
ANSWER: Yes. The only thing that counts in our country in employment or election to office is a person's fitness for the particular job or post. Thousands of cases can be cited where the heads of big factories, institutes, state farms, collective farms, or public organizations are not Party members. For example, the head of Moscow University, Academician Ivan Petrovsky, is not a member of the Party. Neither is the president of the Soviet Peace Committee, the poet Nikolai Tikhonov.

QUESTION: *I'm a teacher and do not belong to any party. I don't suppose I could be a teacher in the Soviet Union. I understand that every teacher there is obliged to be a member of the Communist Party, or isn't he?*
ANSWER: This teacher is mistaken. Party membership is not a prerequisite for working in a school or college. No more than 400,000 of the two million teachers in the country are members of the Communist Party.

QUESTION: *Are the leading Communist Party bodies elected?*
ANSWER: Yes, all Party bodies, from top to bottom, are elected. The Central Committee is elected at a Party Congress once every four years. The leading organs of the Communist Parties of the union republics and the Party committees in territories and regions are elected once every two years. The Party committees of the primary organizations are elected annually. These are all closed elections, and voting is by secret ballot.

QUESTION: *Can Party members challenge persons nominated as candidates to Party organs?*

ANSWER: Yes, they can and do. The rules of the Communist Party of the Soviet Union say, "Every Party member is guaranteed the unlimited right to challenge and criticize candidates."

QUESTION: *Does the composition of the leading Party organs change?*
ANSWER: Yes, it does. The Rules of the CPSU provide for a systematic change and renewal of the leadership. In each election the composition of the Central Committee of the CPSU and of its Presidium is renewed by at least one-fourth. Presidium members as a rule are elected for no more than three successive terms. The composition of the leading organs of the Communist Parties of the union republics and of territorial and regional Party committees is renewed by at least one-third at every election, that of local Party committees or bureaus at plants, factories and offices by at least half. The Rules stipulate that members of these leading Party organs can be elected for no more than three successive terms.

A meeting, conference, or congress of Communists can, if it deems it necessary, elect a Party functionary for a longer term. But in that case he must be elected by no less than 75 per cent of those voting.

f. Some Questions on the Subject of "Freedom"

QUESTION: *Can a Soviet citizen make a will in favor of anyone he wishes?*
ANSWER: Of course, a Soviet citizen has the right to leave his property to anyone he likes—to a private individual or to a public organization, to a church, school, museum, etc. But Soviet law requires that a part of the inheritance go to the children of the deceased under working age, or to an incapacitated wife, mother or father.

QUESTION: *Can a worker leave one job for another or move from one city to another?*
ANSWER: Certainly. All he needs to do is give the customary two weeks' notice. Nothing prevents him from leaving a job that doesn't suit him or from moving to another town.

QUESTION: *Is religious freedom guaranteed in the Soviet Union?*
ANSWER: Yes. Every citizen may follow any faith he chooses. He may change his faith, and he also has the right to follow no religion at all, i.e., to be an atheist. All Soviet citizens have equal rights regardless of their religious faith. Religion is a matter left to the conscience of each person; the state does not intervene in matters of religious faith. More than that, the criminal codes of the Russian Federation and the other

union republics have special articles providing for the severe punishment of those who impede religious rites. Freedom of conscience is guaranteed by the Soviet Constitution.

QUESTION: *Can Soviet citizens criticize members of the government?*
ANSWER: They can and do: at trade union meetings, in the press and in radio broadcasts. Criticism may be directed even at a minister. The Communist Party considers criticism an important spur to progress. The new Party program adopted at the Twenty-second Congress declares that the Party will continue "to foster the most searching criticism and self-criticism as a well-tested working method, as a means of discovering and rectifying mistakes and shortcomings, and as a way of educating the people."

IV

ECONOMIC PLANNING
IN THE U.S.S.R.

"Socialism is inconceivable without . . . planned state organization . . ."

VLADIMIR ILYICH LENIN

"The forty years of experience in socialist construction in the USSR has convincingly proved the advantages of a planned economy over anarchy of production and striving after maximum profit."

NIKITA S. KHRUSHCHEV

"Should the old planning methods be preserved, and given our present rate of growth, in 1980 practically the entire adult population of our country would have to be engaged in the administration and planning spheres. On the other hand, automation of accounting and administrative work, the introduction of electronic machines, will make it possible to solve the problem without undue inflation of the administrative apparatus."

V. S. NEMCHINOV (1894-1964)
FORMER HEAD, LABORATORY FOR THE
APPLICATION OF MATHEMATICAL
METHODS IN ECONOMICS,
ACADEMY OF SCIENCES, U.S.S.R.

In Soviet society, the means of production (the land, the factories, the retail establishments, the banks, the transportation system, etc.) are owned not by private individuals but by society at large, and are operated by the government presumably in the interest of the people. In many ways, such a society can be thought of as a gigantic corporation that encompasses all the means of production—a corporation in which each citizen is an equal shareholder and in which the government acts as the board of directors, operating the corporation for the shareholders. The economic activities of this giant "corporation," just like the activities of any corporation, must be planned in advance. The men in charge must plan what to produce, how

145

many workers and how many machines to employ in different "departments," how much to offer in payment to workers of various degrees of skill and competence, what price to ask for each of the finished products, etc., etc. Production is supposed to be carried on according to plan by paid workers under the guidance and supervision of hired managers—in each of the divisions of large American corporations and in each of the enterprises in Soviet society.

The fundamental difference, then, between a planned economy and what is usually referred to as a free enterprise system, is not that planning is required in one and not in the other, but rather that in the former plans are made for the economy as a whole, while in the latter individuals and business organizations plan only their own activities with the profit motive as a guide and with the forces of demand and supply as the coordinators of economic activity. Whether or not an additional 100,000 TV sets will be produced in a free enterprise society depends upon whether or not the producers expect that they can sell them at a profit. In a planned economy, on the other hand, profitability is of secondary importance. Resources will presumably be allocated for the manufacture of the TV sets if, in the opinion of the planners, their production is in the best interests of society. If "too many" TV sets were produced in a competitive free enterprise economy, sellers unable to sell them all at prevailing prices would put them "on sale"; if the supply were insufficient, sellers, noticing that prospective purchasers were willing to buy more TV sets than available, would be induced to raise prices. In the Soviet Union, prices are changed only by orders from above, but the law of supply and demand still functions. If there were "too many" TV sets on the Soviet market and the government did not lower prices, they would gather dust on the shelves of the stores (since the economic meaning of "too many" is "more than can be sold at the prevailing prices"). If the supply were inadequate, queues would form in front of stores, with eager purchasers lining up to buy before the supply was exhausted.

This brief introduction should make the reader aware of some of the difficulties which beset those whose task it is to plan, supervise, and coordinate the economic activities of an entire nation, especially one of the size and complexity of the U.S.S.R.

In Part A of this chapter, George N. Halm, under *Western Views,* introduces the reader to the general, basic principles of Soviet planning. The Soviet selection is taken from a manual on Marxism-Leninism. In it, the authors (a group of Soviet scholars) present the official Soviet view on the fundamental principles of socialist planning.

While the central planning authorities in Moscow draw up the *overall* plan for the nation, it would hardly be practical for them to make all the *specific* decisions which have to be made for each individual enterprise. Considerable authority is therefore delegated to local managers. However, it is by no means easy to devise an incentive program which would induce these managers to implement efficiently their units' parts in the overall plan. In Part B, one Western and one Soviet economist discuss the wastefulness and inefficiency that is at least partly attributable to present inadequacies in the system of managerial incentives. The authors also evaluate a recent Soviet proposal to improve the prevailing situation—a proposal which has been debated widely and openly in the Soviet Union and which has also received considerable publicity in the West.

A. Fundamental Principles of Central Planning in the U.S.S.R.

WESTERN VIEWS

1. SOVIET PLANNING *

GEORGE N. HALM

Tufts University

. . . The Russian economy is a command economy. The government's command regulates the interdependent actions of producing units on the the basis of one comprehensive plan. Predetermined production quotas and appropriate allocations, rather than competitive buying and selling, are the characteristic feature of this new method of integrating the production process.

The aims of the economy are decided upon by the highest party authorities and not by the consumer. The central plan translates these aims into production targets for the different industries, plants, and collectives and sees that the branches of the economy keep in balance with one another.

Authoritarian central planning means more than the setting of broad

* From *Economic Systems, A Comparative Analysis*, Rev., by George N. Halm, copyright © 1960 by George N. Halm. Reprinted from pp. 244-247 by permission of the author and of Holt, Rinehart and Winston, Inc.

development schemes and production targets; it means the careful quantitative and qualitative enumeration of thousands of items which are needed in the life of a nation, from rolling mills to hairpins, from atomic energy to school equipment and ballet performances. This task is so formidable that it cannot be solved by the central planning agency alone. "It is impracticable for the central authorities to prescribe physically every product and input, or to prescribe some of them—indeed usually most of them—in completely disaggregated terms." [1] To illustrate by a much ridiculed example from the Polish economy: the plan should not endeavor to name the number of sour pickles or of hares to be shot.[2]

The aims of the plan are competitive. Each production target must be limited so that the total of all targets does not exceed the productive power of the nation. And since the factors of production are substitutable only within limits, the production program must be drawn up with reference to the given technical possibilities. Each industry's output depends on an input of intermediary goods which are the output of other industries. How can the plan relate all input and output figures and achieve the coordination of production processes which results in the output of all needed goods in the right proportions?

But even this formulation of the problem is incomplete. The gradual achievement of workable technical interdependence is not sufficient if we want to make the best economic use of the factors of production. Technological interdependence guarantees that the system will function without breakdowns resulting from the development of bottlenecks; however, it does not guarantee the best combination of factors in an economic sense. . . .

The problem would be greatly simplified if for each production process only one technique were available. Actually, however, there is nearly always a choice between different degrees of capital intensity. We remember . . . not only has the social economy to solve the problem of *what* and *how much* to produce; it must also answer the question *how* to produce, i.e., which technique to use.

Through much trial and error the Soviet system has achieved a modicum of technical consistency. But it remains, at least officially, unconscious of the waste which is implied in its emphasis on technology.

This criticism cannot be answered by reference to the fact that Soviet production does not follow the wishes of the consumer; it remains true with respect to any set of preferences. No system can solve its economic problems by recourse to technology. But an autocratic system can pretend, of course, that what it produces is exactly what it wants. It may even pride

---

[1] Gregory Grossman, "Industrial Prices in the USSR," *American Economic Review,* XLIX (May, 1959), p. 59.

[2] Alexander Erlich, "The Polish Economy after October, 1956: Background and Outlook," *American Economic Review,* XLIX (May, 1959), p. 96.

itself in the fact that only the most modern techniques are used, though this statement, of course, is never true for all production processes simultaneously.

Leaving aside all bureaucratic details, we can draw the following simplified outline of Russian planning methods.

First, the authorities decide on such basic issues as heavy versus light industries, location of industries, the development of atomic energy, etc.

With these general directives and the existing production pattern to work with, experts will draw up a tentative plan which translates, as far as feasible, the general development aims into concrete production targets. The interrelation of all production processes makes it imperative that these production targets pass the test of mutual consistency. However, this interrelating of production targets consists mainly in revising and adjusting an already existing production pattern which, in turn, was the result of many previous adjustments.

The planners cannot know all the technical details and cannot give commands in completely disaggregative terms concerning product mix, input mix, the capital intensity of production methods, etc. This kind of specialized knowledge rests with operational managers. These men must be consulted. While they will have no right whatever to question the aims of the plan, they must cooperate in the setting of input and output figures for their industries and plants. Otherwise, they would be placed in the impossible position of having to achieve results which cannot be achieved on the basis of planned allocations.

Tentative plan figures are, therefore, distributed through the administrative channels of the Soviet bureaucracy down to industrial and agricultural producing units. These figures are not yet directives; rather, they are requests for corrections. Corrections and suggestions are then collected through the administrative arteries of the system.

Based on this material, a new plan is drawn up; and this plan, once adopted, becomes the official production program. Its detailed production figures become compulsory instructions. They are commands.

Of course, the final figures which result from this planning procedure cannot possibly be perfect, not even in the limited sense of technical consistency. They rest on assumptions which cannot always be correct. The weather or the terms of foreign trade cannot be ascertained in advance, just as the rise in efficiency per man-hour may elude exact quantitative estimates. For these and other reasons (e.g., human failure) it is vitally important that the execution of the plan be watched constantly so that imbalances can be corrected at the earliest possible time.

It would be wrong, however, to overestimate the difficulties which the planned economy faces in achieving balance in the limited sense of technical consistency. No social-economic system is perfect in this respect, including certainly the capitalist economy with its overinvestment crises, which are nothing but huge disproportions in the development of different branches of the economy. We have to remember, furthermore, that it is possible to create flexibility through the accumulation of reserve stocks, i.e., inventories which make the supply of strategic materials temporarily independent of current production. Finally, figures given for long periods (five years and more) are never more than broad targets or even "ranges." Operational plans are formulated for much shorter periods, and the commands refer to minima for output and maxima for input rather than to rigidly fixed amounts. . . .

SOVIET VIEWS

2. FUNDAMENTAL PRINCIPLES OF SOVIET ECONOMIC PLANNING *

O. V. KUUSINEN AND OTHERS

Soviet Social Scientists, Philosophers, and Authors

The establishment of social ownership in all branches of the national economy completes the transition from capitalism to socialism. Socialism now develops on the basis of large-scale industry and highly mechanised collective farming.

Society itself, the working people themselves, have the opportunity of planning and controlling the production process *of the entire national economy on a country-wide scale.* Under capitalism the organisation of production in a more or less planned way can be achieved only within the limits of an individual enterprise or at most within a single monopoly. But even such planning is constantly upset by the anarchy of production that prevails throughout the national economy. Socialism makes possible planned direction of the entire social production mechanism taken as a whole.

A new era in the history of mankind begins, the era of planned economy. The volume of social production and its structure, the distribution of labour and means of production among various branches of the national

---

* Excerpts reprinted from O. V. Kuusinen and Others, *Fundamentals of Marxism-Leninism: Manual,* 2nd Rev. Ed., Foreign Languages Publishing House, Moscow, 1963, pp. 563 and 568-575.

economy, commodity prices and wage rates—all those no longer come into existence spontaneously. They are planned by society itself, which aims at achieving the greatest possible satisfaction of the needs of its members.

This does not mean, however, that objective laws cease to operate in the economic sphere.

On the contrary, if the conscious management of the economy is to be most effective, socialist society must be guided by the objective laws and must organise its economy in accordance with these laws.

The laws of the new economic formation cannot be mastered at once. Socialist society needs time and experience to comprehend the laws that determine its own development, and to learn to utilise them in its own interest.

The responsibility which under these circumstances rests on the leading bodies in society—both Party and state bodies—is obvious. It is their duty to become proficient in the art of directing the complicated economic organism and to plan all social production in a way which will ensure its uninterrupted growth and a steadily rising living standard for the whole people. . . .

THE MAIN PURPOSE OF SOCIALIST PRODUCTION

The conversion of the means of production into social property radically alters the driving forces and purpose of production.

The purpose of capitalist production is the extraction of profit. The manufacture of a commodity for its own sake hardly interests the capitalist. The question whether the needs of all the members of society are satisfied interests him even less. How to turn the production of any given commodity into a source of profit—that is the capitalist's real preoccupation.

Under socialism the means of production belong to the working people, to society, and it is obvious that the working people cannot exploit themselves. . . .

The whole social product produced every year in the socialist economy belongs to the owner of the means of production—to society, i.e., to the working people, taken as a single national producer collective. . . .

The socialist state considers that its main purpose is the expansion of production in order to provide a continuously rising living standard for the population. This is merely the conscious expression of the objective economic law inherent in socialist production. In economic literature this *basic economic law of socialism* has been formulated thus: the continuous expansion and perfection of production on the basis of the most advanced techniques and collective labour for the purpose of the fullest satisfaction of the constantly growing requirements and the all-round development of all members of society.

The steady rise of the material well-being of the working people in the socialist countries vividly demonstrates the operation of this law. . . .

PLANNED DEVELOPMENT OF THE NATIONAL ECONOMY

With the establishment of social ownership, the laws of capitalist economy cease to operate. As already stated, the new form of property creates its own, new objective laws. The most important of these is the law of planned, proportional development of the national economy.

The Law of Planned, Proportional Development
of the National Economy

In socialist society the national economy is an integral organism, directed by a single will. To ensure harmonious co-ordination and maximum integration of all parts of the country's social production mechanism becomes under these conditions the chief economic requirement. This is expressed in the law of planned, proportional development of the national economy.

What is the essence of this law? First of all, it lies in the fact that the normal functioning of socialist economy requires definite relationships or *proportions* between its different branches. Furthermore, in a socialist society the establishment and maintenance of these proportions can and must take place *in a planned way,* that is as a result of the predetermined action of the socialist state and its planning bodies.

The *objective character* of the law of planned, proportional development lies in the fact that these proportions in the national economy cannot be arbitrarily established according to someone's wish or fancy, but are governed by necessary requirements, the infringement of which leads inevitably to the disorganisation of the social production process. . . .

Let us consider for a moment that society or its state organs guided by the best intentions wanted suddenly to increase sharply the volume of consumption omitting however to arrange in good time for a corresponding increase in production. As a result the existing stocks of commodities would be rapidly exhausted. The same would happen if the relationship between consumption and accumulation of resources earmarked for the expansion of production were to be arbitrarily changed. A reduction in the share of accumulation will inevitably slow down economic development and subsequently bring it to a halt, leading to a rapid consumption of basic capital and to the disorganisation and decline of the whole of economic life. An excessive increase in the rate of accumulation, however, may weaken the material incentive of those engaged in production and ultimately affect the rate of growth of labour productivity. Nor can one disturb with impunity the proportions between wage rates and the level of labour productivity, between the total monetary income of the population and the volume of trade, etc.

In addition to those already enumerated, many other branches of production and distribution exist which cannot function normally unless certain proportions are observed. Thus a balance must be maintained between the basic branches of the national economy, such as industry, agriculture and transport. Incalculable difficulties threaten if any one of them falls behind.

Definite relationships are required in the development of the heavy and light, the extractive and manufacturing industries. A faster rate of development of heavy industry ensures the advance of all branches of the economy. Similarly the raw-material and power industries must expand faster than the manufacturing industries, and create the necessary reserves for their advance. Proper proportions have to be maintained also with regard to the distribution of industry among separate economic districts, and specialisation and co-operation of production. The economy will not work smoothly either unless a correct ratio is established between the number of skilled personnel required in the national economy and the country's training facilities.

Hence it is an important task of socialist society to maintain the wide range of proportions in the national economy.

Someone may say that a certain proportionality in the development of production is required in any economic system, including capitalism. That is in fact so. But under capitalism the necessary economic relationships are established spontaneously by way of abnormal fluctuations and disproportions, crises and recessions. The position becomes still more complicated because monopolies impede the spontaneous flow of capital from one branch to another. Capitalist economy staggers blindly, stumbling and falling, incurring enormous expenses while it gropes its way towards the proportionality demanded by objective economic laws.

Matters are entirely different in a socialist society, where the law of planned, proportional development has come into effect, where in Engels' words, "socialised production upon a predetermined plan becomes henceforth possible." For the first time in history people possess everything required to achieve the maximum co-ordination of the social production process and to control it in a rational way. The fact that all the means of production are social property and production is planned and directed from a single centre, has created unprecedented opportunities for the maximum economy in the expenditure of material and labour and for a high productivity of social labour.

Socialist society gains enormous advantages from mastering the economic law of planned, proportional development. This applies to the national economy as a whole as well as to each of its parts, to any industrial enterprise, mine or collective farm. The smooth functioning of each link, each part of the apparatus of production is a condition for the smooth working of the whole economic machinery of socialism. That is why in socialist economy each worker plays such an important part, whatever job he is doing. . . .

It is the task of the socialist system of planning to take into account in good time the changes which are taking place, to introduce the necessary corrections into the economic plans, and to forestall the appearance of disproportions in the economy, or at any rate to eliminate them speedily should they still occur.

Tasks and Methods of Planning

Planning in the socialist state is a process in which elements of scientific research and economic organisation are closely interwoven. Correct planning demands a thorough knowledge of the economy and of the objective laws governing its development, and the ability to look ahead. Nor is an effective guidance of the economy possible without a well-established system of economic accounting and statistics. Lenin wrote: "Accounting and control—that is the *main* thing required for 'arranging' the smooth working, the correct functioning of the *first phase* of communist society."

The demands of the law of planned development have found their expression in the economic plans drawn up by the state planning bodies in accordance with directives issued by the Communist Party and the Government. Planning bodies exist in the centre as well as in the administrative and economic districts and directly at the enterprises. Proceeding from the tasks confronting the society and carefully taking stock of existing resources and possibilities, the planning bodies work out current and long-term plans for 5, 7 or more years. After these plans have been widely discussed by the population and confirmed by the supreme organ of the socialist state, they become law.

The participation of the workers themselves and the fact that the plans are compiled on the basis of the general experience accumulated in the course of productive work guarantee that the national economy is guided along correct lines. The economic activity of the socialist state rests on Lenin's principles of *democratic centralism*. This means that planning proceeds not only from the top downwards but also from the bottom upwards. Centralised state planning is combined with socialist democracy, with the independence and initiative of the enterprises in economic operations, with the creative activity of the working masses. So-called "counterplans"—i.e., plans amplified by proposals introduced by the workers, engineers and technicians of the enterprises and supplemented in accordance with their wishes—were widely current in the Soviet Union as far back as the first five-year-plan periods. After the reorganisation of management in industry and agriculture carried through in 1957,[1] local experience, initia-

---

[1] Under the 1957 reform, there were set up more than 100 regional economic councils. The control over most industrial enterprises in the U.S.S.R. was transferred from central ministries to these newly created *sovnarkhozy*. In November, 1962, the number of *sovnarkhozy* was reduced and their respective territories enlarged accordingly. [Editor's note.]

tive and suggestions are more than ever taken into consideration in planning practice.

It would, however, be wrong to assume that the great advantages inherent in socialist, planned economy automatically ensure its success. The *law* of planned development of the national economy must not be confused with the actual *planning* itself. Though the economic law unfailingly operates—in the sense that its effect will be felt inevitably—planning may be correct or incorrect, precise or very approximate. Hence the method and system of planning must be continuously improved, the scientific, technical and economic basis of the plans strengthened, and the plans constantly checked and corrected in the light of experience, of the most advanced practice. Only in that case will planning satisfy the actual requirements of a planned economic development.

The historic success of the Soviet economic plans and the results achieved by the People's Democracies in conducting their planned economy, prove that socialist society is mastering the law of planned, proportional development to an ever increasing extent and following it more closely in its day-to-day practice.

It is self-evident that the *objective* advantages which socialism obtains on the basis of the law of planned development only become reality through the practical activity of the working people in socialist society. To compile a good plan for economic development is not enough, it will remain a scrap of paper unless implemented by selfless labour. It is not sufficient to know that socialism is the most economical system; without a daily struggle for economy the advantages of socialism will not be fully utilised, they can even be completely wasted in case of gross negligence. *Only the creative work of all members of society can transform the enormous potentialities of socialism into reality.* The economic and organisational activity of the socialist state and its organs plays a decisive part in this respect. Not only are the production targets for the collectives of working people set by the state, it also organises their work to ensure that they are reached. . . .

B. Managerial Incentives, Success Indicators, and Efficiency: Ills and Proposed Remedies

WESTERN VIEWS

3. MANAGERIAL INCENTIVES AND ENTERPRISE EFFICIENCY: SHOULD PROFIT BE THE BASIC INDEX?

HARRY G. SHAFFER
The University of Kansas

On September 9, 1962, *Pravda* published a proposal by Yevsey G. Liberman, until then a little-known professor at the Kharkov Engineering and Economics Institute.[1] The *New York Times* referred to Liberman as "a heretic . . . obviously influenced by capitalist experience"; Radio Free Europe tagged his plan "notably revisionist—and rational"; but in the Soviet Union his proposal called forth a stormy controversy which, for weeks on end, filled the pages of the leading Soviet newspapers and economic journals, and monopolized the agenda at numerous official and semi-official meetings and conferences. Some of those who participated in these debates saw in Liberman's proposal the greatest contribution to progressive Marxism since Lenin re-interpreted some of the basic theories of Karl Marx; others took a somewhat more skeptical view of what, at least at the surface, appeared to be a deviation from Communist ideology; yet others dubbed Liberman's plan a threat to the very survival of socialist central

---

* Reprinted from Harry G. Shaffer, "A New Incentive Plan for Soviet Managers," *The Russian Review*, Oct., 1963, pp. 410-416, by permission of the publisher.

[1] Although little-known in the West, some Soviet sources assert that Ye. G. Liberman (E. J. Lieberman in some English transliterations) was well-known in the Soviet Union. (See, for example, p. 164.) [Editor's note.]

planning and predicted that its adoption would spell a return to capitalist modes of production. Long before its official publication in *Pravda,* Liberman's plan had been given substantial backing by the Soviet Academy of Sciences' influential "Learned Council for Problems of Scientific Principles of Planning." But the controversy did not quiet down until Khrushchev himself, on November 19, 1962, endorsed some of Liberman's ideas, called on the planning agencies and the Economic Institute of the U.S.S.R. Academy of Sciences to examine the proposals further, and advocated that experiments along the lines proposed by Liberman be carried on. Ten days later, even the chairman of the "orthodox" East German State Planning Commission came out for the proposed plan. Yet, Liberman's recommendations, if adopted, would amount to nothing less than the end of specific, detailed planning from Moscow, the use of profits as the basic indicator of a plant's efficiency, the utilization of the profit motive as the exclusive incentive to induce Soviet managers to perform more efficiently, and greatly enhanced freedom for these managers to make decisions affecting their plants. What deficiencies in the Soviet planning mechanism, what serious inadequacies in Soviet enterprise efficiency, would warrant such drastic measures?

Many a visitor to the Soviet Union has wondered why the nation that placed the first man in orbit, that has built up a military might second only to that of the United States, and that graduates more engineers every year than any other country on earth does not seem capable of mass producing door knobs that keep doors closed or faucets that do not leak. One of the reasons for this apparent contradiction is certainly the low priority placed on the production of consumer goods. At least part of the explanation, however, lies in a system of incentives for Soviet managers that encourages the continuation of obsolete production techniques, the output of low quality consumer goods, wastefulness, and the misallocation of productive resources.

To make the interests of Soviet managers identical with those of Soviet society at large, their income is closely tied to the successful and efficient completion of the objectives assigned to them by the Plan. While managers in various industries or plants may get rewards for increasing labor productivity, decreasing unit costs, economizing on one or another scarce raw material, etc., the main achievement indicator is total output. Hence, the Soviet manager's take-home pay (and incidentally also his professional reputation and even the income of his employees) depends largely upon the extent to which he fulfills or overfulfills the "output plan."

Where "output" can be clearly specified, the performance of the enterprise can be evaluated fairly easily. In the case of a completely homogeneous product, output is readily measurable (pure gold in ounces, electricity in kilowatt-hours, etc.). Again, in the case of highly technical and expensive machinery or equipment, the Soviet government has little choice but to give production specifications in minute detail. But one central planning agency obviously cannot give detailed instructions to thousands upon thousands of producing units, turning out consumer goods in a multitude of sizes, shades, patterns, styles, designs, and qualities. "Output" must be defined in more general terms—and that is where the problem starts!

Whenever orders are given in units of weight, managers find it easiest to fulfill their output plan by making goods unnecessarily heavy. Thus, writing paper or roofing materials become too thick, screws and bolts are manufactured predominantly in larger sizes. The Soviet humor magazine *Krokodil* once carried a cartoon, showing a nail factory which had fulfilled its output plan by producing one single nail, the size of the plant, suspended from the ceiling. To give the orders in square meters of writing paper or in millions of nails would have the opposite, equally undesirable, effect, as paper would then be too thin or nails available in smaller sizes only. During the past year or two, the pages of the Soviet press have been full of examples of frustrating observations and experiences reported by loyal party members, despairing customers, and irate government officials: A truck pool in Moscow province whose output plan is measured in ton-kilometers is reported to be sending some of its trucks on long runs to such far away cities as Kharkov or Minsk; a customer complains that his automobile tire is inadequately repaired and is told by the shop operator that a better repair job would take more time which would prevent the shop from meeting its output quota of 13,500 tire repairs; a lady waits for hours in a beauty parlor for her permanent while other ladies who come in for a shampoo and set are taken ahead of her, because at the government-decreed price the beauty parlor finds it difficult to meet its quota expressed in rubles by giving permanents; the manager of a state retail store finds it disquieting that one of his suppliers sends him dozens upon dozens of ladies' undergarments, all in one color and in but two or three sizes—an easy way to fulfill an output plan specified in numbers of slips and panties! Since the workmanship, as a rule, cannot be measured precisely, many a quantitative output plan is fulfilled at the expense of perfection. But while complaints about the shoddy quality of consumers goods are an everyday occurrence, harried planners also encounter the opposite situation: One children's clothing factory, for instance, met its output expressed in thousands of rubles of merchandise by putting expensive fur collars on boys' overcoats.

Under the present incentive system, Soviet managers are also under direct inducement to conceal the productive capacities of their plants and to operate their enterprises at less than full capacity. Since their bonuses (which make up a very substantial part of their total income) depend primarily upon their fulfillment or overfulfillment of the output plan, they have a financial interest in getting an easy plan. On the other hand, to greatly overfill the output quota, although momentarily profitable, would be ill advised. As each year's output plan is determined by adding a certain percentage to the output achieved by the plant during the preceding year, gross overfulfillment would inevitably result in gross readjustment of the following year's target.

By the same token, the introduction of new techniques usually represents a drain on the pocketbook of the Soviet executive and of his workers. Since innovating and retooling require time and effort, they ordinarily involve a temporary reduction in output with obvious consequences on bonuses. Should the new machines fail to augment output, once they have been installed, nothing has been gained. Should they increase productivity, not much has been gained either, as far as the plant manager's take-home pay is concerned, because a more exacting output target is assigned to the plant at the earliest possible moment. Attempts to remedy the situation by granting special bonuses for fulfillment of an "innovation target" have not improved the situation very much. Obviously, a ten per cent increase in the *number* of inventions is no indication of their economic importance, and, in any case, significant inventions are not easily developed according to a preconceived plan. Is it any wonder that the pages of *Pravda* and *Izvestia* frequently depict the trials and tribulations of exasperated Soviet inventors in their attempts to get their inventions adopted?

With regard to the acquisition of machinery and equipment, the Soviet manager, in one way, is in an enviable position, compared with his American peer: neither he nor his company is charged for any equipment allocated to his enterprise by the planning authorities. But, on the other hand, to procure a piece of machinery, a tool, or even a spare part when needed can become a real problem. Under these circumstances, the Soviet manager, primarily interested in fulfilling or overfulfilling the output plan, is obviously under strong temptation to get hold of all the equipment he possibly can, irrespective of immediate or even anticipated needs. As a result, innumerable machines rust idly in storage rooms in a nation which places high priority on rapid industrialization. At the beginning of 1962, uninstalled equipment in the U.S.S.R. equalled approximately the total quantity of such equipment included in the production plans for the entire year.

To overcome such inadequacies as the ones described above, Yevsey G. Liberman proposed a new approach. Under his scheme the central planning authorities would still decide the types of goods to be produced, set quantitative output targets, and specify delivery dates. However, most other decisions, such as number of workers to be hired, wages to be paid, production techniques to be employed, etc. would be made by each plant manager for his own enterprise. Each enterprise would submit its own "profit plan," and profits would become the exclusive basis for managerial bonuses (although different standards would have to be set up for different branches of industry, or even for firms within one industry operating under different natural or technological conditions). Higher incentive premiums would be paid for planned than for excess profits in order to give enterprise directors a financial stake in "bidding high." As a further inducement for managers to reveal their plants' true productive capacities and to introduce economically sound innovations, output targets would be kept unchanged for several years, thus removing apprehension that honesty and competent, profitable operation would be penalized by more stringent output assignments. To discourage the hoarding of machinery and equipment, the rate of profit would be computed as a percentage of total fixed and working capital, and the incentive premium scale would rise with an increase in the rate of profit. Since bonuses would not be paid for total output *per se,* and since unsaleable or rejected goods would yield no profits—and therefore no bonuses—the production of unwanted items or of poor quality goods would presumably be strongly discouraged.

Liberman readily admits that his proposal is but a tentative blueprint, subject to revisions, modifications, and improvements. Undoubtedly, many shortcomings will become apparent, many problems will be ironed out, and many alterations will be introduced, as experience is gained through experiments now being carried out in the Kharkov area where Liberman heads the economic laboratory of the regional council.

Some Western commentators see in Liberman's proposals a major step in the direction of a capitalist, free enterprise system. Such an interpretation, however, is surely unwarranted. Although the role of profits and of the profit motive might be traceable to "bourgeois" social science, nothing in the plan should be taken as an indication of an eventual return of the means of production to private ownership, or of a weakening of the foundations of socialism in the U.S.S.R. Profit, while of predominant importance as a measuring rod of efficiency at the enterprise level, is in no way meant to be the determining influence in the central planners' major economic decisions; and the envisaged purpose of the profit motive is only to induce those who administer the local producing units to carry out more efficiently their part of the over-all Plan.

Liberman's plan could probably play an important role in improving the efficiency of Soviet economic performance but Khrushchev, apparently hesitant to delegate too much authority to local enterprise directors, has called for further study and experimentation. However, as Soviet economic life increases in complexity, detailed planning from the center will necessarily become ever more difficult. It therefore seems a reasonable prediction that reforms à la Liberman are in the offing in the U.S.S.R. in the not too distant future.

Be that as it may, the greatest significance of the Liberman proposals lies perhaps neither in their bearing upon the question of the private versus the public ownership of the means of production nor in their prospective impact upon economic efficiency in the U.S.S.R. Their major significance, rather, may well lie in the fact that they arose in the course of frank criticism of long-standing government policies and planning operations, and that they led to an open and uninhibited debate over the feasibility of a revision of Soviet planning procedure, so drastic that in the days of Stalin no one would have dared to propose it.

SOVIET VIEWS

4. WHAT SOVIET ECONOMISTS DISCUSS AND WHY *

ALEXANDER BIRMAN
Doctor of Science, Economics

The Soviet press devotes a great deal of space to economics. Newspapers and magazines constantly publish long articles and letters to their editors under such intriguing titles as "Obstacles or Jumping-Off Ground?" "Pros and Cons," "The State Plan and Tires," etc. Why all the discussion? After all, the country is doing well, and the seven-year plan is being fulfilled and overfulfilled.

What has happened is that *the Soviet Union's economy has entered a qualitatively new phase.* Having accumulated vast reserves and resources, our people have set out to create the material and technical basis of communism. There is even a period set for getting this colossal task done— twenty years. The country is carefully checking to see if everything is all right, if anything needs adjustment.

The Twenty-second Congress of the Communist Party of the Soviet Union, held last year, called for radical improvements in planning, for planning on a twenty-year scale. To meet this injunction that life itself dictates, Soviet economists are making a critical analysis of accumulated experience and methods in present use. This is what all the discussion is about.

As usual, "Russian experts" abroad lost no time clamoring about the "crisis" in Soviet planning. Alas, we must disappoint those who enjoy anti-Soviet sensationalism. In the course of the discussion no one had any misgivings about the Soviet economy or about the validity of economic

* Reprinted from *USSR*, Dec., 1962, p. 7, by permission of the publisher.

planning. The principles of socialist planning have been tested in practice and sufficiently proved by the Soviet Union's achievements.

The single national economic plan opens and continues to open new economic horizons for us. Firstly, it guarantees a rational distribution of the national income and concentrates effort in the most critical cultural and economic areas. Our country, one of the most backward in Europe before the Revolution, has developed to the point where it can use more than one-fifth of the national income—several times as much as the United States—for accumulation purposes. The national economic plan has eliminated crises and made for an unprecedented rate of economic growth.

Then there is the territorial distribution of productive forces. Could the economy have put the wealth of Siberia, the Far North, Central Asia and the Far East at the service of the country without a plan? And what about the unparalleled development of culture and science in a land where only four decades ago eight out of every ten people were illiterate? And the rapid and steady rise in living standards?

We witnessed many of the great achievements of human genius in this century; planned economy is certainly one of them. We have reason to be proud that the Soviet Union is the home of scientific planning.

The present discussion is about new ways and methods of planning, ways and methods appropriate to the new, higher level of national economic development.

Just as it is necessary to adjust certain details and parts of a newly created machine, so it is necessary, after the adoption of the control figures of the Soviet twenty-year plan, to find the best methods of planning and the best ways of implementing the plans. And for that the problems created by the unusually rapid development of our economy must be thoroughly analyzed. These are some of the problems.

Talking with drivers who were hurriedly and carelessly trucking pre-fabricated parts to a construction site, Oleg Antonov, well-known aircraft designer (one of the first to speak in the press on the need for better planning), discovered that their work quota was figured in ton-kilometers. Under the circumstances it is only natural that drivers (and transport companies too) are most interested in long-distance hauls. But what about short distances—just as important for the national economy—in housing construction, for example? Nevertheless the automobile and other transport companies have made it a practice to figure in ton-kilometers. Proceeding from this, Antonov moved on to a much more important question: Wasn't it about time to make plan indices that took into consideration the interests of the country as a whole and not only the interests of individual enterprises?

What is involved is much more than the problem of assessing the work done by truckers and transport companies. As a matter of fact, our methods of and criteria for planning date to the thirties and forties, when the country was going through the stormy process of industrialization, to a time when most branches of industry had to be built practically from scratch. Under those conditions it was sufficient to work out plan indices that would make it possible to determine, roughly and especially in quantitative terms, how well a given enterprise was doing and on this basis to define its future tasks.

The problem can be solved quite simply in mines and other enterprises where production is homogeneous: the job there is to mine so and so much coal. But transport is not coal, and the problem is much more complicated. It is even more complicated in the chemical and textile industries that manufacture dozens and even hundreds of different items at the same time, or in an engineering plant with a huge and variegated production program. To reduce these commodities to one denominator, one must perforce resort to a conventional gauge. Lathes and metal goods are usually assessed in tons; other types of goods, in rubles.

And that is where we have, or at any rate can have, a contradiction between what is "profitable" for an enterprise and what is really essential for the socialist economy, whose ultimate goal, let us keep in mind, is to satisfy as completely as possible the needs of all the members of society.

If the plan is figured in tons, then the heavier the lathe, the easier it is to fulfill the plan. And yet the consumer, and consequently society as a whole, has no use for extra-heavy lathes. If the plan for a furniture factory is figured in rubles, an unscrupulous manager may be tempted to manufacture 10 sets at 100 rubles each instead of 100 sets at 10 rubles.

These problems have long worried our economists and managers of enterprises.

What is the best way out? It is clear that the plan should be based on indices that would best satisfy the interests of the consumer and stimulate production along the lines required by society. But how are the efforts of each enterprise to be directed at the same time?

Dozens of proposals have been submitted in the course of the discussion: how to stimulate enterprises to fulfill their plans, how to combine planning with material incentives to workers, etc. Unfortunately space prevents us from dealing with each proposal in detail. The majority agree that it would be impossible to find an index that would fit the many branches of industry. It seems necessary to work out improved, specific methods of planning and calculation for the different branches, areas and, perhaps, even types of production.

At the same time another problem arises: How are all these specific methods suitable for planning the manufacture of each given item to be united into the sort of whole without which the State Planning Committee cannot work, without which nationwide registration and control are impossible?

It would be desirable to have only a few basic indices, perhaps only one. Is it possible for profit to be a generalized criterion of the activity of an enterprise?

Professor E. Lieberman, well-known Kharkov economist, raised this question in an article in *Pravda*. Using mathematical methods and computing machines, he spent several years analyzing the work of dozens of engineering plants in Kharkov, one of the country's biggest industrial centers. He draws this conclusion: Although the production program of each enterprise is different and changeable, although technological progress affects each enterprise differently, it is possible to establish a more or less constant and stable correlation of production indices.

The optimal index is profit, Professor Lieberman says. On the one hand, it is organically linked with the entire activity of the enterprise, for each success and each failure is reflected in the profits. On the other hand, profits depend very little on changes in the production list.

Professor Lieberman's proposal, published simultaneously in *Pravda* and the magazine *Problems of Economics,* gave rise to a lively debate. But before I discuss the proposal, I should like to say a few words about the reaction it has evoked abroad.

Western economists regard Professor Lieberman's proposal as nothing short of "renunciation" of socialist principles, "renunciation" of the planned economy, as a return to the "old" and "natural" stimulus of the capitalist economy. This is obviously wishful thinking, for profit categories in socialist conditions have nothing in common with those under capitalism.

Firstly, the means of production in the USSR belong to the people, to society, and consequently the fruits of production do not go to individuals or private companies but to the whole society. Therefore the aim of production is not profit but the satisfaction of the needs of all the people, of society as a whole. Secondly, prices in the USSR do not shift spontaneously with the market but are fixed by the state; profit is not a consequence of profiteering, temporary boom or of buyers being deluded by high-pressure advertising.

When Soviet people talk of profit, they mean that part of the national product (national income) which remains at the disposal of society and is spent in three ways: to raise living standards, expand the economy and build new enterprises; to pay for free medical treatment, social insurance, etc.; and to meet administrative and defense expenses.

Professor Lieberman and his many followers do not suggest profit as the main index because they regard it as an end in itself. They do not at all propose that the branches that make the most profit be developed first.

Soviet economists look at the problem from an entirely different point of view. They think of profit as a convenient, generalized index which makes it possible to assess the work of an enterprise from every angle. There is general agreement that with the rise of labor productivity and reduction of production costs the government must periodically cut prices (which would correspondingly decrease the profits of the enterprise). A socialist society, since it is both producer and consumer, does not have to "enrich" itself at its own expense.

Professor Lieberman's opponents claim that profit cannot be the *only* criterion for assessing the work of each enterprise because there are other factors beside efficiency that determine how much profit an enterprise makes. In fixing prices and, consequently, predetermining the level of profit, the government cannot ignore such economic factors as correlation of supply and demand, significance of a given type of goods, necessity of stimulating or limiting its consumption (alcoholic beverages, for instance), etc.

For instance, with the price policy followed in the Soviet Union, factories that make children's footwear or clothes will always be less profitable than the regular footwear or garment factories, not because they are less efficient but because prices of children's footwear and clothes are deliberately fixed low. Likewise in the interests of the consumers, low prices are fixed for mineral fertilizers, many raw and finished materials, textbooks and other items.

Everyone agrees that whatever proposal is ultimately adopted, it will have to be tested. Economic experiments take time. But there is no reason for undue haste—the Soviet economy, I repeat, is advancing steadily and at a very high rate.

We can say now, even without predicting the decision that will finally be made, that the shortcomings and obstacles in planning and economic management revealed in the course of the discussion will be eliminated.

This will permit our enterprises and our whole socialist economy to make fuller use of available resources, to move along at an even faster rate, to satisfy the needs of the people even more fully. We shall thus fulfill one of the most important tasks set us by the new Party program: to achieve the best results at the least possible cost to our society and all its members.

V

PEACEFUL COEXISTENCE AND THE ECONOMIC CHALLENGE

"Mankind must put an end to war—or war will put an end to mankind."

JOHN F. KENNEDY

"Every gun that is made, every warship launched, every rocket fired signifies, in the final sense, a theft from those who hunger and are not fed, those who are cold and are not clothed. We pay for a single fighter plane with a half-billion bushels of wheat. We pay for a single destroyer with new homes that could have housed more than 8,000 people. . . . is there no other way the world can live?"

DWIGHT D. EISENHOWER

"Let us prove in practice whose system is better. This is our appeal to the statesmen of capitalist countries. Let us compete without war."

NIKITA S. KHRUSHCHEV

"The heart and soul of the general line of peaceful coexistence pursued by the leaders of the Soviet Communist Party is Soviet-U.S. collaboration for the domination of the world."

RED NEW CHINA NEWS AGENCY
(NCNA)

In June, 1963, L. F. Ilyichev, Secretary of the C.P.S.U.[1] Central Committee, warned the Capitalist world that it "is confronted by the alternatives of either accepting peaceful coexistence of states with different social systems or perishing beneath the debris of war." [2] While these and similar warnings issued periodically by high Soviet government and Party officials may represent attempts to intimidate the West, they also appear

[1] Communist Party of the Soviet Union.
[2] *Pravda*, June 19, 1963. Translated in *The Current Digest of the Soviet Press*, July 3, 1963, p. 7.

166

to reflect a conviction on the part of Soviet leaders that international disputes can no longer be solved on the field of battle. It is highly debatable whether or not the Soviet Union *ever* considered it necessary to spread communism by aggressive war, since Marx had predicted the inevitable collapse of the Capitalist order due to internal "contractions." [3] But even if the Soviet Union ever did contemplate aggressive warfare against a Western alliance, the advent of the nuclear age seemed to impose the necessity of peaceful coexistence upon both East and West, as the only alternative to a war that could easily end in the total destruction of all contenders.

While there appears to be rather widespread (although by no means unanimous) agreement throughout the world that a nuclear holocaust must be averted at almost any cost, the question of just exactly what the Soviets mean by "peaceful coexistence" is a different matter altogether. Does it mean that the Soviet Union would oppose any kind of war, even a war of "liberation" of colonial people against the parent country? Does it mean that the Soviet Union has given up the entire idea of the class struggle, the rebellion of the "exploited class" against the "exploiters"? The selections in Part A of this chapter are intended to introduce the reader to different views on what the Soviet Union means by "peaceful coexistence."

The first selection below has been taken from the official Programme of the Communist Party of the Soviet Union, adopted by the 22nd C.P.S.U. Congress in 1961. It represents the official position of the U.S.S.R. on the "principle of the peaceful coexistence of states with different social systems, put forward by Lenin."

Under *Western Views,* C. M. Woodhouse interprets the Soviet meaning of peaceful coexistence as a policy of stirring up trouble by all methods short of a war that would directly involve the Soviet Union. Fedenko, next, attempts to prove that contrary to Soviet declarations Lenin did not really advocate peaceful coexistence as a permanent policy, and that only the awareness of the catastrophic consequences of a nuclear war induced Khrushchev to retreat from Lenin's position. [4]

Isaac Deutscher, under *Western Marxist Views,* although by no means uncritical of the U.S.S.R., offers a considerably more favorable appraisal of Soviet intentions and prospects. [5] He maintains that the Soviet Union appears to have a much greater economic interest in peaceful coexistence than the West since for her the armament race means an irrational waste of resources, while the West seems to view an unproductive expenditure as

---

[3] See Chapter I above.

[4] The Chinese Communists, incidentally, would agree with Fedenko that Khrushchev's course of peaceful coexistence almost at any price is quite contrary to Lenin's teachings.

[5] It should be stressed that Deutscher, while a Marxist, has been a determined opponent of Stalinism for over thirty years; that he was expelled from the Communist Party in 1932; that for more than twenty years he has not been affiliated with any political party, group, or sect; and that he, therefore, speaks only for himself.

"a boon in disguise." Deutscher believes that under conditions of peaceful coexistence the Soviet Union would present a real challenge to the Capitalist world. He sees this challenge not merely as an economic rivalry in terms of "who will outproduce whom and when" but also as a contest that might find the U.S.S.R. a strong contender for supremacy on issues such as shorter working hours or enhanced opportunities for advanced education. Deutscher acknowledges that the West is ahead as far as political freedom is concerned; but even here he foresees prospects for increased freedom in the U.S.S.R. However, Deutscher contends, if the West only "learns to face the future instead of clinging to the past," it has nothing to fear from the challenge, and it may even gain in the end if and when competitive coexistence gives way to cooperative emulation.

In the first selection under *Soviet Views,* three Soviet specialists in international law assure the West that the Soviet Union has no subterfuge in mind when she proclaims peaceful coexistence as the cornerstone of her foreign policy. Peaceful coexistence, the authors proclaim, means "international law in action," means noninterference in one another's internal affairs, and must exclude any attempt to export revolution or counterrevolution. And the authors couple a demand for general disarmament with a proclamation of faith in the ultimate victory of Communism over Capitalism.

For the past several years, the Soviet leaders have challenged the Capitalist world in general and the United States in particular to an economic race under conditions of peaceful coexistence to "prove" that their system is superior. American social scientists may point out that in the field of agriculture the United States simply is not racing since American farmers are already producing more than the American public is able to consume; that the United States does not erect as many new dwelling places per month as the Soviet Union because there is no housing shortage in the U.S.A.; that while there are millions of unemployed at the present time, unemployment compensation, in many instances, is still higher than the income of the Soviet worker who does have a job; and that, after all, the really important difference between the United States and the Soviet Union does not lie in the field of production but in the area of individual freedom. The United States may be unwilling to accept the challenge altogether—and yet, the race is on. It is on, as far as the uncommitted third of the world is concerned, as far as the hungry lands are concerned, as far as the newly created, less developed nations are concerned. It is on as far as all those impatient hundreds of millions are concerned whose main interest consists in finding the fastest possible way to increase their productive capacity and living standards.

The exact rate of growth of the Soviet Union from the end of World War II through the 1950's may be a matter of dispute, but that this rate was *substantially* higher year after year than that of the United States has not been contested by any serious scholar, East or West. Should the Soviet growth rate continue to exceed that of the U.S.,[6] it can obviously be only a question of time until the Soviet Union makes good on its promise to overtake the most advanced Capitalist nation in the world, the United States, in per capita output. There is disagreement among Western scholars in regard to the outcome, but Soviet writers are confident that the Soviet Union will surpass the United States and that this will demonstrate conclusively the superiority of Communism and ensure its eventual victory over Capitalism. (The Chinese Communists, by the way, consider naive Khrushchev's faith that victory in the economic race will be sufficient to make the "imperialists" give up their positions without a violent struggle which might well go beyond the limits of an internal revolution.)

Part B of this chapter deals with the economic challenge implied in the Soviet concept of peaceful coexistence. In the first selection under Part B, Abram Bergson expresses great doubt that the Soviet Union will be able to maintain her rate of growth which he estimates as around six percent annually during the decade following Stalin's death (as compared with Soviet claims of about ten percent). While Bergson warns that the Soviet economic challenge should not be underestimated, he believes that it is not quite as great as has been widely assumed.

Jan S. Prybyla, on the other hand, cautions us not to become complacent. Dealing with the Soviet strategy of economic development, he foresees the possibility that the U.S.S.R. may well be able to maintain high rates of economic growth for many years to come.

On the Soviet side, V. Pokatayev and Y. Joffe discuss the economic growth of the U.S.S.R., compare it with that of the United States, and proclaim absolute confidence that Soviet rates of growth will not experience any substantial decrease, that time is on their side, and that the Soviet Union will surpass the United States by about 1970 in *total* agricultural production and in *per capita* industrial output.

Early in 1964 the United States Central Intelligence Agency, in the first news briefing in its history, assessed Soviet economic performance so low that it called forth not only violent Soviet denials but also a prolonged controversy among Western Soviet experts. So challenging is this CIA report, and so important is its implication for the future course of Soviet economic development that a separate "supplement" to this chapter is devoted to it.

In the first selection under Chapter V, "Supplement" to B, the CIA's published report (a summary statement of the agency's "maiden venture into publicity," as one commentator called it) is reproduced in full.

In the article under *Western Views* the various parts of the CIA re-

---

[6] The Soviet growth rate did drop considerably in 1963 (and perhaps even in 1962). For a wide variety of views regarding the extent of the drop, see selections 9-12 in this chapter.

port are discussed and the reactions of Soviet experts, East and West, are summarized.

Victor Perlo, under *Western Marxist Views,* calls the CIA report a "mountain of lies," in which he discovers only one "grain of truth," namely that during the early 1960's the Soviet growth rate has been somewhat smaller and the American rate considerably larger than during the decade of the 1950's. This, he admits, will postpone the day on which the USSR will catch up with the United States. But Perlo ridicules as an "habitual device" allegations that the Soviet economy is in a state of crisis, and he advises the United States to concentrate her efforts on the protection of her own people from both unemployment and discrimination and what he considers the imminent danger of either recession or inflation.

K. Valentino, under *Soviet Views,* questions the competence of the CIA to make international economic comparisons, asserts that proper methods of calculation show Soviet economic growth to be about twice as great in 1963 as claimed by the CIA, and maintains that a period much longer than one or two years is needed for any meaningful comparison between the rate of growth of a Socialist and a Capitalist economy.

A. Peaceful Coexistence

1. PEACEFUL COEXISTENCE AND THE STRUGGLE FOR WORLD PEACE *

EXCERPT FROM THE PARTY PROGRAM ADOPTED BY THE 22ND CONGRESS OF THE COMMUNIST PARTY OF THE SOVIET UNION

The C.P.S.U. considers that the chief aim of its foreign-policy activity is to provide peaceful conditions for the building of a communist society in the U.S.S.R. and developing the world socialist system, and together

---

* Reprinted from *Programme of the Communist Party of the Soviet Union Adopted by the 22nd Congress of the C.P.S.U. October 31, 1961,* Foreign Languages Publishing House, Moscow, 1961, pp. 53-59.

with the other peace-loving peoples to deliver mankind from a world war of extermination.

The C.P.S.U. maintains that forces capable of preserving and promoting universal peace have arisen and are growing in the world. Possibilities are arising for essentially new relations between states.

Imperialism knows no relations between states other than those of domination and subordination, of oppression of the weak by the strong. It bases international relations on diktat and intimidation, on violence and arbitrary rule. It regards wars of aggression as a natural means of settling international issues. For the imperialist countries diplomacy has been, and remains, a tool for imposing their will upon other nations and preparing wars. At the time of the undivided rule of imperialism the issue of war and peace was settled by the finance and industrial oligarchy in the utmost secrecy from the peoples.

Socialism contrasts imperialism with a *new type of international relations*. The foreign policy of the socialist countries, which is based on the principles of peace, the equality and self-determination of nations, and respect for the independence and sovereignty of all countries, as well as the fair, humane methods of socialist diplomacy, are exerting a growing influence on the world situation. At a time when imperialism no longer plays a dominant role in international relations, while the socialist system is playing an increasing role, and when the influence of the countries that have won national independence and of the masses of the people in the capitalist countries has grown very considerably, it is becoming possible for the new principles advanced by socialism to gain the upper hand over the principles of aggressive imperialist policy.

For the first time in history, a situation has arisen in which not only the big states, but also the small ones, the countries which have chosen independent development, and all the states which want peace, are in a position, irrespective of their strength, to pursue an independent foreign policy.

The issue of war and peace is the principal issue of today. Imperialism is the only source of the war danger. The imperialist camp is making preparations for the most terrible crime against mankind—a world thermonuclear war that can bring unprecedented destruction to entire countries and wipe out entire nations. The problem of war and peace has become a life-and-death problem for hundreds of millions of people.

The peoples must concentrate their efforts on curbing the imperialists in good time and preventing them from making use of lethal weapons. *The main thing is to ward off a thermonuclear war, to prevent it from breaking out.* This can be done by the present generation.

The consolidation of the Soviet state and the formation of the world socialist system were historic steps towards the realisation of mankind's age-old dream of banishing wars from the life of society. In the socialist part of the world there are no classes or social groups interested in starting a war. Socialism, outstripping capitalism in a number of important branches of science and technology, has supplied the peace-loving peoples with powerful material means of curbing imperialist aggression. Capitalism established its rule with fire and sword, but socialism does not require war to spread its ideals. Its weapon is its superiority over the old system in social organisation, political system, economy, the improvement of the standard of living and spiritual culture.

The socialist system is a natural centre of attraction for the peace-loving forces of the globe. The principles of its foreign policy are gaining ever greater international recognition and support. A vast *peace zone* has taken shape on earth. In addition to the socialist countries, it includes a large group of non-socialist countries that for various reasons are not interested in starting a war. The emergence of those countries in the arena of world politics has substantially altered the balance of forces in favour of peace.

There is a growing number of countries that adhere to a policy of neutrality and strive to safeguard themselves against the hazards of participation in aggressive military blocs.

In the new historical epoch the masses have a far greater opportunity of actively intervening in the settlement of international issues. The peoples are taking the solution of the problem of war and peace into their own hands more and more vigorously. The anti-war movement of the masses, which takes various forms, is a major factor in the struggle for peace. The international working class, the most uncompromising and most consistent fighter against imperialist war, is the great organising force in this struggle of the people as a whole.

It is possible to avert a world war by the combined efforts of the mighty socialist camp, the peace-loving non-socialist countries, the international working class and all the forces championing peace. The growing superiority of the socialist forces over the forces of imperialism, of the forces of peace over those of war, will make it actually possible to banish world war from the life of society even before the complete victory of socialism on earth, with capitalism surviving in a part of the world. The victory of socialism throughout the world will do away completely with the social and national causes of all wars. *To abolish war and establish everlasting peace on earth is a historic mission of communism.*

General and complete disarmament under strict international control is a radical way of guaranteeing a durable peace. Imperialism has imposed an unprecedented burden of armaments on the peoples. Socialism sees its duty towards mankind in delivering it from this absurd waste of national wealth. The solution of this problem would have historical significance for mankind. By an active and determined effort the peoples can and must force the imperialists into disarmament.

Socialism has offered mankind the only reasonable principle of maintaining relations between states at a time when the world is divided into two systems—the principle of the peaceful coexistence of states with different social systems, put forward by Lenin.

Peaceful coexistence of the socialist and capitalist countries is an *objective necessity* for the development of human society. *War cannot and must not serve as a means of settling international disputes.* Peaceful coexistence or disastrous war—such is the alternative offered by history. Should the imperialist aggressors nevertheless venture to start a new world war, the peoples will no longer tolerate a system which drags them into devastating wars. They will sweep imperialism away and bury it.

Peaceful coexistence implies renunciation of war as a means of settling international disputes, and their solution by negotiation; equality, mutual understanding and trust between countries; consideration for each other's interests; non-interference in internal affairs; recognition of the right of every people to solve all the problems of their country by themselves; strict respect for the sovereignty and territorial integrity of all countries; promotion of economic and cultural co-operation on the basis of complete equality and mutual benefit.

Peaceful coexistence serves as a basis for the peaceful competition between socialism and capitalism on an international scale and constitutes a specific form of class struggle between them. As they consistently pursue the policy of peaceful coexistence, the socialist countries are steadily strengthening the positions of the world socialist system in its competition with capitalism. Peaceful coexistence affords more favourable opportunities for the struggle of the working class in the capitalist countries and facilitates the struggle of the peoples of the colonial and dependent countries for their liberation. Support for the principle of peaceful coexistence is also in keeping with the interests of that section of the bourgeoisie which realises that a thermonuclear war would not spare the ruling classes of capitalist society either. The policy of peaceful coexistence is in accord with the vital interests of all mankind, except the big monopoly magnates and the militarists.

The Soviet Union has consistently pursued, and will continue to pursue, the policy of the peaceful coexistence of states with different social systems.

The Communist Party of the Soviet Union advances the following *tasks in the field of international relations*:

to use, together with the other socialist countries, peaceful states and peoples, every means of preventing world war and providing conditions for the complete banishment of war from the life of society;

to pursue a policy of establishing sound international relations, and work for the disbandment of all military blocs opposing each other, the discontinuance of the "cold war" and the propaganda of enmity and hatred among the nations, and the abolition of all air, naval, rocket, and other military bases on foreign territory;

to work for general and complete disarmament under strict international control;

to strengthen relations of fraternal friendship and close co-operation with the countries of Asia, Africa, and Latin America which are fighting to attain or consolidate national independence, with all peoples and states that advocate the preservation of peace;

to pursue an active and consistent policy of improving and developing relations with all capitalist countries, including the United States of America, Great Britain, France, the Federal Republic of Germany, Japan, and Italy, with a view to safeguarding peace;

to contribute in every way to the militant solidarity of all contingents and organisations of the international working class, which oppose the imperialist policy of war;

steadfastly to pursue a policy of consolidating all the forces fighting against war. All the organisations and parties that strive to avert war, the neutralist and pacifist movements and the bourgeois circles that advocate peace and normal relations between countries will meet with understanding and support on the part of the Soviet Union;

to pursue a policy of developing international co-operation in the fields of trade, cultural relations, science, and technology;

to be highly vigilant with regard to the aggressive circles, which are intent on violating peace; to expose, in good time, the initiators of military adventures; to take all necessary steps to safeguard the security and inviolability of our socialist country and the socialist camp as a whole.

The C.P.S.U. and the Soviet people as a whole will continue to oppose all wars of conquest, including wars between capitalist countries, and local wars aimed at strangling people's emancipation movements, and consider it their duty to support the sacred struggle of the oppressed peoples and their just anti-imperialist wars of liberation.

The Communist Party of the Soviet Union will hold high the banner of peace and friendship among the nations.

WESTERN VIEWS

2. THE SOVIET MEANING OF "PEACEFUL COEXISTENCE" *

C. M. WOODHOUSE

Author, Member of British Parliament for Oxford

. . . Lenin expressly said on a number of occasions that the existence of the Soviet Republic and the capitalist states side by side for any length of time was unthinkable. So far as I can trace, the first Soviet leader to use the term 'peaceful coexistence' was Malenkov in 1929, and he also declared it to be impossible. On the other hand, Stalin repeatedly expressed his belief in peaceful coexistence, both before and after the second world war. That obviously should give us food for thought: if Stalin believed in it, then clearly 'peaceful coexistence' cannot mean what most ordinary people in the West would naturally presume it to mean, which could be roughly translated as 'live and let live'.

All recent pronouncements by Soviet leaders and official spokesmen go to show that this is indeed so. The meaning of peaceful coexistence in its Soviet interpretation is most clearly shown in the communiqué of the conference of 81 Communist parties in Moscow in December 1960 and in the new programme of the Soviet Communist party published in July 1961. The context of the two documents is slightly different, since they are concerned in the first instance with external and internal problems respectively. But the general tenor of both is much the same. Both presuppose a continuation of peaceful coexistence with the capitalist world, but neither has any difficulty in reconciling that relationship with the promotion of revolution and violence within that world. There was nothing ironic, in the Soviet view, about the coincidence that on the day the new party programme was published there also took place a spectacular naval

---

* From the answer of The Hon. C. M. Woodhouse to the question asked by the editors of *Survey:* "What are the prospects of 'coexistence' for the sixties?" Excerpts reprinted from *Survey*, April, 1963, pp. 48-50, by permission of the publisher.

review at Leningrad, complete with nuclear submarines, rocket-firing cruisers, and belligerent speeches by the Commanders-in-Chief.

A few quotations may help to show that these are not mere paradoxes. The 1960 communiqué reiterates the dogma of the aggressive nature of capitalism, but adds that 'real forces have appeared that are capable of foiling its plans of aggression: war is not fatally inevitable'. Although the document does not refer explicitly to the nuclear deterrent, contemporary publications of a quasi-official character show that a doctrine similar to that of the West is in fact accepted by the Soviet government. That would in any case be the inescapable conclusion both from the new series of Soviet nuclear tests in 1961 and from the Cuban adventure in 1962. So far the inferences are encouraging: the unthinkability of nuclear war implies the inevitability of peaceful coexistence. But we are then confronted with the definition of that relationship as (to quote Khrushchev himself) 'a form of intense political, economic, and ideological struggle between the proletariat and the aggressive forces of imperialism'. This definition is repeated in different ways in the 1960 communiqué; and both that document and the party programme show in detail how 'the grim struggle between two ideologies, communist and bourgeois', is to be fought out. It is indistinguishable from the cold war.

Peaceful coexistence is therefore a dynamic and not a static relationship. It does not mean a reconciliation between 'socialism' and 'capitalism', but 'an intensification of the struggle'. Socialism is 'continually sapping and destroying imperialism, leading to its weakening and collapse'. It is still the task of 'the international revolutionary movement' to help the working class in capitalist countries, and in newly emerging ex-colonies, to overthrow their bourgeois governments, if necessary by force. 'Where the exploiting classes resort to violence against the people, the possibility of non-peaceful transition to socialism should be borne in mind.' Such is the plan for the 1960's: such is peaceful coexistence. At the same time, and in the same documents, there is set forth a policy of non-interference in the internal affairs of independent countries and of 'improving and developing relations with all capitalist countries with a view to safeguarding peace'.

The theoretical reconciliation of what seem, in Western terms, to be contradictions, is quite simple in Marxist terms. It rests upon the doctrine that relations between states are one thing, relations between classes or between ideas are quite another. But we cannot be seriously expected to accept such a reconciliation, and the fact remains that there are two fundamentally distinct interpretations of peaceful coexistence current in the world. Consequently it is not true that 'there is no third possibility' apart from the two alternatives of destructive war and peaceful coexistence. There are in fact three possibilities: war, peaceful coexistence in the Soviet sense, and peaceful coexistence in the Western sense. Since the second is in fact a verbal subterfuge concealing the continuation of a policy of 'making mischief by all methods short of war involving the Soviet Union in open hostilities' (as the cold war was once defined in a Chatham House publication), it is obvious that the object of Western policy must be to bring about the third possibility rather than either of the other two. . . .

3. PEACEFUL COEXISTENCE: KHRUSHCHEV'S RETREAT FROM LENIN'S POSITION *

P. FEDENKO

Member, Learned Council, Institute for the Study of the U.S.S.R., Munich, Germany

The New Program of the Soviet Communist Party, adopted by the Twenty-Second Congress in October 1961 states:

In the socialist part of the world there are no classes and social groups interested in unleashing wars. By outstripping capitalism in a number of important branches of science and technology, socialism has provided the peace-loving peoples with powerful material means for curbing imperialist aggression . . .

Socialism offers to mankind the only sensible principle for relations between states under the conditions of the division of the world into two systems —the principle of peaceful coexistence of states with different social structures advanced by V. I. Lenin.

The same section of the program lays particular emphasis on the fact that

. . . peaceful coexistence of socialist and capitalist states is an objective necessity for the development of human society. War cannot and must not serve as the means for resolving international disputes.

The compilers of the Program cite Lenin as a champion of the peaceful coexistence of socialism and capitalism. Yet it should be noted that the 1903 Program of the Russian Social Democratic Workers' Party, in the compilation of which Lenin took an active part, makes absolutely no mention of international politics or problems of peace and war. The only point in this program which relates even indirectly to this problem is the call to replace regular armed forces with universal armament of the people. The 1919 Program of the Russian Communist Party, on the other hand, which

* Excerpts reprinted from P. Fedenko, "Lenin's Views on War and Peaceful Coexistence," *Bulletin, Institute for the Study of the U.S.S.R.*, March, 1963, pp. 27-36, by permission of the publisher.

Lenin compiled for the Eighth Party Congress, devotes a great deal of attention to international politics and war, both international and civil. For a long period these problems occupied an important position in Lenin's analysis of the political development of the world in the first twenty-five years of the twentieth century. Under the influence of the works of the English economist Hobson on modern imperialism and the analysis of "finance capital" by the German economist Rudolf Hilferding, Lenin became persuaded that wars were inevitable during the era of "finance capital." This conviction is embodied in the 1919 Program, which states:

> During the era of imperialism imperialist wars inevitably occur, wars for markets, for spheres of capital investment, for raw materials and manpower, that is, for world dominion and for power over small and weak peoples.

But against the power of capital, the program observed, there stood the movement of the toiling masses, whose interest lay in the maintenance of international peace and, since the bourgeoisie was incapable of ensuring peace between states, the exploited toiling masses with the proletariat at their head would inevitably transform international war into civil war against the bourgeoisie. Civil wars in individual states lead "inevitably" to revolutionary wars; "proletarian countries" are forced to defend themselves against foreign intervention and similarly peoples oppressed by imperialist states wage revolutionary wars for their own liberation. The program rejected pacifist slogans, international disarmament, courts of arbitration and the like under capitalism on the grounds that they not only constituted a reactionary utopia but were in fact a downright deception of the workers, and concluded that "only a proletarian Communist revolution can extract mankind from the *impasse* created by imperialism and imperialist wars." . . .

While spending part of World War I in Switzerland, Lenin frequently repeated his conviction that wars were inevitable so long as capitalism existed. In a pamphlet, *Socialism and War,* published in August 1915, he asserted: "We . . . realize the impossibility of eliminating war without eliminating classes and creating socialism." And later: "Under capitalism there are times when no other means of restoring the lost balance are possible than crises in industry and wars in politics." . . .

Lenin called on the working classes of the belligerent countries to oppose the War by every possible means, since he considered World War I an unjust war for which the bourgeoisie of both sides were responsible. His attitude toward revolutionary wars was different, since he considered these just. In 1916, he expressed his sympathy with revolutionary wars by admitting the possibility of wars between socialism victorious in one country and other, bourgeois or reactionary, countries. . . .

Lenin regarded national liberation wars as just and expressed his sympathy for oppressed peoples in their struggle for independence. In 1916, he wrote that "national wars against the imperialist powers are not only possible and probable, they are inevitable and progressive, revolutionary. . . ."

Lenin did not change his attitude toward war even after the 1917 revolution in Russia. He exploited the general war-weariness of the population as propaganda for an immediate peace and by means of an armed uprising seized power; he described his Party government as a "dictatorship of the proletariat and the poorest peasantry." Having assumed dictatorial power in Russia, Lenin immediately set about implementing his plan to bring the world war to an end by means of a world proletarian revolution:

One of our next tasks is to bring the war to a speedy conclusion. But in order to end this war, closely linked as it is with the present capitalist structure, it is clear to everyone that it is essential to overthrow capitalism itself.

On December 19, 1917, the Commissariat for Foreign Affairs published an appeal on these lines. The appeal declared that the Soviet government was of the opinion that existing capitalist governments were incapable of concluding a democratic peace: "Only the revolutionary struggle of the toiling masses against existing governments can bring such a peace nearer." The appeal also stated that, by entering into peace negotiations with the Central Powers, the Soviet government was trying to bring the war to an end, while on the other hand wishing to use every means to break the dominance of capitalism and seize political power. . . .

Thus, according to Lenin, one of the ways of eliminating capitalism was a revolutionary war of the proletariat. Similarly, the liberation wars of colonial peoples, by undermining the foundations of capitalism in the mother countries, were to facilitate the growth of revolutionary attitudes among the proletariats of these countries and thus accelerate the socialist revolution. At the same time, Lenin did not lose sight of his original hopes for further wars between the imperialist powers, which must also lead to the overthrow of capitalism. In the draft Party program adopted at the 1919 congress, Lenin wrote:

A correct understanding of the causes, importance and aims of this revolution requires a clarification of the nature of capitalism and the inevitability of its development toward Communism through imperialism and the imperialist wars which accelerate the downfall of capitalism.

Thus, Communism is a derivative of capitalist development, which passes through an "accelerating" stage of imperialist wars . . .

Lenin spoke with even greater conviction of the inevitability of wars under capitalism in July 1920:

Without the revolutionary overthrow of capitalism, no international arbitration courts, no talks on reduction of armaments, no "democratic" reorganization of the League of Nations can save mankind from new imperialist wars. . . .

These excerpts from the speeches and articles of Lenin give a clear idea of his views on the coexistence of a Communist state with countries of a different political shade. The present Soviet leaders are driven to all manner of shifts in order to adapt Lenin's views to the requirements of the policy of "peaceful coexistence." While it is possible to find references to the coexistence of the Soviet state with countries possessing different political and economic systems in the speeches and articles of Lenin, it should be remembered that Lenin's declarations regarding coexistence were based on tactical considerations: the desire to conceal his real plans and intentions behind empty phrases about the Soviet government's imaginary desire for peace.

This policy was followed by Lenin in interviews with representatives of the foreign press. In December 1919, for instance, he told a reporter of the *Chicago Daily News* that the Soviet government was prepared to guarantee absolute non-intervention in the internal affairs of foreign states. Yet in an article published in *Pravda* on February 28 and March 1, 1918, he spoke out in favor of his government's intervention in the internal affairs of all states: "The interests of the international revolution require that the Soviet regime, having overthrown the country's bourgeoisie, should assist this revolution, but should choose the form of assistance in accordance with its powers." Thus, the principle of Soviet government intervention in the internal affairs of other states remains unshaken; only the forms of intervention may be modified according to the balance of forces, the international situation and the state of affairs in the individual countries concerned.

With the object of misleading foreigners as to Soviet international policy, Lenin spoke of his desire for peace with a correspondent of the *New York Evening Journal* in 1920:

Our plans in Asia? The same as in Europe: peaceful coexistence with the peoples, the workers and peasants of all nations who are awakening to a new life. The basis for peace with America? Let the American capitalists leave us alone. We will leave them alone.

Despite these peaceful sentiments addressed to the capitalists, Lenin continued to stand by his conviction that "wars are inevitable because of private property." The logical outcome of such an understanding of the situation was Lenin's desire to disrupt capitalist society by all means in his power. The coexistence of a socialist state with countries of another order could, in Lenin's eyes, be no more than a respite or temporary stage lasting until his state had gained sufficient strength to seize capitalism by the scruff of the neck and finish with it once and for all.

Lenin's sporadic statements about peaceful coexistence of the Soviet state with capitalist countries were merely a smoke screen behind which the Communist leaders might gather strength and prepare for the decisive attack on world capitalism. Stalin remained true to Lenin's belief in the impossibility of coexistence between countries of the socialist camp and capitalist states. . . .

How is one to explain the retreat of the present Communist leaders under Khrushchev from the positions of Leninism in international policy? Why does Khrushchev so insistently preach a policy of peaceful coexistence between countries of the socialist camp and states of the capitalist world, even going so far as to give spurious interpretations of Lenin's views on the subject? The reasons for this change in tactics are to be found in the advances of military technology. Even if the Soviet Union were victorious in an atomic war against the capitalist camp, the catastrophic consequences of such a war would leave the Communist leaders with no hope of creating Communism on the ruins of civilization. The new Party Program states that "support for peaceful coexistence is also in the interests of the bourgeoisie, who realize that thermonuclear war would not spare even the ruling classes of capitalist society." The authors of the program do not mention that the new ruling class of the Soviet camp would likewise not remain invulnerable in the event of atomic war, but it is this that has prompted the Soviet leaders to carry out a revision of Lenin's theories on war. The *rapprochement* between the Soviet Union and Yugoslavia, whose government long since abandoned Lenin's belief in the inevitably of a new world war, is in line with this policy. . . .

There are grounds for believing that the leaders in the Kremlin and members of the "new class" realize the danger of thermonuclear war to themselves. The more they become convinced that thermonuclear war does not provide them with any chance of victory, the greater will be the possibility of genuine peaceful coexistence, but a peaceful coexistence not on Lenin's terms.

WESTERN MARXIST VIEWS

4. EAST AND WEST: IMPLICATIONS OF COEXISTENCE *

ISAAC DEUTSCHER
Author, Social Scientist

'Peaceful coexistence'—so much has already been said about it that the term has become threadbare. It remains meaningful nevertheless. Whether we are aware of this or not, peaceful coexistence has long been a fact of the international situation. True, twice since the October Revolution attempts have been made to prevent or disrupt coexistence: first, immediately after 1917, when the Western powers intervened in Russia and fought Bolshevism, while Bolshevik Russia believed in the imminence of international revolution; and then during the Second World War, when Nazi Germany refused to 'coexist' with the Soviet Union (and was unable to 'coexist' with the bourgeois democracies of the West either). Apart from these two very important intervals, peaceful coexistence has gone on for decades.

There are, of course, quite a few varieties of coexistence. Antagonistic social systems may confront each other in intense hostility but without resorting to arms; or they may live side by side and ignore each other, although it is difficult to visualize such a situation between régimes the antagonism of which is of a fundamental nature and has assumed world-wide scale. There may be various modalities of coexistence in friendly or hostile neutrality. And, finally, even governments which are ideologically poles apart may co-operate and conclude alliances. In the last forty years we have run through this whole gamut. Following the years of the anti-Bolshevik intervention, there were times, during the late 1920s and early 1930s, when East and West tried to ignore one another and to live in mutual isolation. The Second World War brought the

---

* Reprinted from Isaac Deutscher, *The Great Contest: Russia and the West* (1960), pp. 64-74 and 78-83, by permission of the author and of Oxford University Press.

alliance between the Western democracies and Russia. But the alliance was ridden with latent tensions, which subsequently came to the surface and led to the cold war. We have now reached the stage when it becomes more and more difficult and dangerous to persist in this kind of cold war and more and more urgent to find, if possible, an easier and more co-operative relationship.

The Russians declare frankly that they envisage peaceful coexistence as a competitive contest between the opposed social systems, a contest which should be conducted in the economic sphere and by political means but from which war and the threat of war, implied in the present arms race, should be excluded. This is the so-called Soviet challenge to the West. What are its implications, and prospects?

The Soviet Union, we know, is at present the world's second industrial power and it aspires to attain economic parity with the United States and then to become, in a decade or so, the world's wealthiest industrial nation. As the Soviet rate of industrial expansion is now generally recognized to be much higher than the American, it is very probable that the Soviet Union will indeed become the industrial equal of the United States in the relatively near future. Although Soviet standards of living may still remain below the American ten years from now, they are certain to have risen above Western European standards. This will be a tremendous achievement for a people whose standards were not so long ago closer to those of China or India than of Western Europe.

But what is involved here is not merely comparative statistics of production and consumption. The question is not just who will outproduce whom and when. If this were all, the prospect would not have even part of the dramatic tension it obviously has. We would then still have to expect a great shift in the world's balance of power. But similar shifts, on a smaller scale, have occurred in the past, without creating comparable social, political, and ideological problems. Till the close of the nineteenth century Britain was the world's industrial workshop. Then the United States and Germany caught up with her and surpassed her. The shift that is now in progress is different in kind as well as scale. When Germany and the United States caught up industrially with Britain, their success did not place a question mark over the social system prevailing in Britain. The two nations had achieved their ascendancy within a framework of social relationships and institutions very similar to, and largely modelled on, those which had predominated in Britain. On both sides of the Atlantic capitalism was in its heyday. The attainment of industrial maturity by new nations demonstrated only the vitality of bourgeois society and its immense capacity for expansion. Britain was weakened as the world empire; but in her very reverse there triumphed the principle that underlay her organization.

The economic ascendancy of the Soviet Union tends to place a huge question mark over the structure of Western society. Theoretically, the question mark is not new. Socialism at large and Marxism in particular have disputed the rationality of the bourgeois order for more than a century. Even before 1848 Marx and Engels claimed that capitalist enterprise was increasingly impeding the development of productive resources because it could not function without boom and slump and without making the rich richer and the poor poorer. They saw in this the manifestation of the anarchy of capitalism and looked ahead to the time when capitalism would have to give place to a new order based on public ownership and representing a superior social organization. But for over a century this has been, as far as Western society is concerned, abstract theory; the prolonged theoretical onslaught on the 'bastions of capitalism' could not shake them. Whatever its record of exploitation and oppression, whatever the anarchy of its trade cycles and the destructiveness of its wars, Western capitalism has developed its productive resources beyond what either its critics or even its apologists had imagined as possible. The working classes have in varying degrees participated in the resulting benefits and have consequently placed their hopes on reforms within the capitalist system rather than on its revolutionary overthrow.

Even the Russian revolution was unable to change this situation. True, its first victories sent a fever through Western society and aroused a panic in the possessing classes. But subsequently the Russian revolution itself seemed to disprove the Marxist critique of capitalism and to restore the self-confidence of the West. The 'building of socialism' had been initiated in one of the world's most backward and poverty-stricken countries, with the result that for a long time the Bolshevik régime was unable to deliver the goods socialism had promised. The Soviet levels of production remained far below Western levels; and so did the Soviet standards of living, not to speak of the standards of civil liberties. Despite its slumps, Western capitalism continued by and large to demonstrate its vitality and efficiency, while Russia appeared to provide the evidence of the inefficiency of socialism. (I am here speaking of 'social efficiency' in the broadest sense which includes economic productivity and social and political freedom.) Russia had through the revolution deprived herself of the advantages of capitalism without as yet availing herself of the advantages of socialism.

It is now clear that this was a period of transition. In the fifth decade of the revolution, having undergone forcible industrialization, the Soviet Union is reaping the first benefits of socialism. This at once carries the Marxist critique of bourgeois society from the sphere of theory into that of practice. In the years to come the merits and de-merits of Western social and political institutions are going to be subjected to new and stern scrutiny. The old question of social versus private ownership of the means of production is being re-opened in a new manner. The Soviet inheritors

of the Marxist case need no longer argue primarily from the social inefficiency of capitalism *per se*. They may well grant that Western capitalism
has proved to possess far greater staying power and adaptability than
Marxism had assumed. But they point out that capitalism, even in its
most modern and advanced variety, is still proving to be a less efficient
form of social organization than is even the not so very advanced socialist
or quasi-socialist system of the Soviet Union. They now argue, in other
words, that Western capitalism will succumb not so much—or not directly
—because of its own crises and inherent contradictions as because of its
inability to match the achievements of socialism.

This is how the Marxist argument is at present being re-formulated
in the Soviet Union. (For reasons of doctrinal orthodoxy this modification of the Marxist critique of capitalism is being carried out implicitly
rather than explicitly.) The argument may still seem far-fetched to people
in the West. But its influence on the political thinking of the underdeveloped nations, who form the majority of the human race, is unmistakable. To them the unparalleled rapidity of the industrial rise of the
Soviet Union already suggests that they themselves are more likely to
achieve a similar rise on the basis of public rather than private ownership.

But even the wealthiest nations of the West will have to ask themselves anew just how much scope for progress is left within their present
structure of society. It is true that within it they have achieved their relatively high standards of living and won their political liberties. But where
do they go from here? Can the Western nations secure full employment
as the normal condition of their economy? Can they secure an indefinite
continuation of their post-war prosperity? Even if they can, this will allow
them merely to maintain a rate of progress which has become manifestly
inadequate in comparison with the Soviet rate and inadequate also in
relation to the requirements of the present upheaval in science and technology. Are the Western nations socially equipped to absorb and assimilate
the now unfolding permanent revolution in technology? Can private enterprise keep pace with state enterprise in technical innovation? These questions are at the heart of the Soviet challenge to the West.

It is one of the Soviet claims that the stimuli for their economic
growth are, so to speak, built-in in the public ownership and national
planning of industry. Considerations of national, not of private or sec-
tional, profit determine the uninterrupted and vigorous rhythm of economic
activity. True, the record of post-war prosperity in the West may suggest
that the Western economy too has, on the basis of private enterprise, succeeded in overcoming the anarchy of the old trade cycle; and that it is
no longer subject to the spontaneous alternation of boom, slump, and
depression. But is it not too early to take this for granted? It should not
be forgotten that in the industrial history of the West there were some
trade cycles marked by only the mildest of ups and downs. One may find

a parallel to the present long-lasting prosperity in the steady development of the German economy in the Bismarck era, when for nearly a quarter of a century, from the early 1870s till the late 1890s, German industry knew no severe slump. This aroused the most optimistic hopes and convinced even many socialists that the Marxist critique of capitalism was out of date. Subsequently, however, the German economy found itself once again in the throes of most violent trade cycles, with very steep ups and downs.

Are Keynesian economic controls (assuming that governments adopt them in time) enough to prevent a similar sequel to the present period of prosperity? The practical evidence of the efficacy of such controls in a situation tending towards a deep slump has yet to be produced. Nor should the view be taken for granted that armament can have or has a continuously stimulating effect on economic activity. Armament may cut both ways: it may stimulate the general demand for goods and investment; but, in certain circumstances, it may restrict them both. Even if this were not so, it would be manifestly dangerous for any nation to rely for its prosperity on armament booms. Such a nation would be like a well fed man who every day takes his large red beefsteak with a small admixture of poison—he gets all the proteins and calories he wants and looks healthy and hale; but he is slowly destroying himself. A prosperity based on nuclear armaments is deceptive; those who believe in it implicitly take a defeatist view of the economic future of the West. I do not think that armament has been so decisive a factor in the post-war economic upsurge. But I cannot help being struck by a contrast between Western and Soviet thinking on this point. While in the West opinion has become, as it were, conditioned to treat armament as a stimulus to economic growth and well-being, in the East opinion is conditioned to see it as a brake on growth and a drain on prosperity. While in the West all too often the thought of a slackening of the arms race conjures up memories of the 1930s and fears of poverty and unemployment, the Russians, on the contrary, think confidently of the quickening tempo of their advance and of the prosperity that would come within their reach if only they could rid themselves of the burdens of armament.

This difference shows itself at all levels, in the policies of governments and the reasonings of the 'man in the street'. The West has accustomed itself to view the most unproductive kind of economic activity as a boon in disguise, while the East recognizes it for what it is—the irrational waste of immense resources and energies. It would be ominous for the West to embark upon the new phase of competitive coexistence in this frame of mind. The effective Western answer to the Soviet challenge can lie only in a genuine demonstration of superior efficiency, that is, of the West's ability to secure, without the 'help' of armament, full employment and continuously rising standards of living, and to secure these while preserving and enlarging its heritage of political freedom. Can Western society, as at present constituted, meet the Soviet challenge in this way?

I have referred to the social and international consequences of the permanent technological revolution now in progress. It may be said that this has to some extent replaced the Marxist prospect of a permanent social revolution. But is the upheaval in technology not preparing another upheaval in social relations? The new technology tends to outgrow our inherited institutions and to render obsolete the frameworks within which we have been accustomed to act, think, and live our lives. It grows above the head of private property. Even in the West atomic power has not been the child of private enterprise. It has been the child of state enterprise. Henceforth nearly every act of the technological upheaval is likely to strengthen the trend towards public ownership and enterprise; the gigantic scale of the new inventions and scientific ventures puts these beyond the resources of private investment. What business concern will undertake to finance the exploration of outer space and face the risks involved in a host of other tremendously expensive pioneering projects which are now maturing in the scientists' minds and laboratories? A state which has the command of the nation's industrial resources is in a far better position to cope with these tasks; and this has been a decisive reason why the Russians have been able partly to overtake the West despite the fact that the West is still so much wealthier. Of their smaller wealth the Russians have been able to make a more concentrated and effective use.

Purposeful and concentrated use of resources is inherent in a nationalized and planned economy. It need not necessarily be achieved at the expense of consumer interests and by a government exercising absolute power, although in Russia it was so achieved in the course of a long period of time. The Russian pattern was part and parcel of 'primitive accumulation', that is of forcible industrialization carried out amid an overall scarcity of resources, and amid the political tensions characteristic of a post-revolutionary period. Since they left that initial phase behind, the Russians have been increasingly able to satisfy consumer needs and at the same time to go on investing on an ever larger scale; and they have started to rid themselves of absolutist government, which far from being the *sine qua non* of the progress of their planned economy, has proved to be an obstacle to it. The more rational and concentrated use of resources in a nationalized economy follows from the organic integration of its elements. This by itself immensely accelerates technological progress. To take one example: no Soviet concern or group of concerns can reserve for itself the advantages of any new invention or innovation and withhold these from others—new methods of production benefit the whole industry much more quickly than normally happens under private enterprise. No commercial secrecy sets up its own iron or plastic curtains between various sectors of industry (although bureaucratic rigidity may to some extent obstruct the spread of new 'know-how').

Another aspect of the problem, bound to become increasingly important in competitive coexistence, is the relatively greater ability of a nationalized economy to modernize its equipment. Technological revolution necessitates replacement of equipment on an unprecedented scale. Other things being equal, the ability of any economy to carry this out in time depends on the strength of the vested interests tied to obsolescent industries. The development of atomic fuel will reduce the importance of coal and petrol. Enormous investments in these industries will become 'prematurely' depreciated. Will those who stand to lose thereby not obstruct the development of atomic fuel in the West? Will the Russians, unimpeded by such obstruction, not jump ahead once again in this all-important field? Significantly, the prospect of the industrial replacement of the old fuels by atomic energy is already being treated by the Russians with far greater urgency than is customary in the West, where the prospect is seen as rather remote.

Automation raises a parallel issue. Some Western industrialists who have had a glimpse of its progress in the Soviet Union maintain that already automation is being carried out there on a scale larger than that attempted in the West. Of course, automation releases great masses of labour. A continuously and rapidly expanding economy can re-deploy and re-employ redundant labour more easily than can be done in a stagnant industry or in one that expands slowly. In addition, the Russians train their labour in a way calculated to endow it with industrial mobility: workers are trained in several skills so as to be able to shift from job to job. How is the West going to handle this problem? . . .

I have dwelt until now on the economic issues of competitive coexistence. These have so far been foremost in the Western mind. Much though Western statesmen, politicians, and commentators may despise dialectical materialism (or what passes for it), they are, I am afraid, inclined to approach competitive coexistence in a narrowly materialistic spirit. Yet it cannot be repeated often enough that the chief issue is not who will outproduce whom and when, or even who will eventually have the higher standards of living, important though all this is. Ultimately the challenge is a spiritual one. Even now the fields in which the West finds it most difficult to match the Soviet advance are those of social policy and education. The Russians are completing their transition to the 35–40-hour week in industry (the 35-hour week has been introduced in mining and other dangerous or difficult occupations); and they plan a further reduction to 30–35 hours between 1964 and 1968. Western Europe is working long hours. Even in England only a few trade unions are just beginning to demand a 40-hour week. The workers often compensate for the long hours by economizing their energy and working slowly and sluggishly. Western European industry is in no mood to introduce (or re-introduce) the 40-hour week. When the Russians do go over to 30–35 hours, will even North American industry be inclined to emulate this example? Yet the working classes of the West will certainly grow increasingly aware of the disadvantage under which they will be placed. Here is the greatest challenge in social policy with which the West is going to be confronted.

As to education, we know that the Russians train many more engineers and technicians than does any Western country, including the United States. They have developed a unique system of extramural adult education. And above all their social and educational policies are closely interlinked. While social policy aims at the continuous shortening of working hours and at lightening the burdens of productive work, educational policy envisages an unprecedented spread and improvement of educational facilities. It is this that gives social and cultural sense to the shortening of hours in industry. The worker, as he leaves his factory after a shorter day, is being enabled to make civilized use of his leisure. He does not fall a prey to commercialized entertainment and to the stultifying vulgarities of a sensational press and television. True, his leisure is all too often spoilt by assaults of dogmatic propaganda. It used to be said of the English Puritans that they made people eat bread with religion, and people could not stand it. Stalinism has made the Russians eat bread with ideology. Under Khrushchev they have more bread and less ideology, but they are still being stuffed with a lot of stodgy dogma. Indigestible as this is, it has at least the redeeming feature that it does not lower in the working man the level of his human interests as much as our commercialized 'mass media' do. Despite all their faults the Russian 'mass media' tend to instruct minds rather than to stunt them; they try at least to develop in people a sense of social community and solidarity; and sometimes they do it on a level of seriousness which should be the envy of the West. Whatever may be said in criticism of the Soviet 'way of life', it does not produce the Lonely Crowd.

Nor should we underrate the appeal that the vision of future achievement has on the mass of the people. It gives them what may be described as an anti-Orwell image of 1984. The Russians are encouraged to expect that by that time they may obtain a working day of not more than four or even three hours. Is this a wild dream? I do not think so. Technological advance should allow the reduction of the working day even to three or two hours before the end of this century. About a hundred years ago the idea of a six- or seven-hour day would have seemed wild to our ancestors; yet labour-saving machinery has made it possible to reduce the working day by half and to multiply the wealth of the industrial nations. In all probability, the next forty years will bring progress in labour-saving far greater than that achieved in the last hundred years—and with it the possibility of a reduction of the present working day by at least one half. With only two to three hours' work in an automated industry man would indeed cease to 'eat his bread in the sweat of his brow'; and if the educational system expands as the 'socially necessary' productive labour shrinks, then equal opportunity for all *will* become a reality.

The time of universal academic education may not be so very far off—it may perhaps come even before the end of this century. Again, we should not shrug this off as a pipe dream: did not the idea of universal secondary education seem 'impossible' even at the beginning of this century?

With the work for his livelihood occupying only a small part of his active life, man will be able to spend the rest of his time pursuing intellectual and aesthetic interests, studying, enjoying art, exploring the universe, engaging in sport, and so on. The division of society into the toilers and the leisured classes would then vanish; and with it could disappear the divorce and the gulf between intellectual work and manual labour. The former would cease to be the privilege of a minority, the latter—a dire necessity and a curse for the mass of mankind.

Of course, this is no new ideal. But hitherto ideal and reality have been poles apart; and no path could be seen leading to Utopia. Now at last, the Russians think, technological progress and social and educational developments do begin to throw a solid bridge between the realities of today and the vision of the future.

This is an inspiring vista, and no pooh-poohing it will diminish its attraction. Has the West something better, more realistic, or more inspiring to offer? This is the greatest single question of competitive coexistence.

Of course, there is freedom, political freedom, in the West; and this is absent from the Soviet Union and the communist-ruled countries. The moral importance of this contrast can hardly be overrated. But I do not think that the contrast will last indefinitely. The Russians have already discovered that they need freedom, if only to be socially efficient. In the years to come they will be discovering that the doses of freedom their rulers grant them are too small and meagre. They will clamour for more and, I think, the rulers will have to meet the demand. As I see it, the coming decade will bring a gradual, or not so gradual, enlargement of civil liberty, although there will also be temporary setbacks and there may occur dramatic clashes between the rulers and the ruled.

These prospects will affect competitive coexistence. Hitherto the West has won many a moral and political battle against Russia because Russia was a tyranny and the goddess of freedom fought on the Western side. In the West were also the big industrial battalions. Now Russia is forming and marshalling her big industrial battalions; and the new Soviet generation longs to see the goddess of freedom in its camp; and it may yet tempt her over there. And then the moral advantage the West has so far enjoyed may dwindle.

There are various ways in which the West can face this multiple challenge. It may react with fear and panic; or it may respond with courage and enterprise. It may cling to outdated institutions and social forms; or it may embark upon a bold search for new modes of organization and upon radical changes in the framework of society. The West still has tremendous assets. It has an industrial start over the Soviet bloc: after all, it is still the Soviet aspiration to catch up with the United States. The advantage of political freedom, though far from intact, is still with the West. The West is richer in cultural tradition—its cultural heritage is older and more varied than Russia's. With such assets, if only it does not dissipate them, if only it puts them to the proper use, and if it guards against panicky as well as wishful thinking, the West should have nothing to fear and should be well able to hold its ground. If only the West learns to face the future instead of clinging to the past, the challenge will hold no threat to it; and—who knows?—competitive coexistence may yet change from the bitter competition it is into co-operative emulation. This certainly is the only hope. The alternative may be mutual extermination.

I would like to conclude my remarks with the words which the Dafoe Foundation, as whose guest I have had the honour to speak here, uses as the text of its activities, words written by J. W. Dafoe, the great Canadian editor:

> I am convinced [he wrote], it is the faith by which I live, that all these difficulties arise from conditions that are temporary, and that we are moving irresistibly by the discoveries of science, by the ingenuity of man, by the necessities of our life, to the condition of a world community of peace in which there will be harmonious cooperation between great nations and small nations.

These words evoke a melancholy reflection. Dafoe wrote them in the year 1930; nine years later what was to have been 'a world community of peace' was engulfed in the Second World War. Yet I think that Dafoe's words have lost nothing of their truth—their message has become even more urgent. The Second World War was the last occasion when the Great Powers could still clash in arms without annihilating themselves and mankind. We dare not afford a repetition; we dare not allow, in this nuclear age, the hope expressed by Dafoe to be frustrated once more. We must see to it that the difficulties with which we are confronted do indeed prove temporary; and that the 'discoveries of science, the ingenuity of man, and the necessities of our life' do indeed 'lead us to a condition of a world community of peace'. Dafoe said: 'it is the faith by which I live'. We must know that only if we *act* on that faith shall we live at all.

SOVIET VIEWS

5. PEACEFUL COEXISTENCE AND INTERNATIONAL LAW *

YE. A. KOROVIN
Director, International Law Department,
Moscow State University

F. I. KOZHEVNIKOV
Director, International Law Department,
Institute of Foreign Relations

G. P. ZADOROZHNY
Professor of International Law

Many generations to come will remember with deep gratitude those who in our era of swift and revolutionary break-up of social relations and of radical advances in the life of peoples and states pointed out to mankind the only correct way to avoid a nuclear-missile catastrophe and to ensure lasting peace on earth.

The finest minds of humanity dreamed in the past, too, of the advent of lasting peace on earth, but their projects were only a utopia, since at the time there was no real force capable of making this wonderful dream a reality.

Such a force has appeared in the 20th century, and it is called communism. . . .

The 22nd Congress of the C.P.S.U. emphasized again and again that the peaceful coexistence of states with different systems is an objective necessity for the development of human society. . . . The Party Program says that peaceful coexistence serves as the foundation for peaceful competition between socialism and capitalism. . . .

* From *Izvestia*, April 18, 1962. Excerpts reprinted from the translation in *The Current Digest of the Soviet Press,* published at Columbia University, May 9, 1962, pp. 8-9, by permission of the publisher. Copyright 1963 by the Joint Committee on Slavic Studies.

The capitalist countries should now be no less interested than the socialist countries in removing the danger of war and strengthening peaceful coexistence. . . .

Following the slick example of John F. Dulles, who called peaceful coexistence a "cunning term" that the West should beware of, the ideologists of anticommunism are trying to distort the Leninist principle of peaceful coexistence, which is the general line of Soviet foreign policy, and to prove that peaceful coexistence allegedly has nothing in common with generally recognized principles of international contact.

Refuting inventions of this kind, N. S. Khrushchev has said: "We are profoundly aware that without observance of the norms of international law and fulfillment of accepted commitments there can be no trust in relations among states, and without trust there can be no peaceful coexistence. Consistently upholding the principle of peaceful coexistence, we shall continue to come out in defense of the norms of international law in relations among states."

Peaceful coexistence is inconceivable without international legality. Peaceful coexistence is international law in action.

Peaceful coexistence does not mean simply rejecting the use of force, the absence of war or a state of temporary insubstantial truce but the maintenance and development among the states of the two world systems of all-round political, economic and other relations, including trade, personal contacts and exchange of cultural values.

Peaceful coexistence means ensuring sovereignty, territorial inviolability, political independence and equality of all peoples and states, respect for systems chosen by the peoples, and recognition of the right of every people to choose, in conformity with its sovereign will, one or another form of government, as well as a new socio-economic system, without interference in one another's internal affairs and without export of revolution and counterrevolution. It should be emphasized in this connection that the Punta del Este resolution, endeavoring to present revolutionary Cuba as a regime "incompatible with the principles of the inter-American system," is in crying contradiction to the elementary requirements of international legality. The U.S. policy toward Cuba is export of counterrevolution.

All conditions exist in the present epoch for the full victory of the principles of peaceful coexistence and international law over the aggressive imperialist policy that flouts international law.

The Soviet Union, the entire mighty camp of socialism, played a decisive role in creating these conditions.

V. I. Lenin was the founder of the doctrine of peaceful coexistence between the two systems as an objective necessity of historical development following the Great October Socialist Revolution. He carefully formulated the idea of peaceful coexistence. He wrote about the "inevitability of *agreement*" between the capitalist system of ownership and the socialist system "as equal with equal." Yet J. V. Stalin, in a talk with H. Stassen in 1947, alleged that Lenin had been the first to voice merely "the thought of cooperation between the two systems." Molotov, in a letter to the 22nd Party Congress, went so far as to allege that Lenin had never spoken of peaceful coexistence at all. . . .

The 20th, 21st and 22nd Party Congresses confirmed with new force that the Leninist principle of peaceful coexistence was and remains the general line of Soviet foreign policy.

N. S. Khrushchev, consistent fighter for peace and friendship among peoples, has rendered a great service in developing and substantiating the principles of peaceful coexistence. His reports to the Congresses of the C.P.S.U., his speeches at the United Nations and other pronouncements have been a further development of Lenin's doctrine of peaceful coexistence as it applies to the specific present-day historical epoch.

It is well known, for instance, that at the United Nations N. S. Khrushchev substantiated the thesis that general and complete disarmament is the most effective means for implementing the policy of peaceful coexistence and the victory of the cause of peace. In his speeches at the 14th and 15th sessions of the U.N. General Assembly, N. S. Khrushchev proposed a plan for destroying within a brief period all means of warfare by all states under strict international control, which would make war in effect impossible. The United Nations approved the Soviet idea of general and complete disarmament, and the task today is to implement this idea as soon as possible.

Thus the idea of ensuring general disarmament is now not only the demand of all peace-loving nations, of all people of good will on earth, but it is indivisibly linked with the principles of contemporary international law and has become one of its generally accepted norms.

Even in conditions of disarmament, however, tranquility and the triumph of international legality will not be ensured in the world if there is no genuine equality between peoples, if the last vestiges of colonialism on earth are not done away with. As is known, on the initiative of the Soviet delegation headed by N. S. Khrushchev, the 15th session of the General Assembly adopted in 1960 the historic declaration on the eradication of colonialism.

For peaceful coexistence it is also necessary that the states of the two world systems do everything within their power to settle urgent international problems peacefully, taking into account the legitimate interests of all sides. . . .

The realization of all these measures will provide the peoples with the opportunity of calmly engaging in creative work under conditions of peaceful competition between the two systems, in the course of which the system that provides mankind with a better life, that more fully satisfies his material and spiritual needs, will in the end win out. The peoples, as the creators of history and the masters of their destinies, have sovereign rights issuing from international law, in the first place the right to take the cause of peace into their own hands and to determine their destinies by their own lights. . . .

The forces of communism, which have inscribed on their banner the deliverance of all people from the horrors of war and from any form of exploitation and the affirmation on earth of Peace, Labor, Freedom, Equality, Brotherhood and Happiness for all peoples, are filled with confidence in their complete and final victory over capitalism in conditions of peaceful coexistence and competition between the two systems.

B. The Economic Challenge

WESTERN VIEWS

6. THE GREAT ECONOMIC RACE *

ABRAM BERGSON
Harvard University

. . . Khrushchev, in seeking to "bury us," is prepared to vary his tactics as circumstances permit. But in the economic field he has pursued steadfastly the imperative he inherited from Stalin: by outpacing the U.S.A. economically, the U.S.S.R. must eventually supplant us as the world's first industrial power. How are the Russians progressing in their "economic competition" with us? What are their future prospects?

Stalin died March 5, 1953. For the years that followed, through 1961, the Soviet government claims that the U.S.S.R. increased its national income at an average rate of 9.7 per cent a year. Independent Western calculations, however, place the correct figure at somewhere around six per cent, which is still a rapid pace. While it is certainly not unprecedented

* Reprinted from *Challenge,* The Magazine of Economic Affairs, published by the Institute of Economic Affairs, New York University, March, 1963, pp. 4-6, by permission of the author and the publisher.

in Western experience, the Soviet growth rate compares favorably enough with that of the U.S. for recent years—about 2.7 per cent over the last few cycles.

In expanding their output in recent years, the Russians have been able to rely only to a very limited extent on increases in *employment* of labor. Industrial expansion has been achieved principally through increases in *output per worker*. Moreover, available population projections indicate that employment is not apt to increase any more rapidly in the coming years than it has in the recent past. In fact, there is a good chance that the rate of increase will decline. In hourly terms, however, the Soviet government might avoid such a trend if it should decide to postpone the promised reduction in the workweek to 35 hours by 1964-68. It follows that the growth in output will depend, as it has in the recent past, primarily on productivity increases. What are the prospects for such increases?

Any serious appraisal must consider, to begin with, that, because of the limited amount and quality of natural resources, production in the U.S.S.R., as elsewhere, is subject to diminishing returns. While these limitations will be felt throughout the Soviet economy, in the years ahead they are especially apt to be felt in agriculture—for the U.S.S.R. in terms of soil and climate is not nearly as well endowed agriculturally as its great land surface might suggest. The Russians' recent experience in farming is a dramatic reminder of this fact. I refer, in particular, to the already reduced returns on the vast new acreage cultivated during 1955-58. Thus, in Tselinnyi Krai, the heartland of this acreage, even dubious official figures show that the grain harvest, which was not especially high to begin with, has steadily declined. It was 14.3 million tons in 1958, 13.9 million in 1959, 12.9 million in 1960 and 10.3 million in 1961.

Furthermore, in expanding their output lately, the Russians have still been able to borrow new technology from the West and to extend to industry in general borrowed technology which previously had been used only in advanced enterprises. This "advantage of backwardness," however, is no longer as important as it was in the Thirties, and as the Soviet economy continues to advance, its role will decline even further. Of course, the U.S.S.R. now has a large corps of scientists and engineers of its own, one which can even stand comparison with that of the U.S.A. In addition, the Soviet government is devoting large and increasing sums to research. Therefore, as opportunities to profit from foreign technology dwindle, self-generated innovation will be something of an offset.

Closely related to but not the same thing as the state of technology is "economic efficiency." To weigh from this standpoint the impact of the extraordinary changes in economic organization, principles and procedures that have occurred since Stalin is a difficult task. But by all accounts the Soviet planning system still leaves much to be desired with respect to economic efficiency. And the succession of reforms at least attests to the fact that the government is seriously concerned with exploiting such "hidden reserves." Moreover, the government has also seen fit recently to allow Soviet economists a degree of discretion to explore and debate alternative techniques that was unheard of under Stalin. Even branches of "bourgeois" economic theory, such as "input-output analysis" and "linear programming," are no longer beyond the pale.

By implication, even though it is faced with diminishing returns from natural resources and slowing technological progress, the U.S.S.R. may still be able to avoid a reduced rate of productivity increase by raising economic efficiency. In trying to accomplish this through their planning system, however, the Russians will be treading new and as yet unexplored ground, and how much they will be able to achieve still remains to be seen.

As output has expanded, so too has variety, and partly for this reason the task of planning has become more complex. Accordingly, the Russians may have to improve their economic organization even to hold their own with regard to efficiency, to say nothing of raising it.

I have been referring to the efficiency of the economic system generally. In the agricultural sector, chiefly because of the use of the state farm in the execution of the new lands program, the notorious collective farm is no longer as important as it once was, but it is still predominant. And avowedly the government will continue to rely heavily on it in the coming years. When we consider the U.S.S.R.'s adverse natural endowment, we can see that the Soviet collective farm is not quite as inefficient as is often supposed, but future gains in this regard should be modest.

There are indications, however, that the government at long last is preparing the ground for the transformation of the collective into state farms. Among other things, in place of their customary cooperative shares, collective farm members are increasingly being paid a money income of a sort very much like the money wage of state farm employees. Because of differences in capital and quality of land, the comparison of state farm and collective farm productivity is a complex matter. Soviet economists probably are correct, however, in maintaining that the state farm is often superior to the collective farm, particularly in the growing of grain. But to what extent the higher productivity would survive the conversion of the collectives into state farms, especially if the conversion is abrupt, is another matter.

In general, how much progress will be realized regarding agricultural efficiency will depend very much on the prudence and restraint exercised with regard to farm policy and administration. These are qualities which the arbitrary and impatient Soviet government has thus far found it difficult to realize.

One of the principal reasons for the rapid rise of labor productivity

NATIONAL INCOME PROJECTIONS: U.S. AND U.S.S.R.
(AS % OF U.S. NATIONAL INCOME, 1960)

	U.S. With Annual Increase of		U.S.S.R. With Annual Increase of	
	3.0 Per cent	4.0 Per cent	5.0 Per cent	6.0 Per cent
1960	100.0	100.0	48.0	48.0
1970	134.4	148.0	78.2	86.0
1980	180.6	219.1	127.3	153.9

in the past has been the authoritarian political control exercised over the volume of capital investment. One must be highly optimistic to suppose that this will not persist.

Indeed, given such control, one might wonder whether through its exercise alone the government could not offset or more than offset any and all forces making for a slowdown in the growth of the economy. But it should be borne in mind that the Soviet stock of fixed capital already is growing at an extraordinary rate—in the Fifties by some 11 per cent per year. Even maintaining this high tempo, to say nothing of increasing it, will be a difficult task. This could not be accomplished merely by maintaining the present share of national income devoted to new capital investment. Rather the government would have to continually raise this share.

While this important fact is still not always understood, it becomes obvious when one considers that capital stock has been growing much more rapidly than output and that this is the chief reason that it has been possible to increase output at a rapid pace to begin with. As we saw, the growth in the employment of labor has only been modest.

Thus, in order for the capital stock to expand as in the past, the share of income going to capital investment would have to rise even if in the future output continued to grow at the past tempo. If output should slow down because of retarding forces elsewhere, the rate of investment would have to rise still more.

This leads to the conclusion that the share of national income available for consumption would have to fall. If the rate of growth of income should be maintained or not decline much, total consumption could still increase, for even a declining share of a growing pie can increase absolutely. There might also be an increase in per capita consumption. But the gains in the latter would have to be modest and no doubt would only seem more so to a people who have waited so long and have lately been led by their government to expect so much as have the Russians.

Thus suppose even that there should be no retarding forces elsewhere, so that with the capital stock growing no more rapidly than before, output should continue in the future to grow at six per cent. If allowance is made for the investment needed currently to assure this continued expansion of the capital stock by 11 per cent, according to a crude calculation, consumption per capita during the Sixties might rise by 2.3 per cent, or $9 to $12 a year, from the 1960 level of, say, $400 per capita. This would be respectable progress, but the result would hardly be the affluence that has been promised. If because of retarding forces elsewhere output should tend to grow less rapidly than six per cent, consumption would increase still less.

In deciding its future investment policy, the Soviet government must consider such possible consequences. As we may judge from the continuing stress on "heavy" compared with "consumer goods" industries, it already has determined to increase further the rate of investment, but how much is a momentous matter which it no doubt will decide currently only in the light of the circumstances of the time.

Reference has been to consumption exclusive of communal services, particularly education and health care. What of the latter items? How these might vary in the future is conjectural, but for purposes of the above calculation they are taken to increase proportionately with national income. Hence, with their inclusion in consumption, this category might grow somewhat more rapidly than was indicated. Actually, under its new program the party has committed itself to expand sharply the scope of communal services in the coming years. Among other things, housing in time is to be supplied free of charge instead of (as is now done) at a nominal rental. But such rearrangements would be purely financial and could not affect at all the underlying realities of the matter, particularly the total supply of consumer goods and services of all sorts that will be made available.

For purposes of the hypothetical calculation, I also assume that defense outlays will increase proportionately with national income. Should they fail to do so, there would necessarily be additional productive resources available for either consumption or investment, as the government might wish. And resources available for these purposes would only be greater if at long last defense expenditures were curtailed absolutely. In short, for the U.S.S.R., defense outlays are onerous, and it can only gain economically from disarmament. On the record to date, however, there is little basis to suppose that the Soviet government might determine its future policy on disarmament simply on this basis.

In sum, we can hardly forsesee with any accuracy the future course of the Soviet economy. But it should be difficult for the Russians in the coming years to maintain the six per cent growth rate in output they have realized since Stalin. Still we must assume that they will continue to outpace the U.S.A., at least for some years to come, but more likely the margin by which they do so will tend to diminish.

At this juncture, prospects for a sharp acceleration of the U.S. growth rate do not seem as bright as they did in November, 1960, but a quickening expansion of the labor force is in prospect. Partly for this reason many U.S. economists feel that in the coming years the U.S. economy might grow by at least 3.5 per cent a year. If this tempo is realized, the margin between the Soviet and U.S. rates of increase will narrow more.

In any event, if the Russians ever are to achieve the economic superiority over the U.S. that they seek, it will not be soon. This emerges clearly enough from the hypothetical projections of national income in the two countries as shown in the table on page 198. All figures, including those for the U.S.S.R., are expressed as percentages of the U.S. national income in 1960.

We must not underestimate the Soviet economic challenge, but it is not quite as serious as many in the West have supposed. The threat will be less should we manage to accelerate our own growth above its recent sluggish tempo.

7. COMPETITIVE COEXISTENCE AND SOVIET GROWTH *

JAN S. PRYBYLA

Pennsylvania State University

THE NATURE OF THE SOVIET CHALLENGE

The nature of the Soviet challenge is essentially economic. It lies in the Soviet Union's ability over the years to achieve and sustain high rates of growth, and—subject to rather minor qualifications—to continue growing rapidly in the future. High rates of growth and the ability to sustain such rates, plus a reasonably sure prospect of future rapid growth, are extremely tempting to countries in which economic development has been very slow or negligible. These countries comprise today more than two-thirds of the world's population. The Soviet economic challenge is an invitation for the underdeveloped countries to follow the Soviet example, as to both the strategy of development and the tools used for putting that strategy into effect.

* Reprinted from *Pennsylvania Business Survey*, July, 1962, pp. 4-7, by permission of the author and the publisher.

Strategy and Tools

It is important to distinguish carefully between the Soviet *strategy* of economic development and the *tools,* or institutional arrangements, used to implement that strategy. One reason for stressing this distinction is that, although Soviet strategy appears to be very attractive and rapidly gaining acceptance in noncommunist underdeveloped countries, the Soviet tools are both less tempting and less current in those areas.

It is true that in Marxist-Leninist ideology the strategy and tools are closely linked, and that adoption of the one implies acceptance of the other; but it may be validly argued that this close association is an element of provincialism and an important obstacle to adoption of that doctrine by countries with leaders reared in the western tradition. One may wish to see in one's country high rates of investment in the engineering industries without being enamoured of regional economic councils, the ministerial system of administrative control, or the collective farms.

The Soviet *strategy* of economic development includes:

1. Steep rates of capital formation;
2. Stress on allocation of resources to industry;
3. Stress, within the industrial sector, on development of those branches which have a high pay off in growth (*i.e.,* the engineering or "heavy" industries);
4. Relatively low priority for development of the so-called "non-productive" sectors of the economy (housing, trade, urban facilities) and, to a lesser extent, of agriculture, transport, and communications;
5. Widespread adoption of capital-intensive technology, particularly at levels at which such technology can most easily be implemented.

The Soviet *tools* for implementing this strategy include:

1. Centralized total planning which includes pre-eminently the central allocation of resources;
2. Unquestioning obedience to instruction from above enforced by an elaborate system of administrative and party control; [1]
3. The nationalization of practically all enterprises;
4. The collectivization of agriculture;
5. A totalitarian political system with, at its core, a quasi-military organization inappropriately called "party."

Each of these components of strategy and tools could be broken down much further and other items should, no doubt, be added. The sample given here is representative of what is involved.

Many noncommunist underdeveloped countries have the option to choose the Soviet strategy of economic development. The challenge of com-

[1] This includes the principle of economic accountability (*khozraschet*), and the principle of unity of authority (*edinonachalie*).

petitive coexistence, insofar as western economists and statesmen are concerned, consists of devising ways and means of combining that strategy with non-Soviet, nontotalitarian tools. The great challenge of the coming decades will be the ability of the West to offer the economically underdeveloped countries of the world a theory of economic development in which Soviet-type rates of growth will be combined with institutional arrangements capable of preserving the more important features of democratic processes. It is a fine question of the degree of "command" (and the manner of implementing that command) compatible with western-type democracy.

The running is good since, for all their achievements, the Soviet Union and more generally the communist world have not, as yet, produced a comprehensive theory of economic development. What they do offer is the practical Soviet example plus an increasingly strained ideology. The ideology is for the most part an incisive critique of rather passé capitalism. Both in that aspect and in its optimistic (but very general and often inaccurate) description of socialist reality and prospects, the ideology is mainly useful as an inspirational gadget, an instrument for mobilization of the masses. It is not a widely applicable theory of economic development, nor a blueprint for action. The Soviet practical example is in the nature of a package offer, not acceptable in all its details even within the communist bloc, as witness the revisionist efforts in Poland, Hungary, China and elsewhere. This revisionism consists essentially in pruning some of the more parochial Soviet arrangements.

It is impracticable in this short space to discuss both the Soviet strategy and the tools of that strategy. I shall attempt to deal only with the former—not because it is the more important but because it happens to be more attractive to many underdeveloped countries and more misunderstood in our part of the world. The enthusiasm with which some leaders of non-communist underdeveloped countries have at times approached the Soviet strategy of economic development has often led to Western reaction branding such leaders as "Marxists," an attitude neither helpful nor constructive.

SOVIET GROWTH

In spite of serious conceptual difficulties (which have been ably discussed elsewhere and, what is more significant, have been in part resolved), it is useful to evaluate Soviet economic growth by comparing it with that of the United States. The comparison is certainly of interest from the standpoint of international relations and as such is made much of in the communist world.

Gross National Product
Since 1929 (excluding "abnormal" war and purge years), the Soviet gross national product has grown at an average annual rate estimated by

various authors at between 5 and 7 per cent. The U. S. long-term annual average growth in GNP has been between 3 and 4 per cent. Between 1950 and 1958, the U. S. gross national product increased at an average annual rate of 2.9 per cent, while that of the Soviet rose at an average rate of between 6 and 7 per cent—more than double the U. S. rate.

It may validly be argued that such fine comparisons are rather illusory because of the conceptual difficulties involved. There is, however, little doubt that the Russians have managed to sustain high rates of growth and that these rates have been substantially higher than those achieved by the United States.[2]

It is still sometimes argued that such a comparison is not very instructive since the Soviets started from a much lower base, and hence any given absolute addition to output will represent a much higher *rate* of growth for the U.S.S.R. than for the United States. This argument usually has a corollary to the effect that when the Soviet GNP gets closer to that of the United States, the Soviet growth rate will tend to taper off.

I believe this argument and its corollary to be defective and dangerous. In the first place, a differential in the rate of growth of the magnitude just described will mean that the Russians will catch up with us rather rapidly, a prospect which is bound to have far-reaching repercussions in the international field. Second, the assertion that Soviet output in absolute terms is vastly inferior to ours is rapidly becoming obsolete and incorrect in a number of key industrial sectors: iron ore, steel, machine tools, coal, and lumber are cases in point. Moreover, the total Soviet annual *volume* of capital investment is presently about equal to the U. S. peak investment effort; Soviet industrial investment is presently greatly in excess of the U. S. annual industrial investment, and, since that investment is apparently efficient, the annual expansion of Soviet industrial capacity appears to be in excess of the American. In addition, the Soviet output of producers' durable equipment had, in 1959, achieved parity with the U. S. output and Soviet output of industrial producers' equipment in 1958 was equivalent in value to the U. S. peak, which was achieved in 1957.

There are, of course, fine problems of valuation to be taken into account, and these may, indeed, cause some modification in the estimates. They do not, however, invalidate the conclusion that in a number of key economic sectors the Soviet effort is at present either at par with or ahead of the relevant U. S. effort. Even in construction the U.S.S.R. in 1959 had reached a volume equal to about 70 per cent of that of the United States.

There remains the contention that the rapid growth of the Soviet economy has been a function of a given stage of development; and that

[2] The calculations of Soviet GNP growth rates are based on a sector-of-origin approach. This involves aggregating estimated increases of output in the main sectors of the economy into an index weighted according to the relative importance of the sectors in the national product in 1955.

now that this stage is over the rate of growth will tend to slacken.

It has been shown, I believe conclusively, in a series of studies by American and British economists [3] that there is no compelling reason inherent in the Soviet command economy why this should happen. The fundamental objective of that economy is power through rapid growth; this objective is formulated outside the economy—it is essentially a political decision to which economic expression is given by directing a relatively high proportion of resources to investment and by following a particular strategy of investment. There is no evidence at the present time that Soviet thinking on this score has changed appreciably. On the contrary, the evidence of the long-term plans as currently formulated points to a continuing heavy investment effort and a continuation of the growth-intensive pattern of investment. The thesis of some sort of automatic tapering off of the growth rate once a certain stage of development has been reached seems to me to be invalid if it rests on a mere projection to the circumstances of a command economy of the experience of market-oriented economies. In fact, given the rapid growth of the Soviet economy and the decision to continue that growth, the task of raising the rate of investment so as to offset any decline in the productivity of capital without excessively squeezing the consumer should become easier rather than more difficult with the years.

It may be argued that as the Soviet Union begins on an increasing scale to assume international economic responsibilities both within the communist world and outside it, the competition for resources (as between domestic investment and foreign aid) will tend to exert some drag on Soviet growth—the more so since Soviet aid predominantly takes the form of exports of producers' durable goods (including complete plants). There is some evidence that Soviet aid to China has had some such effect. A rising defense effort may also be assumed to work in this direction. These, I would suggest, are rather marginal factors. In fact, Soviet aid to the noncommunist underdeveloped countries by concentrating on a few objectives of a rather spectacular nature (steel mills, power plants, dams) may outweigh any slowing down of the Soviet rate of growth by its impact on the thinking of those largely responsible for the economic destinies of those countries. The application of the Soviet strategy of economic development abroad *via* foreign aid is certainly a more convincing and efficacious way of spreading the Soviet economic gospel than the prolix rehashing of Marx by party ideologists.

What of the United States? It is well to recall that while the Soviet Union possesses a definite set of economic objectives of which rapid growth

---

[3] See, for example: Joseph A. Kershaw, M. Gardner Clark, Walter Galenson and John M. Montias in *Study of the Soviet Economy* (Indiana University, 1961); Alec Nove, *The Soviet Economy* (Praeger, 1961); Nicolas Spulber, *The Soviet Economy* (Norton, 1962).

is in itself the most important (with increased political power and rising consumer welfare as welcome byproducts), the objectives of the American economy are much more elusive and infinitely more difficult to define. The objectives are elaborated *en marchant,* so to speak; they emerge from the constant interaction of changes in private and public consumption and the supply of investment funds. The net effect over time appears to have been a clear stress on consumer welfare; in fact, in catering to high consumption the American economy has been successful even beyond the wildest dreams of nineteenth century utopians. As it is, industrial capacity in the United States is not being fully utilized at the present time, and the question naturally arises as to the ends for which future growth is desired. Thus while noting the need for more rapid growth from an international "balance of power" standpoint, there is the further necessity of giving careful consideration to the directions which that growth should take. Perhaps the concept of planning for growth is not irrelevant in this context.

Structure of Soviet Investment

It is clearly insufficient to stop at an examination of rates of growth of gross national product, since such rates conceal significant inequalities in the rates of growth of the various components of the total product. Such differences may be important from the standpoint of the power of an economy. A disaggregation of the gross national product into the industrial and agricultural sectors reveals that Soviet industrial production in the years 1927/28 to 1940 and again from 1950 to 1958 grew at an average annual rate of roughly 9 per cent.[4] In recent years U. S. industrial output has grown at an average annual rate of about 4 per cent. I am, of course, fully aware of the inadequacy of such comparisons involving as they certainly do highly complex problems of, among others, the choice of representative periods. Whichever way one looks at it, there looms the inescapable conclusion that the Soviet rate of industrial growth has been significantly above the American, with the U. S. business cycle working to the advantage of the Soviet Union. In agriculture, however, the picture is rather different. Although conceptual difficulties here are even greater, it is fairly clear that the Soviet Union has had over the years a very hard time raising gross agricultural output at rates which would keep up with those relevant to the natural increase in population.

An explanation of these phenomena can be found in the specific pattern of the Soviet investment effort. Although it is not a complete explanation, it has, at least, the merit of pinpointing the major clues. With the exception of war years, the Russians have typically devoted well over 20 per cent of their gross national product to investment (excluding identifiable military expenditures). The significance of this is that not only

---

[4] See: Kaplan and Moorsteen, "An Index of Soviet Industrial Output," *The American Economic Review,* Vol. L, No. 3, June 1960.

has the rate of capital formation been high but it has been sustained at high levels throughout the Soviet period (war years excepted). Furthermore, within the investment sector, primacy has been given consistently to capital formation in industry. While in the United States some 50 to 60 per cent of total investment is typically allocated to housing, services, and socio-cultural projects, in the Soviet Union the proportion of these is nearer one-third. Taking the period 1950-1959, and on the basis of 1955 U. S. dollars, the share of industry in total U. S. capital investment has been about 30 per cent, while the share of industry in total Soviet capital investment has been about 50 per cent. Moreover, within industrial investment, the Russians have overwhelmingly stressed acquisition of equipment in those branches in which pay off is high in terms of growth, *i.e.,* in the producers' goods branches. Of total industrial investment in that period, only 10 to 15 per cent was allocated to the consumer goods industries. It is only fair to point out that in view of the rapidly rising absolute amount of GNP, the Russians will be able to raise consumption in the coming decade by about 5 per cent per year, without devoting any larger share of their total resources to the consumer sector.

With this in mind, it is possible to conclude that in view of the much more lopsided pattern of capital formation in the U.S.S.R. as compared with the United States, the Soviet economy has over the years exhibited relatively high rates of growth and rather low consumption levels, and will continue to do so for some time, while the U. S. economy has tended to show relatively high levels of consumption accompanied by modest rates of growth. It should also be added that unless American industrial investment shows a marked increase in coming years, the Soviet investment effort in the 1960's is very likely to be double that of the United States.

From a western standpoint, the outstanding weakness of the Soviet economy may appear to be its relative neglect of the consumer. It is, however, important to remember that from the standpoint of underdeveloped countries this argument loses much of its force. High consumption of the U. S. type is not only difficult to picture, but it may be—in fact, is—regarded as somewhat unethical in a number of cases. The argument of high growth rates is easily grasped and internalized in the economically underdeveloped parts of the world. It should be added, parenthetically, that the Soviet consumer himself tends to compare his living standards not with those of the American consumer but with his own of ten or fifteen years ago. Such a comparison is on the whole encouraging to him.

Space limitations prevent examination of other aspects of the Soviet investment pattern and preclude touching on the problem of the changing nature of the Soviet tools of development. Since the agricultural problem in the U.S.S.R. has attracted widespread attention in our part of the world, it should perhaps be pointed out that in recent times the Russians began to make a genuine effort in this direction. The share of agriculture in total investment reached a peak in 1955 and declined somewhat thereafter. However, it continues to absorb the annual absolute increases in the volume of investment and is directed at increasing output and releasing labor for industrial employment. This is an interesting development in view of the fact that hitherto the rapid Soviet industrialization effort was accompanied by relatively modest absorption of population from agriculture. In this respect the Soviet strategy of development reveals a rather serious weakness from the standpoint of many underdeveloped countries, saddled as they are with rural overpopulation and underemployment.

EPILOGUE

A brief summary of this kind cannot, quite obviously, lead to any hard-and-fast conclusions. My purpose has been merely to raise a number of issues and, more important perhaps, to present a plea against the kind of optimistic and rather ill-informed thinking which, I suspect, is still much too common outside a narrow circle of economists and "Soviet area specialists."

Although a great deal of excellent work has been done on the Soviet economy, the knowledge so gained is still largely confined to a narrow group, while intelligent public opinion has to make do with slogans about the inevitable superiority of private enterprise backed by "healthy competition." Even though we may be convinced of the superior nature of our type of economic organization, it is certainly not out of place to understand that there is nothing inevitable about it and that its power to convince two-thirds of mankind must ultimately depend on its mettle proven in that peculiar variety of struggle known in current political jargon as "competitive coexistence."

SOVIET VIEWS

8. PEACEFUL COMPETITION: U.S.S.R.—U.S.A.*

Y. POKATAYEV

Candidate of Economic Science; Specialist on Economic Competition between the U.S.S.R. and the U.S.

Y. JOFFE

Senior Scientific Staff Member, Institute of Economy, U.S.S.R. State Planning Committee

THE MEANING OF ECONOMIC COMPETITION

"When I really feel gloomy I think that five years from now they will be obviously superior to us in every area. But when I am optimistic I feel it will take ten years for them to achieve this position."

J. B. WIESNER, PROFESSOR AT THE
MASSACHUSETTS INSTITUTE OF TECHNOLOGY

Walter Lippmann, commentator of the *New York Herald Tribune,* once said that the challenge to competition with the Soviet Union appeared on the horizon of the United States only in the mid-1950's.

He was wrong. The capitalist countries were challenged to this competition immediately after the victory of the socialist revolution in Russia. It is something else that for a long time capitalism did not take up this challenge, pretending not to notice it.

But capitalism inevitably had to accept this challenge, because it is a challenge made by history, a challenge made by progress. It is a product not of ill-will on the part of the Communists, but of the eternal striving for a better life, and better forms of social organisation.

* Excerpts reprinted from Y. Pokatayev and Y. Joffe, *Peaceful Competition: U.S.S.R.—U.S.A.* (published by Soviet Booklets, London, Jan., 1963), by permission of the publisher.

It would be wrong to assume that this is the first case in history of coexistence and competition between differing social and economic systems. Long before the birth of socialism the slave system and feudalism, and later feudalism and capitalism existed side by side. The present opponents of socialism would do well to recall the indignation with which the supporters of monarchy received bourgeois revolutions, with what contempt the nobility and the clergy treated the "upstarts", the capitalists. Yet though tradition and power were on the side of the former it was the capitalists who won. Why?

Because the capitalist system of economy proved more efficient. It made possible the development of human society, science, technology and culture much faster than under feudalism.

Capitalism, however, is far from being an ideal system of society. Insecurity and unemployment, crises and anarchy of production, corruption and general moral degradation—these are intrinsic features of capitalism, which long ago made intelligent people think and impelled humanity to search for more rational and humane forms of organisation. These explorations first led to the birth of the doctrine of socialism and then to the establishment of socialist parties, the struggle for the socialist revolution and finally to the formation of socialist states.

When the Soviet Union set out to lay the foundations of a planned economy, the principal capitalist countries were far ahead of it in the development of the productive forces. The United States, Britain, France and Germany had diversified integrated economies; they had accumulated large resources of metal, equipment, buildings and houses, and had built up their transport facilities and trade. In other words, history gave the capitalist economy a lead of many years.

This complicated the task of socialism, because at first it had to overtake the capitalist countries in the economic sphere. Perhaps that is the reason why spokesmen of the capitalist world for a long time tried "not to notice" the challenge of socialism. But it was there, whether they wanted it or not.

At the end of 1958, the British journal *Economist* wrote that the Communists have a very strong faith in the future. The slogan of overtaking the United States was formulated already at the time when Soviet industry was in its infancy. Only in recent years did this slogan lose the semblance of complete infeasibility.

Acceptance of slogans is up to people, of course. Some accept them, others do not. But even if there had been no slogans at all, competition between the Soviet Union and the United States would have taken place just the same, because it is an objective process that does not depend on the will or desires of people.

When two differing social systems exist side by side they inevitably compete to prove their superiority. The principal part is played by economic competition, because ultimately the system which gives the people more of the good things of life and satisfies their requirements more fully, is the better system.

And so, economic competition between socialism and capitalism is an objective historical process, in the course of which countries belonging to different systems demonstrate their potentialities in developing the productive forces, in raising the standard of living of the people, in advancing science, technology and culture.

The term "threat" has recently become a vogue-word with western economists and political leaders when discussing the economic competition between the Soviet Union and the United States. This word is used to frighten people.

But is an expansion of production and improvement of the living standards of the people a threat? Do not measures which improve the people's welfare benefit them? It is only the capitalists who will have to give up part of their profits to improve the lot of the people that may be the losers in the course of economic competition.

Competition in raising the living standards of the people requires tremendous resources and efforts. It is incompatible with war preparations which require huge outlays that burden the working people, on the one hand, and poison their lives and make the future uncertain, on the other. Consequently, economic competition must be peaceful and preclude any business based on war or war preparations.

The socialist countries are vitally interested in developing and strengthening peaceful forms of coexistence between the two different social systems. From the first days of the October Revolution, Lenin pointed out, ". . . our attention and all our efforts were concentrated on achieving a transition from relations of war with the capitalist countries to peaceful and trade relations".

Coexistence and peaceful economic competition have nothing in common with the cold war, as some leaders in the West claim. In this competition, the Soviet Union and the other socialist countries aim to demonstrate in practice the colossal opportunities which socialism brings the working people. This aim cannot be achieved by a trade war, economic blockade, the arms race, or by inflicting harm on the people in the capitalist countries. The only thing needed is peace and good-neighbourly relations among the peoples.

Western economists often say that the Soviet Union seeks to overtake the United States because the American level of development is the highest achievement of mankind and, moreover, the things the Soviet Union seeks to attain have already been achieved in the United States.

This is untrue. Having entered into competition with the United States, the Soviet Union regards its own achievement of the American level of economic growth merely as a stage in building communist society, because this level is certainly not the limit of advance of the productive forces.

At the Twenty-First Congress of the C.P.S.U., N. S. Khrushchev said: "We are competing with America, but we do not regard America as a standard of economic development. . . . When we win in this economic competition with the United States, we shall only have completed the initial phase of the building of communism. The economic level reached in this phase will not be the end of our road, but only a halfway station, at which we shall overtake capitalism's most developed country, leave it behind and push ahead."

At the Twenty-Second Congress, the Communist Party of the Soviet Union outlined the prospects of the country's economic development in 1961-80 and adopted the new Programme of the C.P.S.U., the programme of building communism which ensures society an abundance of the good things of life.

Specifying the dates of our future progress we say: by the end of the 1960's the Soviet Union will exceed any capitalist country for the level of economic development. But this is not the ultimate goal of the Soviet people. They look farther ahead, they want and will achieve more. The main aim, the main economic task of the Soviet Union is to build the material and technical basis of communism.

A DECISIVE STAGE

"Two generations ago people debated the question whether a socialist economy could possibly work. History removed that question from the agenda. The last generation changed the question to whether the Soviet economy could work at all efficiently. . . . My discussion takes for granted that the Soviet economy is reasonably efficient."

J. BERLINER, AMERICAN ECONOMIST,
SYRACUSE UNIVERSITY.

The economic competition of the two systems began with the victory of the Great October Revolution. But it proceeded under quite unequal conditions for the competing sides. The Soviet Union inherited an extremely backward economy from tsarism. At the same time the capitalist world spared no effort in raising obstacles to the economic development of the land of Soviets. The young Soviet republic was subjected to the military intervention of the biggest Western powers (the United States, Britain, France, etc.) who sought to destroy the state of the workers and peasants who had just overthrown the monarchy. Having failed to achieve their ends by force of arms, the imperialist countries continued the struggle against the Soviet Union by economic means, intensifying the economic blockade which was introduced during the period of military intervention in 1918-22. In these conditions the Soviet people had to deny themselves many things in order to restore the national economy with their own hands, by their heroic labour and without any outside help, and to begin closing the gap which separated young Soviet Russia from the leading capitalist countries. It is clear what tremendous efforts the Soviet people had to exert to overcome these handicaps.

The Soviet Union made a gigantic leap from backwardness to progress, becoming a country with a powerful industry, advanced science and high culture.

In 1913, Russia was a poor country with a low level of economic development. It was equipped with modern machinery to an extent that was one-fourth of the British, one-fifth of the German and one-tenth of the American level. The production of machinery in Russia in 1913 was only one-fortieth that in Germany and one-thirty-third that in the United States. Russia imported more than one-third of the industrial equipment she needed. The country lacked many industries altogether.

The economic backwardness of Russia was intensified by the First World War and the Civil War which inflicted colossal damage and brought the country to the verge of economic ruin.

TABLE 1

PER CAPITA PRODUCTION IN 1913

		Russia	*U.S.A.*
Electric power k.w.h.		14	260
Coal	lb.	451	11,693
Steel	"	66	719
Cement	"	24	358
Paper	"	3.1	75.2
Cotton fabrics yards		14.1	63.25

TABLE 2

INFLUENCE OF WORLD WAR I ON THE ECONOMY OF THE U.S.S.R.
AND U.S.A.

(1920 compared with 1913 in per cent (1913 = 100)

	U.S.S.R.	*U.S.A.*
Industrial production	14	116
Electrical energy	26	277
Coal	30	115
Steel	5	135
Cement	2	108
Cotton fabrics	4	112
Agricultural production	67	117

In 1920 industrial output dropped 86 per cent as compared with the pre-war level, while in Western Europe the decline was only 22 per cent. In 1921, the Soviet Union accounted for only 0.5 per cent of the world industrial output. Such was the economic situation in the period when the socialist mode of production came into being.

The Second World War wrought colossal destruction on the Soviet economy. Direct losses caused by the destruction of property alone amounted to 680,000 million old roubles, which according to the official rate of exchange in those years, was equivalent to 170,000 million dollars, or nearly one-seventh of the present national wealth of the United States.

Notwithstanding all this, the Soviet Union in a brief period advanced to second place in the world for industrial and agricultural production and to first place in various spheres of science and technology.

To see how fast the Soviet Union is reducing its lag behind the United States let us examine the dynamics of their production in recent years. For this purpose we will take three major indices of the rate of production growth: the relative increase in output, absolute increase and the time needed for achieving a definite level of output.

In the last decade (1951-60) industrial production in the U.S.S.R. more than trebled, with the average annual rate of growth being 11.7 per cent. During the same period industrial production in the United States increased by only 45 per cent and the average annual rate of growth was 3.8 per cent.

For major items the rates of growth in the U.S.S.R. and the United States were as follows:

AVERAGE ANNUAL RATES OF GROWTH IN THE OUTPUT OF MAJOR INDUSTRIAL ITEMS IN 1954-61 (PERCENTAGE)

Item	Soviet Union	United States
Steel	8.0	−1.4
Oil	15.4	1.4
Electrical Power	11.7	6.8
Cement	15.6	2.3
Woollen fabrics	6.9	−1.8
Leather footwear	8.1	1.7
Sugar	7.4	2.6

In the 1950's a new feature came into the economic competition of the U.S.S.R. and the U.S.A.—the Soviet Union began to outstrip the United States not only for relative rates of growth but also for actual increase in output.

In 1954-61 the absolute average annual increase in the output of major industrial goods in the U.S.S.R. and the United States was as follows:

Item	Unit of measurement	Soviet Union	United States
Pig iron	Million tons	2.9	−1.1
Steel	" "	4.1	−1.3
Coal	" "	21.2	−8.4
Oil	" "	14.2	−4.8
Electric power	Million k.w.h.	22,400	44,700
Cement	Million tons	4.4	1.1
Cotton fabrics	Million square feet	159.7	648.4
Woollen fabrics	Million linear feet	60.4	−16.8
Leather footwear	Million pairs	25.5	9.8
Sugar	Thousand tons	331	87

Lastly, here is a comparison of how many years each competing side needed to raise production by the one and the same magnitude.

YEARS NEEDED TO RAISE THE OUTPUT OF VARIOUS GOODS

	United States	Soviet Union
Steel, from 27 to 65 million tons	30 years (1912-41)	10 years (1951-60)
Pig iron, from 10 to 47 million tons	38 years (1904-41)	" "
Oil, from 38 to 148 million tons	22 years (1915-36)	" "
Electric power, from 91,000 million to 220,000 million k.w.h.	21 years (1927-47)	" "
Cement, from 10 to 45 million tons	42 years (1912-53)	" "

Of course, with present-day technology it is easier to double the production of steel or electric power and less time is needed than in the 1930's or 1940's, but even making an allowance for this factor, the contrast between the time needed by the socialist economy and the capitalist economy remains great.

The gap in the provision of the population with consumer goods is being reduced at a similarly fast pace. So far the Americans are better provided with consumer goods and housing than the Soviet people, but *the standard of living in the Soviet Union is rising much faster than in the United States and for all sections of the population.*

In the last decade the correlation between the output of some consumer goods in the United States and the Soviet Union has changed as follows:

OUTPUT IN THE SOVIET UNION, PER CENT OF THE U.S. LEVEL

	1950	1960
Cotton fabrics	32.4	60.7
Woollen fabrics	36.6	132.0
Leather footwear	38.8	70.2
Refrigerators	1.2	15.5
Washing machines	0.007	27.8
TV sets	0.16	30.2

So far the lag is biggest in durable consumer goods: TV sets, refrigerators, washing machines, cars, etc. The reasons for this lag are various.

The material requirements of people can be grouped as follows: (1) food; (2) clothing and footwear; (3) housing; (4) household goods and articles that meet cultural requirements.

In the United States the satisfaction of these requirements has proceeded in a definite sequence.

The Soviet Union has to solve all these problems almost simultaneously. After the war it was essential to restore agriculture in the shortest time, to provide the people with food and industry with the necessary raw materials (cotton, wool, hides, etc.). It was necessary to solve one of the most intricate problems, which, in effect, has still not been solved in any country, the housing problem. What made this task so complicated was not only the small and neglected housing inherited from pre-revolutionary Russia. During the last war more than six million buildings were destroyed, while the rapid development of industry swiftly increased the urban population.

The Soviet Union sets itself the task of ensuring a high standard of living not only for separate groups but for the entire people—a population of 221 million or about sixty million families. To fully satisfy their requirements in durable goods, it is necessary to bring up the number of both TV sets and refrigerators in use to 60 million. This is a huge undertaking, but the task is being accomplished successfully.

Of course, when starting from scratch it is not difficult to arrive at high rates of growth. But the important thing is that the production of durable consumer goods continues to increase at higher rates as compared with other manufactured goods. In 1961, for example, total industrial output increased 9.2 per cent and the production of steel 8 per cent, while the output of TV sets rose 13 per cent, furniture 16 per cent, refrigerators 30 per cent and washing machines 44 per cent.

The American writers Pearson and Anderson write in their book *U.S.A.—Second Class Power?* that the emergence of Russia from the wheelbarrow age into the atomic age is the greatest miracle of our epoch.

What is the source of this "miracle"? Perhaps favourable market conditions for the development of the Soviet economy? No. This is denied even by such a man immune to sympathies for communism and the Soviet Union as Allen Dulles, former chief of the U.S. Central Intelligence Agency. He points out that people who minimised Soviet achievements arrived at the conclusion that there was nothing unusual in Soviet industrial progress. Such people claim that the United States had scored the same achievements at a comparative stage of development. . . . Such conclusions ignore the unusually favourable conditions which promoted the growth of the United States before the First World War. The point is, Dulles stresses, not only that these factors no longer exist in the United States, but that they have never existed for a long period in Russia.

We should add to this that of the forty-five years the Soviet state has been in existence, nearly two decades have been taken up by wars and the restoration of the war-wrecked economy, while in the United States war years have been periods of the fastest economic growth and, moreover, no enemy soldier has ever trodden American soil.

If, notwithstanding all this, the Soviet Union was able to advance to second place in the world after the United States, this once again proves that the social system in the U.S.S.R. is the source of this "miracle". The socialist system has raised the organisation of production to a qualitatively new level.

The capitalist system of economy signified a big step forward in the organisation of production. It created large enterprises with a scientific division of labour and organisation of production within them. As a result the scale of production rose sharply, labour productivity increased and costs declined. But when regarded in the light of the entire national economy, capitalism remains a system of disunited production units.

Yet, the present level of division of labour, contemporary machinery and technology of production imperatively dictate the need for organising a *single production process for the whole of society,* that is, the application of all the methods of rational management, to the economy as a whole.

This has been attained under socialism. All production units are linked together and this makes it possible to develop science and technology in a planned way, to organise the training of labour and to utilise it fully. All this, in turn, enables society to plan for five, ten and even twenty years ahead, without fearing crises or depressions. Thus, the Soviet people themselves are the makers of their future.

Having assumed the function of directing production, the socialist state at the same time undertook to protect the lives and health of the members of society, to raise the educational and cultural level.

Free medical service at home, in polyclinics and hospitals, free services at mother and child welfare centres, the provision of pensions to all aged workers, four-month maternity leaves, paid holidays, a wide network of nurseries, kindergartens, summer camps and holiday homes—all this guarantees Soviet citizens the satisfaction of their most vital needs.

Now a new decisive stage has arrived in the economic competition between the Soviet Union and the United States. . . .

SOVIET UNION—UNITED STATES, 1960

"If Soviet world power and prestige have risen so high on such a relatively small economic base compared to ours, one can only look forward with foreboding . . ."

HARRY SCHWARTZ, FROM THE REPORT OF THE JOINT ECONOMIC COMMITTEE OF THE U.S. CONGRESS.

Calculations of the time which the Soviet Union needs to reach first place in the world for level of production do not involve magic. They are understandable and accessible to everyone.

If you want to find out how much time you need to overtake a man who is ahead you have to establish

(1) The distance separating you.

(2) The speed at which you are both travelling.

This is also the case in the present competition. What is the distance separating the U.S.S.R. from the United States as regards *volume of production?* Statistical organisations of the Soviet Union have made the following calculations. They established how much coal, electric power, footwear, fabrics, motor vehicles, etc., are produced in the U.S.S.R. and the United States. These figures were collected for 400 major industrial items. Then the prices of these items were estimated, taking into account the differences in quality. These 400 items do not cover the entire output of industry which produces hundreds of thousands of items. Only the principal, decisive and most representative goods were taken, goods which make up more than 50 per cent of the total value of industrial output. The value of these items was calculated twice: in Soviet prices and in American prices. In both cases the same results were obtained—the volume of Soviet industrial production was 60 per cent of the United States level.[1] The population of the United States is approximately 20 per cent smaller than that of the U.S.S.R. (18 per cent to be more exact). Consequently, per capita production in the U.S.S.R. now amounts to 50 per cent of the U.S. level.

At the plenary meeting of the Central Committee of the C.P.S.U., held in November 1962, Nikita Khrushchev pointed out that the growth of industrial production exceeds the planned targets for the 7-year plan. In

---

[1] It should be pointed out that one recent American study estimated the 1960 industrial output of the Soviet Union as 75 percent of the U.S. level. See: Alexander Tarn and Robert W. Campbell, "A Comparison of U.S. and Soviet Industrial Output," *American Economic Review*, LII, September, 1962, pp. 703-727. For a similar estimate see Peter Wiles, "Economic Growth," *Survey*, April, 1963, p. 82. [Editor's note.]

the first four years of the period (1959-62), the following had been produced over and above the targets: textiles—1,400 million yards; knitted goods—189 million articles; leather footwear—88 million pairs; TV sets—617,000; washing machines—413,000, and so on. At the same time Khrushchev pointed out the need for "additional measures to be taken to accelerate the production of consumer goods".

It was relatively easy to calculate the volume of agricultural production in the U.S.S.R. and the United States because twenty to twenty-five commodities (grains, industrial crops, animal products, vegetables and fruit, etc.) account for 90-95 per cent of the total value of agricultural production. These calculations showed that the level of agricultural production in the U.S.S.R. was about 75-80 per cent of the U.S. level and per capita production about 70 per cent of the U.S. level.

Thus, in 1960 the U.S.S.R. produced almost 20 per cent of the world industrial output and approximately 60 per cent of the level of industrial output in the United States. . . .

ON WHOSE SIDE IS TIME?

"Continuation of their rapid industrial growth makes increasingly credible the Soviet claims for overtaking the U.S. levels of industrial production at some future date."

JOHN HARDT, FROM A REPORT OF THE JOINT
ECONOMIC COMMITTEE OF THE U.S. CONGRESS.

The next problem is the correlation of the rates of growth of production in the Soviet Union and the United States.

To determine the rates of growth for the United States it is necessary to use past records. What period should be taken as a basis for such calculations? Here the most diverse suppositions can be made. We think that the United States will probably develop at the same rate as in the past eight years, after the end of the Korean war. The following are the points in favour of such a supposition.

This was a normal, typical period for American industry. There were no wars or other outside circumstances to influence the industrial rates of growth.

During this period there were two recessions in the United States: in 1954 and in 1958. In 1961 the growth rate was 1 per cent. This, of course, was not much, but production increased and did not decline. In general, in the past 100 years there were sixty-five years of growth and thirty-five years of decline. In other words, on the average, for every three years there was one year of recession. The proportion was about the same in the last eight years.

Some American economists claim that American industry in the 1960's will grow at an annual rate of 3 and even 4 per cent. Is this correct?

True, during the Second World War U.S. industry developed at a fast pace. At the beginning of the war the United States had huge reserves of productive capacity, colossal stocks of raw materials and fuel and millions of unemployed which, coupled with a swift rise in the demand, ensured high rates of growth. But there are no grounds for expecting the United States to be able to increase the growth rates by half or to double them as compared with the last eight years.

The home market in the United States is restricted by the slow growth of effective demand of the population. Big hopes were placed in military expenditure, but they were not justified. Moreover, in future an ever greater part of the military appropriations will go for research and for missiles. But such outlays cannot provide an impetus for the expansion of all production.

Hopes for an expansion of foreign trade are similarly groundless. In general exports do not play a big part in the U.S. economy. In face of the keen struggle for markets which flared up in recent years, the United States has no grounds for expecting an increase of exports big enough to bring about a telling increase of output.

Thus, it will be more proper to hold that rates of growth in the United States most likely will remain the same as in the last eight years, that is 2.3 per cent annually (during the entire post-war period—1945-61 —the rate was 1.8 per cent). Even if we assume that in future this rate would increase somewhat, to 2.5 per cent annually on the average, in 1961-70 industrial output in the United States will increase by 28 per cent and in 20 years by 65 per cent.

During the past eight years agricultural production increased at a rate of 2 per cent annually. If this rate is preserved production will grow by 22 per cent in ten years and by 45 per cent in twenty years.[1] We proceed from the assumption that the level of agricultural production in the United States is considerably above the effective demand and expect the efforts of the government to curtail production to be successful.

What will be the economic rates of growth in the U.S.S.R.?

Most Western economists do not deny the high growth rates in the Soviet Union. But many of them (Rostow, Nutter, Allen in the United States, Klaus in West Germany and others) claim that these rates do not depend on the social and political system in the Soviet Union, are not connected with the public ownership of the means of production in our country but are explained by the stage of development at which the U.S.S.R. now stands. High rates of growth they assert, are inherent in the initial phases of industrial development. But when a country becomes highly industrialised, like the United States or Britain, growth rates fall sharply. That is why the Soviet Union too, in their opinion, faces low growth rates and periodic recessions in future.

[1] The 20-year figure should be 49 per cent. [Editor's note.]

"Your future," they say, "is our present . . ."

To begin with, all supporters of this "theory" carefully avoid analysing the continuity of production growth in the socialist countries and
the cyclical development of the economy in the capitalist countries. But how
can one speak seriously about rates of growth without examining the
problem of continuity of development. In the message on the country's
economic situation, sent by President Kennedy to the U.S. Congress in January 1961, he pointed out that of the fifteen post-war years the United States
spent seven years in recessions and recovery after recessions.

The same cyclical development prevailed in the past in the countries
which are now building socialism. Czechoslovakia had seven years of
recession and stagnation between 1921 and 1938 when it was a capitalist
country, yet in the sixteen post-war years it has not known a single year of
recession. This equally applies to Poland, Hungary, Rumania, and to any
country which has taken the socialist road.

If the rates of growth depend on the stage of development, then, evidently there must have been periods in the history of the United States
when it developed as fast as the U.S.S.R. is developing now? But it is impossible to find such periods in the history of the United States. It is twenty
years since the United States reached the level of production at which the
U.S.S.R. stands now. What were the rates of growth of the United States
in 1930-40? About 1 per cent annually! Suppose the United States reached
the present level of the Soviet Union not twenty or twenty-five years, but
thirty years ago? Can we name a period in the history of the United States
when it developed at the rates usual for the Soviet Union—10 per cent
annually? Even in the best and remotest times these rates over a prolonged
period have never exceeded 5 per cent annually in the United States. . . .

It is known that in the U.S.S.R., agriculture has lagged behind the
requirements of the economy, and its progress has been subjected to severe
and just criticism. This, of course, does not mean that Soviet agriculture
is in a state of stagnation or decline. In 1954-61 agricultural production
increased at an annual rate of 6 per cent as compared with 2 per cent of
the United States.

But these rates do not suit the Soviet Union. Why? First of all because
they do not meet the country's requirements which are swiftly rising in view
of the rapid growth of cities and industry. These rates also do not correspond to the possibilities inherent in large-scale socialist agriculture
equipped with modern machinery.

Energetic steps are now being taken to bring up the rates of growth of
agriculture to those of industry, that is to raise them from 6 per cent to
9-10 per cent annually.

Some Western economists think that Soviet industrial rates of growth
will slow down in view of the increase in the volume of production. . . .

What is true in such arguments? Is there a connection between the level of production and rates of growth? There is. It is manifested in that the bigger the level of production, the more efforts a country has to exert with the *given technology* to maintain high rates of growth. We stress: with the given technology. This is the crux of the matter.

If the technique of production and construction were to stand still, there would be much truth in such arguments. But technology marches ahead and what yesterday seemed a dream is reality today.

Here is an example. Before the last war it was held, and rightly so, that steel production in the Soviet Union could grow by 2-3 million tons annually. Not that the Soviet Union could not build furnaces with a bigger capacity. But if you build open-hearth or Bessemer furnaces with a capacity of 2-3 million tons, you at the same time must build blast furnaces of corresponding capacity, increase the production of coke for open-hearth and blast furnaces, expand the capacity of coal mines, iron ore mines, the capacity of rolling mills, the capacity of the engineering and other metal-consuming industries.

But in post-war years technology has made a big step forward and at present, even taking into account the definite "chain reaction" which an increase in steel production sets off, it can be raised annually not by 2-3 million tons, but by 5-6 million tons. It took two or three years to build a blast furnace before the war, while now the job is completed in six months. The sinking of mines and collieries has also been accelerated several times over. Thus, within a few years it will be possible, without any great complications, to commission annually capacities for 15-20 million tons, although today this task is beyond the strength of any country.

The experience of the U.S.S.R. shows that as production grows and technology progresses the possibilities for increasing output are multiplied. A bigger volume of production cannot be an obstacle to maintaining high rates of economic growth in future as well.

A LOOK INTO THE FUTURE

"Between now and 1970 a decisive test will take place."
W. W. ROSTOW, AMERICAN ECONOMIST.

Taking into account the increase in the country's labour resources, the available material resources, the scale of new construction, the introduction of new technology and many other factors influencing the scale of production, Soviet planners have calculated that in 1970 industrial production in the U.S.S.R. will rise approximately 2.5 times as compared with 1960.

Consequently, since Soviet industrial production in 1960 was 60 per cent of the U.S. level, in 1970 it will amount to 150 per cent (60 × 2.5), or 50 per cent higher than the present U.S. level.

During this period industrial output in the United States will grow by 28 per cent. Since the population of the Soviet Union will be about 20 per cent greater than in the United States and since Soviet industrial output will be bigger than that in the United States by the same 20 per cent, it may be assumed that by approximately 1970 the U.S.S.R. will exceed the United States in per capita industrial production as well.

Of course, American industry may develop somewhat faster than we expect (or perhaps slower) and then the date will be shifted by one or two years in either direction. But this is of no essential importance: on the scale of history this in infinitesimal.

In agriculture the Soviet Union will surpass the United States for total production in 1961-70 and also for per capita output of major agricultural products. True, for some commodities (fruit and citrus fruit) the lag will continue for a certain time, but later it, too, will be ended.

By 1980 industrial production in the U.S.S.R. should rise six times as compared with 1960 and exceed the present level of the United States 3.6 times. Should U.S. industrial output reach 65 per cent above the present level by 1980 the Soviet Union would then exceed the American level twice over.

By 1980 Soviet industrial production will be 20 per cent higher than in all the countries of the world at present and almost twice as high as in all the non-socialist countries today.

TOTAL SOVIET INDUSTRIAL OUTPUT IN 1980 AS COMPARED
WITH THE INDUSTRIAL OUTPUT OF ALL THE COUNTRIES OF THE
NON-SOCIALIST WORLD IN 1960

Item	Unit of measurement	U.S.S.R. in 1980	Non-Socialist World in 1960
Electric power	Million kwh	2,700,000-3,000,000	1,870,000
Oil	Million tons	690-710	889
Coal	" "	1,180-1,200	1,083
Steel	" "	250	239
Mineral fertilisers	" "	125-135	74
Synthetic resins and plastics	" "	19-21	6.5
Cement	" "	233-235	227
Fabrics	" square feet	214,000-235,000	406,000
Grain	" tons	300-315	550
Wool	" "	1.0-1.1	2.0
Raw cotton	" "	10-11	21
Sugar beet	" "	98-108	76
Potatoes	" "	156	133
Milk	" "	170-180	245
Meat	" "	30-32	40

Such are the prospects for the near future. . . .

The economic competition between the U.S.S.R. and the United States is not only in the interests of the Soviet people. Undoubtedly it is they, above all, who will gain from the effort to achieve a higher economic development than the United States and, ultimately, a higher living standard. But the American people, too, will be the gainers.

Soviet people are confident of victory, not because they hope for catastrophic upheavals in the U.S. economy, but because they are deeply convinced of the advantages of communist society. Should U.S. leaders in the course of the competition devote more attention to the development of a peaceful economy and not to war production, this would only be welcomed by the Soviet people.

Peaceful economic competition can ease the international situation and help normalise relations between the Soviet Union and the United States.

At present U.S. ruling circles have, to all intents and purposes, banned Soviet-American trade relations. But this has no adverse effect on the Soviet Union. It had concluded long-term trade agreements with Italy, Britain, West Germany and other European countries to supply the goods they need and, in turn, to buy what it needs. Businessmen of these countries are farsighted. They are strengthening trade relations with the U.S.S.R., well aware that with a slowing-down in business activity and keener struggle for markets, such relations are very advantageous to them.

The expansion of trade relations between the U.S.S.R. and the United States would strengthen the U.S. economy, create an additional market for a number of American goods which cannot be sold at home, would load up plants, and reduce unemployment. This would help create the calm and businesslike atmosphere in the world which is so lacking at present.

Economic competition is of benefit to both the Soviet and American peoples, because it is bound up with peaceful coexistence. Economic competition is peaceful competition and hence states will be able to use the funds now designated for military purposes as an additional source of expansion of peaceful production.

In the course of this competition the peoples will be able to judge which social system is the better.

"Supplement" to B. The Controversial CIA Report: A New Assessment of Soviet Economic Strength

9. SOVIET ECONOMIC PROBLEMS MULTIPLY *

CENTRAL INTELLIGENCE AGENCY

In the past few years, Moscow's aggressive foreign policy has been accompanied by boasts of overtaking and surpassing US production by 1970, thus in Khrushchev's words, defeating capitalism without war. However, an analytical review of recent Soviet economic performance compared with that of the US supports just the opposite conclusion—namely, that the Soviet Union is falling behind in the economic race.

The first years of Khrushchev's leadership were marked by a series of successes. The expansion of planted acreage through the New Lands program gave agriculture its first real lift since 1937. Economic growth was rapid—probably better than 6 percent a year for the 1950-59 period as a whole, aided by cuts in armed forces personnel and in military spending which took place in 1956 and 1957.

While housing continued to be very tight, there were noticeable improvements in living standards, particularly in foodstuffs but also in consumer goods as compared with the late Stalin years.

After 1959, however, economic growth began to slow appreciably. The rate of expansion of fixed investments, upon which growth depends, was not maintained. With annual increases in investment cut in half, falling to between 4 and 5 percent in 1962-63, a sharp curtailment in economic growth was inevitable. In 1962, Soviet gross national product was about $260 billion, or 47 percent of that of the US. Because the differ-

---

* Reprinted from the published CIA summary statement of Jan. 9, 1964 by permission of the Central Intelligence Agency.

ences in the rate of growth have narrowed, little change in this proportion is expected over the next few years.

To a great extent Soviet economic difficulties stem from a series of programs too ambitious for available resources. With a gross national product less than half that of the US, the Soviet leadership has invested in new plant and equipment amounts nearly as large as investment in the US and has maintained a military-space program approaching in real cost that of the US.

Much of the blame for recent reductions in the rate of growth falls on the sharp increase in Soviet defense spending, which between 1959 and 1963 increased by about one-third. However, the problem centers less on the total size of defense outlays than on the diversion of scarce, critical resources—both manpower and materials. The military "bite" was particularly severe on the best scientific and engineering talent, on the most skilled construction specialists, and on the associated high-quality materials and components. The costs of increased military efforts showed up in shortfalls in industrial investment, especially in the chemicals industry, and in the gross underfulfillment of the Soviet plan for automation and modernization in industry.

Although the slowdown in industrial output has had its effect, the serious decline in economic growth in 1962 and 1963 is largely due to the failures in agriculture.

A necessary corollary of the headlong rush to develop heavy industry was the neglect of agriculture. Starved for investment funds, agriculture was faltering badly by the time Stalin died. Khrushchev succeeded, at very small cost, in temporarily reversing the downward trend. The New Lands put more grain into Soviet stomachs, into livestock, and into foreign markets—perhaps most importantly from the standpoint of political stability, into the European Satellite countries to make up deficits in their own laggard farm output. But the returns from the vast new acreage plowed up in 1955-58 proved to be temporary. Once the original soil moisture and fertility were used up, output fell off. In 1963, a severe drought in the traditional farming areas, as well as in Kazakhstan and Siberia, resulted in a near disaster. Output on a per capita basis in 1963 was about 10 percent below that of 1958. Total agricultural output declined some 4 percent in 1962 and probably more than 4 percent in 1963.

The plight of Soviet agriculture is further illustrated by the composition of the Soviet diet. In total calories, the average Russian citizen is not far behind his American counterpart. But 70 percent of the Soviet diet consists of grain and potatoes, compared to 28 percent in the U.S. Only 25 percent of the Soviet diet consists of quality foods—livestock products, vegetables, and fruits.

The impact of a short grain crop on this pattern of diet is obvious. Bread for human consumption must be curtailed. Livestock herds must be reduced. There is plenty of recent evidence on the disappearance of flour from stores, of distress slaughtering of livestock, and of the elimination of free bread from factory cafeterias.

The revolution of rising expectations applies in the Soviet Union as well as in other parts of the world and Khrushchev recognizes this is a more serious problem for his regime than it was in Stalin's day. Rising food prices, shortages of meat and bread, a decline in housing construction, and small gains in the output of consumer durables are sources of growing consumer dissatisfaction.

The Soviet leaders are now calling for a solution to the agricultural problem and for a faster increase in certain consumer goods through the expansion of the chemical and related industries. They appear determined to commit the very substantial resources required. As formally presented by Khrushchev on 9 December at the Central Committee plenum, the new program calls for tripling production of chemicals by 1970. Among the specific goals of the program are production increases in fertilizers from 20 million tons to 70 million to 80 million tons in 1970.

Khrushchev apparently recognizes that the needs of this new program will clash with those of other claimants. He has implied that the resources earmarked for the expansion of the chemical industry will come in part from the overall growth of the economy, from imports, and from the diversion of funds from communal services and housing construction. He has also noted the need to study possible reductions in the strength of the armed forces.

Although the Soviet economy, given more favorable agricultural weather, may be able to rebound from last year's growth of 2.5 percent, the prospects for recovery to a sustained growth rate equal to that of the 1950's are not bright.

In an attempt to maximize industrial investment, the Soviet Union is turning to the West for greatly expanded credits and far more liberal repayment terms than the present 5 years. Moscow's gold position today is viewed as little better than minimal, with reserves of less than $2 billion.

A chronic inability to generate enough exports to the West to cover rising imports has resulted in a continuous drain on gold balances. Soviet gold sales in 1963 amounted to $400 million to $500 million, compared with recent annual production of about $150 million to $175 million— production which incidentally is very high cost even by Soviet standards.

The accelerated outflow of gold in 1963-64 is a direct response to the payment requirements generated by purchasing nearly 10 million tons of grain in the Free World. The import requirements for chemical machinery and equipment, largely to produce fertilizers, will exceed several hundred million dollars a year, and could be $2 billion in total.

Hence, the current Soviet push for new foreign credits and extended repayment terms is directly related to Moscow's desire to prevent the chemical program from impinging too directly on the production of military end items. In 1962-63, new medium-term credits from the industrial West amounted to about $300 million annually. However, payments on principal and interest for past loans left only a small net balance in 1963. With the growth of traditional Russian exports slowing down or declining in virtually all major categories—petroleum, timber, grain—increased credits represent the only promising means of financing substantially larger imports of machinery.

While the Soviets have been seeking larger credits from the West, the cost of their own economic aid program to the less developed countries also has been steadily rising. New extensions of credit in 1963 did not exceed $200 million, compared with more than $800 million in 1959; however, drawings against Soviet credits have continued to increase, approaching $400 million in 1963 (exclusive of drawings against military credits).

In summary, the Kremlin leadership for several years has been trying to do too much with too few resources. This living on borrowed capital, improvising cheap but temporary solutions to basic problems such as agriculture, and chronically neglecting balanced development to push ahead spectacularly on a narrow range of goals has finally caught up with the Soviet Union. A nearly disastrous crop failure in 1963 was not the root cause of Moscow's current economic difficulties; what it did was to bring to a head the many underlying problems of the Soviet economy and force a reconsideration of the pattern of resource allocation.

WESTERN VIEWS

10. SOVIET ECONOMIC PERFORMANCE: THE CIA REPORT RE-EXAMINED *

HARRY G. SHAFFER

The University of Kansas

In a sensational news release on January 9, 1964, the U.S. Central Intelligence Agency painted a rather dismal picture of the Soviet Union's economic performance and prospects, ascribing her economic difficulties primarily to failures in agriculture, to the diversion of scarce resources for increased defense expenditures and, in general, to "a series of programs too ambitious for available resources." The center and the most controversial part of the news release (which was reportedly based on a study by CIA Soviet area specialists) was the assertion that the Soviet growth rate dropped from "probably better than 6 percent a year" during the 1950's [1] to 2½ percent in 1963.

Since the CIA did not back up its assertions with supporting evidence and failed to indicate how the figures had been computed, the motives, objectivity, and correctness of the reports have been challenged abroad as well as in the United States. A very few non-U.S.-government experts have lent support to the CIA study (for example Peter Wiles of Brandeis University [2] and G. Warren Nutter of the University of Virginia [3]) but the

---

* Reprinted from the *Kansas Business Review*, August, 1964, by permission of the publisher.

[1] In Congressional hearings the average annual growth rate of the USSR from 1950-1960 was given as 6.8 percent. See Stanley H. Cohn, "The Gross National Product in the Soviet Union: Comparative Growth Rates," *Dimensions of Soviet Economic Power,* Hearings, Joint Economic Committee, Congress of the United States, Dec. 10 and 11, 1962, p. 75.

[2] Peter Wiles' study was referred to in *The New York Times* of Feb. 10, 1964. This author had the opportunity to see the full-length study in which Wiles reached the conclusion that the Soviet growth rate in 1963 was only 1 percent. Without going into the mathematics of his computations, it should be stated that they are based on such highly questionable assumptions as assigning to a cow a weight equal to two pigs or four sheep and include entire columns of figures labelled "guessed."

[3] In a Radio Free Europe Special from Washington, dated February 19, 1964, Nutter was reported to have testified at hearings conducted by the House of Representatives Subcommittee on Europe that Russia's *industrial* growth has been even less than estimated by the CIA.

majority of Western academicians have at least doubted if not outright denied the validity of the CIA's conclusions. For instance, Nicholas Spulber of City College, New York City said that he was "baffled" and "just cannot believe it" [4]; Robert Campbell of Indiana University commented that the difference between the present and the previous CIA estimates was "fantastic" [5]; and Werner Klatt of the Royal Institute of International Affairs, London, considered the CIA growth rate figure of 2½ percent "highly improbable." [6] In a somewhat more cautious vein, Warren Eason of Syracuse University stated incredulously that he would have to look at the report "long and hard"; Abram Bergson of Harvard University expressed surprise but felt that he could not rule it out completely; and Herbert Levine, at present also at Harvard University, was "very surprised" but "not too skeptical," [7] and he counseled Americans to "be cautious when they interpret statistics on the Soviet economy released . . . by the Central Intelligence Agency." [8]

University professors were not the only ones critical of the CIA findings. For instance, Leon Herman, Senior Specialist on Soviet Affairs at the Library of Congress, warned that "we must avoid extremes; we tend to either describe them as four feet tall or eight feet tall," [9] and a Washington correspondent reported that the CIA's news briefing "raised so many protests and eyebrows here that the move is unlikely to be repeated for a long, long time." [10] *The* (London) *Economist* held that "the validity and also the consistency of some of the figures can be seriously challenged" [11]; a correspondent reported from London that British Intelligence disagreed not only with the CIA's conclusions but even with some of the factual estimates [12]; another correspondent at United Nations headquarters in New York disclosed that "a sampling of opinion among delegates . . . indicates . . . considerable scepticism" [13]; and, according to Soviet sources, a *New York Herald Tribune* correspondent wrote from Geneva that "the CIA facts have not been accepted in Europe." [14]

Soviet reaction to the CIA Report was as could have been expected: The CIA statements were referred to as simply "another anti-Soviet fabrica-

[4] Harry Schwartz, *The New York Times,* Jan. 9, 1964.
[5] *Ibid.*
[6] Werner Klatt, "Output and Utilization of Foodstuffs in the Soviet Union," Paper delivered at the International Symposium on *Soviet Agriculture: The Great Debate,* on February 21, 1964, at the Institute for the Study of the USSR, Munich.
[7] The last three comments were reported by Harry Schwartz, *op. cit.*
[8] *The Christian Science Monitor,* Jan. 13, 1964.
[9] Bernard Gwertzman, *The Washington Evening Star,* Jan. 17, 1964.
[10] Tom Lambert, *Herald Tribune,* Jan. 13, 1964.
[11] Jan. 18, 1964, p. 189.
[12] Flora Lewis, *Washington Post,* Jan. 19, 1964.
[13] Earl Foell, *The Christian Science Monitor,* Jan. 11, 1964.
[14] *Moscow News,* Feb. 8, 1964.

tion," [15] and as a "concoction of the country's major political organization" which "even the American press could not swallow" [16]; the CIA was accused of "misleading the American taxpayer who finances it," and it was asserted that the Agency had once again "made a laughing stock of America." [17] Khrushchev, at the February Plenum of the Central Committee of the CPSU, had this to say about what he called the "ill-fated 'documents' of the U.S. Central Intelligence Agency":

What can we say on this point? Well, Messrs. imperialists, you indulge in whatever illusions you like: we don't care about it one way or another. Things must be pretty bad for you if you have to resort to such deceptions. You want to impress on the peoples of your countries that socialism isn't as good as they say. But there are people all over the globe—and their number is rising all the time—who are beginning to see clearly what socialism is bringing to man, what heights the development of productive forces is soaring to under socialism.[18]

There seems to be little disagreement, even in the English-speaking world, that the motives which induced the CIA to grant the first general news briefing in its history were primarily political in nature. The CIA's purpose was labeled as "unashamedly propagandistic," [19] and the figures released by the Agency as "suspect . . . presented for political reasons no less brazenly than Khrushchev's boasting." [20] It was asserted that "the task which the CIA has cut out for itself . . . is to convince manufacturers and bankers in Western Europe that Russia is a poor credit risk," [21] and that even "American businessmen regard the CIA estimates as largely aimed at trying to discourage Europeans from extending credit to the Communists." [22] Other observers saw the CIA's "maiden venture into publicity" as an attempt to "improve the agency's public 'image,' somewhat spattered by its roles in the Bay of Pigs Cuban incident and in South Vietnam," [23] or, alternately, as an attempt to "tarnish an 'image' of the Soviet Union in underdeveloped countries." [24]

While the CIA's decision to grant its first press interview at this strategic moment has certainly not been devoid of political motives, it should in all fairness be pointed out that not all previous CIA research

[15] Moscow Radio Broadcast in Turkish to Turkey, monitored on Jan. 10, 1964 by Radio Liberty.

[16] Moscow Radio Broadcast in English to the United Kingdom, monitored on Jan. 22, 1964 by Radio Liberty.

[17] Moscow Radio Broadcast in English to Eastern North America, monitored on Jan. 18, 1964 by Radio Liberty.

[18] *Daily Review of the Soviet Press,* Feb. 15, 1964, p. 23.

[19] Victor Zorza, *The Guardian,* Jan. 23, 1964.

[20] Edward Crankshaw, *The New York Times Magazine,* March 1, 1964.

[21] Ben Weberman, *New York Herald Tribune,* Jan. 19, 1964.

[22] Sam Dawson, *Washington Star,* Jan. 14, 1964.

[23] Tom Lambert, *Herald Tribune,* Jan. 14, 1964.

[24] Edwin Dale, *New York Times,* Jan. 9, 1964.

has been confidential or secret, and that scholarly, non-propagandistic, unclassified CIA studies on the USSR have been freely available for several years.[25] This paper will contain no speculation on the CIA's motives; rather an attempt will be made to determine what implications, if any, can be drawn from the CIA study in regard to the future prospects of Soviet economic development. First, however, the validity of the CIA Report, significantly entitled "Soviet Economic Problems Multiply," should be examined.

Although most criticism of the CIA's statistical findings was directed at the estimate of Soviet growth rates, a few preliminary words should be said on some other aspects of the Agency's report, i.e., on its comparisons of U.S. and U.S.S.R. gross national products, and on its appraisal of the extent of Soviet gold reserves and gold production.

The CIA's assessment of Soviet gross national product (GNP) as 47 percent of United States GNP is probably reasonably close, perhaps a few percentage points below most previous Western estimates.[26] Official Soviet sources give Soviet *industrial* output for 1963 as 65 percent of U.S. *industrial* output.[27] But the advantage of the United States over the Soviet Union is greater in the case of gross *national* product (which is equal to the total value of *all goods and services* produced)[28] than in the case of gross *industrial* product (which equals the total value of only the *material goods produced by industry*), partly because there are many services "produced" in the United States which a Soviet-type Socialist system would either not utilize at all or utilize only to a very limited extent (such as, for instance, the services of stockbrokers, real estate salesmen, and advertising copy writers). Exact comparisons of Soviet and United States gross national product are complicated, since Soviet national income analysis does not include a GNP concept at all, and since in Soviet national income computations only material goods but not "unproductive" services

---

[25] Among recent studies, see for instance the CIA's *Survey of Soviet Economists and Economic Research Organizations* (1960, revised 1963); *Comparisons of U.S. and Soviet Population and Manpower* (1960); *Developments in the Organization and Planning of Soviet Industry* (1961); *Recent Developments in Soviet Agriculture* (1962).

[26] Stanley H. Cohn, for instance, using geometric means of Soviet and United States quantity weights for conversion rates, arrives at a 235.5 billion current dollar figure for the USSR's 1960 GNP, as compared with 504.4 billion dollars for the United States. (See Stanley H. Cohn, *op. cit.,* p. 76.) This would make the Soviet output for 1960 46.7 percent of that of the United States, and the Soviet Union has undoubtedly gained some ground during the subsequent two-year period.

[27] See, for example, Khrushchev's address to the February 1964 Plenum of the Central Committee of the Communist Party, *Daily Review of the Soviet Press,* Feb. 15, 1964, p. 24.

[28] To be more precise GNP is a measure of the total value of all *finished* goods and *direct* services (with some exceptions such as illegal goods or the services of housewives performed in their own homes), avoiding all double counting and adjusting for changes in inventories.

are counted.[29] Comparisons are further complicated by the necessity of converting either Soviet output into dollar values or United States output into rubles, and by the fact that different results are obtained depending upon which of the methods is used.[30] Neither of these two methods is in itself more "correct" than the other, nor would the use of some type of "average" have any greater theoretical justification; but for an intelligent evaluation one should know what method the CIA used in its computation. This, unfortunately, was not disclosed.

The CIA reported present Soviet gold holdings as less than 2 billion dollars and Soviet gold production as between 150 and 175 million dollars annually. Both figures are well below previous Western estimates, which in general have ranged from 4 to 10 billion dollars for Soviet gold reserves and from 350 to 600 million dollars for per annum Soviet gold output.[31] The U.S. Bureau of Mines, for instance, estimated Soviet gold production for 1962 at about 12 million ounces, representing a value of 420 million dollars.[32] Since the CIA has failed to reveal its sources of information, it is difficult to evaluate its figures. The Soviets have ridiculed them but have not given any of their own, which has been taken by some observers as tacit consent.[33] Others have deduced from various aspects of Soviet behavior (shortage of gold teeth, the reintroduction of harsher punishments for speculation in gold, reluctance to purchase foreign goods for gold, etc.) that the CIA figures might not be too far off.[34] But all such "evidence" is

[29] Vladimir N. Starovskyi, Director of the Central Statistical Administration, USSR, computed Soviet National Income for 1963 as 60 percent of that of the United States in *Pravda,* March 14, 1964. His computations, most assuredly, have been based on the Soviet concept of "national" income. Since in the United States national income is derived from GNP (and therefore includes services) Starovskyi had to make a substantial downward adjustment in the U.S. figure in order to make it what he considered comparable to the national income of the USSR.

[30] To illustrate: Bread and potatoes, which make up a larger part of the Soviet than of the American diet, are relatively low priced in the USSR and relatively higher priced in comparison with other goods in the United States, while meat and eggs, of greater importance in the American diet, are more plentiful and cheaper in the United States. Converting, for comparison's sake, the Soviet output into dollars (which essentially answers the question: How much would the Soviet output be worth in the United States?) would therefore be relatively more favorable to the Soviet Union, while converting the U.S. output into rubles (which essentially answers the question: How much would the U.S. output be worth in the Soviet Union?) would slant the comparison towards the United States.

[31] *Neue Züricher Zeitung,* Fernausgabe, Jan. 21, 1964 in an article dealing with a report of the 1963 world gold production and supply, published by the First National City Bank of New York in the January issue of *Monthly Economic Letter.*

[32] *Wall Street Journal,* March 2, 1964.

[33] For example, Alfred Zauberman, "Soviet Economists Versus CIA," *European Service, General News Talk,* Jan. 20, 1964, p. 3.

[34] *The Economist,* Jan. 18, 1964, for instance, finds the CIA gold production figures "acceptable, on grounds of logic," but feels that the correctness of the 2 billion dollar gold reserve claim is "anyone's guess" (p. 190). Flora Lewis from the Washington Post Foreign Service, on the other hand, reports from London that the British estimates of current gold reserves coincide with the CIA's. *Washington Post,* January 19, 1964.

rather circumstantial. Once again one can only wish that the CIA had substantiated its assertions, for how else can one effectively counter the Soviet contention that "they have amused the whole world: they have ascribed the loss of gold reserves in the United States . . . to the Soviet Union." [35] In any case, even if the figures were correct, 2 billion dollars in gold reserves is not only quite considerable in absolute amount, but even as percentage of total imports it exceeds that of most other countries in the world. As to gold production, there are indications that it is on the increase [36] and there can be little doubt that it *can* be increased further (albeit at rather high costs) if the Soviet government decides to divert resources for that purpose.[37]

The CIA's contention that the Soviet growth rate had dropped to 2½ percent ran into trouble with Western Soviet experts from the outset. To a considerable degree, the immediate, extremely unfavorable reaction of the overwhelming majority of the experts was due to an error in reporting. The official CIA news release talked about a fifty percent drop in the Soviet Union's "annual increases in investment" in 1962-63, and about a "serious decline in economic growth in 1962 and 1963," but it gave a figure of 2½ percent *only for "last year's growth,"* i.e. *1963*. Unfortunately, some CIA officials talked with a few reporters before the printed summary report was released at the Agency's Virginia headquarters on January 9, 1964. As a result, the 2½ percent growth rate became "less than 2½ percent," the period to which it presumably applied was changed from 1963 to 1962 *and* 1963, and it was reported as such by *New York Times* correspondents Harry Schwartz and Edwin Dale [38] and reiterated by U.S. Under Secretary of State George Ball.[39] After that, the contention that the low rate applied to both 1962 and 1963 was attributed to the CIA by newspapers East and West.[40]

To the best knowledge of the author, with the exception noted in footnote 41 below, no Western economist who specializes in the Soviet economy has claimed that the 1962 Soviet growth rate was as low as 2½

[35] Victor Mayevskyi in *Pravda,* Jan. 15, 1964.

[36] *Wall Street Journal,* March 2, 1964.

[37] At the Party Presidium plenum in March 1964 Khrushchev implied that it may not be economically advisable to increase gold output in the USSR. "One should ask oneself," Khrushchev said, "whether it is easier to mine gold or to process timber," since either gold or wood pulp could be used to pay for foreign imports. (Khrushchev's comment was quoted by Paul Wohl in *The Christian Science Monitor,* March 16, 1964.)

[38] *The New York Times,* Jan. 8, 1964; repeated by both men, *The New York Times,* Jan. 9, 1964.

[39] Reuters, Jan. 9, 1964. Embargoed for automatic release Jan. 10.

[40] See, for instance, *The Christian Science Monitor,* Jan. 13, 1964; *Business Week,* Jan. 18, 1964; *The Economist,* Jan. 18, 1964; *People's World,* Jan. 25, 1964; *New World Review,* March 1964; *Izvestia,* Jan. 14, 1964; *Moscow News,* Feb. 8, 1964.

percent.[41] But as to 1963, is the CIA's estimate of 2½ percent correct; are those Western and Soviet sources right who believe that the growth rate was about twice that high; [42] or are perhaps those justified who consider the CIA estimate as too high? [43]

To a great extent, the answer to this question depends upon the way in which the statistical information has been interpreted, weighted, and utilized. Comparing two economies is a difficult and tricky business in any case.[44] The problems are multiplied when one deals with a country such as the USSR where some statistical information is unobtainable and therefore somewhat conjectural (for example total expenditure on atomic weapons) and where other statistical revelations must be taken with a grain of salt (for example percentage increases of peasants' real income). Moreover, the Soviet Union, which rarely shows balanced growth among its various sectors, experienced extraordinarily uneven rates of development in 1963. Not only was a disastrous setback in agriculture accompanied by a respectable increase in the industrial sector (8.5 percent according to Soviet sources),[45] but there were great fluctuations even within each sector. (The output of washing-machines, for instance, increased by 27 percent while the output of sewing machines decreased by an equivalent percentage.)[46] Under such circumstances, the choice of weights to be assigned to the various sectors and sub-sectors of the economy has a considerable effect, enabling statisticians East and West to deflect results to some degree in any desired direction.

Without wishing to get into the polemic over the "exact" or the "correct" growth rate for 1963, one may state fairly safely that it has dropped considerably as compared with previous years, but a "serious

---

[41] The Joint Economic Committee of the United States Congress gave the Soviet growth rate for 1962 as 2.2 percent but qualified its estimate by stating that "If no imputation is made for agricultural rent on the grounds that no Soviet data is available for an adjustment and that some rent payment may be included in the evaluation even though not explicitly costed," the rate would be 3 percent. *Annual Economic Indicators for the U.S.S.R.*, Joint Economic Committee, Congress of the United States, Feb. 25, 1962, pp. 94-95.

[42] See, for instance, *The Economist*, Jan. 18, 1964; R. R. Gill, *Radio Free Europe/Munich, Background Information USSR*, Jan. 27 and Feb. 27, 1964; Vladimir N. Starovskyi in *Izvestia*, Jan. 13, 1964; *Moscow News*, Feb. 8, 1964; Anushan A. Arzumanyan in *Pravda*, Feb. 24, 1964.

[43] For example Peter Wiles and G. Warren Nutter, cited above.

[44] See, for instance, "Comparing United States and Soviet Economies: Problems and Methodology," and "Comparisons of United States and Soviet National Income and Gross National Product," (Chapters 2 and 3 respectively) in Harry G. Shaffer, *The Soviet Economy: A Collection of Western and Soviet Views*, Appleton-Century-Crofts, New York, 1963.

[45] *Pravda*, Jan. 24, 1964.

[46] See Alec Nove, "Soviet Economy's Uneven Development," *The Times*, Feb. 2, 1964.

decline" for 1962, or a "steadily dropping growth rate during the 1960's" is much more questionable. Official Soviet sources gave the national income in billions of rubles for 1960 as 146.6, for 1961 as 152.9, for 1962 as 165.1 [47] and now for 1963 as 173.[48] This amounts to growth rates of 8, 7, 8 and 4.9 percent respectively for those four years. It appears that an arithmetic error crept into the percentage computation for 1962, which was given as 6 instead of 8 percent in the official publication in which the income was also given in billions of rubles,[49] and the error was subsequently carried, apparently unnoticed, into further Soviet and Western publications.[50] In all probability, the ruble figures are the arithmetically correct result of Soviet computations and, to the extent to which they are accepted, any theory of a "continuous decline" in Soviet growth rate would be defeated. Should one, however, make the unlikely assumptions that the percentage figure for 1962 was correct and the ruble figure in error, then national income in 1962 would have been only 162.1 billion rubles, which would give a 6.7 percent growth rate for 1963. (Under this assumption, notice, the growth rate would have increased by 0.7 percent from 1962 to 1963. It should also be pointed out that if ruble figures were somewhat exaggerated, growth rates would not be affected so long as the exaggerations were equal, percentagewise, each year.)

Although the CIA asserted that "the Soviet Union is falling behind in the economic race," the final evaluation of future possibilities was phrased more carefully. The statement that ". . . the Soviet economy, given more favorable agricultural weather, may be able to rebound from last year's growth of 2.5 percent," but that "the prospects for recovery to a sustained growth rate equal to that of the 1950's are not bright," certainly does not imply that the USSR will not be able to recover from the 1963 (or 1962-63?) slackening of her economic growth. Yet the entire tone of the CIA release called forth predictions that "Soviet growth rates over coming years will remain distinctly unglamorous" [51]; that the Soviet economy is so badly off that without large-scale, long-term credits from the West, "deep cuts" in Soviet defense expenditures will be necessary; and—in a less extreme form—that "the Soviet growth rate *could* well rise to around 4 percent or 5 percent . . . *in a few years.*[52] But more cautious voices have warned that "it would be unwise to project from the last two

---

[47] *Narodnoye Khozaistvo,* 1960, pp. 152-53; 1961, pp. 597-98; 1962, p. 482.

[48] *Pravda,* Feb. 24 and 25, 1964.

[49] *Narodnoye Khozaistvo,* 1962, p. 481.

[50] See, for instance, *Izvestia,* Jan. 13, 1964; *Moscow News,* Feb. 8, 1964; Zauberman, *op. cit.,* p. 2; *The Economist,* Jan. 18, 1964, p. 189.

[51] Walt Rostov, Chairman of the U.S. State Policy Planning Council, addressing the Business International Chief Executives Round Table in a prepared address. Reported by Reuters, Jan. 9, 1964; embargoed for release, Jan. 10.

[52] The last two views are presented as two schools of thought among U.S. officials by *Business Week,* Jan. 18, 1964, p. 31. Emphasis mine.

years," [53] that the CIA figures "give no permanent indications of how the economy will develop from now on," [54] and that with good weather the 1964 growth rate could go to 6, 7, or 8 percent.[55]

Before venturing an estimate in regard to the prospects for future economic development in the Soviet Union, one should take a brief look at some of the major factors which are likely to impede and some which are likely to promote a high rate of economic growth in the Soviet Union.

Adverse Factors

1. With the second decade of the postwar era coming to a close, increasing investments will be required merely to replace worn-out and obsolete machinery and equipment.

2. The shift to the production of more sophisticated goods may well slow down growth rates. There seem to be strong indications that an increase in the production of chemicals, for instance, is more likely to cause difficulties and to lead to bottlenecks than would an increase in the production of steel.

3. As Soviet economic life becomes more complex, the problems of central planning multiply to such an extent that, in the words of Soviet Academician V. S. Nemchinov, "Should the old planning methods be preserved, and given our present rate of growth, in 1980 practically the entire adult population of our country would have to be engaged in the administration and planning spheres." [56] (Nemchinov is confident, however, that the increased use of mathematical computers will obviate the necessity of an augmentation in the planning apparatus.)

4. Having worked hard and sacrificed much, the Soviet people are demanding more and better things *now*. This "revolution of rising expectations" is gradually resulting in an increasing emphasis on the production of consumer goods. As early as 1961, Khrushchev allegedly proclaimed that with heavy industry built up, it was no longer necessary to give it priority.[57] Although the production of capital goods has continued to re-

[53] Abram Bergson, quoted by Harry Schwartz in *The New York Times*, Jan. 9, 1964.

[54] Herbert Levine, quoted by Richard Neff in *The Christian Science Monitor*, Jan. 13, 1964.

[55] A "Pentagon Economist," quoted by Bernard Gwertzman in *The Washington Evening Star*, Jan. 17, 1964.

[56] V. S. Nemchinov, "Society Can Be Run Along Scientific Lines," *World Marxist Review*, April, 1963, p. 48.

[57] *The New York Times*, July 31, 1961 reported that Khrushchev made this statement in impromptu remarks on May 20, 1961 at a reception preceding the opening of the British Trade Fair in Moscow. See also Naum Jasny, "Plan and Superplan", *The Future of Communist Society* (Walter Laqueur and Leopold Labedz, editors), Frederick A. Praeger, Inc., New York, 1962, p. 34; also Leopold Labedz, "Ideology and Utopia, The New CPSU Program," *Survey*, October, 1961, p. 20. Khrushchev's alleged remark, by the way, has never been published in the USSR.

ceive priority, Khrushchev's recent attacks on the "metal-eaters," [58] and Academician Anushan A. Arzumanyan's still stronger (although carefully worded) plea for equal or even faster growth of consumer than of capital goods [59] indicate that the time of extreme sacrifices by present generations for the sake of rapid growth rates and of higher living standards in the future has come to an end in the USSR.

5. A decrease in the length of the workday and the workweek was provided for in the last Party Program [60] and is apparently being enacted gradually, although somewhat more slowly than originally anticipated. Increased leisure will have to be compensated for by a combination of increases in hourly productivity and in the working force, since otherwise not merely the rate of growth but total output *per se* would be diminishing.

Favorable Factors

1. A more realistic approach to agriculture and particularly a willingness to allocate more resources for investment in agriculture is likely to pay off in terms of overall economic growth. More than any other single factor, it was the extremely serious crop failure in 1963 which was responsible for the low rate of economic growth. The U.S. Department of Agriculture is already predicting the high probability of a "near-normal grain crop" in the USSR for 1964 (and, parenthetically, a well above normal crop for the Eastern European countries).[61] Increased emphasis on fertilizer, on irrigation projects, on agricultural equipment, and on enhanced material incentives for collective farmers will certainly show its effects in years to come. Western agricultural experts seem to be in fairly general agreement that improvements in Soviet agricultural output are not likely to come as rapidly or to be as far reaching as anticipated by Soviet leaders, but neither is it probable that the 1963 crop disaster will be repeated soon.[62] And even a normal or almost normal crop could be rea-

---

[58] One of Khrushchev's most recent attacks, against those who still cry for "steel, more steel" was included in his marathon speech to the Central Committee Plenum on Feb. 14, 1964, *Daily Review of the Soviet Press*.

[59] *Pravda*, Feb. 24 and 25, 1964.

[60] The complete text of the Program can be found in *The New York Times*, August 1, 1961; in *Marxism*, edited by Arthur P. Mendel, Bantam Pocket Books, 1961, pp. 371-468; in *Program of the Communist Party of the Soviet Union, Adopted by the 22nd Congress of the CPSU, Oct. 31, 1961*, Crosscurrent Press, 1961; and in many other places. For substantial excerpts and Western and Soviet interpretations, see Harry G. Shaffer, *op. cit.*, Chapter IV.

[61] *Foreign Agriculture*, March 9, 1964.

[62] This, at least, appeared to be the consensus of opinion among Western experts who assembled for a symposium on Soviet agriculture at the Institute for the Study of the USSR at Munich, Germany, February 20-22, 1964. (See Harry G. Shaffer, "Problems and Prospects of Soviet Agriculture," *Radio Free Europe/Munich, Non-Target Communist Area Analysis Department*, Feb. 24, 1964, pp. 2-3.)

sonably expected to spell a considerable growth rate for 1964, and substantial growth rates thereafter, since most sectors of Soviet *industry* continue to overfulfill their fairly ambitious targets.

2. There appears to be a definite trend in the direction of a more
rational allocation of productive resources. One may argue that the industrial price reform now in progress in the Soviet Union and scheduled to
take effect on January 1, 1965 is but a stopgap measure and at best a
poor substitute for market determined factor allocation [63]; that the use of
mathematics and of electronic computers for the purpose of improving
planning efficiency is still in its infancy; that the utilization of the profit
motive, of market forces, and of enhanced material incentives is still essentially in the discussion and experimentation stage; and that the willingness
of the central planners to delegate adequate decision-making power to
local enterprises is still to be proven. Yet, the winds seem to be blow-
ing in the direction of greater "revisionism" and Khrushchev's willingness
to "learn from the capitalists" [64] is interpreted by most Western economists
as likely to lead to enhanced productive efficiency and hence to augmented
growth rates.[65]

3. Increased trade with countries outside the Soviet Bloc will enable
the Soviet Union to exchange commodities in the production of which
she has a relative advantage or which are relatively less urgently needed,
for commodities produced in other countries in the production of which
the Soviet Union is relatively less efficient or which she needs relatively
more urgently.

4. The postwar crop of babies is beginning to hit the labor market,
and the previously reported general labor shortage appears to be on the
decline (although certain types of skilled and professional workers are still
rather scarce and in some areas, such as Siberia, manpower shortage still
poses very serious problems). While the total number of births in the immediate post-war years was well below that of the prewar years (due to
the extremely severe losses of the war), it was well above that of the war
years proper. The industrial working force, as a matter of fact, has been
increasing well above Soviet expectations. The 1958 Plan provided for
66.5 million "workers and employees" (excluding collective farmers) by
1965 while present expectations are that the labor force by next year will

[63] For an outline of the industrial price reform now in progress, see *Eco-
nomicheskaya Gazeta,* Jan. 18 and Feb. 29, 1964.

[64] Khrushchev's report to the Party Central Committee Plenum (*Pravda,* Nov.
20, 1962); also Khrushchev's address to the Party Central Committee Plenum on
Feb. 14, 1964 (see, for instance, *Soviet News,* Feb. 14, 1964, p. 74). In both cases he
attributed to Lenin the original statement that Communists should be willing to
learn from the Capitalists.

[65] For percentage decreases in production costs of industrial goods during the
last few years see for instance Vladimir Smolyansky's (Novosti Press Agency)
"Letter to the Editor," *The New York Times,* March 11, 1964; page 4 in the International Edition.

exceed 76 million.[66] The number of graduates from secondary schools more than doubled from 1962 to 1963 [67] but alarmed parents discovered that those offspring who became school dropouts (most frequently unskilled and around 16 years of age) had difficulty finding jobs. So serious, as a matter of fact, did the situation become that the government issued a decree requiring that a certain percentage of the working force of each factory consist of minors.[68] In a recent article, the Soviet ideological journal *Kommunist* predicted that the Soviet population, now about 226 million, will reach 280 million by 1980.[69]

In attempting to predict the future course of Soviet economic development, one has to take account not only of present economic conditions in the USSR but also of factors, such as those discussed above, which will tend to exert an influence, either positive or negative, upon the rate of Soviet economic growth. Since there is no one "correct" or "right" way to ascertain the relative significance of any of these, predictions must necessarily be somewhat speculative.

With this reservation in mind, then, it is the author's considered "guestimate" that the Soviet Union will not be able to fulfill its overall

[66] *The Economist*, Jan. 18, 1964, p. 193. It should be pointed out that roughly 1.4 million of the increase is accounted for by a statistical change involving the reclassification of members of industrial cooperatives (artels)—of collective entrepreneurs, so to speak—to state workers. Additional workers were added to the labor force statistically, although not *de facto*, by the conversion of collective farms (kolkhozi) into state farms (sovkhozi). Yet, even after taking these into account, the "overfulfillment of the plan" is quite spectacular. Vladimir N. Starovskyi gives the percentage increase in the labor force, corrected for statistical reclassifications, as 4.1 percent annually for the 1959-63 period, as compared with 3.8 percent for 1954-58 (*Pravda*, March 14, 1964).

[67] R. R. Gill, *Radio Free Europe/Munich, Background Information USSR*, Jan. 27, 1964, p. 7.

[68] *Trud*, Jan. 12, 1964. The minimum quota, apparently set according to local conditions, varied from region to region between three and five percent.

[69] *Kommunist*, March 1, 1964. It should be pointed out that the relative adequacy of the Soviet labor supply is a controversial matter. For a recent report of a severe labor shortage in the USSR, see for instance Ray Vicker, *Wall Street Journal*, March 4, 1964. In a scholarly article ("Soviet Economic Growth: Perspectives and Prospects," *The Quarterly Journal of Economics and Business*, Spring, 1964, pp. 57-67), Jan S. Prybyla points to the recent decline in the Soviet birth rate and discusses the labor shortage as one of the obstacles to Soviet growth. However, it is far too early to predict a long-run decline in the birth rate; the population increase (birth minus death) has by no means shown a pattern of continuous decline during the past decade and, although dropping in 1961 and 1962, has kept well above the 1940 figure; and Prybyla's own reference to the "notoriously wasteful use of labor in . . . agriculture," indicates a potentially quite important addition to the industrial labor force, once efficiency of agricultural production has been enhanced. (For statistical tables of birth and death rates in the USSR, see *Narodnoye Khozaistvo*, 1962, p. 30.) Emily Clark Brown maintains that the problem of manpower shortage in the U.S.S.R. is "improving not worsening" (*Problems of Communism*, May-June, 1964, p. 83), but Jay B. Sorenson, in reply, asserts that "a shortage of manpower and a high level of unemployment exist simultaneously." (*Ibid.*, p. 85.)

plan for 1970 and for 1980 (as outlined in the 1961 Party Program), and that she, therefore, will not be able to catch up with the United States, or at least not as rapidly as Soviet leaders had predicted. On the other hand, future years are likely to be considerably better for the USSR than 1963. The 1963 crop failure will certainly have some adverse effects on the food and some light industries, and the 1963 slaughter of vast numbers of animals (brought on by the shortage of animal feed) boosted meat production in that year but will hamper it for at least the following two years; however, the expected recovery from the poor harvest of 1963 will in all likelihood more than offset such unfavorable influences on economic growth. The Soviet Union's 1964 overall growth rate will therefore probably be well above 6 percent (measured by U.N. standards) [70] and thereafter average growth rates, although less than during the 1950's, are likely to be respectable.[71] But this means that the Soviet Union will eventually "catch up" with the United States, unless United States growth rates (fairly low during the late 1950's and through 1961, and better but still inadequate during 1962 and 1963) rise well above their present level. Therefore, unless this prediction about the prospects of Soviet economic development proves incorrect, only a high rate of economic growth in the United States could enable her to stay ahead in the economic race.

[70] The 1964 issue of the ECE (United Nations Economic Commission for Europe) annual review of economic conditions gave the 1963 growth rate of Soviet national income as 4 percent. (Reported by UPI from Geneva; embargoed for release, April 29, 1964.)

[71] It should be noted that the Soviet Twenty-Year Plan itself provided for decreasing growth rates. "The national income of the USSR," the Plan states, "in the next ten years will increase nearly 150 percent, and about 400 percent in twenty years." This, notice, would amount to a drop in the growth rate from 150 percent for the first decade to 100 percent for the second.

WESTERN MARXIST VIEWS

11. THE CIA'S PROPAGANDA BOMBSHELL *

VICTOR PERLO
Economist, Author

At its first formal press conference, the Central Intelligence Agency
. . . announced the results of "exhaustive research": that Soviet economic
growth had declined to a rate of only 2.5 per cent per year in 1962 and
1963, while in the last three years the U.S. rate had increased to 5 per
cent per year. Thus, "the United States is widening the gap . . . each year,
and this widening is expected to continue" (*N. Y. Times,* Jan. 8). Ergo,
capitalism has won the economic competition with socialism.

This is supposedly a conclusion based on the labors of "several hundred analysts." But unlike genuine research reports, absolutely no supporting calculations or explanations of method were provided. Nor was this
justified as needed to protect secret sources. The CIA specified that main
reliance was on published material.

The CIA top researchers themselves were not publicly identified,
perhaps to protect their reputations. In any case, the material is typical of
the published work of G. Warren Nutter, University of Virginia Professor
of Economics, who is notorious for his absurd underestimates of the Soviet
economy. Nutter claims that the USSR is relatively more backward than
Tsarist Russia! He has been chastised by fellow-economists at public meetings for his dubious methods.

Business Week, in its article repeating the CIA position, charted the
CIA estimates for 1962 and 1963 as a continuation of Nutter's estimates
for the previous year. Finally, in a letter to the *New York Herald Tribune*
(Feb. 3), Nutter takes issue with the negative press and academic reactions
to the CIA "findings."

It seems that either the material was prepared for the CIA by Nutter
or by some secret, ideological twin.

---

* Excerpts reprinted from the *New World Review,* March, 1964, pp. 13-18 by
permission of the author and the publisher.

We must evaluate its conclusion, then, on the basis of official data for both countries, which are accepted at face value by United Nations experts, and, so far as Soviet statistics are concerned, admitted to be close to reality by most Western specialists. Knowing something of the weaknesses of both countries' statistics, this writer considers that comparisons of official data yield results without a pro-Soviet bias.

Comparisons of industrial production are most valid, because it is the key sector, and both countries measure about the same things. The Soviet growth in the past three years was, respectively, 9, 9.5, and 8.5 per cent, for a very consistent average of 9 per cent per year. The United States growth was, respectively, 1, 7.7, and 5.1 per cent for an average of 4.6 per cent per year. The Soviet growth was higher in each single year, twice as high on the average, and incomparably steadier. The three-year period is a reasonable one for the comparison, because it embraces a full cyclical swing in the United States.

American researchers prefer comparisons of gross national product, although its measurement involves much crude estimation and subjective evaluation; and techniques differ radically in the two countries. The gross social product (as it is called in the USSR), increased an average of 6 per cent per year in the same period (5 per cent in 1963). The increase in the United States averaged 3.9 per cent.[1] Both figures are in constant prices. However, unlike the Soviet figures, American statistics include services, most notably, for the period under review, rapidly rising military expenditures. Exclusion of private and government services, giving data more comparable to the Soviet statistics, leaves a rise of 3.2 per cent per year for the U.S., or again about half the Soviet rate.[2]

The CIA stresses Soviet farm difficulties. Still, the sharp drop in the Soviet 1963 grain crop was partly counterbalanced by a sensational record cotton crop, bumper potato and vegetable crops, and higher livestock output. Over the past three years farm output in both countries increased insignificantly, less than one per cent per year. But over the past decade— a more meaningful stretch for agriculture—the average gain was 4.6 per cent per year in the USSR, 1.4 per cent per year in the U.S.A., or three times as fast in the former country.

As a welfare indicator, the physical volume of retail sales in the USSR, adjusted for price changes, increased 5 per cent per year during the three year period ending 1963, as compared with 3 per cent per year in the United States. The per capita contrast is sharper.

[1] Readers might wonder how the CIA dared to exaggerate the published American average, using 5 percent instead of 3.9 percent. That agency took the three-year gain from the beginning of 1961—at the bottom of the recession—to the booming end of 1963. A cheap statistical device indeed!

[2] Also, in the Soviet weighting system, agriculture counts for 17 percent of the gross social product, as compared with 4 percent in the American system. So the comparative lag in agriculture, which applies in both countries, holds back the calculated total growth rate more in the USSR than in the USA.

The grain of truth beneath the CIA mountain of lies is that the Soviet growth rate in this cycle has been somewhat slower, and the American growth rate considerably faster, than in the two previous cycles, extending from 1953 to 1960. Here is not the place to analyze the causes of these changes. Their combined effect is, that while the Soviet economy grew 3-4 times faster than the American economy in 1953-60, it grew twice as fast in 1960-63. If this changed relationship continues, the USSR will catch up to the United States in per capita production 5-10 years later than the 1970 date set as a goal by Premier Khrushchev in 1958, but still well within the century during which the late President Kennedy regarded the U.S. lead as secure. . . .

A HABITUAL DEVICE

Again and again official propagandists crow about alleged Soviet economic crises and failures. Each time they remain silent when events prove them wrong.

In 1958, when the Seven-Year Plan was launched, prevailing publicity claimed its certain failure, in whole or major part. A year or two ago, the experts claimed it had failed and had been "scrapped." Yet, it has been overfulfilled, in industrial output, each year, and in the five years so far industrial output increased 58 per cent instead of the 51 per cent scheduled. Concerning recently revised targets for 1964-1965, the final years of the plan, *the Economist* commented: "A quick comparison of the old and new figures suggests that Russian industry (but not agriculture) has been steered smoothly towards its appointed destination, slightly faster than originally laid down." However, it continued, consumers were "somewhat neglected" along the way.

In 1959, Allen Dulles, then CIA chief, predicted that the Soviet Union would not reach 60 per cent of American industrial output before 1970. Actually it has reached 65 per cent of American industrial output seven years earlier. This poor prediction does not prevent the present CIA chief from the more extravagant claim that Soviet production is now "less than half" the U.S. level, and will not gain on it at all in the future.

In 1957 *Fortune* featured an alleged Soviet economic crisis. In a brilliant rejoinder Academician Eugene Varga showed that the Soviet economy was flourishing, and warned that the place to look for a crisis was in the United States, where one was ripening and might be starting at that very moment. And, indeed, an American recession began just as the rejoinder was published.

I do *not* think we are entering a crisis at this moment. But the lesson remains applicable. American officials would serve the public better not by inventing "crises" in the Soviet Union, but by acting to protect people from existing mass unemployment and discrimination, and from the dangers of either recession or speedy price inflation, both of which are imminent in the present course of economic events. . . .

SOVIET VIEWS

12. THE TRUTH ABOUT THE CIA STUDY *

K. VALENTINOV

The Central Intelligence Agency of the United States recently made a startling "discovery." If we are to believe it the Soviet Union's economic growth in the last two years has been less than 2.5 percent annually, well below the rate of the United States. The CIA reported this at a press conference, in an analytical study of the economic situation in the Soviet Union.

The CIA estimates claim that while the Soviet Union's annual rate of economic growth was 2.5 percent, in the USA the figure was 5 percent. Somebody apparently thought even this "comparison" inadequate. So, a few days ago, US press tycoon Hearst, Jr. who calls himself a friend of John McCone (head of the CIA) declared that the American economy was growing five times as fast. . . .

CIA KEEPS CALCULATIONS SECRET

For our part we shall question the CIA's competence to make international economic comparisons. One might also think that the CIA had some special reasons for not revealing the sources and the methods used in its exercises in statistics.

A fundamental requirement for any international comparison is comparability of statistical indices. But the CIA is using the concept of gross national product, an index used in the United States to determine the rate of growth. The Soviet Union does not use this index at all. The Soviet Union operates with the indices of the gross value of material production and of the national income, and these are far from being identical with the gross national product used in the United States.

* Excerpts reprinted from an article originally published under the title "The Objective of the CIA Study," in *Moscow News*, February 8, 1964.

The gross value of material production represents the total gross production of all enterprises engaged in material production, the national income represents this production minus the replacement fund. The American conception of gross national product is somewhat closer to the Soviet national income index.

However, the gross national product in the United States is much wider in scope if it is judged by the number of components. Besides the national income it covers wear and tear, and expenditure on personal services. So, to achieve complete comparability it is necessary either to recalculate the US index using the Soviet method, or vice versa, to recalculate the Soviet index using the American method. The extent of the divergence of the two indices is clear from the example of a recalculation for 1961. In that year the US gross national product, according to official data, was 518,200 million dollars and after a recalculation using the Soviet method, which was undertaken for the sake of an objective comparison, it was slashed by more than 40 percent and represented 306,000 million dollars. . . .

Now, if for the sake of objective comparison the American figures are recalculated using the Soviet method, the rate of growth in the USA—of its national income—would prove to be much smaller and for the last two years would be not five percent as the CIA claims, but something like 4 percent per annum. The methods for making such a recalculation are dealt with exhaustively in the relevant literature.

On the other hand, the Soviet gross social product has increased 6 percent in 1962 and 5 percent in 1963. Last year industry exceeded its programme of growth for gross and net production. As for agriculture, the Soviet Union fell short of its programme owing to unfavourable weather conditions. However, during the past five years our gross social product has increased by 39 percent. The national income reveals approximately the same rate of growth, i.e. a higher rate than in the United States.

Although the CIA has not disclosed its methods of calculation it is perfectly clear that it has been "comparing" incomparables, exaggerating the rate of the USA growth and underrating the Soviet rate. This is the worth of the CIA percentages, which have been plucked from the blue, to say the least, as was ironically remarked by V. Starovsky, Corresponding Member of the Academy of Sciences of the USSR and head of the Central Statistical Board of the USSR.

RATE OF NATIONAL INCOME:
USSR—8.7%; USA—2.4%

Furthermore the CIA compares the past two years. This is a mistake in itself, because one cannot compare the rate of growth of a capitalist economy against that of a socialist economy on the basis of one or two years only. Capitalist economies develop unevenly, in cycles and therefore a choice of the rate of growth for one or two years at random might be neither characteristic nor correct for the required comparison. True enough, the rate of USA's economic growth during the past two years, though falling behind the USSR, may still be recognised as relatively high. This is a transient development due to a favourable phase of the economic cycle, state control, etc. We believe that these exceptional conditions are not characteristic and cannot be used as a basis for forecast.

It would be much more correct to use the rates of growth for fairly long periods of time, when the influence of opposing factors is equalised. For instance, the average growth rate of the national income in the USA calculated on the same basis as that of the USSR for the decade 1954-1963 was 2.4 percent, while in the USSR it was 8.7 percent, i.e., 3.5 times as much.

During the past decade . . . considerable shifts in our favour have taken place in all the most important economic indices. While industrial production in the USSR amounted to 33 percent of that in the USA in 1953 and 47 percent in 1957, it was about 65 percent in 1963.

Ten years ago the Soviet Union was ahead of the United States only in the flour and cereals industry and the sugar industry. Today, the Soviet Union is producing more than the United States and is holding first place in the world for the gross production of iron ore, coal, coke, for gross output in a number of engineering industries (including machine building and farm-machinery manufacture), cement, window pane, prefabricated ferro-concrete, wood pulp, and for total production of sawn timber, woollens, butter, sugar and several other items. . . .

VI

LIVING STANDARDS
IN THE U.S.S.R.

"The C.P.S.U. sets the historical task of achieving in the Soviet Union a living standard higher
than that of any of the capitalist countries."

PROGRAM OF THE COMMUNIST PARTY
OF THE SOVIET UNION ADOPTED BY
THE 22ND CONGRESS OF THE C.P.S.U.
OCTOBER 31, 1961.

A dictionary of economic terms defines "standard of living" as "the
relative scale of consumption enjoyed by an individual or group of individuals." [1] To increase the standard of living of her people, the Soviet
Union would thus have to increase the goods and services available for
consumption. However, in a country which utilizes all its productive facilities as best it can, an increase in the production of any one commodity can
be brought about only at the expense of some other commodity. If the
Soviet Union decided to increase her output of agricultural products, she
could do so by shifting workers from the cities to the farms, thus assuring
that every pound of grain be harvested from the fields. But the increase
in output thus attained might not warrant its costs in terms of other products which the workers could produce if they remained in the city. From a
long-range point of view, for instance, it might be more advisable to utilize
the manpower for the purpose of erecting factories and plants capable of
turning out tractors and mineral fertilizer which, in years to come, might
increase agricultural output considerably while releasing additional manpower from the farms for the production of yet other commodities. But
such a decision, note, would mean that the people would need to tighten
their belts while the plants and factories were being built! [2]

[1] Byrne J. Horton, Julien Ripley Jr., and M. B. Schnapper, *Dictionary of Modern Economics,* Public Affairs Press, Washington, D.C., 1948, p. 313.

[2] This is necessarily a somewhat simplified discussion. It does not take into consideration, for instance, the possibility of increasing productive efficiency by means
such as education (which would involve the utilization of resources for the building
of schools, the training of teachers, etc.) or by improving the planning mechanism
and the incentive structure. But issues such as these are covered, to some extent, in
other chapters. (See, for example, Chapter IV on Economic Planning and Chapter
VII on Soviet Education.)

247

Throughout her history, the Soviet Union has been faced with the alternative of devoting more of her resources (1) to an immediate, albeit small, increase in consumers' goods (for instance food), or (2) to an increase in the production of producers' goods (goods used in the production of other goods, for instance tractors) which could subsequently bring about a greater increase in the output of consumers' goods (food), or (3) to an increase in the production of producers' goods (such as machinery used in the production of tractors) which could in time increase the production of other producers' goods (tractors) which in turn could eventually facilitate a yet greater increase in the production of consumers' goods (food). Throughout her history, the Soviet Union has consistently made her decision in favor of concentrating her efforts on increasing her productive capacity, rather than her immediate output of consumers' goods. But it would obviously be nonsensical to make the increase in productive capability an end in and of itself. Has the concentration on producers' goods, then, already begun to pay off in terms of increasing living standards? And what are the prospects for the immediate and the long-run future?

To some extent, the answers to these questions depend upon just what one means by "living standards." While Western economists usually restrict their definition to encompass only such items as could be included in real, per capita consumption,[3] Soviet social scientists frequently take into account such nonmeasurable indicators as the cultural level of the population, the opportunity to obtain work, the incidence of sickness, and the level of health care.[4] It should be pointed out that in comparing living standards some non-Soviet experts, in recent years, have also begun to pay attention to abstract factors which cannot be measured in terms of money.[5]

No matter how one measures it, there is no denying that the living standard of the Soviet citizen today is considerably higher than it was at the time of Stalin's death. It is also considerably higher than the living standard of the inhabitant of any other country in Asia, Africa, and Latin America, with the possible exception of Israel, especially if one accepts

---

[3] By "real" consumption is meant the actual goods and services consumed (as distinguished from monetary expenditures for consumption). Comparisons of real consumption from one year to another can be made by adjusting monetary consumption outlays for changes in the price level; and comparisons of the real consumption (or real income) of nations are statistically possible although it is by no means easy to make them truly meaningful. In this connection it should be pointed out that in making such comparisons the Soviets place special emphasis on (and Western observers often under-emphasize the importance of) the U.S.S.R.'s "public consumption fund." (See footnote 2, page 137, above.)

[4] See, for instance, a summary of the report by M. R. Eidelman, "Comparing Indices of Living Standards of the U.S.S.R. and the U.S.A.," *Vestnik statistiki* No. 6, June, 1963. Excerpts translated in *The Current Digest of the Soviet Press,* November 13, 1963, pp. 11-12.

[5] In a report to the Economic and Social Council of the United Nations in 1954, for instance, a group of experts enumerated several "abstract" factors (such as "working conditions" and "human freedoms") as having a bearing on standards of living. (See pp. 252-253 below.)

the Soviet proposal to compare incomes of workers only, i.e., to exclude from any comparisons those classes in society which derive their income from the ownership of wealth, rather than from their labor. On the other hand, it is generally conceded by Soviet economists that overall living standards in the U.S.S.R. still lag somewhat behind those of most of the Western European nations, and that the United States is still far ahead. However, as we shall see, Soviet and Western Marxist authors maintain that the Soviet Union has already surpassed the United States in *some* of the indicators of living standards and will surpass her in overall levels of income and consumption in the not-too-distant future.

In the first selection of this chapter, Imogene Erro notes some improvements, but considers the overall lot of the Soviet consumer still rather depressing, both in terms of the quantity and of the quality of consumers' goods available. Future gains, she predicts, will be gradual and production problems will increase in complexity as Soviet light industry expands.

Glovinsky, in the second selection below, compares the U.S.S.R. and the U.S.A. on the basis of many "indicators" of living standards, including even such indices as the availability of basic drugs and the extent of "human freedoms," and he rates the Soviet Union low man on the totem pole on all counts.

A picture rather different from the one in the first two selections is painted by Victor Perlo under *Western Marxist Views*. Perlo does not deny that the average citizen in the United States now has a greater purchasing power than his Soviet peer, but he finds the actual difference far from overwhelming if one takes into account the collective noncash income of the Soviet worker. He also considers the "average" less significant in the U.S. than in the U.S.S.R. since the range of income is smaller in the Soviet Union while in the United States extremes of wealth and poverty are averaged into a not-too-meaningful figure of "per capita income." Perlo concludes that barring radical reforms in the United States or major complications in the international arena, another dozen years will find the socialist lands well ahead of the capitalist world in living standards.

In the Soviet selection, Y. Pokatayev and Y. Joffe lend full support to Perlo's arguments. By 1980, they predict, real per capita income of workers in the Soviet Union will exceed that of workers in the United States by 75 percent, and this advance in living standards will be accompanied by such significant and beneficial socio-economic changes as great reductions in the length of the work day, substantially increased disability pensions, and a carefree and secure old age.

WESTERN VIEWS

1. THE LOT OF THE SOVIET CONSUMER *

IMOGENE ERRO

Author, Specialist on Consumption in the U.S.S.R.

SUMMARY

In the U.S.S.R., which now ranks as a leading world power, the consumers' share in the total product of industry is still too small to satisfy their basic requirements, in spite of the gradual rise in the level of living that has been achieved. Under the existing system of priorities for investment funds and other resources since 1950, light industry has grown more slowly than total industry and slower still compared with the machine-building branch of heavy industry. Nevertheless, by 1960, light industrial production had grown to 2.5 times the level in 1950, almost doubling the output of textiles, more than doubling the output of leather footwear and hosiery, and increasing at an even faster rate the output of knitwear and sewn garments. Still these goods were far from adequate when measured either by consumer satisfaction or by the official standards for optimum consumption.

Presently light industry, growing at a rate below that needed to reach the 1965 goal, is producing half the textiles and only a little more than half of leather footwear needed to reach the norms which Khrushchev has pledged to achieve by 1970. Even the production required by the 7-year plan, should it be reached, is still far short of supplying the prescribed norms as shown by the following data per capita.

	1961	1965 plan	Consumption norm [1]
Textiles (square meters)	29.9	35.2	58.1
Leather footwear (pairs)	2.0	2.2	3.5

* Excerpt reprinted from Imogene Erro, "Trends in the Production of Consumer Goods," *Dimensions of Soviet Economic Power,* Materials prepared for the Joint Economic Committee, Congress of the United States, 1962, pp. 388-389.

[1] Soviet planners have set up so-called scientific norms for consumption of basic commodities produced by the light and other consumer industries. But the list of commodities considered "really necessary" is extremely limited by comparison with the wide range of goods available, for example, in the average U.S. department store. Although the Soviet norms for food approach U.S. quantitative consumption levels, norms for textiles and clothing are generally lower.

As for apparel, Soviet consumers are receiving much more factory-made clothing than they did in earlier years. Retail sales of sewn garments in 1960 were almost 80 percent above the 1955 level, whereas sales of fabrics in that period increased only 30 percent, indicating that as the supply of factory-made clothing increases, the need for sewing at home and by private seamstresses and tailors is diminishing.

Besides the radios and sewing machines which are fairly common throughout the U.S.S.R., many urban householders in recent years have acquired their own television sets, refrigerators, and washing machines. However, the appliances are of poor design, low quality of construction, and undependable operation to the extent that many of them would not be salable in Western markets. By 1965 Soviet officials estimate that for each five urban households there will be one refrigerator; for each three urban households, one washing machine; and of all Soviet households, urban and rural, half will have sewing machines. Few plants specialize in household appliances, production being relegated instead to subsidiary shops of machine-building plants that specialize in other types of machinery.

Soviet light industry recently has suffered a decline in rate of growth, falling from an increase of 9 percent in 1959 to an increase of 4 percent during the first 6 months of 1962 over the corresponding period in 1961. The present rate of growth thus is below the 6 percent average annual increase required to meet the 1965 goal and is also below the 7 percent achieved annually in the preceding 7-year period. Contributing heavily to the decline in rate of growth are shortages of raw materials and failures in achieving the investment plans.

That Soviet agriculture may be unable adequately to meet the requirements of the textile industry in the future is a probability which planning officials apparently accept. The output of agricultural fibers recently has increased at a declining rate, increases for both cotton and wool falling in 1960 and 1961 far below the increase achieved in 1959. Light industry thus must rely more heavily on the nonagricultural types of textile fibers —rayon and the various types of synthetic fibers which are now being developed.

The low technological level at which Soviet light industry operates is reflected by high inputs of labor and a relatively low investment of capital. Light industry's share of investment, even when combined with the food industry, is still below the shares, respectively, of the machine-building, ferrous metallurgical, and oil and gas industries for both the 7-year plan and the 7-year period preceding it. Because of its technological lag, the Soviet light industry compares poorly with that in the United States, the annual output per Soviet production worker amounting to less than half of that of his U.S. counterpart. To help in raising the level of technology, the U.S.S.R. is importing modern machinery and equipment from firms in

Western countries—mainly the United States, the United Kingdom, West Germany, and others—as well as from the East European satellites.

On balance, the Soviet consumers' lot has improved gradually over time, but the prospects are that future gains also will be gradual in spite of the growing desires of consumers for more and better goods. Soviet light industry, which continues to build gradually on achievements of past years, is becoming increasingly burdened with problems of expansion. To increase the capacity for production and to provide enough raw materials to support it, is the task of the present and of the future.

2. THE PROBLEM OF RAISING THE LIVING STANDARD IN THE U.S.S.R.*

E. GLOVINSKY (1894-1964)

Former Deputy Director and Senior Researcher, Institute for the Study of the U.S.S.R., Munich, Germany

One of the goals of the new Soviet Party Program is to achieve a higher standard of living in the Soviet Union than in any capitalist country. This is to be done in two stages; by 1970 the welfare of the population is to be raised to the level where all will be assured of a "material sufficiency"; between 1970 and 1980 "an abundance of material and cultural goods will be guaranteed for the entire population" and "Soviet society will come very close to implementing the principle of distribution according to need." This is to be achieved, on the one hand, by raising the individual pay of workers "according to the quantity and quality of their labor," and on the other, by extending free social services "irrespective of the quantity and quality of labor." As a result of this policy, the Party Central Committee asserts that in the next ten years the real income of a worker will almost double and in the next twenty will rise by 200 to 250 percent. During the same period, the real income of collective farm workers should rise even more—by more than 100 percent in ten years and more than 300 percent in twenty.

Of course, it is not only real income which determines a standard of living. In a report to the Economic and Social Council of the United Nations

* Excerpts reprinted from *Bulletin, Institute for the Study of the USSR,* March, 1962, pp. 35-39, by permission of the publisher.

in March 1954, a special commission of experts proposed the following list of factors as having a bearing on standards of living:

1. Health, in particular demographic conditions;
2. Food and diet;
3. Education, in particular literacy and technical qualifications;
4. Working conditions;
5. Level of employment;
6. Level of consumption and savings;
7. Transportation facilities;
8. Living accommodation, in particular provision of public services;
9. Clothing;
10. Recreational facilities;
11. Social security;
12. Human freedoms.

Certain of these factors relate directly to real income, but others are abstract factors which cannot be expressed in monetary terms. However, leaving the latter aspect aside for the moment, let us first make a comparison of real incomes in the Soviet Union and in the United States, the country which is generally accepted as having the highest standard of living in the world at the present time.

Soviet commentators frequently accuse Western researchers of misusing averages, arguing that where there are large differences in income such figures distort the truth. To avoid this charge, we will therefore limit our comparison to the largest and most important category of the working population, industrial workers. It should be borne in mind that Soviet statistics include under this heading white-collar as well as other workers —"workers and employees."

At the present time, workers and employees in the Soviet Union number 62 million, and this figure should rise to 66,500,000 by 1965. The great majority (60 million by 1965) earn up to 100 rubles per month. Thus, it may be assumed that the average pay of 90 percent is in the region of 80-90 rubles per month. . . . To this must be added the value of those services such as education, medical care, pensions and day nurseries which are provided free by the state and also the subsidies on housing, which amount to some 60 percent of the cost of providing and maintaining living accommodation. In 1960, the value of public services amounted to 24,500 million rubles, while personal expenditure totaled 93,700 million rubles. Taking the number of persons engaged in the national economy to be about 100 million, this represents a *per capita* outlay of approximately 245 rubles per year, or 20 rubles per month. The statistical yearbook *The National Economy of the USSR in 1960* puts the figure at 380 rubles per year, but this has been obtained by dividing the total sum by the number of workers and employees engaged in industry, which is hardly an accurate calculation, since such benefits as free medical care and free education are enjoyed by other workers as well. However, as industrial workers certainly benefit more from these public services (the value of which is sometimes termed "socialized pay") than, say, workers on collective farms, it would be fair to set the figure for industrial workers at 300-324 rubles per year, or 25-27 rubles per month. Thus, the average monthly remuneration of a Soviet industrial worker, including his "socialized pay," amounts to 107-117 rubles, or on a weekly basis 25-27 rubles.

In the United States, average weekly rates of pay are as follows: in manufacturing industries—$90.39; in coal mining—$94.46; and in the building industry—$148.45. For the sake of comparison, we will take the figure for the manufacturing industries, i.e., $90.39. From this must be deducted various taxes, which a Soviet worker either does not pay or will cease to pay very shortly. According to Soviet sources, which tend to ex-aggerate, American workers pay approximately 12 percent of their income in direct taxes. If one assumes that the American worker does not receive anything equivalent to the Soviet "socialized pay" (in fact this is not alto-gether true), one is left with a net weekly wage of $72-73.

Direct comparison of the purchasing power of the dollar and the ruble is difficult, if not impossible. The official exchange rate since January 1961 has been 90 kopeks to the dollar. However, an official exchange rate, even where a currency is convertible (which the Soviet ruble is not) does not always reflect the purchasing power of that currency. One thing at least is clear, and that is that the purchasing power of the ruble is considerably less than that of the dollar, as the following table of comparative prices of certain foodstuffs shows:

	Price per Kg in the USSR (Kopeks)	Price per Kg in the USA (Cents)
White Bread	19–29	46
Wheat Flour	27	25
Potatoes	7	15
Beef	140	178
Pork	205	195
Lard	230	44
Butter	260–290	168
Margarine	139	59
Eggs (each)	7	6
Sugar	94–106	26

Of the items listed, it is possible to buy more bread, potatoes and beef for one ruble than for one dollar; otherwise, the dollar possesses a very favorable margin of purchasing power. We do not intend to extend this comparison of buying power to manufactured consumer goods, since this would involve allowing for the quality of the goods, but in this field too there is good reason to suppose that such items are cheaper in the

United States. However that may be, on the basis of the foodstuffs listed above, it would appear that the ratio of the purchasing power of the dollar and ruble is about 3 : 2. This means that in order to catch up with his American colleague's purchasing ability the Russian worker would need to raise his income, not from 27 rubles to 72 rubles weekly, but to 108 rubles, an increase of 300 percent. According to the new Party Program, only an increase of 250 percent is envisaged in the next twenty years, so that the basic target of achieving a higher standard of living than any capitalist country within that period is clearly impossible.

It should be borne in mind that there are also other factors with which the Soviet Union will have to contend in its efforts to outstrip the capitalist world. First, there is no reason to suppose that the United States economy will mark time for the next twenty years and there will be no rise in the standard of living. The Soviet Party Central Committee asserts that a socialist economy achieves higher rates of development than a capitalist one, but to date this has only been true of the capital goods industry; it applies neither to the consumer goods industry nor to agriculture.

Second, there is the closely related question of whether it is even possible to raise incomes in the USSR to the extent envisaged by the Party. This involves enabling the population to buy foodstuffs, clothing, footwear and other consumer goods both in larger quantities and of better quality; providing more comfortable and spacious living accommodation and also a sufficiency of various public utilities and services. Most of these problems, however, depend directly for their solution on agriculture, which provides most of the raw materials not only for foodstuffs but also for many manufactured consumer goods. The rough estimates of the future rate of growth of agricultural production made by Khrushchev at the Party Congress are, in the light of 30 years' experience of "socialist" agriculture, far from valid. An increase of 200-300 percent or more in the output of certain agricultural products could be made possible only by a complete reorganization of the agricultural system: doubling grain output, for example, could only be achieved either by bringing more virgin land under cultivation, which is not being done at the moment (the areas already under cultivation will require such a large outlay of labor and capital in the near future that any extension of the scheme is unlikely to be profitable), or by doubling yields on existing acreage. In view of the fact that yields have not risen by more than 20 percent since the Revolution, it seems unlikely that Soviet agriculture will be capable of achieving this latter goal.

Third, turning to other items that figure either in the list of amenities promised by the new Party Program or in the list of factors considered by the United Nations' experts to have a direct bearing on standards of living, such benefits as the provision of free medical care are of little value so long as druggists and hospitals have insufficient supplies of basic drugs. Food should not only contain the necessary number of calories, but also be tastefully cooked and served. Too many criticisms of the unpalatable food and the oppressive atmosphere and unhygienic conditions prevailing in communal dining halls have appeared in the Soviet press to suggest that they meet these requirements. The Party assures the people that by 1980 public transportation facilities will be free, but this does not in itself mean that they will be either adequate or convenient (quite apart from the fact that the Soviet citizen might well prefer to travel to and from his work in his own private automobile). Then there are all the everyday facilities, taken for granted in many Western countries but markedly absent in the Soviet Union. Standing in line for goods—an almost inevitable feature of a centralized distribution system—wastes a large part of workers' free time. The adequacy of living accommodation is not determined solely by the amount of rent a person or family has to pay, but also by the area of living space and the condition in which the building is maintained. It can hardly be claimed that 5.8 square meters of living space, the average per head for the urban population in the Soviet Union in 1958, is sufficient for present-day man. Security in old age depends not only on the size of pensions, but also on whether a person possesses savings, other valuables, his own home and furniture, etc.

Again, there is bound to be a great difference between the standard of living in a country where incomes have already been at a high level for a considerable time and a country where a high level has only recently been attained. In the United States, for instance, the time is long since past when the majority of the population were only able to afford the bare means of existence.

In conclusion, *à propos* of that factor which the United Nations experts termed "human freedoms," it must be pointed out that, so long as there is a totalitarian regime in the Soviet Union, such freedoms will always enjoy a very low priority and this must inevitably have an adverse effect on the living standards of its population.

WESTERN MARXIST VIEWS

3. THE WORLD'S HIGHEST LIVING STANDARDS *

VICTOR PERLO
Author, Economist

COMPARISON OF LIVING STANDARDS

Today the U.S. has the highest average living standard of any major country. Per capita consumption of goods and services is now (1960), about twice as large as in the USSR. But there is much more to living standards than this statistical comparison. The hostile tradition in this country is to stick to statistics, distort them, and thereby grossly exaggerate the difference in living standards. AFL-CIO President George Meany, for example, charges that per capita consumption in the USSR is only 20% of that in the United States.

A typical method is to compare store prices and monthly wages in the two countries, and then publish figures showing how the poor Russian worker has to slave for many hours to buy something his American brother can buy with a few minutes' labor.

These calculations usually suffer from plain statistical fudging. They pick absurdly low estimates of Soviet wages, and exaggerate the length of the Soviet working day. The main trick, however, is to omit the collective, noncash income of the Soviet worker.

When the higher stage of communist society is reached, all goods and services will be distributed without cash payment. Elements of that form of distribution have existed in the USSR from its earliest stages, and they are expanding continuously. Already, according to Soviet estimates, one-third of people's real incomes consists of the value of goods and services distributed free of charge and of subsidies which cut prices of other items to nominal levels.

* Reprinted from Victor Perlo, *USA and USSR: The Economic Race,* 1960, pp. 72, 74-78, and 80-81 by permission of the author and of International Publishers Co., Inc.

Recently, for the first time, an American university economist [Lynn Turgeon] attempted a realistic comparison of living standards in the two countries. He took social consumption into account, at least partly, and reasonably estimated Soviet families' income levels. . . .

He estimates the average family income at $435 monthly in the U.S., 1,400 rubles monthly in the USSR. From the American income $55, or 13%, are deducted for direct taxes, leaving $380. These take 85 rubles, or 8% of the Soviet family's income, leaving 1,315 rubles. Then there are the costs that the normally-situated family cannot avoid, rent and electricity, doctor bills, travel to work, insurance premiums. These absorb $200, or more than half of the American family's after-tax income. But they are in the social consumption area in the USSR, where they take only 195 rubles, or 15% of after-tax income.

So the American family has left only $180, or 41% of its gross earnings, for food, clothing, durable consumers goods, personal care and recreation—for everything one goes into a store and buys, for everything where one has a consumer's choice, for most of the items which make up the "American standard of living." The Soviet family has 1,120 rubles, or 80% of its earnings, left for these purposes.

Now, Turgeon notes, the Soviet family has for free spending 6.2 times as many rubles as the American family has dollars. So, he considers, if Moscow store prices in rubles were 6.2 times higher than New York store prices in dollars, each family would have equal purchasing power. Actually, the price ratios are usually higher—about 10 to 1. So the Soviet family still has less free purchasing power, but not by an overwhelming margin.

A number of factors enter into a proper comparison of living standards which reduce the significance of the American advantage in per capita supply of consumers goods.

The most appropriate comparison should be between the standards of working people in both countries. A very substantial proportion of all consumers goods and services are absorbed by the very wealthy in the U.S. The upper fifth get ten times as much income as the lower fifth. Leaving out the upper fifth, which include the capitalists and the upper crust generally, the average income of the remainder of the population is only 70% of the "average" U.S. income. The range in incomes in socialist society is much narrower, and all people work. And the average consumption of working people in the United States, is—as suggested by the above figures —considerably below the per capita consumption of the entire population.

The contrasts in poverty are also significant. According to the typical Congressional studies, roughly 40 million Americans or over one-fifth of the population, are poverty-stricken. There are also poor people in the Soviet Union, including the unskilled non-industrial urban workers and the least productive collective farmers. But poverty has cruel aspects in America which are not duplicated in the Soviet Union. In our country millions of families of unemployed and extremely low-paid workers suffer from cold and hunger. They do not starve or freeze, but they are certainly undernourished on the relief food, and many are the children who stay home from school in wintertime for lack of adequate clothing while others go to school to get their only meal of the day. In the Soviet Union even poor people are adequately, if plainly, fed and clothed. In America there is more housing space per capita than in the USSR. But one-fourth to one-third of the population live in wretched, unsanitary, unsafe, dilapidated slums, and these slums are spreading in American cities. In the Soviet Union there is still a severe housing shortage, but, in the words of the well-known financial advisor Roger Babson: "There are no slums in Russia such as are in our large cities."

Also, poverty in America is concentrated among especially oppressed and exploited national minorities, and is associated with segregation and other evils. These features are wholly lacking in the USSR.

In important respects Soviet living standards are already considerably higher than those of American workers. Mainly, these are in the area of security, health and welfare services. The United States still has nothing like the full cradle-to-grave "welfare state" of the USSR. Consider medical services. To begin with, there are many more doctors, hospital beds, and other medical facilities per capita in the USSR than here. Still more important, they are available to everybody, without discrimination, and without charge. In America, really adequate medical service is a privilege of the wealthy. Recent publicity highlights the fact that medical costs, never more than partially covered by group insurance schemes, are sky-high and steadily rising. The people's medical and death expenses leaped from $3.5 billion in 1940 to $6.9 billion in 1946 and about $20 billion in 1960. This is more than people spend for personal care, education, religious and welfare activities, foreign travel and remittances combined.

The Soviet Union also offers far more in education, and better quality in education, than the United States. Moreover, Soviet education is available to all equally, with ability being the only criterion for admission to higher institutions. In the United States colleges, and especially graduate schools, are still much more accessible to the propertied classes. Every Soviet graduate has a choice of jobs awaiting him in his chosen field. Here, college graduates, especially Negroes, often are unable to obtain employment in their profession.

There is simply nothing in the United States to compare with the nurseries to take care of small children of working mothers, the prolonged periods of before-and-after maternity leave with full pay, the low-cost availability of vacation resorts and children's camps for Soviet workers and their families.

All cultural objects, such as books, theaters, and records, are far more plentiful and cheaper in the Soviet Union than in the United States.

Old-age pensions in the USSR average 70% of wages, 100% for those at the low income levels, as compared with an average of 25-30% in the United States.

Finally, how can one value the liberation of the Soviet worker from that scourge of capitalism—unemployment? Or the freedom of fear from repossession of his car, or eviction from his home when he loses his job?

This side of the equation is too often wholly ignored by American comparative studies and publicity. It does not negate the fact that the *average* American worker still is better off in material things than his Soviet counterpart, but it certainly modifies the fact, and helps make it clear why the Soviet people consider attainable by 1970 the highest living standard in the world.

WHO WILL LIVE BETTER BY 1970?

At the 5% per year rate of increase projected in the Seven-Year Plan, real wages in the USSR will rise 80% over the 1958 level by 1970. This may be regarded as a minimum. During the first year of that plan production and labor productivity increased more than provided by plan by several percentage points. Immediately part of that added performance was translated into an acceleration of planned gains in living standards. New goals for production of durable consumers goods were established, providing for the doubling and tripling of output of major types by 1962.

At an increase of 6% per year in real wages, the gain by 1970 will be about 100%; at 7% per year, it will be 125%. Considering real wages in the USSR in 1958 at one-half the American level, according to definitions customary here, it appears that by 1970 real wages in the Soviet Union will be in the approximate range of U.S. real wages of 1958. The extent of increase in American real wages in the interval is, of course, uncertain. If the snail's pace of the past decade is continued, they will not be very much higher than at present. And if the current big business anti-union offensive is successful, they may be lower.

Average real incomes of workers' families in the two countries will probably be close together in 1970. Soviet families, however, will be far ahead in all other factors making up living standards, considering their dramatic plans for accomplishment and the lack of such by those in power in America.

A few years before 1970, the Soviet workweek will establish a new historic low, 15% below ours. This will signify a great advantage in Soviet living standards, unless American workers themselves win decisively the campaign for a 35-hour week.

The Seven-Year Plan provides for 22 million housing units, enough to comfortably house 88 million people. Considering the undoubling that will take place, more than half the Soviet population, and the mass of the urban population, will enjoy new or improved housing. During the first year of the Seven-Year Plan, the housing goal was substantially exceeded with about 3 million units built. Long before 1970, the housing shortage, which had been the most glaring weakness in Soviet living standards, will be completely overcome.

Here housing construction remains in the range 1-1.5 million units per year, and most of it is replacement housing for those already adequately housed.

By 1963-65 wages of the lowest categories of workers in the USSR will be raised 70-80%, as compared with an average rise of 26% in money wages. By then, the purchasing power of the minimum wage in the Soviet Union will be close to the average wage of only a few years ago. At the same time, there is a spreading move to raise the income level of collective farmers to that of city workers. Prominent in this is the payment of monthly regular advances on incomes to collective farmers, computed on the basis of 80% of their estimated earnings for the year. No such sweeping combination of crop insurance, price and income parity, and living advances against farm production in process, has even been approached in proposals made in this country.

Probably by 1965, and certainly by 1970, the last vestige of poverty will be gone from the USSR. Unfortunately, there is no such improvement projected in governing quarters in the U.S. Nor is there any plan to end unemployment, provide free medical care, or otherwise improve matters in those respects where Soviet living standards are already well ahead of ours.

A decade hence American workers will still be better supplied with automobiles, and perhaps a few other items. But these will be exceptions among the whole range of items in which Soviet standards will be up to or above those applicable to American workers. Balancing the statistical and non-statistical features, it does appear that by 1970 working people's living standards in the USSR will be higher than in the United States—unless a new constellation of political forces is able to accomplish major reforms here in the meantime. . . .

THE HISTORICAL PERSPECTIVE

Those who boast about the superiority of American living standards as evidence of the superiority of capitalism refuse to view the matter in historical perspective.

In 1913, when there was no socialist power anywhere, the American workers had the highest real wages in the world, while the Russian workers had the lowest real wages of any major power. The masses of the Russian people were peasants still close to serfdom, existing on the verge of starvation, and in famine years experiencing it. A minority were city workers with an average wage of 21 rubles a month (about $11).

If the average American worker consumes twice as much as the average Russian today, he consumed five or ten times as much in 1913, when both countries were capitalist.

Secondly, no country in modern history suffered so much from foreign and civil wars as the USSR in the first 28 years of its existence. To multiply the living standards of the people the Soviet Union had to do it several times over. Here is the history since 1917.

1917-21—Civil war, foreign armed intervention and famine—90% economic destruction.
1921-28—Restoration of wartime damage.
1928-32—Beginning of socialist industrialization; kulak (rich peasant) destruction of 50% of livestock.
1932-38—Peaceful development of economy and living standards.
1938-41—All efforts to prepare for defense against Hitler fascism.
1941-45—World War II; 40% economic destruction.
1945-50—Repairing war damage.
1950-53—Some improvement, living standards only gradually gain because cold war at its peak (Korean War, McCarthyism, Pentagon threats) forced military effort to expand.
1953-59—Peaceful development of economy and living standards.

So far the USSR has had 12 years of more or less unhampered economic development, 7 years of limited development owing to international or domestic tensions; and 23 years of war or repairing war damage.

The fact that the Soviet people did endure sacrifices while building socialism, that the rise in their living standard was not steady, but underwent several setbacks, is due to this particular history of the pioneer country of socialism.

No state of an earlier social system could have survived such adversities, as no state of capitalism could have defeated the enemy which killed 20 million and occupied the most productive parts of the country.

The first socialist state not only survived, but in the limited peaceful time at its disposal became the second industrial power of the world, and multiplied living standards of the population several times.

Today the balance of world power has shifted so that the forces of reaction cannot harass or damage socialist countries to anything like the extent the Soviet Union had to endure. The only exception would be a nuclear war, which of course would render meaningless economic comparisons between what was left of the two rival civilizations.

Otherwise, socialism can go ahead in living standards with comparative freedom from outside interference. That so much has been accomplished in a dozen years of only "normal" stress and strain, explains why the Soviet people are so confident of the future. They and their leaders have ample grounds for believing that, with other socialist lands, they can emerge far ahead of the capitalist world in living standards and all other economic measures in another 12 years of comparatively clear sailing internationally.

SOVIET VIEWS

4. THE SOVIET UNION WILL SURPASS ALL CAPITALIST NATIONS IN PER CAPITA INCOME AND LIVING STANDARDS *

Y. POKATAYEV

Candidate of Economic Science; Specialist on Economic Competition between the U.S.S.R. and the U.S.

Y. JOFFE

Senior Scientific Staff Member, Institute of Economy, U.S.S.R. State Planning Committee

MACHINE TOOLS OR BUTTER?

"Clearly, the Soviets are increasing not only the output of heavy industry, but also raising the living standard."

M. GOLDMAN
FOREIGN AFFAIRS, JULY, 1960

When the Civil War ended and the Soviet Union went over to peaceful construction it began in the first place to restore agriculture and light industry. It was necessary to feed and clothe the millions of hungry and ragged people. But even then, in the early 1920's, it was clear that the further development of agriculture and light industry depended on heavy industry.[1]

Indeed, to increase agricultural output it was necessary to extend the sown areas, to raise crop yields and the productivity of livestock, and

---

* Excerpts reprinted from Y. Pokatayev and Y. Joffe, *Peaceful Competition: U.S.S.R.–U.S.A.* (published by Soviet Booklets, London, Jan., 1963), pp. 29-31 and 35-39, by permission of the publisher.

[1] In this connection, "heavy industry" refers to producers' goods industry, i.e., industry turning out machinery and equipment. [Editor's note.]

for this machinery and chemicals—the output of heavy industry, were needed.

The same things are needed for the development of light industry, construction and transport. In the final analysis it is machinery, metals and chemicals that are vital for a country's development.

The experience of the Soviet Union and other highly industrialised countries shows that the possibility of rapid development of industry and agriculture is directly connected with high rates of growth of heavy industry.

The Soviet Union is building on a huge scale. Housing construction in the U.S.S.R. has outstripped in volume that in any other country. Clearly all this requires the production of a colossal quantity of machinery, equipment, metal, building materials, etc.—the output of heavy industry.

Without a developed heavy industry it is impossible to build up an economy which could give the population the highest living standard in the world, and this is the cardinal aim of industrial development in the U.S.S.R.

Lastly, an analysis of the development of industry in all countries without exception shows that the building up of an industry to meet the country's requirements, is possible only if heavy industry grows still faster. This is an economic law of development of society irrespective of its social nature. More than that, calculations show that in all industrially developed countries, such as the U.S.S.R., the United States, Britain, West Germany and France, the share of heavy industry in total industrial output is approximately the same, ranging from 60 to 70 per cent. The Soviet Union is no exception in this respect.

But is it true that the rapid development of heavy industry in the U.S.S.R. leads to a neglect of consumers' interests? First of all, the correlation of rates of growth in heavy and light industry is constantly changing in the U.S.S.R. Suffice it to examine the following figures to understand the direction of these changes. During the first Five-Year Plan (1928-32) the growth rates of heavy industry were 2.3 times higher than in light industry; during the second Five-Year Plan (1933-37) they were 50 per cent higher, and in 1950-58, 20 per cent higher. Under the Seven-Year Plan (1959-65), as in the next twenty years, this proportion will remain about the same. It should be noted that on the whole Soviet light industry grows five times faster and the food industry four times faster, than those of the United States.

Not so long ago textiles and footwear were the main branches of light industry. The situation is now changing: ever greater importance is acquired by durable goods: refrigerators, TV sets, washing machines, etc. The production of these goods is growing rapidly and the task has been set of equipping every family with one of each of these machines.

Heavy industrial plants can be divided into two groups. The first consists of plants which manufacture machinery and equipment for heavy industry itself; the second, plants which manufacture machinery and equipment for light industries, for the food industry, for agriculture, housing construction, for cultural and public services.

When the Soviet Union was laying the foundation of a modern heavy industry its efforts were concentrated on developing the first group of plants to the utmost, limiting capital investments in the second group. The situation is now changing radically. In the next twenty years plants of the first group have to increase output six times and of the second group, thirteen times. The development of heavy industry will be increasingly subordinated to the task of raising the material and cultural standards of the people.

Lastly, some foreign economists refer to the high proportion of accumulations in the national income of the U.S.S.R.

For many years such accumulations accounted for one-quarter of the national income of the U.S.S.R. and consumption, for three-quarters. Between 1950 and 1960 the national income increased 2.7 times, the annual rate of growth being 10.4 per cent. With an unchanging correlation between accumulation and consumption in the national income, this means that the consumption fund and accumulation fund increased annually by 10 per cent and the per capita consumption fund, taking into account the increase of the population, grew by 7-8 per cent annually.

In the United States, according to official figures, the proportion of accumulation is about 10 per cent and the share of consumption 90 per cent. Between 1950 and 1960 the national income increased by 35 per cent, that is, the average annual rate of growth was 3.1 per cent. Consequently, the consumption fund per capita rose annually by about 1 per cent.

In what country is the dynamics of consumption higher—where the proportion of accumulation is 25 per cent of the national income and the per capita consumption fund rises annually by 7-8 per cent as in the U.S.S.R., or in a country like the United States where the accumulation accounts for 10 per cent, but the consumption fund rises on the average by only 1 per cent? The answer is clear—in the Soviet Union! . . .

NOT BY BREAD ALONE

"The long-term prospect offers grounds for asserting that if the volume of consumption by the Soviet people continues to grow at the same rate as now, it will exceed U.S. level." [2]

PETER WILES, ECONOMIST, OXFORD UNIVERSITY

So far we have discussed how production will grow.[3] But the important thing is to know not only how many per cent it will increase

---

[2] Retranslated from the Russian.

[3] This refers to the first part of *Peaceful Competition: U.S.S.R.–U.S.A.* Extensive excerpts from it have been reprinted as selection V. 8 above.

annually, but *what this will give the people*. We must ascertain for what purpose production is being developed.

Under socialism this development is subordinated to the interests of the people, which is attested to by facts and figures. Between 1950 and 1961 the national income rose by 183 per cent in the U.S.S.R. and by 37 per cent in the United States.

The real incomes of factory and office workers in the U.S.S.R. per employed person increased annually on the average by 5.5 per cent, while in the United States, according to the most optimistic estimates, they rose slightly more than 1 per cent. Production of consumer goods in the U.S.S.R., per capita, more than doubled and the volume of state and co-operative retail trade increased 3.5 times. All this shows the advance in the standard of living of the Soviet people.

To analyse the prospects of competition between the Soviet Union and the United States it is necessary to define the concept "standard of living of the people" and the system of indices characterising it.

By standard of living we understand the degree of satisfaction of man's material and spiritual requirements. This includes food, clothing, footwear and other consumer goods, housing, education, medical service, sports, the opportunity for work and recreation and for developing man's finest abilities.

A comparison of the standard of living of the working people in the U.S.S.R. and the United States is a very intricate task because of the deep social differences, essential distinctions in the economic and climatic conditions and also national traditions. That is why a thorough analysis of all the main aspects of the life of the working people in the U.S.S.R. and the United States is needed. It cannot, of course, be made in a booklet of this size, but the main tendencies can be indicated.

At present the Soviet Union still lags behind the United States in per capita consumption levels and the general level of per capita real incomes. But the Soviet people already enjoy benefits which are inaccessible to the working people in the capitalist countries. These are the absence of exploitation, unemployment, crises and racial or other discrimination. Confidence in the future, free education, free medical aid, low rents, etc., are all very real benefits. All these are elements of the standard of living which ensure the moulding of the finest human traits and the all-round development of each member of communist society.

What are the prospects of the Soviet people as regards the further improvement of their standard of living?

No matter what indices are used in measuring the standard of living in the U.S.S.R. and the United States, the consumption fund in the national income of both countries must be compared. In 1961, the total consumption fund amounted to 233,000 million dollars in the United States and about 115,000 million dollars in the U.S.S.R., i.e., 50 per cent of the American level.

But the consumption fund in the U.S.S.R. does not include the substantial part of their incomes which Soviet working people get from public funds. These funds are distributed free of charge and irrespective of work done. They go towards health services, education, pensions, and other free services. These are the so-called "socialised" wages—approximately one-third of all wages. On the other hand, the consumption fund in the United States includes a huge total spent by the rich on luxury articles.

If all this is taken into account the gap is reduced noticeably. The consumption funds of the Soviet Union in 1961 actually amounted not to 50 per cent, but to more than 60 per cent of the American level.

Soviet economists calculate that the entire consumption of an average Soviet family (food, rent, public utilities, education, medical aid), taking into account the public funds, amounted in 1961 to more than half of the average American level.

Making use of the great advantages in growth rates of the national income and the incomes of the working people, the Soviet Union will soon close the gap altogether.

The process will be as follows. By 1970, real per capita incomes of the Soviet working people will double. This means that a Soviet family will have the same real income as the family of an average American worker, and higher than that of the working people in the West European capitalist countries. But there will be this other big difference. All Soviet people without exception will have security and sufficiency. For the first time in history, insufficiency will be completely and finally eliminated.

By 1980 per capita incomes in the U.S.S.R. will be 3.5 times higher than at present.

The U.S.S.R. pays great attention to developing the public consumption funds. By 1980 they will rise more than tenfold, from 24,500 million roubles in 1960 to 255,000-265,000 million roubles. To give an idea of the immensity of this sum, let us recall that in 1961 all the outlays of the American population for the purchase of goods, for transport, education and medical service amounted to about 300,000 million dollars, which corresponds approximately to 270,000 million roubles. In other words, in 1980 the Soviet state will give its citizens free of charge, a volume of benefits which is equivalent to all that the American people now buy for money. If we bear in mind that in 1980 the public funds will make up approximately half of the incomes of the population, while the other half will consist of wages, it will be clear that the consumption fund of the Soviet people will be almost twice as large as the present consumption fund of the American population. If account is taken of the larger population of the U.S.S.R., in 1980 real per capita incomes in the Soviet Union will exceed the present level of incomes of the working people in the United States by 75 per cent.

The British weekly paper *Tribune* writes that this seems fantastic.

But the programme of 1903 drawn up by a small group of emigrées whom everyone ridiculed seemed even more fantastic, while in 1919 hardly anyone expected the Soviet government to last more than a few months . . .

Tribune adds that there are no weighty grounds for doubting that in 1981 the Soviet economy will be able to provide the goods and services promised by the new programme, because it is a planned economy. . . .

The growth of incomes will also be ensured by expanding the output of consumer goods. In 1980 per capita consumption will increase as follows compared with 1960: clothing and footwear, approximately 3.5 times; household goods and articles for cultural requirements, 5.5 times. In 1970 state and co-operative retail trade in town and country will increase 2.5 times as compared with 1960, and in 1980, 5 times.

But the important thing is not only the figures of growth. Together with the advance in the standard of living major social changes will take place.

As a result of the rise in incomes the category of lower-paid workers will also vanish because the incomes of workers in the lower brackets will be swiftly brought up to the level of the middle and higher brackets.

Lastly, the shorter working day and longer holidays will give the people new opportunities for rapid cultural and technical advance. Communist society will be confronted with the task of creating conditions for the development of all the individual capabilities of each person. The harmonious combination of labour, aesthetic and scientific education of man, proceeding from his individual inclinations, is the aim of communist society.

The completely free maintenance of all incapacitated persons will be ensured and pensions will be increased. In the second decade it will be possible to go over gradually to a single system of pensions for all incapacitated persons. It will be of no importance at what job a person works. What will be important is that he works honestly, giving all his energies to the ideals and interests of humanity. Therefore, in old age he will have the right to the same care and security as any other member of society. Thus, one of the ideals of humanism, the universal equality of people, will be fully realised.

The housing shortage will be ended. Each family will be provided with a well-appointed house or flat free of charge.

Such in brief are the prospects for the rise in the well-being of the Soviet people which will enable them to enjoy a standard of living higher than that in any capitalist country.

VII

EDUCATION IN THE U.S.S.R.

"The socialist system offers unlimited opportunities for all-round development of personality and for creative endeavor. Socialism opens up greater prospects for scientists, engineers, and technicians, for our intellectuals, for every Soviet man and woman, than the capitalist system."

NIKITA S. KHRUSHCHEV

"A student is not a vessel to be filled but a lamp to be lighted."

ALEXANDER D. ALEXANDROV
RECTOR, LENINGRAD UNIVERSITY

From the very outset, and especially since the death of Stalin, the Soviet government and the C.P.S.U. have placed great emphasis on education. In the days of the Tsars four out of every five children, according to Soviet sources, never attended school.[1] The figure may be exaggerated, but there can be little doubt that the Russian population was preponderantly illiterate or semiliterate in 1917, and that higher education was reserved primarily for the upper classes. During the 1962-63 academic year, on the other hand, compulsory eight-year schooling was made universal throughout the U.S.S.R., and in 1963 the total number of students in general education reached forty-one million.[2] What is the reason for this emphasis on education? How does education, and especially higher education, fit into the framework of Marxist-Leninist ideology? What is the role reserved for it in the Soviet Union's long-range Plan? What does a higher education mean, in terms of prospective life income and career opportunities to the Soviet citizen as compared with the citizen of the United States?

Marx, Engels, and Lenin proclaimed repeatedly, and their followers have reiterated incessantly that two primary conditions have to be met during the preparatory stages before a society of perfect Communism can become a reality. First, the economic base for Communism has to be

[1] *Soviet Weekly,* May 7, 1963, p. 11.
[2] *Pravda,* December 11, 1962. Translated in *Problems of Economics,* December, 1962, p. 14.

269

created; in other words, productive capacity has to be increased so as to lay the economic foundation for a society of material abundance for all. Secondly, and equally important, man has to be transformed into a social being to make possible the creation of a society in which each individual contributes according to his ability without coercion, inspired only by his desire to serve society, and in which he takes from the common stores what he needs, without any inclination to accumulate or to grow rich at the expense of his fellow men. Present-day Soviet leaders never tire of stressing that education has to assume the major role in bringing about these two primary conditions: rearing the physicists, chemists, biologists, mathematicians, agronomists, engineers, etc. without which a rapid increase in productive facilities would be impossible and molding the "New Soviet Man," a task which, in the words of Party Secretary L. F. Ilyichev, "the party regards . . . as the most difficult work of communist transformation." [3]

Education is of relatively greater importance to Ivan than to John, since Ivan's position in life, his career opportunities, his income are more likely to depend upon the successful accomplishment of his educational goals. Not that education is unimportant to John, since an ever-increasing number of jobs, and especially higher positions, require at least a college degree. Yet, if he fails to complete his higher education, John is not necessarily relegated to a life of relative poverty. He does have other opportunities—opportunities not open to his Soviet peer. Ivan, unlike John, cannot inherit his father's business, "go into business" for himself, speculate on the stock exchange, nor earn a decent income by "going into politics" (since even the members of the Supreme Soviet keep their regular jobs and, while the Supreme Soviet is in session, receive the same pay as they do during the rest of the year). Because Ivan's income, in his native land, depends largely upon what he DOES and has practically no relation to what he OWNS, preparation for higher positions (i.e., education) takes on special significance.

Part A of this chapter consists of an exposition of Western and Soviet views on Soviet education in general; Part B deals with Soviet higher education.

To introduce the reader to the various opportunities open to the young Soviet citizen in search of an education, the first selection depicts graphically the Soviet educational ladder, from nursery school to the university.

Under *Western Views,* Nicholas DeWitt analyzes critically the Soviet educational system, concentrating on comparisons between the Soviet Union and the United States.[4] DeWitt acknowledges considerable achievements

---

[3] *Pravda,* June 19, 1961. Translated in *The Current Digest of the Soviet Press,* July 3, 1963, p. 10.

[4] Readers interested in more detailed comparisons of U.S.S.R. and U.S. school curricula are advised to consult Professor DeWitt's original paper. Space limitations, unfortunately, precluded the inclusion of the entire paper herein.

but also finds much to criticize in the objectives and the accomplishments of the Soviet system of education.

Under *Soviet Views,* S. G. Strumilin, recognized "Dean of Soviet Economists," evaluates Soviet education primarily in terms of the economic benefits which Soviet society has derived from its investment in education. Strumilin's paper contains much informative, factual material and his analysis shows rather conclusively that the investment in public education has proven profitable both to the individual recipients and to the Soviet nation.

In the next selection under *Soviet Views,* N. I. Boldyrev discusses the role of the Soviet school as an institution dedicated to the teaching of "the moral code of the builders of Communism"—to the rearing of the "New Soviet Man." But this "New Soviet Man": can he be created? Man's selfishness, his desire to accumulate, his urge to reserve the best and the most for himself and perhaps his family—are these not characteristics of human nature that can never be altered by any environmental factors or educational processes? And lying, cheating, stealing, killing—have these not been aspects of every human society from the beginning to present days? Most Utopians have expressed the belief that, given the right conditions and the right preparation and training, man can be elevated to undreamed-of heights of moral behavior. Most Western social scientists, on the other hand, have discarded as unrealistic any serious reference to the perfectibility of man. The last selection under Part A of this chapter is a condensation from the official textbook used in a social science course in Soviet schools. Marxism has *scientifically* proved, the authors of the textbook proclaim and the Soviet students learn, that once the economic and political conditions are ripe (and they are in the Soviet Union today!) man *can* be perfected.

Under Part B of this chapter, Seymour M. Rosen and V. P. Elyutin present *Western Views* and *Soviet Views* respectively on higher education in the U.S.S.R. In their analyses, as would be expected, Rosen is somewhat critical and Elyutin quite enthusiastic. In some respects the two selections are complementary, since a substantial part of Rosen's paper deals with the planning and supervision of higher education by the Communist Party and the Soviet government, a topic not elaborated on in Elyutin's piece, while the latter covers at somewhat greater length some of the fields of study at institutions of higher learning, a topic not included in the excerpts reprinted from the former.[5]

[5] Rosen's paper contains detailed listings of hundreds of Soviet higher education specialties. Space limitation, however, precluded the reproduction of the complete, thirty-five-page paper.

A. The Structure, Goals, and Achievements of the Soviet System of Education

1. THE SOVIET EDUCATIONAL LADDER

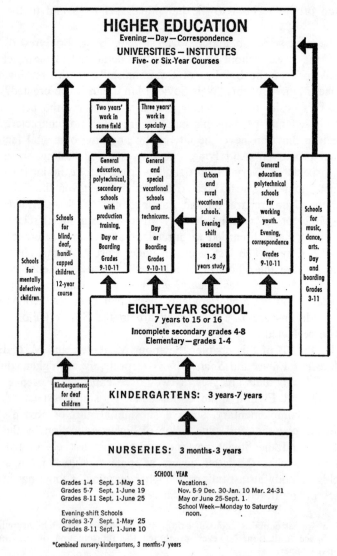

HIGHER EDUCATION
Evening — Day — Correspondence
UNIVERSITIES — INSTITUTES
Five- or Six-Year Courses

Two years' work in some field

Three years' work in specialty

General education, polytechnical, secondary schools with production training. Day or Boarding Grades 9-10-11

General and special vocational schools and technicums. Day or Boarding Grades 9-10-11

Urban and rural vocational schools. Evening shift seasonal 1-3 years study

General education polytechnical schools for working youth. Evening, correspondence Grades 9-10-11

Schools for blind, deaf, handicapped children. 12-year course

Schools for mentally defective children.

Schools for music, dance, arts. Day and boarding Grades 3-11

EIGHT-YEAR SCHOOL
7 years to 15 or 16
Incomplete secondary grades 4-8
Elementary — grades 1-4

Kindergartens for deaf children

KINDERGARTENS: 3 years-7 years

NURSERIES: 3 months-3 years

SCHOOL YEAR

Grades 1-4	Sept. 1-May 31	Vacations.
Grades 5-7	Sept. 1-June 19	Nov. 5-9 Dec. 30-Jan. 10 Mar. 24-31
Grades 8-11	Sept. 1-June 25	May or June 25-Sept. 1.
		School Week—Monday to Saturday noon.
Evening-shift Schools		
Grades 3-7	Sept. 1-May 25	
Grades 8-11	Sept. 1-June 10	

*Combined nursery-kindergartens, 3 months-7 years

SOURCE: Elizabeth Moos, *Education in the Soviet Union*, 1963, p. 30. Reprinted by permission of the publisher, the National Council of American-Soviet Friendship, New York.

WESTERN VIEWS

2. EDUCATION AND THE DEVELOPMENT OF HUMAN RESOURCES IN THE U.S.S.R.*

NICHOLAS DEWITT
Indiana University

Throughout the world today, fundamental changes are taking place in the assessment of conditions under which social and economic progress is achieved. The traditional approach to the problem of economic growth assigned well-nigh an exclusive role to the accumulation of material wealth as a precondition to industrial development. This emphasis is giving way to new trends in economic thinking.

It is being acknowledged now that in advanced societies, as well as in underdeveloped countries, long-term social and economic progress is conditioned not so much by the mere availability of physical capital as by investment in human capital. There is a worldwide awareness that the strategy of economic development must be firmly rooted to the strategy of the development of human resources. The real bottleneck in achieving targets for rapid economic expansion is viewed to be the quality of human resources, which is determined largely by education.

Recognizing that education is the main tool in the development of human resources required to augment the strategic capability of a nation, Soviet planners have for the last four decades been busily engaged in a buildup of skilled and high-level professional manpower, particularly the training of specialists in science and technology. From the very inception of their plans for rapid economic expansion in the late 1920's, they have emphasized that it was education, the training of cadres of specialized personnel, which would decide the outcome of the Soviet industrialization

* Excerpts reprinted from Nicholas DeWitt, "Education and the Development of Human Resources: Soviet and American Efforts," *Dimensions of Soviet Economic Power,* Materials prepared for the Joint Economic Committee, Congress of the United States, 1962, pp. 233-268. The paper was prepared by Dr. DeWitt in his capacity as consultant to the National Science Foundation, Scientific Personnel and Education Studies Section.

drive. For this reason, Soviet educational planning has been to a large degree future oriented, so as to create an abundant stock of technological manpower to suit the growing needs of the expanding economy.

The purposes of education in any country are shaped by the nature of the particular society, by its cultural heritage, and its political, economic, and social institutions, and—to a greater or lesser extent—by the "world outlook" upon which the society is based. In emphasizing the Communist commitment to education, it must be recognized that Soviet society is a planned society and that, as such, the Government of the U.S.S.R. operates a centrally planned economy requiring, in turn, a certain optimal combination of human skills. Ever since Lenin declared that education should be a weapon for moving society forward on the road to communism, the Soviet leaders have used the educational system to serve the state and to help attain its goals. . . .

Elementary education and junior secondary education are nearly universal in the U.S.S.R. It is on the secondary and higher education levels that the major differences between the Soviet and American educational efforts are evident. In the United States about 90 percent of the secondary-school-age population are actually enrolled in schools. In the U.S.S.R. only about one-half of the respective levels are found in educational establishments. If we were to consider only the regular upper secondary grades (8-10) of Soviet schools, about one-third of the age group were in attendance. While in the United States about one-fourth of the college-age population is enrolled in institutions of higher learning, the corresponding proportion in the Soviet Union is only 6 percent. In the Soviet case, however, if part-time education enrollments are considered, the rates of attendance would obviously increase. . . .

The result of the educational effort of a country can be measured in various ways. One of these measures is the educational attainment of the population (and the labor force as its component). . . .

Partly because of the relative youth of the Soviet Union's mass education efforts, and to a great extent because of deliberately more selective educational policies, in 1959 over one-half of the Soviet adult population had had less than 4 years of schooling. In the United States in the same year more than half of the adult population had had up to 11 years of schooling. The estimated median number of years of schooling completed by the adult population in the Soviet Union was about 3.8, and the estimated mean was 4.7 years. In the same year in the United States the median number of years of schooling completed by the adult population was 10.9, and the mean was 10.3. The U.S.S.R. curve was heavily skewed toward the lower levels of educational attainment, while the U.S. distribution of population by level of educational attainment, by contrast, closely approached a normal distribution curve.

In historical perspective, then, and in terms of the median number of years of schooling completed, the U.S.S.R. achieved in 1959 what the United States achieved at the turn of the century. . . . In terms of the number of persons with partial or completed secondary education, the Soviet Union in 1959 stood where the United States stood in 1930. And in terms of the population of higher education graduates, the Soviet Union in 1959 was in a position reached by the United States in 1940. The lag of the U.S.S.R. behind the United States in terms of the levels of educational attainment does not deny the Soviet Union's rapid progress in the course of the last few decades; indeed, the *rates* of growth of the educated component of the population in the U.S.S.R. were considerably higher than in the United States. Nevertheless, the level of educational attainment of the Soviet population is presently still significantly lower compared to the United States. . . .

The U.S.S.R. follows the practice—a common one in many countries —of having a standard curriculum in its general education primary-secondary schools; this is to say that all students, as they progress through school, generally take the same subjects. There are some variations between urban and rural schools, for purposes of allowing participation in agricultural or industrial work, and small variations between Russian-language and native-language schools. In the main, unlike the U.S. system where determination of curriculum is on a State or local basis, and students have latitude in choice of subjects, students in the U.S.S.R. all receive about the same amount of instruction in basic subjects.

The functional emphasis in Soviet primary and secondary education is a relatively recent development. Until the mid-1950's, primary and secondary schooling was intended primarily to lay the groundwork for higher education, weeding out the less competent and providing those of demonstrated ability with a foundation of general academic knowledge (particularly in the sciences). Since then, however, first through a process of piecemeal adjustment and then by radical institutional reform, primary and secondary schools have become institutions for turning out students who, in addition to having academic preparation, are trained in labor skills and ready for employment.

Soviet pedagogical theorists distinguish five basic components of primary and secondary "general education." These elements incorporate the theoretical aims of Soviet general education and are supposedly embodied in educational practice:

1. *Physical education,* aimed at developing health and physical strength through curricular instruction and/or extracurricular participation in sports.

2. *Esthetic education,* aimed at developing appreciation of "artistic realism" among all students and/or mastery of a "performing arts skill" by those who are particularly gifted.

3. *Mental education,* aimed at the mastery of all subjects of instruction; the development of a conscious scientific and materialistic outlook; mastery of the dialectical method; and orderly and systematic study and thought habits.

4. *Polytechnical education,* aimed at developing a specific manual skill; detailed familiarity with methods and techniques of production of a given type; and a general knowledge of production techniques and the organization of socialist industry.

5. *Moral education,* aimed at creating a "conscious Communist morality," the elements of which are: conscious discipline; Soviet patriotism and proletarian internationalism; dedication to the goals of the community, the state, and the Communist Party; dedication to socialist labor; and acceptance of approved common rules of conduct and etiquette.

Because the Communists themselves declare that their educational system is, first and foremost, oriented toward the development of the ideal personality—"the new Soviet man"—many Western observers have emphasized *"moral education"* of the Communist type as being the most important. This does play an important role in the educational process, to be sure; but it does not necessarily shape the content of education. Until the mid-1950's the content of Soviet education reflected a dominant emphasis on academic education; since then, the dominant influence has been *polytechnical education,* with specific vocational preparation in the upper grades. Physical education and, in particular, esthetic education have had relatively small roles. . . .

In the new 11-year school [1] the Soviet student must take a standard set of academic subjects, with language and literature and mathematics being taught in all grades. History and geography begin in grades 4 and 5, respectively, and continue through grade 11. Science courses are introduced gradually beginning in grade 4 and continue through grade 11. Activity subjects—physical education and music—are required in all grades. Manual training is required in both the elementary grades and in grades 5 to 8. As in the past, there are no electives as far as academic, activity or manual training subjects are concerned. The only option the

---

[1] Under the 1958 reform, the ten years of schooling required to complete one's general education were extended to eleven years, and the seven year minimum of schooling to eight years. In August, 1964, the 11-year program was again reduced to 10 years, primarily by cutting down on the production training hours in grades 9 to 11. Since those who started their 10th or 11th school year in September, 1964 continued according to their originally scheduled curriculum, the changeover will not be fully effectuated until the 1966-67 school year. [Editor's note.]

student may exercise is in grades 8 to 11, when he may select one of a number of alternatives in the fundamentals of production and specific trade skill training.

As of January 1961, the U.S.S.R. had a total stock of about 4.5 million higher education graduates, some 80 percent of whom were gainfully employed in the national economy. This total stock of professionals was about one-half the aggregate number of U.S. college graduates with bachelor and higher degrees. About 73 percent of the 8.5 million higher education graduates in the United States were gainfully employed in the national economy. The Soviet stock was composed of 48 percent female (as compared with about 40 percent for the United States). Moreover, most of the Soviet female professionals (87 percent) were gainfully employed in the national economy, versus 56 percent of U.S. women college graduates. The Soviets thus had an advantage, not only in the proportion of women professionals, but also in the degree of their utilization in the economy. The Soviet stock of professionals was also substantially younger: 48 percent of them in the 20-to-34 age group, as compared with about one-third in this age group in the United States.

While the United States had a substantial 2-to-1 advantage over the U.S.S.R. in terms of total stock, the pattern of employment of this stock was radically different in the two countries. . . . Among the historical trends to be particularly noted is the expansion of professional employment in the research and development establishments of the Soviet Union. In the decade of the 1950's, the expansion of professional employment in agriculture and trade, two bottleneck areas of the Soviet economy, should be especially noted. Despite this, the 20-year trend indicates that the two dominant branches of professional employment in the U.S.S.R. have remained industry and education. . . .

The pattern of employment of Soviet professional graduates by field of former training indicates the high concentration of such graduates in employment sectors coinciding with the fields for which they were trained. Indeed, the majority of Soviet graduates trained in engineering are concentrated in industry, research, and related fields. Likewise, the majority of graduates trained in education fields are employed in the public education sector. The majority of physicians are engaged in public health establishments. This pattern of employment suggests that not only initial placement policies (which assign graduates for a 3-year employment period in a place designated by the planning organs) but general employment policies of the Soviet regime concerning specialized professional manpower have been relatively effective in retaining professionals in those branches of activities for which they were specifically trained.

The radical differences in the pattern of employment of Soviet and

American higher education graduates may be further evidenced by the following data:

	Percent of graduates employed	
Branch of Economy	*U.S.S.R.*	*United States*
Manufacturing, construction, transportation, and communication—including research and development	27	28
Agriculture	4	3
Trade and distribution	1	21
Government administration	14	13
Education	43	22
Public health	11	13

These data indicate that over one-fifth of U.S. college graduates worked in trade and distribution, reflecting its consumption-oriented activities, while in the U.S.S.R. only 1 percent was thus employed. The proportion of higher education graduates employed in education was twice as high in the Soviet Union (43 percent) as in the United States (22 percent), reflecting another basic feature of the Soviet effort—emphasis on education as a crucial feedback mechanism for the buildup of its specialized manpower potential. In sum, then, this pattern of the deployment of Soviet professional manpower is a reflection of the radically different patterns of the orientation of human activities in the two economies, with the Soviet strategy still being aimed primarily at industrial expansion and the development of the human resources required for its attainment.

Another dimension in the deployment pattern of specialists is the performance of functions. Although the above data on the employment of Soviet professionals indicate that the majority of specialists are employed in those industry sectors of the economy for which they were trained, the general problem of actual on-the-job utilization remains an unexplored one. Similarly, for the United States, the question of actual utilization of college graduates, in relation to their former fields of training and performance of professional functions, stilll calls for serious study. In general, it is apparent that in the U.S.S.R., in the absence of generalists, Soviet technical specialists have many functions in various industrial administrations, management, and government. About one-half of all Soviet engineers are engaged either in managerial positions in industry directly, or in the management of research and development, or in government administration. About one-third of Soviet physicians employed in the health sector of the economy actually combine their practice with managerial functions. Almost two-thirds of all agricultural specialists are employed in management. Such use of technical specialists in managerial positions, which in the United States are often filled by liberal arts and business administration graduates, tends to decrease the numerical imbalance in the stock of technical graduates between the United States and the U.S.S.R.

RETROSPECT

The development of Soviet education and specialized manpower resources should be viewed mainly in the context of total Communist advances—political, economic, social, and cultural. There is a much closer integration of educational and manpower policies with economic and political objectives in the Soviet totalitarian society than in other modern industrial nations whose policies are based on pluralistic values. Soviet education derives its strength and, by the same token, its weaknesses, from the fact that it is centrally planned and directed by the state.

In the Soviet Union a high premium is placed upon technical and specialized, rather than general, excellence. Science and technology are particularly recognized as the foundation of national strength, and consequently they receive emphasis on all levels of the educational effort. Secondary schooling provides the base for early (and mandatory) exposure to the sciences and technology, from which select individuals are chosen for professional education. The quality of Soviet professional training in scientific, engineering, and applied fields today is, on substantive grounds, comparable to that offered in the West. This is not true, however, of all fields—especially where political intervention is heavily felt or where exclusively applied objectives prevail.

With the numerical expansion of the stock of higher education graduates, the question of the adequacy of their specialized training becomes increasingly important. In recent years the exceedingly narrow specialization of Soviet professionals has been curtailed somewhat, though it still remains more pronounced than in the West. With the advent of the new phase of Soviet industrial expansion—accelerated technological change and the accelerated development of automation in which the narrow specialties of engineer and industrial technician training may prove quite insufficient and inadequate for the more sophisticated needs of the Soviet industrial economy—perhaps a broader professional education of Soviet specialists may become a necessity.

Many qualitative reservations, however, become less significant in view of the quantitative gains made by Soviet professional education over the last three decades. The planners have succeeded in increasing spectacularly the rate of producing specialists. Higher education is still accessible to a substantially smaller proportion of the Soviet population than is the case in the United States. Instead of making higher educational opportunity widely available, the Soviet regime has concentrated its efforts on the development of the specialized manpower needed to further its longrun economic and military goals. As a result, in recent years the number of higher education graduates in the sciences and various applied fields—engineering, agriculture, and medicine—has exceeded substantially (by a factor of 2 or 3 to 1) the rate of training such specialists in the United States.

At the recent 22nd Party Congress, Mr. Khrushchev reiterated the Communist regime's longstanding commitment to the expansion of Soviet education, forecasting a higher education enrollment of 8 million by 1980, as compared with the current 2.6 million students in Soviet institutions of higher learning. The United States had an enrollment of 4 million in higher education in the fall of 1961; by 1980, it will probably reach 8.5 million. If these targets are achieved by 1980, the Soviet Union will probably catch up with the United States in total enrollments in higher education. Whether or not these targets are actually achieved, however, the strong Soviet effort in developing human resources and in training professional specialists, particularly in science and engineering, will undoubtedly continue, posing a serious challenge in the longrun struggle between democracy and totalitarianism.

SOVIET VIEWS

3. THE EFFECTIVENESS OF EDUCATION IN THE U.S.S.R.*

S. G. STRUMILIN

*Academician, Academy of Sciences
U.S.S.R.*

Public education in the USSR is organized so that instruction and character training of the rising generation are closely linked with life, with productive labor, thus enabling the adult population to combine production work with further training and education in accordance with their personal inclinations and the requirements of society. Basing public education on these principles, as the Party Program stipulated, promotes the shaping of harmoniously developed members of communist society and, thereby, the solution of one of the most important social problems, namely, elimination of the essential differences between mental and physical labor.

But alongside these long-term aims in the sphere of social policy, public education in the USSR serves the country's immediate tasks as well, being a powerful lever for economic progress and high rates of growth in labor productivity. . . .

In the countries where private capital rules it is only natural that businessmen should invest only in areas that promise them a sufficiently high rate of profit, irrespective of any other effects of these investments on other persons or the whole of society. . . .

It is clearer in the socialist countries—where private capital and its changing concomitants are non-existent—than anywhere else that a high rate of profitability cannot serve as a sufficiently precise and objective yardstick of the effectiveness of capital investments. This is so, first of all, because when we spend social accumulations we must take into account their overall effect, that is, for the whole of society, whereas the rate of profitabil-

* From *Ekonomicheskaia Gazeta,* April 2, 1962. Translated in *Soviet Education,* April, 1962, pp. 3-11. Excerpts reprinted from the translation by permission of the publisher.

ity always measures only that part of the effect accruing to a particular enterprise.

Under socialism the only yardstick of the total effect of investments is the increase in the productivity of social labor that they bring, for this not only increases the accumulations of an enterprise but lowers the cost of the given product for the whole of society.

Labor productivity, as we know, is determined by various circumstances, but we can regard as the most important a high level of technology and the amount of electric power per unit of labor. Today, when automation and telemechanics are being introduced into production on an ever wider scale and cybernetics and electronics are being successfully applied, it is possible to say that *the application of science is now becoming the decisive factor in the powerful growth of society's productive forces. But this means that the achievements of science must become the property of larger and larger sections of the population.* That cannot be done without very substantial capital outlays for school instruction and out-of-school education for the working people on a national scale. The most advanced machinery yields nothing until it is fully mastered by those who have to operate it. The more complicated and expensive the machinery, the broader the range of knowledge without which it is easier to ruin it than operate it, the more important it is to have a rational system of public education, and the more fruitful are the capital investments in it.

This is borne out by the Soviet Union's entire experience of planning. In tsarist times practically the whole population of Russia was illiterate. The workers' and peasants' government literally had to begin its cultural mission by teaching the many millions of workers and peasants to read and write. As early as December 26, 1919, the Soviet Government issued a decree on the abolition of illiteracy among the entire adult population of the republic up to the age of 50. Although all of two decades were required to accomplish this objective, the results were quite satisfactory. In 1924 the country was given another important goal: a ten-year program for expanding the school system was submitted for the consideration of the State Planning Commission. Its aim was universal, obligatory, free education of all children. . . .

Naturally, highly skilled and highly productive workers increase not only their own earnings but also the social product of their labor, and at the same time the total volume of the national income grows in equal measure. Therefore, by comparing society's outlays on school education with the additional increase in the national income which these outlays yield, we can determine the effectiveness of public education. According to calculations made in 1924, an outlay of 1.622 billion rubles would be required to reorganize elementary education and increase school enrollment from 4,000,000 pupils to over 8,000,000 in the course of ten years. However, by the end of this period the increase in the national income resulting from the higher work skills of the children taught in those years amounted to more than 2 billion rubles, after only five years of their work. This increase more than covered all the outlays.

Actually, the Soviet Union's first major planned task in public education was solved, in the main, by the beginning of 1934. Universal obligatory education was introduced everywhere, and the cities had seven-year education. The new Party Program adopted in 1961 sets the following tasks: to effect, in 1960-1970, compulsory *secondary* general and polytechnical *eleven-year* education for all children of school age in both urban and rural localities, and to provide facilities so that everyone who wishes to study can obtain a *higher* education, either studying full time or combining work with study. What the Soviet Union has achieved to date in the sphere of public education can be judged from the few general figures which follow.

In 1960 the number of pupils in the Soviet Union's elementary schools —1st to 4th grades—was 18,600,000. School enrollment among the corresponding age groups is sufficiently complete, and further growth in the number of pupils in this category obviously cannot exceed the current increase of new generations of children. This makes all the more noticeable the rapid growth in pupils of the older age groups receiving general and specialized schooling in the 5th to 10th grades of the secondary schools and technical schools, and of students in the higher schools. A comparison with the tsarist school system (on the present territory of the Soviet Union) reveals the following growth in school enrollment (in thousands):

	Secondary Schools			Total	
			Universities		
Year	*General*	*Specialized*	*and higher*	*Absolute*	*%*
	5th to 10th grades		*technical schools*		
1914	506	36	112	654	22
1930	2,042	587	288	2,917	100
1940	13,796	975	812	15,583	534
1950	14,612	1,298	1,247	17,157	588
1960	17,392	2,060	2,396[1]	21,848	749

[1] The 1961 figure was 2,600,000.

From 1930 to 1960 the population of the USSR increased by only 39%, while enrollment in the 1st to 4th grades of elementary school increased 7.5 times in those 30 years and 33 times compared with 1914. In other words, the training of personnel so needed by the national economy went ahead at a rapid rate. There was also an increase in the number of students finishing secondary schools and higher schools each year. The number of teachers, doctors, engineers and scientists grew. The total graduating classes of general and technical secondary schools and higher schools also increased. Here are some figures showing this growth in the USSR since the revolution as compared with the maximum figures in tsarist Russia (counting the area within the present frontiers of the Soviet Union):

NUMBER OF STUDENTS GRADUATED
(IN THOUSANDS)

Types of Schools

	1914	1930	1940	1950	1960
General secondary	—	48	277	284	1,055
Secondary technical	4.9	61.4	237	314	484
Universities and higher technical schools	10.7	43.9	126	177	343
Total (in thousands)	15.6	153.3	640	775	1,882
(in %)	—	100	417	506	1,228

In the early years of the planned reconstruction of Soviet industry it seemed to many that machines were the decisive factor. However, it proved so difficult for untrained workers to learn to operate the machines that, in the interests of the machinery, a new slogan had to be advanced: cadres decide everything. That is why the expansion in the school training of personnel in the ten years from 1930 to 1940 was so great. In the subsequent decade military adversities slowed down this growth. But from 1950 to 1960 we again see a big growth in the number of skilled persons trained in schools: an increase of 140% in those ten years, not counting the number trained at factory schools, trade schools and the like. Altogether, from 1918 to 1960 the Soviet national economy received 4,781,000 specialists from higher educational institutions and 7,744,000 from secondary technical schools, making a total of 12,525,000. The number trained in the past ten years alone is 6,755,000, or 54% of the total trained since the revolution.

The tremendous amount of work put into eliminating illiteracy should also be taken into account. From 1920 to 1939 more than 57,500,000 illiterate and 38,500,000 semi-literate adults finished schools or courses for the elimination of illiteracy. In addition, the number of children who finished the four-year elementary schools and the seven-year incomplete secondary schools in the 12 years from 1924 through 1935 were 23,800,000 and 7,100,000 respectively, or a total of 30,900,000. . . .

In the 20 years from 1939 to 1959, a period which includes the war years, the population of the USSR grew from 190,700,000 to 208,800,000, an increase of 18,100,000, or 9.5%. The gainfully employed population grew from 88,000,000 to 99,000,000, or by 12%, while the number of persons with a secondary or higher education rose by 43,000,000, or by 270%, notwithstanding the wartime losses. An even bigger rise in the number of secondary and higher school graduates—by 335%—was registered among the gainfully employed population. Even among the industrial workers and collective farmers, that is, persons engaged chiefly in physical labor, the proportion of secondary and higher school graduates increased from 4.3 to 31.6%; among industrial workers they comprise not less than 38.6% of the total, the figure rising to 53.5% in the metallurgical and metal-working industries, 64% in the printing trades, and a still higher percentage among workers in some other fields.

Of those persons with a higher education, engineers and agronomists are of particular importance to the national economy. In total number of these the USSR has long since held first place in the world. As of December 1, 1960, more than 1,115,000 engineers and 1,931,300 graduate technicians, that is, upwards of 3,000,000 engineers and technicians were employed in our national economy. Nevertheless, not fearing an overproduction of these specialists, Soviet schools graduated another 120,000 engineers and 250,000 technicians in 1960, and plan a further expansion of their training. The United States, by comparison, had some 525,000 engineers in 1960 and the number graduated annually in recent years has not exceeded 38,000.

The elimination of mass illiteracy and the introduction of universal obligatory four-year elementary schooling provided a broad foundation for the development of secondary and higher education. However, in 1940 there were still no less than 62,000,000 citizens, excluding schoolchildren, who had not received a seven-year education. By 1960 the number was no more than 38,000,000. Thus, the relative number of persons with a low level of education is sharply decreasing, while the average educational level is rising rapidly, and ten years from now, with the implementation of universal eleven-year secondary education, will increase still faster.

The older workers with the lowest educational level will go on pension—more than 20,000,000 in the next ten years—and more than 30,-000,000 young people will replace them from the secondary and higher schools. Thus, even in the sphere of material production the labor force, besides possessing advanced technology, will have a solid background of knowledge. Considering the fact that the annual number of persons finishing complete secondary and higher schools has more than doubled in the past ten years and reached a total of about 2,000,000 per year in 1961, it is not difficult to calculate that in the next 10 years the personnel from the Soviet intelligentsia will grow by at least 30,000,000, and in the next 20 years by from 70,000,000 to 80,000,000.

In the West, with their market conditions, such a growth would create the threat of a grave overproduction of manpower in all occupations involving intellectual labor, would result in greater unemployment, and sharply reduce wages in the corresponding fields. In a planned economy such dangers do not exist. All citizens of the USSR are guaranteed the right to work. They are the masters of their own destiny. They are threatened neither by unemployment nor a cut in earnings, since the country's production plans provide beforehand for a feasible rise in labor productivity, the reduction in the work day that becomes necessary in this connection, the possible rise in money wages commensurate with the growth of the national income, as well as for a rise in the real standard of living of all working people.

The expansion of public education has been accompanied by a growth in state appropriations for this item that is proportionately bigger than the growth of USSR budget expenditures as a whole. . . . Expenditures on education went up from 2.25 billion rubles in 1940 to 5.7 billion in 1950 and 10.3 billion in 1960, in terms of the new ruble. . . . Parents do not pay anything for the instruction of their children. . . .

Accompanying the expansion of public education was an increase in the economic effect already directly connected with it. This refers, first of all, to a rise in the wages of workers whose qualifications had risen. . . . Under socialism earnings are scaled to stimulate every worker and engineer to obtain knowledge, to improve his qualifications. This, in turn, leads to higher earnings for workers and specialists. . . .

By raising workers' qualifications we increase, proportionately, the product they create for society and the payment for their labor. For instance, according to the 1959 statistics on the national income of the USSR, for every 100 rubles earned by workers in material production there was created no less than 88 rubles' worth of surplus product, which went into the country's funds of social consumption and accumulation. Therefore, in studying the effectiveness of education and the profitability of the capital investments made in it, we must include in the effect that share of the surplus product which is created as a result of the rise in workers' qualifications.

From 1940 to 1960 the national income of the USSR grew from 33.5 billion rubles to 146.6 billion, in constant prices, that is, by 338%, or by 113.1 billion rubles in 1961 prices. The number of persons engaged in producing it increased in those 20 years from 54,600,000 to 68,400,000, that is, by only 25%. But the rise in the qualifications of the labor force through secondary and higher education also has to be taken into account. . . .

Another major factor in the growth of the national income from the standpoint of consumption is the extent to which workers are equipped with instruments of labor which contribute to higher productivity. As a yardstick of this we can take the growth of productive capital, in constant prices, per unit of labor as a first approximation. From 1940 to 1960 the value of the Soviet Union's fixed productive capital increased from 55.7 billion rubles to 173.9 billion rubles, that is, it more than trebled in these 20 years. If the number of workers remains constant, each per cent of increase in this capital generally yields, as a result of the growth in the technical equipment of labor, a proportionate growth in its output. However, if there is a simultaneous growth in the number of workers and the technical equipment of labor, its effect on production grows in proportion to the product of these two factors. . . . Nevertheless, the part played by labor of higher qualifications in the sum total registered in our table is a very big one. . . . If the total national income in 1960 was 146.6 billion rubles, in current prices, 23% of which came through a rise in the qualifications of the labor force, in terms of money this share was no less than 33.7 billion rubles.

Such is the economic effect yielded by secondary and higher education in the USSR. It can be compared with the current state expenditures on education and with the fixed capital in education, science and art embodied in the construction and equipment of the corresponding institutions, since in the final analysis not only the schools but also the theaters, art galleries, zoological gardens and polytechnical museums all serve the same aim of educating the working people and raising their qualifications. According to data of the Central Statistical Administration, the value of this capital was 1.205 billion rubles in 1930, 4.370 billion in 1940, 5.388 billion in 1950, and 16.237 billion in 1960, all these figures being in current prices. Amazing though this growth is, the increase in the effectiveness of labor as a result of secondary and higher education proceeded at a still faster rate. A comparison with even the total outlays on all types of schools in the country gives the following picture of this steadily-growing effectiveness:

EFFECTIVENESS AND PROFITABILITY OF PUBLIC EDUCATION IN THE USSR
(IN BILLIONS OF RUBLES, IN CONSTANT PRICES)

	1940		1950		1960	
Indices	*Absolute*	*%*	*Absolute*	*%*	*Absolute*	*%*
A. Fixed capital in education, etc.	4.37	100	5.39	123	16.24	372
B. Effectiveness of education: Increases in national income	5.39	100	11.31	210	33.72	626
Current yearly outlays	3.13	100	4.25	136	10.30	329
Excess of income over outlay	2.26	100	7.06	312	23.42	1,036
The same in % of fixed capital	52	—	131	—	144	—

Although the fixed capital in education, social science and art increased from 1940 to 1960 even faster than in the sphere of material production, and current outlays on education more than trebled, in constant prices, the increase in the national income resulting from secondary and higher education in those years was more than six-fold, while the net profit, after deduction of the current outlays, went up ten-fold. As a result, the economic profitability of the investments in this area of cultural development exceeded, on the average for the whole country, all the other indices we know of. . . .

Such an effect from public education will probably come as quite a surprise to many people, all the more so since it is not registered in any official reports. Nor does everyone clearly understand all the sources of such rapid rates of growth of the national income in the productive sphere as a result of the increase in the number of educated workers, since the incomes of the most highly educated personnel—those employed in the fields of science and culture—are not counted at all in the national income as a whole.[2] However, as their numbers grow, the indirect influence of their labor on the size of the national income from the standpoint of consumption is becoming more and more significant. Indeed, every schoolteacher passes on his knowledge to hundreds of pupils, and this helps to raise the productivity of their labor in material production. Soviet doctors help to improve the health of the working population and to prolong its working capacity by decades, and therefore they too—if not themselves, then through the hands of their patients—increase the general scale of the material values produced. As for scientists, now that science is becoming a direct productive force in our country their labor has grown still more important. . . .

Many great minds, from Euclid to Lobachevsky, from Pythagoras and Archimedes to Newton and Einstein, from Heraclitus and Aristotle to Kurchatov, have enriched science, and the fruits of their creative efforts will continue to serve mankind for thousands of years to come. However, the truths which it took Euclid a lifetime to evolve are assimilated in some three years, along with dozens of other subjects, by our schoolchildren. As for Newton's binomial theorem or Mendeleyev's Periodic Table of the Elements, schoolchildren learn them in a matter of hours. Today's schoolchildren are tomorrow's workers, and the incomparable ease with which they master all the hard-won fruits of science allows us to regard these fruits as sheer gifts.

In present-day industry, with its rapidly developing automation and electronics, knowledge is becoming especially valuable. Today the main thing is not so much brawn and toil-hardened hands but the cultural and technical level of the worker at the lathe and automatic line. For this reason science is now becoming a direct productive force, and it can be stated that its effectiveness will increase immeasurably.

Achievements in public education in the USSR in the past few decades have contributed greatly to the introduction of science directly into produc-

---

[2] In the Soviet Union national income is defined as the total of all incomes earned (or expenditures incurred) in the production of material tangible goods. In the United States, on the other hand, the total of all incomes earned is counted, irrespective of whether they are earned in the production of material goods or in the performance of direct services. [Editor's note.]

tion and to the heightening of its effectiveness as a special productive force of living labor. Another very important contributing factor in this respect is that Soviet workers, regarding themselves not as servants of production but as its masters, are extraordinarily eager to improve their qualifications; tens of millions enthusiastically vie among themselves for higher productivity; from their ranks come millions of gifted inventors and rationalizers of production.

Their successes are promoted by the fact that science enjoys higher prestige in the USSR than anywhere else in the world. "Advancing without science is the same as a blind man trying to walk without a guide: you will stumble all the time," say our people. This keen observation has now become a part of folk wisdom. "Science is our compass," says Comrade N. S. Khrushchev. "Organizing people and moving forward by that compass—such is the course towards victory." As the whole of our Soviet experience has shown, this guiding principle really assures brilliant results.

Our cultural revolution and economic progress are closely intertwined. Our investments in public education are so profitable because they serve the cultural requirements of the working masses and are in accord with the objective demands of the socialist economy. In this process the cultural factor reveals its economic effectiveness more and more strikingly.

4. TO HELP CREATE THE NEW SOVIET MAN: ONE OF THE PRIMARY TASKS OF THE SOVIET SCHOOL *

N. I. BOLDYREV

Head, "Foundations of Education Department," RSFSR Academy of Pedagogical Sciences' Research Institute of the Theory and History of Pedagogy

The new Program of the Communist Party of the Soviet Union formulates, for the first time, the moral code of the builder of communism, outlines the ethical requirements of our society, and indicates the basic moral traits of the new man. The moral code of the builder of communism

* From *Sovetskaia pedagogika*, 1962, No. 6. Translated under the title "The Moral Code of the Builders of Communism—the Basis for the Moral Upbringing of the Rising Generation," in *Soviet Education*, Jan., 1963, pp. 42-49. Excerpts reprinted from the translation by permission of the publisher.

is justly regarded as the theoretical foundation for the moral upbringing of our people and, first and foremost, of the rising generation.

In his report to the 22nd Party Congress on the Party Program, N. S. Khrushchev said: "The generation of communism must be molded from childhood; it should be cared for and tempered in its youth; we must see to it that none are crippled morally, that is, become victims of incorrect upbringing and bad examples. If young plantings of fruit trees are damaged in any way, a great deal of work is needed to have them come up right, and even then these efforts are not always successful. The same may be said of the new generation."

The molding of the new man with the new ethic is a most important duty of the Soviet school, family, and society. The training of all children, adolescents and youths and girls for life and work in a communist society requires that greater attention be paid to moral upbringing.

Our country has reached a high level of economic, socio-political and spiritual development, and the Party has set the gigantic task of educating the entire population in the spirit of scientific communism. As the Program of the CPSU indicates, all members of the society are called upon to consciously build their lives along communist lines.

The moral code includes the basic standards of behavior. After these standards become assimilated and are practiced in everyday behavior, they become moral qualities, attributes of the personality, and characterize the moral make-up of people. The aim of moral upbringing is to convert the moral standards and principles into the main personality traits of the new man.

Lenin called the fundamental standards of human morality the elementary rules for life in a community, and pointed out that they evolved over centuries and millennia. In our country, such moral categories as honesty, truthfulness, simplicity, and modesty are elementary rules of human society. Their observance is a prerequisite for proper relations between people. . . .

The Communist Party considers it one of its most important tasks to educate our people in the spirit of proletarian internationalism. The formation of the world socialist system, the joint effort for peace, the struggle against colonialism, the uncompromising attitude towards the enemies of communism, and the strengthening of friendship and brotherhood among all nations require a further improvement in the rearing of the rising generation in the spirit of internationalism. Devotion to the ideas of communism involves love of man and of all mankind. It is not by chance that the Party Program considers the development of proletarian internationalism as one of the tasks involved in the development of communist consciousness. . . .

Reorganization of the schools so as to ensure their ties with life, and the combining of instruction with productive labor create favorable conditions for developing in the pupils a communist attitude toward labor for the good of society. Proceeding from the principles of the moral code of the builder of communism, our schools are paying much greater attention to schooling the pupils in the preservation and growth of public wealth. A great deal of work is now being done to safeguard school property and to make and preserve school visual aids. The pupils concern themselves with the care of equipment at collective farms and industrial enterprises, as well as with the preservation of nature. The application of this moral principle in practice helps to do away with survivals of the consumer psychology in individual children, adolescents, young men and women. In our day it is particularly important to educate schoolchildren so that their requirements are reasonable, and at the same time to develop their abilities in a definite sphere. These are important tasks of education. Until recently many of our schools hardly paid any attention to this matter.

The building of communism gives every person various duties which must be fulfilled not mechanically, but with a deep understanding and awareness that they are needed by society; they must be fulfilled in accordance with the inner promptings of the heart. A high sense of public duty is a most important principle of the moral code of the builder of communism. Among schoolchildren it is revealed in their attitude toward studying and their assignments, toward socially useful and productive labor, and toward school procedures. . . .

Genuine conditions are being created in the period of transition from socialism to communism for implementing more completely and consistently the lofty moral principles: "One for all and all for one," and "Man is to man a friend, comrade and brother." . . .

The enemies of communism are unable to deny the reality of the fulfillment of the economic program of communist construction. But they dispute the possibility of rearing a new man. The bourgeois ideologists do a great deal of talking and writing about the "unchangeable nature" of man. They are trying to prove that such negative traits as selfishness, cruelty, money-grubbing, lust for profits, greediness and the like will always be characteristic of man. Day in and day out the young people in the imperialist countries read in the newspapers, magazines and books that the world is on the brink of disaster and that, therefore, the concepts about morality, honesty and humanism are outdated. The foreign reactionary press claims that progress is possible only in the material sphere, but, as regards the sphere of morality, mankind is doomed to mark time forever, since the moral qualities of a man allegedly cannot be changed.

Life in a socialist society, the molding of a new man in our country and in the countries of the socialist community refute these inventions completely. . . .

Now, when we are at the near approaches to communism, the moral make-up of the man of the future becomes ever clearer. In the period of the direct building of communism, the basic principles of communist morality have acquired not only theoretical but practical significance as well. That is why the necessity arose to formulate and systematize the basic ethical standards of man's behavior in the form of a definite moral code. This code includes only the main standards of behavior, which are usually called ethical principles and are not decreed from above or established administratively, but reflect what has already been mainly achieved and is being practiced. . . .

The key to the moral upbringing of schoolchildren lies in the organization of their varied activities. The lofty moral principles of our society are comprehended and become personal convictions primarily in the process of labor for the common good. At the 3rd Komsomol Congress, Lenin urged the youth to ". . . devote their labor and energy to the common cause. This is communist upbringing. Only in such work does a young man or woman become a real communist. They become communists only if they are able to achieve practical success as a result of this work."

Active participation by schoolchildren in collective work helps to transform the ethical principles into personal convictions. This has been demonstrated and confirmed by the experience in shaping the communist convictions of the rising generation in the Soviet Union, as well as in the countries of the socialist camp. . . .

The upbringing of children in the spirit of the humane principles of the moral code is promoted not only by socially useful labor, but also by all kinds of school work, various club activities and games, physical training and sports, as well as amateur art activities. Proper organization of the pupils' activities and, first and foremost, their participation in feasible socially useful labor make it possible to eliminate any gap between the consciousness and behavior of the pupils, between their words and deeds. . . .

When organizing various activities for the pupils, our schools give preference to collective forms of these activities. . . . When working in the collective, the schoolchildren are imbued with broad social interests, devote their energies and abilities to the common cause, and as a result, become enriched spiritually, develop and acquire lofty moral qualities.

Under present conditions it is particularly important to expand the sphere of action of the moral factor in the life of school, which gradually will become an ever more democratic institution. . . . We must resolutely discard the authoritarian approach to upbringing, and renounce administration by injunction and unnecessary supervision and tutelage of the pupils. Thought should be given to the idea of transferring to the pupils' organizations the functions of maintaining discipline and order in school.

The system by which upper-grade pupils independently perform duty assignments has fully justified itself. Maintaining order during intervals, keeping the school premises clean, and helping teachers to better organize the teaching process give the pupils a feeling of greater responsibility for the organization of life at school. Simultaneously, their moral experience becomes broader and richer.

The time has come to give the agencies of the pupils' collectives greater rights and independence in drawing up and implementing plans of socially useful work, in organizing cultural and sports activities, and in discussing matters concerning any breach of discipline or order by individual pupils at school, at an enterprise or in public places. All this will undoubtedly help the pupils to accumulate experience while at school, as well as to acquire the knowledge and habits needed for active participation in the agencies of communist self-government. . . .

The extensive use of positive examples in the process of education promotes the pupils' assimilation of moral principles and the transformation of these principles into personal convictions. Everything that is new and progressive finds support and is widely disseminated in our country. The images of our advanced contemporaries constitute a powerful factor in instilling communist views and convictions. The labor exploits of the communist work teams and communist shock workers, the selfless fulfillment by Soviet people of their public duty—all this teaches the pupils to think and act in a communist way, to observe the lofty principles of communist morality. . . .

Dry, abstract conversations on moral themes which do not deal with our splendid reality should be eliminated from school activities. There are always people at the neighboring factory or collective farm where the pupils work whose deeds and behavior vividly reflect the lofty qualities of communist morality. The newspapers and radio have daily reports about the labor heroism, courage, integrity, honesty, and modesty of Soviet people. The thoughtful teacher will always find an opportunity to tell the children about these things in a clear and interesting way, to arouse in them a desire to emulate what is best and progressive in our life. . . . It has become a tradition in many schools to organize gatherings at which pupils meet the best workers from the local enterprises, state and collective farms; exhibitions and displays are also organized on such themes as "Men of Labor" and "Be Like Them." . . .

The volunteer public order squads, numbering over four million persons, are successfully combining struggle against violators of public order with important work in education and re-education. They see to it that children and young people behave properly in public places, help in intelligently organizing the leisure time of those schoolchildren who are without supervision, involve them in interesting occupations, and protect them from baneful influences.

The public takes an active part in setting up prolonged-day schools and groups. Many schools now provide free meals for the pupils at the expense of collective farms and public organizations, and Young Pioneer and Komsomol camps of work and recreation are being organized.

In this way the sphere of public influence on the upbringing of children and young people is widening. Engels' remark that, with the triumph of socialism, ". . . care of children and their upbringing will become a public affair: society will concern itself with all children equally," is coming true.

The moral make-up of the rising generation is being shaped not only as a result of purposeful influences, but also under the influence of the environment. A man with new ethics is being educated by the socialist way of life as a whole and by all the objective conditions taken together. The communist work teams bring to school not only a new, more perfect organization of labor, but also provide new examples of behavior at work, at home and in daily life, thus performing educational functions. The efforts of school Komsomol and Young Pioneer organizations to establish close contact with the communist work teams and shock workers deserve support.

This friendship helps pupils in upper grades to prepare themselves for work in communist work teams, for conscientious and voluntary labor for the good of society.

The new conditions of life and work bring forth new standards and rules of behavior. As we advance toward communism, society will make ever greater demands on its members. Moral purity will become an inherent quality, and voluntary observance of the rules of living in a communist society will be a matter of conscience for every member of society. That is why it is necessary even now to strive to have the principles of the moral code of the builder of communism become an inner need, a guide to action for all the working people in our society. This means that the moral upbringing carried on at school should embrace all pupils, and each one individually, at all stages of their development. . . .

The upbringing of the rising generation on the basis of the moral code of the builder of communism is one of the main, central tasks of the Soviet school. The lofty and humane principles of the moral code must be gradually transformed into inviolable and vital rules for each schoolchild, must become his customary behavior traits.

5. YOU *CAN* CHANGE 'HUMAN NATURE' *

Equality cannot be established until man treats man as friend and brother. Nor can happiness come to him who is poor of spirit, a stranger to the joy of knowledge, deaf and blind to the beauty of art.

While building communism, in other words, society must prepare its members for it, give them the noblest qualities, and help them cleanse themselves of all that blackens human dignity.

Is this feasible?

No! say the bourgeois sociologists and moralists. Man is a low creature by his very nature.

For thousands of years he has been urged not to kill, not to steal, not to cheat and yet blood is shed throughout the world as before, robbery flourishes and brother continues to betray brother.

It is possible—they say—to adjust people partially to communal life, to train them to keep within the framework of superficial decencies, but the brute in man can never be eradicated, nor can he ever be rid of his vices.

CONFIRMED BY HISTORY

We reply: That isn't true! Man can be re-educated. The founders of Marxism proved scientifically that the social life of people shapes their consciousness, and this truth has been confirmed by the history of mankind.

For two or three thousand years people have hardly changed in appearance. If an ancient Roman were to turn up among us dressed in modern clothes he would pass unnoticed in the crowds. But the spiritual world of our contemporary is not only incomparably richer than that of his ancient counterpart, but far richer even than that of a man a century ago.

---

* Abridged from G. H. Shakhnazarov (Editor), *Social Sciences* (a new, official textbook used in a social science course in Soviet schools). Translated in and reprinted from *Soviet Weekly*, May 2, 1963, p. 8, by permission of the publisher.

As for vices, these will inevitably die away once the social conditions that have produced them shall have been removed.

Private property and the exploitation of man by man—these are the chief conditions making for vices.

Nor is it only the objective conditions of social life in the capitalist world that breed the relations of "the war of all against all."

That war is furthered, too, by the whole of bourgeois ideology, glorifying the cult of the "superman" who can set his foot on the throat of his rivals, who can rise to power and riches through deceit and cruelty.

This was most frankly and cynically expressed in the theories of the fascists. The German philosopher Nietzsche, ideological forerunner of fascism, prophesied the new era of the "superman," who would flood the world with blood and reduce all mankind to slavery.

The revolution of the consciousness is, of course, the most complex of all revolutions. But it will nevertheless succeed where the very conditions of life objectively further psychological change and the triumph of the new communist morality.

The controversy about man and his destiny has long passed from theory to practice.

On the socialist side of the world, the communist understanding of man's essence is firmly established.

Man is no slave of the elements, but the builder of his own happiness and master of nature; he is no mere grain in the whirlpool of social storms, but a maker of history.

The entire set-up of our existence is a school for the rearing of the new man.

STINTS NOTHING

Socialist society stints nothing to give everyone the opportunity to receive an education to acquire a speciality, to develop his gifts and employ them fruitfully.

Nor is society concerned with this only because "everything for man" is one of his main slogans. The more educated people are and the wider their outlooks, the more they will be able to give to society.

The fact that the economic and political system of socialism furthers the all-round development of the individual by no means implies that the revolution in the consciousness is something that can happen spontaneously.

Society cannot rely entirely on the objective factors and wait until these have done their work, but must strive to hasten the process of reshaping the consciousness by every ideological means.

The schools, literature, art, the press, radio, television, and all the other means of influencing the minds and hearts of the people are tirelessly propagating the heroism of labour, the ideas of collectivism and humanism, and inculcating those features worthy of the man of communism.

Now that we have actually begun to build the communist society, communist rearing of the working people has come to be the basic task of the party and all social organisations.

B. Soviet Higher Education

WESTERN VIEWS

6. HIGHER EDUCATION IN THE U.S.S.R.*

SEYMOUR M. ROSEN

Specialist in Comparative Education for the U.S.S.R. and Eastern Europe, Office of Education, United States Department of Health, Education, and Welfare

I. PLANNING AND SUPERVISION

The scope, as well as the content, of the activities of the 739 Soviet higher educational institutions, their 146,900 staff members, and 2,395,500 students are subject to planning and control by the central Communist Party and Soviet Government. As demonstrated in the educational reform of 1958, the Communist Party in Moscow initiates major changes for the educational system throughout the country and issues policy statements jointly with the Council of Ministers of the U.S.S.R., the central government executive body. The U.S.S.R. Supreme Soviet, the central Soviet legislative body, then issues the educational laws based on joint decisions of the party and the Government. Thereafter, the Supreme Soviets of the 15 constituent republics follow with laws for the educational apparatus

* Excerpts reprinted from *Dimensions of Soviet Economic Power,* Materials prepared for the Joint Economic Committee, Congress of the United States, 1962, pp. 269-303.

in each republic, closely modeled upon the law issued by the central legislative body. On the whole, the wording of the local laws is identical with that of the central government law, with minor variation to suit local conditions.

Central planning and operational control are implemented through a Communist Party and government executive hierarchy which form a chain of command from Moscow to each higher educational institution.

The party chain extends downward from the Central Committee's Section for Science, Higher Educational Institutions and Schools, through equivalent sections of the party apparatus in the 15 republics, to party offices located within each higher school.

The Government hierarchy extends from the Ministry of Higher and Specialized Secondary Education, U.S.S.R. Council of Ministers, through the 15 republic ministries and committees concerned with higher education, and laterally through the government ministries actually supervising the higher schools (which may not always be the higher education ministries).

The annual budget of each higher educational institution is decided by the central government within the framework of total State expenditures for the whole Soviet economy. Appropriation requests are submitted by the individual higher school through local government channels, and appropriations are considered within the framework of the budget for the constituent republic's Council of Ministers.

According to a statement by one Soviet university president, Rektor Sadykov of the Central Asian University in Tashkent, made in October 1961, Soviet universities are lavishly financed by the State, receiving all the funds they request as needed to execute their programs. The higher schools receive additional funds by fulfilling orders for applied research for local industrial establishments and ministries. As much as half of the budget of each higher institution is devoted to research. . . .

To some extent the current Soviet higher educational system represents a trend toward decentralization in administration, as distinct from overall planning and control. Until 1959, the immediate higher education authority for all higher schools throughout the country (with the exception of the Ukrainian S.S.R. which had its own ministry in the field) was the U.S.S.R. Ministry of Higher Education in Moscow.

Since 1959, new higher education bodies have been established in each republic, having dual subordination to the republic Council of Ministers and the U.S.S.R. Ministry of Higher and Secondary Specialized Education. . . .

Immediate supervision of Soviet higher schools is not limited to the established higher education ministries and committees in each republic. In fact, less than half of the higher schools of education (333) are supervised by higher education agencies. The majority (376) are under the authority of agencies of the Government directly concerned with the fields of specialized training. Thus, for example, nearly all the medical institutes are under the republic Ministries of Health; most of the institutes training specialists in agriculture are under the republic Ministries of Agriculture; transportation and communication institutes are under various related Government agencies, and higher pedagogical schools are generally under the republic Ministries of Education rather than those of Higher Education.

This pattern conforms closely with the often reiterated Soviet concept that education must be "linked with life," and it, therefore, tends to develop a system of higher schools that is responsive to short-range state economic requirements and cultural pressures, as well as to various shifts to meet new needs as defined by the operating economic agencies of the state.

Besides the designated higher education authority for each republic, there are more than a dozen other agencies involved directly in supervising Soviet higher educational institutions. . . .

II. PRODUCTION OF SPECIALISTS

The broad purpose of Soviet higher education is to provide specialists, appropriately trained but also well indoctrinated in Communist doctrine, to meet the objectives defined by the State's leaders in the economic, scientific, social, and cultural fields.

The vast majority of higher education students in the Soviet Union pursue narrowly specialized curricula which provide the theoretical base for their fields of specialization, and "broadened" only by the required courses in Communist ideology and a foreign language.

The Soviet system of higher education has no equivalent to a liberal arts education. Even the 40 Soviet universities, which accommodate only some 10 percent of the total Soviet student body in Soviet higher schools, are concerned with the production of specialists, trained intensively in a single field of the natural sciences, social sciences, or humanities.

About 90 percent of the Soviet higher school students are enrolled not in the universities, but in the 699 specialized institutes, which produce skilled engineering and other professionals in some narrow field of industry, agriculture, economics, or in medicine, pedagogy, and other fields.

In general, the universities provide the theorists and scholars, while the institutes provide the professionals in their respective applied fields to meet the specific, planned needs of the Soviet economy and society.

Student admission quotas are made, students are enrolled, and graduates are assigned work, according to specialty classification. . . .

In all, there are 303 higher education specialties. Of this number, 217, or 71 percent, are in the field of industrial (including construction, transport, and communications) agricultural, and broadly economic activities. Less than 10 percent are indicated as university specialties, a figure which may in fact be somewhat higher than indicated because of the reporting methods used.

This bending of the higher education system to the purpose of producing specialists to serve the indicated requirements of the economy is reflected in other statistical series. Of the 739 Soviet higher educational institutions, 349, or 47 percent, are specialized institutes for industry, agriculture, and economics. Student enrollments in these fields number 1,387,-300 (1960-61 school year), or 57 percent of the total higher education enrollment.

The number of students training in engineering specialties (1,080,535 in 1960-61) is 49 percent of the total number of students enrolled in Soviet higher schools. In 1960, engineering graduates numbered 120,132, or 35 percent of the total of 342,050 graduates, and engineers were already 31.5 percent of the total number of specialists working in the Soviet economy.

The current Soviet 7-year plan, "Control Figures for the Development of the National Economy," confirmed at the 21st Communist Party Congress, calls for almost doubling (1.9 times) the number of engineering graduates during the 1959-65 period as compared with the preceding 7-year period, and the graduation of 1.5 times more agriculture specialists. Higher education graduations as a whole are scheduled to increase 1.4 times, providing 2,300,000 [1] specialists as compared with 1,700,000 in 1952-58. The profile of the Soviet higher education, therefore, will continue to be that of a system weighted toward training specialists for industry and agriculture.

The greatest increase in the number of engineers, through 1965, according to the 7-year plan control figures, will be in chemical technology, automation, computing techniques, radio electronics, and other new technological fields.

III. PART-TIME HIGHER EDUCATION

Slightly more than half of Soviet students in higher education are studying in part-time programs. In the 1960-61 school year 1,240,000 of the 2,395,500 higher students were in evening divisions of higher schools or studying by correspondence. The remainder (1,155,500) were in regular daytime programs. In 1961-62, 1,436,000 of the total of 2,639,000 students in higher education were studying "without interrupting their permanent jobs," or part time.

Over 40 percent of Soviet higher students are in correspondence pro-

---

[1] The total number of higher education graduations for the first 3 years of the 7-year plan is 1,005,100. The official Soviet figures are 338,000 graduations in 1959, 342,100 in 1960, and 325,000 in 1962.

grams, which have been the major source of increased enrollments in Soviet higher education for the past decade. Regular daytime enrollments have remained almost stationary since the 1955-56 school year. Soviet plans are to accelerate even further part-time education as the principal means of higher educational training.

The "Program of the Communist Party of the Soviet Union, Adopted by the 22d Congress of the C.P.S.U., October 31, 1961," published in Moscow in 1961 by the Foreign Languages Publishing House, states (quoting the complete section of the program entitled "Higher and Secondary Special Education"):

In step with scientific and technical progress, higher and secondary special education, which must train highly skilled specialists with a broad theoretical and political background, will be expanded.

Shorter working hours and a considerable improvement in the standard of living of the entire population will provide everyone with an opportunity to receive a higher or secondary special education if he so desires. The number of higher and secondary specialized schools, evening and correspondence schools in particular, as well as higher schools at factories, agricultural institutes (on large state farms), studios, conservatories, etc., must be increased in all areas of the country with the support of factories and trade unions and other social organizations. The plan is to considerably increase every year the number of students at higher and secondary specialized schools; special education will be afforded to tens of millions of people.

Correspondence training is offered in the Soviet Union through special correspondence institutes, officially accredited as higher educational institutions, and by the correspondence divisions of the regular higher educational institutions.

Twelve of the seventeen Soviet correspondence institutes are in the city of Moscow with branches throughout the Russian Republic. Eleven of the seventeen schools are subordinate to republic higher education authorities, the other to government ministries concerned with related specialties. The overwhelming majority of the correspondence institutes (14 of the 17) are in the industrial, agricultural, and economic fields. The remaining three are devoted to pedagogy and law. . . .

Those enrolled in correspondence and evening courses are granted periods of leave from work with pay for consultation, preparation for state examinations, and diploma work. The relevant regulations of the Council of Ministers, effective since the 1959-60 school year for students in correspondence and evening higher educational institutions (VUZy), are the following:

(1) For first- and second-year students, 20 calendar days' leave in evening VUZy (faculties, divisions), and 30 calendar days in correspondence VUZy.

(2) For third and later years, 30 calendar days' leave in evening VUZy and 40 calendar days in correspondence VUZy.

(3) Thirty calendar days' leave for preparation for state examinations.

(4) Four months' leave for preparation and defense of diploma project.

(5) For 10 months prior to beginning of completion of diploma project, 1 workday free a week at half pay.

Correspondence and evening students may receive an additional month's leave without pay in their senior years for orientation in production work related to their chosen specialty, and for preparation of materials for their diploma project.

The trend in Soviet higher education is toward a gradual merger of part-time education, full-time education, and related on-the-job training. The current educational reform, aimed at "connecting school with life," has affected higher education by incorporating substantial on-the-job training into the regular school programs, thereby lengthening the period of study.

The line between full-time and part-time education is also being obscured by the development of a new type of Soviet higher school, called the plant school for higher technical education (*Zavod-VTUZ*). These higher technical schools, the first of which were established in 1960, are located within and are a part of major Soviet industrial plants. Although not designated as part-time institutions, they are organized "on the basis of the evening divisions" of regular higher schools and the courses of study, combining regular studies with factory work and specialized training, extend from 6 months to a year beyond those of regular higher schools.

The *Zavod-VTUZ* is equipped from the factory facilities and maintained by the factory, and "the plant itself, its shop, and all its production processes will be the capital base for full-fledged training and educational and scientific and technical work."

Specialists in the plants form at least part of the teaching staff, and its professors and instructors perform research in line with each plant's industrial production plan.

As of 1961, there were five plant schools for higher technical education, functioning in the Moscow automobile plant named for I. A. Likhachev, the Leningrad metallurgical plant, the Rostov plant for agricultural machine building, the Penza plant, and the Dneprodzerzhinsk metallurgical plant. . . .

On the basis of a continued survey of Soviet professional education literature, along with the regular Soviet press, it is evident that part-time education, and particularly correspondence training, provides an education of a caliber below that of a regular daytime course of study at a school of higher education. Soviet educators and the Communist Party press have expressed concern over the lack of textbooks and methods literature for correspondence students, the concentration of correspondence and evening higher schools in Moscow (a particular difficulty for correspondence students), the lack of "material and technical" facilities (laboratories, libraries) as well as equipment for correspondence and evening students. The substantial dropout of students each year, the weakness of graduating students in the theory of their specialties, and the fact that experienced teachers avoid work with correspondence students pose other problems of concern. One Soviet publication states that in the libraries of educational institutions correspondence students can obtain books only after the needs of students in the full-time departments have been fully met.

These and other problems of the evening and correspondence school system are enumerated in Soviet sources, with a view toward their improvement, and it is probable that innovations such as the *Zavod-VTUZ* are an attempt to overcome defects in this increasingly dominant form of Soviet higher education.

SOVIET VIEWS

7. HIGHER EDUCATION IN THE U.S.S.R.*

V. P. ELYUTIN

USSR Minister of Higher and Specialised Secondary Education

ACHIEVEMENTS IN HIGHER EDUCATION

. . . In 247 towns in the U.S.S.R. there are now 739 institutions of higher learning with a total student body of 2,600,000.

In the Soviet years higher schools have been opened in 226 towns. The spread of higher education has been particularly intensive in the Urals, Siberia, the Far Eastern regions, Kazakhstan and Central Asia. For instance, there used to be only four higher educational establishments in the eastern areas of the country, whereas now there are 204. In the 1914-15 school year there was not a single college or university on the present-day

* Excerpts reprinted from V. P. Elyutin, D. Sc., *Higher Education in the U.S.S.R.* (published by Soviet Booklets, London, Nov., 1962), by permission of the publisher.

territories of the Byelorussian, Uzbek, Kazakh, Azerbaijan, Lithuanian, Moldavian, Kirghiz, Tajik, Armenian and Turkmen republics. Today each of the republics has higher schools, including universities, which train specialists from among the local population.

The Soviet higher schools give training in all fields of knowledge. Education in the humanities, science and technology, agriculture and medicine has achieved particularly great development.

TRAINING OF SPECIALISTS AT EDUCATIONAL ESTABLISHMENTS OF VARIOUS TYPES

Types of educational establishments	1914-1915 academic year		1961-1962 academic year	
	Number of schools	Enrolment	Number of schools	Enrolment
Industrial, civil engineering, transport and communications	18	24,900	206	1,140,000
Agricultural	14	4,600	96	270,000
Economics and law	15	11,400	51	182,000
Education, art and cinematography	52	81,500	288	847,000
Medicine, physical culture and sports	6	5,000	98	195,000
Total	105	127,400	739	2,634,000

Since 1917 our higher schools have graduated more than 5 million young specialists; 8 million have finished specialised secondary schools.

This steadily brings new contingents of personnel with secondary school and college training into the national economy. It is indicative that the higher educational establishments of the Soviet Union have a student body more than double that of all the capitalist countries of Europe put together. The U.S.S.R. has long since forged ahead of all the capitalist countries of the world, including the United States, in the training of engineers. The number of diploma'd engineers employed in the national economy of the U.S.S.R. has grown from 47,000 in 1928 to 1,236,000 at present, or more than twice as many as in the United States.

The U.S.S.R. possesses trained personnel belonging to all nationalities inhabiting the country. In tsarist Russia there were practically no trained specialists among the Uzbeks, Kazakhs, Kirghiz, Tajiks, Turkmenians, and so on. Those nationalities did not have an intelligentsia of their own. Today one out of every four of the inhabitants there has a secondary or higher education. Compared with 1914, school enrollment in Turkmenia has increased forty-fold, in Kirghizia fifty-fold, and in Uzbekistan eighty-five-fold.

Special mention should be made of the fact that the Soviet system has emancipated women and given them complete equality, making them active participants in the building of a communist society. Of the 8,800,000 persons with a specialised secondary education or a higher education employed in the national economy in 1961, a total of 5,200,000, or 59 per cent, were women.

Women make up 29 per cent of all diploma'd engineers. They comprise 39 per cent of agronomists, livestock experts, veterinaries and sylviculturists, 75 per cent of doctors, and 65 per cent of teachers and other workers in the cultural fields.

At present 43 per cent of the higher school student body are women. There are 129,000 women researchers, 36 per cent of the total number in the country. Some 80,000 women hold the scientific degree of Doctor or Master of Science. This is 27 per cent of the total number of researchers with degrees.

As facts and figures show, a great deal has been accomplished in the sphere of higher education in the Soviet Union. A great deal more, however, is to be accomplished in the coming twenty years, during which the material and technical basis of communism is to be built. The higher schools have "to train highly-qualified specialists possessing broad theoretical and political horizons," declares the Programme of the Communist Party of the Soviet Union.

That is the direction in which the higher schools are now developing, both qualitatively and quantitatively. By 1980 the student body will number 8 million, that is, approximately 5.4 million more than in 1961. The average annual increase in number of students (300,000) will in itself be nearly twice as great as their total number in France or the Federal German Republic.

It now becomes more important than ever to make the standard of training still higher, for a communist society presupposes the all-round, harmonious development of citizens. Particular importance attaches to the social sciences, the teaching of which gives specialists a knowledge of the objective laws of history and the riches of human thought. One's spiritual world is also enriched by a broader knowledge of foreign languages and a study of the culture of other nations.

GENERAL INFORMATION

The higher schools can be divided into three main groups: universities, polytechnical institutes, and specialised institutes or colleges.

The vast majority of higher schools in the Soviet Union are maintained by the state, their funds coming out of the State Budget. Insignificant exceptions are a few schools of higher learning which belong to co-operatives or public organisations.

There are three forms of higher education: full-time study; evening study, where the student works in a factory or office in the daytime and attends classes at the college in the evening; study by correspondence. In the latter case the student is sent the study material and assignments and appears at the college only to take examinations. Sometimes all three forms are found at a single college. The diplomas issued by the higher schools have the same validity irrespective of the college or the form of education.

Administratively and economically the higher schools are under Union Republic jurisdiction. Some specialised higher schools are under definite ministries. For example, the higher schools of the transport services are supervised by the Ministry of Railways. To co-ordinate the work of the higher schools, however, guidance of their research and teaching procedure, no matter under whose jurisdiction they come, is in the hands of the Ministry of Specialised Secondary and Higher Education of the U.S.S.R.

The Union Republics, incidentally, have complete independence in deciding questions of major importance in higher education. This ensures that the higher schools accord with the interests of the various nationalities.

Higher schools embody the principles both of individual responsibility and of collective leadership.

Each higher school is headed by a Rector who has several pro-Rectors to supervise instruction, research and maintenance. Under the chairmanship of the Rector is the Learned Council, which is composed of the pro-Rectors supervising instruction and research, the deans of the faculties, the heads of chairs, and a number of instructors. Public organisations at the higher school participate in the work of the Council through one of their leading members. Representatives of industrial establishments, institutions or organisations belonging to the field for which the higher school trains personnel are also appointed members of the Council.

The Councils have broad terms of reference in many differing spheres of activity. They examine questions of instruction and teaching methods, summarise the teaching experience of the chairs, faculties and college as a whole, confer the status of teaching assistant, and discuss candidates for the status of assistant professor and professor. The Councils at the largest higher schools have the right to hear the presentation of theses for the degree of Master of Science and Doctor of Science, to confer the degree of Master of Science, and to recommend confirmation of the degree of Doctor of Science they have conferred.

The Rector approves the research plan, which includes both theoretical problems of a general scientific nature and immediate problems of technological progress in industry and other spheres of the national economy, as well as the application of completed research.

Higher schools publish the scientific studies of members of their teaching staffs, lecture courses, manuals for classroom and laboratory work, books of problems, instructional handbooks, curricular guides on methods, research papers, pamphlets presenting scientific facts in popular form, and so on.

A faculty at a higher school organises the training of personnel in one or several related specialties. It is headed by a dean chosen from among the professors of the faculty's leading specialties. The dean is in direct charge of the instruction and research carried on by the faculty. He is responsible for fulfilment of curricula and study programmes, organises the instructional and educational work in the faculty, and supervises the efficient procedure of studies. He maintains discipline and arranges guidance of the students' practical training.

At the larger higher schools the faculties have their own Councils under the chairmanship of the dean. Faculty Councils have approximately the same functions as the Learned Council of a college. The larger Faculty Councils have the right to hear the presentation of theses.

The basic unit at a higher school is the chair, which carries on instruction and guides teaching methods and research in one or several closely allied subjects. At the head of a department stands a professor who guides the work of the laboratories and study rooms, delivers lectures in the basic subject, directs the work of the teaching staff of professors, assistant professors and instructors, and supervises the standard of their lectures. He likewise directs all aspects of the work done by undergraduates as well as the training of postgraduates and improvement of the qualifications of the teaching staff.

Members of the chair usually include professors, if courses of lectures are delivered, assistant professors, instructors and teaching assistants. The chair usually has laboratory assistants.

The head of a chair and its professors are selected, as a rule, from among applicants with the rank of professor or the degree of Doctor. Assistant professors are chosen from among the applicants with the rank of assistant professor or holding the degree of Master of Science.

Selection of instructors is done by the Learned Council either of the faculty or the college.

The chair functions according to a plan of work for the entire academic year that has been approved by the Rector. The plan covers instruction, research and methodological work. It includes the writing of new textbooks and study manuals, guidance of the student and scientific clubs and societies, and guidance of post-graduate training. Improving the scientific qualifications of professors and instructors holds an important place in the work of the chair.

Meetings of the chair, which are held once or twice a month, discuss the progress of class instruction, hear reports on scientific topics or teaching methods, review the research done by chair members, the manuscripts of textbook and manuals, the outlines of future lectures on major problems in the lecture courses, and the further development of laboratories and study rooms. Plans for theses by chair members are discussed; postgraduates report on their progress, and research papers are read.

Industrial leaders—chief engineers and technicians at industrial establishments and mines, heads of factory laboratories, and agronomists at state farms, collective farms, and farm experiment stations may report on scientific or technical topics at chair meetings. Speakers may also be front-rank workers and farmers, who describe their experience on the job, and also address the students from time to time.

Members of the teaching staff return the favour by giving assistance to industrial establishments, taking part in their research, and helping to develop (at times assuming complete direction) new manufacturing processes, new designs of machines, appliances, etc.

The higher schools are very active in solving important problems of a scientific nature: improving production through application of the latest achievements in science and engineering, finding ways of reducing the cost of industrial goods or buildings, and of all-round economic development of the region in which the school is located.

Lively scientific and engineering contact is thus maintained between the higher schools and industry. This contact has developed greatly since the war as collaboration between scientists and production workers.

Every higher school has its public organisations to which undergraduates, professors, instructors and other staff members belong.

Universities
These grew up through the decades and the centuries as major centres of research and instruction. They train highly-qualified specialists for scientific and cultural-educational institutions, establishments of the national economy, the secondary and higher schools, and the state apparatus. In addition, they carry out large research programmes.

In tsarist Russia there were thirteen universities, with a total enrolment of only 43,000. Today there are forty universities with a student body of roughly 250,000 in the U.S.S.R.

The universities train specialists in such fields as physics, chemistry, mathematics, mechanics, biology, geology, geography, philology, history, philosophy, economics and law. They differ in number and types of departments and specialities. . . .

Moscow University, now the country's largest educational and research centre, was founded in 1755 on the initiative of the great Russian scientist Mikhail Lomonosov and according to his design. . . .

Moscow University today has thirteen faculties and 214 chairs. It comprises four research institutes, 250 laboratories, 163 study rooms, eight research training stations, three museums, botanical gardens and four astronomical observatories.

The six faculties of natural sciences (mechanics and mathematics, physics, chemistry, biology and soil science, geography and geology) are situated in the new buildings on Lenin Hills. The six faculties of the humanities (history, philology, philosophy, economics, law and journalism and the Institute of Oriental Languages) are housed in the old buildings on Mokhovaya Street.

In addition, the university has a preparatory department for foreign students, where they learn enough Russian to be able to attend lectures, classes and seminars.

Moscow University has a staff of more than 2,800 professors, instructors and research workers. These include thirty-five members of the Academy of Sciences of the U.S.S.R., and more than fifty Corresponding Members of the Academy. There are 419 professors, with doctorates, and 1,063 assistant professors, holding M.Sc. degrees. . . .

The university now has an enrolment of more than 22,000, including about 8,000 students of evening and correspondence departments who are going through the university course without dropping their regular work. In addition, 2,000 post-graduate students, some of them part-time, are preparing for scientific or teaching careers. . . .

The course of study in the science faculties is five-and-a-half years; in the faculties of the humanities it is five years. Instruction is based on a unity of educational and research work.

University education in the Soviet Union gives students a broad background of general knowledge. The graduate must not only have a sound knowledge of theory in his own field but also a thorough grounding in the basic sciences as well as in a number of related sciences.

The student's last year at the university is spent chiefly in working on his diploma thesis, which represents a small research project. His university course ends with the presentation of the thesis at a meeting of the department and the taking of state examinations.

Moscow University has spacious buildings and well-equipped laboratories. The new buildings on Lenin Hills cover an area of more than 400 acres. With a floor space of over 4.9 million square feet, they have 25,000 rooms, of which 5,700 comprise student hostels. The university library numbers more than 5 million books, magazines and annual files of newspapers, in Russian and foreign languages. . . .

Technical Colleges

The Soviet Union's technical colleges train engineers in almost 200 subjects. They can be divided into two groups: polytechnical and specialised.

The polytechnical institutes hold a prominent place among the Soviet Union's technical higher educational establishments. As a rule, they have many departments and give a wide variety of training.

For instance, the Leningrad Polytechnical Institute, one of the country's largest schools of this type, has nine faculties, consisting of metallurgy, mechanics and machine-building, electrical machinery, power engineering, physics and mechanics, hydraulic engineering, and radio engineering. Each covers related subjects. The radio engineering faculty, for example, provides training in the following fields: radio physics, industrial electronics, dieletrics and semi-conductors; the faculty of metallurgy trains engineers specialising in iron and steel, non-ferrous metals, the science of metals, foundry production, pressure treatment of metals, and so on.

All in all, forty-two subjects are being taught there to 10,000 students of the day department and more than 800 in the evening department. The teaching staff numbers 860 professors and instructors. With its more than 200 laboratories fitted out with up-to-date instruments and apparatus, the institute provides facilities for extensive laboratory and research work, in which both teaching staff and students participate. The structure of other polytechnical establishments is similar to that of the Leningrad institute. . . .

The other type of technical higher educational establishments, the colleges, usually train specialists for a certain industry. There are, for instance, colleges of metallurgy, mining, civil engineering, chemical engineering, transport, and so on. As a rule, the colleges have fewer departments and give training in fewer specialities than the polytechnical institutes. Here are two examples. The Dniepropetrovsk Mining College, which trains engineers for the coal industry, has faculties of geological prospecting, mining, mining machinery and mine construction. There are ten specialities in all, and the student body numbers 3,900. The Novosibirsk College of Civil Engineering has five faculties and trains engineers in seven subjects.

The division of technical higher educational establishments into polytechnical institutes and specialised colleges is not quite exact. There are a number of technical colleges which occupy a position halfway between the two. For instance, the Moscow Power Institute, while nominally a specialised college, has a number of faculties, ten in all, which give training in twenty-six subjects. . . .

There are now 206 technical institutions of higher learning as compared with only sixteen in 1914. Their geographical distribution has also changed. The number of cities having such schools has increased from nine in pre-revolutionary Russia to sixty at present. Technical higher schools have been set up not only in big cities but also in new industrial districts, where they are much closer to the given industries.

Agricultural Education

The training of specialists for agriculture is carried out exclusively by agricultural colleges.

The high level of mechanisation and the emphasis on scientific farming in the U.S.S.R. resulted in an enormous demand for specialists, and the country's network of agricultural higher schools was considerably expanded to meet this demand. In pre-revolutionary Russia there were only sixteen such schools, with a total student body of 5,000, whereas today the Soviet Union has ninety-six agricultural colleges attended by 270,000 students.

Training is conducted along three main lines: agronomy, livestock raising and veterinary medicine, and farm mechanisation.

The Timiryazev Agricultural Academy in Moscow, for instance, has faculties of agronomy, fruit and vegetable cultivation, agrochemistry, and animal husbandry and economics, and they give training in eight specialities. Since the agricultural colleges are distributed more or less evenly throughout the country it is possible to relate their curricula and syllabuses to key problems of agriculture in the respective areas (that is, to the areas in which most of the students will work after graduation).

The agricultural colleges strive to dovetail instruction with the specific features and requirements of the collective farms and state farms in the given zone. The experimental and training facilities of the colleges are undergoing broad expansion. More than sixty state farms have now been turned over to them. For instance, the Karavayevo State Pedigree Livestock Farm has been turned over to the Kostroma Agricultural College, which today has an experimental training farm with 28,575 acres of land, about 2,000 head of beef and dairy cattle, more than 1,200 pigs, and some 10,000 head of poultry. Students learn agricultural production not from charts and tables but first hand. This yields good results. At the same time, they are being given a more thorough grounding in agricultural theory than formerly.

The agricultural colleges are becoming research centres which render practical assistance to the collective and state farms.

Economics

The Soviet Union's economists have a broad field of activity. They generalise new phenomena in the economic life of society, study national-economic problems, seeks ways and means of making the most efficient use of the country's material and manpower resources, improve methods of planning and organising industrial and agricultural production, elaborate the principles of rational distribution of the productive forces, and analyse technical and economic problems relating to the building of a communist society.

Specialists in the spheres of economics, commerce and finance are trained primarily at colleges of economics. In addition, economists of the highest qualification receive their training in the economics faculties of a number of universities as well as in the economic engineering faculties of some of the technical higher schools. All in all, training in these fields is given at twenty-seven colleges of economics, fourteen universities and sixty-seven industrial and agricultural colleges.

The various subjects taught may be combined under the following headings: political economy, the economics of industry, transport, agriculture and finance, planning and industrial accounting.

Law

The measures being carried out by the Soviet state to further strengthen socialist legality and raise the efficiency of the state apparatus, call for highly-educated lawyers.

These are educated at colleges of law and in the law faculties of universities. Besides studying such special subjects as law, economics, the political sciences and philosophy, future lawyers learn how to conduct research in the fields of law and government.

The number of students in the law colleges and the law faculties of the universities is about 40,000, more than half of whom are correspondence students.

Teacher Training

With the exception of two small private colleges tsarist Russia did not have any higher educational establishments for the training of teachers. In the U.S.S.R. today these form one of the largest groups of higher schools. There are some 200 teacher-training colleges with a total enrolment exceeding 500,000.

These colleges prepare teachers for Grades V to XI of secondary school and teachers of general-education subjects for specialised secondary schools.

Several years ago we closed down the teacher-training junior colleges, which were an intermediate stage between specialised secondary education and higher education, since they did not provide a sufficiently high level of training. The best teacher-training junior colleges were made into full-fledged colleges. Simultaneously, a number of teacher-training colleges became faculties of universities. This considerably raised the standard of training secondary school teachers.

In the near future teachers for all schools without exception will be trained at higher educational establishments only.

The teacher-training colleges are fairly evenly distributed throughout the various republics of the Soviet Union. Together with the universities they provide all the secondary schools, including those where instruction is conducted in languages other than Russian, with the requisite number of teachers.

Medicine

In 1914 Russia had only eight higher schools of medicine. All of them were situated in central Russia, and they graduated no more than 1,000 to 1,500 doctors a year.

Immediately after the Soviet system was established the medical colleges were given the job of training enough highly-qualified doctors to meet the requirements of the whole population of the Soviet republics. By 1922 the number of medical colleges had grown to twenty-six, and today there are eighty of them, with a total student body of more than 170,000. The geographical distribution of medical colleges has been changed. Remote regions where there were never any doctors, to say nothing of higher schools of medicine, today have medical colleges which train highly-qualified doctors.

Medical students are trained in the following specialities: therapy, pediatrics, hygiene, dentistry and pharmaceutics. The course of study is six years. To help doctors to keep abreast of the latest medical findings there is a network of advanced training courses and institutes, most of them attached to medical colleges.

The medical colleges of the U.S.S.R. annually graduate about 25,000 doctors, thereby ensuring the population expert medical care which is rendered free of charge.

Higher education in the field of physical culture and sport has undergone extensive development in the U.S.S.R. Doctors and teachers specialising in physical training study at eighteen colleges attended by a total of about 18,000 students.

The Arts

Pre-revolutionary Russia had only seven establishments giving a higher education in the arts. The U.S.S.R. now has forty-seven, with a student body of more than 20,000. Among them are twenty-two conservatories of music, twelve theatrical and stage-designers' colleges, an institute of cinematography, a college of architecture, several art academies and art colleges, several institutes of applied and decorative art, industrial art schools, and a literary institute.

Many prominent personalities of the Soviet art world teach at these colleges and institutes.

INSTRUCTION AND CHARACTER BUILDING

Various kinds of teaching methods are used in Soviet higher schools. Their underlying aim is to develop the students' individual inclinations and abilities to the utmost. Theory and practice go hand in hand.

The theoretical side of a subject is taught through lecture courses and during laboratory and classroom work, including exercises, seminars and discussion sessions. The proportion of the above elements varies, depending chiefly on the type of subject. For instance, of the 5,200 hours devoted to the study of physics at Moscow University, lectures take up 2,100 hours, laboratory work about 1,700 hours, and classroom work and seminars about 1,400 hours.

Attendance at lectures and classes in Soviet higher schools is obligatory. The curriculum is divided into two terms: the autumn term, from September 1st to January 23rd, and the spring term from February 7th to June 30th. The termination of lectures and classes in each term is followed by an examination period of three to four weeks (not more than five examinations). There are two vacations a year: in winter, from January 24th to February 6th, and in summer, from July 1st to August 31st.

Studies follow a timetable approved by the rector of the college or university. The manner in which subjects are studied, their sequence and their interconnection, are laid down by the curriculum. The curriculum contains from forty to fifty subjects grouped according to the following cycles: social-economic, general scientific, and specialised. Some technical higher schools have a general engineering cycle which occupies quite a substantial place in the training of engineers.

In the training of broad specialists the curriculum stipulates that a large number of hours be devoted to general scientific and general engineering subjects. The distribution of hours according to the various cycles at technical colleges is as follows: up to 40 per cent for the general scientific subjects, from 25 to 40 per cent for the general engineering, from 20 to 25 per cent for the specialised, 8 per cent for the social-economic, and about 3 per cent for sports. At some colleges, those training civil engineers, for example, the specialised cycle accounts for about 40 per cent of the total number of hours in the curriculum.

Scholastic progress is assessed at examinations. Marks are based on the fullness of the answers given to questions on examination cards. In a number of subjects examinations are preceded by course credit tests. A student who fails in a course credit test is not permitted to take the examination in that subject. Each student has a record card in which all the subjects in the course are listed and next to them the marks he receives for course credit tests and examinations. Marking is based on a four-degree system: Excellent, Good, Satisfactory, Unsatisfactory.

End-of-year examinations are conducted only by professors and assistant professors, while course credit tests may be given by teaching assistants and instructors as well.

Many courses at technical higher schools include designs and drawings or course projects. These represent the first independent application by the student of the theoretical knowledge he has acquired. After completing a subject and turning in the required drawings and designs, the student starts upon his course project, whose size, topic and nature are determined by the chairs, depending on the subject.

The student works on his course project independently. The role of the instructor is limited to giving advice and to verifying the project; the rule is for the instructor not to interfere with the student's independent work or to furnish him with ready-made solutions to problems that arise; instead, the instructor should strive to develop the student's creative abilities to the utmost.

At colleges and universities which give training in the humanities, students are required to submit course papers in the main subjects. The student works for a term or a whole year on a paper dealing with a topic chosen from a list supplied by the chair.

To provide the students with a sound theoretical background, the chairs offer elective courses; a student may take up one or several elective courses during a year.

Practical training on the job is an organic part of the instruction procedure. It occupies a prominent place in the curriculum.

To bring education closer to life and to actual production, the higher schools have re-examined the entire content of the instruction procedure, in which productive work by the students, in various forms and during various periods of instruction, has been organically included.

Training in the general scientific and general engineering subjects—mathematics, mechanics, physics, etc.—has been made broader and deeper. Practical laboratory work in mathematics and mechanics has been introduced in order to acquaint students with modern computer techniques.

The following new courses have been introduced into all technical curricula: Fundamentals of Industrial Electronics, Mathematical Machines and Programming, New Materials in Technology, and the Uses of Atomic Energy in the National Economy. The general engineering and specialised subjects are being taught at a higher scientific level than before. The training of specialists in the economics of specific fields and the organisation of production planning has been improved.

The final stage in the course of study at a Soviet higher school is the diploma project, for which twenty to twenty-five weeks in the academic year are set aside.

The choice of topics for diploma projects at technical higher schools is broad and varied. As a rule, a student is assigned to design a complex machine or installation, such as a diesel locomotive, motor lorry, aircraft, factory, shop, mine or power station, depending on his speciality. The project has to consist of from ten to fifteen standard-sized sheets of drawings with from 100 to 120 pages of accompanying texts and calculations.

The practice followed in some specialities (for example, those taught at universities) is to assign diploma theses, which are short pieces of independent research. Technical higher schools, however, prefer diploma projects in order to give the student an opportunity to complete and consolidate his training as an engineer.

Diploma projects pursue primarily instructional aims. The topics, however, deal with concrete problems that arise in industry, the transport and communications services, in construction, and so on, and not infrequently they are used by industrial establishments or building organisations when modernising their plant or manufacturing processes. For example, more than half the students in the graduating class of the Bauman Higher Technical School in Moscow do diploma projects on topics suggested by industrial establishments. Last year's graduating students at the Moscow Institute of Architecture submitted twenty-six diploma projects dealing with the layout and construction of collective farm and state farm communities. Over the past few years students of this institute have been helping to build up the Rassvet Collective Farm on the basis of plans they themselves drafted.

All this brings instruction closer to practical work; moreover, in a number of cases the diploma projects find application in industry or agriculture and have a substantial economic effect.

A great deal of attention is paid in the higher schools to research work. In their last years of study, undergraduates take part in scientific investigations carried out by the chairs and laboratories, design machines and study economic indices. Nearly every higher school has its student scientific society and its technical clubs, which have a total membership of over 300,000 students.

Student designing teams have become highly popular in the last few years; there are now more than 250 of them in the higher schools. Many examples could be given of the successful designing and drafting these teams have done on orders from industrial establishments. One of the teams designed a number of important machines that have been put into production.

The best pieces of student research are awarded money prizes, certificates of honour and medals, and are printed in scientific journals.

The system of public education in the U.S.S.R. is linked up with the tasks of building a communist society. This system shapes the student's materialistic world outlook, equips him with deep and systematic knowledge, and develops his capabilities.

Besides imparting knowledge and giving experience to students, the higher schools give them a standard of ethics, teach them to work conscientiously, and instil in them a sense of social duty, intolerance of violations of the public interest, a spirit of collectivism and comradely mutual assistance, moral purity, a striving for simplicity and modesty in public and private life, and a hatred of injustice, parasitism, dishonesty, careerism and money-grubbing.

The instructional procedure in the higher schools is designed to give the student a thorough knowledge of the basic laws of development of nature and society and to teach him how to apply them correctly and creatively in his life and work.

Social and economic subjects play a big role. Irrespective of the specialities they have chosen all students take courses in the history of the Communist Party of the Soviet Union, political economy, and philosophy.

The training of specialists at higher schools is carried out in accordance with the requirements of a planned socialist economy and culture. Hence, graduates are never faced with the problem of where to find work. They know that the rapid development of the economy ensures opportunities of applying the skills and knowledge they have acquired.

In good time the Rector receives offers of positions for the members of his graduating class. The young people make their choice at a sitting of a state commission of which the Rector is chairman, in the presence of representatives of the establishments offering the positions.

Before taking up his position the young specialist is given a month's holiday during which he receives his regular state scholarship. Graduates moving to a new place of residence are paid moving and relocation allowances for themselves and their families.

Like full-time study at higher schools, part-time education, at evening or correspondence colleges, faculties or departments, is free of charge, the necessary funds being appropriated from the State Budget. Correspondence students do not pay for the aids which are sent them, nor for their textbooks, which are supplied them by the correspondence college library. Neither do they pay any examination fees.

The Government gives special privileges to persons who maintain a satisfactory scholastic record while continuing at their regular jobs. First and second year students at correspondence colleges receive an additional thirty-day paid leave of absence from their jobs during which they do their laboratory assignments and take tests and examinations. After that they get an additional paid leave of forty days every year until they graduate.

Correspondence students receive a paid leave of four months to prepare and present their diploma projects. In their last years of study they are given one free day a week, for which they receive 50 per cent of their regular wage. If they wish, students may have another one or two free days a week but those days are unpaid.

The state pays 50 per cent of the cost of railway or bus fares to the college when a correspondence student goes for laboratory sessions or to take tests and examinations.

PART-TIME STUDY

There are people who for one reason or another were unable to obtain higher education when they were young. They went to work, married and had families. It would be unfair not to provide higher educational opportunities for the most capable of these people.

Part-time education is therefore extensively promoted in the Soviet Union. A large system of evening and correspondence higher schools and faculties has been set up to enable people to get a college education in their spare time, without discontinuing work.

All in all, there are thirty independent correspondence and evening colleges and more than 900 correspondence and evening faculties and departments, with a total enrolment of over 1,400,000, that is, more than half of the entire student body.

Many Soviet higher educational establishments have three sections: a day department, with full-time study, an evening department for people who work and live in the same town as the college, and a correspondence department for out-of-towners who combine work with study and come to the college twice a year to take examinations.

Evening and correspondence faculties of colleges as well as branches of correspondence colleges have been set up at large industrial establishments and construction projects.

In recent years faculties of general technology have been established at a number of colleges. Their curricula provide for general scientific and general engineering training in a group of trades during the first three years, regardless of the field in which the student is going to major.

This form of organisation makes it possible to bring correspondence courses closer to the places where the students live and work and to provide better facilities for study.

Evening and correspondence studies help people to improve their qualifications faster. Here are a few examples. . . .

Educational establishments of a new type, known as factory-colleges, general technical faculties, college-state farms, and people's universities and studios, are now arising. A good deal of experience in the organisation of factory-colleges has been accumulated at such huge establishments as the Likhachov Automobile Plant in Moscow, the Leningrad Metal Works and the Rostov Farm Machinery Works. The instructional procedure at these schools is based on a week of college study alternating with a week of work on the job combined with independent spare-time study or a small number of evening lectures and classes. This combination of practice and theory is already bearing fruit.

Expansion of the network of college-state farms will be equally important. Some agricultural colleges are already being transferred from towns to state farms and experimental farms. This will help to develop a new type of agricultural college which will be more closely connected than ever before with the field of its activity.

The Soviet system of correspondence and evening education is to undergo further development in the near future. What we are concentrating on now is theoretical training. Since the students have a thorough knowledge of practical work, they will study fulltime during their last two years or so at college in order to acquire a fuller mastery of methods of research and designing. . . .

Besides training new specialists for the national economy and cultural fields the higher schools help to improve the technical proficiency and cultural level of the specialists already employed, as well as of factory and office workers. The higher schools provide all citizens having the requisite educational background with an opportunity to study separate groups of subjects within the scope of the college syllabus, or all the subjects that make up a given speciality. Anybody who wants to can obtain a college or university education, or even obtain two college diplomas.

As the country develops and labour productivity rises, the working day will gradually be reduced. This will give the working people still greater opportunities to acquire an education. . . .

VIII

FREEDOM AND DEMOCRACY
IN THE U.S.S.R.

> "Democracy for the vast majority of the people, and suppression by force, i.e., exclusion from democracy, of the exploiters and oppressors of the people—this is the modification of democracy during the *transition* from Capitalism to Communism.
>
> "Only in Communist society, when the resistance of the Capitalists has been completely broken, when the Capitalists have disappeared, when there are no classes . . . only then a really full democracy, a democracy without any exceptions, will be possible and will be realised."
>
> VLADIMIR ILYICH LENIN

According to Marxist-Leninist theory, the state by its very nature must always be an apparatus of coercion, used by the ruling class to keep all other classes subdued.[1] Patricians, feudal lords, absolute monarchs, in turn, utilized the agency of the state to oppress all other classes, and so did the bourgeoisie which built new societies on the ruins of the old. The overthrow of the Capitalist order and the subsequent transfer of power from the bourgeoisie to the proletariat cannot bring in its wake an immediate end to all oppression either, since during the dictatorship of the proletariat the last vestiges of Capitalism must be wiped out once and for all, in order to enable society to embark on its transition to Communism. However, during this preparatory stage, political power (the power to oppress) is no longer in the hands of the wealthy few! For the first time in history the workers (the vast majority) have taken over the reins of government and are able to enjoy democratic rights and freedoms. The bourgeoisie (the small minority), having lost political power, has now become the oppressed class. For the time being, then, there are still oppressors and oppressed. Only in the final stages of perfect Communism, when there are no longer any class distinctions will *all* people:

gradually become accustomed to the observance of the elementary rules of social life that have been known for centuries and repeated for thousands of

[1] See p. 33 above.

320

years in all school books; they will become accustomed to observing them without compulsion, without subordination, without the special apparatus for compulsion which is called the state.[2]

Perfect freedom and *perfect* democracy are thus impossible, according to Marxist-Leninist theory, so long as there is any state at all. But on the other hand, as the transitional stage of the dictatorship of the proletariat moves in the direction of Communism, as class distinctions begin to disappear and the state itself begins to "wither away," freedom and democracy are supposed to become *more* perfect, *more* complete. Since the leaders of the Soviet Union have now proclaimed that socialism has been achieved, that the road to Communism is open, and that Communism shall have been attained essentially by 1980, an extension of more democratic rights and freedoms would be quite in keeping with accepted ideology. The Program of the C.P.S.U. adopted by the 22nd Party Congress in 1961 proclaims: "The Party regards the perfection of the principles of socialist democracy and their rigid observance as a most important task. . . . The transition to Communism means the fullest extension of personal freedom and the rights of Soviet citizens. . . ."[3] Is Soviet society, then, taking rapid strides in the direction of enhanced freedoms and of greater democracy?

To a great extent, the answer to the question depends upon exactly what one means by the terms "freedom" and "democracy." Contrary to rather widely-held views, these terms are not easily definable. Nowhere in the world is one completely free to do as he pleases. In the United States, a man is not free to drive his car as fast as he wishes, to practice medicine without proper accreditation, to be married to two or three pretty girls simultaneously, to advertise his flourishing marihuana cigarette business by giving free samples to high school boys, or to do any of a million other things prohibited by law. Even the meaning of "freedom of speech" is limited by court interpretation. "The most stringent protection of free speech would not protect a man in falsely shouting 'fire' in a theater and causing a panic," wrote Justice Oliver Wendell Holmes in a Supreme Court decision which effectively restricted freedom of speech in cases where it would result in a "clear and present danger."[4]

Is the answer, perhaps, that "freedom" means and ought to mean an individual's right to do as he pleases as long as his actions do not bring harm to others? This may seem acceptable, but who is to determine what is and what is not harmful to one's fellow man or to society? The United States and the Soviet Union are in full agreement that the "freedom" to purchase and to sell human beings on the market is not a freedom that ought to be legally permitted (although no federal law prohibited slavery

[2] V. I. Lenin, *State and Revolution,* New York, International Publishers Co. Inc., 1932, p. 74.

[3] Reprinted in Harry G. Shaffer, Ed., *The Soviet Economy: A Collection of Western and Soviet Views,* New York, Appleton-Century-Crofts, 1963, pp. 86-87.

[4] Schenck v. United States of America, 249 U.S. 47, 1919, p. 52.

in the United States during the first eighty-four years of her existence as a "free and democratic" nation). The United States and the Soviet Union are *not* in agreement, however, as to whether the freedom of an individual to own productive property and to earn a profit from such ownership is harmful to society. What to the former appears to be a constitutional if not an inalienable right, important for the economic well-being of the nation and vital for the maintenance of individual freedom, is in the eyes of the latter nothing but a continuation of the age-old "exploitation of man by man," clothed in modern dress. And as we have already seen above,[5] and shall see in greater detail in this chapter, "freedom *from* wage slavery, poverty, social inequality, insecurity . . ." are considered essential "freedoms" by Marxists, but are not recognized as such by supporters of the Capitalist ideology.

If "freedom" is difficult to define and has different meanings for different individuals, the same holds true for "democracy." To believers in the American type of democracy, a one-party system, by definition, can never be democratic. But Khrushchev sees it differently:

The candidates of the bloc of Communists and non-Party people who have been nominated for the Supreme Soviet by millions of working people are factory and state farm workers, collective farmers, scientists, doctors, teachers, writers, engineers, agronomists, representatives of our country's armed forces, and Party and trade union officials. Each candidate for Deputy works on a specific sector of Communist construction and is inseparably linked with the life of the people. And it cannot be otherwise, for the Soviets are agencies of true people's rule to which the people elect their finest sons and daughters, entrusting to them the sum total of power in the country.[6]

The two major parties in the United States, on the other hand,

. . . both represent the interests of the exploiting classes. Therefore at election time there is bickering between various candidates representing the monopolists, the factory and plant owners—that is, the class whose domination the Soviet people ended back in 1917. The chief difference between the Republican and Democratic Parties in the U.S.A. is the fact that the Republican Party's emblem is an elephant and the Democratic Party's a donkey. You can imagine how limited a choice confronts the American voter.[7]

It is undeniable that great changes have taken place in the Soviet Union since the days of Stalin, when footsteps in the hall were sufficient to make a man tremble in his own home. But whether these changes are merely superficial or truly fundamental, whether they are temporary or likely to be permanent, and whether or not they show promise of leading to further improvement—these are matters on which observers are by no

---

[5] P. 49, for example.
[6] From a campaign speech by Nikita S. Khrushchev, *Pravda*, March 17, 1962. Translated in *The Current Digest of the Soviet Press*, April 25, 1962, p. 4.
[7] *Ibid.*

means in complete agreement, as we have seen in several selections above. Where does the Soviet Union stand today, as far as "freedom" and "democracy" are concerned? What is likely to be her future course? It is hoped that the nine selections in this chapter representing a wide variety of views, will lead to a better understanding of these issues.

In the first two selections below, Edmund Whittaker gives his interpretation of what Soviet Marxists mean when they talk about "freedom," and Anatol Rapoport shows how difficult it is even for well-meaning American and Soviet citizens to communicate when they discuss "democracy" in their respective countries.

William N. Loucks, next, points out how difficult it is to determine objectively whether the Soviet system is "democratic" or "undemocratic," but, in conclusion, states that "we do not believe that the substance of real democracy can flow through the existing forms and processes."

Arthur E. Adams, in the fourth selection under *Western Views,* sees some degree of democracy emerging in the Soviet Union, both within the Communist Party and within the governmental apparatus.

The next selection, from the writings of Ezra Taft Benson, represents the extreme anti-Communist, anti-Soviet view. To Benson, communism is a "truly diabolical" system "opposed to all that we hold dear as a free and God-fearing people." And upon his return from a trip "behind the Iron Curtain" he described "Russia and the other communist-run countries" as "a world of suffering, despair, slave-labor camps, fear, betrayal, and lost human rights." But Konrad B. Krauskopf, in the last selection under *Western Views,* recounts how he embarked on a trip to the U.S.S.R. with the expectation of encountering a society somewhat similar to the one described by Benson, and how within a few days, "in one aspect after another, my stereotype fell apart." Krauskopf found that the Soviet geologists with whom he had prolonged contact simply did not act like "denizens of a slave state," that they and the people in the Soviet Union in general had attained a certain degree of freedom and democracy, that they considered their freedoms and democratic rights in many respects superior to those offered by Western countries, and that they showed a "deep enthusiasm for Communism."

Giuseppe Boffa has spent many years in the Soviet Union as the chief correspondent of the Italian paper, *L'Unità.* In the selection taken from his *Inside the Khrushchev Era,* reprinted under *Western Marxist Views* below, he states unequivocally that "the socialist world is a democratic world, and in many aspects of democracy . . . clearly superior to the so-called 'free world.'" Moreover, Boffa sees the Soviet Union progressing towards "the most authentic civilized democracy the world has ever seen—the absolute democracy of Communism."

The first selection under *Soviet Views* consists of the "fundamental rights" of Soviet citizens and of "the electoral system" of the U.S.S.R., as provided for in articles 118 to 128, and 134 to 142, respectively, of the Soviet Constitution. A comparison with the corresponding sections of the Constitution of the United States will divulge some interesting similarities but also some revealing differences. (It goes without saying that although a written constitution is theoretically the fundamental law, its significance in the last analysis depends upon the way it is transformed into living reality by the proper legislative, judicial, and executive authorities.)

In the final selection of this chapter, V. Denisov explains the Soviet view that "Communism Stands for Freedom." He first elaborates on the Communist position that "freedom" is a meaningless concept unless it is based on guarantees of material welfare and economic security: "As Anatole France pointed out, the millionaire and the pauper are equally free to sleep under the arches of a Seine bridge—but the former prefers to live in his mansion, while the latter does not have any choice." Denisov, then, attempts to show how the transfer of the means of production from private to public ownership has made socialist society "free in the deepest and fullest sense of the word," since the people have become the "masters of the country." And he predicts the further development of Soviet society towards a future so bright that people everywhere will adopt the Communist way of life, "not by military force or conquest . . . (but) of their own free will," once they have come to realize its advantages.

WESTERN VIEWS

1. WHAT SOVIET MARXISTS MEAN BY "FREEDOM" *

EDMUND WHITTAKER

Colorado State University

The Russian Marxists have interpreted freedom somewhat in the manner defined in the categorical imperative of Immanuel Kant, which stated that freedom should be exercised only so far as its use did not deny

* Reprinted from Edmund Whittaker, *Schools and Streams of Economic Thought,* 1960, by permission of the author and of Rand McNally & Company.

like freedom to others. The Russians have also interpreted freedom partly in the Hegelian sense: a moral person achieves his freedom in association with others; he will want things that are for the common good. The Marxists of Russia believed that private enterprise capitalism failed to achieve freedom in these senses. The manner in which the capitalist exercised his freedom denied like freedom to others. Differing class interests led to social conflicts, and the common good was not attained. Therefore the capitalist system must be destroyed. A Communist system must pursue the ultimate aim of want satisfaction for everyone, and it must end exploitation. With these ultimate purposes in view, it became moral to hinder or prevent want satisfaction of some kinds and for some people, when such satisfaction lessened or postponed the chances of ultimately satisfying the wants of all. Presumably, the need for coercive government would disappear (as Marx forecast) only when the entire society had been taught to be moral, in the sense in which moral is defined here. People then would be entirely free and their exercise of freedom would be compatible with the good of the whole. Until that stage is reached, freedom must be limited. This limitation applied to freedom of criticism; if such freedom went so far as to stand in the way of the ultimate attainment of want satisfaction for all and the end of human exploitation, it was immoral. Criticism which furthered the achievement of these objectives, however, presumably was to be desired. Such seems to have been the view of the Russian followers of Karl Marx.

2. WHAT IS DEMOCRACY? *

ANATOL RAPOPORT

University of Michigan

American newspapers insist that the United States is a democracy and that the Soviet Union is a tyranny. The Soviet jurist Vyshinsky in his book on Soviet law declares that the Soviet Union is a "million times more democratic" than the most democratic of the "bourgeois" countries. Who is right? Who is wrong? Instead of asking such a question, let us see this verbal fight in terms of a communication process. Are the Americans and the Russians communicating when they call their respective countries "democracies" and their neighbors' countries "tyrannies"?

How does the conviction "United States is a democracy" arise? To

* Reprinted from Anatol Rapoport, *Science and the Goals of Man,* 1950, pp. 46-47, by permission of the author and of Harper & Row, Publishers. Copyright, 1950, by Harper & Row, Publishers.

begin with, this conviction is implied in the Constitution, where it is stated that the power of government of the United States resides in the elected representatives of the people. The Russians too have a constitution, where it is stated that the power of government resides in the elected representatives of the people. Democracy is implied in many other aspects of American life, frequent election, unrestricted criticism of government officials and of the party in power, free education, frequent examples of "successful" careers, etc., etc. The Russian also has many of these things to show. Elections are also frequent. Government officials are not only criticized but often actually "purged," educational opportunities are widespread, and so are "successful" careers (from lathe worker to factory director, from peasant to party functionary, etc.).

"But," says the American newspaper editor, "this is only sham. You may have elections, but there is only one list of candidates to choose from. Your successful careers depend not only on ability but also to a great extent on conformity to the party line, etc., etc."

"On the contrary," says the Russian journalist, "it is your democracy that is a sham. You have two parties, but they both represent the capitalists. You disfranchise many of your people because of the color of their skin. Your successful careers are often the rewards not of public service but of unscrupulous methods and profiteering at the expense of other people's misery, etc., etc."

Let us consider this argument about democracy as a discussion in good faith, not as a camouflage for "I am afraid of you and I hate you." Why do such arguments fail to effect agreement? Inasmuch as they contain no value judgments, they seem to be built on assertions about things. The controversy is not about which country is "better" or more "moral" (such a controversy would be about the speakers, not about the countries), but about which is the more "democratic." Such an argument is an attempt to reduce a controversy about values into a more objective discussion, presumably about "facts." We have seen cases where resolution of controversies becomes easy once the argument is reduced to questions of fact and facts are produced (see Chapter I). Here the opponents apparently agree on basic "values" (democracy is good). They try to be objective. They try to cite only facts. Still they get nowhere. The discussion invariably degenerates into a certain pattern:

"We have achieved universal literacy."

"Ah, but you are told what to read. Now, *we* have freedom of expression."

"Ah, but most of your press is controlled by monopoly interests. *We* have *n*-tupled our production."

"By using forced labor. We still have the world's highest standard of living."

"And lynchings." . . .

3. IS THE SOVIET GOVERNMENT-PARTY SYSTEM "DEMOCRATIC"? *

WILLIAM N. LOUCKS

Wharton School, University of Pennsylvania

To say that "sovereignty resides in the Communist party" may, perhaps, not be the same as saying that the system is *basically undemocratic* —at least in certain senses of the latter phrase. The person who issues the latter challenge at the Soviet system must be prepared to defend the precise definition of the term *democratic* upon which his contention is based. The literature of political theory offers ample proof that defining *democracy* is a disconcerting task. While the mind of the Western world is inclined to define it in terms of the specific institutions and processes which by tradition and intimate contact it has come to believe synonymous with that concept, a little critical reflection will show that democracy cannot be conceived of entirely in terms of electoral eligibility and rules of representation in legislative assemblies. Democracy, as a meaningful term, must refer to the substance rather than the form. In short, it must refer to the degree of response of government institutions and processes to the popular will.

Defining democracy in such terms gives it a certain fundamental and yet subtle character which reveals the careless and loose manner of its customary use. The existence or nonexistence of democracy in *this* sense cannot be tested by reviewing the mechanical structure and processes of government. Response to popular will lies much deeper than these. Effective and infallible means for ascertaining its presence or absence in a given situation have not as yet been invented. Hence, it is almost meaningless to say that the Soviet system is "undemocratic" or that the government leaders are remaining in power "undemocratically." Who, if anyone, has made observations sufficiently numerous and objective to enable him to say that the currently prevailing policies and practices of the govern-

* Reprinted from William N. Loucks, *Comparative Economic Systems*, Sixth Edition, 1961, pp. 438-441, by permission of the author and of Harper & Row, Publishers, Inc. *Copyright* © 1938, 1943, 1948, 1952, 1957, by Harper & Row, Publishers. *Copyright* © 1961 by William N. Loucks.

ment of the Soviet Union are not in accord with the popular will of the Soviet citizens?

Without any implication that they constitute conclusive or even substantial proof of the dominance of the popular will in the policies of the Soviet Union, several facts are worthy of note in this connection. These are generally agreed to by students of Soviet affairs. First, there exists in the Soviet Union an intricate web of connecting links through which Communist party leaders, if they care to do so, may sample mass opinion. In this maze of connections are the following: the party organization itself which, despite probable domination by its leaders, affords some potential channels whereby opinion may travel up as well as down; the elaborate elected government bodies stretching from the local soviets to the Supreme Soviet of the U.S.S.R.; the network of trade-union organizations whose membership includes practically all the workers in large-scale industries; and a variety of cultural and other types of organizations which are linked to the party leadership in numerous ways at numerous places.

Second, it is significant that neither in the immediate prewar nor the postwar period is there any apparent widespread dissatisfaction with the existing regime. Despite the censorship imposed upon outgoing information, there are various ways in which reports of dissatisfaction, if it existed, could be expected to leak out. Numerous newspaper and periodical correspondents have left the country apparently not expecting to return. Hence, they have written freely and, while they have criticized many features of the Soviet system, they have denied the existence of popular dissatisfaction with it. Whether this reflects merely the power of a "police state" to quell any expression of dissatisfaction or represents a basic approval by Russian popular will of the Soviet regime's policies will have to be determined by him who feels competent to define the "popular will" and to establish means of ascertaining its devious modes of expression.

Nevertheless, it is true that certain forms which are commonly assumed to be the outward evidences of democracy within have not been developed. In general, they include freedom to organize legally recognized political parties representing all manner of opposition to government policies currently holding sway; the right and privilege of choosing from among independently nominated candidates the officials who are to enact, interpret, and execute the laws of the land, and who are to administer justice; and the right of, and facilities for, criticizing openly, either independently or as organized groups, the current *policies and practices* of a government. Nowhere have these generally accepted requisites of real democracy been completely possessed by any people. This, however, is beside the point. The question is this: Has the Soviet Union in any real sense or substantial measure created these forms and instilled into them the spirit and vitality necessary to their realistic, even though imperfect, functioning? If it has not, by what other objective evidence can a measure of real democracy be *proved* to exist?

The student must not be misled by the promises of the constitution. This document grants to the citizens of the Soviet Union "freedom of speech; freedom of the press; freedom of assembly, including the holding of mass meetings; freedom of street processions and demonstrations. These civil rights are ensured by placing at the disposal of the working people and their organizations printing presses, stocks of paper, public buildings, the streets, communications facilities and other material requisites for the exercise of these rights." In defining the political rights of the citizen, the Constitution further provides that "voting at elections of deputies is secret. . . . The right to nominate candidates is secured to public organizations and societies of the working people: Communist party organizations, trade unions, cooperatives, youth organizations and cultural societies." While these constitutional provisions apparently grant liberal civil and political rights to every citizen, it is notable and of the utmost importance that he is not given the right to organize politically outside of, or in opposition to, the Communist party. Without this right he is politically helpless. Whatever civil liberties he thinks he has are only in reality those which the single legal party admits are derived from the words contained in the constitution, and even these words qualify the granting of civil liberties by the phrase *in order to strengthen the socialist system.* What such phrases mean may be the subject of academic debate, but, in effect, no interpretation aside from that of the Communist party leaders has any practical significance in the Soviet Union.

The realities are quite different from the high-sounding constitutional phrases. Never does a candidate other than one from, or approved by, the Communist party stand for election. Assemblies which presumably are legislative meet to approve decisions made by more restricted bodies, which in turn approve decisions made by still smaller bodies, which eventually derive their policies from the Presidium of the Central Committee—the innermost sanctum of the Communist party. Within the party the major decisions appear to flow from the top down, from the few to the many. Strategic government bodies such as the State Planning Committee, the State Bank, and the Council of Ministers unquestionably are completely dominated by the party. The same is true of the court system and the powerful Procurator General of the Soviet Union and his extensive subordinate staff. American newspaper correspondents are unanimous in their opinion that the Soviet press is controlled and utilized by the existing regime for propaganda purposes. This control is relaxed only enough to permit the principle of "self-criticism" to bring to light *detailed* failures to carry out economic policies and achieve industrial goals. It never extends to a free discussion of *policies.*

Clearly these are not the attributes of a real democracy as that concept has substantive meaning for the mind of the Western world. The essence of the situation is that, aside from a revolution, there is no means whereby the existing government can be replaced, nor is there any means of installing another party in place of the Communist party. Whether real democracy in a basic but subtle sense may inhabit the bones and sinews of the Soviet system, despite our inability to see it through our concepts, will be a matter upon which students of the Soviet Union may disagree. However, we do not believe that the substance of real democracy can flow through the existing forms and processes. Indeed, this fact casts some doubt on whether it is legitimate to call the system "socialist." . . .

4. DEMOCRATIC FERMENT BEHIND
THE CURTAIN *

ARTHUR E. ADAMS

Michigan State University

While the West continues to speak of "Soviet totalitarianism," the leaders and writers of the Soviet Communist Party boast ever more loudly that the Party is being "democratized." The truth is that the Soviet Communists have indeed taken significant steps toward "liberalizing" party practices. This evolution toward democracy has already had incalculable consequences inside the Party. It has also profoundly altered the relationships between the Soviet Party and its satellites in Eastern Europe. These developments are favorable to our interests, and we can no longer afford to dismiss them as Communist hokum. We need to examine them closely and ponder how they may be made to serve the cause of peace and freedom.

Events at the Twenty-second Congress of the Party (October, 1961) dramatically marked the most recent stages in the trend toward "liberalization," a trend which has its roots in a fundamental dichotomy of Communist thought. Lenin, the father of the Party, was, on the one hand, fiercely committed to democracy and individual liberty, and, on the other, to the absolute authority of the Party's Central Committee. Democratic notions received short shrift from Stalin, who focused his attention solely upon the aggrandizement of his own personal authority. Only with his death in

* Reprinted from *The Progressive*, August, 1962, pp. 13-14 by permission of the author and the publisher.

March, 1953, and Lavrenti Beria's removal from power three months later was the balance at least partially redressed.

Collective leadership, first under Malenkov, then under Khrushchev, repudiated Stalin's technique of government-by-terror. Denouncing Stalin's cult of personality—meaning his refusal to recognize any law higher than his own bloody caprice—Khrushchev, in the now-famous "secret speech" of 1956, ushered in a new era. Terror largely gave way to persuasion, arbitrary violence to government by law. With the extensive de-Stalinization proceedings at the Twenty-second Congress five years afterward the Party surpassed all previous efforts to sponge away the taint of Stalin's autocracy.

The new Party Statutes, adopted at the Congress, embody important "liberal" innovations and concretely express the Party's "democratic" intentions. These statutes are regarded as fundamental law. Every one of the 9,716,000 Party members is obliged to study them carefully and to be guided by their precepts. Thus their significance for the Party thought and practice can hardly be exaggerated.

These "liberal" innovations arise from the leaders' realization that the Party must adapt itself to changing conditions within the Soviet Union. The ever-increasing complexity of Soviet economic, scientific, and intellectual development demands a comparable growth of well-trained, responsible, and imaginative people who can make the system function with the highest possible degree of efficiency. The days are long gone when aggressive Bolshevism alone qualified a man to run the steel industry, as are the days when a single tyrant could effectively drive the whole Soviet machine by blood purges, exile, and mass slaughter. Khrushchev wants more initiative, more personal responsibility, more people actively participating in the work of piloting Soviet society toward the goals of material abundance he calls "Communism." He considers these goals attainable only if those in the ranks of the Party think for themselves and take a larger role in government Party affairs.

The new Statutes open with a declaration that the bases of all party work are Leninist norms. These are defined as collective leadership; "the comprehensive development of inner-party democracy"; the development of "activeness and initiative among all Communists"; the further development of "criticism and self-criticism." These norms are not new in themselves. They have received growing emphasis since Stalin's death, but their appearance in the Statutes as the formal principles that are to govern all Party work give them new importance. So, too, certain changes in the Statute articles give the Leninist norms significance they have not had before.

Party members now enjoy the right "to discuss freely questions of Party policies and practical activities at party meetings and in the Party press," and "to introduce motions; openly to express and uphold an opinion until the organization has adopted a decision." The pertinent new words here are "freely" and "openly." It should be noted, however, that the last phrase is the crux of what the party calls "democratic centralism." This means that while Ivan and Sergei are now ordered to discuss "freely" and "openly," they are expected, when the Party has reached its decision, to stop arguing at once and fall into line like well-disciplined marines. Democratic centralism represents the predominant centralist current of Communist thought, the Leninist roadblock to genuine democratization within the Party. Practically speaking, however, this principle does not preclude the limited expansion of democratic procedures.

Extending the right of every card-carrying Ivan and Sergei to criticize, the new Statutes also make it somewhat safer for them to do so. Punishments for willful suppression of criticism have been increased to include expulsion from the Party. Bosses at all levels are thereby brought under increased control from the ranks. The old Statutes allowed Party members to "address questions, statements, or proposals to Party leaders at every level." Now they enjoy a specific new right: "to demand an answer on the substance of their address." Although it is hard to imagine Ivan rising in the new assembly hall of the Kremlin to call Khrushchev to account, he will undoubtedly do so at lower levels, when petty officeholders overstep their legal powers or try to cover up mistakes.

In a frontal attack upon tenured Party bosses and the bureaucratic power they amass, new articles provide for the regular turnover of elected Party officials. Specifically, in the supreme Party bodies (the Central Committee and its Presidium), one-quarter of the membership must be newly elected at each regular election. At intermediate Party levels the figure is one-third, and in all primary Party organizations the rate of replacement is half. Tenure is limited to three successive terms for the upper levels, two for the primary level. Exceptions will be made for key men who have given the Party distinguished service, provided they win three-quarters of the votes of their electorate by secret ballot. Party offices have thus been opened to a far greater number of people than ever before. Khrushchev seems committed to make these rules work because he wants a more vigorous Party.

The Statutes call flatly for more public participation in Soviet governmental affairs and charge the Party with "developing the initiative and activeness of the masses as a necessary condition for the gradual transition from a socialist state system to Communist self-government." This is a concise summary of an extensive treatment given by the Party's new "Program" to the problem of helping the people to learn how to govern themselves. The Statutes further instruct party organizations to help "the working people to develop skills in administering state and public affairs."

The Party's professed determination to extend democracy to the people was repeated by Khrushchev in his speech of April 25, on the drafting of a new Soviet Constitution. The main tasks of the future Constitution, he said, will be: "to raise socialist democracy to a still higher level, to provide even more solid guarantees for the democratic rights and freedoms of the working people, to guarantee strict observance of socialist legality, to prepare the conditions for the transition to public, Communist self-government."

Altogether, the changes in the Party Statutes certainly do not mean that the Soviet Communist Party may become democratic overnight. Democratic centralism, expressing the leaders' determination to make all important decisions and to demand absolute obedience from every subordinate body, has not been whittled down one jot. And—let there be no doubt about this—government in the Soviet Union is still a one-party monopoly. Yet, clearly, the leaders hope to effect some degree of democratization. For the sake of efficiency they are willing to share with their followers the increasingly complex burden of ruling the Soviet Union.

The dilemma is obvious: By encouraging the growth of democratic procedures, the leaders doom themselves to a running battle to keep within bounds the very forces they unleash. They would like to tell Ivan, Sergei, and all other Party members: "Criticize thus far, but no further. Think critically to this point; then become obedient robots." But men who learn to reason in the political arena cannot easily stop thinking at a signal; men who become skilled in city and provincial government cannot easily ignore stupidities in national administration.

The new Statutes place democratic centralism in jeopardy. Millions of Ivans and Sergeis will do their best to implement them. As they discuss local problems, their ultimate questions will be: "Why did the Kremlin take this or that action? Why can't we, who know the local situation best, make such decisions for ourselves? Why don't the central authorities ask our advice? Why do they cling to old policies when new conditions demand change?" . . .

5. NO FREEDOM UNDER COMMUNISM *

EZRA TAFT BENSON
*Former United States Secretary of
Agriculture*

All over the world the light of freedom is being diminished. Across whole continents of the earth freedom is being totally obliterated.

Never in recorded history has any movement spread its power so far and so fast as has socialistic-communism in the last three decades. The facts are not pleasant to review. Communist leaders are jubilant with their success. They are driving freedom back on almost every front.

We are in the midst of continuing international crisis—crisis constantly being stirred up by communist world expansion. The outlook for world peace and security is dark indeed. The gravity of the world situation is increasing daily. The United Nations seems unable to settle the troubles of the world. In truth we are faced with the hard fact that the United Nations, now largely dominated by communist countries, their sympathizers and the so-called neutrals, seems to have largely failed in its purpose. Yes, the days ahead are sobering and challenging. . . .

A deadly conflict between good and evil is constantly going on in the world. Some people may try to gloss it over, but the fact remains that one-third of the world's people live in the grip of a political and philosophical system that is truly diabolical.

We must never forget exactly what communism is. Communism is far more than an economic system. It is a total philosophy of life—atheistic and materialistic and utterly and completely opposed to all that we hold dear as a free and God-fearing people.

Where communism prevails, faith, freedom, morality, and religion wither.

The major communist objective, make no mistake about it, is to destroy any society that adheres to the fundamentals of spiritual, economic, and political freedom—the integrity of man. . . .

Suppose for a moment that this country fell under communist control. What would be the fruits of this calamity? First, the true seat of government would immediately be removed from Washington to Moscow. Wil-

* Excerpts reprinted from Ezra Taft Benson, *The Red Carpet*, 1962, pp. 15, 25, 27-28, 44, and 51, by permission of Bookcraft Inc.

liam Z. Foster, the former head of the Communist Party in the United States, said this: "When a communist heads the government of the United States—and that day will come just as surely as the sun rises—the government will not be a capitalistic government but a Soviet government, and behind this government will stand the Red Army to enforce the dictatorship of the proletariat."

What would this mean to you and me in our daily lives?

Could you own your own homes? Your living quarters would be assigned to you and you would pay rent to the state as ordered.

The farms of America are famed world wide. Most of them have been family owned and operated for two centuries. Under communism could you own your own farms? Your farms would be collectivized and become the property of the state and you would work them under orders from the state. You would be moved off the land into community centers or communes, and you would go out from there to work the fields—not YOUR fields, mind you, but the state's. This is what has happened in Russia, China, and other communist nations.

Could you start a business and hire people to work for you? To do so would make you criminals.

Could you work where you pleased? You would work when, where, and how you were told—and the government would do the telling. No farm organizations, chambers of commerce, labor unions, Rotary, Elks, and similar organizations as we now know them would be permitted to exist.

What would happen to your bank accounts? All above a small sum would be confiscated. The rest would be state-controlled for you. The state would take over your insurance.

Except for a few closely personal items, you would have no property to leave to your families when you die.

You could travel around the country only with police permission.

You could not travel abroad or marry a foreigner without the specific approval of the state.

You could not even write freely to friends in other countries.

Under communism our private colleges would cease to exist. Our children would go to the schools selected for them, and only so long as the state permitted. Lenin said, "give us a child for eight years and it will be a Bolshevik forever."

Teachers would be free to teach only what the state authorized. Foster said, "Our teachers must write new school textbooks and rewrite history from the Marxian viewpoint."

To belong to a church would be sure to bring discrimination and penalties of many kinds against you and your families. The great majority of church buildings would become state museums or warehouses. . . .

I have been behind the Iron Curtain. There the American visitor gets a strange feeling—an awareness of the fear of the people when they live under the totalitarian shadow of oppression.

I have been asked if, based on my experience and travels across this country and to countries behind the Iron Curtain, do I still hold the same views on the importance of freedom that I did when I first became Secretary of Agriculture.

I certainly do. Perhaps with an even stronger conviction after visiting Russia and the other communist-run countries. . . .

Everywhere there is tragedy and despair resulting from their loss of freedom. It was heart-rending to see people who had lost not only their worldly possessions but their God-given freedom.

Now why is this so? It is not because the Russian people are not good people. I found it easy to love them. My heart went out to them. Generally speaking they have about the same desires in their hearts as we have. They love their families, they love their homes, they want to raise their standard of living and do what is right. They want to live at peace with their neighbors. They want to be brothers with all mankind.

But the Russian people are operating under a diabolical system which is economically, socially and spiritually unsound and which cannot produce the fruits that can be produced under a system of freedom.

This communistic, totalitarian system is forced upon the Russian people by their Marxist-Leninist masters exercising the powers of a police state. Our visit to Russia was moving beyond any description—because it evidenced the tragedy and hardship that follow when individuals become pawns of the state. What we saw behind the Iron Curtain left us more deeply impressed than ever before with the privileges and blessings of freedom. There is darkness behind the Iron Curtain. It is indeed a world of suffering, despair, slave-labor camps, fear, betrayal, and lost human rights.

6. RUSSIA A "LAND OF THE FREE"? *

KONRAD B. KRAUSKOPF **

Stanford University

In our usual stereotype of the ordinary Russian citizen, we tend to think of him as an essentially unhappy man, steeped in Communist propaganda but dimly aware that life could be better elsewhere, resigned to the regimentation and monotony of existence under the Soviet regime because of fear that any deviation will be brutally punished. If he is intelligent and well educated, so goes the stereotype, he must be doubly unhappy because he sees more vividly the restrictions on his freedom and the hollowness of Communist pretensions. If he has had the good fortune to visit the West or to talk with Westerners, he must envy the free people beyond the Iron Curtain and yearn to escape from the slavery of his communist world. This sort of stereotype is nurtured by the publicity given in our press to occasional Russians who do flee their country, and by the prominence accorded news stories that contain any hint of dissatisfaction among the Russian populace.

With this kind of image in mind, I set off for a month's visit to the Soviet Union last March. Under an exchange-of-scientists program arranged by the national academies of the two countries, I was expected to visit laboratories and talk with scientific colleagues about current research and educational problems. Our conversations, I was sure, would be limited to these subjects. For me to ask questions about political or social problems would be indiscreet, and might mean serious trouble for my hosts and possibly even for myself. Perhaps I would get hints of underlying dissatisfaction, but on the surface I would hear only the familiar meaningless phrases of the current party line.

It took no more than a couple of days in Moscow to convince me that something was wrong. The Russian geologists simply were not acting like denizens of a slave state. On the contrary, they seemed relaxed, con-

* Reprinted from *Stanford University Bulletin*, Series 14, Number 4, Winter, 1961, by permission of the author and the publisher.
** Konrad B. Krauskopf is an academic rarity: a two-Ph.D. man. He won the first in Chemistry at U.C.-Berkeley in 1934 and the second in geology at Stanford in 1939. This unusual combination has led him to, among other things, the high honor of membership in the National Academy of Sciences.

fident, happy in their work—very much like Americans, in fact. The resemblance to Americans impressed itself upon me increasingly during my stay. The Russians I met had the same way of looking at things, the same sense of humor, the same easy informality and hospitality that I was accustomed to at home. They live in a big country, and I could feel it in their optimism and expansiveness. They are sure that the world is making progress, that life will be better a generation hence. These were not at all the attitudes I had expected to find in a communist land.

But this was only the beginning. Very rapidly, in one aspect after another, my stereotype fell apart. The first afternoon, for example, I was asked pointblank what Americans thought about the situation in Cuba. In some confusion I expressed my misgivings about discussing politics, and the Russians found this highly amusing. They were willing to grant that freedom to discuss politics was an innovation of recent years, but they seemed genuinely surprised that an American was not aware that the restriction had been lifted. From that time on I talked politics whenever scientific discussions flagged. The Russians were not only willing but eager to exchange views, almost as if they had been starving for the opportunity. We talked just as freely as I would have in America, on a variety of subjects which were often embarrassing to both sides; we talked in laboratories, in restaurants, on the street, in private homes, and always with no sign of apprehension on the part of the Russians. The conversations were made possible by an exceptionally able interpreter, a man who had spent three years of his childhood in New York and knew the American idiom well enough to convey shades of meaning back and forth. In the course of these talks I learned a great deal about how one group of Russians view the world around them, and discovered that their opinions had very little resemblance to the stereotype I had carried with me from the West.

These opinions are well worth listening to. Many are opinions with which we cannot agree; some are based on faulty or incomplete information; some arise clearly from the long indoctrination in communist ideology to which every Russian is subjected. Nevertheless they are the views of intelligent and thoughtful men, men who have made an honest effort to examine the issues that divide our troubled planet. It is not easy for us to imagine ourselves in their place, to evaluate their problems and to see how they have arrived at their conclusions, but we must make some effort to understand their point of view if we are to deal with them. And deal with them we must, for these men are an influential group in Soviet society. It is opinions like these that Russian scientists will bring to international conferences, and will spread abroad when they are asked by their government to serve as technical advisers in underdeveloped countries.

Basic to the world view of the Russian geologists is a deep enthusiasm for communism. They admit readily enough that their government has made mistakes, that communism has by no means solved all of its problems, that they sometimes envy the higher standard of living in Western lands, but they do not consider these admissions to be serious criticisms of the Communist regime. If communism has not yet brought Utopia, this serves only as a spur to greater effort.

Whence comes such enthusiasm? In part, I am sure, it is gratitude for benefits received: many geologists have come from humble origins, and say proudly, "I am the son of a worker," with the implication that only under communism could a worker's son rise so high. But the enthusiasm has deeper roots than this. In large measure it is a sense of mission, of almost religious dedication to a great cause, of being part of a movement that they believe will make the world a better place. The ideals of communism, however much we in the West think of them as perverted by an oppressive dictatorship, live on in the minds of these scientists.

Most surprising to me among the opinions of my Russian acquaintances was the idea that their government has given them freedom in large and increasing measure. Far from acting like slaves, these geologists boasted of their freedom, maintaining even that in some respects freedom under communism is superior to that in the West. They seemed genuinely puzzled by the assurance of Westerners that true freedom exists only outside the Soviet world. The apparent contradiction arises largely from the difference in the *kinds* of freedom that seem particularly important on the two sides of the Iron Curtain.

Perhaps uppermost in the minds of my Russian friends when they spoke of freedom was freedom of opportunity—opportunity to get an education and then to work at a job and in a place of one's own choosing. Every Russian, I was repeatedly told, as part of his elemental rights is guaranteed a free education up to the limit of his abilities—and the opportunity does not depend on the size of his father's fortune or the color of his skin. If a Russian is trained in a profession he is expected to work in it for a few years (this seems reasonable inasmuch as the state has paid for his schooling), but subsequently, according to my informants, he can change employment as he wishes.

Freedom of discussion is another prized possession of the Russians, perhaps especially prized because it has been granted so recently. A Russian is still not permitted to publish articles critical of the government or to make critical speeches, but in private conversations he may express his views freely, as our talks abundantly witnessed. Another recent development, I was told, is freedom from fear of arbitrary arrest and imprisonment without trial. Political deviation, according to my informants, is no longer punished by imprisonment unless it goes to extremes, and the notorious Siberian camps have been emptied of political prisoners.

Freedom from fear of economic insecurity is an accomplishment in which the Communists take pride, for the government guarantees employment, medical care, and old-age support. So accustomed were my friends

to regarding continuous employment as a basic right that they found unemployment in Western states hard to comprehend. "How can a country
as rich as the United States permit six million people to be unemployed?"
I was often asked. Joblessness in the eyes of these Russians is a relic of
barbarism.

In some areas of freedom, of course, the Westerner has clear superiority. Notable among these is freedom to obtain information. Except for
broadcasts from the BBC and the Voice of America, to which they may
now listen, the Russians are limited to news as it is sifted and interpreted
by their government and by Communist governments elsewhere. Most of
the news is distorted and some is deliberately withheld: the people I talked
with, for example, had very incomplete knowledge about the Hungarian
uprising of 1956, and were almost wholly ignorant of the current situation
in Germany. A Westerner, moreover, can obtain easily, as his Russian colleagues cannot, critical discussions in his own language of important issues
from many points of view. My friends were at least partly aware of these
restrictions on their freedom, and were unhappy about them—though perhaps not as unhappy as we might expect them to be. They explained the
restrictions as a result of political inertia: in the past, when Russia was
weak, control of information from the outside world was necessary; now
that the country has become strong the restrictions should be lifted, but
politicians are slow to change their ways.

Freedom to travel is another Western prerogative that Russians envy.
A Soviet citizen is allowed to travel widely in his own country and in some
of the satellites, but he can cross the Iron Curtain only as a member of
carefully picked official delegations. This limitation of their freedom my
acquaintances found particularly onerous. They felt that it could be justified at present by Russia's need to conserve foreign exchange, but they confidently predicted that the restriction will be lifted as economic conditions
improve.

A Westerner would count among his valued privileges the freedom
to expand a business venture as he sees fit. In Russia, it was explained to
me, expansion beyond the size of a family group is possible only by persuading local authorities that a new government corporation should be
formed. My friends were not aware of this circumstance as a restriction on
their freedom, because it is axiomatic under communism that no individual
can hire someone to work for him without being guilty of "exploiting" the
labor of another.

Freedom to choose candidates for public office should, seemingly, be
another place where the Westerner would have the better of the argument,
but this is a difficult subject to discuss because words are used in different
senses. It is almost impossible, for example, to explain to a Russian what
"free election" means. "How can you call your elections 'free'," he will ask,
"when no candidate can get his name on the ballot unless he has powerful

financial backing, and when the opinion of the electorate is molded by the expenditure of incredible sums for radio and television broadcasts?" In Russia, he will explain, candidates are discussed openly and thoroughly in meetings of the local soviets; once a candidate is selected by this process and is approved by the Party, the electorate rallies behind him and gives him the 99 per cent majority which always seems so ludicrous in American eyes. My acquaintances seemed quite sincere in regarding this way of choosing candidates as actually more democratic than the American method.

In all these many aspects of freedom, Russian geologists find only a few areas where they concede superiority to the West, and these, they feel, are balanced by the areas where they claim their own brand of freedom is more extensive. Very probably, of course, members of other professions—artists and writers, for example—would feel the Communist restrictions on freedom more acutely. But in considering the problems of Russian-American relations, it is important for us to realize that at least one group of educated Russians finds life full and satisfying under the Soviet system, so much so that the Western variety of freedom has little attraction for them.

When our talk turned to the relations between Russia and the rest of the world, a sharp difference in the image that each side holds of the other complicated our arguments. The Westerner regards the Russians as controlled, for the most part without their knowledge, by an oligarchy of rapacious and malevolent men who seek constantly to foment world revolution. The Russian is equally convinced that the West (which means really America, for in Russian eyes all other Western countries are American satellites) is being victimized by a small group of profit-mad "monopolists" who pull the strings that control government, press, and radio, and who try to instigate wars in order to sell munitions.

The contrast in our images of each other became particularly evident when we discussed parts of the world where communism and capitalism are currently in sharp conflict. In southeastern Asia, for example, my geological friends picture their country as the defender of the workers and peasants against corrupt ruling classes which have exploited the people mercilessly for thousands of years. The Soviet Union is not intervening but only is sending material and advisers to the people's armies to counter the military aid which Western monopolists give the exploiters in order to protect their investments. If I objected that the West also is interested in the people's welfare, I was met by queries as to why we then support petty dictators, and why American monetary aid always finds its way into the pockets of the wealthy classes. If I maintained that the West was trying to preserve the people's freedom, I was taunted with the old questions, "Freedom for what? To starve? To have their labor exploited for another five thousand years?" If I suggested the desirability of free elections, the answer came back: "How can there be free elections when the people are ignorant and their votes will be bought by the exploiters?" My acquaintances seemed to have a naive faith in the benign intentions and infinite wisdom of their government, and a deep suspicion of the purposes of the capitalist nations—much as we in the West ascribe noble motives to our own governments and see nothing but evil in the Communist leadership.

Except for their suspicions of our government and especially of supposed unscrupulous financiers behind it, the Russians talked with were uniformly well disposed toward Americans. They genuinely admired our high standard of living, our efficient industries, and our scientific accomplishments. They are eager for scientific exchanges and scientific cooperation with Americans. Many times I heard the wish expressed that our governments could patch up their differences so that Russians and Americans could get better acquainted. Russian geologists share the convictions of their leaders that communism will eventually dominate the world, but for the present they see no reason why communism and capitalism should not exist side by side in peaceful competition. Above all, they do not want war. It is ludicrous, or tragic, or terribly frustrating, according to one's mood, to hear a Russian scientist say fervently, "How happy the world could be, if only America weren't so belligerent!"

Of course, I have asked myself many times whether I was the target for an elaborate propaganda stratagem, but this hardly seems likely. Since my interpreter and I were traveling alone, we were in close personal touch with Russian scientists in their laboratories, clubs, and homes. It seems to me impossible that their unfailing enthusiasm for their country and its government could have been feigned. After all, they were geologists, not actors. My whole purpose, then, in writing this article has not been to sustain in any way their point of view, but rather to show as forcefully as I can that an intelligent and influential segment of the Russian population is sincere in its loyalty to communism, and that we in the West must take account of this in our efforts to combat the spread of communist influence.

WESTERN MARXIST VIEWS

7. SOVIET DEMOCRACY *

GIUSEPPE BOFFA
Chief Correspondent of L'Unità **

. . . The Socialist world is a democratic world, and in many aspects
of democracy—the freeing of man from class exploitation, class injustice,
class inferiority—is clearly superior to the so-called "free world." However modern the capitalist state and however refined its instruments of
political control, the reality of the class struggle remains. The Soviet worker
is free in a way that the French or the American worker can never be.
The Soviet worker is free of a thousand restrictions to which a capitalist
worker is subjected, not necessarily by law, but by economic pressures,
customs, and habits. Those restrictions under capitalism, which flow from
the threat of unemployment, the difficulty of getting an education, the fear
of illness—all these are unknown to the Soviet worker. They must be kept
in mind even when considering the political limitations on democracy
imposed on Soviet workers in past periods.

In its daily life, Soviet society bears a vigorous democratic imprint.
There are few distinctions apparent between one man and another, a
great simplicity in social relations, a strong disapproval of any small manifestation of the abuse of power. There isn't much use comparing this daily
Soviet democratic reality to the constitutional guarantees in other countries, which are often most present where economic privilege is strongest.

The apologists of the "free world" ignore all development of Soviet
democracy. Development implies at least that some kind of democracy
exists, and these apologists maintain there is no democracy in the USSR,
no democracy of any kind, at any time, not before and not after the
Twentieth Congress, not with Lenin, not with Stalin, not with Khrushchev.
These apologists regard the restoration of a capitalist system in the Soviet

* From Giuseppe Boffa, *Inside the Khrushchev Era,* 1959, pp. 192-206. Published
in Italy under the title *La Grande Svolta.* Excerpts reprinted from the translation by
Carl Marzani, by permission of Marzani & Munsell, Publishers.
** *L'Unità* is the official daily paper of the Communist Party of Italy.

Union as the only way to restore democracy in that country. Naturally the Soviets reject any such definition of the word *democracy*. In these terms the choice is not between democracy and non-democracy but between capitalism and socialism, and that choice was made forty years ago. It is impossible to understand Soviet events, and impossible to discuss seriously the USSR, unless people agree that some kind of democracy does exist in the Soviet Union, that its structure already represents a form of government by the people themselves. This structure is evolving and must evolve further, but it is functioning.

The pressure for greater democracy does not come from the outside world; it comes from within Soviet society itself. Its origin lies in the progress of socialism. Whatever problem you examine, the problem of democracy is involved. It is involved in the bonds between the nations of the USSR, in the new industrial expansion, the kolkhoz reforms, the raising of the standard of living, the diffusion of culture. In a sense one could almost say that the Socialist system, as built by the Soviets, is the most democratic in the world because it wants more democracy than any other country. The Socialist system has introduced forms of popular control where they do not exist in other countries—in the armed forces, for example (this was the basis of the clash with Marshal Zhukov). It has introduced forms of popular control in economic production, which has always been the preserve of individual despotism. The real substance of Soviet democracy is found in the economic field. . . . The problem of further development in industry and agriculture is the problem of greater democracy, greater participation of the people in the management of the enterprises as the direct result of the public ownership of those enterprises. During the debate on agricultural reforms, Khrushchev said, "Leninism teaches us that while we advance toward communism, we must manage the economy on an ever more democratic basis." Lenin has said that real democracy would begin only with socialism, and the democracy which exists, the "beginning," is evolving and will evolve over time. . . .

For forty years the Soviet people have seen the Communist Party at their head. The results of its long revolutionary guidance are far from small. It has prestige and it has experience. The Party has remained a vanguard force: first the vanguard of a victorious class, then the vanguard of an internal clash, and finally the directing nucleus of the entire society. Through many battles, from the Civil War to the Twentieth Congress, it has attracted to itself the most politically conscious and committed part of the population. Outside the Party millions of people participate consciously in public life and between them and the Party there exists a continual osmosis. Every year new elements enter the Party, which remains the most alive organism in the country. The most interesting debates, like those following the Twentieth Congress, take place inside the Party. Besides its function as guide, it has a truly representative role and these two functions come not only from the Constitution but from the actual political life of the country and from the Party's real, earned authority. In Socialist democracy its role is essential.

It is impossible to imagine Soviet society without the Communist Party. Its direction is a guarantee of progress towards communism which could only fail as the result of a profound crisis of the whole country which put in jeopardy not only its future, but its past. Such a situation is unthinkable. The exercise of the Party's guidance is not a question of more or less democracy; it is a question of whether socialism exists or not. How this direction is exercised is, of course, subject to change under different historic conditions. When the country was making the great effort of industrialization, the Party's direction was detailed and present even in administrative questions; everywhere it took direct responsibility by virtue of its discipline and firmness. Today that is no longer necessary. Two aspects of its activity are decisive for developing a greater and greater democracy—its internal life and its ties with the people. The Twentieth Congress acted as a renovating force on both these aspects.

Wherever there is production and social activity the Party is present. Through its active members it knows the problems and needs of the country. On its internal functioning depend the evaluation of this knowledge and its elaboration into an effective and just political line. Everybody, therefore, is interested in the Party. From within, the Party began the correction of Stalin's errors, which, together with the most harmful manifestations of the "cult," had begun inside the Party. Even such an internal matter as the recruitment of new members is a matter of general political concern. For example, at the Twentieth Congress it was proposed that the percentage of workers and farmers in the Party should increase. Admissions and expulsions are solemn actions, which require a vote and have a certain public character.

The Party has its own democratic internal life. Communists gather regularly, have discussions, elect committees, take decisions, control, watch and, not infrequently, vote out of office this or that leader. In Moscow the Party publishes a periodical of the Central Committee, *Party Life,* which concerns itself with the questions suggested by its title. It is one of the most interesting Soviet publications, because it gives a picture of a political world in motion, its debates, conflicts, polemics. In all the great events of these past years, the role of the Party organizations at the grass-roots level has been anything but passive. Restricted documents and information have been put at their disposal on many occasions. After the most important decisions, the Party leaders go to local meetings to discuss personally the various positions. In the clash with the Molotov-Malenkov group, both Khrushchev and Bulganin appeared before a meeting of the Moscow "activists." Khrushchev led the fight; the other supported the "four." Both had to speak, answer questions. For the ex-premier this meeting fore-shadowed his retirement, since he was unable to explain his behavior. The next day Mikoyan spoke to the Communists in the University of Moscow. Other leaders were in other important cities. Kaganovich himself was present at the Party meeting in the factory where he was a member when his condemnation by the Central Committee was discussed. A similar work of clarification took place when Marshal Zhukov was dismissed.

The activity of the Central Committee crowns the work of the Party, giving the political orientation to the entire country. It used to have two statutory meetings a year, which were regularly held after 1953. The sessions were raised to four in 1957 and then to six in 1958. A meeting, or "plenum," puts in motion a vast mechanism of consultation and dis-cussion. There is a preparatory phase, when experts are questioned, opinions are sought, recommendations are received from below, and resolu-tions are drawn up. Then there is the executive phase, when the local committees and cells check up on decisions taken and put into effect. . . .

Often after the Twentieth Congress the question was raised as to whether Soviet democracy would not have to create new institutions. This question was particularly discussed abroad, where, to tell the truth, most people didn't even know which were the existing institutions. Obviously some changes were necessary and were made in the following years, but they were not the essential concern. The point was that there were plenty of institutions—Party, press, unions, co-operatives, mass organizations, Soviets, discussion groups, committees, and associations of all kinds. They may have had defects, but they constituted a great system of democratic institutions. The problem was not to add new ones, but to assure the func-tioning of the old ones. Even to see if new organisms were necessary, it was first essential to revitalize the existing ones. There were no miraculous solutions for the problems raised by the Twentieth Congress and it was naïve to think, as occurred here and there outside the USSR, that the key to all progress was in this or that institution: Soviets, unions, or "workers councils." What was needed was an advance along the entire front and the Soviets sought a harmonious development of all the instruments they had which could articulate the political system.

What happened in the field of production is a good example. The functions reserved by the state in the USSR are in great part the economic functions, so that when Khrushchev spoke of the "increasingly democratic" management of the economy he was emphasizing the basis and direction of the political life of the country. In industry we saw new forms emerge, but first we saw the fuller utilization of existing forms. The "permanent assemblies of production" were a new organism, but no one thought of them as a magic formula capable of exhausting all the democratic poten-tials in the factories. On the contrary, their introduction served as an aspect of renewed union activity. The first concern was to utilize the vast possibilities of mass participation in management which the unions embody. In the process, the idea of the "assemblies" was developed. The same observations apply to agriculture. Federations of kolkhozes are being discussed, but the first thought was to stimulate the democratic instruments already existing—collective management, kolkhoz assemblies, village Soviets, and district Soviets. Without this democratic impetus, it would be difficult to conceive of vertical federations.

The organizations which can best assure mass participation in self-government are those which already unite the great masses of people, the social organizations which, whatever their names, will take the place of the state under communism. These are the unions, the Komsomol, and the co-operatives. To prepare them for the day when the state will disappear is to give them tasks now which were hitherto state tasks. Isn't this what is happening in giving unions greater powers of control? Or when the Komsomol is offered control over some of the most important economic enterprises in the country? Tomorrow those organizations will have a determining role in choosing students for the universities. Already physical education and sports, which have been until recently under the control of the state, have passed under the control of these organizations. Something similar but on a vaster scale is being prepared in the organization of culture (theaters, cinemas, artistic centers) since there is talk of dissolving the Ministry of Culture.

Other similar changes can occur. This gradual shift of state functions to social organisms becomes decisive when it touches tasks which have been hitherto coercive in nature—enforcement of public law and order. The direct intervention of society—the self-control of groups and individuals—instead of the state in these matters means that the coercive aspect will be diminished and the role of civic and Socialist conscience increased. In recent years the direction has been unmistakable and shown in the reduction of the staffs of the coercive organs. The security organs of the state have been notably restricted and diminished; the numerical strength of the "militia" has been cut. At the same time volunteer groups are appearing or expanding; the popular militia and neighborhood courts, which are responsible for public law and order, use methods of prevention, correction, education, and, where necessary, methods of punishment. Where state agencies are still functioning in these areas, they are being controlled by social organizations. It is a long range program, which is bound to accompany the evolution of Soviet society. It is useless, therefore, to expect startling changes. The important thing is that the tendency is here, operating day after day, year after year.

To deepen this work of "democratization," all the social organizations have to live a more intense internal life. This is the theme of all the associations in public life. It may be that new associations will prove necessary. Some types have emerged in the last few years; of other kinds there is no discussion. Outside of an antifascist committee there is no women's organization in the USSR. It has always seemed superfluous, because women share public life equally with men. The rights of men and women in the USSR are completely equal. Yet because of its Socialist emancipation, Soviet women represent one of the great democratic forces of the country, and they will probably develop an autonomous expression which will better utilize their great capacities.

The fundamental organs of Soviet power also emanate from the people. The Twentieth Congress had an intense discussion about them. How do they function today? At the apex of the state is the Supreme Soviet of the USSR. Since its sessions have begun to take place regularly, they are awaited with intense interest. The announcement of their convening produces in foreign observers the expectation of a political event. Their parliamentary activity has increased. Together with the discussion of the budget, the discussion of the plans also takes place, so that the deputies can examine each year the major problems of the national economy. In the debates deficiencies are revealed, new requirements, new unsuspected resources. The session of February, 1957, paid special attention to housing and to the industrial reform which was soon introduced. All the new laws, from the decentralization of the legal organs to the sale of machines to kolkhozes, were passed by the two Soviet Chambers in any but a formal manner. There is a new custom of international debates, from which have emerged some important initiatives in foreign policy, such as the suspensions of atomic tests. The work of the public sessions is prepared in commissions, where the laws are often originally written; for example, in 1957 the law concerning the new structure of the Supreme Court of the USSR was being discussed. Thanks to the work of the commission on this legislation, the tribunals on transportation were eliminated, thus ending the last vestige of special courts in the USSR.

The sessions of the Supreme Soviet take place twice a year according to the Constitution. They are usually short, a few days, a week at the most. It remains to be seen whether the pressure of legislative work will lengthen their sessions or require more frequent meetings. Already there are suggestions for enlarging the parliamentary commissions, creating new ones, and co-ordinating their work. It is true that the Supreme Soviet is seen as a deliberative body, and its work is facilitated by the legislative activity of the various republics. Also, its decisions are always the final step in a long elaboration through the various organisms of the country. So perhaps longer sessions are not necessary, although one could wish for a more intense activity to close gaps which have come to light in Soviet law. Socialist legality means not only scrupulous observance of the law, but a constant enrichment of the law itself.

. . . The Soviets do not measure the validity of their elections by the standards that bourgeois countries use. Those who boast of the American electoral choice between two candidates—who have few, if any, differences between them—are faced by the Soviet thinker with the fact of the careful selection of the candidate in the USSR and the social composition of deputies. In the Congress of the USA there are no workers or farmers who came directly from factories or fields. In the Supreme Soviet half of the deputies work directly in production. Three per cent of the American Congress are women; in the Supreme Soviet twenty-seven per cent are women. To the three Negroes of the American Congress the Soviet contrasts the massive representation of its various nationalities; the colored nations are subject to no discriminations whatsoever. The West smiles at the high percentages of the votes cast for single candidates. But voting should be related to specific places, times, and conditions. In the USSR, where the vote is preceded by a long discussion at all levels, the elections have always had, and still have, the character of a plebiscite, of a common front against the old world. I don't see why their democratic character should be contested. After all, whenever the Soviet Union has been in danger, the plebiscite of the ballots has been confirmed by the plebiscite of arms.

The USSR can now afford to discuss whether its elections should continue to have a unitary character or whether they cannot make a major contribution to internal debates. The elections are seen as a way of attracting more and more citizens to a more active participation in the direction of the state. The electoral campaign is already the activity for which the Party "mobilizes" the most; it is the event through which the single citizen receives an accounting and an explanation of various conditions. Unity against an external enemy must remain, but is the single candidacy any longer necessary? There are electoral methods whereby the choice of a candidate or of a deputy permit a judgment and a debate on the issues before the country, facilitating solutions of problems by making more citizens conscious of them. What these methods would be— more names, a longer examination of candidates offered from below, etc. —only the Soviets can decide. Meanwhile, there is a demand that the constitutional provision for the recall of deputies who are not doing their job should be implemented and regularized.

Some experimentation began to take place in the elections of local Soviets in March, 1957. In practice, every organism in the area has the right to designate candidates. It's an excellent system, but often the choice takes place within a restricted number of people. In 1957 the names of candidates went through a longer examination and discussion; some were immediately vetoed by the factories. That electoral campaign had a specific issue—to better the work of the Soviets. Born of three Revolutions, the Soviets constitute a powerful democratic instrument of over a million deputies, which will soon be a million and a half, as well as millions of other militant volunteers. They too received a strong impulse from the Soviet Congress and are in a phase of great activity. Their powers cover all public life—from housing to stores, from schools to transportation, from public health and public order to local industry. There are still many defects in their functioning; their discussions are often formalistic, their questionings rare, and their control over their executives still insufficient. Moreover, even when they function well, with lively discussions and efficient decisions (which is more and more the case), the average citizen doesn't know it because the newspapers don't report the news well—not that long stories are lacking, but they are too long, cold, aseptic, without life, and without the ability to sharpen the more essential and interesting points.

The press is a democratic instrument of unquestioned value. The editions of the daily newspapers in the USSR are much greater than the French, not to mention the Italian, and yet they are not enough to satisfy the great demand. The strength of the Soviet press lies not so much in the great central dailies, but in the numerous regional papers, with editions of two or three hundred thousand, in the periodical press of the district, in the weeklies in the factories, and in the wall newspapers. This dense network is an immense arena for debate and criticism, and a powerful lever for democratic control. In newspaper offices of the provinces are capable newspapermen. All papers are today open to critical correspondence, to warnings from readers, and to discussion articles. Their satirical section is usually the best written. Yet despite the demand for newspapers, they are one of the main objects of criticism by the people, because they are still edited in a heavy manner, they are not sufficiently interesting, and the news items are still comparatively scarce. Even in the best papers the reader does not find all he wants to know about the life around him.

It is not at all impossible that Soviet democracy may find new forms necessary to its development. One of the original forms, typical of a Socialist state, is the habit, which has spread widely in the last few years, of discussing publicly throughout the whole country the more important legislation. This method has a precedent—the discussion around the Constitution of 1936. In these last few years, however, it has assumed a true consultative character, rather than being simply a referendum. Suggestions, changes, new ideas are sought and desired. Six great projects have been discussed since the Twentieth Congress: the sixth Five Year Plan, the law on pensions, the reorganization of industry, the reform of the Machine and Tractor Stations, the educational reform, and the Seven Year Plan. Each time there was a refinement of method, so that the last debates have been those most productive of ideas. They have shown clearly how many people there are in the country who think for themselves on the great issues before the country, and who have developed through the great battles of socialism a mentality capable of dealing intelligently with great state problems. Such methods of vast public examination cannot be used for all legislation, but only for the most important. For other legislation more narrow forms of debate tend to be developed. For example, in developing a plan for the cultivation of cotton or for automation in industry, meetings are called of experts and other interested people, from technicians to scientists, from ministers to skilled workers. The important thing is that these meetings do take place regularly.

On the whole, Soviet democracy is in a phase of expansion. It is clear that there are still problems, that many of its instruments need improvement, that there are gaps, that certain organs function badly, that much clarification is needed. All true. But from the Twentieth Congress on, we have seen an impetuous development of democratic attitudes, a clearing of the road to popular initiative which is the basic element of Socialist democracy. This is the most important fact about Soviet life today, and the tasks begun are being daily carried forward.

Expansion and struggle are present in all aspects of public life; in the Party, the unions, the Soviets. They are present in small specific problems. Let me give a detailed example. One of the democratic forces in the Soviet press is the network of worker correspondents and farmer correspondents, who regularly send to their papers small articles on achievements or critical articles on bad work, deficiencies, problems, etc. Their activity is traditional in the Russian movement and it was a characteristic of Bolshevik newspapers even before the Revolution. After the Twentieth Congress this activity sharply increased. There were conferences of correspondents and the press received their articles more hospitably. The activity of these correspondents is extremely useful but they are still employed in a hit-or-miss way and there are instances of reprisals against them. Here is a struggle for democracy following upon an expansion of it. Something similar has happened to the direct contact between organizations and the citizen. After the Twentieth Congress, the Party has insisted that every letter, every request, every criticism must have a thorough answer. Since then workers are writing to their deputies, their managers, their papers, and other public organisms. Their letters refer to personal cases, but often they contain proposals and criticisms of wider import. Often, however, the answers given still retain a formalistic and bureaucratic character. There are still offices where the man in the street is not allowed to enter, whereas Lenin demanded that in all Soviet institutions the door should be open to all. Here is another area of democratic struggle.

Everything is new in the experience that the Soviets are accumulating. The tasks are new, the participation of the masses in government is new, the instruments to realize this participation are also new. The Soviets are not now "discovering" democracy, as the West would have it; actually they are moving further away from capitalist democracy. The more sophisticated enemies of socialism admit that a political evolution is taking place in the USSR and go on to say that under the influence of industry and education the USSR will sooner or later reach the apex of democracy—Western bourgeois democracy. This, for example, is the opinion of Prime Minister Macmillan. In reality, the Soviets are moving further and further away from capitalistic democracy and moving toward the most authentic civilized democracy the world has ever seen—the absolute democracy of communism. How near or how far the Soviets are from this goal it is impossible to say, but on this road the USSR has advanced further than any other country in the world.

SOVIET VIEWS

8. THE SOVIET "BILL OF RIGHTS" AND THE SOVIET ELECTORAL SYSTEM *

(ARTICLES 118-128 AND 134-142 OF THE CONSTITUTION OF THE U.S.S.R.)

Chapter X: FUNDAMENTAL RIGHTS AND DUTIES OF CITIZENS

Article 118

Citizens of the U.S.S.R. have the right to work, that is, the right to guaranteed employment and payment for their work in accordance with its quantity and quality.

The right to work is ensured by the socialist organization of the national economy, the steady growth of the productive forces of Soviet society, the elimination of the possibility of economic crises, and the abolition of unemployment.

Article 119

Citizens of the U.S.S.R. have the right to rest and leisure.

The right to rest and leisure is ensured by the establishment of an

---

* Reprinted from *CONSTITUTION (Fundamental Law) Of the Union of Soviet Socialist Republics,* Foreign Languages Publishing House, Moscow, 1962, pp. 95-104 and 107-112.

eight-hour day for industrial, office, and professional workers, the reduction of the working day to seven or six hours for arduous trades and to four hours in shops where conditions of work are particularly arduous; by the institution of annual vacations with full pay for industrial, office, and professional workers, and by the provision of a wide network of sanatoriums, holiday homes and clubs for the accommodation of the working people.

Article 120
Citizens of the U.S.S.R. have the right to maintenance in old age and also in case of sickness or disability.

This right is ensured by the extensive development of social insurance of industrial, office, and professional workers at state expense, free medical service for the working people, and the provision of a wide network of health resorts for the use of the working people.

Article 121
Citizens of the U.S.S.R. have the right to education.

This right is ensured by universal compulsory eight-year education; by extensive development of secondary general polytechnical education, vocational-technical education, and secondary specialized and higher education based on close links between school, and life and production; by the utmost development of evening and extra-mural education; by free education in all schools; by a system of state grants; by instruction in schools being conducted in the native language, and by the organization in the factories, state farms and collective farms of free vocational, technical and agronomic training for the working people.

Article 122
Women in the U.S.S.R. are accorded equal rights with men in all spheres of economic, government, cultural, political and other social activity.

The possibility of exercising these rights is ensured by women being accorded an equal right with men to work, payment for work, rest and leisure, social insurance and education, and by state protection of the interests of mother and child, state aid to mothers of large families and unmarried mothers, maternity leave with full pay, and the provision of a wide network of maternity homes, nurseries and kindergartens.

Article 123
Equality of rights of citizens of the U.S.S.R., irrespective of their nationality or race, in all spheres of economic, government, cultural, political and other social activity, is an indefeasible law.

Any direct or indirect restriction of the rights of, or, conversely, the establishment of any direct or indirect privileges for, citizens on account of their race or nationality, as well as any advocacy of racial or national exclusiveness or hatred and contempt, are punishable by law.

Article 124

In order to ensure to citizens freedom of conscience, the church in the U.S.S.R. is separated from the state, and the school from the church. Freedom of religious worship and freedom of anti-religious propaganda is recognized for all citizens.

Article 125

In conformity with the interests of the working people, and in order to strengthen the socialist system, the citizens of the U.S.S.R. are guaranteed by law:

a) freedom of speech;
b) freedom of the press;
c) freedom of assembly, including the holding of mass meetings;
d) freedom of street processions and demonstrations.

These civil rights are ensured by placing at the disposal of the working people and their organizations printing presses, stocks of paper, public buildings, the streets, communications facilities and other material requisites for the exercise of these rights.

Article 126

In conformity with the interests of the working people, and in order to develop the organizational initiative and political activity of the masses of the people, citizens of the U.S.S.R. are guaranteed the right to unite in public organizations: trade unions, co-operative societies, youth organizations, sport and defence organizations, cultural, technical and scientific societies; and the most active and politically-conscious citizens in the ranks of the working class, working peasants and working intelligentsia voluntarily unite in the Communist Party of the Soviet Union, which is the vanguard of the working people in their struggle to build communist society and is the leading core of all organizations of the working people, both public and state.

Article 127

Citizens of the U.S.S.R. are guaranteed inviolability of the person. No person may be placed under arrest except by decision of a court or with the sanction of a procurator.

Article 128

The inviolability of the homes of citizens and privacy of correspondence are protected by law.

Chapter XI: THE ELECTORAL SYSTEM

Article 134

Members of all Soviets of Working People's Deputies—of the Supreme Soviet of the U.S.S.R., the Supreme Soviets of the Union Republics, the Soviets of Working People's Deputies of the Territories and Regions, the Supreme Soviets of the Autonomous Republics, the Soviets of Working People's Deputies of the Autonomous Regions, and the Area, District, city and rural (stanitsa, village, hamlet, kishlak, aul) Soviets of Working People's Deputies—are chosen by the electors on the basis of universal, equal and direct suffrage by secret ballot.

Article 135

Elections of deputies are universal: all citizens of the U.S.S.R. who have reached the age of eighteen, irrespective of race or nationality, sex, religion, education, domicile, social origin, property status or past activities, have the right to vote in the election of deputies, with the exception of persons who have been legally certified as insane.

Every citizen of the U.S.S.R. who has reached the age of twenty-three is eligible for election to the Supreme Soviet of the U.S.S.R., irrespective of race or nationality, sex, religion, education, domicile, social origin, property status or past activities.

Article 136

Elections of deputies are equal: each citizen has one vote; all citizens participate in elections on an equal footing.

Article 137

Women have the right to elect and be elected on equal terms with men.

Article 138

Citizens serving in the Armed Forces of the U.S.S.R. have the right to elect and be elected on equal terms with all other citizens.

Article 139

Elections of deputies are direct: all Soviets of Working People's Deputies, from rural and city Soviets of Working People's Deputies to the Supreme Soviet of the U.S.S.R., are elected by the citizens by direct vote.

Article 140

Voting at elections of deputies is secret.

Article 141

Candidates are nominated for each constituency.

The right to nominate candidates is secured to public organizations and societies of the working people: Communist Party organizations, trade unions, co-operatives, youth organizations and cultural societies.

Article 142

It is the duty of every deputy to report to his electors on his work and on the work of his Soviet of Working People's Deputies, and he may be recalled at any time upon decision of a majority of the electors in the manner established by law.

9. COMMUNISM STANDS FOR FREEDOM *

V. DENISOV

Deputy Editor-in-Chief, Novosti Press Agency

*"Capitalism is the road of suffering for the people.
. . . Socialism is the road to freedom and happiness for the people."*

FROM THE PROGRAMME OF THE C.P.S.U.

The year 1961 saw many historic events, but the Twenty-Second Congress of the Communist Party of the Soviet Union was the most important of them all.

Why has the Congress had such repercussions throughout the world?

The reply to this question is to be found in the new Programme of the C.P.S.U., adopted by the Congress—a programme for the building of a communist society in the Soviet Union.

This Programme is a scientifically-based document, which opens up real and splendid perspectives for building a society in which all peoples will live in freedom, security and happiness. In this lies the source of its appeal.

The future of mankind depends on the outcome of the competition taking place in the world of today between the two social systems—socialism and capitalism. Victory in this contest will go to the social system that

* Excerpts reprinted from V. Denisov, *Communism Stands for Freedom* (published by Soviet Booklets, London, Aug., 1962), by permission of the publisher.

provides men and women with the greatest material and spiritual advantages, creates real conditions for the full development of the human personality, and establishes a real "kingdom of freedom".

WHAT IS FREEDOM?

> *"The entire life of socialist society is based on the principle of broad* democracy. . . . *Socialist democracy includes both political freedoms—freedom of speech, of the press and of assembly, the right to elect and to be elected, and also social rights—the right to work, to rest and leisure, to free education and free medical services, to material security in old age and in case of illness or disability; equality of citizens of all races and nationalities; equal rights for women and men in all spheres of political, economic and cultural activity. Socialist democracy, unlike bourgeois democracy, does not merely proclaim the rights of the people, but guarantees that they are really implemented."*
>
> FROM THE PROGRAMME OF THE C.P.S.U.

When people in Western countries read these lines in the Programme of the Soviet Communist Party, they may object that all political parties talk about freedom. The United States describes itself as the "free world" and the "champion" of freedom. But communists reject what the capitalists call freedom. They declare that only socialism can provide real freedom —freedom for all.

Which is right?

History has already given the answer.

Communists do not only promise freedom in their Programme. They also explain what they mean by freedom. And—what is perhaps the best argument—the Soviet Communists, who were the first in the world to build socialism and have now set about building communism, have shown in practice that the new social system liberates working people from all forms of oppression and exploitation, and provides the most favourable social conditions for every man and woman to obtain real, tangible and not merely formal opportunities for free and all-round development.

Man has today achieved such a level of maturity that people no longer acquiesce in the absence or limitation of freedom. "Life without liberty is worthless," said Romain Rolland, the great French writer. Mankind possesses no prouder or more sacred word than "freedom". The history of mankind is the history of the struggle for liberation.

Many great sacrifices have been made for the cause of freedom. But its universal triumph has yet to be achieved. There are still nations fettered by the chains of colonialism.

Hunger and poverty still threaten the lives and health of certain sections of the population in many parts of the world, even in economically advanced countries. Scientists have invented many miraculous medicines —but epidemics still flare up, killing or crippling many people. Millions of families still live in slums.

Can large-scale unemployment, the lack of opportunities for young people to get an education or a trade, the banning of progressive political parties and the peace movement supporters, or the disfranchisement of large sections of the population for reasons of colour or property qualifications—all to be found in the capitalist world—be considered compatible with "freedom"?

In the light of such facts, how is one to understand freedom? What is it that freedom should give to the individual and to society as a whole? Where is the borderline between genuine and false liberty, between freedom for the few and freedom for all?

The rights and liberties of citizens may be solemnly proclaimed in a country's constitution, which describes those rights and liberties as "inalienable" and "natural". But is it sufficient to possess a right in order to enjoy it? The formal possession of a right is not enough; it must be confirmed materially. Otherwise, equality means merely formal equality in the eyes of the law, while man's actual status in society is determined solely by his wealth. As Anatole France pointed out, the millionaire and the pauper are equally free to sleep under the arches of a Seine bridge—but the former prefers to live in his mansion, while the latter does not have any choice. Society can give its members genuine freedom only if it can first and foremost guarantee their material welfare and economic independence. The degree to which any society is free is indicated by the material foundations of the freedom it extends to its citizens. . . .

Working people, who make up the vast majority of society, . . . need . . . first and foremost, freedom from want and oppression, freedom from fear for the morrow and for the future of their children. That is the principal freedom, the foundation of genuine economic and social freedom for the mass of the people. "Freedom of speech, of ideas and of conscience can acquire significance only given the freedom to live. . . . Therefore to judge whether or not freedom exists in a given society, it is first of all necessary to see whether there is unemployment there, how people are ensured the means of existence, how social security is given effect, and whether life is maladjusted. . . . If the basic freedoms are not provided in a society, it cannot, in essence, be considered free, no matter how many non-basic freedoms are provided," writes the Japanese philosopher Yanagida Kenzuro.

The most extensive and lavishly proclaimed freedom is worthless unless it has a material basis. Under such "freedom" man has only two alternatives—to fall into line, or starve.

The yardstick of genuine freedom is the existence of the economic basis necessary for the unhampered enjoyment of freedom by every member of society.

LIBERATED LABOUR—THE FOUNDATION OF ALL FREEDOMS

> *"Soviet society ensures the real liberty of the individual. The highest manifestation of this liberty is man's emancipation from exploitation, which is what primarily constitutes genuine social justice."*
>
> FROM THE PROGRAMME OF THE C.P.S.U.

Like all revolutions, the Socialist Revolution in Russia in October, 1917 took place under the banner of Freedom. But it differed fundamentally from all previous revolutions.

For centuries people thought that rule by some and enslavement for others was something eternal, preordained by the will of the gods and their representatives on Earth. Dynasty followed dynasty, forms of rule changed, one government succeeded another—but the unjust organisation of society, its division into masters and servants, into rulers and ruled, continued unchanged.

The October Socialist Revolution was great because it gave flesh and blood to a genuine communist understanding of the word Freedom, and because it created the conditions for the refashioning of society on entirely new and just principles. Its triumph ushered in a new epoch in the history of mankind: for the first time in history, the basic wealth once owned by a handful of private proprietors passed into the possession of the entire working people. . . .

Our socialist society is a united family of working people enjoying equal rights. Wealth, national origin, or position are neither privileges nor obstacles to a Soviet man. All Soviet people have equal rights and at the same time are in duty bound to work according to their abilities, and are paid according to the work done.

For whom do Soviet workers, peasants, or intellectuals work? It is with a sense of pride that every Soviet citizen can reply, and say that he is working for himself, for his family, and for the welfare of society as a whole. It cannot be otherwise, for under socialism each man's place of employment is the property of the people as a whole. . . .

The abolition of private property and the transfer of all the wealth of society to the people as a whole as publicly-owned property means not only that each individual is freed from exploitation and oppression, but also the emancipation of all society from the anarchy of production, economic crises and other ruinous phenomena inherent in the capitalist system.

Some Western sociologists like to depict the unorganised, chaotic nature of the capitalist economy as almost the supreme manifestation of freedom. But it is common knowledge that "private enterprise" has long been a fiction, not only because so much wealth is required to take advantage of that freedom—wealth which no man can earn by his own labour—but also because the monopolies that now dominate almost all branches of the capitalist economy prevent any freedom of enterprise.

The scientific organisation of the socialist economy on the basis of over-all plans for the national economy has opened up great prospects for the development of the productive forces, the advancement of science and technology, and the continuous growth of social wealth and consequently of the well-being of all. . . .

Under socialism, the whole of society has become free in the deepest and fullest sense of the word; consequently each member of society enjoys genuine freedom—freedom for all cannot but mean freedom for each. It cannot be otherwise, for a genuinely civilised society can have no aims other than those of the individuals that go to make up that society. It is only by serving each man and giving effect to his aspirations that society justifies its purpose. Socialist society is that sort of society, because it has created conditions in which each individual enjoys unlimited opportunities for the development of his abilities and the satisfaction of his ever-growing needs. These conditions include, above all, the guaranteed right to work and leisure, free education and medical aid, the steady reduction of working hours and the wide development of housing and cultural development.

The entire policy of the Communist Party and of the Soviet Government is prompted by concern for the welfare of the individual. "Everything in the name of man, for the welfare of man" is the slogan of the C.P.S.U., and the law of socialist society.

After a long study of the Soviet Union, Dr. Hewlett Johnson, the Dean of Canterbury, wrote that the socialist world had long ago created wider opportunities for freedom and the all-round development of the individual than had ever been achieved in capitalist society.

He went on to point out that the road to freedom which in socialist society began with food and clothing and the right to education for all classes and all nationalities, continued with the right to work, which is guaranteed to all.

Freed from dependence on the will and whims of private owners, Soviet workers have legal and other guarantees of employment. The Soviet citizen does not have to accept just any kind of work to support himself and his family. "Situations vacant" notices for jobs of all kinds are to be seen outside factories and elsewhere. . . .

One of the most important conditions for the free development of the individual that socialism provides is the opportunity for all to acquire a skill or profession in accordance with their interests and inclinations. Our system of education and vocational training, free and therefore accessible to all, is in the forefront of the Soviet state's attention. The desire to acquire knowledge and improve qualifications and education in every way is encouraged. . . . Study and the improvement of the cultural level of the masses is not only highly beneficial to society as a whole, it is also a most important means of raising the political consciousness and activity of each individual, whose creative possibilities and fields of interest are broadened in consequence. . . .

There is also another rung in the ladder of freedom—the ever greater leisure provided by the reduction of working hours. Man's life is not limited to work alone: he needs rest and leisure for self-education and recreation. . . .

Technological advances and higher labour productivity make it possible for socialist society constantly to reduce working hours. Within the next ten years Soviet factory and office workers will go over to a six-hour day—five hours in mines and occupations injurious to health. Then during the following ten years working hours will be still further reduced, and the Soviet Union will become a country with the shortest, most productive and best paid working day in the world. Workers will have considerably more free time for rest, studies, sport, cultural activities and travelling. This reduction in working hours will be accompanied by a rise in standards of living. Thus, science and engineering, which under socialism are directed towards peaceful and creative ends, become a most important factor contributing to emancipation of the individual, to his physical and intellectual development.

Free labour is a source of joy and pleasure. The life of Soviet people is steeped in this atmosphere. The worker who engages in emulation with his comrades and at the same time helps them, the innovator who introduces an efficiency proposal and helps to secure its wide application in production, the inventor of new machines which help boost productivity and make work easier—all these are genuinely creative individuals in the new and genuinely free communist world. Freedom from want in socialist society means not only economic, material freedom, but also spiritual freedom, since it emancipates man from oppressive fears and worries, and is a source of optimism and enthusiasm.

Freedom of labour must be reinforced by freedom to use the benefits created by that labour. "From each according to his ability, to each according to his labour" is the just principle that operates in socialist society. In the U.S.S.R. labour is the chief criterion in appraising the individual, in determining his material reward and moral encouragement. There is no hereditary capital or office. Each man gains his position in society freely, by his own efforts in accordance with his knowledge, abilities, energy, and experience.

The Socialist principle of distribution of wealth in accordance with work for the common good ensures an all-round increase in incomes and their fair distribution. It means that each man and woman has an incentive to increase social production. The cash payment each worker gets by labour in no way represents the total amount of the material values at his disposal. An increasing role is being played by social consumption— free medical aid and other services. . . .

The Soviet Communist Party's new Programme sets an historic aim— that of . . . securing the complete satisfaction of the material and cultural needs of each man and woman.

With the achievement of the aims set by the Soviet Communist Party's Programme as regards the improvement of the material welfare of the people, the Soviet Union will make considerable strides towards the implementation of the communist principle of distribution according to need. The transition to distribution according to need will mean emancipation, it will signify each man's complete liberation from all material cares, and equal opportunities for all to devote their powers and abilities to creative labour.

On the basis of advanced science and technology, the maximum productivity of labour, an abundance of all kinds of foodstuffs, and the elimination of any distinctions between mental and physical labour, between life in towns and in the countryside, man in communist society will be fully emancipated from slavish dependence on the caprices of Nature. Communism will, in fact, mean a tremendous leap from the "kingdom of necessity" into the "kingdom of freedom", in which the individual will have unlimited opportunities to display his abilities and talents in any field.

This society of freedom has already set out upon its triumphant march. Its outline can be distinctly traced in Soviet life today.

The Communist Party of the Soviet Union has solemnly proclaimed that the present generation of Soviet people will live under communism!

THE PEOPLE ARE MASTERS OF THE COUNTRY

"The transition to communism means the fullest extension of personal freedom and the right of Soviet citizens. *Socialism has brought the working people the broadest guaranteed rights and freedoms. Communism will bring the working people further great rights and opportunities.*"

From the Programme of the C.P.S.U.

"The Soviet Communists are capable of keeping their promises and providing the people with everything inscribed in the new Programme . . . with the exception of individual freedom," was how the French newspaper *Combat* reacted to the publication of the Soviet Communist Party's Programme. A similar statement was made by Andrew Berding, U.S. Assistant-

Secretary of State, who admitted that the Soviet Union's material achievements in recent years had been considerable but, he went on, this progress had been achieved at the expense of other, higher values which Americans greatly regret.

Some people, of course, have a curious understanding of freedom. Often those who accuse Soviet Communists of "crushing" freedom and "infringing" the rights of the individual consider that Franco's régime in Spain and Salazar's bloodstained dictatorship in Portugal are "free", approve the policy of terror and repression in Angola, and make no protest against the atrocities committed by the colonialists in the Congo and elsewhere. Can we really say that countries in which a man can be insulted, manhandled and even killed just because his skin is black, countries in which demonstrations of unemployed and needy war veterans are dispersed by police baton-charges and tear-gas, countries in which progressive organisations are banned, and Communist Parties are outlawed, are "free"?

There are no masters or slaves, exploiters and exploited, oppressors and oppressed, in a communist society. In our country there is not, and there cannot be, any "freedom" to exploit workers or oppress other nations, "freedom" to bribe the press and buy the votes of Congressmen, "freedom" to preach racialist doctrines or atomic war.

Precisely because it does not provide any such "freedom" socialist society is genuinely democratic, the most humane, just and free society in the world. . . .

Lenin's ideal of the widest, constant and decisive public participation in the running of the socialist state has found practical embodiment in the Soviets of Working People's Deputies. As elected organs of popular rule, the Soviets express the will of the working masses, implement their policies and defend their interests. They are all-embracing mass organisations which draw in practically all working people. The fact that over 1,800,000 citizens are deputies to the Soviets, and that the work of their standing and temporary commissions is carried on by millions of people representing all sections of society demonstrate the genuinely democratic nature of the socialist system.

Soviet citizens play a free and equal part in the formation of all organs of power, ranging from local Soviets to the Supreme Soviet of the U.S.S.R. There are no property, racial or other restrictions on Soviet voting rights, and they are genuinely universal. At the last elections to the Supreme Soviet, for instance, about 140 million electors cast votes—almost the entire adult population.

Critics of the Soviet Union cite as alleged proof of the absence of free elections the fact that candidates as a rule enjoy general and full support from the voters.

But it may well be asked whether it is in fact possible to force the people of a huge multi-national state to vote against their own will and interests, when there is universal and equal suffrage by secret ballot (whose existence none deny)? The question alone demonstrates the absurdity of such allegations.

The genuine freedom of Soviet elections consists first and foremost in the fact that candidates are nominated by the workers themselves, from among themselves. This fact plays a vital role in the political activity of Soviet electors, in their unanimous support of their candidates. Let us see for whom Soviet electors vote.

Of the 1,378 deputies in both chambers of the last Supreme Soviet, 831 were workers and peasants. The rest were representatives of the working intellectuals—teachers, doctors, actors, Party functionaries and public figures. Were you to pay a short visit to the Kremlin Palace, where the supreme organ of Soviet power conducts its sessions, you would see a well-known dairy farmworker sitting next to a celebrated academician, and a coalminer next to a writer with a world-wide reputation. People from all parts of our great country gather in this hall.

Socialist democracy ensures not only the fullest representation of the people's interests in the organs of power. It also ensures popular control over their activities. All deputies are obliged to report regularly to their electors. If the latter think that the deputy is not performing his duties in a satisfactory manner, they can have him replaced at any time. The right to recall deputies is a principle of the people's sovereignty recorded in the Constitution.

Soviet deputies are not merely professional parliamentarians. They are active participants in production, politics and the cultural activities of the people. Combining their duties as deputies with work in various fields of life, these representatives of the people are always among the people, and are close to the interests and needs of the workers. . . .

People sometimes ask whether difficulties and conflicts do not arise in the U.S.S.R., and why it is that Soviet factory and office workers never go on strike. Does not this mean, they ask, that there is no freedom? Of course, difficulties often arise, for the Soviet Union was the first country in the world to build socialism and start building communist society. Pioneers never have an easy time, and they carry a special responsibility. However, the Soviet Union is successfully coping with all the difficulties and obstacles because the people are the masters and because all state affairs are decided with the active participation of all the workers and exclusively in their interests. The Soviet government is serving the people, for it comes from the thick of the people, draws its support from the people, has no interests other than those of the people and is concerned with the people's welfare.

In one of his speeches N. S. Khrushchev said:

"At present the standard of living and the workers' wages are rising with every year in the Soviet Union. There have been no strikes, and no demands put forward by the workers. However, our State Planning Committee took stock and reported to the government that it was possible to go over from an eight-hour working day to a seven-hour working day without any cuts in wages, and the government passed a decision and published it in the press. . . .

"Has there been any similar instance in a capitalist state or a capitalist enterprise of the owner of a mine or factory inviting the workers and telling them 'from such and such a date I am going to cut your working hours and raise your wages'? Were such a capitalist to appear, he would probably be taken to a mental hospital to have his sanity certified, to find out whether he was sane. Why is that? Because such a step clashes with the very essence of the capitalist system, is impossible and unthinkable under capitalism. In our socialist state, however, it is normal and natural."

It is sometimes alleged in the West that Soviet people are unable to express their opinions, because all the means of propaganda belong to the state. All Soviet newspapers, radio and TV stations do belong to the state. But the point is: What kind of state? The U.S.S.R. is a country in which all power belongs to the workers. So the press, radio and so on likewise belong to the workers.

Like any other freedom, freedom of speech cannot be regarded as having some kind of metaphysical value, regardless of social conditions. It is a means to an end. More than any other world outlook, communism realises the tremendous importance and impact of the spoken and written word.

It is a great misfortune if a man's body is in chains. But it is no less a deprivation if his mind and thoughts are under lock and key. No government in the world can prevent a man from thinking whatever he wants. But to think and have to be silent, to be unable to voice one's thoughts, is a great deprivation because of man's social nature. That is why freedom of speech and ideas is important, not only for brainworkers, for professional ideologists and publicists but for the ordinary people. The very existence and development of socialist society are unthinkable without the spiritual freedoms. That is because socialism and communism come into being as a result of the conscious, creative activities of the masses. Communism cannot be built by coercing the will of those who build it, that is to say, of the working masses, but only through the education and persuasion of those masses, through drawing them into active participation in the life of society.

Newspapers and magazines, radio and TV, and all other propaganda media are the property of society, so that any citizen can make use of them.

Moscow newspapers alone receive over a million letters a year. Some are published, while the rest are carefully investigated. Press criticism never remains unanswered. No matter to whom it is addressed—rank-and-file executive or cabinet minister—there is an explanation and a report on the steps taken to eliminate shortcomings.

The spirit of criticism and self-criticism pervades the activities of all organisations and institutions in socialist society. It is an unalienable part of the political and social atmosphere. Every man has the right to contribute to decisions on all state affairs, both important and insignificant. This freedom and this right are not looked upon as a personal matter, but as one of social significance.

Who, on the other hand, controls the press and other propaganda media in the West? The press lords and the big radio and TV corporations, or corporations representing the capitalist state—that is, the capitalist class as a whole. Anyone, of course, is "free" to start a newspaper—anybody, that is, who has the money.

This sort of "freedom of the press" is a mockery, a privilege that cannot be exercised by the vast majority of people.

The Soviet people have the last word in deciding all important affairs of state. Many questions of home and foreign policy are discussed by the whole people. Issues which have been the subject of nation-wide discussion during recent years include the draft laws on the reorganisation of industrial management, on pensions and on the further development of the education system, and the national economic seven-year plan. During the nation-wide discussion of the new draft of the Communist Party's Programme more than 500,000 meetings were held attended by over 70 million people, with 4,600,000 putting forward proposals and suggestions. More than 300,000 letters were sent to newspapers and magazines and to Party and government bodies.

It is not only through the Soviets that the Soviet people take part in the government of their country. They also take part through the numerous voluntary public organisations—the trade unions, the Young Communist League, writers' and artists' unions, and other voluntary organisations. . . .

The activities of the trade unions, whose membership embraces practically all factory and office workers in the country, are characteristic. Soviet trade unions enjoy extensive rights and have extensive powers as regards the protection of the rights and interests of the workers. Trade union bodies take an active part in industrial management, and handle all social insurance, for example.

Without the consent of the trade unions, no management can revise production quotas, introduce overtime or dismiss an employee. Standing production commissions have been elected by the workers at factories and on construction sites and state farms. These commissions enjoy the same rights as the management in examining technical problems, raising labour productivity, improving quality, allocating funds for welfare and other purposes, and in other matters. . . .

All Soviet citizens enjoy full political and civic rights. Soviet democracy is not marking time, but is constantly developing along lines charted in the new Programme.

Conditions for the gradual withering away of the state and the transition to communist self-government by the people, are being created in the process of the full-scale construction of communism. The management of the affairs of society will pass from official organs of state power into the hands of society as a whole. That will lead to the disappearance of a special category of people engaged exclusively in government. Every citizen will help run the affairs of society. There will no longer be any need of coercion by the state, since all human actions and activities will be governed by a high sense of civic duty, by public opinion and communist morals. This process is already taking place: many functions that used to be the prerogative of state organs have been transferred to social bodies. The maintenance of public order, the safeguarding of citizens' rights and interests, supervision of cultural and medical services and of sports and physical culture—in all these fields the part played by voluntary bodies is becoming decisive. A corresponding steady reduction in the size of the state apparatus is taking place.

This is why the Programme stresses the need to draw ever-wider sections of the population into public activities, to enhance the role of social organisations in running all public affairs, and to develop socialist democracy to the utmost.

"All-around extension and perfection of socialist democracy, active participation of all citizens in the administration of the state, in the management of economic and cultural development, improvement of the government apparatus, and increased control over its activity by the people constitute the main direction in which socialist statehood develops in the period of the building of communism."

This section of the Programme indicates the main direction in which the Soviet state is developing. All measures implemented by the Party are designed to encourage the initiative of the Soviet people, the creators and masters of the new society.

AN ESSENTIAL CONDITION OF DEVELOPMENT

> *"Socialism lifts the people out of darkness and ignorance and gives them access to modern culture. The intelligentsia is offered ample opportunities for creative effort for the benefit of the people. . . . In the period of transition to communism, creative effort in all fields of culture becomes particularly fruitful and accessible to all members of society."*
>
> FROM THE PROGRAMME OF THE C.P.S.U.

In March 1960 the French newspaper *Combat* published an article, headlined "The Real Nature of the Soviet System". Although its author,

Professor Emile Giraux, admitted that the Soviet régime "has spread education and culture over the whole country" and that the U.S.S.R. "today stands at the head of world scientific progress," he immediately went on to allege that there is no freedom of the spirit in the U.S.S.R., no "freedom of expression of thought. . . . We feel both admiration and indignation".

But no government in the world can order its scientists to think on instructions from above, and at the same time be sure that science will advance.

". . . Can a system built on slavery," N. S. Khrushchev asked Americans during his visit to their country, "ensure such an unprecedented flourishing of science and art as we have in our country?

"The culture of Rome, like that of Greece, perished because it was based on slave labour which fettered the forces, will, and liberty of people. Science and art can reach a flourishing state only given the widest freedom of the individual and freedom of society."

Creative freedom is one of the basic results of society's transformation on socialist principles. This freedom, which is materially and morally encouraged by the state, is not just for some "intellectual élite"; it is for millions of ordinary people in the new society. . . .

The right to education is one of the most important guarantees of future freedom that any country can give its citizens as education always leads to freedom of thought. Socialism has created the most advanced system of universal and free education, universal literacy and culture. . . .

Millions of Soviet people take part in amateur music, drama, dancing and other groups. In all there are about 600,000 such groups in the U.S.S.R., with a membership of over 9 million. These are a reservoir from which thousands of gifted actors, singers, musicians and artists emerge. Examples include ballerina Maya Plisetskaya, tenor Sergei Lemeshev, cinema actor Sergei Bondarchuk, and film director Sergei Gerasimov. Their achievements are a logical consequence of the new social system.

Never, even during the Renaissance, has there been such a rich harvest of talent as in the Soviet Union today.

The flourishing of science, literature and art is irrefutable evidence of the existence of genuine creative freedom and freedom of thought in the U.S.S.R. . . .[1]

The advance of science, literature and art and the growing participation of the general public in the development of culture and in its full enjoyment will be a most important factor in bringing about the flourishing of human personality. By freeing man from worry about his daily bread, communism will help him fully to appreciate all that is noble and beautiful.

Karl Marx wrote that in communist society man will preserve all the wealth that has been amassed while at the same time regaining his genuine

[1] The question of freedom in Soviet literature and art is dealt with in greater length in Chapter IX below. [Editor's note.]

"humaneness", which had been lost. People of the future will not have to sacrifice time and effort in the struggle for existence, the struggle for liberty and peace on earth. Their efforts and abilities will be directed towards creating things that are beautiful and noble.

COMMUNISM—THE BRIGHT FUTURE
OF ALL MANKIND

"When the Soviet people will enjoy the blessings of communism new hundreds of millions of people on Earth will say: 'We are for communism!' It is not through war with other countries, but by the example of a more perfect organisation of society, by rapid progress in developing the productive forces, the creation of all conditions for the happiness and well-being of man that the ideas of communism win the minds and hearts of the masses."

FROM THE PROGRAMME OF THE C.P.S.U.

Writing of the perfect social system of the future, Theodore Dézamy, the French humanist, wrote in the early years of the nineteenth century: "There exists one goal, an ultimate goal, to which all desires and actions of man are directed. That ultimate goal is the free, normal and all-round development of our being, the full satisfaction of all our needs (physical, intellectual and moral), in a word, an existence most in keeping with our nature." Many years before that, the Englishman Thomas More, the Italian Campanella, and the Frenchmen Saint Simon and Charles Fourier painted alluring pictures of life in a future society, in which all wealth would belong to the people, who would be equal and free workers, each giving according to his ability and rewarded according to his needs.

But for many years people did not know what practical steps should be taken to achieve this free and happy society. All the ideas and projects were fanciful dreams, mere utopias.

It was Marx and Engels, leaders and ideologists of the working class, who founded the science of communism. That science demonstrates that capitalism must yield place to a new social system which will put an end to exploitation and poverty, inequality and oppression, war and violence, a society in which the free development of each will be a condition of the free development of all.

Lenin developed the science of communism under new historical conditions, and founded the mighty revolutionary party of Communists. This party led the peoples of Russia in the assault against the old reactionary régime, an assault which ended in complete victory. From that moment, communism ceased to be just a scientific theory; it became a material force.

A socialist society—the first phase of communism—has been in existence in the Soviet Union for many years. The C.P.S.U. has published its Programme for the full-scale building of a communist society in the U.S.S.R. This Programme deals with all aspects of the building of communism, ranging from the laying of the material and technical basis of communism to the education of the new people of communist society.

Communism has already become reality. It is bringing a new social system and a new life to many nations, a new culture and a new type of man. The eyes of millions of oppressed and exploited people all over the world are turned towards communism, because they see that it will bring them a new and radiant future.

Sooner or later the ideas of communism will triumph all over the world—but not by military force or by the conquest of other countries by the Soviet Union. The ideas of Communism will triumph because they will create a society providing the highest standard of living in the world and a way of life founded on the greatest justice, a society that will ensure every material and spiritual benefit.

History will settle the dispute between the two opposing social systems of today. All mankind wants it to be resolved through peaceful competition between the two systems.

When all nations realise the advantages of communism, they will themselves, of their own free will, give preference to this new social system.

"I shall not call you to communism, if you yourselves do not want to follow that path," N. S. Khrushchev said in one of his speeches. "Only those can come to communism who understand what communism is, what grand vistas it opens up to the peoples. If you are following the capitalist path it means that you have not yet realised it. But we shall hope that in the course of time you will understand the advantages of the communist system, and will come to communism without my calling you!"

IX

THE POSITION
OF THE CREATIVE ARTIST
IN SOVIET SOCIETY

"In the Soviet workers' and peasants' republic the . . . special sphere of art, must be imbued with the spirit of the class struggle of the proletariat for the successful achievement of the aims of its dictatorship—the overthrow of the bourgeoisie, the abolition of classes, and the abolition of all exploitation of man by man."

VLADIMIR ILYICH LENIN

"Workers of literature, the theater, cinema, music, sculpture, and painting are called upon to raise ever higher the ideological-artistic level of their art and to continue to be active helpers of the party and state in the communist education of the working people. . . ."

"It may be asked: 'And who is to be the judge, who will decide whether or not ideological work is going in the right direction?' The Party is the judge, the Party and the people; all ideological work, every production of literature and art, must serve their interests, the cause of communism!"

NIKITA S. KHRUSHCHEV

"Nobody, no matter how capable and shrewd he may be, can impose his will on an artist, telling a man how to write a poem, how to create music, how to paint."

PALMIRO TOGLIATTI (1893-1964)
SECRETARY GENERAL OF ITALY'S COMMUNIST
PARTY (1947-1964)

According to the present Soviet interpretation of Marxist-Leninist doctrine, the Soviet Union has achieved socialism and is now embarking on the last leg of its journey towards perfect communism, with its promise of abundance and freedom for all. All hands on deck are to be used to speed the ship on its chartered course, and the winds of increased freedom are to be the source of power (since Stalinist pressures have been adjudged more likely to blow up the engine than to provide the necessary steam). Under such circumstances, what is the position of the creative artist? What are the duties, the responsibilities, the rights, and the privileges of present-day Soviet writers, painters, sculptors, composers, and film-makers?

The Program of the C.P.S.U. adopted by the 22nd Party Congress in 1961 stated clearly that creative artists in the Soviet Union are expected to play their role in building a Communist society:

Soviet literature and art, imbued with optimism and dynamic communist ideas, are great factors in ideological education and cultivate in Soviet people the qualities of builders of a new world. They must be a source of joy and inspiration to millions of people, express their will, their sentiments and ideas, enrich them ideologically and educate them morally.

The highroad of literature and art lies through the strengthening of their bond with the life of the people, through faithful and highly artistic depiction of the richness and versatility of socialist reality, inspired and vivid portrayal of all that is new and genuinely communist, and exposure of all that hinders the progress of society.[1]

In spite of the unanimous adoption of the Party Program, the speeches delivered at the Congress gave evidence of a wide discrepancy of views in regard to the ideological diversity and the liberalizing trends of the creative arts—trends that had been on the increase since the death of Stalin. While all speakers paid lip service to the destruction of the Stalin cult as a great accomplishment of the Party and of its leader, Nikita Sergeyevich Khrushchev, some speakers, such as Gribachev, Kochetov, and even Suslov, powerful members of the Central Committee Presidium, took a strong stand against "revisionism" and demanded an end to the production of works that were not ideologically acceptable. But different voices were also heard at the Congress. Outstanding among them was that of Alexander Tvardovsky, liberal editor-in-chief of *Novy mir,* who declared unequivocally that Soviet art needed to be freed of the lingering traces of Stalinism and that the most essential criterion of a work of art was its artistic quality and not the good intention of the artist.[2] The trend towards liberalization in Soviet literature and art seemed to continue throughout 1962. Books, poems, and newspaper and magazine articles were published that bore little resemblance to "socialist realism" (discussed below), abstract paintings were exhibited in many galleries throughout the U.S.S.R. to the bewilderment of some viewers and the delight of others, and jazz became the craze of the younger generation. But the "orthodox" opposition con-

[1] *Programme of the Communist Party of the Soviet Union,* Foreign Languages Publishing House, Moscow, 1961, pp. 118-119.
[2] D. Burg, "Conflicting Currents in the Soviet Cultural World," *Bulletin, Institute for the Study of the USSR,* February 1962, pp. 54-55.

tinued its fight against the "revisionists." Demands for more strictly enforced conformity of creative artists at long last seemed to carry the day when Khrushchev went to visit the Manezh Gallery on December 1, 1962, where in three side rooms dozens of abstract and semi-abstract paintings were on exhibition. Khrushchev was aghast. Such pictures, he said, "make you wonder whether they were painted by the hand of a man or daubed by a donkey's tail." [3] And addressing some of the offending artists he thundered: "You've gone out of your minds, and now you want to deflect us from the proper course. No, you won't get away with it. . . . Gentlemen, we are declaring war on you." [4]

The Soviet press took up the battle cry, meeting followed meeting, speech followed speech, all echoing the demand for "no peaceful coexistence in the field of ideology," attacking modern art, jazz, and, finally, turning their attacks against certain ideologically "incorrect" trends in Soviet literature.

Among those most bitterly attacked was a young poet by the name of Yevgeny Yevtushenko [5] who had won popular acclaim in the Soviet Union such as is rarely bestowed upon a poet. Thousands of people thronged to parks or arenas when Yevtushenko was scheduled to recite his poetry, and editions of 100,000 copies of his books have been reported sold out within 48 hours.[6] Abroad, Yevtushenko had become a good will ambassador for the Soviet Union, liberal and outspoken in his views, yet never altering his proudly stated contention that he was and would forever remain a devout Communist.

The first of Yevtushenko's poems reprinted below takes its title ("Babi Yar") from a ravine on the outskirts of Kiev in which were found the remains of the entire Jewish population of the city—more than one hundred thousand men, women, and children—slaughtered by the Nazis during the war. In this poem, Yevtushenko decried the lack of a monument to the memory of the Jewish victims of Nazi brutality at Babi Yar, and he identified himself with them:

> "Every old man who was murdered here
> > is I
> and I am every child who was murdered here."

Yevtushenko published "Babi Yar" in September 1961, just prior to the meeting of the 22nd Party Congress. No sooner had the poem appeared in the pages of *Literaturnaya gazeta,* than the denunciations began: "What

---

[3] *Pravda*, December 2, 1962. Translated in *The Current Digest of the Soviet Press,* December 26, 1962, p. 20.

[4] Quoted in Leopold Labedz, "A Chronicle of the Chill," *Partisan Review,* Spring, 1963, p. 99. Also quoted as a "document of whose authenticity we are convinced" in *Encounter,* April, 1963, p. 103.

[5] Notice that in some transliterations from the Soviet alphabet, the letter "Y" is dropped at the beginning of his given, and sometimes also at the beginning of his last name.

[6] Patricia Blake, "New Voices in Russian Writing," *Encounter,* April, 1963, p. 28.

sort of a true Russian are you, when you have forgotten your own people? Your soul has grown as narrow as your trousers, and empty as a stairwell," read a poem by Alexey Markov entitled "My Answer," published just a few days later in the official organ of the Writers' Union of the R.S.F.S.R.,[7] and aimed apparently at Yevtushenko's implication that the horrors of the Nazi terror in the Soviet Union were primarily a Jewish tragedy.

This was only the beginning. The attacks against Yevtushenko continued. In one of the speeches delivered at the 22nd Party Congress, the editors of *Literaturnaya gazeta* (where "Babi Yar" had first been published) were accused of "cheap sensationalism." [8] Khrushchev personally censured Yevtushenko because he had "disclosed ignorance of historical facts" since at Babi Yar not only "the Jewish population fell victim to the fascist crimes" but also "many Russians, Ukrainians and Soviet people died there at the hands of the Hitlerite executioners." Furthermore, Khrushchev stressed, there was no need to raise any doubts as to the treatment of Jews in the Soviet Union (the poem "Babi Yar" surely implies the persistence of antisemitism) since "from the days of the October Revolution the Jews in our country have had equality with all other people of the U.S.S.R. in all respects." [9]

In the fall of 1962, Yevtushenko flung another challenge into the faces of the "orthodox." In a poem entitled "Stalin's Heirs," reprinted below right after "Babi Yar," he warned that some of Stalin's heirs consider his retirement temporary, and that as long as his heirs still roam the earth, "it will seem to me that Stalin is still in the Mausoleum."

While space limitations preclude the inclusion of more of Yevtushenko's writings, it should be pointed out that his "sins" were numerous. He defended abstractionism,[10] he spoke up for some of the artists who had come under attack, and, worst of all, he published his "Precocious Autobiography" as a serial in the French *L'Express*,[11] in violation of a 1958 Central Committee ruling that Soviet authors were not to publish material outside the U.S.S.R. unless it had previously been cleared for publication inside the Soviet Union.[12]

---

[7] *Literatura i Zhizn*, September 24, 1961. Translated by Mirra Ginsburg in *The Russian Review*, July, 1962, p. 237. Ginsburg's piece, entitled "Evgeny Evtushenko" is a translation of a chapter from a book on Soviet literature by Vera Alexandrova.

[8] D. Burg, *op. cit.,* p. 55.

[9] N. S. Khrushchev, "High Ideological Content and Artistic Mastery are the Great Force of Soviet Literature and Art." (Speech) *Pravda* and *Izvestia*, March 10, 1963. Translated in *The Current Digest of the Soviet Press*, April 10, 1963, p. 11.

[10] See Khrushchev's reference to it in *ibid.*, p. 7.

[11] For an English-language condensation of Yevtushenko's "A Precocious Autobiography," see the *Saturday Evening Post*, August 10—August 17, 1963, pp. 46-69.

[12] For a more detailed discussion of the Yevtushenko affair, see, for instance, Priscilla Johnson, "The Regime and the Intellectuals: A Window on Party Politics," *Problems of Communism, Special Supplement*, September-October, 1963, p. XVI-XIX. Although large excerpts from this article are reprinted under *Western Views* below, this particular section was one of those that had to be omitted, due to space limitations.

Khrushchev admonished Yevtushenko not to be afraid and to admit his mistakes.[13] Although Yevtushenko had vowed on Poetry Day, October 8, 1961, to an enthusiastic crowd at the Mayakovsky Monument in Moscow that "I will be firm to the end, I'll not be turned into a fawning sycophant," [14] he reconsidered and recanted. But when Yevtushenko confessed his "errors" before the Plenary Session of the Board of the U.S.S.R. Writers Union in March, 1963, he restricted his remarks almost exclusively to his "Autobiography." Moreover, his words sounded more like an explanation than a recantation. "The tone of his speech," Pravda commented, "clearly indicated that Ye. Yevtushenko did not realize the crux of his mistakes, either in the matter of the publication of the "Autobiography" or in several of his poems." [15]

While most of the attacks were directed against younger creative artists (Yevtushenko was barely thirty at the time), at least one of those most severely reprimanded was a writer of the older generation, Ilya Ehrenburg, born in 1891, who has been contributing to Soviet literature for several decades. In March, 1963, Khrushchev referred to Ehrenburg's novel "The Thaw" (published in 1954) as one of the works which gave an "incorrect, one-sided interpretation of events and phenomena connected with the cult of the individual and of the essence of those fundamental, radical changes that have taken place and are taking place in the social, political, and spiritual life of the people since the 20th Party Congress." [16] However, it was primarily Ehrenburg's autobiography that came under attack, his memoirs published in installments in *Novy mir* under the title "People, Years, Life," beginning in the late summer of 1960. A selection from these memoirs is reprinted below.

Ehrenburg was strongly censured for having stated in his memoirs that Stalin's abuses of power were known to many (including himself), who could do nothing but live "with their teeth clenched." L. F. Ilyichev, Secretary of the Party Central Committee, was among those who pointed an accusing finger at the renowned Soviet author. "We all spoke and wrote thus at the time," said Ilyichev, referring to Ehrenburg's praise of Stalin. "But we were not hypocritical. We believed and wrote. You, on the other hand, did not believe, but you wrote anyhow. These are different positions." [17] Ehrenburg, moreover, was taken to task for having written favorably in his memoirs about the simultaneous existence of many literary schools of thought (including even expressionists and nothingists) during the early days of the regime, and for advocating the recognition of the co-

[13] N. S. Khrushchev, "High Ideological, etc. . . .", *op. cit.,* p. 7.

[14] Mirra Ginsburg (translator), *op. cit.,* p. 237.

[15] *Pravda,* March 29, 1963. Translated in *The Current Digest of the Soviet Press,* April 17, 1963, p. 6.

[16] N. S. Khrushchev, "High Ideological, etc. . . .", *op. cit.,* p. 11

[17] *Pravda,* March 9, 1963. Translated in *The Current Digest of the Soviet Press,* April 3, 1963, p. 6.

existence of different schools in contemporary Soviet art. "Comrade Ehren-burg is making a gross ideological error," admonished Khrushchev, "and we are under obligation to help him to see this."[18] But Khrushchev and others levied most of their attacks against Ehrenburg (and against other creative artists, for that matter), because he painted "everything in gloomy colors"—a major deviation from the accepted line of "socialist realism."

"Socialist realism," to be sure, is not any specific, single line of liter-ary or artistic form or approach, but refers, instead, to the place of art within the social structure of society. "The primary assumption of Socialist Realism," explains a recent article in a Western Marxist journal, "is that art is subordinated to politics and that therefore art is to be judged by the ethical criteria of political unity." [19] In the first selection under *Western Views,* A. Gaev attempts to clarify the meaning of "socialist realism." In his article, Gaev emphasizes the application of the concept to Soviet paint-ing, but his explanation would be equally applicable to sculpture, poems, novels, motion pictures, or other works of creative art.

The recent campaign against unrestrained artistic freedom in the So-viet Union reached its height during the period from December 1, 1962 (when Khrushchev launched his attack against modern art at the Manezh Gallery) to June, 1963 (when the Central Committee Plenum convened to decide upon the official party line in regard to the extent of freedom to be granted to Soviet creative artists, and the degree of toughness to be applied to deviationists). Priscilla Johnson, in the second selection under *Western Views,* reviews the highlights of the campaign during that half-year period. That those Western observers who foresaw a "move back in the direction of Stalinism," [20] had erred in their appraisal seemed indicated by Ilyichev's relatively mild speech at the June, 1963 Central Committee Plenum, when he warned that it would "not be in the spirit of our party" to excommunicate or relegate "to the ranks of the hopeless and incorrigible" those who had made "artistic and ideological mistakes." [21]

Some liberals, such as Tvardovsky, had all along resisted pressures to conform. Many other liberals, Miss Johnson concludes, may have been con-vinced by the failure of the campaign against deviationist trends in art and literature that "in some circumstances resistance pays." Daniel Bell, in the final selection under *Western Views,* briefly examines the question of why the drive for conformity was launched in the first place and he also reaches a somewhat optimistic conclusion: "It is one step backward and two steps forward—to freedom."

[18] N. S. Khrushchev, "High Ideological, etc. . . .", *op. cit.,* p. 7.

[19] Marc Schleifer, "Arts and Socialist Realism," *Monthly Review,* November, 1963, p. 372. The *Monthly Review* classifies itself as "an independent socialist maga-zine."

[20] See, for example, Elden Griffith, "Mr. K's turn toward Stalinism," *Saturday Evening Post,* June 1, 1963, p. 73.

[21] See p. 402 below.

While the campaign was at its height, Soviet leaders made strong statements concerning the necessity of protecting socialist realism in Soviet art and literature from the damaging effects of "bourgeois ideology." The selection under *Soviet Views* consists of excerpts from the speeches of Khrushchev, Ilyichev, and Podgorny, delivered during the first six months of 1963, and also includes a brief statement by the Board of the U.S.S.R. Writers' Union.

By the end of the summer, it had become evident that the campaign had lost most of its steam. Many sectors of the International Communist Movement, including Italy's powerful Communist Party and Cuba's Castro government, had refused to go along; and more pressing events such as the Sino-Soviet split and the unexpectedly small grain crop had begun to occupy the Soviet leaders' minds. By the early fall there was no longer any doubt that the moderates had won the battle. The recantations had been few and for the most part unconvincing; artists who had been under attack, some of them by Khrushchev himself, remained in the Party and in important positions (newspaper editor, motion picture director, etc.); Yevtushenko had gone to Cuba during the summer to make a new movie: [22] Ehrenburg had written several articles and seen them published [23] (including a new appeal for artistic freedom [24]); and Tvardovsky had recited in public and then published a poem that was referred to in the West as "the most outspoken work to appear since Stalin's death." [25]

[22] Reported in *Radio Free Europe/Munich, Non-target Communist Area Analysis Department, Background Information USSR,* July 31, 1963, p. 3. Nine new poems by Yevtushenko have been published in the second issue of *Moskva* for 1964, six others in the August 20, 1964 issue of *Novy mir.*

[23] See, for instance, *Soviet Weekly,* September 5, 1963, p. 11 and September 13, 1963, p. 7.

[24] See, for example, Max Haywood, "The Literary Purge in Retrospect," *Survey,* October, 1963, p. 62.

[25] It should be pointed out that as early as May, 1963 when Tvardovsky, in an interview with United Press International Correspondent Henry Shapiro, not only pointed out that *Novi mir* had published the last installment of Ehrenburg's memoirs (it was published *after* Khrushchev's criticism of the author and his work) but restated, moreover, his intention of continuing to publish the works of "new writers" among whom he specifically mentioned some who had been subject to severe criticism during the height of the campaign. (For Tvardovsky's statement in English translation see, for instance, *Current Soviet Documents,* June 3, 1963.)

1. TWO POEMS AND AN AUTOBIOGRAHY: THREE MAIN TARGETS OF OFFICIAL SOVIET CRITICISM

a. Babi Yar *

EVGENY YEVTUSHENKO
Soviet Poet

There are no memorials at Babi Yar.
As a rough tombstone the cliff-face rises sheer.
I feel afraid.
                    Today, when standing here,
I'm as full of years as the Jewish people are.
Today it seems to me
                    that I'm a Jew.
Through ancient Egypt, wandering still, I go,
and, hung upon the Cross, I die anew;
the nails' stigmata in my flesh I show.
It seems to me that Dreyfus
                              here I am laired.
The petit-bourgeois
                    denounce me, judge my case.
I press behind the jail-bars
                              ringed and snared,
baited
    and slandered,
                    spat on in disgrace,
While the fine ladies, flounced in brussels-lace,
screech as they poke their parasols in my face.
It seems to me
              I'm a boy in Byelostok.

---

* From *Literaturnaya gazeta*, Sept., 1961. Reprinted from the translation in the *Anglo-Soviet Journal*, Spring, 1962, pp. 15-16, by permission of the publisher.
    We have seen several translations—some sacrificing the form and freely rendering the imagery; others over-literal and destroying the poetry—and none has been wholly satisfactory. In this translation made for the *Anglo-Soviet Journal*, Jack Lindsay has endeavoured to retain Yevtushenko's verse form and remain faithful to his imagery. (Editors, *Anglo-Soviet Journal*.)

Blood gushes, soaks the floor, and spreads about.
The braggarts of the tavern run amok,
belching a heat of vodka and onions out.
Booted aside, what can I do? I plead
in vain with the trampling pogromists, who swear
and bellow:
    Save our Russia! Smash the Yids!
A chandler beats my mother senseless there.
O my Russian people!
     well I know
       that you,
deep in your hearts, look past each narrow claim
and love all men. The dirty-handed crew
call with no right at all on your pure name.
I know how good is my native land, how base
the antisemites
    who, with a solemn air,
themselves *The Russian People's League* declare
without one twitch of a nerve across the face.
It seems to me
    I am Anna Frank today
limpidly frail
    as a bud on April's bough.
I love.
  And I have no need of phrases now.
Only,
  look at me, friend with friend, I pray.
How little can we smell,
     how little see.
No greenery left,
    no sky left in this place.
But much we still can do.
    O tenderly,
still in a dark room, friend with friend, embrace.
Someone is coming?
    Have no fear. The steps
are spring's.
    For spring is near, and on our tracks.
Come to me.
    Quickly give me up your lips.
Someone breaks in the door!
     No, the ice cracks.
The grasses rustle on Babi Yar's bleak gap,
and down, the trees in judgment
     sternly stare.

All things scream silently.
                    I remove my cap
and feel
          how greyness slowly fills my hair.
And I am only
                    a soundless unending sigh
over the thousands on thousands buried near.
Every old man who was murdered here
                              is I;
and I am every child who was murdered here.
No part of me
              will ever forget this call.
Let the International
                above us sweep
when earth's last antisemite of them all
for all eternity is buried deep.
No Jewish blood runs in my blood, it's true;
and yet the antisemites, every one,
with bitter rancour hate me
                    as a Jew.
And therefore
          of Russia I'm a trueborn son.

Translated by Jack Lindsay.

b. Stalin's Heirs *

YEVGENY YEVTUSHENKO **
Soviet Poet

The marble was silent.
    The glass glistened silently.
The guards stood silent,
    Bronzing in the sun.
But the coffin gave off a faint vapor.
    Breath leaked through a crack
When they took it through the Mauso-
    leum doors.
The coffin slowly floated past,
    Its corners touching the bayonets.

He too was silent—
                too!—
    But frighteningly silent.
Sullenly clenching
    Embalmed fists,
Inside, the man pretending death
    Pressed against the crack.
He wanted to remember all those
    Who were carrying him out:
Young Ryazan and Kursk recruits,

* From *Pravda*, Oct. 21, 1962. Reprinted from the translation in *The Current Digest of the Soviet Press,* Oct. 31, 1962, by permission of the publisher.
** This poem is by the same author as "Babi Yar" above. The difference in the spelling of the first name is the result of different transliteration from the Russian alphabet. Reproductions in this volume keep the same transliteration as the original translation from which the selection is reprinted.

So that afterward somehow
> He might gather the strength for a
> sally
And rise from the earth
> And get at these rash persons.
He had thought of something.
> He had merely nestled down for a
> rest.
And I appeal to our government
> With the request
To double,
> To triple
> > The guard at this slab
So that Stalin may not rise,
> And, with Stalin,
> > the past.
I am not speaking of that treasured,
valorous past
Which was Turksib,[1]
> Magnitka [2]
> > And the flag over Berlin.
Here
> I mean by the past
The ignoring of the people's welfare,
> The calumnies,
> > The arrests of the innocent.
We sowed honestly.
> We poured steel honestly
And we marched honestly,
> Lining up in soldiers' ranks.
But he feared us.
> Believing in a great goal, he did not
> believe
That the means
> Should be worthy of the great goal.
He was farsighted.
> Skilled in the laws of battle,
He left many heirs on the face of the
globe.
I dream
> that a telephone has been placed
> in the coffin:

Stalin sends his instructions
> to Enver Hoxha.
Where else does the line from the cof-
fin run?
No—Stalin has not given up.
> He considers death
> > remediable.
We rooted him
> out of the Mausoleum.
But how to root Stalin
> out of Stalin's heirs?!
Some of the heirs snip roses in retire-
ment
> and secretly consider
> > the retirement temporary.
Others
> even condemn Stalin from the plat-
> form,
But themselves
> at night
> > pine for the old days.
Evidently not for nothing do Stalin's
heirs today
> suffer heart attacks.
They, once his lieutenants,
> do not like these times
When the camps are empty
> And the halls where people listen
> to poetry
> > Are crowded.
The Party
> ordered me
> > not to be quiet.
Let some repeat over and over:
> "Relax!"—I cannot be
> > calm.
As long as Stalin's heirs exist on earth
It will seem to me
> that Stalin is still in the Mauso-
> leum.

[1] The Turkestan-Siberian Railroad, completed in 1930.
[2] The Magnitogorsk Iron and Steel Combine, one of the great construction projects of the First Five-Year Plan.

c. Retrospect on Russia *

ILYA EHRENBURG
Soviet Author

Right now I feel like looking back, giving some thought to that early tangled skein of hopes and doubts.

I have said elsewhere that history is not made by magic edict; neither is it made according to that irrefutable logic which gives science its basic strength. As a youngster I had often heard it said in the P. G. Smidovich group that the road to socialism would be found by the proletariat of the world's most highly industrialized nations.

In 1946 a worker who lived in the "Iron Mirgorod," in other words, in Detroit, asked me, "Why do you keep talking about American capitalists, about monopolies, about exploitation? Do you think we aren't aware of all this? Of course we are. But still we with our capitalists live better than you without capitalists. . . ." An absence of class consciousness? Of course. But that isn't the whole story; it's a whole different attitude toward life, the cult of creature comforts, fear in the face of achievement, of sacrifices, of the unknown.

Be that as it may, the first country where the socialist revolution was successful was Russia with its backward economy. Two out of three citizens of the young Soviet republic signed their names with an x. I had occasion in 1918 to spend some time in villages in the Moscow and Tula Provinces. In the peasant huts you found plush-upholstered armchairs, gramophones, even pianos either taken from country estates or acquired from city people in trade for a sack of potatoes. But the people still lived the pre-Revolutionary peasant existence described by Chekhov and Bunin. There was a great deal of cruelty, ignorance, darkness. They burned libraries. They hated the townspeople ("parasites") and there were those who rejoiced because the towns were starving. Perhaps this explains at least in part the bewilderment which at times overwhelmed the intelligentsia and which found expression in some of Gorky's writings.

The young people who had come to the cities and were caught up in the maelstrom of events easily accepted the over-simplified concepts of the "prolet-cult" extremists, the future members of the "On Guard" group. More than once I heard people say, "Why complicate things? The intelli-

---

* From Ilya Ehrenburg's memoirs, *People, Years, Life*. Excerpts translated in *The Soviet Review*, July, 1961, pp. 3-40. Reprinted from Chapter 25 of the translation by permission of the publisher.

gentsia is so much offal. You've read the paper? Then everything is clear. The why's and wherefore's are just bourgeois talk. . . . Why bother your head about it. . . ."

In the fall of 1920 V. I. Lenin had this to say to the members of the Young Communist League: "If a Communist took it into his head to brag about communism on the basis of ready-made conclusions, without having done a great deal of hard, serious, important work, without having examined the facts which he is under obligation to approach and consider critically, he would be a sad sort of Communist indeed. And such superficiality would unquestionably be disastrous."

I have already spoken of the thirst for knowledge which in those days took hold of millions of young men and women. The people opened their first primer. Now I must also speak about those who taught them their ABC's, who lectured on history or geology, who saved books from burning, museum buildings from vandalism, who, probably half-starved most of the time, continued to defend culture—about Russia's intelligentsia. I am now speaking, of course, not about that section of it which went abroad and there tried to vilify its own people, but about those who, having accepted the October Revolution, at the same time remained full of doubt. When you reread the early stories of Vsevolod Ivanov, Malyshkin, Pilniak, H. Ognev, the first poems of Tikhonov, it becomes clear that these doubts stemmed from a desire to approach critically those same facts of which Lenin spoke.

On Strastnaya Place there hung a poster: "Hail electrification!" Under it Yesenin once read me the monologue of Pugachev which began, "Oh Asia, Asia, blue region covered with salt, sand and lime. . . ." It was a good poem. But it isn't the poetry I am thinking of now. Criminal bands roamed the countryside. In the villages the food collection details were being fired on. The fields lay fallow. Homeless children wandered around railroad stations. The cities were hungry. The mortality rate increased rapidly.

All this seems ancient history now. "Blue Asia" is in the process of becoming industrialized, with the Soviet Union helping her. If toward the end of the 1930's some Western politicians still persisted in calling our country "a colossus with feet of clay," they were soon to be convinced that the "colossus' " feet were thoroughly solid.

. . . When I look at Moscow today I can hardly realize that this is the city where I spent my childhood. You go to Vnukhovo Airport and each time you marvel—you see not just houses, but whole streets and developments mushrooming on the way.

True, our people are better at making jet airplanes than pots and pans; but in time they will learn how to make pots too. For the moment the Western politicos can talk of nothing but the ballistic feet of the "colossus."

By nature I am one of those known as doubting Thomases. (The adjective may be misleading. Thomas was deeply faithful and, according to Christian legend, bore up well under torture; but he could never take things on faith—he wanted to verify everything that others told him, that is, to approach facts critically.) During the years which I am now remembering—1920-1921—I had plenty of doubts, but those doubts were nothing like the talk of people who were sure that Russia was disintegrating, that the Varangians, bearers of order, would eventually come, that everything would end with the establishment of a moderate-liberal bourgeois system. There was one thing about which I was in no doubt whatever—the victory of the new socialist order.

Life was frightening: there was dried fish for food, there were broken sewer pipes, bitter cold, epidemics. But I knew, as did all those whom I considered my friends, that the people, having beaten the interventionists, would also beat the chaos. Julio Jurenito, as he speaks about the marvelous city of the future, all steel, glass and organization, exclaims, "That's how it's going to be! I speak of it here in pauperized, ruined Russia, for it is not those who own a superabundance of stones that shall build, but those who dare strengthen these unbearably heavy stones with their own blood. . . ."

My doubts were not in relation to thoughts of houses, but thoughts of the people who would inhabit them. In Yuri Olesha's play the heroine draws up two lists: on one side are the "benefits" of the Revolution and on the other its "crimes." Later she recognizes her mistake, and the play is entitled *The List of Benefits*. I made no such lists—neither on paper nor in my mind. Life is more complex than beginning logic, many crimes may lead to benefits, and there are also benefits which are potentially crimes.

(Speaking of the darker side of our life people are prone to add, "the hangovers of capitalism." Sometimes this is true, sometimes not. Bright light intensifies shadows and good may bring some evil in its wake. Let me take a most glaring example—bureaucracy; V. I. Lenin wrote of it in his time and our newspapers continue writing about it forty years later. Is this paper-work dropsy, this hypertrophy of those who register, verify, authenticate, pass judgment—is this merely a hangover? Is not such an ailment —which in time can and must disappear—connected with the development of the organization, the accounting and control of production, in other words, with that which is progressive and correct?)

I remember how the cleaning woman in the military-chemistry school, a young country girl, used to sing a *chastushka* [topical verses]: "I'll make trouble for myself, I'll go to the toilet without a pass, I'd be glad to get a pass, but there's no one can issue one." I laughed when I heard it, then I started to think about it.

The worker knows very well that a machine, no matter how complicated, is man-made and made to serve man.

Of course I was first and foremost concerned with the fate of art. A diagram which hung in the office of V. I. Bryusov not only amazed but rather frightened me. Literature seemed to be a lot of squares, circles, diamonds—screws in a giant machine.

I once admitted my doubts to Lunacharsky. He answered that communism must lead not to sameness but to variety, that artistic creativity must not be made to conform to one pattern. Anatole Vasilievich went on to say that there exist Derzhimordas [1] who have no understanding of the nature of art. A year later he wrote a piece for *Pechat i Revolutsia (The Press and the Revolution)* in which he used the same definitions. After saying that during the period of transition censorship is inevitable, he continued, "But the person who says, 'Let there be an end to all these foolish myths about freedom of speech; under our communist system state direction over literature is appropriate, censorship is not just a hideous feature of the transition period but inherent in a well-ordered, socialized socialist existence'—the person who from this draws the conclusion that criticism as such must become a kind of denunciation or else a kind of forcing of artistic creativity into primitive revolutionary molds will merely prove, if you scratch him a little, that under his communist cloak there sits a Derzhimorda and that, be he given the least bit of power, he will get nothing out of it except the pleasure of bullying, playing the petty tyrant and especially of pushing others around."

. . . During those years we all of us were romantics, even though we were ashamed of the word. I was at odds not with the epoch, but with myself. My ideas were far from clear. I was all for industrial esthetics, for a planned economy, abhorring the chaos, the hypocrisy, the surface gilt of capitalism (mine was not a book knowledge of it); yet more than once I asked myself what would happen in the new, more rational and just society to the diversity of human character; and wouldn't those perfected machines whose praises I now was singing supplant art, and wouldn't technology crush those sometimes vague but precious human emotions?

Forty years later I published in *Komsomolskaya Pravda* a letter from a young Leningrad girl. She spoke about a fine engineer who was contemptuous of art, indifferent to the tragedy of Manolis Glezos, equally cold to his mother and his comrades, and who considered love an anachronism in the atomic age. In that same issue I read a letter from a specialist in cybernetics: he made fun of any girl capable of "crying into her pillow," of anyone who in our time admires the music of Bach or the poetry of Blok.

Many of my doubts of the year 1921 were naive and were later taken care of by life itself; many, but not all. . . .

What I feared most was indifference, the mechanization not of industry but of human emotions, of art losing its vitality. I knew that the forest would grow tall and kept thinking about the fate of the warm, living tree,

---

[1] Derzhimorda (literally, "shut your trap") is the policeman in Gogol's *The Inspector General*. The name has become a byword for ignorance and intolerance.

with its complicated root system, its unique branches, its heartwood rings.

Quite possibly those thoughts came to me because at the age of thirty I was about to take the examination to earn the right to call myself a writer. Of course I did not suspect what problems were ahead of me. But it was clear to me that it was not merely a matter of how to build a novel or turn a phrase. In one of his letters Chekhov said that the business of the writer is to take up for humanity. This may sound simple, but actually it is very hard. . . .

. . . A man, a writer may guess and understand a great deal, but certainly not everything. You see your own gray hair in the mirror when you shave, but to look into the future is far more difficult. It took me a long time to understand that a great many tough crossings still lay ahead and that the wind would not die down so long as the heart continued beating. . . .

WESTERN VIEWS

2. SOCIALIST REALISM IN ART *

A. GAEV

Expert on Soviet Literature

. . . The function of Soviet art is summed up in the phrase "socialist realism." Probably not even its author, Maxim Gorky, foresaw the future that was in store for this expression in the Soviet theory of art. For almost thirty years, it has occupied a firm place in Soviet terminology, has been repeated times without number at all levels of propaganda and rhetoric, from the tribunes of the Kremlin to amateur art clubs in factories, and is duly defined and explained in the Soviet dictionaries and encyclopedias. The whole of Party policy in the sphere of art is founded on the compulsory observance of the requirements of "socialist realism": not one branch of art is allowed to depart from them. . . .

The best evidence for the true essence of "socialist realism" is furnished by those works of art which follow this method and which are rec-

* Excerpts reprinted from *Bulletin, Institute for the Study of the USSR,* February, 1962, pp. 20-29 by permission of the publisher.

ognized by the Soviet authorities as "achievements" of socialist art. Last year, the artist M. Khmelko attempted to rejoice the hearts of the Soviet authorities with an enormous canvas on which he had long been engaged. The picture, entitled "Congress of the Builders of Communism," is the work of an experienced and obsequious hand. On the dais of the celebrated Georgievsky Zal in the Kremlin stands the inspired and paternally smiling figure of Nikita Khrushchev, who, evidently having just completed a speech, is caught in a dynamic oratorical pose. Behind him is a full-length, life-size portrait of Lenin, also in the act of delivering a speech. There is a great deal in common to be observed between the postures and even facial expressions of the two men, although Lenin is bald while the artist's foreshortening has concealed Khrushchev's bald patch with a touch of noble gray hair. The steps leading up to the dais are occupied by people who, having abandoned their seats in the hall, are applauding with their gaze fixed on the orator. The entire group of delegates is a picture of awe-filled rapture and admiration. Behind Khrushchev one may recognize without difficulty the figures of Voroshilov, Mikoyan, Furtseva, Suslov, Malinovsky, Kozlov and others . . . In the center stands Khrushchev, pointing the way to Communism.

The canvas is an equal blend of vivid color and loyal devotion. The artist has done his best to give the episode historical significance. Clearly, he had to spend much time and effort over the study of dozens of photographs, for the majority of figures depicted are real people. One finds writers, headed by Mikhail Sholokhov, well-known academicians, heroes of socialist labor, inventors and, of course, leading officials from the various republic Party organizations. Careful to satisfy all possible political demands, the artist portrays a number of figures in national costume, thus emphasizing the "unity in rapture" of these representatives of all the peoples of the Soviet Union. . . .

The main requirement [for "socialist realism"] is as follows: "Art must first of all be a mirror for all the people reflecting the victorious march of Communism." As a result, a prominent place in Soviet art is taken by the representation of political events in which Party leaders always appear. It is essential that the episode depicted should demonstrate the link between these leaders and representatives of the people or even whole groups of the people. Khmelko's picture is only one of many examples. . . .

Quantitatively speaking, another type of picture is more important than these, namely pictures whose content is obviously determined by the Central Committee's injunction that art should reflect the life of the people —as the Party leaders see it. An enormous number of pictures is devoted to labor, to the daily life of factory workers, builders, miners, collective farmers, fishermen and so on. Many of them portray well-known shock workers engaged in their work. . . . Women are very often portrayed, but, significantly enough, hardly ever when engaged on typically feminine tasks such as sewing, laundering, cooking, operating telephone switchboards, nursing children or a patient, etc. Instead, we find women on the building sites, in factory workshops or in the mines. (Admittedly, artists are not guilty here of distorting the truth.) Finally, it may be added that a large number of pictures in this category are devoted to the cultivation and development of the virgin lands and industrially undeveloped areas, particularly Siberia. . . .

All this is naturally also true of the treatment of life on the collective farms: here it only remains to point out the emphasis laid upon the aspect of mechanization—the plowing up of the virgin lands, the work of tractor and combine drivers and truck operators on the lands of Kazakhstan.

The main feature of all these pictures dedicated to labor is their portrayal of work as a heroic feat performed by celebrated shock workers or as a joy indulged by ordinary workers and collective farmers who are known to no one. There is no sign of work conceived as drudgery, as a tedious or exhausting *corvée*.

The next category, in quantity and also political significance, consists of paintings on war and other heroic subjects. In recent years, only a small number have been devoted to the Revolution or the Civil War. Most of them relate to World War II and are designed to demonstrate Soviet patriotism. . . . The numerousness of paintings in this category is due, not to the undoubted fact that the war produced many cases of courage, self-sacrifice and patriotism, but to the official policy of maintaining a militant patriotic spirit and demonstrating the country's military preparedness rather in the spirit of the phrase "Keep your powder dry!" Socialist realism forbids all portrayal of the unheroic aspect of war. If Soviet officers and men are depicted, there must be no suggestion that any are seized with fear. If there are any corpses, they must continue posthumously to urge the others on until their last bullet is spent. And, of course, there must be the political slant: it may be the figure of a commissar, a slogan or banner displayed in a prominent position, or simply the title of the picture. However he does it, the artist must use his ingenuity to fulfill this requirement.

In spite of the vivid portraiture required in Soviet painting and sculpture, photographic exactitude is out of place in socialist realism. . . . What socialist realism requires is not photography, but what the photographic lens cannot see. It is, in fact, essentially associated with the dressing up, the prettifying of reality, or the neglect of reality in favor of a deceptively attractive propagandist unreality. The negative aspects of a subject which are unavoidable in photography are in Soviet art made use of only to bring out the more clearly what has intentionally been brought under focus. It is very difficult, for example, to obtain a photograph of a workman performing strenuous physical work while retaining a joyful facial expression. For the artist, it is easy, even if he wants to preserve the lifelikeness of a portrait. . . .

Landscapes form, as always, an important part of Soviet painting. It would seem difficult to subject landscape painting to political demands, but even here there are requirements presented by socialist realism. The artist has to approach Nature with an ideological rule, since not every landscape is equally acceptable. The note required is optimism: "There is painting that is optimistic in its essence, painting which teaches joy." The article in which this remark occurs describes the work of the painter Aleksandr Gerasimov and compliments him on his optimistic landscapes, quoting as examples the paintings "After the Rain" and "From the Window." . . .

One may ask: Wherein lies these pictures' optimism? How can one portray a wintry road in a mountainous district or the late fall in cheerful colors? The answer lies in some small detail. In Panteleev's painting, for example, far beyond the cheerless, desolate road, beyond the horizon, one can discern in the gray sky the tiny form of an airplane in flight. Burzyantsev's picture of a rather gloomy landscape is enlightened by a glimpse in the distance of a three-storied building with a tall chimney, the smoke from which testifies that life is there.

Still less favor is bestowed in Soviet art upon the *genre* of still life, and for this socialist realism is undoubtedly responsible. After all, it is far from easy to convey the heroic side of Soviet labor or construction when painting fruit, flowers, pottery or the like disposed on a table.

Quantitatively speaking, *genre* painting is very poorly represented, in contrast to the past. . . . Only a very limited number of pictures on such subjects were shown at the various exhibitions which have been organized in the last two or three years. . . .

Many themes have all but disappeared from the canvases of Soviet artists. This applies above all to historical subjects. History begins with the year 1917, and anything that occurred before that date rarely appears. We find only themes that are obviously revolutionary—risings, strikes, episodes from the lives of members of the "Narodnaya volya" organization, the social-democrats and, of course, the 1905 Revolution. Even these pictures are few, however, and are mostly used as illustrations to historical texts. Another rarity are representations of family life, for the family has here given way to the "collective." There is also no reflection of commercial life—not even the kolkhoz bazaar.

It is impossible to find pictures where man is depicted as a contemplator. He has to be doing something, and not alone at that. Even such an ordinary occupation as taking a solitary walk is ignored by Soviet artists of the recent past. Hunting and fishing have also been largely abandoned as subjects, presumably again because of the necessity of not showing people outside their occupational pursuits, free of immediate cares and alone with themselves.

One looks in vain in Soviet portraits for drunkards, hooligans, truants from work, brawlers, *stilyagi,* people with vicious characters. There are no religious believers, still less persons of clerical status—priests, rabbis, mullahs or sectarians: all these persons, embraced by the single term "survivals of the past," are relegated in their entirety to the caricaturists. People with moral vices, however numerous they may be in real life, cannot figure in pictures fulfilling the demands of "socialist realism." The artist is deprived of the right to expose or accuse: consequently, breakers of the law are excluded from his choice of subject, even those who are already serving their legal punishment. In addition, trials at court, legal investigations and the like are inadmissible. All this is clearly due to the principle that the Soviet artist may not depict negative types of humanity: he must show that Soviet society consists of healthy, honest and life-loving people conforming entirely to the Communist ethic. It is significant that during all the twenty years that religion has been officially allowed in the USSR not one artist, to judge by pictures displayed at exhibitions, has depicted an open church, mosque or other place of worship.

Another aspect of life that one does not see on the canvas is that of disease: there are no portraits of the sick, the starving, the dying or the crippled, although there are more war invalids, for example, in the USSR than in any other country.

Finally, all modernist, abstract and in general "left-wing" art is banned. This ban, being absolute, goes much further than the limitations imposed on the choice of *genre,* etc., that we have been discussing: the flat rejection of the "left-wing" art of the free world is merely one more way of attacking this free world. . . .

3. THE REGIME AND THE INTELLECTUALS *

PRISCILLA JOHNSON

*Author, Journalist, Expert on
Contemporary Soviet Literature*

More than a year ago,[1] while their conservative hetmen were off on a tour of the provinces, a group of writers in Moscow skillfully wielded the secret ballot to elect eight of their young and liberal members to the board of the Moscow writers' organization. . . . By last autumn the liberals of both art and literature had racked up such a string of successes

* Reprinted from *Problems of Communism, Special Supplement,* Sept.-Oct., 1963, by permission of the United States Information Agency.
[1] In the early spring of 1962. [Editor's note.]

that they may well have suffered that Communist feeling of "dizziness from success." In the field of art, there had been a few books and articles defending modern, even abstractionist, trends in painting, even occasional exhibits of modern painting and sculpture. On the literary front the liberal gains had been more spectacular and even more far-reaching. In 1962 the conservatives were foiled in at least two attempts to disband the liberal Moscow writers' organization. Later that year Yevgeni Yevtushenko and Vasili Aksionov, symbols of the spirit of youthful liberalization, were elected to the editorial board of the journal *Yunost*. . . .

And yet there were signs all summer and fall that, chastened as it might be, the conservative impulse in the arts was anything but dead. In July the party theoretical journal *Kommunist* published an unsigned article "On the Attitude Toward the Literary Heritage of A. V. Lunacharsky." Naming no names, the article seemed aimed against those, such as Ilya Ehrenburg, who had cited the views of Lenin's Commissar of Enlightment to justify a lenient party policy in the arts. During the same month, July, the literary journal *Zvezda* printed a scurrilous, politically motivated attack on the alleged "leftism" of the 29-year-old poet Andrei Voznesenski. . . .

There is little doubt that these conflicting trends in literature, one liberal, the other conservative, only reflected a far more fundamental split in the political sphere—above all, the struggle by bureaucrats left over from the Stalin era to hang onto their power and positions. On October 21, with scarcely any warning, *Pravda* published a poem by Yevgeni Yevtushenko called "Stalin's Heirs." In the poem, Yevtushenko called upon the Communist Party "to double, to triple" the guard at Stalin's grave "lest Stalin rise again and, with Stalin, the past." . . . On the day "Stalin's Heirs" appeared, the newspaper *Komsomolskaia pravda* published still another poem by Yevtushenko, "Fears." This poem celebrated the end of terror. Neither poem had been published before, although they had been known to exist for some time.

Then, in November, the literary journal *Novyi mir* [2] appeared, containing Alexander Solzhenitsyn's remarkable and powerfully understated story, "One Day in the Life of Ivan Denisovich." A moving description of life in a Soviet prison camp under Stalin, the story was bound to stir up a public sentiment that those responsible for the crimes of the Stalin era must now be brought to account. Its publication seemed to be a signal that destalinization was about to be carried deeper than ever before. . . . In a speech on November 23, Khrushchev revealed that it was he who had authorized publication of Yevtushenko's "Stalin's Heirs" and Solzhenitsyn's "One Day in the Life of Ivan Denisovich." Other members of the Soviet

[2] Note the different transliteration of *Novi mir* and of Ilyichev below. [Editor's note.]

leadership, he revealed, had suggested cuts in the story, but he had over-ruled them on the ground that "no one had the right to alter the author's version."

Khrushchev's speech was never made public. Only a few days after it was delivered, he himself appeared to set in motion a dramatically reversed policy toward the arts. . . .

Already, as the plenary session adjourned [Nov. 23, 1962] it an-nounced the creation of a special Ideological Commission of the Central Committee, to be headed by Leonid Ilichev. It was the purpose of the new commission to see to it that ideological activity be not relaxed but stepped up during the forthcoming period of attention to economic reforms.

An initiative had meanwhile been undertaken by Stalin's heirs in the hope of retrieving their position. While the Central Committee was meet-ing between November 19 and 23, it received a petition "from a large group of artists" complaining of growing "formalist trends in art" and ask-ing the party to intervene. This was the first step in a long chain which was to see party conservatives destroy the recent liberal trend in art, then literature, in an attempt to halt the process of destalinization and upset the balance of power inside the party Presidium itself. . . . Let us look at the second link in the chain that led to action.

Art for the Party's Sake

On Monday evening, November 26, a semi-private exhibit of art that by Moscow standards was avantgarde, opened in the barn-like studio of a 38-year-old art teacher named Eli Beliutin. . . .

On Thursday evening, November 29, a second exhibit of modern art was to take place in the Yunost Hotel in Moscow. Hours before it was to open, the show was mysteriously postponed. Later, it was cancelled alto-gether. In the meantime, the work at the Beliutin studio was suddenly summoned to the huge Manezh gallery, where a retrospective exhibit, "Thirty Years of Moscow Art," of 2000 canvases and sculptures in now fashionable variations of the official, socialist realist style, had been under-way for nearly a month. The works from Beliutin's were not hung with the rest, but placed in three separate rooms. . . .

On Saturday afternoon, December 1, Nikita Khrushchev, accom-panied by four Presidium members and several members of the party Secretariat, paid a surprise visit to the Manezh. Khrushchev's reaction . . . [was one of] violence and crudity. . . . To certain high-ranking cultural officials, not to mention . . . the Beliutin painters who also were on hand, Khrushchev's negative reaction, let alone his violence, came as a total surprise. For hadn't Khrushchev authorized the release of a volume of liberal writing, *Tarusskie stranitsy,* in 1961, after his officials had con-fiscated it? And weren't his words of praise on opening the glassily modern

Pioneer Palace only the summer before on record? There was, then, a "myth" of Khrushchev's liberalism, and it seemed not altogether lacking in foundation.

As anyone who has trailed him on visits to Western exhibitions is aware, Khrushchev appears genuinely to detest modern painting and sculpture, as distinct from functional architecture. Thus, those who had instigated his visit to the Manezh and who stood by him, making disparaging remarks about the modernistic paintings, probably counted on an outburst of profanity and were prepared to use the visit for their own ends. In the post-Cuba atmosphere, with supporters of moderate policies in every sphere on the defensive, these conservatives were primed to carry the consequences very far indeed. They were lucky in their timing. The panic that seized them over "Ivan Denisovich" coincided neatly with an inner-party recoil after Cuba.

Thus, within hours after Khrushchev's explosion at the Manezh, the campaign for "ideological purity" in art was under way. The papers came out with editorials demanding, among other things, that all unions of artists, writers, composers, film and theater workers be merged into a single one so as to prevent nonconformity in the future; old-time bureaucrats came back into prominence, and some were elected to important positions. Yet the liberals took action as well. Undeterred by the thought that criminal charges of "factionalism" might later be raised against them, at least three groups of intellectuals now sent protest petitions to the Central Committee. A group of young abstract painters declared in a letter that they were seeking their way in "socialist art," and that without such searches there could be no progress. A group of seventeen eminent artists and scientists, in a message addressed directly to Khrushchev, pleaded with him "to stop the swing in the representational arts to past methods which are alien to the whole spirit of our times." The signatories of this letter included two Nobel Prize-winning scientists, Igor Tamm and Nikolai Semionov, as well as the writers Konstantin Simonov, Ilya Ehrenburg, Kornei Chukovski and Veniamin Kaverin, the sculptors Konenkov and Favorski, the composer Dimitry Shostakovich, the film maker Mikhail Romm, and others. A similar letter, but one which appeared to go even farther, calling for " 'peaceful coexistence' of all trends in art," was also dispatched. According to one source, this letter was later withdrawn. According to others, one or more signatures were withdrawn. The very fact, which later came to light, that Alexei Surkov, former head of the Writers' Union and persecutor of Boris Pasternak, was one of the original signatories of this letter, is a sign how deep the dry rot of liberal ideas had penetrated even those on whom the party had hitherto been able to rely as sturdy zealots of conformity.

Speeches and Discussions

At a meeting on December 17 between party leaders and 400 writers, artists and other intellectuals at the Pioneer Palace on Lenin Hills, the first phase of the new campaign came to a head. The gathering was addressed by Khrushchev in a speech that has not been published. The main address, however, said to have been ten hours long, was given by Ilichev. Art, he said, must be militant. It must inculcate "Communist Party spirit." . . . Yet the truly striking note in Ilichev's speech was its defensiveness. "It is considered inconvenient," he complained, "and unfashionable to defend correct party positions; one might get the reputation of being, so to say, a reactionary and a conservative." Unwittingly, he disclosed just how much pressure the regime was under to allow greater freedom of expression. There are people, he admitted, who are demanding an end to all censorship: "Exhibitions without juries, books without editors, the right of the artist to display without an intermediary what he wishes. 'Let us create as we ourselves wish,' these people say. 'Do not restrict us.' "

Again and again, so that it is almost a leitmotif, he lamented the influence of the West on Soviet art. In so doing, he showed just how vulnerable the party itself is to praise of its artistic exports abroad, and how skillfully the liberals have used their renown in the West to bolster their standing at home.

Compared with such speeches in the past, however, Ilichev's tone, at least in the published text, was mild. . . . Furthermore, some of the informal exchanges that took place at the meeting—of which the outside world learned subsequently—are as remarkable for what they reveal about Khrushchev's own feelings as for what they tell of the intellectuals' resistance to party interference in art. Thus Ilya Ehrenburg cited the cases of Picasso and Mayakovsky to show that modern artists need not, as the party insists, be political reactionaries. The sculptor Ernst Neizvestny reportedly said to Khrushchev: "You may not like my work, but it has the warm support of such eminent Soviet scientists as Kapitsa and Landau." Khrushchev replied: "That's not why we admire Kapitsa and Landau." Yevtushenko rose to Neizvestny's defense in a chivalrous exhibition of loyalty. "He came back from the war with 14 bullets in his body," he declared. "I hope he will live many more years and produce many more fine works of art." To which Khrushchev replied: "As they say, only the grave corrects a hunchback." It was Yevtushenko's turn to deliver an admonition: "I hope, Comrade Khrushchev, we have outlived the time when the grave was used as a measure of correction." Stunned at first, the audience burst into applause. Even Khrushchev joined in. These displays of solidarity within the liberal camp, irrespective of medium, help explain why the campaign was so quick to spread from art into literature.

A stormy intervention of Khrushchev on anti-Semitism was occasioned

by Shostakovich's choice of Yevtushenko's poem "Babi Yar" as the theme
for the first movement of his new Thirteenth Symphony. There is no anti-
Semitism in the Soviet Union, Khrushchev declared. . . . In the aftermath of Khrushchev's statement, Yevtushenko agreed to add several new
lines to "Babi Yar."

January, [1963] on the whole, was a time of paradox, of patent in-
decision at the top. The press saved its fire for "formalism" in the fine
arts. Writers were criticized less as writers than as patrons of modern art.
Yet, on January 17, an exhibit of 300 canvasses by the French painter
Fernand Léger, an abstractionist who had the grace to be a Communist
as well, opened at the Pushkin Museum, where it ran for three months
before being shipped back to Paris. The young poets were giving as many
public readings as ever, and the much-criticized Bulat Okudzhava was
permitted to perform with his guitar before a crowd of 10,000 at the Sports
Palace. Valentin Kataiev and the playwright Viktor Rozov left for the
United States as planned, and Yevtushenko slipped off on a visit to West
Germany and France. Before leaving, he fired a rather defiant poetic
parting shot,[3] which seems to reflect inner turmoil over the lines he had
been prevailed upon to add to "Babi Yar."

In the fine arts there were signs of stubborn resistance even from the
public, to say nothing of the artists themselves. . . . Firm as most writers
proved to be in their opposition when the campaign later turned full force
against them, it is the artists who were the most silent and stubborn of
all. . . . The recantations were few and far between. . . .

Attack from the Right

Toward the end of January, the campaign took a sharp break. From
now on it was aimed first of all at the writers. . . .

The opening stage of the literary drive reached its climax a few days
after when *Izvestia*[4] mounted a blistering attack by Yermilov on Ilya
Ehrenburg—primarily for the latter's assertion, in his memoirs published
in *Novyi mir,* that he and other Soviet citizens had been perfectly well
aware during the 1930's that millions of Stalin's victims were innocent,
but that they had been compelled to live with "clenched teeth" and be
silent. Yermilov vehemently denied this. No one, he insisted, unless he
enjoyed some special "advantage," was aware at the time that the arrests
were largely a frameup. Those rare individuals who happened to know
that a particular victim was innocent "fought, and fought not with silence."
The point, of course, was that if a journalist like Ehrenburg knew, what
about high-ranking officials, like Khrushchev, who even then held respon-

[3] Ye. Yevtushenko, "My Ideology," *Izvestia,* Jan. 8, 1963.
[4] Jan. 30, 1963.

sible posts in the party? Were they too cowardly to take steps against the slaughter? Or were they knowingly helping to carry it out?

Ehrenburg lost no time replying. He took issue with Yermilov that people "fought" the arrests of the 1930's: "I was not present at a single meeting at which people took the floor to protest the arbitrary persecution of comrades whose innocence they never doubted. Not once did I read an article of protest."

Izvestia printed Ehrenburg's reply, but only with another attack by Yermilov and a note from the editors supporting the attack. . . .

Immediately after the initial assault on Ehrenburg, *Izvestia* set out to chasten two other members of the older generation who had protected the talented but mettlesome young. The victims were Alexander Tvardovski, editor of *Novyi mir,* and Boris Polevoi, editor of the journal *Yunost.* Mildly, *Izvestia* scolded Tvardovski for publishing Alexander Yashin's story "Vologda Wedding"—a shocking picture of poverty, brutality and superstition in a Russian village after 47 years of Soviet rule. Tvardovski did not reply for three and a half months. Then, in an interview with UPI correspondent Henry Shapiro, he called Yashin's story "excellent" and "full of poetry." He added that the story "was, in my opinion, unjustly attacked in the press." These words were deleted from *Pravda's* account of the interview.[5] . . .

The Peak of the Campaign

It was an apprehensive gathering of 600 writers, artists and other intellectuals who met in the Kremlin's Sverdlov Hall on March 7 to hear the party leaders speak once again. In Paris, Yevtushenko had received an urgent cable on February 28 summoning him home for the meeting. He left on March 4 on the last flight that could deliver him to Moscow on time. . . .

Ilichev was the first major speaker. Acknowledging that the discussion touched off on December 1 was by now "a national debate," he conceded that the party's drive had been greeted by skepticism, silence and open protest. Some people, he admitted, were fearful that there would now be "creative stagnation" and "suppression of innovational searches in art." Some "have not merely misunderstood, but continue stubbornly to defend their mistaken views." . . .

The brunt of Ilichev's speech fell on Ehrenburg. Like Yermilov, he accused the elderly writer of enjoying special protection from Stalin. Hadn't Ehrenburg himself, he asked, quoting some of Ehrenburg's flights of prose, praised Stalin in 1951? As if anticipating that this weapon might one day be turned against himself, Ilichev added: "We all spoke and wrote

[5] The words are taken from the UPI text distributed abroad—they constitute the only discrepancy between the UPI and *Pravda* versions. . . .

thus at the time without being hypocritical. We believed and we wrote. And you, it turns out, did not believe, but wrote. These are different positions!" . . .

The main speech of the two-day meeting was that of Nikita Khrushchev. This was the speech that at last brought home to Moscow intellectuals the full ferocity of the campaign that had been mounted against them. . . .

Khrushchev's references to Ehrenburg were particularly venomous. . . . Another author whom Khrushchev selected for especially sharp reproof was Viktor Nekrasov. . . . Toward no one was Khrushchev so equivocal as toward Yevtushenko. In one passage he accused Yevtushenko along with Ehrenburg of "a gross ideological error" in liking some contemporary art. Praising him for his speech of December 24-26, however, Khrushchev gave the poet a bit of fatherly advice: "To hold dear the trust of the masses and not to seek cheap sensation, not to bow to the ideas and tastes of the philistines." He made the poet's "Babi Yar" the occasion of the longest public statement he has ever given on Soviet anti-Semitism ("We do not have a Jewish question, and those who dream it up are singing a foreign tune.") . . .

At the moment of Khrushchev's speech, Yevtushenko already was under attack in the press. The attacks did not say so, but it was known in Moscow that the poet had consented to serialization of his five-part autobiography in the French weekly *L'Express,* beginning on February 21. Whether the party would make an issue of the autobiography was a subject of speculation in the Soviet capital. As Khrushchev spoke, however, he must have been aware of the contents of at least two installments of the autobiography. Thus, Khrushchev's speech suggests that he hoped to preserve intact his most famous roving ambassador abroad, the young man who had come to symbolize the new and more liberal image of the USSR. . . .

Even before the meeting was over, it was clear that conservatives were still dissatisfied and wanted the drive to go farther. . . .

Main Target: The Young
. . . On March 26, a plenary meeting of the board of the USSR Writers' Union opened in Moscow, amid rumors at home and abroad that the moderate liberal Alexander Tvardovski was to be replaced as editor of *Novyi mir* by Yermilov and that the position of Konstantin Fedin as head of the Writers' Union might also be in jeopardy. In its reports of the meeting, significantly, *Literaturnaia gazeta* featured two photos each of Fedin and Tvardovski, giving the lie to the rumors and showing that both men had powerful moderate support. . . .

The speeches reflected the enormous pressure which Yevtushenko and Voznesenski were now under—Aksionov was out of town—to make a clean breast of their sins and offer up their hearts to the party. Nor was public pressure by any means the whole story. More privately they were told that in future they would not be published at all unless they accepted the right of the party to direct their work.

Another kind of threat was in the air as well. The atmosphere in Moscow by now was one of fear. There was a feeling that control had somehow been lost, that anything might happen, including a swing back to Stalinism. It is perfectly possible that Voznesenski and Yevtushenko were led to believe that their confessions were needed to forestall precisely such an eventuality.

It was not too great a surprise, therefore, when the slender, boyish figure of Andrei Voznesenski rose to the podium facing the assembled writers. What followed was concise, only 114 words, and one of the more remarkable statements in the annals of Russian recantations:

It has been said at this plenum that I must not forget the stern and severe words of Nikita Sergeievich. I shall never forget them. I shall not forget not only these severe words, but also the advice which Nikita Sergeievich gave me. He said: "Work." I do not justify myself now. I simply wish to say that for me the main thing now is to work, work, work. What my attitude is to my country, to communism, what I myself am, this work will show. (*Pravda,* March 29.)

To recant at all is, of course, to concede. But here at least was no extra word, no shade of capitulatory meaning that could be sliced off and exploited. . . .

Yevtushenko's recantation is a measure of the ambivalence of the man. Alternately defiant and abject, it was published only in part, and hence misrepresented. How grossly, we do not know. According to some sources, the poet defended himself and even counterattacked. Characteristically, he vigorously defended his colleague Neizvestny. . . . In those portions of the statement that appeared in the Soviet press, Yevtushenko confined himself to the autobiography. He did not apologize for writing, or even for publishing it. He did not repudiate what he had actually written. On the contrary, he said that it contained much that is "serious and mature." But he added, "I see now that it has much that is superficial and immodest. My most serious mistake is that I forgot about the morals of the bourgeois press, and for this I was cruelly punished." He had been the victim, he claimed, of distortions and misleading headlines by the editors of *L'Express*. He concluded:

I have committed an irreparable mistake. I feel heavy guilt on my shoulders. . . . I have lived through and felt a lot in these days. It is a lesson to me for my whole life. I want to assure the writers' collective that I fully understand and realize my error, and will try to correct it by all my future work.

To judge by reports of travellers, so unyielding was the mood of many Moscow young people that they greeted Yevtushenko's and even Voznesenski's statement with anger, disappointment, dismay. The idols were damaged although not, apparently, shattered. The conservative writers at the plenum were dissatisfied, too, albeit in a very different way. Having wrung even a slight admission of fault from the poets, they now were anxious to break them entirely. . . .

Volte-Face?

. . . It was in late March and early April that the storm showed real signs of getting out of hand. Shortly thereafter, however, the clamor against Yevtushenko and the other young writers subsided. We have only two clues as to the answer, one having to do with protests by Communist parties abroad, the other with stresses inside the Soviet leadership itself.

In late March or early April, at the height of the campaign against the young writers, all foreign Communist newspapermen stationed in Moscow had been summoned to a meeting. There, the editor of a leading Soviet literary journal showed them a "dossier of the accused." In language reminiscent of the purge era, the "dossier" spoke of an "opportunist fraction," from Yuri Kazakov ("this descendant of Ivan Bunin") to Yevtushenko, in the tradition of "that dubious political personality, Boris Pasternak." The dossier termed Yevtushenko's autobiography (shades of *Dr. Zhivago!*) a "blasphemy on the October Revolution."

This effort to prepare foreign Communist opinion for further draconian action seems to have fallen flat. One elderly Communist at the meeting said it sounded like Zhdanovism to him. A Cuban rose to defend Yevtushenko, a national hero in his country. The correspondent of the Italian Communist newspaper *L'Unità,* Pancaldi, wrote a critical dispatch. The French were silent. . . . Finally, on the eve of the elections to be held in his country on April 30, Palmiro Togliatti, head of the Italian Communist Party, made a statement disavowing the drive. . . . By early April, as we have seen, there seemed to be a danger that the wave of reaction inside the Soviet Union might be getting out of control. The adverse response of foreign Communist leaders may well have given a strong argument to moderates who wanted the campaign to go no further.

Apparently . . . the marked easing of the drive against the intellectuals in April, like the early stages in November, reflected high-level maneuvering inside the Soviet party and the influence of Communist parties abroad. On April 20, Khrushchev was back at his desk in the Kremlin. In a strong speech to industrial workers on April 24, he once again asserted the control of the party center over both left and right. He made it clear that coercion—the method being urged by the right—as a method of dealing with recalcitrants, was out, with the regime relying on maximum moral pressure instead, with the hope that the conscience of the individual writer or artist would coincide with the will of the party: "Poets and writers, too, ought to criticize our shortcomings. The only thing that counts is from what positions this is done and for what end—to assert what is new and Communist, or to deny it."

Nearly three weeks later, *Pravda* published the aforementioned interview of Alexander Tvardovski with UPI correspondent Henry Shapiro, in which the editor of *Novyi mir* congratulated the Central Committee and Khrushchev personally for their "broadmindedness" in approving publication of "One Day in the Life of Ivan Denisovich"; rather gently chided Yevtushenko and Voznesenski (whom he called "poets who are young not so much in age as in skill," adding that "a poet should have a fate, not a career"); and lent his support to all his authors who were under fire. . . .

In a statement in the April issue, which appeared only in May, the editorial board of *Novyi mir* went beyond Tvardovski's statement, granting that the criticism directed at Ehrenburg's memoirs by Khrushchev and Ilichev, was "just, and we bear our share of responsibility," and also conceding that Khrushchev's remarks about Nekrasov (about whom Tvardovski, an old and close friend, had kept silent) had been "correct." Apparently, the acceptance of criticism of Nekrasov was the price of continuing to publish his work. For the editors specifically announced that Nekrasov and other writers who were under fire—Yashin, Tendriakov, and Aksionov—were at work on new manuscripts, and that *Novyi mir* would stick to its 1963 publishing plan, including these authors.

Uncertainty—and Resistance

If the *Novyi mir* statement was a sign that party pressure was still heavy, an editorial in *Pravda* on May 19 gave new evidence that extreme militancy had at least given way to sober second thoughts. In a statement somewhat reminiscent of Khrushchev's speech to Soviet writers of May 1959, *Pravda* now proclaimed that the party saw "no need to watch over every step" by the intellectuals, "to explain in detail how to write a book, stage a play, make a film, compose music. Setting forth the main aim of creative work, the party urges the masters of literature and art to creative boldness and independence." If not a complete about-face, this statement at least represented a major shift in position compared with the speeches of March 8. . . .

On the eve of the Central Committee session, *Pravda* began publishing "One Hundred Anwers" to a questionnaire it had sent to writers inquiring about their current work. The aim of the exercise, no doubt, was to give the impression that Soviet literature was in a healthy state. It is not known how many writers who received the questionnaire failed to reply, or indeed how much pressure they were under to answer. Certain omissions, nonetheless, are striking. Missing were the names of Surkov, Tvardovski, and, for that matter, Kochetov. Sholokhov—who, like the Soviet Union's other famed novelist, Leonid Leonov, had refused to publish a word in favor of the party campaign—was represented by a single, surly sentence. The only liberal to reply was Aksionov. As the Central Committee session drew close, the liberal "conspiracy of silence" continued remarkably firm. . . .

The Long-Awaited Plenum

. . . Khrushchev, in a speech delivered at the Central Committee Plenum that opened on June 18, . . . warned that the "weakening of the class war in the international arena" could drive him to more extreme measures. Gogol's hero, Taras Bulba, recalled Khrushchev darkly, "killed his own son, Andrei, for going over to the side of the enemy. Such is the logic of the struggle." . . .

In spite of the specter of physical force, however, Khrushchev's speech was milder in some respects than that of March 8. He was at pains to avoid a frontal assault on the entire intellectual milieu or on individuals who might prove to be rallying points, singling out, besides Nekrasov, only the film director Mikhail Romm for criticism. He gave pointed praise to Fedin, Sholokhov and, significantly, Tvardovski. On the one hand, the hint of force; on the other, the hope of conciliation.

The most revealing part of Khrushchev's speech dealt with destalinization. He defended the wisdom of destalinization against charges by his critics that the campaign had destroyed respect for authority and was responsible for the crisis between "fathers and sons." . . .

Elsewhere in his speech Khrushchev addressed himself to the proposals to tighten organizational control over the arts. He was lukewarm to the idea of setting up a single union in place of the present unions of artists, writers and so on. He had no objection to the continued existence of separate unions, he indicated, so long as their work did not collide with the party line. On the other hand, he was favorably disposed to the creation of a single publishing enterprise. . . .

Nothing so clearly illustrates the improvised quality of the plenum, the lack of the old, Stalin-style coordination, than Khrushchev's remarks on the suggested changes in publishing and on the single union of creative artists. With Khrushchev one of the last to speak, the others, apparently unaware that he was going to give it his blessing, scarcely mentioned the proposed publishing reform at all. Several, on the other hand, spoke up for the single union, to which he was to indicate indifference. Those in favor included Ilichev; the Secretary of the Leningrad City Party Committee, G. I. Popov; and the head of the Composers' Union, Tikhon

Khrennikov. The final decree adopted by the session made no reference to either proposal. . . .

The plenum was notable for the absence of Kochetov—he was expected in England on a tourist visa, but his arrival, if it actually occurred, went unreported—as well as for the failure of Yuri Zhukov, Alexander Prokofiev, and others identified with the harshest stages of the campaign, to address the gathering. Extremes were avoided. So, too, were decisions. Furtseva's vigorous defense of the success of Soviet cultural contacts with the West was another sign, a more positive one, of the softening of the drive. . . . And the choice of the outspoken film director Grigori Chukhari as a speaker may even have been a gesture of conciliation toward the liberals.

Ilichev's three-hour speech, while scarcely conciliatory, refrained nevertheless from naming names or giving gratuitous offense. Careful to strike a balance in nearly everything he said, he was at pains not to challenge the entire intellectual milieu as the speeches of March 7-8 had done. Thus, in speaking of those who yearn to be free of party intervention, he added:

But let us all remember that we are speaking of Soviet artists, people who are politically close to us. Our task is not to excommunicate them but to help them understand their artistic and ideological mistakes. It would not be in the spirit of our party to relegate creative workers who have made mistakes to the ranks of the hopeless and incorrigible.

In tougher passages, he called upon the editors of *Yunost, Novyi mir,* and *Neva* to explain their publishing errors. Finally, he warned his audience against thinking that it had all been a " 'temporary' campaign, destined soon to pass, that 'all will be forgotten' and that it is possible in the meantime to sit it out and be silent. It won't do! The party is waging not a campaign but a consistent struggle."

What of the Future?

How the party is to wage this "struggle," however, neither Ilichev nor any speaker at the plenum could say. The resolution adopted at the session contained not a single concrete proposal. If the events of last winter prove anything, it is that maintenance of "ideological purity" in the arts—whatever that means—is rarely at the center of party attention for long. Occasionally, owing to a juncture of political circumstances, it can briefly become so. . . .

The greatest lesson of the campaign, however, is that it is not only possible to defy the demands of the extremists but that in some circumstances resistance pays. A correlation already exists between public opinion and the power struggle inside the Communist Party. Thus, the "conspiracy of silence" of the writers and artists and the backing they received from other intellectuals clearly shored up the arguments of the party moderates that force was no answer; used against symbolic individuals, or on a wide enough scale to be effective, it would entail too great a sacrifice of public support.

Conversely, within hours after the recantations of Yevtushenko and Voznesenski on March 29, the right wing was howling for more. By encouraging the demands of the extremists, the recantations had heightened the pressure on all of the liberal left, and hence even on the party center. Far from appeasing the attack, they fed it. Quick to realize that their apologies had been not only unnecessary, but a *political mistake* as well, the poets refused to go farther.

For several years now the wisest and most experienced of the liberals, such as Tvardovski, have been aware that to resist—when it can be done— is to strengthen the position of moderates inside the party. Having accomplished the feat of holding out, often under heavy pressure, Tvardovski and his like may even, on occasion, have been *rewarded* for their resistance by support from moderate elements at the top. What the Tvardovskis have understood all along, the 1962-63 cultural drive may now have taught others. . . .

4. THE EROSION OF SOVIET IDEOLOGY *

DANIEL BELL

Columbia University

. . . Ehrenburg was the chief whipping boy of Nikita Khrushchev's recent, 15,000-word speech on ideology and the arts.[1] Of course, at the age of 72 Ehrenburg has little to fear personally. At worst, the final chapters of his memoir will not be published during his lifetime; but he will have the secret satisfaction of knowing that sometime, somewhere they will doubtless appear after his death. Yet what of the entire generation of young Soviet poets, painters, writers, dramatists and film makers who had begun to show a resurgence of creative power? What is their fate now that another "merciless champion of progress" has spoken?

* Excerpts reprinted from *The New Leader*, April 15, 1963, pp. 18-23, by permission of the author and of the American Labor Conference on International Affairs, Inc.

[1] The speech was delivered on March 7 and 8, 1963 at a Kremlin conference. [Editor's note.]

In reading Khrushchev's speech, one is struck first by his brutal language and emotional vehemence in confronting specific works of modern art. The sculptures of Ernst Neizvestny (who, ironically, has been hailed by John Berger, the English New Left art critic and a rancorous opponent of abstract art, as the leader of a new humanism) he called "revolting concoctions" and "deformities." The paintings of B. Zhutovsky ("who eats the bread of the people, and how does he repay the people?") he described as "horrible rot and dirty daubs." Abstract artists he dismissed as "perverted people who, as the phrase goes, have a screw loose, and [produce] shameful hackwork insulting to the feelings of human beings."

The second notable aspect of the speech is the insistently reiterated declaration of ideological war in the realm of art. In concluding different sections, Khrushchev comes to such formulations as:

• "Who is not with the workers and peasants is inevitably against them."

• "Strictly speaking, there is no non-partisanship in society. He who advertises his non-partisanship does so in order to conceal his disagreement with the Party's views and ideas, in order to recruit supporters."

• "We take class positions in art and emphatically oppose the peaceful coexistence of Socialist and bourgeois ideology. Art enters into the sphere of ideology. Those who think that Socialist Realism and formalistic, abstract trends can live peacefully side by side in Soviet art inevitably sink to a position alien to us, the position of peaceful coexistence in the field of ideology."

To put the question in the style of Bolshevik didacticism, what does all this mean? Why attack abstract art? Why single out for rebuke, by name, Ehrenburg, Konstantin Paustovsky, Viktor Nekrasov, Yevgeny Yevtushenko, Andrei Voznesensky and Marlen Khutsiev? And why at this time?

There are, I think, three underlying problems which explain this singular statement of Khrushchev's. One is the "conflict of generations" in Soviet society. The second is the culpability of the present Soviet leadership for the Stalin purges. The third is the "erosion of ideology" among the Soviet intelligentsia. These three elements, together with the desire to be left alone to do one's work, add up to a wholesale demand on the part of liberal intellectuals that all remaining vestiges of Stalinism—including the right of the Party to impose a uniform artistic style—be eliminated. . . .

To sum up: Khrushchev's pressure for cultural orthodoxy will not go so far as Stalin's. For one thing, the present-day Soviet intelligentsia has a built-in defense: If the pressures become too extreme, the question can be publicly raised whether such measures do not smack of Stalinism, and this would put Khrushchev himself on the defensive. Moreover, Khrushchev is quite sensitive, as Stalin was not, to public opinion outside the USSR. One of the charges against Valentin Katayev, Nekrasov and other intellectuals who have traveled outside the USSR is that they were too "outspoken" and thus gave "ammunition to the enemy." Khrushchev also does not want to lose the support of the intellectuals; Stalin simply did not care and was contemptuous of them.

Finally, Khrushchev has staked his "place in history" as the man who ended Stalinism, and this itself puts a limit on his actions. Mindful of the way the cultural pressures in Poland and Hungary quickly translated themselves into political demands, Khrushchev has called a halt to cultural experiments. But they cannot be held down indefinitely. The desire, not to "imitate" the West, but to become part of the general cultural community is as strong among Soviet artists and writers as it is among the country's scientists. In this area, then, Chekhov's reflection still applies, although the emphasis is different: It is one step backward and two steps forward—to freedom.

SOVIET VIEWS

5. SOCIALIST REALISM IS THE ONLY PATH

a. *"Peaceful Coexistence in the Field of Ideology Is Treason"* *

NIKITA S. KHRUSHCHEV

Former First Secretary, Central Committee of the Communist Party of the Soviet Union and Former Chairman of the U.S.S.R. Council of Ministers

The press and radio, literature, painting, music, the cinema and the theater are a sharp ideological weapon of our party. . . .

Abstractionism, formalism, which some of its advocates are suggest-

* From a speech by N. S. Khrushchev delivered on March 8, 1963, at a meeting of Party and Government Leaders with workers in Literature and Art. Published in *Pravda* and *Izvestia,* March 10, 1963. Excerpts reprinted from the translation in the *Current Digest of the Soviet Press,* published at Columbia University, April 10, 1963, pp. 7-10, by permission of the publisher. Copyright 1963 by the Joint Committee on Slavic Studies.

ing should be given the right to exist in socialist art, is one of the forms of bourgeois ideology. . . .

Peaceful coexistence in the field of ideology is treason against Marxism-Leninism and betrayal of the cause of the workers and peasants. Soviet society is now at a stage in which there has been achieved full and monolithic unity of all the socialist nations of the country and all strata of the people—workers, collective farmers and the intelligentsia—who are successfully building communism under the guidance of the Leninist Party. . . .

Each citizen of our country, no matter who he is—worker or collective farmer, scientist or writer, artist or composer—all are sons and daughters of their people and cannot imagine themselves outside the life of the people, outside their creative activity. Party spirit and kinship with the people in art do not contradict each other; they comprise a united whole! . . .

We call upon those who are still straying to consider their errors, to understand the nature and sources of these errors and to overcome them, and together with the Party in united ranks, under the red banner of Marxism-Leninism, to participate actively in the building of communism and to multiply the successes of socialist culture, literature and art. . . .

b. *"Abstractionism: A Path for Bourgeois Propaganda"* *

FROM A REPORT OF THE BOARD OF THE U.S.S.R. WRITERS' UNION

Abstract art, which dulls man's sensibilities, spreads disgust with and mistrust of life and ideologically and morally disarms the working people, is of use only to the bourgeois and anticommunist forces. The indulgence of abstractionist tendencies here means opening up a path for bourgeois propaganda. . . . This same harmful idea is also served by the recogni-

---

* From *Sovetskaya kultura*, April 11, 1963. Excerpts reprinted from the translation in *The Current Digest of the Soviet Press*, published at Columbia University, May 8, 1963, p. 16, by permission of the publisher. Copyright 1963 by the Joint Committee on Slavic Studies.

tion of the right of formalism to coexist with socialist realism in our Soviet art and by the support of so-called "left" tendencies by I. Ehrenburg and some other writers.

The Party has decisively rebuffed the idea of peaceful coexistence in the field of ideology by showing that behind this idea there lies a plan for revision of our principal ideological positions. . . .

c. "An Uncompromising Struggle Against Bourgeois Ideology" *

N. V. PODGORNY

Member, Central Committee Presidium, Communist Party of the Soviet Union

Bourgeois propaganda each day pours mud on the countries of the socialist system, grasps at every slightest one of our faults and shortcomings to use them against the Soviet people, to reduce at least somehow the power of attraction of the ideas of communism and conceal the truth of the great victories of the builders of the bright new life. . . .

It is necessary to realize firmly that as long as capitalism continues to exist, the struggle on the ideological front will be, as always, a fierce and uncompromising class struggle. There can be no coexistence of the two ideologies. The Party is waging an offensive on a broad ideological front. The chief task of the offensive is the communist upbringing of all Soviet people, a merciless struggle against bourgeois ideology, against any of its manifestations in our life, against the survivals of capitalism in the minds of people. This offensive must grow and mount with each day and each hour on all its sectors.

We must depose the capitalist mode of life, expose the cunning of bourgeois ideology, defend Soviet people by every means against its corrupting influence. It is necessary to arm every toiler and the young people with the Marxist-Leninist interpretation of what is going on in the world, carry it to their hearts and minds and intensify the conscious participation of the masses in communist construction.

In the great and noble work of the ideological upbringing of our people . . . a particularly responsible role belongs to our literature and art. . . .

* From *Pravda Ukrainy,* April 10, 1963. Excerpts reprinted from the translation in *The Current Digest of the Soviet Press,* published at Columbia University, May 1, 1963, p. 16, by permission of the publisher. Copyright 1963 by the Joint Committee on Slavic Studies.

d. "Literature and Art Are a Mighty Weapon" *

L. F. ILYICHEV

Secretary, Central Committee, Communist
Party of the Soviet Union

The Party is vigorously . . . steering the development of literature and art along the path shown us by V. I. Lenin, the path of service to the people building communism. Winning the battle for communism calls for conquering people's minds, hearts and souls. We must therefore keep our ideological weapons in good order, must constantly perfect them and remove the slightest bit of rust from them.

And literature and art are a mighty weapon, a most important means of communist education. . . . Our art is called on to inspire the people to labor in the name of communism, to wage war on shortcomings in our work, to encourage our friends and to smite the enemies of communism unerringly.

Every worker is helping, to the extent of his abilities, to build the great edifice of communism, is laying his share of the bricks. . . . The contribution that every poet, novelist, composer and artist makes to the common cause is in the final analysis measured by whether his work has found favor with and proved useful to the people, whether it gives them joy, helps them in their daily lives, in their work, in the building of communist society.

What other, higher criterion can there be, how else can the creative work of our artistic intelligentsia be judged? ! . . . .

An impassioned struggle for the triumph of the most humane and just society on earth—communism—is the principal mission of literature and art in our day.

We cannot but welcome searchings after new forms for the artistic reflections of life. . . . Those who think that socialist realism and creative searchings are mutually exclusive are mistaken. But . . . formalism and

* From various speeches delivered by L. F. Ilyichev, originally published in *Pravda*, December 22, 1962; *Sovetskaya kultura*, Jan. 10, 1963; *Pravda*, June 21, 1963; and *Pravda* and *Izvestia*, June 29, 1963. Translated respectively in *The Current Digest of the Soviet Press*, published at Columbia University, January 16, 1963, pp. 16-21; February 6, 1963, pp. 7-13; July 3, 1963, pp. 5-12; and July 10, 1963, pp. 7-17. Excerpts rearranged and reprinted from the translation by permission of the publisher. Copyright 1963 by the Joint Committee on Slavic Studies.

abstract art are not searches for new forms but the revival of old forms discarded by life, they are a concession to bourgeois ideology, surrender of our ideological positions. . . .

Can it be that it does not occur to any of the young people professing abstractionism to ask why journalists hostile to us hunt them out and interview them? Yet if they thought about it for even a moment they would be convinced that their abstract daubing is deeply tinted with the paint of politics. Perhaps it is appropriate here to recall A. Bebel's famous adage: If the enemy praises you, ponder what stupidity you have committed; what is he praising you for? . . .

Our Soviet reality can be viewed in various ways.

One way is to view it with the scornful, hostile eye of the bourgeois journalist, to go grubbing in back yards, to picture the contents of the garbage can as most characteristic of our lives. . . .

The truly Soviet artist or writer cannot approach life this way, has not the moral right to do so. He is obliged to see our shortcomings, which are sometimes very grave, not in order to sneer or become panic-stricken, however, but in order to expose them and thus help overcome the short-comings and the difficulties on the way to the great goal. But most important: He is asked to have keen eyes for and to help consolidate by all available means—including the sharp weapon of satire—those new, grow-ing, communist features that express the very essence of our life as it develops, as it progresses.

We must always remember that the chief task of Soviet literature and art is the highly artistic depiction of the positive aspects of our so-ciety's development, the shoots of the new, the communist in our lives. . . .

Soviet literature and art are called on to portray the Leninist path—a difficult path, but the only right one—that our country has followed and is confidently continuing to follow toward communism. The Soviet people want not an idyllic but a heroic art, revealing the grandeur of the achieve-ment and the beauty of spirit of the builders of a new world. Our people want truthful works of art with a lofty and inspiring civic message. . . .

Our party has been giving its backing to truthful works of the most sharply critical purpose if written from a constructive point of view and imbued with the ideals of our society. . . .

Some comrades would have us believe, however, that efforts are being made to obstruct criticism of the negative features of our life, that the Party does not endorse or encourage works that have a critical orienta-tion. Such assertions are untrue, as are the allegations that socialist realism demands the prettifying of reality, the smoothing over of contradictions, rosy complacency, philistine smugness, etc.

No, the highest criterion, the core of socialist realism is artistic and social truth, however harsh it may be. . . .

So it is not a question of skirting negative features in our life; they exist, and the Party is taking the lead and setting an example in eradicating them.

The point is that while boldly exposing everything that stands in our way, we must not strike at Soviet society itself. We must differentiate between life-asserting works of sharp critical orientation, which rouse and inspire people to combat shortcomings, and works that are decadent, alarmist and slanderous, that sow lack of faith in Soviet society and weaken the force and energy of the people in the struggle to achieve communism.

Socialist realism affords wide opportunity . . . for creative competition of the most diverse artists—the adherents of the generalizing-romantic, the strictly analytical and other stylistic currents in our art. Without this community there cannot be development of our Soviet literature, of our Soviet art.

But does this mean that we are . . . for "peaceful coexistence," among such opposite ideological trends in art as socialist realism and abstractionism, which in the final analysis reflect not only opposed positions in esthetics and ideas but also opposed political, class positions?

We must make this utterly clear:

There has not been and cannot be peaceful coexistence between socialist ideology and the ideology of the bourgeoisie. The Party has opposed and will continue to oppose bourgeois ideology and all of its manifestations. Following Vladimir Ilyich Lenin's directives, it has always defended and will go on defending the Party nature of literature and art. . . .

In ideology the battle with the bourgeois world goes on and does not cease for a moment, a struggle for the souls and hearts of people, particularly young people, a struggle to shape them, these young people, a struggle over what they will take from the past and carry into the future. We have no right to underestimate the danger of subversion by bourgeois ideology in the sphere of literature and art, just as in other spheres.

The idea of coexistence in the sphere of ideology is in actuality nothing but betrayal of the interests of Marxism-Leninism, of the interests of socialism.

We must wage an active offensive on all fronts of communist construction, and the ideological front has been and still is one of the most important in the struggle for the victory of communism. . . .

The Soviet land is on a great march; it is preparing the decisive battle for communism. Therefore it is quite natural that the Party should consider it necessary to raise the level of ideological work, to make it correspond to the social and economic changes that have taken place in all spheres of the life of Soviet society in recent years. . . .

The highest criterion and the very core of socialist realism is the truth of life expressed in artistic images from the positions of the communist world view. . . .

The people expect works from the writers and artists that depict all the variety of life, people at various levels of social and moral awareness, but they want the portrayals to be accurate and to emphasize the things in our reality that are basic, leading. The chief heroes of the art of socialist realism are people who are actively engaged in the transformation of life, who are moving forward, who—in V. I. Lenin's words—are "a country's flower, its strength, its future."

It is especially important to emphasize the educative role of the positive hero when we speak about art for children and young people.

Only works that vividly reveal the high and noble truth of our life, the heroism and romanticism of the revolutionary struggle of the Soviet people for a new society, can fire young hearts with a desire to accomplish feats, can inculcate a feeling of active and effective love for the great homeland and can attract the young through the inspiring example of the older generations. . . .

As far as the legend about a "crisis in Soviet art" is concerned, it looks very stupid. Indeed, how can there be talk of a depression or crisis when works written by masters of Soviet art of all generations are winning the hearts and souls of honest people throughout the world? It often happens that those who howl about the decline of art in the Soviet Union begin to speak a different language after they have been to one of our best theaters, heard one of our musical organizations or seen one of our best films.

In evaluating the state of artistic creativity in our country, we must not indulge in self-disparagement. We have things to be proud of. We have a great socialist art and a great socialist literature. . . .

The Party sharply criticizes writers and artists who have made mistakes, who have strayed from the true path. There can be no retreats or compromises in matters of ideology. But all of us remember that we are talking about Soviet artists who are, as a rule, politically close to our people. The task is not to "excommunicate" them but rather to help them understand their ideological and artistic errors, to help them put their talents fully at the service of the people and the cause of communism. It would not be in the spirit of our party's policy to place creative workers who have made mistakes in the category of hopeless cases and incorrigibles.

We must avoid all prejudice, must remember that the struggle is not against people but for people and against bad ideas.

X

SOVIET LAW

"The Party's objective is to enforce strict observance of socialist legality, eradicate all violations of law and order, abolish crime and remove all the causes of crime. . . .

"Higher standards of living and culture, and greater social consciousness of the people, pave the way to the abolition of crime and the ultimate replacement of political punishment by measures of public influence and education."

PROGRAM OF THE COMMUNIST PARTY
OF THE SOVIET UNION ADOPTED BY THE
22ND CONGRESS OF THE C.P.S.U.,
OCTOBER 31, 1961

"Our ideological opponents do not believe in the power of man, in the possibility of his education and re-education. The education of man, the eradication of crime, is unquestionably a long and complex process, but the entire experience of education in the Soviet Union and the other countries of the socialist camp utterly refutes the assumptions of the bourgeoisie."

G. Z. ANASHKIN,
CHAIRMAN OF THE CRIMINAL COLLEGIUM
OF THE USSR SUPREME COURT

There is no one universally accepted definition of "law." In 1938 the Institute of Law of the U.S.S.R. Academy of Sciences drafted this definition:

Law is the aggregate of rules of behavior expressing the will of the dominant class . . . and also of the customs and rules of society sanctioned by the state power, the application of which is ensured by the coercive force of the state with the object of defending, consolidating and developing social relations and forms which are advantageous and welcome to the dominant class.[1]

[1] *Voprosy teorii gosundarstva i prava* (Problems of the Theory of State and Law), Moscow, 1949, p. 84. Cited in English translation in A. Yurshenko, "The Present Soviet Interpretation of Law," *Bulletin, Institute for the Study of the USSR,* September, 1962, p. 14.

In a more recent work, Professor N. G. Aleksandrov states that "law is always the 'elevation to the status of law' [2] (i.e., of a universally binding rule of behavior) of the will of those classes in whose hands in fact, in accordance with the economic relations prevailing in the society concerned, state power resides." [3] Webster's Collegiate Dictionary, on the other hand, defines law as "the binding custom or practice of a community; rules of conduct enforced by a controlling authority." In one way or another, many Western texts state that law defines the rights and duties of members of the society which are guaranteed and enforced respectively by the coercive powers of the government or ruler.

The Soviets, then, conceive of law as an expression of the will of the ruling class, while most Western legal thinkers maintain that law, at least in Western democracies, to a very high degree reflects the will of a majority if not all of the citizens. Both are in agreement that law has meaning only if it is backed by the coercive powers of what in Marxist-Leninist terminology is usually referred to as "the state." Western legal thinkers, however, assume the necessity of a government or ruler, while the state in Marxist-Leninist ideology is supposed gradually to wither away during the dictatorship of the proletariat, since in the final stages of perfect (classless) Communism there will be no classes who have need of the powers of the state to oppress other classes.[4] By definition, law and the entire legal structure of society would therefore have to wither away also. Does this mean, then, that there will be no transgressions at all once a completely Communist society has been established? Does it mean that each and every citizen will have become a "New Soviet Man" in the truest sense of the word? [5] Lenin does not go quite that far, but he does maintain that no special legal apparatus will be necessary; anyhow, with the elimination of the economic cause of crime—"want and poverty"—crimes will be rare and will eventually disappear altogether:

We are not Utopians and we do not in the least deny the possibility and inevitability of excesses on the part of *individual persons,* nor the need to suppress *such* excesses. But, in the first place, no special machinery, no special apparatus of repression is needed for this; this will be done by the armed people itself, as simply and as readily as any crowd of civilised people, even in modern society, parts a pair of combatants or does not allow a woman to be outraged. And secondly, we know that the fundamental social cause of excesses which consist in violating the rules of social life is the exploitation of the

---

[2] The repetition of the word "law" in the definition of "law" is a result of the translation since in the Russian original the terms *pravo* and *zakon* (law, statute) respectively are used.

[3] N. G. Alexandrov, *Pravo i zakonnost v period razvernutogo stroitelstva kommunizma* (Law and Legality in the Period of the Large-scale Construction of Communism), Moscow, 1961, p. 11. Cited in English translation, Yurshenko, *op. cit.,* p. 15.

[4] See especially Chapter I above.

[5] For a discussion of the creation of the "New Soviet Man," see especially Chapter VIII above.

masses, their want and their poverty. With the removal of this chief cause, excesses will inevitably begin to *"wither away."* We do not know how quickly and in what succession, but we do know that they will wither away.[6]

According to the 1961 Party Program and to the repeated declarations of all Soviet leaders, Soviet society has now achieved socialism and has embarked on the final lap of its journey towards Communism. Is there any indication, then, that crime has decreased in the Soviet Union, that the need for law and for law enforcement has diminished, that courts have become more liberal, and that, in the words of the Party Program, "the . . . replacement of political punishment by measures of public influence and education" has been started? Harold J. Berman under *Western Views* and A. F. Gorkin and N. Mironov under *Soviet Views* discuss these and related questions.

Berman stresses the changing character of Soviet criminal law. He sees clear evidence of tendencies in post-1953 Soviet law reforms towards the elimination of political terror, the liberalization of procedures, the systematization and rationalization of the legal system, decentralization and democratization of decision making, greater popular participation in the administration of justice, and—since 1961—a return to harsher penalties for "those who will not cooperate in building Communism." Apart from the last, these tendencies are all in a direction which Western observers, generally, would consider desirable. But, Berman concludes, it still remains to be seen whether the Soviet leaders will establish a legal framework that would assure the complete supremacy of law over arbitrary actions by those in power and that would contain adequate guarantees against a reversal of the liberalization and democratization process.

Gorkin attempts to show that Soviet criminal procedure aims at speedy disclosure of crimes, at just punishment for the guilty, and at maximum protection for the innocent. Since the termination of the Stalin cult, he claims, "democratic principles of legal procedure [have been] . . . rigidly adhered to." Gorkin, as well as Mironov in the second selection under *Soviet Views,* emphasizes that the purpose of Soviet criminal law is not primarily retribution but rather the re-education of the guilty; and both discuss the role of the "comrades' courts," which, they assert, use predominantly persuasion and public influence to instill an attitude of obedience to law and of intolerance toward antisocial acts. (In November, 1963, incidentally, the range of cases which comrades' courts are permitted to handle was greatly expanded in the Russian Federation, the largest of the Soviet republics. It is a fairly safe guess that this increase in the power of comrades' courts was approved from above with the intention of extending it to other parts of the U.S.S.R.)

The two selections included in this chapter deal primarily with

---

[6] V. I. Lenin, *State and Revolution,* International Publishers, New York, 1932, p. 75.

criminal law. A new Soviet civil law code came into force on May 1, 1962. The major part of this new code covers various aspects of property rights, such as the right of individuals to own personal property, the right of inheritance, copy and patent rights, the right of creditors to be reimbursed for loss by a defaulting debtor, etc., etc. Because of space limitations and the technical nature of the subject, no selections on Soviet civil law have been included.[7]

WESTERN VIEWS

1. THE DILEMMA OF SOVIET LAW REFORM *

HAROLD J. BERMAN
Harvard Law School

Some years ago black-and-white thinking had so distorted America's vision of the Soviet Union that it was difficult to discuss Soviet law without an elaborate explanation that indeed there is such a thing as law in the Soviet Union; that in the mid-1930's, after a period of legal nihilism and naked terror, Stalin proclaimed the need for "stability of laws" and "socialist legality"; and that the legal system which Stalin established (with Vyshinsky's help) was designed not only to make people obey but also to encourage initiative and responsibility and, above all, to instill a belief in the rightness of the Soviet political, economic, and social order. It may be that today we have outgrown our fire-and-brimstone concept of hell and our primitive notion that the devil rules by fear alone. If so, we are in a better position to assess both the strengths and the weaknesses of Soviet law.

[7] For a good Western selection on Soviet civil law, see T. Davletshin, "Reform of Soviet Civil Law," *Bulletin, Institute for the Study of the USSR,* April, 1962. For a representative Soviet view see, for instance, Semyon Gerson, "In the Interests of Society and Each Citizen," *USSR,* Feb., 1962.

* Reprinted from the *Harvard Law Review,* March, 1963, pp. 929-951, by permission of the author and the publisher. Most footnotes omitted. Copyright © 1963 by The Harvard Law Review Association. With some revisions and with an additional section, this selection has been included as Chapter 2 in Harold J. Berman's *Justice in the U.S.S.R.,* revised edition, 1963, Harvard University Press; also Random House, Vintage paperback.

Such an assessment is of critical importance for us as Americans. We have, strangely enough, a very great stake in the development of Soviet law. That stake is partly physical and partly spiritual. Physically, our very survival depends in part on the extent to which law can exercise a stabilizing influence both on Soviet internal developments and on Soviet foreign policy. The fact that the Soviet people, including the Soviet leaders, believe in law is therefore a cause for us to rejoice. The fact that the law in which they believe differs sharply in certain essential features from the law in which we believe is, by the same token, a cause for us to be greatly concerned. Indeed, never before in our history has the study of a foreign legal system been of such crucial significance to us, for no other people has ever lived so close to us as the Soviets. We are less than a half hour away from them by missile.

But even apart from the danger of atomic war, the destiny of the Soviet Union is intimately related to our own destiny. We are two revolutionary peoples in the world today—two peoples who have a world-wide mission. The struggle between us is only in part a power struggle. More basically, it is a spiritual struggle between two concepts—two developing concepts—of social order, each claiming universal validity. The spiritual struggle is more basic, for however the power struggle ends the spiritual struggle will remain. War would not settle the question of communism, no matter who is "victorious." The survivors of a war would still have to choose between something like the ideals reflected in Soviet law and something like the ideals reflected in American law.

I. THE SIGNIFICANCE OF SOVIET LAW REFORM

The fact that the Soviet concept of social order is not a static but a developing one is dramatically illustrated in the striking changes which have taken place in the Soviet legal system in recent years. Indeed the reform movement in Soviet law is one of the most significant aspects of Soviet social development in the past ten years since Stalin's death.

In interpreting this reform movement, one must start with Stalin—however much the present Soviet leaders would like to expunge his name from the memory of their people. For despite the very substantial changes which they have introduced, the Soviet legal system remains Stalinist in its basic structure and its basic purposes. The organization and functions of the law-making, law-enforcing, and law-practicing agencies—the legislature, the Procuracy, the courts, the administrative organs, the bar—are not essentially different now from what they were when Stalin died. The main outlines of Soviet criminal law and procedure, civil law and procedure, labor law, agrarian law, family law, administrative law, constitutional law, and other branches of the Soviet legal tree, remain basically the same as before.

And if one looks behind the structure to the purposes of Soviet law, it remains a totalitarian law, in the sense that it seeks to regulate all aspects of economic and social life, including the circulation of thought, while leaving the critical questions of political power to be decided by informal, secret procedures beyond the scrutiny or control either of legislative or judicial bodies. It remains the law of a one-party state. It remains the law of a planned economy. It remains a law whose primary function is to discipline, guide, train, and educate Soviet citizens to be dedicated members of a collectivized and mobilized social order.

If this is so, it may be asked, what is the significance of the recent reforms? Indeed, many Western observers have treated each successive development in Soviet law during the past ten years as mere smoke without fire—or even as a smokescreen designed to conceal the absence of any fire. Others have viewed the reforms as half-hearted concessions designed to appease the appetite of the Soviet people without really satisfying their hunger. These grudging responses are reminiscent of Soviet interpretations of American law reforms: the New Deal, we are told by Soviet writers, did not really alter the fundamental nature of the American capitalist system; the Supreme Court decision in the *Segregation Cases* did not end discrimination against Negroes; American law remains "bourgeois."

Viewed from a sufficiently lofty height, the scene never changes. This may only mean, however, that the viewer does not see what is really going on. To give an example: in December 1958 the Supreme Soviet enacted new Fundamental Principles of Criminal Law which, among other things, reduced the maximum period of detention of criminals from twenty-five to fifteen years. This was part of a general movement toward greater leniency in penal policy. In 1961 and 1962, however, the death penalty (which previously had been restricted to certain crimes against the State and to first-degree murder) was extended to various economic crimes, such as bribery of state officials under aggravating circumstances, counterfeiting, illegal transactions in foreign currency, and large-scale theft of state or social property. One of the main reasons for the excessive harshness of 1961-1962 was the disappointment of the Soviet leaders in the results of the excessive softness of 1958, for in fact the rate of serious crimes increased in 1959, 1960, and 1961.[1] The point is that those Western observers who did not take seriously the earlier policy of leniency are in a poor position to evaluate the later policy of repression.

Of course, if the observer abandons all elevation and descends into the midst of the events, he loses all perspective and sees only flux. The foreign journalist in Moscow—and the reader of his articles at home—tend

---

[1] This fact has not been publicly admitted but I heard it stated by the Minister of Justice of the R.S.F.S.R. in a lecture delivered in Moscow on May 3, 1962.

to see a whirling, eddying stream. The only solution is to seek a composite picture, from various perspectives.

Such a composite picture would reveal, I believe, six major tendencies in Soviet law reform since 1953:

First, there has been a tendency toward the elimination of political terror.

Second, there has been a tendency toward the liberalization both of procedures and of substantive norms.

Third, there has been a tendency toward the systematization and rationalization of the legal system.

Fourth, there has been a tendency toward decentralization and democratization of decisionmaking.

Fifth, there has been a tendency to introduce popular participation in the administration of justice.

Sixth, there has been a tendency in the past two years to threaten those who will not cooperate in building communism with harsh criminal and administrative penalties.

A. The Tendency Toward Elimination of Terror

Stalin's system since the mid-1930's was based on a coexistence of law and terror. Law was for those areas of Soviet life where the political factor was stabilized. Terror, either naked or in the guise of law (as in the purge trials of the late 1930's), was applied when the regime felt itself threatened. But these two spheres were not easy to keep separate either in theory or in practice. It was not a peaceful coexistence. In the first place, the borderline shifted: the crime of theft of state property, for example, which was supposed to be dealt with by due process of law, could easily merge with counterrevolutionary crime and thereby become subject to repression by the secret police. In the second place, even though terror diminished after 1938, it continued to have a deleterious effect on the legal system itself. Urgently needed law reforms were delayed and sidetracked because of people's fear of being labeled "deviationist."

A month after Stalin's death in March 1953, his successors began to proclaim the "inviolability" of Soviet law and to denounce "arbitrary procedures" and "violations of socialist legality," particularly in connection with the so-called "Doctors' Plot," which many have supposed Stalin trumped up in the last months of his life as a pretext for a new wave of purges. After the arrest of Beria in July 1953, many of the excesses of Stalinist terror were attributed not to the dictator himself but to his chief of secret police. This deception wore thin, however, and in February 1956 Khrushchev attacked Stalin by name at the 20th Congress of the Communist Party of the Soviet Union, denouncing him for the "cult of personality" and for persecution of loyal party members in violation of their legal rights. In October-November 1961, at the 22nd Party Congress, the attacks on Stalin were renewed with even greater vigor. The inviolability of socialist law was again proclaimed. Vyshinsky's name was added to Stalin's as co-author of a legal system which permitted falsification and distortion of legality for the persecution of people innocent of any crime.

In implementation of these attacks upon the "cult of personality" important steps have been taken since September 1953 to eliminate those features of the preexisting Soviet law which permitted the disguise of terror in legal form.

First, the Special Board of the Ministry of Internal Affairs has been abolished.[2] It was this Special Board which had been the chief instrument of terror. It was a three-man administrative committee—the Russians called it a *troika*—which was empowered by a 1934 statute to send people to labor camps without a hearing, in a secret administrative procedure, without right of counsel and without right of appeal.

Second, the security police have been deprived of the power to conduct investigations of crimes under their own special rules without supervision by the Procuracy.

Third, the special procedures for court cases involving the most serious antistate crimes have been abolished. The laws of 1934 and 1937 permitting persons charged with certain such crimes to be tried secretly, in absentia, and without counsel, were repealed.

Fourth, the military courts, which had previously had a wide jurisdiction over civilians, particularly in the case of political crimes, have been deprived of all jurisdiction over civilians except for espionage.

Fifth, the law permitting punishment of relatives of one who deserts to a foreign country from the armed forces—though they knew nothing of the desertion—has been abolished.

Sixth, Vyshinsky's doctrine that confessions have special evidentiary force in cases of counterrevolutionary crimes—based on the transparently false notion that people will not confess to such crimes unless they are actually guilty—has been repudiated; confessions are now treated as having no evidentiary force in themselves, and the matters contained in a confession must be corroborated by other evidence.

Seventh, Vyshinsky's doctrine that the burden of proof shifts to the accused in cases of counterrevolutionary crimes has also been repudiated. The new Soviet codes place the burden of proving the guilt of the accused squarely on the prosecutor. Although the phrase "presumption of innocence" is avoided in the codes, all that we mean by that phrase is spelled out in Soviet law.

Eighth, Vyshinsky's broad definition of complicity, borrowed from the Anglo-American doctrine of conspiracy, has been repudiated. Innocent

2 The abolition took place in 1953.

association with others who are planning an illegal act can no longer constitute a crime under the new Soviet legislation.

Ninth, the law on so-called "counterrevolutionary crimes" has been slightly narrowed and made a little less vague. The term "counterrevolutionary" has been eliminated and the term "antistate" substituted. The crime of "terrorist acts," which hitherto had been interpreted to include any violent act against a state or party official or, indeed, his close relatives, whatever the motive, has been restricted to murder or serious bodily injury of the official himself committed for the purpose of overthrowing or weakening the Soviet authority. The law on state secrets has been substantially relaxed—though it is still far wider in its scope than we would consider tolerable. And a new list of information constituting state secrets has been enacted which is less broad and more precise than the earlier list.

Finally, there took place from 1953 (or 1955) to 1957 a systematic reexamination of all cases of persons previously convicted of counterrevolutionary crimes and the release from labor camps of the overwhelming majority of such persons as fully rehabilitated.

The restoration of procedural due process of law in political cases is a signal achievement of the post-Stalin regime. The Soviet citizen is now protected against police terror, false charges, and faked trials to a far greater extent than ever before in Soviet history. No longer need he fear the midnight knock on the door as a prelude to transportation to a Siberian labor camp without a fair hearing.

Yet one cannot speak of the total elimination of political terror so long as open opposition to Communist Party policy—the "Party line"—can lead to criminal sanctions, however "objectively" and "correctly" imposed. The 1958 Statute on State Crimes carries over from the earlier law on counterrevolutionary crimes the provision against "agitation or propaganda" directed against the Soviet system. To defame the Soviet political and social system, or even to possess written materials of such defamatory nature, if for the purpose of weakening Soviet authority, is punishable by deprivation of freedom of up to seven years. In 1961, for example, certain leaders of the Jewish community in Leningrad were convicted for the crime of circulating anti-Soviet literature obtained from a foreign embassy, presumably the Israeli. We would call this a denial of "substantive" due process of law.

The law of antistate agitation and propaganda is only one of many features of the Soviet system which keep alive the fear of Soviet citizens that the terror may return. Later I shall speak more fully of this fear, and of some of the conditions which give rise to it. But it is important to stress at this point that the fear of a return to terror is itself a form of terror. Therefore, one must view the developments of the past ten years as reflecting only a tendency—though an extremely important tendency—toward the elimination of terror.

B. The Liberalization of Procedural and Substantive Law

Even apart from political crimes, Soviet law has undergone substantial liberalization in the past ten years. It would be impossible to list the hundreds, indeed thousands, of needed reforms which have been introduced. Let me speak very briefly of some of the most important, first in criminal law and procedure, then in criminal punishment and the system of detention, and finally in some other fields of law.

In criminal law and procedure, the "tightening up" of the rules with respect to burden of proof, evaluation of confessions, and the doctrine of complicity, which have already been mentioned in the discussion of political crimes, have given increased protection to persons accused of other crimes as well. In addition, the right to counsel prior to trial, though still limited, has been significantly extended; the time for supervisory review of acquittals in criminal cases, formerly unlimited, has been reduced to one year; powers of search and seizure have been somewhat restricted; the doctrine of analogy, whereby a person who committed a socially dangerous act not specifically made punishable by law could be sentenced under a law proscribing an analogous act, has been eliminated; penalties have been substantially lightened for many crimes—for example, new laws imposing lighter sentences for petty rowdyism ("hooliganism") and petty theft of state or public property have removed the necessity of many long years in labor camps for conviction of trivial offenses; and some crimes have been eliminated altogether—for example, abortion,[3] absenteeism from work, and quitting one's job without permission. The large-scale amnesties of 1953 and 1957 released all except those sentenced for, or charged with, the most serious offenses.

With respect to the system of detention, a 1957 law eliminated the name "labor camp," substituting "labor colony" for all places of confinement (except prisons, which are used only for temporary detention or, very rarely, for the most serious crimes) and introduced a new regime for prisoners which permits far more leniency in their treatment. Those convicted of less serious crimes are permitted to have their wives (or husbands) visit and stay with them from time to time; they are paid substantial wages for their work and are required to send home allotments to their dependents. Also liberal parole provisions have been introduced.

Liberalization has not been confined to criminal policy. Since 1953, and especially since 1955, there has been a reexamination of every branch of law and a weeding out of many of the harshest features. For example,

---

[3] Any woman may have a legal abortion if she requests it. However, the person performing the abortion is subject to punishment if he lacks a medical education or does not follow established procedures.

a new civil right has been created to obtain a court order for public retraction of a newspaper libel. Equal rights of foreigners under Soviet law have been declared—subject, of course, to statutory restrictions. (It would be interesting to put those two provisions together and to have a suit by a foreigner in a Soviet court demanding a retraction of a newspaper libel against him.) In labor law the rights of trade unions have been enhanced and the procedures for settlement of workers' grievances have been improved. In family law, a new code is expected to be enacted shortly which will, among other things, ameliorate the position of the child born out of wedlock. Similar examples could be multiplied from many other fields of law.

In 1961 and 1962 there has been a contrary trend, away from liberalization, in certain areas. These recent backward steps, however, cannot, yet at least, be considered to have stopped the liberal momentum of the post-Stalin reforms.

C. Systematization and Rationalization

The general tendency toward liberalization of law is, of course, an important supporting buttress of the tendency toward elimination of political terror. For such tendencies to have permanence, however, deeper foundations are required in the legal system as a whole. From that standpoint, the efforts of recent years to systematize and rationalize the Soviet legal system are of great significance.

The Stalin Constitution of December 1936, and the Vyshinsky jurisprudence which surrounded it, rehabilitated the various republican criminal, civil, labor, and family codes of the "New Economic Policy" period of the twenties which had largely fallen into disrepute in the period from 1930 to 1936. Of course the NEP codes, designed for a transition period of mixed capitalism-socialism, were inadequate for the new period of full socialism with its planned economy. The Stalin Constitution therefore called for the creation of all-union codes to replace the earlier republican codes. But until such new all-union codes were adopted, the earlier ones were to prevail, together with the thousands of statutory and administrative changes introduced into them.

During the remaining sixteen years of Stalin's reign, however, new all-union codes were not adopted, although many drafts were produced. Only with the removal of the political and ideological pressure of Stalinist autocracy did it become possible to introduce new codes, and, together with them, a reorganization of the entire system of legal administration.

The first major event in this development was the adoption in August 1955 of a new Statute on Procuracy Supervision. The Procuracy is the cornerstone of the Soviet legal system. It combines functions of our Department of Justice, congressional investigating committees, and grand juries. It not only investigates and prosecutes crimes, but it supervises the entire system of administration of justice, and has power to investigate and protest to higher authorities (whether administrative or judicial) any abuse of law which comes to its attention. Until 1955 it had operated on the basis of a 1922 statute upon which were encrusted many legislative and administrative modifications. The 1955 statute clarified and consolidated its supervisory powers over judicial and administrative acts. Incidentally, the new statute also added sanctions against officials of the Procuracy for negligence in failing to expose illegal practices in places of detention of criminals.

The second major event was the removal of certain aspects of Ministry of Justice control over the courts, and the reorganization of the Supreme Court of the U.S.S.R. and of the republican and regional courts. This took place in 1956 and 1957. The result was a streamlining of the court system and an increase in its independence.

In 1957 the constitution was amended to provide for separate republican codes to be based upon new all-union Fundamental Principles. In December 1958 the Supreme Soviet of the U.S.S.R. adopted a series of Fundamental Principles of various branches of law—Fundamental Principles of Criminal Law, Fundamental Principles of Criminal Procedure, and Fundamental Principles of Court Organization—together with new comprehensive statutes on state crimes, military crimes, and military tribunals. Subsequently, in December 1961, the Supreme Soviet adopted Fundamental Principles of Civil Law and of Civil Procedure. Fundamental Principles of Family Law and of Labor Law are now in preparation; indeed, a statute on the procedure for the hearing of labor disputes adopted in 1957 is itself a systematization of many aspects of labor law.

On the basis of the Fundamental Principles, the various republics have adopted their own new codes of criminal law and criminal procedure and are now in the last stages of work on new codes of civil law and civil procedure.

Of the many other important pieces of legislation of recent years mention should also be made of the 1961 statute on administrative commissions of local municipal councils, which restricted the powers of administrative bodies to impose fines and established a procedure for appealing from such fines; the 1960 statute on state *Arbitrazh,* which reorganized the procedures for hearing the hundreds of thousands of contract disputes which arise each year between state economic enterprises; and the new statutes on the organization of the legal profession in the various republics, which strengthen the independence of the advocate and his responsibility to his client.

Two other items cannot be omitted from this very brief account. The Juridical Commission of the Council of Ministers of the U.S.S.R. has been given the function of determining which laws have lost their force in the light of the new legislation. In the twenty years between 1937 and

1958, the U.S.S.R. Supreme Soviet enacted over 7,000 statutes, edicts, and decrees, and the U.S.S.R. Council of Ministers issued about 390,000 decrees and regulations. Few of these were formally declared to have lost their force. Yet in 1960 only about 15,000 of these approximately 400,000 normative acts actually remained in force. The Juridical Commission has been attempting to cleanse the Augean stables of Soviet legislation by systematically listing, little by little, those laws and other normative acts which are no longer valid.

In connection with this, it is important to note two new laws on the publication of laws. Of the more than 7,000 laws of the Supreme Soviet enacted between 1937 and 1958, only some hundreds were published. Of the 390,000 decrees and regulations of the Council of Ministers, only a few thousand were published. The rest were merely distributed to the appropriate officials concerned with their enforcement and to other authorized persons. A 1958 law requires publication of all acts of the Supreme Soviet. Edicts, decrees, and acts of the Presidium of the Supreme Soviet are required to be published only if they are of "general significance" or have a "normative character." Also a 1959 decree of the Council of Ministers requires publication of all its decrees and orders which are general or normative. The determination of which acts are general or normative and which are not is left to the Presidium and the Council respectively.

The systematization and rationalization of Soviet law is not something which can be accomplished in a few years. Indeed, it is something which must go on continually. The recognition of its importance, and the very great efforts being devoted to it, are an encouraging sign of the determination of the post-Stalin regime to establish a far higher degree of legal security than that which existed in the past.

D. The Tendency Toward Decentralization and Democratization

Khrushchev has committed himself to the view that the harshness of the Stalinist system cannot achieve the purposes of socialism as he envisages it, and that cooperation with the policies of his regime cannot be secured without a systematic and rational legality. Implicit in this conviction, and necessary to its implementation, is the belief in the possibility of a wide decentralization of decisionmaking and a still wider participation of the public in the formulation of issues for decision.

Two qualfications must be made at the outset, however, in discussing the tendency of the post-Stalin period of Soviet history toward greater decentralization and democratization. The first is that there is no sign that the present Soviet leadership has any intention of allowing this tendency to go beyond its power to control it. The limits of decentralized decisionmaking and democratization are set by the central authorities. The second qualification is that this theory of "democratic centralism"— centralization of authority combined with decentralization of operations—

was also Stalin's theory. The difference today is a difference in degree.

The tendency toward decentralization and democratization has been greatly accelerated since Stalin's death, however, by the very nature of the tendencies toward elimination of political terror, toward liberalization, and toward systematization and rationalization of the law. Apart from all other considerations, these tendencies have imposed an absolute requirement of help from hundreds of thousands of people at various levels of the official hierarchy and in various parts of the Soviet Union. In addition, the main purpose of these tendencies—to overcome the rigidities of the system inherited from Stalin, to stimulate local and individual initiative and enthusiasm—has necessitated the enlistment of maximum cooperation from the maximum number of people.

When we think of America we think of 180 million people of diverse outlooks, traditions, and interests, scattered across a great continent which includes not only New York City and Washington, D.C., but also Texas and California and Mississippi and Vermont and a host of other very different kinds of communities. But too many of us, when we think of the Soviet Union, stop with the Kremlin. It should not need demonstration that even if we imagined the entire Soviet population to be a disciplined army, the commander-in-chief would be greatly in need of subordinate units of command with considerable autonomy of action. He could not run the lives of 220 million people, including thirty or forty major nationalities, spread across one-sixth of the earth's surface, by pushbutton from Moscow. When I presented the "pushbutton" theory to a leading Soviet jurist some years ago he merely replied: "It would take too many pushbuttons!"

This is not to say that centralization is not the major fact of the Soviet political and economic system. "Bolsheviks are centralists by conviction." [4] Under Stalin this Bolshevik conviction was strengthened by fear of the "old man," who often urged decentralization but did not hesitate to crack down when it tended toward deviation.

The decision in 1957 to abandon the rule of the 1936 Constitution calling for all-union codes and to substitute a rule calling for separate codes in each of the fifteen Soviet republics, based, however, on all-union Fundamental Principles; the earlier decision to dissolve the all-union Ministry of Justice into separate republican ministries of justice and the later decision to do the same with the Ministry of Internal Affairs; [5] and,

---

[4] I believe this quotation is from Sir John Maynard's book *Russia in Flux* (1948).

[5] The R.S.F.S.R. Ministry of Internal Affairs was recently renamed Ministry of Protection of Social Order (*Ministerstvo Okhrany Obshchestvennogo Porjakdi*). In 1954 the security functions of the earlier all-union Ministry of Internal Affairs had been allocated to the Committee on State Security (KGB) of the U.S.S.R. Council of Ministers.

most important of all, the decision in 1957 to split the economy of the country into about one hundred economic regions, each with its own Council of National Economy, and to divide among these regional councils some of the functions of the former economic ministries with their central offices in Moscow—these decisions in the direction of decentralization were called for by the enormous bureaucratization of Soviet social and economic life, which had become almost too stifling to endure.

Yet decentralization in itself is not democratization; it may be, and to a certain extent it has been, simply a moving of the center to the localities, a stretching of the chain of command. It has also been more than that, however. The lower links in the chain have unquestionably been given more initiative. And even where ultimate decisions have been reserved for Moscow, a far greater hearing has been given to the voices of the localities.

This is illustrated by the process of law reform itself. Khrushchev and his immediate associates could give the word that the time had come for substantial law reforms and could indicate the lines along which the reforms should run. But the word could not become a reality without an enormous effort by the people who would be directly affected by these reforms. These include not only the professional lawyers who would have to draft them and the officials who would have to administer them, but also the various people who would have to live under them.

The comprehensive legislation enacted in recent years has been worked on by representatives of hundreds, indeed thousands, of organizations. All the major governmental agencies have expressed detailed views on their various provisions. There has been endless discussion of them in the universities, in research institutes, in economic organizations of various kinds, in scholarly journals, and in the daily press.

Let me give two bits of testimony concerning this from my personal experience as a resident in the Soviet Union last year. In May, I was visiting a Soviet jurist in Moscow, a law professor who was one of the chief draftsmen of the Fundamental Principles of Civil Procedure adopted last December by the Supreme Soviet of the U.S.S.R. He showed me a large pile of mimeographed pages containing, he said, comments of various organizations on the provisions of the Fundamental Principles when they had been in draft form. Unfortunately, he was not free to allow me to study this valuable document. However, he let me take a quick look at it to see its general nature. It contained such items as: "The State Planning Committee proposes that Section such-and-such be amended in the following manner. . . ." "The Moscow College of Advocates proposes that a separate section be introduced to cover such-and-such." And so it went on for some hundreds of pages.

Then in Leningrad in June, I was invited by a law professor to attend a two-day session of the civil law department of the University at which the drafts of the civil codes of the Russian and the Ukrainian Republics were discussed. About ten people, teachers and graduate students, spent about twelve hours during those two days in the most lively debate, going over the drafts point for point, differing sharply with each other both on matters of technique and on matters of policy. A stenographer took down the discussion in shorthand and the report of it was to be sent to Moscow to be sifted by the subcommittee of the Legislative Proposals Committee of the Supreme Soviet of the R.S.F.S.R. (Russian Republic). I was told that such discussions were taking place in all the twenty or so law faculties of the Soviet Union, in research institutes, in the regional economic councils, in individual large plants, and in many other places.

In addition, popular participation in lawmaking has been stimulated by the expansion of the committee system of the Supreme Soviet of the U.S.S.R. and of the Supreme Soviets of the fifteen republics. Tens of thousands of expert consultants have reported to these committees. And apart from major all-union and republican legislation, there has been a substantial increase in the powers of the local municipal councils and a vast amount of activity of local governmental organizations, involving the participation of literally hundreds of thousands of Soviet citizens.

Of course it would be a mistake to suppose that Soviet federalism and Soviet democracy involve—as ours do—a struggle between opposing political units and groups, a competition for political leadership. In the Soviet Union all power resides in the Communist Party, which remains, as stated in the constitution, the "central core" of all organizations, whether they be state organizations or social organizations. Despite the development of greater intra-Party democracy in recent years, the Party remains a disciplined elite, subservient to its leadership. Decentralization and democratization of decisionmaking in the spheres of government, law, and economic administration is not a threat to Party supremacy; indeed, it is required by the Party as a means of maintaining its supremacy.

Yet Party control is, in a much deeper sense, challenged by the development of autonomous centers of discussion and initiative, even though it remains the "central core" of such centers. One of my strongest impressions in a year of intimate association with Soviet jurists of all kinds is that of their cohesion. Whether they are judges, procurators, Ministry of Justice officials, law professors, research workers, legal advisers of state institutions and enterprises, or advocates, the seventy to eighty thousand jurists of the Soviet Union are bound together by the closest professional ties. They meet together in many different kinds of activity; they discuss and debate common problems; they work together; and they are bound not only by their common legal education but also by their common vested interest in the preservation of legality. As a class, they have grown greatly in importance during the past ten years.

E. Popular Participation in the Administration of Justice

In describing the movement away from political terror, harshness of punishment, chaos and irrationality of legislation, and overcentralization of decisionmaking, one runs the risk of leaving the false impression that the Soviet legal system is becoming just like ours. It is true that Stalin's successors have sought to eliminate the dualism of law and terror which formerly characterized the Soviet system, and in so doing they have taken important steps in the direction of a more humane, more rational, and more democratic legal system. Yet they have sought to do this without abandoning the dynamic revolutionary development of the Soviet state and of Soviet society; indeed, their purpose has been to instill new vitality into that revolutionary development by softening the motive force of fear and strengthening the motive force of common effort, struggle, and enthusiasm. The Soviet people are now being asked voluntarily to make sacrifices which formerly were evoked from them in part by threat of force. No doubt both the leaders and the people are greatly relieved at the decrease in emphasis upon terror and coercion and the increase in emphasis upon the liberal, rational, and democratic elements in their legal system. But these elements are not—for the leaders, at least—ends in themselves but rather a means toward lifting their society to new heights of economic progress, political power and social solidarity.

Law is conceived of as a major instrument for achieving these goals. Law is conceived of, above all, as a means of educating Soviet people to be the type of socially conscious, dedicated members of society which are required if socialism is to be maintained and if communism is to be achieved. This concept of the dynamic function of law in molding not merely the conduct of men but also their morality and their very characters is, in my view, the greatest challenge which Soviet law presents to the world. I wish to consider now, however, only one aspect of this concept, namely, its reflection in recent years in a greatly increased participation of ordinary Soviet citizens—of society, the public, *obshchestvennost'*, as Soviet terminology has it—in the administration of justice.

It is Soviet theory that under communism the functions of state organizations (which operate in part by coercion) will be turned over entirely to social organizations (which operate only by persuasion). In anticipation of this glorious day, the role of social organizations has been greatly increased. Neighborhood and factory meetings have been convened for a variety of purposes and have been given certain semijudicial functions. Also a voluntary auxiliary police force has been organised—the so-called *druzhiny,* or bands—to help keep order; they direct traffic, take drunks into custody, and in general make themselves unpopular among the people on the streets. In addition many special volunteer commissions have been formed and given semiofficial status—to observe conditions in the labor colonies and to make recommendations, to report to municipal councils on housing questions, to report on local observance of "socialist legality," and for a host of similar purposes. Trade unions and the Young Communist League (*Komsomol*) are also considered to be social organizations, and their functions have been extended.

Many of the functions of Soviet social organizations are also performed in the United States by volunteer workers and social organizations. Indeed, no country in the world can match the United States, I would venture to say, in the amount of public-spirited activity of volunteer social organizations. Yet there is a difference in kind between Soviet social organizations and their American counterparts—a difference which is striking. In part it is a difference in the scope of the activities of Soviet social organizations and especially their powers over the lives of their members; in part it is a difference in the amount of official pressure that can be brought upon them, due especially to their links with the State through the Communist Party.

For example, the *Komsomol* organizations in the universities call for student volunteers to work during the summer holidays in the so-called "virgin lands" of the East. The volunteers are recruited, however, by lists posted on bulletin boards, and refusal to go courts expulsion from the *Komsomol* and probably—at least it is so assumed by the students—from the university. A second example may be found in the activities of "comrades' courts," now operating under a recent statute, which meet in apartment houses or in factories to consider minor offenses committed by neighbors or fellow-workers. Their punitive powers are limited to a ten-ruble fine. Mostly they issue reprimands and warnings. However, they may also recommend eviction from the apartment or disciplinary action (including demotion) by the factory management. Such eviction or disciplinary action may be resisted through regular court proceedings, but nevertheless the recommendation of the comrades' court is a serious matter. One other example: Soviet courts sometimes go "on circuit," so to speak, to apartments or factories, to hear criminal cases involving persons in those places. The purpose is to demonstrate to the entire "collective" and to the public the social danger of the offenses charged and to educate people in the requirements of the law. But the tendency to convict and to mete out harsh punishment is very strong when such an educational purpose is in the forefront of the procedure itself.

Some Western students of the Soviet scene have, in my opinion, exaggerated the evils of this kind of new "social justice." One must put oneself in the Soviet situation, where true social cooperation in informal voluntary groups, entirely independent of the State, hardly exists. The comrades' courts that I have seen in action have impressed me by the good spirit with which they act and with which they are received. Especially important is the fact that their powers are very limited and that these limits are enforced by the courts and by the legal system.

The great danger, of course, is the potentiality of abuse of these social organizations by the Communist Party and the State. The still greater danger is the dream of a far-off time when there will be no legal system and no State but only one vast social organization, one vast Communist Party. It is, I am sure, a dream which can never be realized; but so long as it is held it inhibits the achievement of true legal security.

F. The Return to Harsh Criminal and Administrative Penalities

A sixth major tendency in Soviet law in the post-Stalin period is the return in 1961 and 1962 to harsh criminal and administrative penalties against those who refuse to cooperate in building communism.

In May and June 1961, the three largest republics, comprising three-fourths of the Soviet population, finally enacted the notorious antiparasite law which had been first proposed for public discussion in 1957 and later adopted in the smaller republics from 1957 through 1960. This law, in its final form, provides for "resettlement" in specially designated localities, for two to five years, of persons who constitute "antisocial, parasitic elements" and who are not performing socially useful work but are living on unearned income. Persons may be sentenced under this law by the judges of the regular courts in a summary procedure and without the usual guarantees of the criminal law, or else by general meetings in the factories or apartments, with review by the local municipal council.

In 1959 I was told in Moscow by the principal draftsman of the 1958 Fundamental Principles of Criminal Procedure that in his opinion the antiparasite laws contradicted the provision of the Fundamental Principles that no person may be punished for a crime except by sentence of a court; and that there was a good chance they would not be adopted in the three largest republics and that they would be repealed in those republics where they had already been adopted. His optimism proved unjustified. The laws have now been reconciled with the Fundamental Principles on the more-than-tenuous theory that the offender is not being punished for a crime, nor is he being confined; he is simply sent to another place where he must take a socially useful job!

In the first year of the operation of this law in the R.S.F.S.R., as I learned last May at a lecture by the Minister of Justice, 10,000 people in Moscow were charged under the antiparasite law. Eight thousand, he said, received only warnings; 2,000 were sent out of Moscow; of these, only fifteen were subjected to confiscation of property. It may be inferred from the relatively few instances of confiscation that the law is principally a device for getting rid of vagrants and putting them to work.

Also the extension of the death penalty in 1961 and 1962 to a wide variety of crimes, many of them economic crimes not involving violence, reflects the regime's determination to take extreme measures against those who most flagrantly violate the tenets of Communist morality. In a case tried in July 1961, one of the statutes imposing the death penalty was applied retroactively by a special edict of the Presidium of the Supreme Soviet authorizing the retroactive application "as an exception" in the specific case. (The edict was never published as it was not considered to be "of general significance." I was shown it, however, by a member of the U.S.S.R. Supreme Court. There is reason to believe that there were other such cases of retroactive application of the death sentence, specially authorized by similar edicts.) Judging from Soviet press accounts of individual trials probably over 250 Soviet citizens were executed for economic and other crimes in the year from May 1961 to May 1962, and probably an equal or greater number were executed from June to December 1962. One can only say "probably" because Soviet crime statistics are a state secret! (In 1961, forty-three persons were executed in the United States.)

This harsh policy was also reflected in increased penalties for lesser crimes. Soviet jurists have publicly criticized the tendency of some procurators and courts to treat the imposition of the death penalty for serious crimes as a signal for reversing the entire trend toward liberalization.

What significance should we attach to these developments? As is so often the case with violations of basic principles of judicial procedure, the particular individual victims do not command our affection. They were, presumably, scoundrels. It is rather the abuse of the integrity of the legal process that concerns us, for one abuse suggests another.

When I asked how he could explain the decision of July 1961 applying the death penalty retroactively, one leading Soviet jurist replied, "We lawyers didn't like it!"—an answer as interesting for the "we lawyers" as the "didn't like it." Another prominent lawyer told me he did not believe in the use of the death penalty in peacetime in any case. Not only lawyers, however, were concerned about these measures. An engineer said to me when I raised the question of what was so bad about getting rid of the scoundrels: "If they start with scoundrels, what is to stop them from going on to political opponents?" Whether the majority of Soviet citizens make this connection, however, is something that cannot be known. Many, at least, seem to support the regime's new policy of ruthless repression of large-scale economic crimes.

II. CONCLUSION

We have heard much of "the thaw"—to use Ehrenburg's phrase [6]— the unfreezing of Soviet life in the years since Stalin died, the reduction of terror, the increased freedom to criticize, the greater encouragement of individual initiative, the relaxation of tensions. But the *long-range* problem of government in the Soviet Union is whether the Soviet leaders are

---

[6] This is the translation of the title of Ilya Ehrenburg's 1954 novel, *Ottepel'*, which was the first literary expression of the spirit of the post-Stalin era.

willing and able to establish not merely a season, or a climate, or a policy, of freedom and initiative, but also a legal and institutional foundation which will make freedom and initiative secure from their own intervention. Until that problem is solved, the fear of a return to Stalinist terror will haunt the Soviet people, and especially the intellectuals. In research institutes and universities, as well as among educated people generally, debates rage over the "liquidation of the consequences of the cult of personality" which is Party jargon for preventing a recurrence not only of violence but also of all the rigidities that went with it. Nobody—presumably from Khrushchev on down—wants such a recurrence. But nobody can guarantee that it won't happen—if it becomes "necessary."

A Soviet professor said to me: "I am not proud of the book I wrote in 1952. But in those days, if you said anything objective on that subject you would be told, 'Enough!'—and if you persisted you might disappear." Then he paused, and added, "And you know, nine years is a very short time in the light of history!"

Khrushchev has replaced the Stalinist dualism of law and terror by a new dualism of law and social pressure; one is free from arbitrary arrest by the secret police, but one is not free from the social pressure of the "collective"—whether it be the more innocuous pressure of the collective of the neighbors in the crowded apartment houses or the less innocuous pressure of the factory, one's co-workers, or the local Party organization. The new dualism still stands in the shadow of the old.

In 1960 I wrote that "Khrushchev's great contribution to Soviet politics is his belief that terror is inefficient and unnecessary and that, by a common effort of will and enthusiasm, the Soviet people can lift their society to new heights. So far he has been enormously successful. But the doubt remains as to how he will respond to setbacks and crises, whether at home or abroad"; 1961 and 1962 have been years of such setbacks. Domestically, the setbacks in agriculture deeply upset not only the economy but also the confidence of the people; the failure to grant the usual spring price decreases in 1962, followed by drastic increases in prices of meat and butter (30 and 25 per cent respectively), produced a great shock among the city-dwellers. In addition, the renewed attack on Stalin caused great consternation, not only because many people loved Stalin, but also, and more important, because many could not understand what Khrushchev's purposes were: they asked, was he moving Stalin from the mausoleum only to make room for himself? Internationally, there was the split with China, the Berlin crisis, the resumption of atomic tests, the talk of war.

It is not surprising, therefore, that the Soviet leadership responded to discontent at home with a stepping up of social pressure and with such harsh legal measures as the death penalty for economic crimes.

Yet it would be a great mistake to assume that the "thaw" has ended.

Such an assumption underestimates the importance of the legal and institutional changes which have in fact taken place. The law reforms have already counted. They have acquired a momentum which is hard to stop. A vast structure of procedures and rights has been built, and though its foundations need to be greatly strengthened it is not something which can easily be toppled.

The question remains, does the Soviet leadership wish to carry the process of law reform to its conclusion? Is it willing to establish guarantees against the reversal of this process? If it does not do so, it will have great difficulty in maintaining—especially in the face of domestic and international failures—the sustained drive, the sustained will and enthusiasm, which alone can make the Soviet system work. If it does establish such guarantees against a return to arbitrary measures, it will lay a basis for the gradual overthrow of that system.

SOVIET VIEWS

2. THE U.S.S.R. JUDICIAL SYSTEM *

A. F. GORKIN

Chairman, Supreme Court of the U.S.S.R.

The purpose of criminal procedure is the speedy and complete disclosure of crimes, exposure of the guilty and the guarantee of the correct application of the law so that every person who commits a crime shall suffer just punishment and no innocent person shall be held criminally liable and convicted. No one may be held as an accused except on grounds and in the manner established by law.

During the Stalin cult period democratic principles of legal procedure were grossly violated, and the Party frankly and straight-forwardly told of the distortions which took place in that period, holding that the people should know about them so as never again to permit their repetition.

Since eliminating the evil consequences of the personality cult, the Communist Party of the Soviet Union has attentively assured that demo-

* From A. F. Gorkin, *The USSR Judicial System,* Current Soviet Documents, Special Supplement, June 24, 1963. Copyright © 1963 by Crosscurrent Press, Inc. Excerpts reprinted by permission of Crosscurrent Press Inc.

cratic principles of legal procedure are rigidly adhered to, forcefully emphasizing that legality in the activity of judicial bodies is a basic requirement for the administration of socialist justice.

Ensuring the inviolability of the person and strict observance of the law are the following basic legal norms: no person may be placed under arrest except by decision of a court or with the sanction of a procurator; no one may be found guilty and subjected to a criminal penalty except by sentence of a court; all citizens are equal before the law and the court; judicial proceedings are conducted in the language which the persons participating in the trial understand; cases are heard in public; and the accused has the right to defense. . . .

No one, neither state nor public establishments, nor officials may order courts or recommend to them that they hand down a particular verdict in a concrete criminal or civil case. The independence of judges and their subordination only to the law is a constitutional principle. Special regulations provided by law for holding judges criminally liable or taking disciplinary action against them for misdemeanors guarantees the independence of judges and their subordination only to the law. . . .

Soviet law makes it incumbent on the court, procurator, investigator, and the person conducting the inquiry to make sure that the investigation of all the facts in the case is comprehensive, complete and objective, and that aggravating as well as extenuating circumstances are brought out.

The court, procurator and investigator have no right to put the burden of proof on the accused. It is forbidden to force the accused to give testimony by use of violence, threats or any other illegal means.

The rights and duties of participants in a trial are precisely defined by law.

The accused has the right to offer explanations in respect to the charges preferred against him and present evidence; to present motions; to acquaint himself with all the material of the case on the termination of the preliminary investigation; to have defense counsel; to challenge; and to appeal from actions and decisions of the investigating officer, the procurator or the court.

Before the court sitting begins, the court must give the accused the opportunity to prepare his defense. The court is charged with the duty of handing the accused a copy of the indictment not less than three days before the case comes up for trial. This enables the accused to find out exactly what he is charged with and the evidence offered to prove the charges. Failure to hand him a copy of the indictment, or tardiness in handing it to him, is regarded as a gross violation of his right to defense, and the verdict pronounced by a court where such a violation takes place will be set aside.

At the hearing of a case in a sitting of the court, the accused has the same procedural rights as other participants in the trial to present evidence, take part in its examination, and to offer motions, and he has the right to the last plea.

At trials before a court of first instance, cases are heard with the participation of the accused. The trial of a case without the presence of the accused, except in cases provided for by law, is a gross procedural violation and will cause the setting aside of the verdict.

Defense counsel is allowed to participate in the case as soon as the accused is informed that the preliminary investigation has been completed and has been handed all the material of the case for the purpose of allowing him to acquaint himself with it.

Where persons charged with the commission of a crime are minors, or persons who because of physical or mental deficiencies are unable to exercise their right to defend themselves, defense counsel is permitted to take part from the time the charge is preferred.

Defense counsel is either retained by the accused or is appointed by the court where such a request is made by the accused.

From the moment defense counsel is permitted to participate in the case he has the right to interview the accused; to acquaint himself with all the material of the case and copy out needed information; to offer evidence; to present motions; to participate in the court examination; make challenges; to lodge complaints against actions and decisions of the investigator, procurator and court. With the sanction of the investigator, defense counsel may be present during the interrogation of the accused and during other acts of investigation carried out at the request of the accused or counsel. The accused may retain any lawyer to defend him, and the lawyer, once he has undertaken to act as counsel, may not withdraw from the case.

Article 23 of the Fundamentals of Criminal Procedure for the USSR, the Union and Autonomous Republics provides that defense counsel is duty bound to employ all ways and means envisaged by the law to bring out circumstances exonerating the accused or mitigating his liability and to give him the necessary legal aid. Participation by defense counsel in a trial is an important guarantee of a just verdict. When a lawyer defends his client, argues against unfounded charges, he thereby helps to establish the truth.

The procurator participates in administrative sessions of the court and sittings of the court during the hearing of criminal and civil cases, conducts the prosecution on behalf of the state, and initiates and supports civil actions in court. Procurators exercise supervision to ensure that sentences, judgments, rulings and decisions of judicial bodies are legal and well-founded, and that sentences are carried out, by filing appropriate protests with the higher courts.

The law also guarantees the rights of the accused in the later stages of a criminal trial. The law holds it inadmissible to increase the punishment of the accused or to apply to him a law covering a graver crime when the case is reviewed by a court of cassation or by way of supervision.

A review by way of supervision of a guilty verdict or a ruling or decision of the court on the ground that the penalty was too mild or that a law covering a graver crime should be applied to the convicted person, and likewise a review of a verdict of acquittal or an order or decision of the court to quash the case is permitted only within one year from the time they have come into force.

In all courts cases are heard in public except where state secrets are involved. Other cases that may be heard in *camera* are those which concern crimes committed by persons under the age of 16, sex crimes, and cases where it is deemed necessary to prevent the spread of information on the intimate aspects of the lives of those concerned in the case; in all these cases the court must state in its decision that this is the reason for holding the hearing in *camera*. Verdicts in all cases are pronounced in public.

The hearing of cases in public places and the activity of the court under control of the broad masses of the working people favors the performance by the court of its major function, that of education.

Under Soviet criminal law a penalty is not merely a punishment for the crime committed; it also has for its purpose the reform and re-education of convicted persons and the prevention of further crime both on the part of those convicted and on the part of other persons. Punishment is not intended to inflict physical suffering or denigrate human dignity.

The law provides the following types of punishment for penal offenses: corrective labor without deprivation of liberty; fines; public censure; exile; banishment; deprivation of the right to occupy certain posts or engage in certain activity; and deprivation of liberty. Members of the Armed Forces on regular service may be sent to a disciplinary battalion.

A sentence involving deprivation of liberty may not exceed a term of 10 years, except for especially grave crimes and for particularly dangerous habitual criminals, in which cases the sentence may run to 15 years. However, where the person was under the age of 18 when he committed the crime, he may not be sentenced for more than ten years.

Soviet legislation has given up the imposition of exceptionally long terms of deprivation of liberty as that does not serve the purpose of reforming those who have committed a crime.

Suspended sentences are extremely common in judicial practice; where the court, in fixing a penalty involving deprivation of liberty or corrective labor, takes into consideration the facts in the case and the character of the guilty person and deems it inexpedient to have him serve the sentence, it will suspend the sentence. The sentence will not have to be served at all if the convicted person does not again commit a similar criminal offense or one equally grave within a probationary period fixed by the court.

To indicate how widely suspended sentences are given the following figures are offered: in Byelorussia suspended sentences last year made up 12.4 per cent of total sentences passed in cases with a preliminary investigation, and in the Lithuanian SSR, 14.5 per cent.

Until such time as capital punishment is totally abolished, Soviet law permits the imposition of a sentence of death by shooting, as an exceptional measure, for the grave crimes of high treason, espionage, sabotage, terrorist acts, banditry, and premeditated murder under aggravating circumstances.

Under legislation passed in 1961 and 1962 the death sentence may be imposed by courts for especially large misappropriations of state or public property; taking bribes under aggravating circumstances; counterfeiting or the violation of regulations covering foreign currency operations involving large sums, or dealing in foreign currency as a business; rape under aggravating circumstances; attempts at undermining order in places where particularly dangerous habitual criminals and persons convicted of grave crimes are confined, connected with attacks on officials or convicts who are sincerely reforming for the purpose of terrorizing them; and attempts on the life of members of the militia or voluntary public order squads.

Under laws in force, the death sentence may not be imposed on persons under the age of 18 at the time the crime is committed or on women who are pregnant at the time the crime is committed or the sentence is passed. Nor can a death sentence be carried out in the case of a woman who is pregnant at the time set for its execution. . . .

Persons sentenced to deprivation of liberty serve their sentence in corrective labor colonies, and those under 18 in labor colonies for juveniles. Deprivation of liberty by way of imprisonment may be imposed by the court only on those who have committed grave crimes or on particularly dangerous habitual criminals. Such persons who have served not less than half the term of their sentence may, if their behavior has been exemplary, have their imprisonment commuted to detention in a colony by order of the court.

Convicted persons serving their sentence in a corrective labor colony or in prison are given productive work, learn a trade and attend general educational courses. They may send money from their earnings for the support of their families. After serving their sentence they take up a life of honest labor. Local Soviets and economic bodies are charged with finding jobs for them and helping them get settled.

As a result of character strengthening in colonies or prison and the influence exerted by the collective of their place of work, it is rare for released convicts to commit new crimes.

In contrast to some Western countries, there is essentially no organized professional crime in the Soviet Union. Cases of recurring criminality following release are comparatively rare. In judicial practice we have not come across any gangster organizations, proficient bands of robbers and ravishers.

The suspended sentence or commutation of sentence, where the convicted person has by exemplary behavior and honest attitude toward work proved that he has reformed, is of great importance in the remoulding and reeducation of criminal offenders.

Persons convicted for a crime committed when they were under 18 may be released after serving a third of their sentence, and others after serving half or two-thirds of their sentence, depending on the nature and gravity of the crime.

Supervisory commissions, made up of representatives of public organizations function under local Soviets. They keep an eye on the conditions of convicted persons deprived of liberty, help officials of corrective labor colonies carry on character training work among the convicts, and assist those released to find jobs and get settled.

Supervisory commissions have the right to recommend release before termination of sentence or commutation of sentence for convicts.

An important role in the reeducation of convicts is exercised by the patronage of corrective labor colonies by factories and collective farms. Factory collectives arrange lectures for the convicts and talks on current topics, and help the colony and prison administrations to organize cultural activity and vocational training. After serving their sentence many convicts find work in the plant, state farm or collective farm which exercises patronage over the corrective labor colony in which they served their sentence.

Thus the Soviet state, through a whole system of measures carried out by government bodies and public organizations, endeavors to have every person who has committed a crime prove by conscientious labor and exemplary behavior while serving his sentence that he has reformed and take his place in a collective and apply himself to honest labor. The doors are not closed even to those serving sentences for the commission of a grave crime; they can go back to the collective and to their families.

Elected on a democratic basic, Soviet courts are widely supported in all of their activity by public organizations and collectives of working people.

The educational significance of judicial activity is ensured by the fact that all cases are heard in public, with participation of People's Assessors, and the more typical and important cases are heard by the court in sittings held at the factory, collective farm or other establishment where the crime was committed. The press, radio and television are used extensively to report and comment on the trials. In 1962, for example, 24.8 per cent of the criminal cases tried in the Kazakh Republic were heard in outside sittings, and in the Ukrainian SSR, 26.4 per cent.

Legislation of the USSR and of the Union Republics provides for representatives of public organizations to be admitted by the court to participate in the trial as public prosecutors or public defenders, where such a request is made by the public organizations.

Where a particular collective is interested in a case, the trade union, Komsomol and other public organizations of the plant, office or other establishment involved choose, at a general meeting, as public prosecutor a fellow worker with the best reputation. The collective acquaints itself with the nature of the crime committed by their fellow worker, hears what he has to say about it, if he is not in custody, also what people who know him have to say about him, and also listens to a report from a representative of the Procurator's Office and then decides what attitude to take to the criminal offense committed and to the offender.

The public prosecutor has the right to offer evidence, take part in examining evidence, present motions and make challenges, participate in the pleadings, tell the court his opinion as to whether the charges have been proved and as to the social danger of the prisoner at the bar and of what he has done. He may express his view as to the application of the criminal law and the penalty to be imposed and to other questions involved in the case.

The public defender has the right to offer evidence, take part in examining evidence, present motions and make challenges, participate in the pleadings, tell the court what in his opinion are extenuating circumstances or circumstances calling for an acquittal, or why he thinks a milder penalty should be imposed, or the sentence suspended, or the defendant discharged, or ask that the defendant be turned over to the custody of the collective in whose behalf he, the public defender, appears.

In 1962, a public prosecutor appeared in 11.5 per cent of all cases heard in Estonian courts and 12.9 per cent in Ukrainian courts; public defenders appeared in 6.2 per cent of cases heard by courts in the Turkmen Republic, 6.9 per cent in the Moldavian Republic, and 9.9 per cent in the Estonian Republic.

Laws of the USSR and of the Union Republics provide for turning an accused over to the custody of public organizations or collectives of working people. Where a petition to that effect is submitted, the court, the Procurator's Office, the investigator, or the militia (with the consent of the procurator) have the right to quash a criminal case with respect to persons who have committed a crime not constituting a great social danger and who have sincerely repented. In such a case, the accused whose cases have been quashed are turned over to the custody of the public organizations or collectives of working people which have submitted the petition, for the reeducation and reform of the accused.

The public organization or collective of working people takes the steps needed for educating them.

Testifying to the positive effect of this form of reeducating law-breakers and prevention of crime is the fact that of the number of persons turned over by courts or investigating bodies to the custody of public organizations only 1.1 per cent were convicted by People's Courts in 1961 for the commission of a new crime, and 0.5 per cent in 1962, according to statistics for the latter year.

The Soviet court is not merely a state agency of coercion; it is also an agency of education; it has been given the task of combining measures of coercion with measures of persuasion, and is supported in its activity by various forms of public influence.

In addition to hearing cases, judicial workers report on their work to the population, deliver lectures on legal questions, and talks on the state of crime in the particular district or town, and the measures taken to combat it. In 1962, people's judges made 60,698 reports and delivered 204,944 lectures and talks on legal subjects.

In combatting crime the Soviet state proceeds from the proposition that it is better to prevent crime than to impose criminal penalties and reform the law-breaker; and in line with this, side by side with provision for punishment, the public, collectives of the working people, are widely enlisted to help combat crime.

Participation of the public in the struggle against breaches of public order and amoral deeds varies greatly in form. There are the voluntary public order squads, comrades' courts, commissions for the affairs of minors, and so on.

Public order squads are voluntary bodies made up of foremost factory and office workers at plants, offices, and house managements, and collective farmers; they carry on considerable preventive and educational activity. Their method is persuasion, and they take measures to prevent breaches of public order.

An important role in the struggle against violations of labor discipline, amoral deeds and lawbreaking is played by the comrades' courts, which the great Lenin, founder of the Soviet state, called "proletarian courts of honor."

These courts hear cases of violation of labor discipline, of unfitting conduct in public places or at work, of an improper attitude toward parents or toward women, of failure to perform one's duties in respect to bringing up children, of insults, and of other antisocial actions, none of which involve criminal liability.

Comrades' courts may apply the following measures to those found guilty: make them publicly apologize to the injured person or to the collective; issue a comradely warning; issue a public reprimand with or without publication in the press; impose a fine not exceeding 10 rubles, provided the action did not involve violation of labor discipline. A comrades' court may decide that the hearing of the case in public is enough and will not apply any of the measures if the guilty person has sincerely repented, publicly apologizes to the collective or the injured party, and voluntarily makes good the damage inflicted.

Comrades' courts function on the basis of a special statute and are elective public bodies; their task is actively to help in educating people. Their principal task is to prevent lawbreaking and actions harmful to society, to educate people through persuasion and public influence, to create an atmosphere of intolerance toward any and all antisocial acts.

For prevention of lawbreaking by those under age, implementation of measures for combatting neglect of minors, for handling the affairs of children and juveniles and protecting their rights, commissions for the affairs of minors are formed to function under executive committees of district, town, territorial and regional Soviets; they are based on wide participation by the public. They are composed of representatives of trade unions, Komsomol and other public organizations, of educational, health, social maintenance workers, and workers of the Public Order Ministry.

The commissions, working jointly with public education agencies and with the participation of the public, seek out children and juveniles requiring state and public aid, and juveniles who have left school and do not work, find jobs for them or send them back to school, boarding school, or children's homes; they also help parents in rearing children. The commissions keep an eye on the behavior of minors following their return from special character-training institutions or special health and educational institutions, or from a labor colony after serving their sentence; they keep an eye too on those who have received a suspended sentence, or have been released before expiration of their sentence, giving them needed help in character training.

The commissions may bring influence to bear on parents or guardians who fail to give proper attention to the upbringing of children, who create conditions favoring lawbreaking by the children or juveniles.

The commissions are charged with hearing cases of minors under 16 who commit socially dangerous acts. They have the right to ask the court not to impose a penalty, to suspend sentence or apply a milder penalty, or to expunge a conviction before the expiration of the term, or to release the minor before he has served the full sentence, or to commute the sentence.

Measures of an educational and preventive nature against those who violate the rules of the socialist community are carried out also by standing commissions of local Soviets, factory and local trade union committees, parents' committees cooperating with schools, boards of trustees of children's homes and boarding schools, street and house committees, and many other independent organizations of the working people.

Recent years have witnessed the passage, at the request of the working people, following an extensive discussion in the press, of a law for combatting idlers and parasites. Persons doing no socially useful work may be banished from the town or village in which they live by order of a People's Court, or a court made up of a collective of fellow-citizens, so as to make them go to work. These measures are not criminal penalties, and their application is not counted as a conviction and does not entail any other restriction of rights following banishment.

Much attention is given by the courts and the Soviet public to eliminating the causes of and the conditions making for crime; they proceed from the proposition that a person is not born a criminal.

Soviet society can, by exerting its efforts, eradicate the causes giving rise to crime in our country, as they do not stem from conditions of our society but are conditioned by shortcomings in our educational work, the negative survivals of the past, and the still persisting consequences of the war.

The further rise in material security and advance of the cultural level and social consciousness envisaged by the Party Program will make it possible to eradicate crime and eventually to replace state measures by measures of public influence and education. . . .

3. PERSUASION AND COMPULSION IN COMBATTING ANTI-SOCIAL ACTS *

N. MIRONOV

Chief, Department of Administrative Agencies, Central Committee, Communist Party of the Soviet Union.

Most Soviet people are public-spirited and conscientious in their attitude toward work and toward socialist property. Comradely mutual assistance based in a community of interests and a common objective, a spirit of collectivism, mutual respect, an uncompromising attitude toward viola-

* From *Kommunist*, 1961, No. 3. Translated in *The Soviet Review*, September, 1961, pp. 54-65. Excerpts reprinted from the translation by permission of the publisher.

tions of the standards of conduct in socialist society are more and more widespread. The citizen of the future communist society—a cultured, educated human being with advanced ideas, free of the psychology of the bourgeois world—is beginning to emerge.

But vestiges of the old system of exploitation still survive in the minds of some of our people, and these make themselves felt in the behavior of certain individuals through actions hostile to socialist society. One of the holdovers from the past is crime. There are still instances of embezzlement, theft, hooliganism and other crimes which violate the rights and personal security of other citizens.

It goes without saying that the causes of crime and other anti-social acts in our country are not the same as in the capitalist world. There crime is a normal and ineradicable social misfortune, rooted in the very nature of the system itself with its poverty, unemployment and doubtful bourgeois morals. The socialist system, on the other hand, has destroyed the root causes, the permanently operating causes of crime inherent in capitalism. It has created all the prerequisites for its sharp reduction. But socialism has not developed in a vacuum. It still retains traces of the old world. It would therefore be a delusion to believe that crime and other anti-social acts would disappear immediately and of themselves. A long and stubborn struggle is needed to cleanse society of the accumulation of hundreds and thousands of years of decay. For one thing, our people are not isolated from the influence of hostile bourgeois ideology, the propaganda which attempts to revive the private property drive and other customs and habits now alien to us. Nor can we forget the bitter aftermath of the last war. The war itself, which scattered many families and left large numbers of children without parents or proper homes, had a disastrous effect on many people. Later on there were the difficulties of the post-war period of economic recovery.

Yet experience shows that a substantial proportion of the crimes in our society are committed by persons who evade socially useful work and lead a parasitic life. In some regions and republics this group accounts for nearly one-third of all crimes. Drunkenness is another source of crime—especially of the dangerous kind. Not enough is being done to eliminate the factors contributing to lawbreaking. Parasites, drunks and hoodlums do not always face public condemnation. Administrative bodies are not always sufficiently strict.

The Communist Party and the Soviet Government attach exceptional importance to educating the masses to a communist attitude toward work and observance of the socialist rules of behavior. . . .

Party, trade union and public organizations are paying a great deal of attention to combatting infringements of the law. Anti-social acts, no matter what their nature, become increasingly intolerable in a society where every possibility exists for eradicating crime. Success in this area depends above all on utilizing the powerful forces of the public, on efficient work by the militia, the courts and the procurator's office and on ever closer coordination between state bodies and public organizations. The problem arises of how to use persuasion and compulsion together, how to combine measures of a public and educational character with coercive measures.

As we have said, the Soviet State differs in principle from states that existed or now exist in societies composed of antagonistic classes. Violence, compulsion and suppression—political, economic, spiritual and physical —are characteristic of the attitude of the bourgeois state toward the working people. In socialist society the situation is different. Here the state is an instrument in the hands of the people. It defends and protects their interests. The very strength of the Soviet State lies in the political and social awareness of its citizens. Its main method of governing is through persuasion, by educating and organizing. Lenin stressed that point time and again. "First of all, and at all costs, we must persuade, and only then compel."

As socialist society develops, our citizens are more and more drawn into the management of public affairs. A number of functions previously performed by state bodies belong to public organizations. A gradual withering away of state administrative bodies—bodies that carry out functions of compulsion—is now taking place. The public is called upon to play an increasingly important role in safeguarding the rules of the socialist community and to forestall acts detrimental to society.

The Party policy of increasing the role of the public in combatting crime and other violations of socialist standards of conduct is an embodiment of Lenin's idea of organizing a mass campaign among the people to fight against survivals of capitalism. In *How to Organize Competition* Lenin wrote: "The voluntary, conscientious cooperation of the masses of workers and peasants in controlling with revolutionary enthusiasm . . . the rogues, the idlers and the hooligans alone can conquer these survivals of an accursed society. . . ."

It is significant that from the very beginning the fight against crime became a matter which the Soviet people undertook themselves. They formed societies and brigades to help the militia, public-order commissions, youth squads, factory and rural comrades' courts and other voluntary organizations. Today the public is utilizing the experience of those years to work out new forms of combatting lawbreakers. There now exist voluntary public-order squads whose organization received its impetus from a decision of the Central Committee of the CPSU and the Council of Ministers of the USSR, *On the Participation of the Working People in the Maintenance of Public Order,* adopted in March 1959.

The strength of the public-order squads lies in the voluntary, mass-scale participation and active support of the entire population. . . . Squads make it their aim to assure exemplary order in places of public recreation and entertainment. . . . Their fine work has made it possible to reduce the militia [police] posts at motion picture houses and recreation centers and even do away with some of those posts.

The squads are constantly extending their sphere of activity and improving their methods. They now combat drunkenness, illicit distilling of vodka and profiteering. They expose persons who lead a parasitic life and try to eradicate instances of child neglect. . . .

In re-educating lawbreakers public-order squads make wide use of satirical newspapers, leaflets and photograph displays. These, incidentally, are often more effective than administrative measures. Violators beg headquarters not to post their photographs in public.

Not only drunks and hoodlums but hardened criminals are beginning to realize the significance of the voluntary public-order squads. Criminals break laws when they feel they can get away with it but not when they meet organized public rebuff. A hardened recidivist thief, after serving his latest sentence, recently wrote: "The days of our brethren are numbered. The public-order squads are catching us red-handed. Nearly every citizen helps. They make sketches of us and post them for everyone to see. Something unbelievable is going on. . . ."

It is only right that a person who violates the laws and acts to the detriment of society as a whole should be punished. But must criminal punishment be the rule in all cases? By no means. If the infringement is insignificant and does not endanger society, if the offender realizes the harm in his actions and is anxious to atone, if finally the organs of justice are confident that the culprit can reform and that this may be attained without resorting to criminal punishment—that is, by releasing him, placing him in the care of the collective with which he works or studies, and that the collective will be able to influence him—criminal punishment is not indicated. Once the public becomes involved in the fight against lawbreaking, it is possible to bring such persons to light not only *post factum* but beforehand —possibly to prevent crimes by focusing ahead of time on conduct deviating from standards of social behavior.

Prevention of anti-social acts and re-education are effected by both state institutions and public organizations. Discussion of a person's misdemeanor by the group with which he works is a particularly effective form of re-education. Only a hardened criminal, one without either honor or conscience, is capable of deceiving the collective, ignoring the confidence placed in him. As a rule the understandable indignation of fellow-workers, their blunt appraisal of what he has done, and finally the trust they place in him when they decide to vouch for his future conduct, all make a deep impression on the miscreant's mind and compel him to give serious thought to his actions. . . .

Comrades' courts set up at factories, offices, collective and state farms enjoy increasing prestige. Their strength, like that of other public groups, lies in condemnation of misdemeanors in front of the collective. These courts cannot of course hand down a sentence depriving someone of liberty. But an offender in facing it feels he is facing the public conscience. Small wonder that many ask that their cases not be taken up by comrades' courts—they are ashamed to face the judgment of their comrades.

During the past two years collectives of workers, public-order squads and comrades' courts have reformed and returned to useful activity many people who had gone astray, then sincerely repented. In Moscow there are several hundred such persons now being reformed in the collectives at their places of work. Most of them are justifying the trust placed in them. Of the total number of offenders for whom collectives vouched in 1960 less than one per cent repeated offenses. . . .

The fact that persuasion is recognized as the chief method of guiding the masses and the policy followed of drawing the public into the fight against violations of the law does not of course exclude the use of compulsion. Strict observance of laws established in the interests of the whole of society requires more than cultural, educational and organizational work on the part of state bodies and public organizations. It also requires a firm hand by the state authorities in ensuring observance and punishing those who do not wish to observe the law voluntarily. . . .

In order correctly to evaluate the role of compulsion in socialist society, and particularly the role of its severest form, punishment meted out by a court of law, we must bear in mind that this is resorted to only when all other methods have failed or when violation is particularly dangerous to society and its citizens. At the same time compulsion, even in the form of criminal punishment, aims not only at forcing the wrongdoer to observe the law but also at educating him, persuading him by the very act of punishment that it is necessary for laws to be observed. Significantly one of the articles of the Fundamentals of Criminal Legislation of the USSR and the Union Republics declares: "Punishment is not only retribution for a crime; it also pursues the aim of reforming and re-educating the sentenced persons in the spirit of a conscientious attitude toward work, strict observance of the laws, respect for the rules of socialist intercourse, and also the prevention of further crimes either by the sentenced persons or other persons."

In socialist society compulsion therefore remains an important means of eradicating crime. Later on of course every citizen will observe the laws voluntarily, out of deep inner conviction and awareness of moral duty, by force of habit. But until they do, the state must uphold law and order by applying compulsion. It now becomes a matter not of rejecting compulsion but of gradually narrowing the sphere of its application, spearheading punitive measures against imperialist agents, confirmed criminals, dangerous recidivists and others who do not lend themselves to re-education. . . .

Socialist laws must be strictly observed in the fight against infringements of public order. In trying criminals, including dangerous ones, our courts must always take into account not only the circumstances aggravating guilt but also those mitigating it, study the motives and make the punishment fit the crime. But the present process of narrowing the sphere of compulsion and extending that of public influence must not lead to allowing criminals to escape responsibility for what they have done. There must be no going to extremes in such matters. It is important correctly to combine measures of public influence and measures of criminal punishment, starting from examination of the nature of the crime, the character of the criminal and the degree to which he is a menace to society. Soviet people are humane and can forgive those who commit minor infractions of the law. But we must not show leniency or liberalism toward those who deliberately break laws, who commit dangerous crimes, who deceive the collective and scorn public opinion. The criminal who encroaches on the security of society and of the Soviet citizen must not be allowed to escape punishment.

There is little doubt that by combining the efforts of state bodies and public organizations we will succeed in sharply reducing, then completely eradicating crime in our country. Party organs must give constant attention to organizing the fight against violations of law and order. They must look upon this as an important task in the building of communist society.

XI

SOVIET AID TO THE LESS DEVELOPED COUNTRIES: PURPOSES AND ACCOMPLISHMENTS

> "We do not demand military bases and concessions in exchange for our aid, do not impose any enslaving agreements. We do not humiliate young states with 'charity' and do not insult them with degrading credit terms. Our principles are equality of rights and mutual respect."
>
> NIKITA S. KHRUSHCHEV

How often has it been said that the struggle between East and West will eventually be decided in the underdeveloped countries? Perhaps such a view is exaggerated, extreme; yet there can be little doubt that the inhabitants of these lands—one-third of the world's population, still largely uncommitted—are destined to play a major role in the ideological contest that has divided mankind into two great camps (or perhaps three, considering China), each convinced that it alone has found the "right" road which will lead to a better future for all of mankind. In the economic sphere, there is deep significance in the fact that these "underdeveloped" countries are ever more often referred to as the "less developed" countries, the "developing" countries, or the "emerging" nations. In the political world arena, these countries have been rising in power; most of the more than sixty new nations which have joined the United Nations since 1945 (and many of the fifty who were among the original members) come from their ranks. The new nations may not have veto power, their governments may be subject to frequent and often violent changes, yet they hold the balance of power in the Council of Nations. (Were they to vote as a bloc, they could outvote any combination of the developed nations, West and East.)

Yet, in spite of all the progress they have made in recent years, most of the people in these less developed lands are still illiterate, hungry, ill-clothed, ill-housed, disease-ridden, and destined to die decades earlier than their brethren in the United States, Western Europe, or the Soviet

Union—and the gulf between the have and the have-not nations appears to be widening. Their appetites whetted by their increased contacts with the "more advanced" nations, these people are eagerly searching for the best way to achieve rapid economic growth. But, warned U.S. Undersecretary of State George Ball, "Economic development is an intricate and difficult process. It has," he admonished, "proved difficult for the industrialized countries who have gone through it in the past, and it will be so for the newer countries going through it now." [1] The Soviets, however, proclaim that the elimination of colonialization, the socialization of the means of production, and nationwide planning in the interest of society (plus, perhaps, a little financial and technical assistance) would enable any country to do in decades what it took capitalist economies centuries to accomplish. Such assertions often seem plausible to people whose experience with capitalism has not been as gratifying as that of the United States or of Western Europe, especially since the Soviet Union by her own example has proven that her type of economic and political system (in the words of an outstanding Western expert) "has . . . been a means of industrializing a relatively backward country." [2]

Since in her present stage of economic development the Soviet Union herself could well use the raw materials, the machinery, and the technicians which she dispatches to the underdeveloped countries, economic assistance to backward regions represents a real sacrifice to the Soviet people. Yet Soviet aid, although considerably smaller in quantity than that from the West, continues to be forthcoming. Why is the Soviet Union willing to permit this drain on her economic resources, and what have been the effects of that aid on the underdeveloped countries?

The economic and political effects of Soviet aid may be a matter of dispute, but there is little disagreement regarding the answer to the first part of the question. The West is convinced that "the Communists regard their role in history as that of midwives assisting in the birth of Communist societies," [3] and the Soviet Union (who conceives of mankind's ultimate destiny as a world community built along lines of perfect communism) [4] does not conceal its hope that the underdeveloped countries will find their way "through general democratic transformation to (Soviet) socialist transformation".[5] Toward this end they are willing to extend economic aid even to presently non-Communist, nationalist nations; toward this end

[1] Reported widely in the U.S. press. See, for instance, *Washington Evening Star,* March 29, 1964.

[2] Alec Nove, "The Soviet Model and Under-Developed Countries," *International Affairs,* London, Jan. 1961, p. 29.

[3] "Communist Economic Policy in the Less Developed Areas," *Dept. of State Publications 7020, European and British Commonwealth Series 60,* July 1960, p. 5.

[4] See Chapter I above.

[5] *Kommunist,* Sept. 1962. Translated in *The Current Digest of the Soviet Press,* Nov. 7, 1962, p. 14; parentheses added.

they are willing to support (at least morally although not always militarily) the "peoples of the colonial and dependent countries in their justified aspiration and struggle against oppressors." [6]

The authors of the two selections under *Western Views* are also in agreement that the primary purpose of Soviet aid to underdeveloped countries is to discredit the West and to promote what the Soviets consider to be the correct economic and political development of the nations involved. As to the effect of that aid, however, George S. Carnett and Morris H. Crawford in the first selection feel that Soviet aid, relatively small but carefully selective, has quite an impact, and they see no reason to doubt that the Soviet Union will be able to meet her commitments. Leon Herman, on the other hand, points to the great involvement of the newly developing countries in the activities of the world market and expresses his view that the Communist countries do not have enough resources to spare to make the "Soviet alternative" to trade with the West sufficiently attractive.

In the first selection under *Soviet Views,* V. Tyagunenko explains why, in his opinion and in the opinion of the Soviets in general, the people of the underdeveloped countries will not choose the Capitalist path. G. M. Prohorov, finally, presents the official Soviet views regarding the U.S.S.R.'s unselfish aid to the emerging nations, and the economic significance of this aid to the young nations' economic development.

[6] Words in quotes used by Nikolai S. Patolichev, USSR Minister of Foreign Trade, as reported by Richard E. Mooney, *New York Times,* March 26, 1964.

WESTERN VIEWS

1. SOVIET AID TO LESS DEVELOPED COUNTRIES *

GEORGE C. CARNETT

Staff Member, Bureau of Foreign Economic Relations of the Soviet Bloc, Office of Intelligence and Research, U.S. Department of State.

MORRIS H. CRAWFORD

Chief, Bureau of Foreign Economic Relations of the Soviet Bloc, Office of Intelligence and Research, U.S. Department of State.

1. SOVIET MOTIVES

The peoples of Asia, Africa, and Latin America have always been regarded by the Soviet leadership as potential allies in the cause of the Communist revolution. In the early postwar period, and especially during the years 1948-50, the Kremlin encouraged the local Communist parties in the less developed areas to follow militant tactics aimed at bringing about Communist revolutions. As these areas increasingly attained national status and independence, however, Soviet policy became increasingly out of date. New tactics were called for, tactics which would have an appeal to the widespread desire in the less developed areas for national independence and economic expression.

After the death of Stalin in 1953, Soviet policy toward the less developed countries, reflecting the altered world situation, underwent a dramatic change. A new Soviet approach was devised, based essentially on efforts to court the non-Communist bourgeois governments in the less developed countries by a combination of approaches in the political, economic, and

* Excerpts reprinted from *Dimensions of Soviet Economic Power*, Joint Economic Committee, Congress of the United States, December, 1962, pp. 457-474.

cultural fields. Communist state efforts to establish good relations with the governments of the neutralist less developed countries were usually accompanied by a slowing down of the militant, aggressive action in which the local Communist parties had previously been engaged. Country-to-country aid for economic development and the introduction of other facets of modern society have played a key role in the new approach. The Soviet Union in the intervening years has come to regard its foreign aid program as an index of its growing power and role in the world and as an important element in its general support to "national liberation struggles." The very knowledge that it provides an alternative source of economic aid will, the Kremlin hopes, encourage neutral states to be more demanding in their relations with free world nations. Economic assistance also provides the U.S.S.R. with a political entree into countries where its role has hitherto been very limited and lays the groundwork for a more sensitive attitude toward the desires of the Communist countries.

Neutral states are told that acceptance of bloc economic assistance not only is consistent with a true policy of neutrality but also contributes to their ability to follow an independent policy. Those nations which have chosen to remain allies of the free world are told that, by becoming neutral and accepting assistance from the bloc, they would receive more, rather than less, assistance from the free world. Once the bloc has secured a foothold in a country, Soviet officials and their local Communist agents do all they can to discredit free world aid programs and to encourage the local government to reduce and even break off relations with the free world.

Even routine economic features of Soviet aid are designed to complement political intentions of the Soviet approach. Most Soviet assistance is in the form of interest-bearing credits to finance specific projects, in part to give the impression of making businesslike deals and because the Soviets may consider that interest-free loans or grants arouse suspicion as to "strings" in the recipient countries. Obviously the guarantee of repayment with interest, even if at a low rate, makes the assistance virtually free of cost to the U.S.S.R. At the same time, the impression that the low interest rate conveys is that Soviet foreign assistance is "mutually profitable" and that the only reason the free world nations charge higher rates is to reap "capitalist profits."

The use of credits rather than grants also serves as a restraint on the volume of requests, enabling the U.S.S.R. from the outset to limit the overall scope of its aid program with minimum adverse political effects. Finally, the use of credits assures that throughout the repayment period the Soviets will be able to maintain close and continuing relations with the target countries, while some of the exports of the debtor countries are diverted from traditional markets elsewhere, thus depriving the exporting countries of foreign exchange earnings.

2. SCOPE OF AID PROGRAM

Since 1954, the U.S.S.R.'s program of foreign assistance has been enlarged continuously both in size and geographical scope. At the present time it encompasses 25 independent nations in the free world. Initially modest in total annual amounts, credits and grants were extended at an average rate of about $700 million annually during the 1959-61 period. . . .

Five countries—United Arab Republic, Indonesia, India, Afghanistan, and Cuba—account for more than two-thirds of all Soviet aid commitments. The impact potential of smaller lines of credit, however, may be substantial when viewed in the context of the level of the recipient country's investment from domestic sources, recent aid received from free world sources, and general level of technology.

Although its campaign is worldwide in scope, it is apparent that the U.S.S.R. directs its aid where it believes situations exist which lend themselves to exploitation for political, psychological, or even, in a broad sense, strategic gains. In a number of cases Soviet aid overtures have coincided with a strain in the country's relations with the United States or one of its allies. Offers to Greece, Iran, Turkey, and Pakistan provide notable examples of Soviet attempts to use aid as a means of weakening Western defense pacts; but despite much pressure, U.S. allies have accepted only very limited bloc credits. Among the neutralists, Soviet tactics include concentrated efforts in key countries whose regional influence is expected to expand.

3. INTEREST RATES

One of the features of Soviet credits to less developed countries which has attracted great attention has been the low interest rates—typically 2 or 2.5 percent. The interest rate on Soviet credits is presumably politically motivated rather than based on economic calculations. These rates approximate the Soviet state bank's domestic interest rates on short-term loans, although the foreign credits are long-term and for investment purposes. Soviet theory and practice do not even recognize the use of interest charges internally on investment capital. The chronically severe shortage of capital in the U.S.S.R. in relation to planned investment would undoubtedly impose a considerably higher rate than is used in Soviet foreign credits. The Soviets probably regard interest rates as necessary in order to strengthen the credibility of the claim to "stringless" aid. At the same time, interest rates are kept low so as to suggest that the bloc is not taking advantage of less fortunate, capital-shy nations. Higher rates, they insinuate, imply "capitalist profits."

4. REPAYMENT TERMS

Repayment is generally scheduled over a period of 12 years or less, which compares unfavorably with many U.S. Government loans. Many of the major Soviet credit agreements provide for future negotiations to establish lists, prices, and quantities of goods to be delivered in repayment. It is not yet clear just what these provisions imply, but obviously they leave a large area for later bargaining, which may become a source of future friction and possible pressure if the U.S.S.R. should find this opportune.

In its recent deals the U.S.S.R. has agreed to defer repayments until completion of its own deliveries of equipment and services. For the recipients of such assistance, this is attractive because it permits production to begin on Soviet-financed projects before payments are due.

5. CREDITS USED OVER A PERIOD OF YEARS

When the U.S.S.R. extends a line of credit to a less developed country, the plans for its implementation generally are not immediately specified. Project lists may be agreed upon, but even these are subject to considerable revision. . . .

Since most drawings to date under Soviet economic credits have been for survey and design work, and to a much lesser extent for construction or purchases of machinery and equipment, Soviet assistance expenditures are at present a moderate fraction of total aid commitments. The modest level of expenditures, compared with total commitments, also reflects the recency of many of the large extensions of aid. Deliveries under military aid pacts have been rapid, since they generally involve shipment of hardware out of stocks or in current production rather than items requiring special designs.

6. TECHNICAL ASSISTANCE

An extremely important phase of . . . aid programs is the technical guidance provided in conjunction with other assistance. These services are paid for by the recipient. In the first half of 1962 approximately 9,000 Soviet technicians spent a month or more on the job in 25 less developed countries. The U.S.S.R. played host to the majority of the estimated 22,000 technicians and students from the less developed countries who have gone to the bloc for study and training of various types during the last 5 to 6 years.

There has been a continued increase in the size and scope of this aspect of the Soviet aid program. Only 4 years ago, for example, the number of Soviet technicians employed in less developed countries was less than half the present number. The increased activity reflects growing implementation of economic assistance agreements and the conclusion of new accords. . . .

While Soviet technicians as a whole have been careful to avoid the appearance of engaging in subversive activities, this type of assistance provides valuable means for ultimately influencing the nationals of less-developed countries in directions favorable to Communist aims. By sending technicians to countries where they are needed and by providing training both in the U.S.S.R. and in the countries concerned, many key individuals and groups have been brought into contact with the economic and technical achievements of the U.S.S.R. as well as with its culture and its systems of values. The U.S.S.R. has made special efforts to place personnel as advisers to influential officials in key ministries and on important projects.

Approximately 6,700 Soviet technicians were employed on economic projects during 1962. . . .

7. MILITARY ASSISTANCE

By the end of June 1962 the U.S.S.R.'s agreements to supply arms and military training to non-Communist countries provided for military aid of nearly $2.5 billion. The main recipients have been Syria, Egypt, Indonesia, Iraq, Cuba, and Afghanistan. Commitments to Yemen, Guinea, and Mali, which are much smaller, are still of major significance in relation to the size and requirements of the recipient country. . . .

8. SOVIET CAPABILITIES

The rapid and continuing growth of the Soviet economy has given the Kremlin sufficient economic and technological power to meet its commitments under present aid and trade agreements. Moreover, these commitments could be considerably expanded if the Soviet leadership should decide that the political gains justify the diversion of resources from alternative uses within the bloc. Growing experience in implementing projects under agreements concluded in earlier years is adding to the U.S.S.R.'s ability to carry out foreign-aid programs. A growing body of trained technicians and increasing professional expertise are also increasing Soviet capabilities to provide technical services abroad.

Among the factors which are expected to enhance further bloc foreign aid capabilities over the next several years are an acceleration in research on the less-developed areas, with a concomitant increase in highly trained Soviet personnel who have a specialized knowledge of the language, politics, social structure, and economic problems of the country to which they are assigned. Facilities are being greatly expanded for providing academic and technical training for civilians from less-developed countries, and special programs have been set up for military personnel from Africa, Asia, and Latin America. . . .

2. THE POLITICAL GOALS OF SOVIET FOREIGN AID *

LEON M. HERMAN

Senior Specialist in Soviet Economics, Legislative Reference Service, Library of Congress

Anyone who wishes to try his hand at it, can muster a variety of reasons why the Soviet Union ought not to engage in the effort of extending foreign aid outside the Communist bloc. There is, to begin with, the rather obvious reason that the kind of resources that are most in demand for the task of supporting economic development abroad are notoriously scarce within the Soviet Union. These resources are also costly, especially in terms of opportunities foregone; in terms of dislocations caused at home. There is, furthermore, the familiar reason that there are still large and promising regions of the vast Soviet land today that cry out for development and for incorporation into the mainstream of the country's drive toward modernization. There could be mentioned, moreover, the important sectors of the economy that continue to live on short rations of precisely the kind of development capital, physical and human, that is required to sustain foreign economic assistance projects.

In addition, attention could also be called to the urgent needs in the sphere of economic development within the Soviet bloc, especially among Russia's Communist allies in Asia. Then, too, there is an added ideological factor to be considered, namely, that economic aid as a social technique belongs more appropriately in the storehouse of the protagonists of stabilization and reformism rather than in the arsenal of the champions of class antagonism and social revolution.

No matter how persuasive these reasons may appear to the outside observer, however, they have, obviously enough, not carried the day among the present rulers of the U.S.S.R. As we know, the decision to venture into the field of foreign aid outside the bloc was taken by the Soviet inner circle some 8 years ago, for reasons that were sufficiently compelling from their point of view. Since then, the Soviet commitment of resources to foreign aid has grown steadily from year to year, until it has come to encompass

* Excerpts reprinted from *Dimensions of Economic Power*, Joint Economic Committee, Congress of the United States, December, 1962, pp. 475-485.

some 25 countries, scattered far and wide in Asia, the Middle East, and Africa.

What are these compelling reasons that account for the substantial commitment made by the Soviet Union to foreign aid? What are the ascertainable main considerations that have persuaded the Soviet leaders that they can derive more political advantage from the expensive and exposed foreign-aid operation than their economically better endowed competitors in the field; namely, the industrial nations of the West?

I. LENINISM IN ACTION

From time to time, the principal Soviet leaders take occasion in their public statements to provide an explanation of, and thereby to elicit popular approval for, the policy of granting foreign aid to non-Communist countries. In discussing this issue in its broadest terms, they have generally explained foreign aid as a form of practical contemporary application of the basic Leninist principles in international relations. Speaking from the rostrum of the 22nd Congress of the CPSU, in late October 1961, Deputy Premier Anastas Mikoyan justified the official Soviet position on foreign aid in terms of its relevance to the broad international aims of communism:

> The Soviet Union and the other Socialist countries [he said] have entered into the arena of life of these less-developed peoples, bringing their just methods of maintaining economic ties on the basis of equality and their noble intentions of facilitating the advance of these peoples on the road of progress. We were taught this by the great Lenin. This is an example of proletarian internationalism in action under modern conditions.

To the initiated, who made up Mikoyan's audience, his compact political formula told a great deal. It indicated, in the first place, that Stalin's narrow approach to the promotion of the international goals of the Communist movement, with his primary reliance on expansion by military force and by open subversion, had been found wanting by his successors. It told, furthermore, that the party was once again moving in the open sea of international politics, guided by Lenin's bold vision of a "history-making alliance" between the Communist-ruled states and the former colonial peoples. As now frequently paraphrased in the official press, Lenin had forecast that great historic changes could flow from a policy of active economic and political assistance to the former colonial peoples:

> With the support of the countries of socialism, the nations that find themselves in the stage of precapitalist social relationships can bypass the capitalist stage, and the countries having a low level of capitalist development can break with it, can cut short the ordeal of passing through all the stages, and launch upon the building of socialism.

Needless to say, the prospect of a "noncapitalist development" for more than a third of the world's population is a political goal of great attraction to the rulers of the Soviet Union. As they view the course of world events, moreover, such a development appears to them eminently plausible. . . .

The reasons that motivate the Soviet leaders to extend aid to the developing nations are, in short, largely external to the specific needs of the recipients. They do not spring from a desire to bring relief from temporary economic pressures, such as food shortages or balance-of-payments difficulties. Rather, the sights of the Soviet leadership are fixed on finding ways to promote the building of economic institutions likely to produce the "correct" historymaking changes in these countries. They would not be Marxist politicians if they acted otherwise. . . . Just where the journey will ultimately end, according to Soviet doctrine, is a settled matter. All that needs to be arranged, in this light, is to accelerate the speed of the passage.

II. THROUGH THE SOVIET LOOKING GLASS

What is it, we may ask, that makes the Soviet leaders so confident that their direct involvement in the economic development of the new nations will produce the desired far-reaching changes in their internal and external political orientation? The answer can be found in the basic phenomenon that they are economic determinists. Accordingly, they are persuaded that they can discern on the horizon a series of "significant signs." . . .

One of the "significant signs," for example, is the fact that the new nations resort to state enterprise in promoting some sectors of the domestic economy. This may look innocent on the surface, but the net effect of this practice, as the Soviet experts tell them, is—

to reduce the sphere of influence of foreign imperialist exploitation, to strengthen the political independence of the country, to prevent the restoration of colonialism. . . .

The unfolding sequence of events, in fact, looks so favorable to the Soviet experts in this field that they refuse to be alarmed by the evident growth of private capitalist enterprise in the economies of the developing countries. This, too, is adjudged to be a force moving in the "correct" direction. . . . The reason for this sanguine conclusion is given by one expert as follows:

The contemporary world capitalist system rests on the power of the monopolies. The way to bring this system down crashing is by undermining the rule of the monopolies. Everything that inflicts damage upon the monopolies changes the correlation of forces in favor of socialism.

In any event, they regard the economic climate in the new countries to be most unfavorable for private enterprise. All signs within the new nations, as they read them, point not to the entrepreneur but to the state as the principal organizer of economic activity related to development. Among these signs they include: the extreme scarcity of private financial resources; of private access to foreign sources of credit; of private managerial talent. These lacks, coupled with the strong urge to attain rapid growth, as Soviet observers see it, help to push the emerging countries in the direction of state enterprise. This results in ever greater inroads of government direction and regulation of the economy.

These reported tendencies, needless to say, are adjudged by Soviet observers to be both positive and progressive. They see in them a strong kinship to the basic economic method employed in the Communist countries. Such an area of common interest, they stress, needs to be cultivated and enlarged.

At present—

reports one Soviet expert approvingly—

over 40 less developed nations have their own programs for developing the economy . . . In one way or another, they are striving to feel their way toward new forms for the organization of production, to utilize the rich positive experience accumulated by the socialist countries. . . .

It follows that the road to "true, progressive, noncapitalist development" must be paved by some working alliance of proletarian and patriotic forces. This is a goal toward which Premier Khrushchev has given his firm support on more than one occasion. He repeated this advice in his principal address to the 22d party congress, on October 17, 1961, declaring:

The entry of the former colonial and dependent nations onto the non-capitalist path of development, cannot be achieved by the drift of events (*samotiok*). Only the active struggle of the working class, the toiling masses, the union of all democratic and patriotic forces, and the broad national front can lead the nations onto such a road.

At the same time, Khrushchev urged the new nations to bear in mind the "advantages" of reliance upon the Soviet bloc:

They have on their side the nations of the whole world socialist system, which are powerful international forces, endowed with all that is necessary for extending effective moral and material support.

III. THE SELECTIVE APPLICATION OF SOVIET AID

It is not surprising, therefore, that the content of the Soviet aid program is carefully controlled, on the basis of a set of criteria that would help to promote the main official goals of the U.S.S.R. in the field of economic development. Care is generally exercised that the projects selected for support must, to begin with, serve to accelerate those trends in the process of economic and social change in the client countries which the Soviet Government considers to be "positive" in character. For these reasons, Soviet aid in general displays a strong bias, for example, in favor of industrial projects. Nearly 60 percent of all Soviet bloc credit obligations, through 1961, were committed to installations in the field of manufacturing. The promotion of industry helps, of course, to expand the ranks of the proletariat, a process that contributes, in Soviet terms, to the widening of the class base of the local Communist parties. By the same token, it serves to offset the influence of the potentially hostile class, the "national bourgeoisie."

The use of Soviet aid to build production plants, especially in the heavy industrial sector, also helps to project a favorable image of the U.S.S.R. in the new countries. It lends visual proof to a major Marxist theme, namely, that only the U.S.S.R. is willing and able to buttress the "real economic independence" of the emerging nations, a condition, they insist, that is quite impossible of attainment without a domestic heavy industry. In this part of the program, the Soviet dispensers of foreign aid know that they are working to enlist on their side the forces of economic nationalism of the emerging states. . . .

Soviet aid is also selectively applied in still another sense, in the sense that it is directed exclusively toward the state sector in the economy of the recipient country. . . . On this practice in selection rests a great deal of the optimism that marks the official view of the evolving state of affairs within the developing countries. . . . It is counted upon to build up the strength of the "progressive" state sector in its struggle against the "internal enemy," namely, private enterprise. . . .

Still another strategic ingredient of the Soviet aid program is the conspicuous support of technical training in the client countries. This type of project is designed to drive home to the new nations two favorite Soviet themes: (1) that only the Soviet Union is ready to meet their aspirations to acquire the technical skills of modern industry: (2) that Soviet support, financial as well as technical, has no ulterior motives of self-interest: it is offered only for the duration of the period of shortage of "nationally trained cadres."

In a number of countries, therefore, the Soviet Union is building technical institutes as part of its economic aid program. In such cases, they not only supply the equipment but also help to staff the schools with teaching and research personnel. In other instances, where the prospects may be less immediately promising, the Soviet commitment provides for the transmission of technical skills by a less formal instrumentality, namely by the acceptance of local workers for training in the appropriate industrial enterprises of the U.S.S.R.

There is yet another, heavily used route by which the managers of the Soviet aid program offer to guide the interested less-developed countries toward "economic independence." This is the route of the geological survey, followed by prospecting for mineral deposits. The cost of these surveys are, as a rule, covered by the long-term credit from the U.S.S.R., and carried out with the aid of Soviet technical personnel. Hence, there is no current outlay by the recipient country; only a glittering promise of sudden enrichment by means of some important mineral find. At the same time, the Soviet Union stands by, ready to help in the process of extraction, and to defend the resource against "the greed of capitalist interests." As may be expected, this element in Soviet foreign aid occupies a position of great prominence in official commentaries on the subject. Also, the extension of this type of offer is quite prominent in Soviet proposals. Work on geological surveys is going on in a majority of the countries included in the Soviet aid program.

IV. THE LIMITS OF THE SOVIET "ALTERNATIVE"

Everything about the Soviet program—its calculated application, its cost, and expanding scale—leaves little room for doubt that the Communist leaders have a strong and immediate incentive to influence the political direction of economic organization in the developing countries. What they expect to see emerge in the upshot, they tell us, is nothing less than "a radical change in the balance of forces on a world scale in favor of socialism." In order to accomplish this critical shift in the world balance they offer to the new nations an "alternative way," a shortcut to help resolve their domestic and international difficulties. At home, they urge the developing countries to order their economic and political affairs on the basis of Soviet-tested, "non-capitalist" forms of social organization. In regard to their economic needs from abroad, Communist spokesmen also point unhesitatingly in the direction of the Soviet bloc as an "alternative" source for filling their current wants as well as their requirements for long-term economic development.

As a practical matter, however, the foreign economic resources of the Soviet camp can scarcely be qualified as a plausible "alternative." Because of their built-in institutional commitment to autarchy, internal national as well as intrabloc, the Communist countries do not have much to spare for trade with the outside world. . . . In 1961, total world trade was measured by an export figure of $118 billion. . . . The newly developing nations are very much involved in the activities of the world market. . . . As a group, they sell currently some $28 billion worth of commodities in the world market. Of this total, the share of the Soviet bloc as a whole comes to only 4.3 percent. The proportion is roughly the same on the import side: only 4.1 percent of the $30 billion worth of goods imported by the less-developed countries in 1961 came from the Sino-Soviet group of nations. . . .

In the field of trade, the prime objective of the newly developing nations is to employ their export resources in such a way as to help speed up their economic development. To this end, they try to maximize the import of industrial equipment in the course of any given year. Here, too, the preponderant source is the capitalist world market. In 1960, the industrialized nations of the West delivered to the underdeveloped countries a quantity of equipment valued at $7.6 billion. In contrast, imports in this category from the Soviet bloc amounted to less than $300 million in the same year; i.e., a ratio of nearly 25 to 1. . . .

It may be reasonably concluded from the above brief survey, that the Communist leaders' appreciation of the usefulness of economic aid as an instrumentality for improving their power position in general, and their influence among the developing nations in particular, has in no way diminished in recent years. . . .

SOVIET VIEWS

3. THE PEOPLE OF THE UNDERDEVELOPED COUNTRIES ARE AGAINST THE CAPITALIST PATH *

V. TYAGUNENKO

Member, Editorial Office, World's Economic and International Affairs

The ideas of socialism are now penetrating into the most remote corners of the world. The influence of the world socialist system is constantly growing.

Capitalism as a social system has discredited itself in the eyes of the peoples of the former colonies. The best teacher of the masses is their own experience. They are becoming convinced that capitalism not only cannot offer them prospects of social and economic progress but that it is an obstacle to their development. Let us take the problem of the rate of

* Originally published under the title "The Peoples are Against the Capitalist Path," in *Kommunist,* September, 1962. Excerpts reprinted from the translation in *The Current Digest of the Soviet Press,* published at Columbia University, Nov. 7, 1962, pp. 8-9, by permission of the publisher. Copyright 1962 by the Joint Committee on Slavic Studies.

economic growth of the liberated countries. The young states are several decades behind the imperialist powers. Although two-thirds of the population of the capitalist world lives in the economically underdeveloped countries, they produce less than one-twelfth of the capitalist world's mining output and output of base metals and less than one-twenty-fifth of the output of the metalworking industry. Even their share in the capitalist world's output of mineral raw materials and fuel hardly exceeds one-fourth. In the majority of countries the per capita national income is tens of times exceeded by that in the leading imperialist powers. On the average it is lower than it was in the developed countries on the eve of the industrial revolution. Such are the consequences of colonial domination.

The attainment of political independence by the majority of the formerly oppressed countries naturally spurred the rate of their development. Whereas before the second world war the average annual rate of growth of the national product in these countries was within the confines of only 1%, it now reaches 4% a year. The rise of industrial production in the underdeveloped countries also has accelerated substantially, as is seen from the table below.

RATE OF DEVELOPMENT OF INDUSTRIAL OUTPUT (BY GROUPS OF
COUNTRIES AND REGIONS) IN THE CAPITALIST WORLD AT
THE THIRD STAGE OF THE GENERAL CRISIS OF CAPITALISM

	1961 (1955=100)	Avg. Annual % of Growth
Entire capitalist world	124.1	3.7
Industrially developed countries[1]	121.9	3.3
—including:		
North America	105.6	0.9
Western Europe	133.6	4.9
Underdeveloped countries	160.3	8.2
—including:		
Southeast Asia	167.4	9.0
Latin America	140.1	5.8

[1] Composite index compiled on the basis of indices of countries of North America, Western Europe and Japan.

The acceleration of the rate of industrial progress is a direct result of national liberation, of the liquidation of the noneconomic forms of colonial exploitation and of a certain weakening of the economic positions of the monopolies in these countries. Aid from world socialism is of great importance. But the present rates of development clearly are still insufficient to do away with backwardness. After all, if the underdeveloped countries are to catch up with the group of leading capitalist states in total volume of industrial output alone, about 70 to 80 years will be required, given the present ratio of the growth rates. Further, considering that in comparison with the developed capitalist states the population in the countries of Asia, Africa and Latin America is double and that the rates of its increase are also double, it is not difficult to calculate that the abovementioned period will have to be multiplied by several times. And this means that, even at the present slightly faster rates, the liberated countries will need centuries to liquidate the gap in the level of industrial development.

To this day hunger is a common phenomenon for several underdeveloped countries. The rates of agricultural production in Latin America and Southeast Asia are not even keeping pace with the natural population increase. The per capita output of agricultural products (including food products) in these regions is now lower than it was before the second world war.

Life convinces the popular masses that it is impossible to solve the basic national tasks on the path of capitalism. The peoples see that the bourgeoisie, after seizing the dominant economic positions in a number of countries, tries to shift the burdens of economic development first of all onto the shoulders of the working people, while a handful of rich people earn vast wealth. Thus, in the U.A.R. before the reform of July, 1961, according to data published in the press of that country, 390,000 capitalists and landowners, constituting less than 1.5% of the population, had concentrated 35.4% of all income in their hands, while the share of 17,400,000 people, or two-thirds of the population, was slightly more than 16% of the income. Furthermore, almost 3,000,000 people (9% of the country's population) had no sources of income at all and no work. . . .

Another example. In India ten extremely wealthy financial and industrial groups have concentrated in their hands 67% of the country's paid stock capital and are continuing to grow rich. The situation of the working masses is becoming worse. . . .

In explaining the situation in the country, the Indian Communists came to the conclusion: "The basic cause is that an attempt is being made in India to create an independent capitalist economy without taking resolute measures against foreign imperialist capital and without radical agrarian reform; the basic reliance is placed on the big bourgeoisie." Thus from the standpoint of internal development the capitalist path promises no future for the people.

An analysis of the continuing unequal status of the liberated countries in the world capitalist economy leads to the same conclusion. Their economy remains an agrarian and raw-materials annex of the imperialist powers. Trade conditions for the underdeveloped countries have been deteriorating constantly for the past decades. According to the calculations of U.N. experts, on the eve of the second world war they had to export 40% more raw materials to pay for a given amount of finished manufactured goods than 50 years earlier. In the postwar years the difference between prices for raw materials and those for finished manufactured goods continued to increase, despite some fluctuations. It increased by about 23% in the period from 1950 to 1960 alone. Total losses to the underdeveloped countries from the unbalanced exchange through foreign trade channels amount to about $14,000,000,000 to $16,000,000,000 a year. Moreover, the imperialist monopolies pump enormous sums out of the underdeveloped countries in the form of income from their capital investments. These revenues reach $5,000,000,000 a year. Thus, the total annual tribute paid by the underdeveloped countries to imperialism is about $20,000,000,000. The magnitude of this sum can be judged if it is recalled that the gross national product of all the underdeveloped countries taken together was estimated at $117,400,000,000 in 1957. Consequently, the imperialist monopolies annually pump out of these countries a fortune equal to one-sixth of their gross national product. This is real bloodsucking, and it is especially unhealthy for the weakened economic organisms of the young states. It is impossible to liquidate this colonialist exploitation fully without tearing away from the world capitalist economy. . . .

In the contemporary epoch the objective course of historical development is such that it is impossible to move forward without going toward socialism. . . .

4. U.S.S.R. CONTRIBUTION TO THE INDEPENDENT ECONOMIC DEVELOPMENT OF THE DEVELOPING COUNTRIES *

G. M. PROHOROV

Department Head, Institute for Economics of the World Socialist System, Academy of Sciences, U.S.S.R.

We are witnesses of vast changes. which have taken place in the world in the last ten to fifteen years, the most important being the winning of political independence by many underdeveloped countries of Asia and Africa. This, however, is only the first step on the path to true independence.

* Excerpts reprinted from the *Review of International Affairs*, Belgrade, Yugoslavia, Jan. 5, 1963, pp. 16-18, by permission of the publisher.

This entails the building of a highly developed, ramified national economy based on modern industry, which produces, not only consumer goods, but also the most important means of production. Only thus can the winning of economic independence, which is the chief prerequisite of real independence, be ensured.

The colonialism and exploitation practised by foreign monopolists have left deep scars on the newly independent countries, and they are the main cause of their retarded advance. It is therefore quite natural that the peoples of these countries should strive to speed up their economic development and to improve their living standard as far as possible. It is also natural that they should pin their hopes for the achievement of these objectives on the aid and support of the industrial countries.

The monopolist capital of the west seeks to take advantage of the need of the underdeveloped countries to achieve its own aims, to impose new forms of dependence on them, and to continue to exploit them and make high profits out of them. Only in this way can one explain the persistent refusal of the western powers to contribute efficiently to the industrialization of the underdeveloped countries.

The approach of the USSR to these countries is completely different. The peoples of our country view the liberation struggle of the peoples of other countries with deep sympathy and understanding, and welcome the proclamation of the independence of liberated states. The Soviet Union sincerely desires extensive relations and co-operation with the underdeveloped countries in the sphere of their national economies.

The main objective of the Soviet Union in its co-operation with the newly independent states is to contribute as efficiently as possible to their struggle to overcome underdevelopment and to build a highly developed economy as the material basis for the improvement of the living standard of their peoples and the confirming of their independence.

The economic relations of the USSR with the underdeveloped countries are based on the principles of sovereignty and equality, of mutual benefit and friendship among peoples. This means supporting those peoples who are fighting against imperialism and for the achievement of their independence. The friendship and co-operation between the USSR and the less developed countries reflect an objective necessity, and are the result of their common vital interests. The basis of these relations is their common effort to safeguard the peace and security of their peoples, their common interests in the struggle against imperialism and colonialism, their concern for the progress of mankind, and their mutual benefit from economic co-operation and scientific and cultural exchange.

It is the underdeveloped countries that are primarily interested in the promotion of these relations, since they contribute to the stepping up of the development of their national economies, to the strengthening of their position on the world markets and, consequently, to their independence.

The underdeveloped countries which export raw materials are experiencing great difficulties owing to unstable market conditions and the steady deterioration of trade terms. Our country supports the efforts of these countries to achieve the stabilization of prices and the expansion of raw material markets. Unlike the capitalist countries, the Soviet Union, in its trade with the developing countries, does not seek to make profits from the purchase or sale of goods. The chief objective of its foreign trade with such countries is to contribute to their economic progress and the improved supply of goods for their populations. This trade represents an important factor in the development of the national economies of the underdeveloped countries, because it enables them to exchange their export products for machines, equipment and other necessary technical goods, and also to increase their exports.

The Soviet Union maintains trade relations with more than thirty underdeveloped countries of Asia, Africa and South America. The value of the goods exchanged with these countries reached 1,460 million roubles in 1961, or 5.7 times more than in 1955.

In recent years the Soviet Union has considerably increased its imports from the developing countries; these consist of goods normally exported by these countries—a fact that has contributed to the stabilization of their prices, which began to fall rapidly owing to the reduction of imports by capitalist countries in their periods of economic stagnation. This was emphasised in the UN Review of World Economy for 1958.

In return for goods purchased in the countries of Asia, Africa and South America, the Soviet Union supplies these countries with machines and other goods needed for their economic development and the satisfaction of the needs of their population. The share of machines and equipment in Soviet exports to these countries was about 40 per cent in 1961.

It is well-known that the Soviet Union is opposed to discrimination and restrictions in trade prompted by political considerations, and to the artificial barriers which the western powers are placing on the path of progress of world trade. . . .

The underdeveloped countries are making great efforts to step up the pace of their development and solve their present problems more rapidly. Many of these countries are devoting special attention to the problem of industrialization, and more than twenty underdeveloped countries are getting economic and technical aid from the Soviet Union for the construction of modern industries and the development of other branches of economy.

Under the arrangements concluded so far, the Soviet Union will help various underdeveloped countries to construct about 480 industrial enterprises, plants and factories, including 34 steel plants and enterprises of non-ferrous metallurgy, more than 30 factories for the production of machines and the manufacture of metals, oil refineries, electric power plants, and other important factories and plants, many of which will serve as the basis for the construction of new industries.

A number of these countries have made the development of the metallurgical industry one of the main objectives of their economic plans of development. It is therefore natural that the aid of the Soviet Union is especially important in this sphere. Metallurgical plants in India, Indonesia, Iraq, Cuba and Ceylon, with a total capacity of more than 3.5 million tons of steel a year, will make an important contribution to the industrialization of these countries. Machine-producing factories will supply machines and equipment for metallurgical plants, mines, electric power plants, textile factories, and agriculture.

The problem of the exploitation of the national resources of oil and its refining is an important one in many of these countries. In this sphere, too, the Soviet Union extends friendly aid in prospecting and in the construction of oil refineries, and plans have already been made for the construction of refineries with a total capacity of 9 million tons of oil a year.

The electric power plants which are under construction in a number of countries with the aid of the Soviet Union will generate a total of about 20 million KWh of electric power a year. These include plants of such exceptional importance as the Assuan Dam and the electric power plant on the Nile.

The Soviet Union appreciates the efforts of the newly independent countries in connection with the training of technical experts and skilled workers, and in this sphere, too, offers them friendly aid. The Soviet experts transmit their knowledge and experience to the experts and workers of the countries in which they are operating, so that building sites and factory departments frequently assume the aspect of mass schools for the training of national personnel.

Parallel with this, the Soviet Union has extended aid for the construction of 64 institutes, technical and other schools and training centres in the underdeveloped countries. Twenty-two of these schools have already started training national cadres this year. The University of Friendship of Peoples in Moscow, which bears the name of Patrice Lumumba, serves the same purpose, and students from many countries study there. This university trains engineers, agricultural experts, physicians, teachers, economists, and experts in other fields of learning necessary for the advance of economy, science and culture in developing countries.

These countries are in need of credits and loans granted on favourable economic terms and without any political and military conditions or demands; and it is loans of just such a nature that the Soviet Union grants. Their total amount has reached about 3 billion roubles (more than 3 billion dollars); and they are usually granted at 2.5 percent interest. These credits are normally repaid through deliveries to the USSR of the usual export products of the country concerned.

It should finally be emphasized that economic cooperation on a sound basis has proved to be an efficient means for the improvement of political relations among states, and the strengthening of friendship among peoples; and herein lies its great importance.